Morality in Practice

Fourth Edition

Morality
in
Practice

Fourth Edition

Edited by
James P. Sterba
University of Notre Dame

Wadsworth Publishing Company
Belmont, California
A Division of Wadsworth

Philosophy Editor: Tammy Goldfeld
Editorial Assistant: Kristina Pappas
Production Editor: The Book Company
Print Buyer: Karen Hunt
Permissions Editor: Robert Kauser
Designer: Vargas/Williams/Design
Copy Editor: Susan Lundgren
Cover: Lois Stanfield
Compositor: Kachina Typesetting
Printer: Fairfield Graphics

*This book is printed on
acid-free recycled paper.*

International Thomson Publishing
The trademark ITP is used under license

Printed in the United States of America

1 2 3 4 5 6 7 8 9 10—98 97 96 95 94

Library of Congress Cataloging-in-Publication Data

    Morality in practice. / edited by James P. Sterba. —4th ed.
       p.   cm.
    Includes bibliographical references.
    ISBN 0-534-21277-8
    1. Social ethics. I. Sterba, James P.
HM216.M667 1993
303.3'72-dc20   93-5408
                                                CIP

This book is again dedicated to Sonya,
now a teenager, whose sense of what are
moral problems has changed my own.

Contents

III. Abortion and Euthanasia

Introduction   122

IV. Sex Equality

Introduction   208

VIII. Privacy, Drug Testing, and AIDS

Introduction 382

IX. Gay and Lesbian Rights

Introduction 428

X. Animal Liberation and Environmental Justice

Introduction 466

XI. National Health Care
Introduction   514

XII. War and Humanitarian Intervention
Introduction   532

Preface

Moral problems courses tend to teach themselves. It takes a really bad teacher to mess them up. Teachers can mess up a moral problems course in at least three ways:

1. By presenting just one set of views on various topics. Students appreciate the need for fair play here.
2. By encouraging students to hold a crude relativism. Students know that all moral stances are not equally good.
3. By not being relevant to student concerns. Students can reasonably expect that at least an ethics course will be relevant to their lives.

This text enables teachers to avoid (1) by presenting radically opposed selections on all topics. It enables teachers to avoid (2) by suggesting, through the introductions and through the ordering and selection of topics, how some views turn out to be more defensible than others. It enables teachers to avoid (3) by being the only moral problems text that provides readings on a broad range of standard and new topics. In fact, no other moral problems text combines such breadth and depth. In addition, it has to recommend it, the following:

New Features

1. Thirty-three new readings.
2. Three new sections: sexual harassment, national health care, and war and humanitarian intervention.
3. Two sections recast and revised: near and distant peoples, sex equality.
4. All other sections revised.

5. A revised general introduction that provides a background discussion of traditional moral approaches to ethics as well as an accessible answer to the question: Why be moral?

Retained Features

1. Section introductions that help to set out the framework for the discussion and criticism of the articles in each section.
2. Brief summaries at the beginning of each article that enable students to test and improve their comprehension.
3. Each section of the anthology concludes with one or more articles discussing specific practical applications.
4. Suggestions for further reading are found at the end of each section.

In putting together this fourth edition, I have again benefited enormously from the advice and help of many different people. Very special thanks go to my colleague John Robinson, who offered many suggestions that have been incorporated into this edition. Thanks also go to Ken King of Wadsworth Publishing Company, George Calmenson of The Book Company, my wife and fellow philosopher Janet Kourany, and Wendy Donner of Carleton University. I would also like to thank the following reviewers whose suggestions were especially helpful: Elizabeth Anderson, University of Michigan, Ann Arbor; Edward Becker, University of Nebraska, Lincoln; Thomas Carlson, Macalester College; Charles Dresser, Arizona State University; Timothy J. Eves, University of Connecticut; and Justin Schwartz, Ohio State University.

Morality
in
Practice

Fourth Edition

General Introduction

Most of us like to think of ourselves as just and moral people. To be truly such, however, we need to know something about the demands of justice and how they apply in our own particular circumstances. We should be able to assess, for example, whether our society's economic and legal systems are just—that is, whether the ways income and wealth are distributed in society as well as the methods of enforcing that distribution give people what they deserve. We should also consider whether other societal institutions, such as the military defense system, the education system, and the foreign aid program, are truly just. Without investigating these systems and coming to an informed opinion, we cannot say with any certainty that we are just and moral persons rather than perpetrators or beneficiaries of injustice.

This anthology has been created to help you acquire some of the knowledge you will need to justify your belief that you are a just and moral person. For this purpose, the anthology contains a wide spectrum of readings on twelve important, contemporary, practical problems:

1. The problem of the distribution of income and wealth. (Who should control what resources within a society?)

2. The problem of near and distant peoples. (What obligations do we have to near and distant peoples?)

3. The problem of abortion and euthanasia. (Do fetuses have a right to life, and what should we do for the dying and those requiring life-sustaining medical treatment?)

4. The problem of sex equality. (Should the sexes be treated equally, and what constitutes equal treatment?)

5. The problem of affirmative action and comparable worth. (What specific policies are required to remedy discrimination and prejudice?)

6. The problem of pornography. (Should pornography be prohibited because it promotes violence against women?)

7. The problem of sexual harassment. (What is sexual harassment and how can it be avoided?)

8. The problem of privacy, drug testing, and AIDS. (Do programs for drug testing and testing for AIDS violate a person's right to privacy?)

9. The problem of gay and lesbian rights. (What rights should gays and lesbians have?)

1

10. The problem of animal liberation and en-
    vironmental justice. (What should our
    policies be for the treatment of animals
    and the environment?)
11. The problem of national health care.
    (How can our national health care system
    be improved?)
12. The problem of war and humanitarian
    intervention. (What are the moral limits to
    the international use of force?)

Before you get into these problems, however,
you should know what it means to take a moral
approach to these issues and how such an
approach is justified.

The Essential Features
of a Moral Approach
to Practical Problems

To begin with, a moral approach to practical
problems must be distinguished from various
nonmoral approaches. Nonmoral approaches
to practical problems include the *legal approach*
(what the law requires with respect to this
practical problem), the *group-* or *self-interest
approach* (what the group- or self-interest is of
the parties affected by this problem), and the
scientific approach (how this practical problem
can best be accounted for or understood). To
call these approaches nonmoral, of course,
does not imply that they are immoral. All that
is implied is that the requirements of these
approaches may or may not accord with the
requirements of morality.

What, then, essentially characterizes a moral approach to practical problems? I suggest
that there are two essential features to such an
approach:

1. The approach is prescriptive, that is, it
   issues in prescriptions, such as "do this"
   and "don't do that."
2. The approach's prescriptions are acceptable to everyone affected by them.

The first feature distinguishes a moral approach from a scientific approach because a

scientific approach is not prescriptive. The
second feature distinguishes a moral approach
from both a legal approach and a group- or
self-interest approach because the prescriptions that accord best with the law or
serve the interest of particular groups or individuals may not be acceptable to everyone
affected by them.

Here the notion of "acceptable" means
"ought to be accepted" or "is reasonable to
accept" and not simply "is capable of being
accepted." Understood in this way, certain
prescriptions may be acceptable even though
they are not actually accepted by everyone
affected by them. For example, a particular
welfare program may be acceptable even
though many people oppose it because it involves an increased tax burden. Likewise, certain prescriptions may be unacceptable even
though they have been accepted by everyone
affected by them. For example, it may be that
most women have been socialized to accept
prescriptions requiring them to fill certain social roles even though these prescriptions are
unacceptable because they impose second-
class status on them.

Alternative Moral Approaches
to Practical Problems

Using the two essential features of a moral
approach to practical problems, let us consider
three principal alternative moral approaches
to practical problems: a *Utilitarian Approach,* an
Aristotelian Approach, and a *Kantian Approach.*[1]
The basic principle of a Utilitarian Approach
is:

Do those actions that maximize the net utility or satisfaction of everyone affected by
them.

A Utilitarian Approach qualifies as a moral
approach because it is prescriptive and because it can be argued that its prescriptions are
acceptable to everyone affected by them since
they take the utility or satisfaction of all those
individuals equally into account.

To illustrate, let's consider how this approach applies to the question of whether

nation A should intervene in the internal affairs of nation B when nation A's choice would have the following consequences:

Nation A's Choice

	Intervene	Don't Intervene
Net utility to A	4 trillion units	8½ trillion units
Net utility to B	2 trillion units	−2 trillion units
Total utility	6 trillion units	6½ trillion units

Given that these are all the consequences that are relevant to nation A's choice, a Utilitarian Approach favors not intervening. Note that in this case, the choice favoring a Utilitarian Approach does not conflict with the group-interest of nation A, although it does conflict with the group-interest of nation B.

But are such calculations of utility possible? Admittedly, they are difficult to make. At the same time, such calculations seem to serve as a basis for public discussion. Once President Reagan, addressing a group of black business leaders, asked whether blacks were better off because of the Great Society programs, and although many disagreed with the answer he gave, no one found his question unanswerable.[2] Thus faced with the exigencies of measuring utility, a Utilitarian Approach simple counsels that we do our best to determine what maximizes net utility and act on the result.

The second approach to consider is an Aristotelian Approach. Its basic principle is:

Do those actions that would further one's proper development as a human being.

This approach also qualifies as a moral approach because it is prescriptive and because it can be argued that its prescriptions are acceptable to everyone affected by them.

There are, however, different versions of this approach. According to some versions, each person can determine through the use of reason his or her proper development as a human being. Other versions disagree. For example, many religious traditions rely on revelation to guide people in their proper development as human beings. However, although an Aristotelian Approach can take these various forms, I want to focus on what is probably its philosophically most interesting form. That form specifies proper development in terms of virtuous activity and understands virtuous activity to preclude intentionally doing evil that good may come of it. In this form, an Aristotelian Approach conflicts most radically with a Utilitarian Approach, which requires intentionally doing evil whenever a *greater* good would come of it.

The third approach to be considered is a Kantian Approach. This approach has its origins in seventeenth- and eighteenth-century social contract theories, which tended to rely on actual contracts to specify moral requirements. However, actual contracts may or may not have been made, and, even if they were made, they may or may not have been moral or fair. This led Immanuel Kant and contemporary Kantian John Rawls to resort to a hypothetical contract to ground moral requirements. A difficulty with this approach is in determining under what conditions a hypothetical contract is fair and moral. Currently, the most favored Kantian Approach is specified by the following basic principle:

Do those actions that persons behind an imaginary veil of ignorance would unanimously agree should be done.[3]

This imaginary veil extends to most particular facts about oneself—anything that would bias one's choice or stand in the way of a unanimous agreement. Accordingly, the imaginary veil of ignorance would mask one's knowledge of one's social position, talents, sex, race, and religion, but not one's knowledge of such general information as would be contained in political, social, economic, and psychological theories. A Kantian Approach qualifies as a moral approach because it is prescriptive and because it can be argued that its prescriptions would be acceptable to everyone affected by them since they would be agreed to by everyone affected behind an imaginary veil of ignorance.

To illustrate the approach, let's return to the example of nation A and nation B used earlier. The choice facing nation A was the following:

Nation A's Choice

	Intervene	Don't Intervene
Net utility to A	4 trillion units	8½ trillion units
Net utility to B	2 trillion units	−2 trillion units
Total utility	6 trillion units	6½ trillion units

Given that these are all the consequences relevant to nation A's choice, a Kantian Approach favors intervention because persons behind the imaginary veil of ignorance would have to consider that they might turn out to be in nation B, and in that case, they would not want to be so disadvantaged for the greater benefit of those in nation A. This resolution conflicts with the resolution favored by a Utilitarian Approach and the group-interest of nation A, but not with the group-interest of nation B.

Assessing Alternative Moral Approaches

Needless to say, each of these moral approaches has its strengths and weaknesses. The main strength of a Utilitarian Approach is that once the relevant utilities are determined, there is an effective decision-making procedure that can be used to resolve all practical problems. After determining the relevant utilities, all that remains is to total the net utilities and choose the alternative with the highest net utility. The basic weakness of this approach, however, is that it does not give sufficient weight to the distribution of utility among the relevant parties. For example, consider a society equally divided between the Privileged Rich and the Alienated Poor who face the following alternatives:

Nation A's Choice

	Alternative A	Alternative B
Net utility to Privileged Rich	5½ trillion units	4 trillion units
Net utility to Alienated Poor	1 trillion units	2 trillion units
Total utility	6½ trillion units	6 trillion units

Given that these are all the relevant utilities, a Utilitarian Approach favors Alternative A even though Alternative B provides a higher minimum payoff. And if the utility values for two alternatives were:

Nation A's Choice

	Alternative A	Alternative B
Net utility to Privileged Rich	4 trillion units	5 trillion units
Net utility to Alienated Poor	2 trillion units	1 trillion units
Total utility	6 trillion units	6 trillion units

A Utilitarian Approach would be indifferent between the alternatives, even though Alternative A again provides a higher minimum payoff. In this way, a Utilitarian Approach fails to take into account the distribution of utility among the relevant parties. All that matters for this approach is maximizing total utility, and the distribution of utility among the affected parties is taken into account only insofar as it contributes toward the attainment of that goal.

By contrast, the main strength of an Aristotelian Approach in the form we are considering is that it limits the means that can be chosen in pursuit of good consequences. In particular, it absolutely prohibits intentionally doing evil that good may come of it. However, although some limit on the means available for the pursuit of good consequences seems desirable, the main weakness of this version of an

Aristotelian Approach is that the limit it imposes is too strong. Indeed, exceptions to this limit would seem to be justified whenever the evil to be done is:

1. Trivial (e.g., stepping on someone's foot to get out of a crowded subway).
2. Easily reparable (e.g., lying to a temporarily depressed friend to keep her from committing suicide).
3. Sufficiently outweighed by the consequences of the action (e.g., shooting one of 200 civilian hostages to prevent in the only way possible the execution of all 200).

Still another weakness of this approach is that it lacks an effective decision-making procedure for resolving practical problems. Beyond imposing limits on the means that can be employed in the pursuit of good consequences, the advocates of this approach have not agreed on criteria for selecting among the available alternatives.

The main strength of a Kantian Approach is that like an Aristotelian Approach, it seeks to limit the means available for the pursuit of good consequences. However, unlike the version of the an Aristotelian Approach we considered, a Kantian Approach does not impose an absolute limit on intentionally doing evil that good may come of it. Behind the veil of ignorance, persons would surely agree that if the evil were trivial, easily reparable, or sufficiently outweighed by the consequences, there would be an adequate justification for permitting it. On the other hand, the main weakness of a Kantian Approach is that although it provides an effective decision-making procedure for resolving some practical problems, such as the problem of how to distribute income and wealth and the problem of near and distant people, a Kantian Approach cannot be applied to all problems. For example, it will not work for the problems of animal rights and abortion unless we assume that animals and fetuses should be behind the veil of ignorance.

So far, we have seen that prescriptivity and acceptability of prescriptions by everyone affected by them are the two essential features of a moral approach to practical problems, and we have considered three principal alternative approaches that qualify as moral approaches to these problems. Let's now examine what reasons there are for giving a moral approach to practical problems precedence over any nonmoral approach with which it conflicts.

From Rationality to Morality

To begin with, the ethical egoist, by denying the priority of morality over self-interest, presents the most serious challenge to a moral approach to practical problems. Basically, that challenge takes two forms: Individual Ethical Egoism and Universal Ethical Egoism. The basic principle of Individual Ethical Egoism is:

> Everyone ought to do what is in the overall self-interest of just one particular individual.

The basic principle of Universal Ethical Egoism is:

> Everyone ought to do what is in his or her overall self-interest.

Obviously, the prescriptions deriving from these two forms of egoism would conflict significantly with prescriptions following from a moral approach to practical problems. How then can we show that a moral approach is preferable to an egoist's approach?

The Justification for Following a Moral Approach to Practical Problems

In Individual Ethical Egoism, all prescriptions are based on the overall interests of just one particular individual. Let's call that individual Gladys. Because in Individual Ethical Egoism Gladys's interests constitute the sole basis for determining prescriptions, there should be no problem of inconsistent prescriptions, assuming, of course, that Gladys's own particular interests are in harmony. The crucial problem for Individual Ethical Egoism, however, is justifying that only Gladys's interests count in determining prescriptions. Individual Ethical Egoism must provide at least some reason for accepting that view. Otherwise, it would be irrational to accept the theory. But what reason or reasons could serve this function? Clearly, it will not do to cite as a reason some characteristic Gladys shares with other persons because whatever justification such a characteristic would provide for favoring Gladys's interests, it would also provide for favoring the interests of those other persons. Nor will it do to cite as a reason some unique characteristic of Gladys, such as knowing all of Shakespeare's writings by heart, because such a characteristic involves a comparative element, and consequently others with similar characteristics, like knowing some or most of Shakespeare's corpus by heart, would still have some justification, although a proportionally lesser justification, for having their interests favored. But again the proposed characteristic would not justify favoring only Gladys's interests.

A similar objection could be raised if a unique relational characteristic were proposed as a reason for Gladys's special status—such as that Gladys is Seymour's wife. Because other persons would have similar but not identical relational characteristics, similar but not identical reasons would hold for them. Nor will it do to argue that the reason for Gladys's special status is not the particular unique traits that she possesses, but rather the mere fact that she had unique traits. The same would hold true of everyone else. Every individual has unique traits. If recourse to unique traits is dropped and Gladys claims that she is special simply because she is herself and wants to further her own interests, every other person could claim the same.[4]

For the Individual Ethical Egoist to argue that the same or similar reasons do *not* hold for other peoples with the same or similar characteristics to those of Gladys, she must explain *why* they do not hold. It must always be possible to understand how a characteristic serves as a reason in one case but not in another. If no explanation can be provided, and in the case of Individual Ethical Egoism none has

been forthcoming, the proposed characteristic either serves as a reason in both cases or does not serve as a reason at all.

Universal Ethical Egoism

Unfortunately, these objections to Individual Ethical Egoism do not work against Universal Ethical Egoism because Universal Ethical Egoism does provide a reason why the egoist should be concerned simply about maximizing his or her own interests, which is simply that the egoist is herself and wants to further her own interests. The Individual Ethical Egoist could not recognize such a reason without giving up her view, but the Universal Ethical Egoist is willing and able to universalize her claim and recognize that everyone has a similar justification for adopting Universal Ethical Egoism.

Accordingly, the objections that typically have been raised against Universal Ethical Egoism are designed to show that the view is fundamentally inconsistent. For the purpose of evaluating these objections, let's consider the case of Gary Gyges, an otherwise normal human being who, for reasons of personal gain, has embezzled $300,000 while working at People's National Bank and is in the process of escaping to a South Sea island where he will have the good fortune to live a pleasant life protected by the local authorities and untroubled by any qualms of conscience. Suppose that Hedda Hawkeye, a fellow employee, knows that Gyges has been embezzling money from the bank and is about to escape. Suppose, further, that it is in Hawkeye's overall self-interest to prevent Gyges from escaping with the embezzled money because she will be generously rewarded for doing so by being appointed vice-president of the bank. Given that it is in Gyges's overall self-interest to escape with the embezzled money, it now appears that we can derive a contradiction from the following:

1. Gyges ought to escape with the embezzled money.

2. Hawkeye ought to prevent Gyges from escaping with the embezzled money.

3. By preventing Gyges from escaping with the embezzled money, Hawkeye is preventing Gyges from doing what he ought to do.

4. One ought never to prevent someone from doing what he ought to do.

5. Therefore, Hawkeye ought not to prevent Gyges from escaping with the embezzled money.

Because premises 2 and 5 are contradictory, Universal Ethical Egoism appears to be inconsistent.

The soundness of this argument depends, however, on premise 4, and defenders of Universal Ethical Egoism believe there are grounds for rejecting this premise. For if "preventing an action" means "rendering the action impossible," it would appear that there *are* cases in which a person is justified in preventing someone else from doing what he or she ought to do. Consider, for example, the following case. Suppose Irma and Igor are both actively competing for the same position at a prestigious law firm. If Irma accepts the position, she obviously renders it impossible for Igor to obtain the position. But surely this is *not* what we normally think of as an unacceptable form of prevention. Nor would Hawkeye's prevention of Gyges's escape appear to be unacceptable. Thus, to sustain the argument against Universal Ethical Egoism, one must distinguish between acceptable and unacceptable forms of prevention and then show that the argument succeeds even for forms of prevention that a Universal Ethical Egoist would regard as unacceptable. This requires elucidating the force of "ought" in Universal Ethical Egoism.

To illustrate the sense in which a Universal Ethical Egoist claims that other persons ought to do what is in their overall self-interest, defenders often appeal to an analogy of competitive games. For example, in football a defensive player might think that the opposing team's quarterback ought to pass on third down with five yards to go, while not wanting the quarterback to do so and planning to prevent any such attempt. Or to use Jesse Kalin's example:

I may see how my chess opponent can put my king in check. This is how he ought to move. But believing that he ought to move his bishop and check my king does not commit me to wanting him to do that, nor to persuading him to do so. What I ought to do is sit there quietly, hoping he does not move as he ought.[5]

The point of these examples is to suggest that a Universal Ethical Egoist may, like a player in a game, judge that others ought to do what is in their overall self-interest while simultaneously attempting to prevent such actions or at least refraining from encouraging them.

The analogy of competitive games also illustrates the sense in which a Universal Ethical Egoist claims that she herself ought to do what is in her overall self-interest. For just as a player's judgment that she ought to make a particular move is followed, other things being equal, by an attempt to perform the appropriate action, so likewise when a Universal Ethical Egoist judges that she ought to do some particular action, other things being equal, an attempt to perform the appropriate action follows. In general, defenders of Universal Ethical Egoism stress that because we have little difficulty understanding the implications of the use of "ought" in competitive games, we should also have little difficulty understanding the analogous use of "ought" by the Universal Ethical Egoist.

To claim, however, that the "oughts" in competitive games are analogous to the "oughts" of Universal Ethical Egoism does not mean there are no differences between them. Most important, competitive games are governed by moral constraints such that when everyone plays the game properly, there are acceptable moral limits as to what one can do. For example, in football one cannot poison the opposing quarterback in order to win the game. By contrast, when everyone holds self-interested reasons to be supreme, the only limit to what one can do is the point beyond which one ceases to benefit. But this important difference between the "oughts" of Universal Ethical Egoism and the "oughts" found in publicly recognized activities like competitive games does not defeat the appropriateness of the analogy. That the "oughts" found in publicly recognized activities are always limited by various moral constraints (What else would get publicly recognized?) does not preclude their being a suggestive model for the unlimited action-guiding character of the "oughts" of Universal Ethical Egoism.[6]

From Rationality to Morality

Although the most promising attempts to show that Universal Ethical Egoism is inconsistent have failed, the challenge the view presents to a moral approach to practical problems can still be turned aside. It can be shown that, although consistent, the egoist acts contrary to reason in rejecting a moral approach to practical problems.

To show this, let us begin by imagining that we are members of a society deliberating over what sort of principles governing action we should accept. Let us assume that each of us is capable of entertaining and acting on both self-interested and moral reasons and that the question we are seeking to answer is what sort of principles governing action it would be rational for us to accept.[7] This question is not about what sort of principles we should publicly affirm since people will sometimes publicly affirm principles that are quite different from those they are prepared to act on, but rather it is a question of what principles it would be rational for us to accept at the deepest level—in our heart of hearts.

Of course, there are people who are incapable of acting on moral reasons. For such people, there is no question about their being required to act morally or altruistically. But the interesting philosophical question is not about such people, but about people, like ourselves, who are capable of acting self-interestedly or morally and are seeking a rational justification for following one course of action over the others.

Obviously, from a self-interested perspective the only principles we should accept are those that can be derived from the following principle of Universal Ethical Egoism:

Each person ought to do what best serves his or her overall self-interest.

But we can no more defend egoism by simply denying the relevance of moral reasons to rational choice than we can, by simply denying the relevance of self-interested reasons to rational choice, defend the view of pure altruism that the principles we should accept are those that can be derived from the following general principle of altruism:

Each person ought to do what best serves the overall interest of others.

Consequently, in order not to beg the question against either egoism or altruism, we seem to have no other alternative but to grant the prima facie relevance of both self-interested and moral reasons to rational choice and then try to determine which reasons we would be rationally required to act on, all things considered.

In this regard, there are two kinds of cases that must be considered. First, there are cases in which there is a conflict between the relevant self-interested and moral reasons.[8] Second, there are cases in which there is no such conflict.

Now it seems obvious that where there is no conflict, and both reasons are conclusive reasons of their kind, both reasons should be acted on. In such contexts, we should do what is favored both by morality and by self-interest.

Consider the following example. Suppose you accepted a job marketing a baby formula in underdeveloped countries, where the formula was improperly used, leading to increased infant mortality.[9] Imagine that you could just as well have accepted an equally attractive and rewarding job marketing a similar formula in developed countries, where the misuse does not occur, so that a rational weighing of the relevant self-interested reasons alone would not have favored your acceptance of one of these jobs over the other.[10] At the same time, there were obviously moral reasons that condemned your acceptance of the first job—reasons that you presumably are or were able to acquire. Moreover, by assumption in this case, the moral reasons do not clash with the relevant self-interested reasons; they simply made a recommendation where the relevant self-interested reasons are silent. Consequently, a rational weighing of all the relevant reasons in this case could not but favor acting in accord with the relevant moral reasons.[11]

Yet it might be objected that in cases of this sort there would frequently be other reasons significantly opposed to these moral reasons—other reasons that you are or were able to acquire. Such reasons would be either *malevolent* reasons seeking to bring about the suffering and death of other human beings, or *benevolent* reasons concerned to promote non-human welfare even at the expense of human welfare, or *aesthetic* reasons concerned to produce valuable results irrespective of the effects on human or nonhuman welfare. But assuming that such malevolent reasons are ultimately rooted in some conception of what is good for oneself or others,[12] these reasons would have already been taken into account, and by assumption outweighed by the other relevant reasons in this case. And although neither benevolent reasons (concerned to promote nonhuman welfare) nor aesthetic reasons would have been taken into account, such reasons are not directly relevant to justifying morality over rational egoism.[13] Consequently, even with the presence of these three kinds of reasons, your acceptance of the first job can still be seen to be contrary to the relevant reasons in this case.

Needless to say, defenders of rational egoism cannot but be disconcerted with this result since it shows that actions that accord with rational egoism are contrary to reason at least when there are two equally good ways of pursuing one's self-interest, only one of which does not conflict with the basic requirements of morality. Notice also that in cases where there are two equally good ways of fulfilling the basic requirements of morality, only one of which does not conflict with what is in a person's overall self-interest, it is not at all disconcerting for defenders of morality to admit that we are rationally required to choose the way that does not conflict with what is in our overall self-interest. Nevertheless, exposing this defect in rational egoism for cases where moral reasons and self-interested reasons do

not conflict would be but a small victory for defenders of morality if it were not also possible to show that in cases where such reasons do conflict, moral reasons would have priority over self-interested reasons.

Now when we rationally assess the relevant reasons in such conflict cases, it is best to cast the conflict not as a conflict between self-interested reasons and moral reasons but instead as a conflict between self-interested reasons and altruistic reasons.[14] Viewed in this way, three solutions are possible. First, we could say that self-interested reasons always have priority over conflicting altruistic reasons. Second, we could say, just the opposite, that altruistic reasons always have priority over conflicting self-interested reasons. Third, we could say that some kind of a compromise is rationally required. In this compromise, sometimes self-interested reasons would have priority over altruistic reasons and sometimes altruistic reasons would have priority over self-interested reasons.

Once the conflict is described in this manner, the third solution can be seen to be the one that is rationally required. This is because the first and second solutions give exclusive priority to one class of relevant reasons over the other, and only a completely question-begging justification can be given for such an exclusive priority. Only the third solution, by sometimes giving priority to self-interested reasons and sometimes giving priority to altruistic reasons, can avoid a completely question-begging resolution.

Consider the following example. Suppose you are in the waste disposal business and you decided to dispose of toxic wastes in a manner that was cost efficient for you but predictably caused significant harm to future generations. Imagine that there were alternative methods available for disposing of the waste that were only slightly less cost efficient and which did not cause any significant harm to future generations.[15] In this case, you are to weigh your self-interested reasons favoring the most cost-efficient disposal of the toxic wastes against the relevant altruistic reasons favoring the avoidance of significant harm to future generations. If we suppose that the projected loss of benefit to yourself was ever so slight and the projected harm to future generations was ever so great then a nonarbitrary compromise between the relevant self-interested and altruistic reasons would have to favor the altruistic reasons in this case. Hence, as judged by a non-question-begging standard of rationality, your method of waste disposal was contrary to the relevant reasons.

Notice also that this standard of rationality would not support just any compromise between the relevant self-interested and altruistic reasons. The compromise must be a nonarbitrary one, for otherwise it would beg the question with respect to the opposing egoistic and altruistic views. Such a compromise would have to respect the rankings of self-interested and altruistic reasons imposed by the egoist and altruistic views, respectively. Since for each individual there is a separate ranking of that individual's relevant self-interested and altruistic reasons, we can represent these rankings from the most important reasons to the least important reasons as shown in the table below.

Accordingly, any nonarbitrary compromise among such reasons in seeking not to beg the question against egoism or altruism will have to give priority to those reasons that rank highest in each category. Failure to give priority to the highest-ranking altruistic or self-interested reasons would, other things being equal, be contrary to reason.

Of course, there will be cases in which the only way to avoid being required to do what is contrary to your highest-ranking reasons is by requiring someone else to do what is contrary to her highest-ranking reasons. Such cases are sometimes called "lifeboat cases." But while such cases are surely difficult to resolve (may-

be only a chance mechanism can offer a reasonable resolution) they surely do not reflect the typical conflict between the relevant self-interested and altruistic reasons that we are or were able to acquire. For typically one or the other of the conflicting reasons will rank higher on its respective scale, thus permitting a clear resolution.

Now it is important to see how morality can be viewed as just such a nonarbitrary compromise between self-interested and altruistic reasons. First of all, a certain amount of self-regard is morally required or at least morally acceptable. Where this is the case, high-ranking self-interested reasons have priority over the low-ranking altruistic reasons. Second, morality obviously places limits on the extent to which people should pursue their own self-interest. Where this is the case, high-ranking altruistic reasons have priority over low-ranking self-interested reasons. In this way, morality can be seen to be a nonarbitrary compromise between self-interested and altruistic reasons, and the "moral reasons" which constitute that compromise can be seen as having an absolute priority over the self-interested or altruistic reasons that conflict with them.

Of course, exactly how this compromise is to be worked out is a matter of considerable debate. A Utilitarian Approach favors one sort of resolution, an Aristotelian Approach another, and a Kantian Approach yet another. However, irrespective of how this debate is best resolved, it is clear that some sort of a compromise view or moral solution is rationally preferable to either ethical egoism or pure altruism when judged from a nonquestion-begging standpoint.[16]

Individual A		Individual B	
Self-Interested Reasons	Altruistic Reasons	Self-Interested Reasons	Altruistic Reasons
1	1	1	1
2	2	2	2
3	3	3	3
.	.	.	.
.	.	.	.
.	.	.	.
N	N	N	N

The Interconnectedness of Moral Solutions to Practical Problems

Given this justification for following a moral approach to practical problems, we are in a good position to begin examining the twelve practical problems covered in this anthology. Each section contains readings defending radically opposing solutions to the problem at hand, as well as one or more readings discussing specific practical applications. Working through these readings should give you a more informed view about the demands morality places on us with respect to each of these practical problems.

Even if you do not cover all of these practical problems, you should still come to appreciate why a solution to any one of them requires solutions to the others as well. That is to say, the readings on the distribution of income and wealth (in Section I) may help you to characterize a morally defensible system for distributing income and wealth within a society, but you would still not know fully how to apply such a system in a particular society without also inquiring how just that society is with respect to the other problem areas covered by this anthology.

Or suppose justice requires us to provide for the basic nutritional needs of distant peoples as well as for people within our own society. (See the readings in Section II.) Such a requirement would at least restrict the use of nonrenewable resources to satisfy the nonbasic or luxury needs of persons within our society—a use that might otherwise be permitted by a morally defensible system for distributing income and wealth within our society.

Further moral restrictions on the satisfaction of nonbasic or luxury needs could arise from a correct determination of who has a right to life. For example, if fetuses have a right to life, many of us may be morally required to sacrifice the satisfaction of certain nonbasic or luxury needs to bring fetuses to term. If, by contrast, euthanasia can be morally justified, scarce resources that are now used to sustain human life could be freed for other purposes. (See the readings in Section III.)

Justice also may demand that we sacrifice some nonbasic or luxury needs to satisfy the requirements of sex equality and remedy past discrimination, prejudice, and harassment. For example, at the cost of considerable redistribution, we may be required to provide women with the same opportunities for self-development that are now open to men. (See the readings in Sections IV and VII.) We may also be required to turn away qualified candidates for medical schools and law schools so that other candidates who have suffered past injustices may be compensated by admission to these schools. (See the readings in Section V.) Obviously, a radical solution to the problem of pornography prohibiting its distribution would affect those who derive their income from that eight-billion-dollar-a-year industry. (See the readings in Section VI.) Likewise, a radical solution to the problem of privacy, drug testing, and AIDS favoring a strong right to privacy would have a significant impact on the lives of employees generally as well as the incomes of those employed in drug testing. (See the readings in Section VIII.) Recognition of a strong right to privacy would also result in considerable redistribution that would benefit homosexuals by providing them with the same opportunities for self-development as heterosexuals. (See the readings in Section IX.)

Moral restrictions on the satisfaction of nonbasic needs and even on the way basic needs are satisfied could arise from a determination of what obligations, if any, we have to animals and the environment. For example, if vegetarianism were morally required and recognized as such, the impact on our lives would be far-reaching. (See the readings in Section X.)

Similarly, the legitimate costs of health care must ultimately enter into any calculation of who gets to keep what in society. This will require a solution to the problem of national health care. (See the readings in Section XI.)

Finally, as we in the United States are painfully aware at the present time, proposed allocations for distributing income and wealth through social welfare programs can come into conflict with proposed allocations for defense and humanitarian intervention. Many people have argued that when this happens we must sacrifice social welfare programs to meet the requirements of defense and humanitarian intervention, but many other people have disagreed. Obviously, then, to know exactly how your solutions to the other problem areas treated in this anthology should be applied in a particular society, you also need to know what are the moral limits to the international use of force. (See the readings in Section XII.)

Put briefly, what is required (or permitted) by a morally defensible solution to the problem of the distribution of income and wealth within a society will depend on what is required (or permitted) by morally defensible solutions to the problems of near and distant peoples; abortion and euthanasia; sex equality; affirmative action and comparable worth; pornography; sexual harassment; privacy, drug-testing, and AIDS; gay and lesbian rights; animal liberation and environmental justice; national health care; and war and humanitarian intervention. This means that any solution you might devise to one of these problems is only provisional until you can determine solutions to the others as well. And even if you are unable at the moment to devise solutions to all of these practical problems (because, for example, the course you are now taking is only considering some of them), you must still acknowledge that in the final analysis your solutions to these practical problems will have to be interconnected.

Note, too, that acknowledging the interconnectedness of the solutions to these practical problems does not presuppose a commitment to any particular political or moral ideal. For example, whether you tend to be a libertarian, a welfare liberal, a socialist, or anything else, the interconnectedness of the solutions to the practical problems we are discussing still holds true. Individuals who endorse different political and moral ideals will presumably devise different solutions to these practical problems, but the solutions will still be interconnected.

Working through the readings in this anthology will not always be an easy task. Some articles will be clear on the first reading, whereas others will require closer scrutiny. You should also make sure you give each selection a fair hearing, because although some will accord with your current views, others will not. It is important that you evaluate these latter with an open mind, allowing for the possibility that after sufficient reflection you may come to view them as the most morally defensible. Indeed, to approach the selections of this anthology in any other way would surely undermine the grounds you have for thinking you are a just and moral person.

Notes

1. Obviously, other moral approaches to practical problems could be distinguished, but I think the three I consider reflect the range of possible approaches that are relevant to the resolution of these problems.

2. In fact, the debate as to whether blacks are better off now because of the programs of the Great Society has taken a more scholarly turn. See Charles Murray, *Losing Ground* (New York: Basic Books, 1984), and Christopher Jencks, "How Poor Are the Poor?" *New York Review of Books,* May 9, 1985.

3. See Section II of this text and my book, *The Demands of Justice* (Notre Dame: University of Notre Dame Press, 1980), especially Chapter 2.

4. For further argument on this point, see Marcus Singer, *Generalization in Ethics* (New York: Alfred A. Knopf, 1961), Chapter 2, and Alan Gewirth, "The Non-Trivializability of Universalizability," *Australasian Journal of Philosophy* (1969), pp. 123–131.

5. Jesse Kalin, "In Defense of Egoism," in *Morality and Rational Self-Interest,* ed. David Gauthier (Englewood Cliffs, N.J.: Prentice-Hall, 1970), pp. 73–74.

6. For additional reasons why ethical egoism is a consistent view, see my article, "Ethical Egoism and Beyond," *Canadian Journal of Philosophy* (1979), pp. 91–108.

7. "Ought" presupposes "can" here. Unless the members of the society have the capacity to entertain and follow both self-interested and moral reasons for acting, it does not make any sense to ask whether they ought or ought not to do so.

8. For an account of what counts as *relevant* self-interested or moral reasons, see my *How to Make People Just* (Totowa, N.J.: Rowman and Allanheld, 1988) pp. 165–166.

9. For a discussion of the causal links involved here, see *Marketing and Promotion of Infant Formula in Development Countries*. Hearing before the Subcommittee of International Economic Policy and Trade of the Committee on Foreign Affairs, U.S. House of Representatives, 1980. See also Maggie McComas et al., *The Dilemma of Third World Nutrition* (1983).

10. Assume that both jobs have the same beneficial effects on the interests of others.

11. I am assuming that acting contrary to reason is an important failing with respect to the requirements of reason, and that there are many ways of not acting in (perfect) accord with reason that do not constitute acting contrary to reason.

12. Otherwise, they would really fall under the classification of aesthetic reasons.

13. Of course, such reasons would have to be taken into account at some point in a complete justification for morality, but the method of integrating such reasons into a complete justification of morality would simply parallel the method already used for integrating self-interested and altruistic reasons.

14. This is because, as I shall argue, morality itself already represents a compromise between egoism and altruism. So to ask that moral reasons be weighed against self-interested reasons is, in effect, to count self-interested reasons twice—once in the compromise between egoism and altruism and then again when moral reasons are weighed against self-interested reasons. But to count self-interested reasons twice is clearly objectionable.

15. Assume that all these methods of waste disposal have roughly the same amount of beneficial effects on the interests of others.

16. For further argument, see my article, "Justifying Morality: The Right and the Wrong Ways," (Kurt Baier Festschift) *Syntheses* (1987), vol. 1, pp. 45–70.

The Distribution of Income and Wealth

Introduction

Basic Concepts

The problem of the distribution of income and wealth within a society has traditionally been referred to as the problem of distributive justice. Less frequently, this problem has been taken to include the distribution of other social goods (for example, political freedoms such as freedom of speech and freedom of the press), and at times it has been expanded to embrace distribution on a worldwide scale. Most philosophers, however, tend to agree that the distribution of income and wealth within a specific society is at the heart of the problem of distributive justice.

Just as traditionally, a variety of solutions have been proposed to the problem of distributive justice. Before examining some of these solutions, let's observe what they all have in common.

First, even though the solutions may differ as to exactly how much income and wealth people deserve or should rightfully possess, they all purport to tell us what people deserve or what they have a right to possess. For example, some solutions propose that people deserve to have their needs fulfilled, whereas others state that what people deserve or should rightfully possess is what they can produce by their labor.

Second, all solutions to the problem of distributive justice distinguish between justice and charity. *Justice* is what we should do as a matter of obligation or duty, whereas *charity* is what we should do if we want to choose the morally best possible action available to us. Accordingly, the demands of charity go beyond duty. In addition, failure to fulfill the demands of justice is blameworthy, violates someone's rights, and can legitimately be punished. By contrast, failure to fulfill the demands of charity, although not ideal, is not blameworthy, does not violate anyone's rights, and cannot legitimately be punished. Some solutions to the problem of distributive justice give more scope to justice and less to charity, whereas others do just the opposite.

Turning from common ground to disputed territory, solutions offered to the problem of distributive justice have appealed to a number of political ideals. In our times, libertarians have appealed to an ideal of liberty, socialists to an ideal of equality, and welfare liberals to an ideal of contractual fairness.

Libertarianism

Libertarians such as John Hospers (see Selection 1) take liberty as the ultimate political ideal and typically define liberty as "the state of being unconstrained by other persons from doing what one wants." This definition limits the scope of liberty in two ways. First, not all constraints, whatever the source, count as a restriction of liberty; the constraints must come from other persons. For example, people who are constrained by natural forces from getting to the top of Mount Everest do not lack liberty in this regard. Second, the constraints must run counter to people's wants. Thus, people who do not want to hear Beethoven's Fifth Symphony do not feel their liberty is restricted when other people forbid its performance, even though the proscription does in fact constrain what they are able to do.

Of course, libertarians may argue that these constraints do restrict a person's liberty because people normally want to be unconstrained by others. But other philosophers have claimed that such constraints point to a serious defect in the libertarian's definition of liberty, which can only be remedied by defining liberty more broadly as "the state of being unconstrained by other persons from doing what one is able to do." If we apply this revised definition to the previous example, we find that people's liberty to hear Beethoven's Fifth Symphony would be restricted even if they did not want to hear it (and even if, perchance, they did not want to be unconstrained by others) because other people would still be constraining them from doing what they are able to do.

Confident that problems of defining liberty can be overcome in some satisfactory manner, libertarians go on to characterize their political ideal as requiring that each person should have the greatest amount of liberty commensurate with the same liberty for all. From this ideal, libertarians claim that a number of more specific requirements—in particular, a right to life; a right to freedom of speech, press, and assembly; and a right to property—can be derived.

It is important to note that the libertarian's right to life is not a right to receive from others the goods and resources necessary for preserving one's life; it is simply a right not to be killed. So understood, the right to life is not a right to welfare. In fact, there are no welfare rights in the libertarian view. Accordingly, the libertarian's understanding of the right to property is not a right to receive from others the goods and resources necessary for one's welfare, but rather a right to acquire goods and resources either by initial acquisition or by voluntary agreement.

Obviously, by defending rights such as these, libertarians can only support a limited role for government. That role is simply to prevent and punish initial acts of coercion—the only wrongful actions for libertarians.

Libertarians do not deny that it is a good thing for people to have sufficient goods and resources to meet at least their basic nutritional needs, but libertarians do deny that government has a duty to provide for such needs. Some good things, such as the provision of welfare to the needy, are requirements of charity rather than justice, libertarians claim. Accordingly, failure to make such provisions is neither blameworthy nor punishable.

A basic difficulty with the libertarian's solution to the problem of distributive justice as defended by Hospers is the claim that rights to life and property (as the libertarian understands these rights) derive from an ideal of liberty. Why should we think that an ideal of liberty requires a right to life and a right to property that excludes a right to welfare? Surely it would seem that a right to property (as the libertarian understands it) might well justify a rich person's depriving a poor person of the liberty to acquire the goods and resources necessary for meeting his or her basic nutritional needs. How then could we appeal to an ideal of liberty to justify such a deprivation? In Selection 4, James P. Sterba argues that we cannot do so.

Socialist Justice

In contrast with libertarians, socialists take equality to be the ultimate political ideal and contend that the fundamental rights and duties in a society are determined by the ideal of equality. More specifically, socialists defend an ideal that calls for equality of need fulfillment. As Kai Nielson contends (Selection 2), radical egalitarianism is justified because it produces the conditions for the most extensive satisfaction of the needs of everyone.

At first hearing, this ideal might sound simply crazy to someone brought up in a capitalist society. The obvious problem is how to get persons to put forth their best effort if income will be distributed on the basis of individual need rather than individual contribution.

The socialist answer is to make the work that must be done enjoyable in itself, as much as is possible. As a result, people will want to do the work they are capable of doing because they find it intrinsically rewarding. For a start, socialists might try to convince workers to accept lower salaries for presently existing jobs that are intrinsically rewarding. For example, they might ask top executives to work for $300,000 a year rather than $600,000. Yet socialists ultimately hope to make all jobs intrinsically as rewarding as possible so that, after people are no longer working primarily for external rewards when making their best contributions to society, distribution can proceed on the basis of need.

Socialists propose to implement their ideal of equality by giving workers democratic control over the workplace. They believe that if workers have more to say about how they do their work, they will find their work intrinsically more rewarding. As a consequence, they will be more motivated to work, because their work itself will be meeting their needs. Socialists believe that extending democracy to the workplace will necessarily lead to socialization of the means of production and the end of private property.

However, even with democratic control of the workplace, some jobs, such as collecting garbage or changing bedpans, probably can't be made intrinsically rewarding. Now what socialists propose to do with respect to such jobs is to divide them up in some equitable manner. Some people might, for example, collect garbage one day a week and then work at intrinsically rewarding jobs for the rest of the week. Others would change bedpans or do some other slop job one day a week and then work at an intrinsically rewarding job the other days of the week. By making jobs intrinsically as rewarding as possible, in part through democratic control of the workplace and an equitable assignment of unrewarding tasks, socialists believe people will contribute according to their ability even when distribution proceeds according to need.

Finally, it is important to note that the socialist ideal of equality does not accord with what existed in the Soviet Union or Eastern Europe under Communism. Judging the acceptability of the socialist ideal of equality by what took place in those countries would be as unfair as judging the acceptability of the libertarian ideal of liberty by what took place in Chile under Pinochet or South Africa under apartheid, where citizens were arrested and imprisoned without cause. By analogy, it would be like judging the merits of college football by the way Vanderbilt's or Northwestern's teams play rather than by the way Miami's or Notre Dame's teams play. Actually, a fairer comparison would be to judge the socialist ideal of equality by what takes place in countries like Sweden and to judge the libertarian ideal of liberty by what takes place in the United States. Even these comparisons, however, are not wholly appropriate because none of these countries fully conforms to those ideals.

To justify the ideal of equality, Kai Nielson argues that it is required by liberty or at least by a fair distribution of liberty. By "liberty" Nielson means both "positive liberty to receive certain goods" and "negative liberty not to be interfered with," so his argument from liberty will not have much weight with libertarians, who only value negative liberty. Rather, his argument is directed primarily at welfare liberals, who value both positive and negative liberty as well as a fair distribution of liberty.

Another basic difficulty with Nielson's socialist solution to the problem of distributive justice concerns the proclaimed necessity of abolishing private property and socializing the means of production. It seems perfectly possible to give workers more control over their workplace while at the same time allowing the means of production to remain privately owned. Of course, private ownership would have a somewhat different character in a society with democratic control of the workplace, but it need not cease to be private ownership. After all, private ownership would also have a somewhat different character in a society where private holdings, and hence bargaining power, were distributed more equally than is found in most capitalist societies, yet it would not cease to be private ownership. Accordingly, we could imagine a society where the means of production are privately owned but where —because ownership is so widely dispersed throughout the society (e.g., nearly everyone owns 10 shares of major industrial stock and no one more than 20 shares) and because of the degree of democratic control of the workplace—many of the valid criticisms socialists make of existing capitalist societies would no longer apply.

Welfare Liberalism

In contrast with libertarians and socialists, welfare liberals, such as John Rawls (Selection 3), take contractual fairness to be the ultimate political ideal and contend that the fundamental rights and duties in a society are those that people would agree to under fair conditions.

Note that welfare liberals do not say that the fundamental rights and duties in a society are those to which people actually do agree, because these might not be fair at all. For example, people might agree to a certain system of fundamental rights and duties only because they have been forced to do so or because their only alternative is starving to death. Thus, actual agreement is not sufficient, nor is it even necessary, for determining an adequate conception of justice. According to welfare liberals, what is necessary and sufficient is that people would agree to such rights and duties under fair conditions.

But what are fair conditions? According to John Rawls, fair conditions can be expressed by an "original position" in which people are concerned to advance their own interests behind a "veil of ignorance." The effect of the veil of ignorance is to deprive people in the original position of the knowledge they would need to advance their own interests in ways that are morally arbitrary.

Rawls presents the principles of justice he believes would be derived in the original position in two successive formulations. The first formulation is as follows:

I. Special conception of justice
　1. Each person is to have an equal right to the most extensive basic liberty compatible with a similar liberty for others.
　2. Social and economic inequalities are to be arranged so that they are (a) reasonably expected to be to everyone's advantage and (b) attached to positions and offices open to all.
II. General conception of justice
　All social values—liberty and opportunity, income and wealth, and the bases of self-respect—are to be distributed equally unless an unequal distribution of any or all of these values is to everyone's advantage.

Later these principles are more accurately formulated as:

I. Special conception of justice
　1. Each person is to have an equal right to the most extensive total system of equal basic liberties compatible with a similar system of liberty for all.
　2. Social and economic inequalities are to be arranged so that they are (a) to the greatest benefit of the least advantaged, consistent with the just savings principle, and (b) attached to offices and positions open to all under conditions of fair equality of opportunity.
II. General conception of justice
　All social goods—liberty and opportunity, income and wealth, and the bases of self-respect—are to be distributed equally unless an unequal distribution of any or all of these goods is to the advantage of the least favored.

Under both formulations, the general conception of justice differs from the special conception of justice by allowing trade-offs between liberty and other social goods. According to Rawls, persons in the original position would want the special conception of justice to be applied in place of the general conception of justice whenever social conditions allowed all representative persons to exercise their basic liberties.

Rawls holds that these principles of justice would be chosen in the original position because persons so situated would find it reasonable to follow the conservative dictates of a "maximin strategy" and thereby secure for themselves the highest minimum payoff.

Rawls's defense of a welfare liberal conception of justice has been challenged in a variety of ways. Some critics have endorsed Rawls's contractual approach while disagreeing with Rawls over what principles of justice would be derived thereby. These critics usually attempt to undermine the use of a maximin strategy in the original position.[1] Other critics, however, have found fault with the contractual approach itself. Libertarians, for example, have challenged the moral adequacy of the very ideal of contractual fairness.

This second challenge to the ideal of contractual fairness is potentially the more damaging because, if valid, it would force supporters to embrace some other political ideal. This challenge, however, fails if it can be shown, as James P. Sterba argues in Selection 4, that the libertarian's own ideal of liberty, when correctly interpreted, leads to a universal right to welfare usually associated with the welfare liberal's ideal of contractual fairness. But Sterba's argument also raises a problem for the welfare liberal because he shows that recognition of this universal right to welfare leads to the equalization of resources that is characteristic of a socialist state.

Practical Applications

The application of the ideals of libertarianism, socialism, or welfare liberalism to a particular society obviously has basic and far-reaching effects. These ideals have implications for constitutional structure, the control of industry, taxing policy, social welfare programs, property law, and much more. The next two readings in this section are from important United

States Supreme Court decisions to which our three political ideals can be usefully related.

The U.S. Supreme Court, of course, does not view itself as directly applying one or the other of these political ideals to the laws of the land. Rather the Court views itself as deciding whether particular laws accord with the provisions of the United States Constitution. However, most people, including Supreme Court justices, do not clearly separate their views about what are the practical applications of the political ideal they take to be the most morally defensible from their views about what sort of laws accord with the U.S. Constitution. Hence, it is frequently possible to see how commitment to a political ideal is decisive in judicial decision making.

Beyond coming to appreciate how political ideals and their presumed applications function in judicial decision making, it is important that you examine U.S. Supreme Court decisions to determine to what degree the laws of your society accord with the political ideal you take to be the most morally defensible. For you to have good reasons to believe that you are a just and moral person, you need to assess to what degree the laws and institutions of your society are just—in this case, to what degree they accord with the requirements of distributive justice. Examining the two U.S. Supreme Court decisions included in this anthology should serve this purpose well.

In the first decision *(Wyman v. James)*, the majority of the Court decided that the rights of welfare recipients are limited in various ways and in particular that recipients are not protected against mandatory visits by caseworkers. Such a decision would surely seem justified if one believed, as libertarians do, that the provision of welfare is, at best, only a requirement of charity. Welfare liberals and socialists, however, would have difficulty accepting this decision, as did the dissenting justices of the Court.

In the second decision *(Plyler v. Doe)*, the majority of the Court determined that although public education is not a right, it still cannot be denied to the children of illegal aliens because of the pivotal role of education in sustaining our political and cultural heritage. This decision has some affinity with the way welfare liberals and socialists would understand the practical requirements of their ideals; libertarians would probably find themselves persuaded by the arguments of the dissenting justices.

It is important to notice that you can also work backward from your considered judgments about these Supreme Court cases to the political ideal you should favor. Frequently, only by considering the practical applications of alternative political ideals can we clarify our views about which ideal is the most morally defensible.

In the final reading in this section, Peter Marin (Selection 7) paints a vivid picture of the homeless in the United States and asks the relevant question, "What does a society owe its members in trouble, and how is that debt to be paid?" Surely, at least one of our three political ideals must have an adequate answer.

Notice, too, that any fully adequate solution to the problem of distributive justice within a society presupposes a solution to the other moral problems presented in this anthology. In particular, the problem of near distant peoples, which is discussed in the following section, seems to be clearly connected with the problem of distributive justice. We cannot know for sure what resources particular persons within a society should receive unless we also know what obligations persons within that society have to distant peoples.

Note

1. See, for example, my article, "Distributive Justice," *American Journal of Jurisprudence* (1977), pp. 55–79, and John C. Harsanyi, *Essays on Ethics, Social Behavior, and Scientific Explanation* (Boston: D. Reidel Publishing Co., 1976), pp. 37–85.

1. The Libertarian Manifesto

John Hospers

John Hospers explores various ways of understanding the basic libertarian thesis that every person is the owner of his or her own life. According to Hospers, such ownership entails rights to life, liberty, and property. Since these rights are violated by an initial use of force, the proper role of government is said to be limited to the retaliatory use of force against those who have initiated its use. All other possible roles for government, such as protecting individuals against themselves or requiring people to help one another, are regarded as illegitimate by the libertarian.

The political philosophy that is called libertarianism (from the Latin *libertas,* liberty) is the doctrine that every person is the owner of his own life, and that no one is the owner of anyone else's life: and that consequently every human being has the right to act in accordance with his own choices, unless those actions infringe on the equal liberty of other human beings to act in accordance with their choices.

There are several other ways of stating the same libertarian thesis:

1. *No one is anyone else's master, and no one is anyone else's slave.* Since I am the one to decide how my life is to be conducted just as you decide about yours, I have no right (even if I had the power) to make you my slave and be your master, nor have you the right to become the master by enslaving me. Slavery is *forced* servitude, and since no one owns the life of anyone else, no one has the right to enslave another. Political theories past and present have traditionally been concerned with who should be the master (usually the king, the dictator, or government bureaucracy) and who should be the slaves, and what the extent of the slavery should be. Libertarianism holds that no one has the right to use force to enslave the life of another, or any portion or aspect of that life.

From "What Libertarianism Is," in *The Libertarian Alternative* edited by Tibor Machan (1974). Reprinted by permission of the author, the editor, and Nelson-Hall Inc.

2. *Other men's lives are not yours to dispose of.* I enjoy seeing operas; but operas are expensive to produce. Opera-lovers often say, "The state (or the city, etc.) should subsidize opera, so that we can all see it. Also it would be for people's betterment, cultural benefit, etc." But what they are advocating is nothing more or less than legalized plunder. They can't pay for the productions themselves, and yet they want to see opera, which involves a large number of people and their labor; so what they are saying in effect is, "Get the money through legalized force. Take a little bit more out of every worker's paycheck every week to pay for the operas we want to see." But I have no right to take by force from the workers' pockets to pay for what I want.

Perhaps it would be better if he *did* go to see opera—then I should try to convince him to go voluntarily. But to take the money from him forcibly, because in my opinion it would be good for *him,* is still seizure of his earnings, which is plunder.

Besides, if I have the right to force him to help pay for my pet projects, hasn't he equally the right to force me to help pay for his? Perhaps he in turn wants the government to subsidize rock-and-roll, or his new car, or a house in the country? If I have the right to milk him, why hasn't he the right to milk me? If I can be a moral cannibal, why can't he too?

We should beware of the inventors of utopias. They would remake the world according to their vision—with the lives and fruits of the labor of *other* human beings. Is it someone's utopian vision that others should build pyramids to beautify the landscape? Very well, then other men should provide the labor; and if he is in a position of political power, and he can't get men to do it voluntarily, then he must *compel* them to "cooperate"—i.e., he must enslave them.

A hundred men might gain great pleasure from beating up or killing just one insignificant human being; but other men's lives are not theirs to dispose of. "In order to achieve the worthy goals of the next five-year-plan, we must forcibly collectivize the peasants . . ."; but other men's lives are not theirs to dispose of. Do you want to occupy, rent-free, the mansion that another man has worked for twenty years to buy? But other men's lives are not yours to dispose of. Do you want operas so badly that everyone is forced to work harder to pay for their subsidization through taxes? But other men's lives are not yours to dispose of. Do you want to have free medical care at the expense of other people, whether they wish to provide it or not? But this would require them to work longer for you whether they want to or not, and other men's lives are not yours to dispose of. . . .

3. *No human being should be a nonvoluntary mortgage on the life of another.* I cannot claim your life, your work, or the products of your effort as mine. The fruit of one man's labor should not be fair game for every freeloader who comes along and demands it as his own. The orchard that has been carefully grown, nurtured, and harvested by its owner should not be ripe for the plucking for any bypasser who has a yen for the ripe fruit. The wealth that some men have produced should not be fair game for looting by government, to be used for whatever purposes its representatives determine, no matter what their motives in so doing may be. The theft of your money by a robber is not justified by the fact that he used it to help his injured mother.

It will already be evident that libertarian doctrine is embedded in a view of the rights of man. Each human being has the right to live his life as he chooses, compatibly with the equal right of all other human beings to live their lives as they choose.

All man's rights are implicit in the above statement. Each man has the right to life: any attempt by others to take it away from him, or even to injure him, violates this right, through the use of coercion against him. Each man has the right to liberty: to conduct his life in accordance with the alternatives open to him without coercive action by others. And every man has the right to property: to work to sustain his life (and the lives of whichever others he chooses to sustain, such as his family) and to retain the fruits of his labor.

People often defend the rights of life and liberty but denigrate property rights, and yet the right to property is as basic as the other two: indeed, without property rights no other rights are possible. Depriving you of property is depriving you of the means by which you live. . . .

I have no right to decide how *you* should spend your time or your money. I can make that decision for myself, but not for you, my neighbor. I may deplore your choice of lifestyle, and I may talk with you about it provided you are willing to listen to me. But I have no right to use force to change it. Nor have I the right to decide how you should spend the money you have earned. I may appeal to you to give it to the Red Cross, and you may prefer to go to prize-fights. But that is your decision, and however much I may chafe about it I do not have the right to interfere forcibly with it, for example by robbing you in order to use the money in accordance with *my* choices. (If I have the right to rob you, have you also the right to rob me?)

When I claim a right, I carve out a niche, as it were, in my life, saying in effect, "This activity I must be able to perform without interference from others. For you and everyone else, this is off limits." And so I put up a "no trespassing" sign, which marks off the area of my right. Each individual's right is his "no trespassing" sign in relation to me and others. I may not encroach upon his domain any more than he upon mine, without my consent. Every right entails a duty, true—but the duty is only that of *forbearance*—that is, of *refraining* from violating the other person's right. If you have a right to life, I have no right to take your life; if you have a right to the products of your labor (property), I have no right to take it from you without your consent. The nonviolation of these rights will not guarantee you protection against natural catastrophes such as floods and earthquakes, but it will protect you against the aggressive activities *of other men.* And rights, after all, have to do with one's relations to other human beings, not with one's relations to physical nature.

Nor were these rights created by government; governments—some governments, obviously not all—*recognize* and *protect* the rights that individuals already have. Governments regularly forbid homicide and theft; and, at a more advanced stage, protect individuals against such things as libel and breach of contract. . . .

The *right to property* is the most misunderstood and unappreciated of human rights, and it is one most constantly violated by governments. "Property" of course does not mean only real estate; it includes anything you can call your own—your clothing, your car, your jewelry, your books and papers.

The right of property is not the right to just *take* it from others, for this would interfere with *their* property rights. It is rather the right to work for it, to obtain non-coercively, the money or services which you can present in voluntary exchange.

The right to property is consistently underplayed by intellectuals today, sometimes even frowned upon, as if we should feel guilty for upholding such a right in view of all the poverty in the world. But the right to property is absolutely basic. It is your hedge against the future. It is your assurance that what you have worked to earn will still be there and be yours, when you wish or need to use it, especially when you are too old to work any longer.

Government has always been the chief enemy of the right to property. The officials of government, wishing to increase their power, and finding an increase of wealth an effective way to bring this about, seize some or all of what a person has earned—and since government has a monopoly of physical force within the geographical area of the nation, it has the power (but not the right) to do this. When this happens, of course, every citizen of that country is insecure: he knows that no matter how

hard he works the government can swoop down on him at any time and confiscate his earnings and possessions. A person sees his life savings wiped out in a moment when the tax-collectors descend to deprive him of the fruits of his work; or, an industry which has been fifty years in the making and cost millions of dollars and millions of hours of time and planning, is nationalized overnight. Or the government, via inflation, cheapens the currency, so that hard-won dollars aren't worth anything any more. The effect of such actions, of course, is that people lose hope and incentive: if no matter how hard they work the government agents can take it all away, why bother to work at all, for more than today's needs? Depriving people of property is *depriving them of the means by which they live*—the freedom of the individual citizen to do what he wishes with his own life and to plan for the future. Indeed only if property rights are respected is there any point to planning for the future and working to achieve one's goals. *Property rights are what makes long-range planning possible*—the kind of planning which is a distinctively human endeavor, as opposed to the day-by-day activity of the lion who hunts, who depends on the supply of game tomorrow but has no real insurance against starvation in a day or a week. Without the right to property, the right to life itself amounts to little: how can you sustain your life if you cannot plan ahead? and how can you plan ahead if the fruits of your labor can at any moment be confiscated by government? . . .

Indeed, the right to property may well be considered second only to the right to life. Even the freedom of speech is limited by considerations of property. If a person visiting in your home behaves in a way undesired by you, you have every right to evict him; he can scream or agitate elsewhere if he wishes, but not in your home without your consent. Does a person have a right to shout obscenities in a cathedral? No, for the owners of the cathedral (presumably the Church) have not allowed others on their property for that purpose; one may go there to worship or to visit, but not just for any purpose one wishes. Their property right is prior to your or my wish to scream or expectorate or write graffiti on their building.

Or, to take the stock example, does a person have a right to shout "Fire!" falsely in a crowded theater? No, for the theater owner has permitted others to enter and use his property only for a specific purpose, that of seeing a film or watching a stage show. If a person heckles or otherwise disturbs other members of the audience, he can be thrown out. (In fact, he can be removed for any reason the owner chooses, provided his admission money is returned.) And if he shouts "Fire!" when there is no fire, he may be endangering other lives by causing a panic or a stampede. The right to free speech doesn't give one the right to say anything anywhere; it is circumscribed by property rights.

Again, some people seem to assume that the right to free speech (including written speech) means that they can go to a newspaper publisher and demand that he print in his newspaper some propaganda or policy statement for their political party (or other group). But of course they have no right to the use of his newspaper. Ownership of the newspaper is the product of his labor, and he has a right to put into his newspaper whatever he wants, for whatever reason. If he excludes material which many readers would like to have in, perhaps they can find it in another newspaper or persuade him to print it himself (if there are enough of them, they will usually do just that). Perhaps they can even cause his newspaper to fail. But as long as he owns it, he has the right to put in it what he wishes; what would a property right be if he could not do this? They have no right to place their material in his newspaper without his consent—not for free, nor even for a fee. Perhaps other newspapers will include it, or perhaps they can start their own newspaper (in which case they have a right to put in it what they like). If not, an option open to them would be to mimeograph and distribute some handbills.

In exactly the same way, no one has a right to "free television time" unless the owner of the television station consents to give it; it is his station, he has the property rights over it, and it is for him to decide how to dispose of his time. He may not decide wisely, but it is his right to decide as he wishes. If he makes enough unwise decisions, and courts enough unpopularity with the viewing public or the sponsors, he may have to go out of business; but as he is free to make his own decisions, so is he free to face their consequences. (If the government owns the television station, then government officials will make the decisions, and there is no guarantee of *their* superior wisdom. The difference is that when "the government" owns the station, you are forced to help pay for its upkeep through your taxes, whether the bureaucrat in charge decides to give you television time or not.)

"But why have *individual* property rights? Why not have lands and houses owned by everybody together?" Yes, this involves no violation of individual rights, as long as everybody consents to this arrangement and no one is forced to join it. The parties to it may enjoy the communal living enough (at least for a time) to overcome certain inevitable problems: that some will work and some not, that some will achieve more in an hour than others can do in a day, and still they will all get the same income. The few who do the most will in the end consider themselves "workhorses" who do the work of two or three or twelve, while the others will be "freeloaders" on the efforts of these few. But as long as they can get out of the arrangement if they no longer like it, no violation of rights is involved. They got in voluntarily, and they can get out voluntarily; no one has used force.

"But why not say that everybody owns everything? That we *all* own everything there is?"

To some this may have a pleasant ring—but let us try to analyze what it means. If everybody owns everything, then everyone has an equal right to go everywhere, do what he pleases, take what he likes, destroy if he wishes, grow crops or burn them, trample them under, and so on. Consider what it would be like in practice. Suppose you have saved money to buy a house for yourself and your family. Now suppose that the principle, "everybody owns everything," becomes adopted. Well then, why shouldn't every itinerant hippie just come in and take over, sleeping in your beds and eating in your kitchen and not bothering to replace the food supply or clean up the mess? After all, it belongs to all of us, doesn't it? So we have just as much right to it as you, the buyer, have. What happens if we *all* want to sleep in the bedroom and there's not room for all of us? Is it the strongest who wins?

What would be the result? Since no one would be responsible for anything, the property would soon be destroyed, the food used up, the facilities nonfunctional. Beginning as a house that *one* family could use, it would end up as a house that *no one* could use. And if the principle continued to be adopted, no one would build houses any more—or anything else. What for? They would only be occupied and used by others, without remuneration.

Suppose two men are cast ashore on an island, and they agree that each will cultivate half of it. The first man is industrious and grows crops and builds a shelter, making the most of the situation with which he is confronted. The second man, perhaps thinking that the warm days will last forever, lies in the sun, picks coconuts while they last, and does a minimum of work to sustain himself. At the time of harvest, the second man has nothing to harvest, nor does he assist the first man in his labors. But later when there is a dearth of food on the island, the second man comes to the first man and demands half of the harvest as his right. But of course he has no right to the product of the first man's labors. The first man may freely choose to give part of his harvest to the second out of charity rather than see him starve; but that is just what it is— charity, not the second man's right.

How can any of man's rights be violated? Ultimately, only by the use of force. I can make suggestions to you, I can reason with you, entreat you (if you are willing to listen), but I cannot *force* you without violating your rights; only by forcing you do I cut the cord between your free decisions and your actions. Voluntary relations between individuals involve no deprivation of rights, but murder, assault, and rape do, because in doing these things I make you the unwilling victim of my actions. A man's beating his wife involves no violation of rights if she *wanted* to be beaten. *Force is behavior that requires the unwilling involvement of other persons.*

Thus the use of force need not involve the use of physical violence. If I trespass on your property or dump garbage on it, I am violating your property rights, as indeed I am when I steal your watch; although this is not force in the sense of violence, it *is* a case of your being an unwilling victim of my action. Similarly, if you shout at me so that I cannot be heard when I try to speak, or blow a siren in my ear, or start a factory next door which pollutes my land, you are again violating my rights (to free speech, to property); I am, again, an unwilling victim of your actions. Similarly, if you steal a manuscript of mine and publish it as your own, you are confiscating a piece of my property and thus violating my right to keep what is the product of my labor. Of course, if I give you the manuscript with permission to sign your name to it and keep the proceeds, no violation of rights is involved—any more than if I give you permission to dump garbage on my yard.

According to libertarianism, the role of government should be limited to the retaliatory use of force against those who have initiated its use. It should not enter into any other areas, such as religion, social organization, and economics.

Government

Government is the most dangerous institution known to man. Throughout history it has violated the rights of men more than any individual or group of individuals could do: it has killed people, enslaved them, sent them to forced labor and concentration camps, and regularly robbed and pillaged them of the fruits of their expended labor. Unlike individual criminals, government has the power to arrest and try; unlike individual criminals, it can surround and encompass a person totally, dominating every aspect of one's life, so that one has no recourse from it but to leave the country (and in totalitarian nations even that is prohibited). Government throughout history has a much sorrier record than any individual, even that of a ruthless mass murderer. The signs we see on bumper stickers are chillingly accurate: "Beware: the Government Is Armed and Dangerous."

The only proper role of government, according to libertarians, is that of the protector of the citizen against aggression by other individuals. The government, of course, should never initiate aggression; its proper role is as the embodiment of the *retaliatory* use of force against anyone who initiates its use.

If each individual had constantly to defend himself against possible aggressors, he would have to spend a considerable portion of his life in target practice, karate exercises, and other means of self-defenses, and even so he would probably be helpless against groups of individuals who might try to kill, maim, or rob him. He would have little time for cultivating those qualities which are essential to civilized life, nor would improvements in science, medicine, and the arts be likely to occur. The function of government is to take this responsibility off his shoulders: the government undertakes to defend him against aggressors and to punish them if they attack him. When the government is effective in doing this, it enables the citizen to go about his business unmolested and without constant fear for his life. To do this, of course, government must have physical power—the police, to protect the citizen from aggression within its borders, and the armed forces, to protect him from aggressors outside. Beyond that, the government should not intrude upon his life, either to run his business, or adjust his daily activities, or prescribe his personal moral code.

Government, then, undertakes to be the individual's protector; but historically governments have gone far beyond this function. Since they already have the physical power, they have not hesitated to use it for purposes far beyond that which was entrusted to them in the first place. Undertaking initially to protect its citizens against aggression, it has often itself become an aggressor—a far greater aggressor, indeed, than the criminals against whom it was supposed to protect its citizens. Governments have done what no private citizen can do: arrest and imprison individuals without a trial and send them to slave labor camps. Government must have power in order to be effective—and yet the very means by which alone it can be effective make it vulnerable to the abuse of power, leading to managing the lives of individuals and even inflicting terror upon them.

What then should be the function of government? In a word, the *protection of human rights*.

1. *The right to life:* libertarians support all such legislation as will protect human beings against the use of force by others, for example, laws against killing, attempting killing, maiming, beating, and all kinds of physical violence.
2. *The right to liberty:* there should be no laws compromising in any way freedom of speech, of the press, and peaceable assembly. There should be no censorship of ideas, books, films, or of anything else by government.
3. *The right to property:* libertarians support legislation that protects the property rights of individuals against confiscation, nationalization, eminent domain, robbery, trespass, fraud and misrepresentation, patent and copyright, libel and slander.

Someone has violently assaulted you. Should he be legally liable? Of course. He has violated one of your rights. He has knowingly injured you and since he has initiated aggression against you he should be made to expiate.

Someone has negligently left his bicycle on the sidewalk where you trip over it in the dark and injure yourself. He didn't do it intentionally; he didn't mean you any harm. Should he be legally liable? Of course; he has, however unwittingly, injured you, and since the injury is caused by him and you are the victim, he should pay.

Someone across the street is unemployed. Should you be taxed extra to pay for his expenses? Not at all. You have not injured him, you are not responsible for the fact that he is unemployed (unless you are a senator or bureaucrat who agitated for further curtailing of business, which legislation passed, with the result that your neighbor was laid off by the curtailed business). You may voluntarily wish to help him out, or better still, try to get him a job to put him on his feet again; but since you have initiated no aggressive act against him, and neither purposely nor accidentally injured him in any way, you should not be legally penalized for the fact of his unemployment. (Actually, it is just such penalties that increase unemployment.)

One man, A, works hard for years and finally earns a high salary as a professional man. A second man, B, prefers not to work at all, and to spend wastefully what money he has (through inheritance), so that after a year or two he has nothing left. At the end of this time he has a long siege of illness and lots of medical bills to pay. He demands that the bills be paid by the government—that is, by the taxpayers of the land, including Mr. A.

But of course B has no such right. He chose to lead his life in a certain way—that was his voluntary decision. One consequence of that choice is that he must depend on charity in case of later need. Mr. A chose not to live that way. (And if everyone lived like Mr. B, on whom would he depend in case of later need?) Each has a right to live in the way he pleases, but each must live with the consequences of his own decision (which, as always, fall primarily on himself). He cannot, in time of need, claim A's beneficence as his right.

If a house-guest of yours starts to carve his initials in your walls and break up your furniture, you have a right to evict him and call the police if he makes trouble. If someone starts to destroy the machinery in a factory, the factory-owner is also entitled to evict him and call the police. In both cases, persons other than the owner are permitted on the property only under certain conditions, at the pleasure of the owner. If those conditions are violated, the owner is entitled to use force to set things straight. The case is exactly the same on a college or university campus: if a campus demonstrator starts breaking windows, occupying the president's office, and setting fire to a dean, the college authorities are certainly within their rights to evict him forcibly; one is permitted on the college grounds only under specific conditions, set by the administration: study, peaceful student activity, even political activity if those in charge choose to permit it. If they do not choose to permit peaceful political activity on campus, they may be unwise, since a campus is after all a place where all sides of every issue should get discussed, and the college that doesn't permit this may soon lose its reputation and its students. All the same, the college official who does not permit it is quite within his rights; the students do not own the campus, nor do the hired trouble-makers imported from elsewhere. In the case of a privately owned college, the owners, or whoever they have delegated to administer it, have the right to make the decisions as to who shall be permitted on the campus and under what conditions. In the case of a state university or college, the ownership problem is more complex: one could say that the "government" owns the campus or that "the people" do since they are the taxpayers who support it; but in either case, the university administration has the delegated task of keeping order, and until they are removed by the state administration or the taxpayers, it is theirs to decide who shall be permitted on campus, and what nonacademic activities will be permitted to their students on the premises.

Property rights can be violated by physical trespass, of course, or by anyone entering on your property for any reason without your consent. (If you *do* consent to having your neighbor dump garbage on your yard, there is no violation of your rights.) But the physical trespass of a person is only a special case of violation of property rights. Property rights can be violated by sound-waves, in the form of a loud noise, or the sounds of your neighbor's hi-fi set while you are trying to sleep. Such violations of property rights are of course the subject of action in the courts.

But there is another violation of property rights that has not thus far been honored by the courts; this has to do with the effects of *pollution* of the atmosphere.

From the beginnings of modern air pollution, the courts made a conscious decision not to protect, for example, the orchards of farmers from the smoke of nearby factories or locomotives. They said, in effect, to the farmers: yes, your private property is being invaded by this smoke, but we hold that "public policy" is more important than private property, and public policy holds factories and locomotives to be good things. These goods were allowed to override the defense of property rights—with our consequent headlong rush into pollution disaster. The remedy is both "radical" and crystal clear, and it has nothing to do with multibillion dollar palliative programs at the expense of the taxpayers which do not even meet the real issue. The remedy is simply to enjoin anyone from injecting pollutants into the air, and thereby invading the rights of persons and property. Period. The argument that such an injunction prohibition would add to the costs of industrial production is as reprehensible as the pre–Civil War argument that the abolition of slavery would add to the costs of growing cotton, and therefore should not take place. For this means that the polluters are able to impose the high costs of pollution upon those whose property rights they are allowed to invade with impunity.[1]

What about automobiles, the chief polluters of the air? One can hardly sue every automobile owner. But one can sue the manufacturers of automobiles who do not install anti-smog devices on the cars which they distribute—and later (though this is more difficult), owners of individual automobiles if they discard the equipment or do not keep it functional.

The violation of rights does not apply only to air-pollution. If someone with a factory upstream on a river pollutes the river, anyone living downstream from him, finding his water polluted, should be able to sue the owner of the factory. In this way the price of adding the anti-pollutant devices will be the owner's responsibility, and will probably be added to the cost of the products which the factory produces and thus spread around among all consumers, rather than the entire cost being borne by the users of the river in the form of polluted water, with the consequent impossibility of fishing, swimming, and so on. In each case, pollution would be stopped at the source rather than having its ill effects spread around to numerous members of the population.

What about property which you do not work to earn, but which you *inherit* from someone else? Do you have a right to that? You have no right to it until someone decides to give it to you. Consider the man who willed it to you; it was his, he had the right to use and dispose of it as *he* saw fit; and if he decided to give it to you, this is a windfall for you, but it was only the exercise of *his* right. Had the property been seized by the government at the man's death, or distributed among numerous other people designated by the government, it *would* have been a violation of his rights: for he, who worked to earn and sustain it, would not have been able to dispose of it according to his own judgment. If he doesn't have the right to determine who shall have it, who does?

What about the property status of your intellectual activity, such as inventions you may devise and books you write? These, of course, are your property also; they are the products of your mind; you worked at them, you created them. Prior to that, they did not exist. If you worked five years to write a book, and someone stole it and published it as his own, receiving royalties from its sales, he would have stolen your property just as surely as if he had robbed your home. The same is true if someone used and sold without your permission an invention which was the product of your labor and ingenuity.

The role of government with respect to this issue, at least most governments of the Western world, is a proper one: government protects the products of your labor from the moment they materialize. Copyright law protects your writings from piracy. In the United States, one's writings are protected for a period of twenty-seven years, and another twenty-seven if one applies for renewal of the copyright. In most other countries, they are protected for a period of fifty years after the author's death, permitting both himself and his surviving heirs to reap the fruits of his labor. After that they enter the "public domain"— that is, anyone may reprint them without your or your heirs' permission. Patent law protects your inventions for a limited period, which varies according to the type of invention. In no case are you forced to avail yourself of this protection; you need not apply for patent or copyright coverage if you do not wish to do so. But the protection of your intellectual property is there, in case you wish to use it.

What about the property status of the airwaves? Here the government's position is far more questionable. The government now claims ownership of the airwaves, leasing them to individuals and corporations. The government renews leases or refuses them depending on whether the programs satisfy authorities in the Federal Communications Commission. The official position is that "we all own the airwaves": but since only one party can broadcast on a certain frequency at a certain time without causing chaos, it is simply a fact of reality that "everyone" cannot use it. In fact the government decides who shall use the airwaves and one courts its displeasure only at the price of a revoked license. One can write without government approval, but one cannot use the airwaves without the approval of government.

What policy should have been observed with regard to the airwaves? Much the same as the policy that was followed in the case of the Homestead Act, when the lands of the American West were opening up for settlement. There was a policy of "first come, first served," with the government parcelling out a certain acreage for each individual who wanted to claim the land as his own. There was no charge for the land, but if a man had not used it and built a dwelling during the first two-year period, it was assumed that he was not homesteading and the land was given to the next man in line. The airwaves too could have been given out on a "first come, first served" basis. The first man who used a given frequency would be its owner, and the government would protect him in the use of it against trespassers. If others wanted to use the same frequency, they would have to buy it from the first man, if he was willing to sell, or try to buy another, just as one now does with the land.

Laws may be classified into three types: (1) laws protecting individuals against themselves, such as laws against fornication and other sexual behavior, alcohol, and drugs; (2) laws protecting individuals against aggressions by other individuals, such as laws against murder, robbery, and fraud; (3) laws requiring people to help one another; for example, all laws which rob Peter to pay Paul, such as welfare.

Libertarians reject the first class of laws totally. Behavior which harms no one else is strictly the individual's own affair. Thus, there should be no laws against becoming intoxicated, since whether or not to become intoxicated is the individual's own decision: but there should be laws against driving while intoxicated, since the drunken driver is a threat to every other motorist on the highway (drunken driving falls into type 2). Similarly, there should be no laws against drugs (except the prohibition of sale of drugs to minors) as long as the taking of these drugs poses no threat to anyone else. Drug addiction is a psychological problem to which no present solution exists. Most of the social harm caused by addicts, other than to themselves, is the result of thefts which they perform in order to continue their habit—and then the *legal* crime is the theft, not the addiction. The actual cost of heroin is about ten cents a shot; if it were legalized, the enormous traffic in illegal sale and purchase of it would stop, as well as the accompanying proselytization to get new addicts (to make more money for the pusher) and the thefts performed by addicts who often require eighty dollars a day just to keep up the habit. Addiction would not stop, but the crimes would: it is estimated that 75 percent of the burglaries in New York City today are performed by addicts, and all these crimes could be wiped out at one stroke through the legalization of drugs. (Only when the taking of drugs could be shown to constitute a threat to *others,* should it be prohibited by law. It is only laws protecting people against *themselves* that libertarians oppose.)

Laws should be limited to the second class only: aggression by individuals against other individuals. These are laws whose function is to protect human beings against encroachment by others; and this, as we have seen, is (according to libertarianism) the sole function of government.

Libertarians also reject the third class of laws totally: no one should be forced by law to help others, not even to tell them the time of day if requested, and certainly not to give them a portion of one's weekly paycheck. Governments, in the guise of humanitarianism, have given to some by taking from others (charging a "handling fee" in the process, which, because of the government's waste and inefficiency, sometimes is several hundred percent). And in so doing they have decreased incentive, violated the rights of individuals, and lowered the standard of living of almost everyone.

All such laws constitute what libertarians call *moral cannibalism.* A cannibal in the physical sense is a person who lives off the flesh of other human beings. A *moral* cannibal is one who believes he has a right to live off the "spirit" of other human beings—who believes that he has a moral claim on the productive capacity, time, and effort expended by others.

It has become fashionable to claim virtually everything that one needs or desires as one's *right*. Thus, many people claim that they have a right to a job, the right to free medical care, to free food and clothing, to a decent home, and so on. Now if one asks, apart from any specific context, whether it would be desirable if everyone had these things, one might well say yes. But there is a gimmick attached to each of them: *At whose expense?* Jobs, medical care, education, and so on, don't grow on trees. These are goods and services *produced only by men*. Who then is to provide them, and under what conditions?

If you have a right to a job, who is to supply it? Must an employer supply it even if he doesn't want to hire you? What if you are unemployable, or incurably lazy? (If you say "the government must supply it," does that mean that a job must be created for you which no employer needs done, and that you must be kept in it regardless of how much or little you work?) If the employer is forced to supply it at his expense even if he doesn't need you, then isn't *he* being enslaved to that extent? What ever happened to *his* right to conduct his life and his affairs in accordance with his choices?

If you have a right to free medical care, then, since medical care doesn't exist in nature as wild apples do, some people will have to supply it to you for free: that is, they will have to spend their time and money and energy taking care of you whether they want to or not. What ever happened to *their* right to conduct their lives as they see fit? Or do you have a right to violate theirs? Can there be a right to violate rights?

All those who demand this or that as a "free service" are consciously or unconsciously evading the fact that there is in reality no such thing as free services. All man-made goods and services are the result of human expenditure of time and effort. There is no such thing as "something for nothing" in this world. If you demand something free, you are demanding that other men give their time and effort to you without compensation. If they voluntarily choose to do this, there is no problem; but if you demand that they be *forced* to do it, you are interfering with their right not to do it if they so choose. "Swimming in this pool ought to be free!" says the indignant passerby. What he means is that others should build a pool, others should provide the material, and still others should run it and keep it in functioning order, so that *he* can use it without fee. But what right has he to the expenditure of *their* time and effort? To expect something "for free" is to expect it *to be paid for by others* whether they choose to or not.

Many questions, particularly about economic matters, will be generated by the libertarian account of human rights and the role of government. Should government have a role in assisting the needy, in providing social security, in legislating minimum wages, in fixing prices and putting a ceiling on rents, in curbing monopolies, in erecting tariffs, in guaranteeing jobs, in managing the money supply? To these and all similar questions the libertarian answers with an unequivocal no.

"But then you'd let people go hungry!" comes the rejoinder. This, the libertarian insists, is precisely what would not happen; with the restrictions removed, the economy would flourish as never before. With the controls taken off business, existing enterprises would expand and new ones would spring into existence satisfying more and more consumer needs; millions more people would be gainfully employed instead of subsisting on welfare, and all kinds of research and production, released from the stranglehold of government, would proliferate, fulfilling man's needs and desires as never before. It has always been so whenever government has permitted men to be free traders on a free market. But *why* this is so, and how the free market is the best solution to all problems relating to the material aspect of man's life, is another and far longer story.

Note

1. Murray Rothbard, "The Great Ecology Issue," *The Individualist*, 2, no. 2 (February 1970), p. 5.

2. Radical Egalitarianism

Kai Nielson

The fundamental requirement of radical egalitarianism is equality of basic condition for everyone. Kai Nielson justifies this requirement on the grounds that it produces the conditions for the most extensive satisfaction of everyone's needs. He also contends that radical egalitarianism is required by the moral point of view and would lead to two specific principles of justice. Finally, Nielson defends radical egalitarianism on the grounds that it is required by liberty or at least a fair distribution of liberty.

I

I have talked of equality as a right and of equality as a goal. And I have taken, as the principal thing, to be able to state what goal we are seeking when we say equality is a goal. When we are in a position actually to achieve that goal, then that same equality becomes a right. The goal we are seeking is an equality of basic condition for everyone. Let me say a bit what this is: everyone, as far as possible, should have equal life prospects, short of genetic engineering and the like and the rooting out of any form of the family and the undermining of our basic freedoms. There should, where this is possible, be an equality of access to equal resources over each person's life as a whole, though this should be qualified by people's varying needs. Where psychiatrists are in short supply only people who are in need of psychiatric help should have equal access to such help. This equal access to resources should be such that it stands as a barrier to their being the sort of differences between people that allow some to be in a position to control and to exploit others; such equal access to resources should also stand as a barrier to one adult person having power over other adult persons that does not rest on the revokable consent on the part of the persons over whom he comes to have power. Where, because of some remaining scarcity in a society of considerable productive abundance, we cannot reasonably distribute resources equally, we should first, where considerations of desert are not at issue, distribute according to stringency of need, second according to the strength of unmanipulated preferences, and third, and finally, by lottery. We should, in trying to attain equality of condition, aim at a condition of autonomy (the fuller and the more rational the better) for everyone and at a condition where everyone alike, to the fullest extent possible, has his or her needs and wants satisfied. The limitations on the satisfaction of people's wants should be only where that satisfaction is incompatible with everyone getting the same treatment. Where we have conflicting wants, such as where two persons want to marry the same person, the fair thing to do will vary with the circumstances. In the marriage case, freedom of choice is obviously the fair thing. But generally, what should be aimed at is having everyone have their wants satisfied as far as possible. To achieve equality of condition would be, as well, to achieve a condition where the necessary burdens of the society are equally shared, where to do so is reasonable, and where each person has an equal voice in deciding what these burdens shall be. Moreover, everyone, as much as possible, should be in a position—and should be equally in that position—to control his own life. The goals of egalitarianism are to achieve such equalities.

Abridged from *Equality and Liberty* (1985), pp. 283–292, 302–306, 309. Reprinted by permission of Rowman & Allanheld, Publishers. Notes renumbered.

Minimally, classlessness is something we should all aim at if we are egalitarians. It is necessary for the stable achievement of equalities of the type discussed in the previous paragraph. Beyond that, we should also aim at a statusless society, though not at an undifferentiated society or a society which does not recognize merit. . . . It is only in such a classless, statusless society that the ideals of equality (the conception of equality as a very general goal to be achieved) can be realized. In aiming for a statusless society, we are aiming for a society which, while remaining a society of material abundance, is a society in which there are to be no extensive differences in life prospects between people because some have far greater income, power, authority or prestige than others. This is the *via negativia* of the egalitarian way. The *via positiva* is to produce social conditions, where there is generally material abundance, where well-being and satisfaction are not only maximized (the utilitarian thing) but, as well, a society where this condition, as far as it is achievable, is sought equally for all (the egalitarian thing). This is the underlying conception of the egalitarian commitment to equality of condition.

II

Robert Nozick asks "How do we decide how much equality is enough?"[1] In the preceding section we gestured in the direction of an answer. I should now like to be somewhat more explicit. Too much equality, as we have been at pains to point out, would be to treat everyone identically, completely ignoring their differing needs. Various forms of "barracks equality" approximating that would also be too much. Too little equality would be to limit equality of condition, as did the old egalitarianism, to achieving equal legal and political rights, equal civil liberties, to equality of opportunity and to a redistribution of gross disparities in wealth sufficient to keep social peace, the rationale for the latter being that such gross inequalities if allowed to stand would threaten social stability. This Hobbesist stance indicates that the old egalitarianism proceeds in a very pragmatic

manner. Against the old egalitarianism I would argue that we must at least aim at an equality of whole life prospects, where that is not read simply as the right to compete for scarce positions of advantage, but where there is to be brought into being the kind of equality of condition that would provide everyone equally, as far as possible, with the resources and the social conditions to satisfy their needs as fully as possible compatible with everyone else doing likewise. (Note that between people these needs will be partly the same but will still often be importantly different as well.) Ideally, as a kind of ideal limit for a society of wondrous abundance, a radical egalitarianism would go beyond that to a similar thing for wants. We should, that is, provide all people equally, as far as possible, with the resources and social conditions to satisfy their wants, as fully as possible compatible with everyone else doing likewise. (I recognize that there is a slide between wants and needs. As the wealth of a society increases and its structure changes, things that started out as wants tend to become needs, e.g., someone in the Falkland Islands might merely reasonably want an auto while someone in Los Angeles might not only want it but need it as well. But this does not collapse the distinction between wants and needs. There are things in any society people need, if they are to survive at all in anything like a commodious condition, whether they want them or not, e.g., they need food, shelter, security, companionship and the like. An egalitarian starts with basic needs, or at least with what are taken in the cultural environment in which a given person lives to be basic needs, and moves out to other needs and finally to wants as the productive power of the society increases.)

I qualified my above formulations with "as far as possible" and with "as fully as possible compatible with everyone else doing likewise." These are essential qualifications. Where, as in societies that we know, there are scarcities, even rather minimal scarcities, not everyone can have the resources or at least all the resources necessary to have their needs satisfied. Here we must first ensure that, again as far as possible, their basic needs are all satisfied and then we move on to other needs and finally to wants. But sometimes, to understate it, even in

very affluent societies, everyone's needs cannot be met, or at least they cannot be equally
met. In such circumstances we have to make
some hard choices. I am thinking of a situation
where there are not enough dialysis machines
to go around so that everyone who needs one
can have one. What then should we do? The
thing to aim at, to try as far as possible to
approximate, if only as a heuristic ideal, is the
full and equal meeting of needs and wants of
everyone. It is when we have that much equality that we have enough equality. But, of
course, "ought implies can," and where we
can't achieve it we can't achieve it. But where
we reasonably can, we ought to do it. It is
something that fairness requires.

The "reasonably can" is also an essential
modification: we need situations of sufficient
abundance so that we do not, in going for such
an equality of condition, simply spread the
misery around or spread very Spartan conditions around. Before we can rightly aim for
the equality of condition I mentioned, we must
first have the productive capacity and resource
conditions to support the institutional means
that would make possible the equal satisfaction
of basic needs and the equal satisfaction of
other needs and wants as well.

Such achievements will often not be possible; perhaps they will never be fully possible,
for, no doubt, the physically handicapped will
always be with us. Consider, for example,
situations where our scarcities are such that we
cannot, without causing considerable misery,
create the institutions and mechanisms that
would work to satisfy all needs, even all basic
needs. Suppose we have the technology in
place to develop all sorts of complicated life-
sustaining machines all of which would predictably provide people with a quality of life
that they, viewing the matter clearly, would
rationally choose if they were simply choosing
for themselves. But suppose, if we put such
technologies in place, we will then not have the
wherewithal to provide basic health care in
outlying regions in the country or adequate
educational services in such places. We should
not, under those circumstances, put those
technologies in place. But we should also recognize that where it becomes possible to put
these technologies in place without sacrificing
other more pressing needs, we should do so.

The underlying egalitarian rationale is evident
enough: produce the conditions for the most
extensive satisfaction of needs for everyone.
Where A's need and B's need are equally important (equally stringent) but cannot both be
satisfied, satisfy A's need rather than B's if the
satisfaction of A's need would be more fecund
for the satisfaction of the needs of others than
B's, or less undermining of the satisfaction of
the needs of others than B's. (I do not mean to
say that that is our only criterion of choice but
it is the criterion most relevant for us here.)
We should seek the satisfaction of the greatest
compossible set of needs where the conditions
for compossibility are (a) that everyone's needs
be considered, (b) that everyone's needs be
equally considered and where two sets of needs
cannot both be satisfied, the more stringent set
of needs shall first be satisfied. (Do not say we
have no working criteria for what they are. If
you need food to keep you from starvation or
debilitating malnutrition and I need a vacation
to relax after a spate of hard work, your need
is plainly more stringent than mine. There
would, of course, be all sorts of disputable
cases, but there are also a host of perfectly
determinate cases indicating that we have
working criteria.) The underlying rationale is
to seek compossible sets of needs so that we
approach as far as possible as great a satisfaction of needs as possible for everyone.

This might, it could be said, produce a
situation in which very few people got those
things that they needed the most, or at least
wanted the most. Remember Nozick with his
need for the resources of Widner Library in
an annex to his house. People, some might
argue, with expensive tastes and extravagant
needs, say a need for really good wine, would
never, with a stress on such compossibilia, get
things they are really keen about.[2] Is that the
kind of world we would reflectively want?
Well, *if* their not getting them is the price we
have to pay for everyone having their basic
needs met, then it is a price we ought to pay. I
am very fond of very good wines as well as
fresh ripe mangos, but if the price of my having them is that people starve or suffer
malnutrition in the Sahel, or indeed anywhere
else, then plainly fairness, if not just plain human decency, requires that I forego them.

In talking about how much equality is

enough, I have so far talked of the benefits that equality is meant to provide. But egalitarians also speak of an equal sharing of the necessary burdens of the society as well. Fairness requires a sharing of the burdens, and for a radical egalitarian this comes to an equal sharing of the burdens where people are equally capable of sharing them. Translated into the concrete this does *not* mean that a child or an old man or a pregnant woman are to be required to work in the mines or that they be required to collect garbage, but it would involve something like requiring every able-bodied person, say from nineteen to twenty, to take his or her turn at a fair portion of the necessary unpleasant jobs in the world. In that way we all, where we are able to do it, would share equally in these burdens—in doing the things that none of us want to do but that we, if we are at all reasonable, recognize the necessity of having done. (There are all kinds of variations and complications concerning this—what do we do with the youthful wonder at the violin? But, that notwithstanding, the general idea is clear enough.) And, where we think this is reasonably feasible, it squares with our considered judgments about fairness.

I have given you, in effect appealing to my considered judgments but considered judgments I do not think are at all eccentric, a picture of what I would take to be enough equality, too little equality and not enough equality. But how can we know that my proportions are right? I do not think we can avoid or should indeed try to avoid an appeal to considered judgments here. But working with them there are some arguments we can appeal to to get them in wide reflective equilibrium. Suppose we go back to the formal principle of justice, namely that we must treat like cases alike. Because it does not tell us *what* are like cases, we cannot derive substantive criteria from it. But it may, indirectly, be of some help here. We all, if we are not utterly zany, want a life in which our needs are satisfied and in which we can live as we wish and do what we want to do. Though we differ in many ways, in our abilities, capacities for pleasure, determination to keep on with a job, we do not differ about wanting our needs satisfied or being able to live as we wish. Thus, *ceterus*

paribus, where questions of desert, entitlement, and the like do not enter, it is only fair that all of us should have our needs equally considered and that we should, again *ceterus paribus,* all be able to do as we wish in a way that is compatible with others doing likewise. From the formal principle of justice and a few key facts about us, we can get to the claim that *ceterus paribus* we should go for this much equality. But this is the core content of a radical egalitarianism.

However, how do we know that *ceterus* is *paribus* here? What about our entitlements and deserts? Suppose I have built my house with my own hands, from materials I have purchased and on land that I have purchased and that I have lived in it for years and have carefully cared for it. The house is mine and I am entitled to keep it even if by dividing the house into two apartments greater and more equal satisfaction of need would obtain for everyone. Justice requires that such an entitlement be respected here. (Again, there is an implicit *ceterus paribus* clause. In extreme situations, say after a war with housing in extremely short supply, that entitlement could be rightly overridden.)

There is a response on the egalitarian's part similar to a response utilitarianism made to criticisms of a similar logical type made of utilitarians by pluralistic deontologists. One of the things that people in fact need, or at least reflectively firmly want, is to have such entitlements respected. Where they are routinely overridden to satisfy other needs or wants, we would *not* in fact have a society in which the needs of everyone are being maximally met. To the reply, but what if more needs for everyone were met by ignoring or overriding such entitlements, the radical egalitarian should respond that that is, given the way we are, a thoroughly hypothetical situation and that theories of morality cannot be expected to give guidance for all logically possible worlds but only for worlds which are reasonably like what our actual world is or plausibly could come to be. Setting this argument aside for the moment, even if it did turn out that the need satisfaction linked with having other things—things that involved the overriding of those entitlements—was sufficient to make it the case that more need satisfaction all around for *everyone* would be achieved by overriding those entitlements, then, for reasonable people who clearly saw that, these entitlements would not have the weight presently given to them. They either would not have the importance presently attached to them or the need for the additional living space would be so great that their being overridden would seem, everything considered, the lesser of two evils (as in the example of the postwar housing situation).

There are without doubt genuine entitlements and a theory of justice must take them seriously, but they are not absolute. If the need is great enough we can see the merit in overriding them, just as in law as well as morality the right of eminent domain is recognized. Finally, while I have talked of entitlements here, parallel arguments will go through for desert.

III

I want now to relate this articulation of what equality comes to to my radically egalitarian principles of justice. My articulation of justice is a certain spelling out of the slogan proclaimed by Marx "From each according to his ability, to each according to his needs." The egalitarian conception of society argues for the desirability of bringing into existence a world, once the springs of social wealth flow freely, in which everyone's needs are as fully satisfied as possible and in which everyone gives according to his ability. Which means, among other things, that everyone, according to his ability, shares the burdens of society. There is an equal giving and equal responsibility here according to ability. It is here, with respect to giving according to ability and with respect to receiving according to need, that a complex equality of result, i.e., equality of condition, is being advocated by the radical egalitarian. What it comes to is this: each of us, where each is to count for one and none to count for more than one, is to give according to ability and receive according to need.

My radical egalitarian principles of justice read as follows:

(1) Each person is to have an equal right to the most extensive total system of equal basic liberties and opportunities (including equal opportunities for meaningful work, for self-determination and political and economic participation) compatible with a similar treatment of all. (This principle gives expression to a commitment to attain and/or sustain equal moral autonomy and equal self-respect.)

(2) After provisions are made for common social (community) values, for capital overhead to preserve the society's productive capacity, allowances made for differing unmanipulated needs and preferences, and due weight is given to the just entitlements of individuals, the income and wealth (the common stock of means) is to be so divided that each person will have a right to an equal share. The necessary burdens requisite to enhance human well-being are also to be equally shared, subject, of course, to limitations by differing abilities and differing situations. (Here I refer to different natural environments and the like and not to class position and the like.)

Here we are talking about equality as a right rather than about equality as a goal as has previously been the subject matter of equality in this chapter. These principles of egalitarianism spell out rights people have and duties they have under *conditions of very considerable productive abundance*. We have a right to certain basic liberties and opportunities and we have, subject to certain limitations spelled out in the second principle, a right to an equal share of the income and wealth in the world. We also have a duty, again subject to the qualifications mentioned in the principle, to do our equal share in shouldering the burdens necessary to protect us from ills and to enhance our well-being.

What is the relation between these rights and the ideal of equality of condition discussed earlier? That is a goal for which we can struggle now to bring about conditions which will some day make its achievement possible, while these rights only become rights when the goal is actually achievable. We have no such rights in slave, feudal or capitalist societies or such duties in those societies. In that important way they are not natural rights for they depend on certain social conditions and certain social structures (socialist ones) to be realizable. What we can say is that it is always desirable that socio-economic conditions come into being which would make it possible to achieve the goal of equality of condition so that these rights and duties I speak of could obtain. But that is a far cry from saying we have such rights and duties now.

It is a corollary of this, if these radical egalitarian principles of justice are correct, that capitalist societies (even capitalist welfare state societies such as Sweden) and statist societies such as the Soviet Union or the People's Republic of China cannot be just societies or at least they must be societies, structured as they are, which are defective in justice. (This is not to say that some of these societies are not juster than others. Sweden is juster than South Africa, Canada than the United States and Cuba and Nicaragua than Honduras and Guatemala.) But none of these statist or capitalist societies can satisfy these radical egalitarian principles of justice, for equal liberty, equal opportunity, equal wealth or equal sharing of burdens are not at all possible in societies having their social structure. So we do not have such rights now but we can take it as a goal that we bring such a society into being with a commitment to an equality of condition in which we would have these rights and duties. Here we require first the massive development of productive power.

The connection between equality as a goal and equality as a right spelled out in these principles of justice is this. The equality of condition appealed to in equality as a goal would, if it were actually to obtain, have to contain the rights and duties enunciated in those principles. There could be no equal life prospects between all people or anything approximating an equal satisfaction of needs if there were not in place something like the system of equal basic liberties referred to in the first principle. Furthermore, without the rough equality of wealth referred to in the second principle, there would be disparities in power and self-direction in society which would render impossible an equality of life prospects or the social conditions required for an equal satisfaction of needs. And plainly, without a roughly equal sharing of burdens,

there cannot be a situation where everyone has equal life prospects or has the chance equally to satisfy his needs. The principles of radical egalitarian justice are implicated in its conception of an ideally adequate equality of condition.

IV

The principles of radical egalitarian justice I have articulated are meant to apply globally and not just to particular societies. But it is certainly fair to say that not a few would worry that such principles of radical egalitarian justice, if applied globally, would force the people in wealthier sections of the world to a kind of financial hari-kari. There are millions of desperately impoverished people. Indeed millions are starving or malnourished and things are not getting any better. People in the affluent societies cannot but worry about whether they face a bottomless pit. Many believe that meeting, even in the most minimal way, the needs of the impoverished is going to put an incredible burden on people—people of all classes—in the affluent societies. Indeed it will, if acted on non-evasively, bring about their impoverishment, and this is just too much to ask. Radical egalitarianism is forgetting Rawls' admonitions about "the strains of commitment"—the recognition that in any rational account of what is required of us, we must at least give a minimal healthy self-interest its due. We must construct our moral philosophy for human beings and not for saints. Human nature is less fixed than conservatives are wont to assume, but it is not so elastic that we can reasonably expect people to impoverish themselves to make the massive transfers between North and South—the industrialized world and the Third World—required to begin to approach a situation where even Rawls' principles would be in place on a global level, to say nothing of my radical egalitarian principles of justice.[3]

The first thing to say in response to this is that my radical egalitarian principles are meant actually to guide practice, to directly determine what we are to do, only in a world of extensive abundance where, as Marx put it, the springs of social wealth flow freely. If such a world cannot be attained with the undermining of capitalism and the full putting into place, stabilizing, and developing of socialist relations of production, then such radical egalitarian principles can only remain as heuristic ideals against which to measure the distance of our travel in the direction of what would be a perfectly just society.

Aside from a small capitalist class, along with those elites most directly and profitably beholden to it (together a group constituting not more than 5 percent of the world's population), there would, in taking my radical egalitarian principles as heuristic guides, be no impoverishment of people in the affluent societies, if we moved in a radically more egalitarian way to start to achieve a global fairness. There would be massive transfers of wealth between North and South, but this could be done in stages so that, for the people in the affluent societies (capitalist elites apart), there need be no undermining of the quality of their lives. Even what were once capitalist elites would not be impoverished or reduced to some kind of bleak life though they would, the incidental Spartan types aside, find their life styles altered. But their health and general well-being, including their opportunities to do significant and innovative work, would, if anything, be enhanced. And while some of the sources of their enjoyment would be a thing of the past, there would still be a considerable range of enjoyments available to them sufficient to afford anyone a rich life that could be lived with verve and zest.

A fraction of what the United States spends on defense spending would take care of immediate problems of starvation and malnutrition for most of the world. For longer range problems such as bringing conditions of life in the Third World more in line with conditions of life in Sweden and Switzerland, what is necessary is the dismantling of the capitalist system and the creation of a socio-economic system with an underlying rationale directing it toward producing for needs—everyone's needs. With this altered productive mode, the irrationalities and waste of capitalist production would be cut. There would be no more built-in obsolescence, no more merely cosmetic changes in consumer durables, no more fashion roulette, no more useless products and the like. Moreover, the enormous expenditures that go into the war industry would be a thing of the past. There would be great transfers from North to South, but it would be from the North's capitalist fat and not from things people in the North really need. (There would, in other words, be no self-pauperization of people in the capitalist world.) . . .

V

It has been repeatedly argued that equality undermines liberty. Some would say that a society in which principles like my radical egalitarian principles were adopted, or even the liberal egalitarian principles of Rawls or Dworkin were adopted, would not be a free society. My arguments have been just the reverse. I have argued that it is only in an egalitarian society that full and extensive liberty is possible.

Perhaps the egalitarian and the anti-egalitarian are arguing at cross purposes? What we need to recognize, it has been argued, is that we have two kinds of rights both of which are important to freedom but to rather different freedoms and which are freedoms which not infrequently conflict.[4] We have rights to *fair terms of cooperation* but we also have rights to *non-interference*. If a right of either kind is overridden our freedom is diminished. The reason why it might be thought that the egalitarian and the anti-egalitarian may be arguing at cross purposes is that the egalitarian is pointing to the fact that rights to fair terms of cooperation and their associated liberties require equality while the anti-egalitarian is pointing to the fact that rights to non-interference and their associated liberties conflict with equality. They focus on different liberties.

What I have said above may not be crystal clear, so let me explain. People have a right to fair terms of cooperation. In political terms this comes to the equal right of all to effective participation in government and, in more broadly social terms, and for a society of economic wealth, it means people having a right to a roughly equal distribution of the benefits and burdens of the basic social arrangements that affect their lives and for them to stand in such relations to each other such that no one has the power to dominate the life of another. By contrast, rights to non-interference come to the equal right of all to be left alone by the government and more broadly to live in a society in which people have a right peacefully to pursue their interests without interference.

The conflict between equality and liberty comes down to, very essentially, the conflicts we get in modern societies between rights to fair terms of cooperation and rights to non-interference. As Joseph Schumpeter saw and J. S. Mill before him, one could have a thoroughly democratic society (at least in conventional terms) in which rights to non-interference might still be extensively violated. A central anti-egalitarian claim is that we cannot have an egalitarian society in which the very precious liberties that go with the rights to non-interference would not be violated.

Socialism and egalitarianism plainly protect rights to fair terms of cooperation. Without the social (collective) ownership and control of the means of production, involving with this, in the initial stages of socialism at least, a workers' state, economic power will be concentrated in the hands of a few who will in turn, as a result, dominate effective participation in government. Some right-wing libertarians blind themselves to that reality, but it is about as evident as can be. Only an utter turning away from the facts of social life could lead to any doubts about this at all. But then this means that in a workers' state, if some people have capitalistic impulses, they would have their rights peacefully to pursue their own interests interfered with. They might wish to invest, retain and bequeath in economic domains. In a workers' state these capitalist acts in many circumstances would have to be forbidden, but that would be a violation of an individual's right to non-interference and the fact, if it was a fact, that we by democratic vote, even with vast majorities, had made such capitalist acts illegal would still not make any difference because individuals' rights to non-interference would still be violated.

We are indeed driven, by egalitarian impulses of a perfectly understandable sort, to accept interference with laissez-faire capitalism to protect non-subordination and non-domination of people by protecting the egalitarian right to fair terms of cooperation and the enhanced liberty that that brings. Still, as things stand, this leads inevitably to violations of the right to non-interference and this brings with it a diminution of liberty. There will be people with capitalist impulses and they will be interfered with. It is no good denying, it will be said, that egalitarianism and particularly socialism will not lead to interference with very precious individual liberties, namely with our right peacefully to pursue our interests without interference.[5]

The proper response to this, as should be apparent from what I have argued throughout, is that to live in any society at all, capitalist, socialist or whatever, is to live in a world in which there will be some restriction or other on our rights peacefully to pursue our interests without interference. I can't lecture in Albanian or even in French in a standard philosophy class at the University of Calgary, I can't jog naked on most beaches, borrow a book from your library without your permission, fish in your trout pond without your permission, take your dog for a walk without your say so and the like. At least some of these things have been thought to be things which I might peacefully pursue in my own interests. Stopping me from doing them is plainly interfering with my peaceful pursuit of my own interests. And indeed it is an infringement on liberty, an interference with my doing what I may want to do.

However, for at least many of these activities, and particularly the ones having to do with property, even right-wing libertarians think that such interference is perfectly justified. But, justified or not, they still plainly constitute a restriction on our individual freedom. However, what we must also recognize is that there will always be some such restrictions on freedom in any society whatsoever, just in virtue of the fact that a normless society, without the restrictions that having norms imply, is a contradiction in terms.[6] Many restrictions are hardly felt as restrictions, as in the attitudes of many people toward seat-belt legislation, but they are, all the same, plainly restrictions on our liberty. It is just that they are thought to be unproblematically justified.

To the question would a socialism with a radical egalitarianism restrict some liberties, including some liberties rooted in rights to noninterference, the answer is that it indeed would; but so would laissez-faire capitalism, aristocratic conceptions of justice, liberal conceptions or any social formations at all, with their associated conceptions of justice. The relevant question is which of these restrictions are justified.

The restrictions on liberty proferred by radical egalitarianism and socialism, I have argued, are justified for they, of the various alternatives, give us both the most extensive and the most abundant system of liberty possible in modern conditions with their thorough protection of the right to fair terms of cooperation. Radical egalitarianism will also, and this is central for us, protect our civil liberties and these liberties are, of course, our most basic liberties. These are the liberties which are the most vital for us to protect. What it will not do is to protect our unrestricted liberties to invest, retain and bequeath in the economic realm and it will not protect our unrestricted freedom to buy and sell. There is, however, no good reason to think that these restrictions are restrictions of anything like a basic liberty. Moreover, we are justified in restricting our freedom to buy and sell if such restrictions strengthen, rather than weaken, our total system of liberty. This is in this way justified, for only by such market restrictions can the rights of the vast majority of people to effective participation in government and an equal role in the control of their social lives be protected. I say this because if we let the market run free in this way, power will pass into the hands of a few who will control the lives of the many and determine the fundamental design of the society. The actual liberties that are curtailed in a radically egalitarian social order are inessential liberties whose restriction in contemporary circumstances enhances human well-being and indeed makes for a firmer entrenchment of basic liberties and for their greater extension globally. That is to say, we here restrict some liberty in order to attain more liberty and a more equally distributed

pattern of liberty. More people will be able to do what they want and have a greater control over their own lives than in a capitalist world order with its at least implicit inegalitarian commitments.

However, some might say I still have not faced the most central objection to radical egalitarianism, namely its statism. (I would prefer to say its putative statism.) The picture is this. The egalitarian state must be in the redistribution business. It has to make, or make sure there is made, an equal relative contribution to the welfare of every citizen. But this in effect means that the socialist state or, for that matter, the welfare state, will be deeply interventionist in our personal lives. It will be in the business, as one right-winger emotively put it, of cutting one person down to size in order to bring about that person's equality with another person who was in a previously disadvantageous position.[7] That is said to be morally objectionable and it would indeed be deeply morally objectionable in many circumstances. But it isn't in the circumstances in which the radical egalitarian presses for redistribution. (I am not speaking of what might be mere equalizing upwards.) The circumstances are these: Capitalist A gets his productive property confiscated so that he could no longer dominate and control the lives of proletarians B, C, D, E, F, and G. But what is wrong with it where this "cutting down to size"—in reality the confiscation of productive property or the taxation of the capitalist—involves no violation of A's civil liberties or the harming of his actual well-being (health, ability to work, to cultivate the arts, to have fruitful personal relations, to live in comfort and the like) and where B, C, D, E, F, and G will have their freedom and their well-being thoroughly enhanced if such confiscation or taxation occurs? Far from being morally objectionable, it is precisely the sort of state of affairs that people ought to favor. It certainly protects more liberties and more significant liberties than it undermines.

There is another familiar anti-egalitarian argument designed to establish the liberty-undermining qualities of egalitarianism. It is an argument we have touched upon in discussing meritocracy. It turns on the fact that in any society there will be both talents and handicaps. Where they exist, what do we want to do about maintaining equal distribution? Egalitarians, radical or otherwise, certainly do not want to penalize people for talent. That being so, then surely people should be allowed to retain the benefits of superior talent. But this in some circumstances will lead to significant inequalities in resources and in the meeting of needs. To sustain equality there will have to be an ongoing redistribution in the direction of the less talented and less fortunate. But this redistribution from the more to the less talented does plainly penalize the talented for their talent. That, it will be said, is something which is both unfair and an undermining of liberty.

The following, it has been argued, makes the above evident enough.[8] If people have talents they will tend to want to use them. And if they use them they are very likely to come out ahead. Must not egalitarians say they ought not to be able to come out ahead no matter how well they use their talents and no matter how considerable these talents are? But that is intolerably restrictive and unfair.

The answer to the above anti-egalitarian argument is implicit in a number of things I have already said. But here let me confront this familiar argument directly. Part of the answer comes out in probing some of the ambiguities of "coming out ahead." Note, incidentally, that (1) not all reflective, morally sensitive people will be so concerned with that, and (2) that being very concerned with that is a mentality that capitalism inculcates. Be that as it may, to turn to the ambiguities, note that some take "coming out ahead" principally to mean "being paid well for the use of those talents" where "being paid well" is being paid sufficiently well so that it creates inequalities sufficient to disturb the preferred egalitarian patterns. (Without that, being paid well would give one no relative advantage.) But, as we have seen, "coming out ahead" need not take that form at all. Talents can be recognized and acknowledged in many ways: First, in just the respect and admiration of a fine employment of talents that would naturally come from people seeing them so displayed where these people were not twisted by envy; second, by having, because of these talents, interesting and secure work that their talents fit them for and

they merit in virtue of those talents. Moreover, having more money is not going to matter much—for familiar marginal utility reasons—where what in capitalist societies would be called the welfare floors are already very high, this being made feasible by the great productive wealth of the society. Recall that in such a society of abundance everyone will be well off and secure. In such a society people are not going to be very concerned about being a little better off than someone else. The talented are in no way, in such a situation, robbed to help the untalented and handicapped or penalized for their talents. They are only prevented from amassing wealth (most particularly productive wealth), which would enable them to dominate the untalented and the handicapped and to control the social life of the world of which they are both a part. . . .

I think that the moral authority for abstract egalitarianism, for the belief that the interests of everyone matters and matters equally, comes from its being the case that it is *required by the moral point of view.*[9] What I am predicting is that a person who has a good understanding of what morality is, has a good knowledge of the facts, is not ideologically mystified, takes an impartial point of view, and has an attitude of impartial caring, would, if not conceptually confused, come to accept the abstract egalitarian thesis. I see no way of arguing someone into such an egalitarianism who does not in this general way have a love of humankind.[10] A hard-hearted Hobbesist is not reachable here. But given that a person has that love of humankind—that impartial and impersonal caring—together with the other qualities mentioned above, then, I predict that that person would be an egalitarian at least to the extent of accepting the abstract egalitarian thesis. What I am claiming is that if these conditions were to obtain (if they ceased to be just counterfactuals), then there would be a consensus among moral agents about accepting the abstract egalitarian thesis. . . .

Notes

1. See the debate between Robert Nozick, Daniel Bell and James Tobin, "If Inequality Is Inevi-

table What Can Be Done About It?" *The New York Times,* January 3, 1982, p. E5. The exchange between Bell and Nozick reveals the differences between the old egalitarianism and right-wing libertarianism. It is not only that the right and left clash but sometimes right clashes with right.

2. Amartya Sen, "Equality of What?" *The Tanner Lectures on Human Values,* vol. 1 (1980), ed. Sterling M. McMurrin (Cambridge, England: Cambridge University Press, 1980), pp. 198–220.

3. Henry Shue, "The Burdens of Justice," *The Journal of Philosophy* 80, no. 10 (October 1983): 600–601; 606–608.

4. Richard W. Miller, "Marx and Morality," in *Marxism,* eds. J. R. Pennock and J. W. Chapman, Nomos 26 (New York: New York University Press, 1983), pp. 9–11.

5. Ibid., p. 10.

6. This has been argued from both the liberal center and the left. Ralf Dahrendorf, *Essays in the Theory of Society* (Stanford, Calif.: Stanford University Press, 1968), pp. 151–178; and G. A.

Cohen, "Capitalism, Freedom and the Proletariat" in *The Idea of Freedom: Essays in Honour of Isaiah Berlin,* ed. Alan Ryan (Oxford: Oxford University Press, 1979).

7. The graphic language should be duly noted. Jan Narveson, "On Dworkinian Equality," *Social Philosophy and Policy* 1, no. 1 (autumn 1983): 4.

8. Ibid., p. 1–24.

9. Some will argue that there is no such thing as a moral point of view. My differences with him about the question of whether the amoralist can be argued into morality not withstanding, I think Kurt Baier, in a series of articles written subsequent to his *The Moral Point of View,* has clearly shown that there is something reasonably determinate that can, without ethnocentrism, be called "the moral point of view."

10. Richard Norman has impressively argued that this is an essential background assumption of the moral point of view. Richard Norman, "Critical Notice of Rodger Beehler's *Moral Life,*" *Canadian Journal of Philosophy* 11, no. 1 (March 1981): 157–183.

---

3. A Social Contract Perspective

John Rawls

John Rawls believes that principles of justice are those on which free and rational persons would agree if they were in an original position of equality. This original position is characterized as a hypothetical position in which persons are behind an imaginary veil of ignorance with respect to most particular facts about themselves. Rawls claims that persons in his original position would choose principles requiring equal political liberty and opportunity and the highest possible economic minimum because they would be committed to the maximin rule, which requires maximizing the minimum payoff.

My aim is to present a conception of justice which generalizes and carries to a higher level of abstraction the familiar theory of the social

Abridged from *A Theory of Justice* (1971), pp. 11–22, 60–65, 150–156, 302–303. Excerpted by permission of the publishers from *A Theory of Justice* by John Rawls. Cambridge, Mass.: The Belknap Press of Harvard University Press. Copyright © 1971 by the President and Fellows of Harvard College.

contract as found, say, in Locke, Rousseau, and Kant.[1] In order to do this we are not to think of the original contract as one to enter a particular society or to set up a particular form of government. Rather, the guiding idea is that the principles of justice for the basic structure of society are the object of the original agreement. They are the principles that free and rational persons concerned to further their own interests would accept in an initial position of equality as defining the fundamental terms of their association. These principles are to regulate all further agreements; they specify the kinds of social cooperation that can be entered into and the forms of government that can be established. This way of regarding the principles of justice I shall call justice as fairness.

Thus we are to imagine that those who engage in social cooperation choose together, in one joint act, the principles which are to assign basic rights and duties and to determine the division of social benefits. Men are to decide in advance how they are to regulate their claims against one another and what is to be the foundation charter of their society. Just as each person must decide by rational reflection what constitutes his good—that is, the system of ends which it is rational for him to pursue—so a group of persons must decide once and for all what is to count among them as just and unjust. The choice which rational men would make in this hypothetical situation of equal liberty, assuming for the present that this choice problem has a solution, determines the principles of justice.

In justice as fairness the original position of equality corresponds to the state of nature in the traditional theory of the social contract. This original position is not, of course, thought of as an actual historical state of affairs, much less as a primitive condition of culture. It is understood as a purely hypothetical situation characterized so as to lead to a certain conception of justice.[2] Among the essential features of this situation is that no one knows his place in society, his class position or social status, nor does any one know his fortune in the distribution of natural assets and abilities, his intelligence, strength, and the like. I shall even assume that the parties do not know their conceptions of the good or their special psychological propensities. The principles of justice are chosen behind a veil of ignorance. This ensures that no one is advantaged or disadvantaged in the choice of principles by the outcome of natural chance or the contingency of social circumstances. Since all are similarly situated and no one is able to design principles to favor his particular condition, the principles of justice are the result of a fair agreement or bargain. For given the circumstances of the original position, the symmetry of everyone's relations to each other, this initial situation is fair between individuals as moral persons; that is, as rational beings with their own ends and capable, I shall assume, of a sense of justice. The original position is, one might say, the appropriate initial status quo, and thus the fundamental agreements reached in it are fair. This explains the propriety of the name "justice as fairness"; it conveys the idea that the principles of justice are agreed to in an initial situation that is fair. The name does not mean that the concepts of justice and fairness are the same, any more than the phrase "poetry as metaphor" means that the concepts of poetry and metaphor are the same.

Justice as fairness begins, as I have said, with one of the most general of all choices which persons might make together, namely, with the choice of the first principles of a conception of justice which is to regulate all subsequent criticism and reform of institutions. Then, having chosen a conception of justice, we can suppose that they are to choose a constitution and a legislature to enact laws, and so on, all in accordance with the principles of justice initially agreed upon. Our social situation is just if it is such that by this sequence of hypothetical agreements we would have contracted into the general system of rules which defines it. Moreover, assuming that the original position does determine a set of principles (that is, that a particular conception of justice would be chosen), it will then be true that whenever social institutions satisfy these principles those engaged in them can say to one another that they are cooperating on terms to which they would agree if they were free and equal persons whose relations with respect to one another were fair. They could all view their arrangements as meeting the stipulations which they would acknowledge in an initial situation that embodies widely accepted and reasonable constraints on the choice of principles. The general recognition of this fact would provide the basis for a public acceptance of the corresponding principles of justice. No society can, of course, be a scheme of cooperation which men enter voluntarily in a literal sense; each person finds himself placed at birth in some particular position in some particular society, and the nature of this position materially affects his life prospects. Yet a society satisfying the principles of justice as fairness comes as close as a society can to being a voluntary scheme, for it meets the principles which free and equal persons would assent to under circumstances that are fair. In this sense its members are autonomous and the obligations they recognize self-imposed.

One feature of justice as fairness is to think of the parties in the initial situation as rational and mutually disinterested. This does not mean that the parties are egoists; that is, individuals with only certain kinds of interests, say in wealth, prestige, and domination. But they are conceived as not taking an interest in one another's interests. They are to presume that even their spiritual aims may be opposed, in the way that the aims of those of different religions may be opposed. Moreover, the concept of rationality must be interpreted as far as possible in the narrow sense, standard in economic theory, of taking the most effective means to given ends. I shall modify this concept to some extent . . . , but one must try to avoid introducing into it any controversial ethical elements. The initial situation must be characterized by stipulations that are widely accepted.

In working out the conception of justice as fairness one main task clearly is to determine which principles of justice would be chosen in the original position. To do this we must describe this situation in some detail and formulate with care the problem of choice which it presents. It may be observed, however, that once the principles of justice are thought of as arising from an original agreement in a situation of equality, it is an open question whether the principle of utility would be acknowledged. Offhand it hardly seems likely that persons who view themselves as equals, entitled to press their claims upon one another, would agree to a principle which may require lesser life prospects for some simply for the sake of a greater sum of advantages enjoyed by others. Since each desires to protect his interests, his capacity to advance his conception of the good, no one has a reason to acquiesce in an enduring loss for himself in order to bring

about a greater net balance of satisfaction. In the absence of strong and lasting benevolent impulses, a rational man would not accept a basic structure merely because it maximized the algebraic sum of advantages irrespective of its permanent effects on his own basic rights and interests. Thus it seems that the principle of utility is incompatible with the conception of social cooperation among equals for mutual advantage. It appears to be inconsistent with the idea of reciprocity implicit in the notion of a well-ordered society. Or, at any rate, so I shall argue.

I shall maintain instead that the persons in the initial situation would choose two rather different principles: the first requires equality in the assignment of basic rights and duties, while the second holds that social and economic inequalities, for example, inequalities of wealth and authority, are just only if they result in compensating benefits for everyone, and in particular for the least advantaged members of society. These principles rule out justifying institutions on the grounds that the hardships of some are offset by a greater good in the aggregate. It may be expedient but it is not just that some should have less in order that others may prosper. But there is no injustice in the greater benefits earned by a few provided that the situation of persons not so fortunate is thereby improved. The intuitive idea is that since everyone's well-being depends upon a scheme of cooperation without which no one could have a satisfactory life, the division of advantages should be such as to draw forth the willing cooperation of everyone taking part in it, including those less well situated. Yet this can be expected only if reasonable terms are proposed. The two principles mentioned seem to be a fair agreement on the basis of which those better endowed, or more fortunate in their social position, neither of which we can be said to deserve, could expect the willing cooperation of others when some workable scheme is a necessary condition of the welfare of all.[3] Once we decide to look for a conception of justice that nullifies the accidents of natural endowment and the contingencies of social circumstance as counters in quest for political and economic advantage, we are led to these principles. They express the result of leaving aside those aspects of the social world that seem arbitrary from a moral point of view.

The problem of the choice of principles, however, is extremely difficult. I do not expect the answer I shall suggest to be convincing to everyone. It is, therefore, worth noting from the outset that justice as fairness, like other contract views, consists of two parts: (1) an interpretation of the initial situation and of the problem of choice posed there, and (2) a set of principles which, it is argued, would be agreed to. One may accept the first part of the theory (or some variant thereof), but not the other, and conversely. The concept of the initial contractual situation may seem reasonable although the particular principles proposed are rejected. To be sure, I want to maintain that the most appropriate conception of this situation does lead to principles of justice contrary to utilitarianism and perfectionism, and therefore that the contract doctrine provides an alternative to these views. Still, one may dispute this contention even though one grants that the contractarian method is a useful way of studying ethical theories and of setting forth their underlying assumptions.

Justice as fairness is an example of what I have called a contract theory. Now there may be an objection to the term "contract" and related expressions, but I think it will serve reasonably well. Many words have misleading connotations which at first are likely to confuse. The terms "utility" and "utilitarianism" are surely no exception. They too have unfortunate suggestions which hostile critics have been willing to exploit; yet they are clear enough for those prepared to study utilitarian doctrine. The same should be true of the term "contract" applied to moral theories. As I have mentioned, to understand it one has to keep in mind that it implies a certain level of abstraction. In particular, the content of the relevant agreement is not to enter a given society or to adopt a given form of government, but to accept certain moral principles. Moreover, the undertakings referred to are purely hypothetical: a contract view holds that certain principles would be accepted in a well-defined initial situation.

The merit of the contract terminology is that it conveys the idea that principles of jus-

tice may be conceived as principles that would be chosen by rational persons, and that in this way conceptions of justice may be explained and justified. The theory of justice is a part, perhaps the most significant part, of the theory of rational choice. Furthermore, principles of justice deal with conflicting claims upon the advantages won by social cooperation; they apply to the relations among several persons or groups. The word "contract" suggests this plurality as well as the condition that the appropriate division of advantages must be in accordance with principles acceptable to all parties. The condition of publicity for principles of justice is also connoted by the contract phraseology. Thus, if these principles are the outcome of an agreement, citizens have a knowledge of the principles that others follow. It is characteristic of contract theories to stress the public nature of political principles. Finally there is the long tradition of the contract doctrine. Expressing the tie with this line of thought helps to define ideas and accords with natural piety. There are then several advantages in the use of the term "contract." With due precautions taken, it should not be misleading.

A final remark. Justice as fairness is not a complete contract theory. For it is clear that the contractarian idea can be extended to the choice of more or less an entire ethical system; that is, to a system including principles for all the virtues and not only for justice. Now for the most part I shall consider only principles of justice and others closely related to them; I make no attempt to discuss the virtues in a systematic way. Obviously if justice as fairness succeeds reasonably well, a next step would be to study the more general view suggested by the name "rightness as fairness." But even this wider theory fails to embrace all moral relationships, since it would seem to include only our relations with other persons and to leave out of account how we are to conduct ourselves toward animals and the rest of nature. I do not contend that the contract notion offers a way to approach these questions, which are certainly of the first importance; and I shall have to put them aside. We must recognize the limited scope of justice as fairness and of the general type of view that it exemplifies. How far its conclusions must be revised once these other matters are understood cannot be decided in advance.

The Original Position and Justification

I have said that the original position is the appropriate initial status quo which insures that the fundamental agreements reached in it are fair. This fact yields the name "justice as fairness." It is clear, then, that I want to say that one conception of justice is more reasonable than another, or justifiable with respect to it, if rational persons in the initial situation would choose its principles over those of the other for the role of justice. Conceptions of justice are to be ranked by their acceptability to persons so circumstanced. Understood in this way the question of justification is settled by working out a problem of deliberation: we have to ascertain which principles it would be rational to adopt given the contractual situation. This connects the theory of justice with the theory of rational choice.

If this view of the problem of justification is to succeed, we must, of course, describe in some detail the nature of this choice problem. A problem of rational decision has a definite answer only if we know the beliefs and interests of the parties, their relations with respect to one another, the alternatives between which they are to choose, the procedure whereby they make up their minds, and so on. As the circumstances are presented in different ways, correspondingly different principles are accepted. The concept of the original position, as I shall refer to it, is that of the most philosophically favored interpretation of this initial choice situation for the purposes of a theory of justice.

But how are we to decide what is the most favored interpretation? I assume, for one thing, that there is a broad measure of agreement that principles of justice should be chosen under certain conditions. To justify a particular description of the initial situation one shows that it incorporates these commonly shared presumptions. One argues from widely accepted but weak premises to more specific conclusions. Each of the presumptions should by itself be natural and plausible; some of them may seem innocuous or even trivial. The aim of the contract approach is to establish that taken together they impose significant bounds on acceptable principles of justice. The ideal outcome would be that these conditions determine a unique set of principles; but I shall be satisfied if they suffice to rank the main traditional conceptions of social justice.

One should not be misled, then, by the somewhat unusual conditions which characterize the original position. The idea here is simply to make vivid to ourselves the restrictions that it seems reasonable to impose on arguments for principles of justice, and therefore on these principles themselves. Thus it seems reasonable and generally acceptable that no one should be advantaged or disadvantaged by natural fortune or social circumstances in the choice of principles. It also seems widely agreed that it should be impossible to tailor principles to the circumstances of one's own case. We should ensure further that particular inclinations and aspirations, and persons' conceptions of their good, do not affect the principles adopted. The aim is to rule out those principles that it would be rational to propose for acceptance, however little the chance of success, only if one knew certain things that are irrelevant from the standpoint of justice. For example, if a man knew that he was wealthy, he might find it rational to advance the principle that various taxes for welfare measures be counted unjust; if he knew that he was poor, he would most likely propose the contrary principle. To represent the desired restrictions one imagines a situation in which everyone is deprived of this sort of information. One excludes the knowledge of those contingencies which sets men at odds and allows them to be guided by their prejudices. In this manner the veil of ignorance is arrived at in a natural way. This concept should cause no difficulty if we keep in mind the constraints on arguments that it is meant to express. At any time we can enter the original position, so to speak, simply by following a certain procedure; namely, by arguing for principles of justice in accordance with these restrictions.

It seems reasonable to suppose that the parties in the original position are equal. That is, all have the same rights in the procedure for choosing principles; each can make proposals, submit reasons for their acceptance, and so on. Obviously the purpose of these conditions is to represent equality between human beings as moral persons, as creatures having a conception of their good and capable of a sense of justice. The basis of equality is taken to be similarity in these two respects. Systems of ends are not ranked in value; and each man is presumed to have the requisite ability to understand and to act upon whatever principles are adopted. Together with the veil of ignorance, these conditions define the principles of justice as those which rational persons concerned to advance their interests would consent to as equals when none are known to be advantaged or disadvantaged by social and natural contingencies.

There is, however, another side to justifying a particular description of the original position. This is to see if the principles which would be chosen match our considered convictions of justice or extend them in an acceptable way. We can note whether applying these principles would lead us to make the same judgments about the basic structure of society which we now make intuitively and in which we have the greatest confidence; or whether, in cases where our present judgments are in doubt and given with hesitation, these principles offer a resolution which we can affirm on reflection. There are questions which we feel sure must be answered in a certain way. For example, we are confident that religious intolerance and racial discrimination are unjust. We think that we have examined these things with care and have reached what we believe is an impartial judgment not likely to be distorted by an excessive attention to our own interests. These convictions are provisional fixed points which we presume any conception of justice must fit. But we have much less assurance as to what is the correct distribution of wealth and authority. Here we may be looking for a way to remove our doubts. We can check an interpretation of the initial situation,

then, by the capacity of its principles to accommodate our firmest convictions and to provide guidance where guidance is needed.

In searching for the most favored description of this situation we work from both ends. We begin by describing it so that it represents generally shared and preferably weak conditions. We then see if these conditions are strong enough to yield a significant set of principles. If not, we look for further premises equally reasonable. But if so, and these principles match our considered convictions of justice, then so far well and good. But presumably there will be discrepancies. In this case we have a choice. We can either modify the account of the initial situation or we can revise our existing judgments, for even the judgments we take provisionally as fixed points are liable to revision. By going back and forth, sometimes altering the conditions of the contractual circumstances, at others withdrawing our judgments and conforming them to principle, I assume that eventually we shall find a description of the initial situation that both expresses reasonable conditions and yields principles which match our considered judgments duly pruned and adjusted. This state of affairs I refer to as reflective equilibrium.[4] It is an equilibrium because at last our principles and judgments coincide; and it is reflective since we know to what principles our judgments conform and the premises of their derivation. At the moment everything is in order. But this equilibrium is not necessarily stable. It is liable to be upset by further examination of the conditions which should be imposed on the contractual situation and by particular cases which may lead us to revise our judgments. Yet for the time being we have done what we can to render coherent and to justify our convictions of social justice. We have reached a conception of the original position.

I shall not, of course, actually work through this process. Still, we may think of the interpretation of the original position that I shall present as the result of such a hypothetical course of reflection. It represents the attempt to accommodate within one scheme both reasonable philosophical conditions on principles as well as our considered judgments of justice. In arriving at the favored interpretation of the initial situation there is no point at which an appeal is made to self-evidence in the traditional sense either of general conceptions or particular convictions. I do not claim for the principles of justice proposed that they are necessary truths or derivable from such truths. A conception of justice cannot be deduced from self-evident premises or conditions on principles; instead, its justification is a matter of the mutual support of many considerations, of everything fitting together into one coherent view.

A final comment. We shall want to say that certain principles of justice are justified because they would be agreed to in an initial situation of equality. I have emphasized that this original position is purely hypothetical. It is natural to ask why, if this agreement is never actually entered into, we should take any interest in these principles, moral or otherwise. The answer is that the conditions embodied in the description of the original position are ones that we do in fact accept. Or if we do not, then perhaps we can be persuaded to do so by philosophical reflection. Each aspect of the contractual situation can be given supporting grounds. Thus what we shall do is to collect together into one conception a number of conditions on principles that we are ready upon due consideration to recognize as reasonable. These constraints express what we are prepared to regard as limits on fair terms of social cooperation. One way to look at the idea of the original position, therefore, is to see it as an expository device which sums up the meaning of these conditions and helps us to extract their consequences. On the other hand, this conception is also an intuitive notion that suggests its own elaboration, so that led on by it we are drawn to define more clearly the standpoint from which we can best interpret moral relationships. We need a conception that enables us to envision our objective from afar: the intuitive notion of the original position is to do this for us. . . .

Two Principles of Justice

I shall now state in a provisional form the two principles of justice that I believe would be chosen in the original position. In this section I wish to make only the most general comments, and therefore the first formulation of these principles is tentative. As we go on I shall run through several formulations and approximate step by step the final statement to be given much later. I believe that doing this allows the exposition to proceed in a natural way.

The first statement of the two principles reads as follows:

> First: each person is to have an equal right to the most extensive basic liberty compatible with a similar liberty for others.

> Second: social and economic inequalities are to be arranged so that they are both (a) reasonably expected to be to everyone's advantage, and (b) attached to positions and offices open to all.

There are two ambiguous phrases in the second principle, namely "everyone's advantage" and "open to all." Determining their sense more exactly will lead to a second formulation of the principle. . . .

By way of general comment, these principles primarily apply, as I have said, to the basic structure of society. They are to govern the assignment of rights and duties and to regulate the distribution of social and economic advantages. As their formulation suggests, these principles presuppose that the social structure can be divided into two more or less distinct parts, the first principle applying to the one, the second to the other. They distinguish between those aspects of the social system that define and secure the equal liberties of citizenship and those that specify and establish social and economic inequalities. The basic liberties of citizens are, roughly speaking, political liberty (the right to vote and to be eligible for public office) together with freedom of speech and assembly; liberty of conscience and freedom of thought; freedom of the person along with the right to hold personal property; and freedom from arbitrary arrest and seizure as defined by the concept of the rule of law. These liberties are all required to be equal by the first principle, since citizens of a just society are to have the same basic rights.

The second principle applies, in the first approximation, to the distribution of income and wealth and to the design of organizations that make use of differences in authority and responsibility, or chains of command. While the distribution of wealth and income need not be equal, it must be to everyone's advantage, and at the same time, positions of authority and offices of command must be accessible to all. One applies the second principle by holding positions open, and then, subject to this constraint, arranges social and economic inequalities so that everyone benefits.

These principles are to be arranged in a serial order with the first principle prior to the second. This ordering means that a departure from the institutions of equal liberty required by the first principle cannot be justified by, or compensated for, by greater social and economic advantages. The distribution of wealth and income, and the hierarchies of authority, must be consistent with both the liberties of equal citizenship and equality of opportunity.

It is clear that these principles are rather specific in their content, and their acceptance rests on certain assumptions that I must eventually try to explain and justify. A theory of justice depends upon a theory of society in ways that will become evident as we proceed. For the present, it should be observed that the two principles (and this holds for all formulations) are a special case of a more general conception of justice that can be expressed as follows:

> All social values—liberty and opportunity, income and wealth, and the bases of self-respect—are to be distributed equally unless an unequal distribution of any, or all, of these values is to everyone's advantage.

Injustice, then, is simply inequalities that are not to the benefit of all. Of course, this conception is extremely vague and requires interpretation.

As a first step, suppose that the basic structure of society distributes certain primary goods, that is, things that every rational man is presumed to want. These goods normally have a use whatever a person's rational plan of life. For simplicity, assume that the chief primary goods at the disposition of society are rights and liberties, powers and opportunities, income and wealth. (Later on . . . the primary good of self-respect has a central place.) These are the social primary goods. Other primary goods such as health and vigor, intelligence and imagination, are natural goods; although their possession is influenced by the basic structure, they are not so directly under its control. Imagine, then, a hypothetical initial arrangement in which all the social primary goods are equally distributed: everyone has similar rights and duties, and income and wealth are evenly shared. This state of affairs provides a benchmark for judging improvements. If certain inequalities of wealth and organizational powers would make everyone better off than in this hypothetical starting situation, then they accord with the general conception.

Now it is possible, at least theoretically, that by giving up some of their fundamental liberties men are sufficiently compensated by the resulting social and economic gains. The general conception of justice imposes no restrictions on what sort of inequalities are permissible; it only requires that everyone's position be improved. We need not suppose anything so drastic as consenting to a condition of slavery. Imagine instead that men forgo certain political rights when the economic returns are significant and their capacity to influence the course of policy by the exercise of these rights would be marginal in any case. It is this kind of exchange which the two principles as stated rule out; being arranged in serial order they do not permit exchanges between basic liberties and economic and social gains. The serial ordering of principles expresses an underlying preference among primary social goods. When this preference is rational so likewise is the choice of these principles in this order.

In developing justice as fairness I shall, for the most part, leave aside the general conception of justice and examine instead the special case of the two principles in serial order. The advantage of this procedure is that from the first the matter of priorities is recognized and an effort made to find principles to deal with it. One is led to attend throughout to the conditions under which the acknowledgment of the absolute weight of liberty with respect to social and economic advantages, as defined by the lexical order of the two principles, would be reasonable. Offhand, this ranking appears extreme and too special a case to be of much interest; but there is more justification for it than would appear at first sight. Or at any rate, so I shall maintain. . . . Furthermore, the distinction between fundamental rights and liberties and economic and social benefits marks a difference among primary social goods that one should try to exploit. It suggests an important division in the social system. Of course, the distinctions drawn and the ordering proposed are bound to be at best only approximations. There are surely circumstances in which they fail. But it is essential to depict clearly the main lines of a reasonable conception of justice; and under many conditions, anyway, the two principles in serial order may serve well enough. When necessary we can fall back on the more general conception.

The fact that the two principles apply to institutions has certain consequences. Several points illustrate this. First of all, the rights and liberties referred to by these principles are those that are defined by the public rules of the basic structure. Whether men are free is determined by the rights and duties established by the major institutions of society. Liberty is a certain pattern of social forms. The first principle simply requires that certain sorts of rules, those defining basic liberties, apply to everyone equally and that they allow the most extensive liberty compatible with a like liberty for all. The only reason for circumscribing the rights defining liberty and making men's freedom less extensive than it might otherwise be is that these equal rights as institutionally defined would interfere with one another.

Another thing to bear in mind is that when principles mention persons, or require that everyone gain from an inequality, the reference is to representative persons holding the various social positions, or offices, or whatever, established by the basic structure. Thus in applying the second principle I assume that it is possible to assign an expectation of well-being to representative individuals holding these positions. This expectation indicates their life prospects as viewed from their social station. In general, the expectations of representative persons depend upon the distribution of rights and duties throughout the basic structure. When this changes, expectations change. I assume, then, that expectations are connected: by raising the prospects of the representative man in one position we presumably increase or decrease the prospects of representative men in other positions. Since it applies to institutional forms, the second principle (or rather the first part of it) refers to the expectations of representative individuals. As I shall discuss below, neither principle applies to distributions of particular goods to particular individuals who may be identified by their proper names. The situation where someone is considering how to allocate certain commodities to needy persons who are known to him is not within the scope of the principles. They are meant to regulate basic institutional arrangements. We must not assume that there is much similarity from the standpoint of justice between an administrative allotment of goods to specific persons and the appropriate design of society. Our common sense intuitions for the former may be a poor guide to the latter.

Now the second principle insists that each person benefit from permissible inequalities in the basic structure. This means that it must be reasonable for each relevant representative man defined by this structure, when he views it as a going concern, to prefer his prospects with the inequality, to his prospects without it. One is not allowed to justify differences in income or organizational powers on the ground that the disadvantages of those in one position are outweighed by the greater advantages of those in another. Much less can infringements of liberty be counterbalanced in this way. Applied to the basic structure, the principle of utility would have us maximize the sum of expectations of representative men (weighted by the number of persons they represent, on the classical view); and this would permit us to compensate for the losses of some by the gains of others. Instead, the two principles require that everyone benefit from economic and social inequalities.

The Reasoning Leading to the Two Principles of Justice

It will be recalled that the general conception of justice as fairness requires that all primary social goods be distributed equally unless an unequal distribution would be to everyone's advantage. No restrictions are placed on exchanges of these goods and therefore a lesser liberty can be compensated for by greater social and economic benefits. Now looking at the situation from the standpoint of one person selected arbitrarily, there is no way for him to win special advantages for himself. Nor, on the other hand, are there grounds for his acquiescing in special disadvantages. Since it is not reasonable for him to expect more than an equal share in the division of social goods, and since it is not rational for him to agree to less, the sensible thing for him to do is to acknowledge as the first principle of justice one requiring an equal distribution. Indeed, this principle is so obvious that we would expect it to occur to anyone immediately.

Thus, the parties start with a principle establishing equal liberty for all, including equality of opportunity, as well as an equal distribution of income and wealth. But there is no reason why this acknowledgment should be final. If there are inequalities in the basic structure that work to make everyone better off in comparison with the benchmark of initial equality, why not permit them? The immediate gain which a greater equality might allow can be regarded as intelligently invested in view of its future return. If, for example, these inequalities set up various incentives which succeed in eliciting more productive efforts, a person in the original position may look upon them as necessary to cover the costs of training and to encourage effective performance. One might think that ideally individuals should want to serve one another. But since the parties are assumed not to take an interest in one another's interests, their acceptance of these inequalities is only the acceptance of the relations in which men stand in the circumstances of justice. They have no grounds for complaining of one another's mo-

tives. A person in the original position would, therefore, concede the justice of these inequalities. Indeed, it would be shortsighted of him not to do so. He would hesitate to agree to these regularities only if he would be dejected by the bare knowledge or perception that others were better situated; and I have assumed that the parties decide as if they are not moved by envy. In order to make the principle regulating inequalities determinate, one looks at the system from the standpoint of the least advantaged representative man. Inequalities are permissible when they maximize, or at least all contribute to, the long-term expectations of the least fortunate group in society.

Now this general conception imposes no constraints on what sorts of inequalities are allowed, whereas the special conception, by putting the two principles in serial order (with the necessary adjustments in meaning), forbids exchanges between basic liberties and economic and social benefits. I shall not try to justify this ordering here. . . . But roughly, the idea underlying this ordering is that if the parties assume that their basic liberties can be effectively exercised, they will not exchange a lesser liberty for an improvement in economic well-being. It is only when social conditions do not allow the effective establishment of these rights that one can concede their limitation; and these restrictions can be granted only to the extent that they are necessary to prepare the way for a free society. The denial of equal liberty can be defended only if it is necessary to raise the level of civilization so that in due course these freedoms can be enjoyed. Thus in adopting a serial order we are in effect making a special assumption in the original position, namely, that the parties know that the conditions of their society, whatever they are, admit the effective realization of the equal liberties. The serial ordering of the two principles of justice eventually comes to be reasonable if the general conception is consistently followed. This lexical ranking is the long-run tendency of the general view. For the most part I shall assume that the requisite circumstances for the serial order obtain.

It seems clear from these remarks that the two principles are at least a plausible conception of justice. The question, though, is how one is to argue for them more systematically. Now there are several things to do. One can work out their consequences for institutions and note their implications for fundamental social policy. In this way they are tested by a comparison with our considered judgments of justice. . . . But one can also try to find arguments in their favor that are decisive from the standpoint of the original position. In order to see how this might be done, it is useful as a heuristic device to think of the two principles as the maximin solution to the problem of social justice. There is an analogy between the two principles and the maximin rule for choice under uncertainty.[5] This is evident from the fact that the two principles are those a person would choose for the design of a society in which his enemy is to assign him his place. The maximin rule tells us to rank alternatives by their worst possible outcomes: we are to adopt the alternative the worst outcome of which is superior to the worst outcomes of the others. The persons in the original position do not, of course, assume that their initial place in society is decided by a malevolent opponent. As I note below, they should not reason from false premises. The veil of ignorance does not violate this idea, since an absence of information is not misinformation. But that the two principles of justice would be chosen if the parties were forced to protect themselves against such a contingency explains the sense in which this conception is the maximin solution. And this analogy suggests that if the original position has been described so that it is rational for the parties to adopt the conservative attitude expressed by this rule, a conclusive argument can indeed be constructed for these principles. Clearly the maximin rule is not, in general, a suitable guide for choices under uncertainty. But it is attractive in situations marked by certain special features. My aim, then, is to show that a good case can be made for the two principles based on the fact that the original position manifests these features to the fullest possible degree, carrying them to the limit, so to speak.

Consider the gain-and-loss table below. It represents the gains and losses for a situation which is not a game of strategy. There is no one playing against the person making the decision; instead he is faced with several possible circumstances which may or may not obtain. Which circumstances happen to exist does not depend upon what the person choosing decides or whether he announces his moves in advance. The numbers in the table are monetary values (in hundreds of dollars) in comparison with some initial situation. The gain (g) depends upon the individual's decision (d) and the circumstances (c). Thus $g = f(d,c)$. Assuming that there are three possible decisions and three possible circumstances, we might have this gain-and-loss table.

Decisions	Circumstances		
	c_1	c_2	c_3
d_1	−7	8	12
d_2	−8	7	14
d_3	5	6	8

The maximin rule requires that we make the third decision. For in this case the worst that can happen is that one gains five hundred dollars, which is better than the worst for the other actions. If we adopt one of these we may lose either eight or seven hundred dollars. Thus, the choice of d_3 maximizes $f(d,c)$ for that value of c which for a given d, minimizes f. The term "maximin" means the *maximum minimorum;* and the rule directs our attention to the worst that can happen under any proposed course of action, and to decide in the light of that.

Now there appear to be three chief features of situations that give plausibility to this unusual rule.[6] First, since the rule takes no account of the likelihoods of the possible circumstances, there must be some reason for sharply discounting estimates of these probabilities. Offhand, the most natural rule of choice would seem to be to compute the expectation of monetary gain for each decision and then to adopt the course of action with the highest prospect. (This expectation is defined as follows: let us suppose that g_{ij} represents the numbers in the gain-and-loss table, where i is the row index and j is the column index; and let p_i, j = 1, 2, 3, be the likelihoods of the circumstances, with $\Sigma p_j = 1$. Then the expectation for the ith decision is equal to $\Sigma p_i g_{ij}$.)

Thus it must be, for example, that the situation is one in which a knowledge of likelihoods is impossible, or at best extremely insecure. In this case it is unreasonable not to be skeptical of probabilistic calculations unless there is no other way out, particularly if the decision is a fundamental one that needs to be justified to others.

The second feature that suggests the maximin rule is the following: the person choosing has a conception of the good such that he cares very little, if anything, for what he might gain above the minimum stipend that he can, in fact, be sure of by following the maximin rule. It is not worthwhile for him to take a chance for the sake of a further advantage, especially when it may turn out that he loses much that is important to him. This last provision brings in the third feature; namely, that the rejected alternatives have outcomes that one can hardly accept. The situation involves grave risks. Of course these features work most effectively in combination. The paradigm situation for following the maximin rule is when all three features are realized to the highest degree. This rule does not, then, generally apply, nor of course is it self-evident. Rather, it is a maxim, a rule of thumb, that comes into its own in special circumstances. Its application depends upon the qualitative structure of the possible gains and losses in relation to one's conception of the good, all this against a background in which it is reasonable to discount conjectural estimates of likelihoods.

It should be noted, as the comments on the gain-and-loss table say, that the entries in the table represent monetary values and not utilities. This difference is significant since for one thing computing expectations on the basis of such objective values is not the same thing as computing expected utility and may lead to different results. The essential point, though, is that in justice as fairness the parties do not know their conception of the good and cannot estimate their utility in the ordinary sense. In any case, we want to go behind de facto preferences generated by given conditions. Therefore expectations are based upon an index of primary goods and the parties make their choice accordingly. The entries in the example are in terms of money and not utility to indicate this aspect of the contract doctrine.

Now, as I have suggested, the original position has been defined so that it is a situation in which the maximin rule applies. In order to see this, let us review briefly the nature of this situation with these three special features in mind. To begin with, the veil of ignorance excludes all but the vaguest knowledge of likelihoods. The parties have no basis for determining the probable nature of their society, or their place in it. Thus they have strong reasons for being wary of probability calculations if any other course is open to them. They must also take into account the fact that their choice of principles should seem reasonable to others, in particular their descendants, whose rights will be deeply affected by it. There are further grounds for discounting that I shall mention as we go along. For the present it suffices to note that these considerations are strengthened by the fact that the parties know very little about the gain-and-loss table. Not only are they unable to conjecture the likelihoods of the various possible circumstances, they cannot say much about what the possible circumstances are, much less enumerate them and foresee the outcome of each alternative available. Those deciding are much more in the dark than the illustration by a numerical table suggests. It is for this reason that I have spoken of an analogy with the maximin rule.

Several kinds of arguments for the two principles of justice illustrate the second feature. Thus, if we can maintain that these principles provide a workable theory of social justice, and that they are compatible with reasonable demands of efficiency, then this conception guarantees a satisfactory minimum. There may be, on reflection, little reason for trying to do better. Thus much of the argument . . . is to show, by their application to the main questions of social justice, that the two principles are a satisfactory conception. These details have a philosophical purpose. Moreover, this line of thought is practically decisive if we can establish the priority of liberty, the lexical ordering of the two principles. For this priority implies that the persons in the original position have no desire to try for greater gains at the expense of the equal liberties. The minimum assured by the two principles in lexical order is not one that the parties wish to jeopardize for the sake of greater economic and social advantages. . . .

Finally, the third feature holds if we can assume that other conceptions of justice may lead to institutions that the parties would find intolerable. For example, it has sometimes been held that under some conditions the utility principle (in either form) justifies, if not slavery or serfdom, at any rate serious infractions of liberty for the sake of greater social benefits. We need not consider here the truth of this claim, or the likelihood that the requisite conditions obtain. For the moment, this contention is only to illustrate the way in which conceptions of justice may allow for outcomes which the parties may not be able to accept. And having the ready alternative of the two principles of justice which secure a satisfactory minimum, it seems unwise, if not irrational, for them to take a chance that these outcomes are not realized.

So much, then, for a brief sketch of the features of situations in which the maximin rule comes into its own and of the way in which the arguments for the two principles of justice can be subsumed under them. . . .

The Final Formulation of the Principles of Justice

. . . I now wish to give the final statement of the two principles of justice for institutions. For the sake of completeness, I shall give a full statement including earlier formulations.

First Principle
Each person is to have an equal right to the most extensive total system of equal basic liberties compatible with a similar system of liberty for all.

Second Principle
Social and economic inequalities are to be arranged so that they are both:
(a) to the greatest benefit of the least advantaged, consistent with the just savings principle, and
(b) attached to offices and positions open to all under conditions of fair equality of opportunity.

First Priority Rule (The Priority of Liberty)
The principles of justice are to be ranked in lexical order and therefore liberty can be restricted only for the sake of liberty. There are two cases:
(a) a less extensive liberty must strengthen the total system of liberty shared by all;
(b) a less than equal liberty must be acceptable to those with the lesser liberty.

Second Priority Rule (The Priority of Justice over Efficiency and Welfare)
The second principle of justice is lexically prior to the principle of efficiency and to that of maximizing the sum of advantages; and fair opportunity is prior to the difference principle. There are two cases:
(a) an inequality of opportunity must enhance the opportunities of those with the lesser opportunity;
(b) an excessive rate of saving must on balance mitigate the burden of those bearing this hardship.

General Conception
All social primary goods—liberty and opportunity, income and wealth, and the bases of self-respect—are to be distributed equally unless an unequal distribution of any or all of these goods is to the advantage of the least favored.

By way of comment, these principles and priority rules are no doubt incomplete. Other modifications will surely have to be made, but I shall not further complicate the statement of the principles. It suffices to observe that when we come to nonideal theory, we do not fall back straightway upon the general conception of justice. The lexical ordering of the two principles, and the valuations that this ordering implies, suggest priority rules which seem to be reasonable enough in many cases. By various examples I have tried to illustrate how these rules can be used and to indicate their plausibility. Thus the ranking of the principles of justice in ideal theory reflects back and guides the application of these principles to nonideal situations. It identifies which limitations need to be dealt with first. The drawback of the general conception of justice is that it lacks the definite structure of the two principles in serial order. In more extreme and tangled instances of nonideal theory there may be no alternative to it. At some point the priority of rules for nonideal cases will fail; and indeed, we may be able to find no satisfactory answer at all. But we must try to postpone the day of reckoning as long as possible, and try to arrange society so that it never comes. . . .

Notes

1. As the text suggests, I shall regard Locke's *Second Treatise of Government,* Rousseau's *The Social Contract,* and Kant's ethical works beginning with *The Foundations of the Metaphysics of Morals* as definitive of the contract tradition. For all of its greatness, Hobbes's *Leviathan* raises special problems. A general historical survey is provided by J. W. Gough, *The Social Contract,* 2nd ed. (Oxford, The Clarendon Press, 1957), and Otto Gierke, *Natural Law and the Theory of Society,* trans. with an introduction by Ernest Barker (Cambridge, The University Press, 1934). A presentation of the contract view as primarily an ethical theory is to be found in G. R. Grice, *The Grounds of Moral Judgment* (Cambridge, The University Press, 1967).

2. Kant is clear that the original agreement is hypothetical. See *The Metaphysics of Morals,* pt. I *(Rechtslehre),* especially §§ 47, 52; and pt. II of the essay "Concerning the Common Saying: This May Be True in Theory but It Does Not Apply in Practice," in *Kant's Political Writings,* ed. Hans Reiss and trans. by H. B. Nisbet (Cambridge, The University Press, 1970), pp. 73–87. See Georges Vlachos, *La pensée politique de Kant* (Paris, Presses Universitaires de France, 1962), pp. 326–335; and J. G. Murphy, *Kant: The Philosophy of Right* (London, Macmillan, 1970), pp. 109–112, 133–136, for a further discussion.

3. For the formulation of this intuitive idea I am indebted to Allan Gibbard.

4. The process of mutual adjustment of principles and considered judgments is not peculiar to moral philosophy. See Nelson Goodman, *Fact, Fiction, and Forecast* (Cambridge, Mass., Harvard University Press, 1955), pp. 65–68, for parallel remarks concerning the justification of the principles of deductive and inductive inference.

5. An accessible discussion of this and other rules of choice under uncertainty can be found in W. J. Baumol, *Economic Theory and Operations Analysis,* 2nd ed. (Englewood Cliffs, N.J., Prentice-Hall, 1965), ch. 24. Baumol gives a geometric interpretation of these rules, including the diagram used . . . to illustrate the difference principle. See pp. 558–562. See also R. D. Luce and Howard Raiffa, *Games and Decisions* (New York, John Wiley and Sons, 1957), ch. XIII, for a fuller account.

6. Here I borrow from William Fellner, *Probability and Profit* (Homewood, Ill., Richard D. Irwin, 1965), pp. 140–142, where these features are noted.

4. From Liberty to Equality

James P. Sterba

James P. Sterba argues that when a libertarian ideal of liberty is interpreted in the manner favored by libertarians as the absence of interference by other people from doing what one wants or is able to do, it leads to a universal right to welfare. He further argues that the recognition of this universal right to welfare leads to the equalization of resources characteristic of a socialist state. He considers a number of objections to these arguments and finds them wanting.

The central contrast between libertarians and socialists is usually put this way. Libertarians take the ideal of liberty to be the ultimate political ideal from which they claim it follows that nothing more than a minimal or night watchman state can be justified. By contrast, socialists take the ideal of equality to be the ultimate political ideal from which they claim it follows that only a state that socializes the means of production can be justified. Libertarians, however, tend to agree with socialists that when the ideal of equality is interpreted in the manner socialists favor, it would justify a socialist state. Libertarians simply contend that the socialist interpretation of the ideal of equality is arbitrary. Why not interpret the ideal in the manner favored by libertarians as equality before the law or equality of political rights so that the ideal is at least consistent with, if not required by, the libertarian's own ideal of liberty? Why not indeed! But obviously an analogous question could be directed at libertarians. Why not interpret the ideal of liberty in the manner favored by socialists as a positive rather than a negative ideal so that the ideal would justify the greater restrictions of a socialist state?

To either of these questions, no convincing answers seem forthcoming. Both the interpretations of the ideals of liberty and equality favored by libertarians and those favored by socialists appear arbitrary. Consequently, the dispute between libertarians and socialists

Revised from "Peace Through Justice: A Practical Reconciliation of Opposing Conceptions of Justice," in *In the Interests of Peace*, ed. Kenneth Klein and Joseph Kunkel (1990). Reprinted by permission.

seems irresolvable. Yet despite appearances, I wish to argue that this dispute is not irresolvable. Rather I contend that for all practical purposes the dispute can be resolved so as to provide a justification for a socialist state—a justification to which libertarians would have to assent.

Liberty and Welfare

To see that this is the case, suppose we were to interpret the ideal of liberty as a negative ideal in the manner favored by libertarians.[1] So understood, liberty is the absence of interference by other people from doing what one wants or is able to do.

Interpreting their ideal in this way, libertarians claim to derive a number of more specific requirements, in particular, a right to life, a right to freedom of speech, press, and assembly, and a right to property. Here it is important to observe that the libertarian's right to life is not a right to receive from others the goods and resources necessary for preserving one's life; it is simply a right not to be killed unjustly. Correspondingly, the libertarian's right to property is not a right to receive from others the goods and resources necessary for one's welfare, but rather a right to acquire goods and resources either by initial acquisition or by voluntary agreement.

Of course, libertarians would allow that it would be nice of the rich to share their surplus resources with the poor. Nevertheless, according to libertarians, such acts of charity should not be coercively required. For this reason, libertarians are opposed to coercively supported welfare programs.

Now in order to see why libertarians are mistaken about what their ideal requires, consider a typical conflict situation between the rich and the poor. In this conflict situation, the rich, of course, have more than enough resources to satisfy their basic needs. By contrast, the poor lack the resources to meet their most basic needs even though they have tried all the means available to them that libertarians regard as legitimate for acquiring such resources. Under circumstances like these, libertarians usually maintain that the rich should have the liberty to use their resources to satisfy their luxury needs if they so wish. Libertarians recognize that this liberty might well be enjoyed at the expense of the satisfaction of the most basic needs of the poor; they just think that liberty always has priority over other political ideals, and since they assume that the liberty of the poor is not at stake in such conflict situations, it is easy for them to conclude that the rich should not be required to sacrifice their liberty so that the basic needs of the poor may be met.

Of course, libertarians would allow that it would be nice of the rich to share their surplus resources with the poor. Nevertheless, according to libertarians, such acts of charity are not required because the liberty of the poor is not thought to be at stake in such conflict situations.

In fact, however, the liberty of the poor is at stake in such conflict situations. What is at stake is the liberty of the poor to take from the surplus possessions of the rich what is necessary to satisfy their basic needs. When libertarians are brought to see that this is the case, they are genuinely surprised—one might even say rudely awakened—for they had not previously seen the conflict between the rich and the poor as a conflict of liberties.[2]

Now when the conflict between the rich and the poor is viewed as a conflict of liberties, we can either say that the rich should have the liberty to use their surplus resources for luxury purposes, or we can say that the poor should have the liberty to take from the rich what they require to meet their basic needs. If

we choose one liberty, we must reject the other. What needs to be determined, therefore, is which liberty is morally preferable: the liberty of the rich or the liberty of the poor.

I submit that the liberty of the poor, which is the liberty to take from the surplus resources of others what is required to meet one's basic needs, is morally preferable to the liberty of the rich, which is the liberty to use one's surplus resources for luxury purposes. To see that this is the case, we need only appeal to one of the most fundamental principles of morality, one that is common to all political perspectives, namely, the "ought implies can" principle. According to this principle, people are not morally required to do what they lack the power to do or what would involve so great a sacrifice that it would be unreasonable to ask, and/or in cases of severe conflict of interest, unreasonable to require them to abide by.

For example, suppose I promised to attend a departmental meeting on Friday, but on Thursday I am involved in a serious car accident which puts me into a coma. Surely it is no longer the case that I ought to attend the meeting now that I lack the power to do so. Or suppose instead that on Thursday I develop a severe case of pneumonia for which I am hospitalized. Surely I could legitimately claim that I cannot attend the meeting on the grounds that the risk to my health involved in attending is a sacrifice that it would be unreasonable to ask me to bear. Or suppose the risk to my health from having pneumonia is not so serious that it would be unreasonable to ask me to attend the meeting (a supererogatory request), it might still be serious enough to be unreasonable to require my attendance at the meeting (a demand that is backed up by blame or coercion).

What is distinctive about this formulation of the "ought" implies "can" principle is that it claims that the requirements of morality cannot, all things considered, be unreasonable to ask, and/or in cases of severe conflict of interest, unreasonable to require people to abide by. The principle claims that reason and morality must be linked in an appropriate way, especially if we are going to be able justifiably to use blame or coercion to get people to abide by the requirements of morality. It should be noted, however, that although major figures in the history of philosophy—and most philosophers today, including virtually all libertarian philosophers—accept this linkage between reason and morality, this linkage is not usually conceived to be part of the "ought" implies "can" principle. Nevertheless, I claim that there are good reasons for associating this linkage between reason and morality with the "ought" implies "can" principle, namely, our use of the word "can" as in the example just given, and the natural progression from logical, physical, and psychological possibility found in the traditional "ought" implies "can" principle to the notion of moral possibility found in this formulation of the "ought" implies "can" principle. In any case, the acceptability of this formulation of the "ought" implies "can" principle is determined by the virtually universal acceptance of its components and not by the manner in which I have proposed to join those components together.[3]

Now applying the "ought" implies "can" principle to the case at hand, it seems clear that the poor have it within their power willingly to relinquish such an important liberty as the liberty to take from the rich what they require to meet their basic needs. Nevertheless, it would be unreasonable to ask or require them to make so great a sacrifice. In the extreme case, it would involve asking or requiring the poor to sit back and starve to death. Of course, the poor may have no real alternative to relinquishing this liberty. To do anything else may involve worse consequences for themselves and their loved ones and may invite a painful death. Accordingly, we may expect that the poor would acquiesce, albeit unwillingly, to a political system that denied them the right to welfare supported by such a liberty, at the same time that we recognize that such a system imposed an unreasonable sacrifice upon the poor—a sacrifice that we could not morally blame the poor for trying to evade.[4] Analogously, we might expect that a woman whose life was threatened would submit to a rapist's demands, at the same time that we recognize the utter unreasonableness of those demands.

By contrast, it would not be unreasonable to ask and require the rich to sacrifice the liberty to meet some of their luxury needs so that the poor can have the liberty to meet their basic needs.[5] Naturally, we might expect that the rich, for reasons of self-interest and past contribution, might be disinclined to make such a sacrifice. We might even suppose that the past contribution of the rich provides a good reason for not sacrificing their liberty to use their surplus for luxury purposes. Yet, unlike the poor, the rich could not claim that relinquishing such a liberty involved so great a sacrifice that it would be unreasonable to ask and require them to make it; unlike the poor, the rich could be morally blameworthy for failing to make such a sacrifice.

Consequently, if we assume that however else we specify the requirements of morality, they cannot violate the "ought" implies "can" principle, it follows that, despite what libertarians claim, the right to liberty endorsed by them actually favors the liberty of the poor over the liberty of the rich.

Yet couldn't libertarians object to this conclusion, claiming that it would be unreasonable to ask the rich to sacrifice the liberty to meet some of their luxury needs so that the poor could have the liberty to meet their basic needs? As I have pointed out, libertarians don't usually see the situation as a conflict of liberties, but suppose they did. How plausible would such an objection be? Not very plausible at all, I think.

For consider: What are Spencerian libertarians going to say about the poor? Isn't it clearly unreasonable to require the poor to sacrifice the liberty to meet their basic needs so that the rich can have the liberty to meet their luxury needs? Isn't it clearly unreasonable to require the poor to sit back and starve to death? If it is, then, there is no resolution of this conflict that would be reasonable to require both the rich and the poor to accept. But that would mean that libertarians could not be putting forth a moral ideal because a moral ideal resolves severe conflicts of interest in ways that it would be reasonable to ask and require everyone affected to accept. Therefore, as long as libertarians think of themselves as putting forth a moral ideal, they cannot allow that it would be unreasonable in cases of severe conflict of interest *both* to require the rich to sacrifice the liberty to meet some of their luxury needs in order to benefit the poor and to require the poor to sacrifice the liberty to meet their basic needs in order to benefit the rich. But I submit that if one of these requirements is to be judged reasonable, then, by any neutral assessment, it must be the requirement that the rich sacrifice the liberty to meet some of their luxury needs so that the poor can have the liberty to meet their basic needs; there is no other plausible resolution, if libertarians intend to be putting forth a moral ideal.

In brief, I have argued that a libertarian ideal of liberty can be seen to support a right to welfare through an application of the "ought" implies "can" principle to conflicts between the rich and the poor. In the interpretation I have used, the principle supports such rights by favoring the liberty of the poor over the liberty of the rich. In another interpretation (developed elsewhere), the principle supports such rights by favoring a conditional right to property over an unconditional right to property.[6] In either interpretation, what is crucial to the derivation of these rights is the claim that it would be unreasonable to require the poor to deny their basic needs and accept anything less than these rights as the condition for their willing cooperation.

In his book, *Individuals and Their Rights*, Tibor Machan criticizes my argument that a libertarian ideal of liberty leads to welfare rights, accepting its theoretical thrust but denying its practical significance.[7] He appreciates the force of the argument enough to grant that if the type of conflict cases I describe between the rich and the poor actually obtained, the poor would have welfare rights. But he denies that such cases—in which the poor have done all that they legitimately can to satisfy their basic needs in a libertarian society—actually obtain. "Normally," he writes, "persons do not lack the opportunities and resources to satisfy their basic needs."[8]

But this response virtually concedes everything that defenders of welfare rights had hoped to establish. For the poor's right to welfare is not unconditional. It is conditional principally upon the poor doing all that they legitimately can to meet their own basic needs. So it is only when the poor lack sufficient opportunity to satisfy their own basic needs that a right to welfare has moral force. Accordingly, on libertarian grounds, Machan has conceded the legitimacy of just the kind of

right to welfare that defenders of welfare had hoped to establish.

Liberty and Equality

Now it is possible that libertarians, convinced to some extent by the previous argument, might want to accept a right to welfare but then deny that this would lead to anything like a socialist state. At most, libertarians might concede that the previous argument shows that the ideal of liberty supports a welfare state but not a socialist state. This is because at least in an affluent society a right to welfare could be fully secured while inequalities of wealth and privilege incompatible with the socialist ideal of equality remain.

I now hope to show why this line of argument cannot prevail. After all, the fundamental rights recognized by libertarians are universal rights, that is, rights possessed by all people not just those who live in certain places or at certain times. Of course, to claim that these rights are universal rights does not mean that they are universally recognized. Obviously, the fundamental rights that flow from the libertarian ideal have not been universally recognized. Rather to claim that they are universal rights, despite their spotty recognition, implies only that they ought to be recognized at all times and places by people who have or could have had good reasons to recognize these rights, whether or not that they actually did or do so.

Nor need these universal rights be unconditional. This is particularly true in the case of the right to welfare, which, I have argued, is conditional on people doing all that they legitimately can to provide for themselves. In addition, this right is conditional on there being sufficient resources available so that everyone's welfare needs can be met. So where people do not do all that they can to provide for themselves or where there are not sufficient resources available, people simply do not have a right to welfare.

Yet even though libertarians have claimed that the rights they defend are universal rights in the manner I have just explained, it may be that they are simply mistaken in this regard. Even when universal rights are stripped of any claim to being universally recognized or unconditional, still it might be argued that there are no such rights, that is, that there are no rights that all people ought to recognize.

But how would one argue for such a view? One couldn't argue from the failure of people to recognize such rights because we have already said that such recognition is not necessary. Nor could one argue that not everyone ought to recognize such rights because some lack the capacity to do so. This is because "ought" does imply "can" here, so that the obligation to recognize certain rights only applies to those who actually have or have had at some point the capacity to do so. Thus, the existence of universal rights is not ruled out by the existence of individuals who have never had the capacity to recognize such rights. It would only be ruled out by the existence of individuals who could recognize these rights but for whom it would be correct to say that they ought, all things considered, not to do so. But we have just seen that even a minimal libertarian moral ideal supports a universal right to welfare. And I have also argued elsewhere that when "ought" is understood prudentially rather than morally a non-question-begging conception to rationality favors morality over prudence.[9] So for those capable of recognizing universal rights, it simply is not possible to argue that they, all things considered, ought not to do so.

Still, one might grant that there are universal rights, even a right to welfare, that can be supported by the libertarian ideal of liberty but still deny that such rights lead to a socialist rather than a welfare state. But to see why this is not the case, consider what would be required to recognize a universal right to welfare.

At present, there is probably a sufficient worldwide supply of goods and resources to meet the normal costs of satisfying the basic nutritional needs of all existing persons. According to the former U.S. Secretary of Agriculture, Bob Bergland,

> For the past twenty years, if the available world food supply had been evenly divided and distributed, each person would have received more than the minimum number of calories.

Other authorities have made similar assessments of the available world food supply.

Needless to say, the adoption of a policy of supporting a right to welfare for all existing persons would necessitate significant changes, especially in developed countries. For example, the large percentage of the U.S. population whose food consumption clearly exceeds even an adequately adjusted poverty index would have to alter their eating habits substantially. In particular, they would have to reduce their consumption of beef and pork so as to make more grain available for direct human consumption. (Presently the amount of grain fed American livestock is as much as all the people of China and India eat in a year.) Thus, at least the satisfaction of some of the nonbasic needs of the more advantaged in developed countries would have to be forgone, leading to greater equality, so that the basic nutritional needs of all existing persons in developing and underdeveloped countries could be met. Furthermore, to raise the standard of living in the developing and underdeveloped countries will require substantial increases in the consumption of energy and other resources. But such an increase would have to be matched by a substantial decrease in the consumption of these goods in the developed countries, otherwise global ecological disaster would result from increased global warming, ozone depletion, and acid rain, lowering virtually everyone's standard of living.[10]

In addition, once the basic nutritional needs of future generations are also taken into account, then the satisfaction of the nonbasic needs of the more advantaged in developed countries would have to be further restricted in order to preserve the fertility of cropland and other food-related natural resources for the use of future generations. And once basic needs other than nutritional needs are taken into account as well, still further restrictions would be required. For example, it has been estimated that presently a North American uses fifty times more resources than an Indian. This means that in terms of resource consumption the North American continent's population is the equivalent of 12.5 billion Indians. Obviously, this would have to be radically altered if the basic needs of distant peoples and future generations are to be met. In effect, recognizing a universal right to welfare applicable both to distant peoples and future generations would lead to an equal sharing of resources over place and time. In short, socialist equality is the consequence of recognizing a universal libertarian right to welfare.

Still, one might want to press Machan's objection to this argument from liberty to equality, which is that the argument has no practical significance because "persons do not lack the opportunities and resources to satisfy their basic needs." However, this objection is particularly easy to refute once the libertarian ideal is seen to ground a universal right to welfare. This is because there is simply no denying that most of the 1.2 billion people who are living today in conditions of absolute poverty "lack the opportunities and resources to satisfy their basic needs."[11] Yet the objection also fails when we look closely at the poor within our own society. It is estimated that some 32 million Americans live below the official poverty index, and that one fifth of American children are growing up in poverty.[12] Surely many of these Americans also "lack the opportunities and resources to satisfy their basic needs."

It might be objected that this argument falls victim to its own success. If a universal right to welfare requires an equal sharing of resources, wouldn't talented people simply lack the incentive to produce according to their ability when such a right is enforced? But what sort of incentive is needed? Surely there would be moral incentive for the talented to make the necessary sacrifices if the ideal of liberty requires such a right to welfare. Yet, except for those who closely identify with such moral incentives, there would not be sufficient self-interested incentive to accept the equality of resources required by a universal right to welfare. Even so, if it can be shown, as I claim, that morality has priority over self-interested prudence, there is no question of what ought to be done.

In brief, I have argued that when a libertarian ideal of liberty is correctly interpreted, it leads to a universal right to welfare and, further, that the recognition of this universal right to welfare leads to the equalization of resources characteristic of a socialist state. Of course, the libertarian ideal, unlike the socialist ideal, does not directly pursue the goal of equality. Nevertheless, I contend that the practical effect of both ideals is much the same.

Notes

1. See John Hospers, *Libertarianism* (Los Angeles: Nash Press, 1971).

2. Ibid., Chapter 7.

3. I am indebted to Alasdair MacIntyre for helping me make this point clearer.

4. See James P. Sterba, "Is There a Rationale for Punishment?," *American Journal of Jurisprudence* (1984). Vol 29, pp. 29–43.

5. By the liberty of the rich to meet their luxury needs I continue to mean the liberty of the rich not to be interfered with when using their surplus possessions for luxury purposes. Similarly, by the liberty of the poor to meet their basic needs I continue to mean the liberty of the poor not to be interfered with when taking what they require to meet their basic needs from the surplus possessions of the rich.

6. For this other interpretation, see my *How to Make People Just* (Totowa, N.J.: Rowman and Littlefield, 1988), Chapter 5.

7. Tibor Machan, *Individuals and Their Rights* (LaSalle: Open Court, 1989), pp. 100–111.

8. Ibid., p. 107.

9. See *How to Make People Just*, Chapter 9, and the Introduction to this anthology, pp. 5–10.

10. For a discussion of these causal connections, see Cheryl Silver, *One Earth One Future* (Washington, D.C.: National Academy Press, 1990); Bill McKibben, *The End of Nature* (New York: Doubleday, 1989); Jeremy Leggett, ed., *Global Warming* (New York: Oxford, 1990); Lester Brown, ed., *The World Watch Reader* (New York: Norton, 1991).

11. Alan Durning, "Life on the Brink," *World Watch*, 3(2) (1990), p. 24.

12. Ibid., p. 29.

5. *Wyman, Commissioner of New York Department of Social Services v. James*

Supreme Court of the United States

The issue before the Supreme Court of the United States was whether the Fourth Amendment prohibition of unreasonable searches applies to visits by welfare caseworkers to recipients of Aid to Families with Dependent Children. The majority of the Court held that the Fourth Amendment does not apply in this case because the visitation is not forced or compelled, and even if it were, the visitation serves the state's overriding interest in the welfare of dependent children. Dissenting Justices Douglas and Marshall argued that the Fourth Amendment prohibition does apply because the visitation is forced and compelled (although not normally by a threat of a criminal penalty) and because there are other ways of protecting the state's interest in this case. Justices Douglas and Marshall also argued that the decision of the majority is inconsistent with the Supreme Court's rulings with respect to the allocation of benefits in other cases.

Mr. Justice *Blackmun* delivered the opinion of the Court.

This appeal presents the issue whether a beneficiary of the program for Aid to Families with Dependent Children (AFDC) may refuse a home visit by the caseworker without risking the termination of benefits.

The New York State and City social services commissioners appeal from a judgment and decree of a divided three-judge District Court. . . .

The District Court majority held that a mother receiving AFDC relief may refuse, without forfeiting her right to that relief, the periodic home visit which the cited New York statutes and regulations prescribe as a condition for the continuance of assistance under the program. The beneficiary's thesis, and that of the District Court majority, is that home visitation is a search and, when not consented to or when not supported by a warrant based on probable cause, violates the beneficiary's Fourth and Fourteenth Amendment rights. . . .

Plaintiff Barbara James is the mother of a son, Maurice, who was born in May 1967. They reside in New York City. Mrs. James first applied for AFDC assistance shortly before Maurice's birth. A caseworker made a visit to her apartment at that time without objection. The assistance was authorized.

Two years later, on May 8, 1969, a caseworker wrote Mrs. James that she would visit her home on May 14. Upon receipt of this advice, Mrs. James telephoned the worker that, although she was willing to supply information "reasonable and relevant" to her need for public assistance, any discussion was not to take place at her home. The worker told Mrs. James that she was required by law to visit in her home and that refusal to permit the visit would result in the termination of assistance. Permission was still denied. . . .

A notice of termination issued on June 2.

Thereupon, without seeking a hearing at the state level, Mrs. James, individually and on behalf of Maurice, and purporting to act on behalf of all other persons similarly situated, instituted the present civil rights suit. . . .

When a case involves a home and some type of official intrusion into that home, as this case appears to do, an immediate and natural reaction is one of concern about Fourth Amendment rights and the protection which that Amendment is intended to afford. Its emphasis indeed is upon one of the most precious aspects of personal security in the home: "The right of the people to be secure in their persons, houses, papers, and effects. . . ." This Court has characterized that right as "basic to a free society. . . ." And over the years the Court consistently has been most protective of the privacy of the dwelling. . . .

This natural and quite proper protective attitude, however, is not a factor in this case, for the seemingly obvious and simple reason that we are not concerned here with any search by the New York social service agency in the Fourth Amendment meaning of that term. It is true that the governing statute and regulations appear to make mandatory the initial home visit and the subsequent periodic "contacts" (which may include home visits) for the inception and continuance of aid. It is also true that the caseworker's posture in the home visit is perhaps, in a sense, both rehabilitative and investigative. But this latter aspect, we think, is given too broad a character and far more emphasis than it deserves if it is equated with a search in the traditional criminal law context. We note, too, that the visitation in itself is not forced or compelled, and that the beneficiary's denial of permission is not a criminal act. If consent to the visitation is withheld, no visitation takes place. The aid then never begins or merely ceases, as the case may be. There is no entry of the home and there is no search.

If, however, we were to assume that a caseworker's home visit, before or subsequent to the beneficiary's initial qualification for benefits, somehow (perhaps because the average beneficiary might feel she is in no position to refuse consent to the visit), and despite its interview nature, does possess some of the characteristics of a search in the traditional sense, we nevertheless conclude that does not fall within the Fourth Amendment's proscription. This is because it does not descend to the level of unreasonableness. It is unreasonableness which is the Fourth Amendment's standard.

There are a number of factors that compel us to conclude that the home visit proposed for Mrs. James is not unreasonable.

The public's interest in this particular segment of the area of assistance to the unfortunate is protection and aid for the dependent child whose family requires such aid for that child. . . . The dependent child's needs

are paramount, and only with hesitancy would we relegate those needs, in the scale of comparative values, to a position secondary to what the mother claims as her rights.

The agency, with tax funds provided from federal as well as from state sources, is fulfilling a public trust. The State, working through its qualified welfare agency, has appropriate and paramount interest and concern in seeing and assuring that the intended and proper objects of that tax-produced assistance are the ones who benefit from the aid it dispenses. . . .

One who dispenses purely private charity naturally has an interest in and expects to know how his charitable funds are utilized and put to work. The public, when it is the provider, rightly expects the same. . . .

We therefore conclude that the home visitation as structured by the New York statutes and regulations is a reasonable administrative tool; that it serves a valid and proper administrative purpose for the dispensation of the AFDC program; that it is not an unwarranted invasion of personal privacy; and that it violates no right guaranteed by the Fourth Amendment.

Reversed and remanded with directions to enter a judgment of dismissal.

It is so ordered. . . .

Mr. Justice *Douglas,* dissenting. . . .

In 1969 roughly 127 billion dollars were spent by the federal, state, and local governments on "social welfare." To farmers alone almost four billion dollars were paid, in part for not growing certain crops. . . .

Yet almost every beneficiary whether rich or poor, rural or urban, has a "house"—one of the places protected by the Fourth Amendment against "unreasonable searches and seizures." The question in this case is whether receipt of largesse from the government makes the *home* of the beneficiary subject to access by an inspector of the agency of oversight, even though the beneficiary objects to the intrusion and even though the Fourth Amendment's procedure for access to one's *house* or *home* is not followed. The penalty here is not, of course, invasion of the privacy of Barbara James, only her loss of federal or state largesse. That, however, is merely rephrasing the problem. Whatever the semantics, the central question is whether the government by force of its largesse has the power to "buy up" rights guaranteed by the Constitution. But for the assertion of her constitutional right, Barbara James in this case would have received the welfare benefit. . . .

The applicable principle, as stated in *Camara* as "justified by history and by current experience" is that "except in certain carefully defined classes of cases, a search of private property without proper consent is 'unreasonable' unless it has been authorized by a valid search warrant."

In *See* we [decided] that the "businessman, like the occupant of a residence, has a constitutional right to go about his business free from unreasonable official entries upon his private commercial property." There is not the slightest hint in *See* that the Government could condition a business license on the "consent" of the licensee to the administrative searches we held violated the Fourth Amendment. It is a strange jurisprudence indeed which safeguards the businessman at his place of work from warrantless searches but will not do the same for a mother in her *home*.

Is a search of her home without a warrant made "reasonable" merely because she is dependent on government largesse?

Judge Skelly Wright has stated the problem succinctly:

Welfare has long been considered the equivalent of charity and its recipients have been subjected to all kinds of dehumanizing experiences in the government's effort to police its welfare payments. In fact, over half a billion dollars are expended annually for administration and policing in connection with the Aid to Families with Dependent Children program. Why such large sums are necessary for administration and policing has never been adequately explained. No such sums are spent policing the government subsidies granted to farmers, airlines, steamship companies, and junk mail dealers, to name but a few. The truth is that in this subsidy area society has simply adopted a double standard, one for aid to business and the farmer and a different one for welfare.

(Poverty, Minorities, and Respect for Law, 1970 Duke L. J. 425, 437–438.)

If the welfare recipient was not Barbara James but a prominent, affluent cotton or wheat farmer receiving benefit payments for not growing crops, would not the approach be different? Welfare in aid of dependent children, like social security and unemployment benefits, has an aura of suspicion. There doubtless are frauds in every sector of public welfare whether the recipient be a Barbara James or someone who is prominent or influential. But constitutional rights—here the privacy of the *home*—are obviously not dependent on the poverty or on the affluence of the beneficiary. It is the precincts of the *home* that the Fourth Amendment protects; and their privacy is as important to the lowly as to the mighty.

I would sustain the judgment of the three-judge court in the present case.

Mr. Justice *Marshall,* whom Mr. Justice *Brennan* joins, dissenting.

. . . The record plainly shows . . . that Mrs. James offered to furnish any information that the appellants desired and to be interviewed at any place other than her home. Appellants rejected her offers and terminated her benefits solely on the ground that she refused to permit a home visit. In addition, appellants make no contention that any sort of probable cause exists to suspect appellee of welfare fraud or child abuse.

Simply stated, the issue in this case is whether a state welfare agency can require all recipients of AFDC benefits to submit to warrantless "visitations" of their homes. In answering that question, the majority dodges between constitutional issues to reach a result clearly inconsistent with the decisions of this Court. We are told that there is no such search involved in this case; that even if there were a search, it would not be unreasonable; and that even if this were an unreasonable search, a welfare recipient waives her right to object by accepting benefits. I emphatically disagree with all three conclusions. . . .

. . . In an era of rapidly burgeoning governmental activities and their concomitant inspectors, caseworkers, and researchers, a restriction of the Fourth Amendment to "the traditional criminal law context" tramples the ancient concept that a man's home is his castle. Only last Term, we reaffirmed that this concept has lost none of its vitality. . . .

. . . [I]t is argued that the home visit is justified to protect dependent children from "abuse" and "exploitation." These are heinous crimes, but they are not confined to indigent households. Would the majority sanction, in the absence of probable cause, compulsory visits to all American homes for the purpose of discovering child abuse? Or is this Court prepared to hold as a matter of constitutional law that a mother, merely because she is poor, is substantially more likely to injure or exploit her children? Such a categorical approach to an entire class of citizens would be dangerously at odds with the tenets of our democracy. . . .

Although the Court does not agree with my conclusion that the home visit is an unreasonable search, its opinion suggests that even if the visit were unreasonable, appellee has somehow waived her right to object. Surely the majority cannot believe that valid Fourth Amendment consent can be given under the threat of the loss of one's sole means of support. . . .

In deciding that the homes of AFDC recipients are not entitled to protection from warrantless searches by welfare caseworkers, the Court declines to follow prior case law and employs a rationale that, if applied to the claims of all citizens, would threaten the validity of the Fourth Amendment. . . . Perhaps the majority has explained why a commercial warehouse deserves more protection than does this poor woman's home. I am not convinced; and, therefore, I must respectfully dissent.

6. *Plyler v. Doe*

Supreme Court of the United States

The issue before the Supreme Court was whether a Texas statute that withholds from local school districts any state funds for the education of children who were not "legally admitted" into the United States and that authorizes local school districts to deny enrollment to such children violates the Equal Protection Clause of the Fourteenth Amendment. Justice Brennan, delivering the opinion of the Court, argued that the Texas statute did violate the Equal Protection Clause. He contended that although public education is not a right granted to individuals by the Constitution (Marshall dissenting), given the "pivotal role of education in sustaining our political and cultural heritage" and the economic benefits that accrue to Texas from the presence of illegal aliens, petitioners had failed to establish a legitimate state interest in denying an education to illegal aliens. In dissent, Chief Justice Burger with whom Justices White, Rehnquist, and O'Connor joined, argued that although the Texas statute is unwise and unsound, it is not unconstitutional. Burger contended that although illegal aliens are included within the category of persons protected by the Equal Protection Clause, the Texas statute does bear "a relation to a legitimate state purpose," especially in view of the fact that the federal government sees fit to exclude illegal aliens from numerous social welfare programs.

. . . In May 1975, the Texas Legislature revised its education laws to withhold from local school districts any state funds for the education of children who were not "legally admitted" into the United States. The 1975 revision also authorized local school districts to deny enrollment in their public schools to children not "legally admitted" to the country. . . . These cases involve constitutional challenges to those provisions.

[*Plyler v. Doe*] is a class action, filed in the United States District Court for the Eastern District of Texas in September 1977, on behalf of certain school-age children of Mexican origin residing in Smith County, Tex., who could not establish that they had been legally admitted into the United States. The action complained of the exclusion of plaintiff children from the public schools of the Tyler Independent School District. The Superintendent and members of the Board of Trustees of the School District were named as defendants; the State of Texas intervened as a party-defendant. After certifying a class consisting of all undocumented school-age children of Mexican origin residing within the School District, the District Court preliminarily enjoined defendants from denying a free education to members of the plaintiff class. In December 1977, the court conducted an extensive hearing on plaintiffs' motion for permanent injunctive relief. . . .

The District Court held that illegal aliens were entitled to the protection of the Equal Protection Clause of the Fourteenth Amendment, and that [this section] violated that Clause . . .

The Court of Appeals for the Fifth Circuit upheld the District Court's injunction. . . .

The Fourteenth Amendment provides that "[n]o State shall . . . deprive any person of life, liberty, or property, without due process of law; nor deny to *any person within its jurisdiction* the equal protection of the laws." . . . (Emphasis added.) Appellants argue at the outset that undocumented aliens, because of their immigration status, are not "persons within the jurisdiction" of the State of Texas, and that they therefore have no right to the equal pro-

tection of Texas Law. We reject this argument. . . .

. . . The Equal Protection Clause was intended to work nothing less than the abolition of all caste-based and invidious class-based legislation. That objective is fundamentally at odds with the power the State asserts here to classify persons subject to its laws as nonetheless excepted from its protection.

Although the congressional debate concerning . . . the Fourteenth Amendment was limited, that debate clearly confirms the understanding that the phrase "within its jurisdiction" was intended in a broad sense to offer the guarantee of equal protection to all within a State's boundaries, and to all upon whom the State would impose the obligations of its laws. Indeed, it appears from those debates that Congress, by using the phrase "person within its jurisdiction," sought expressly to ensure that the equal protection of the laws was provided to the alien population. Representative Bingham reported to the House the draft resolution of the Joint Committee of Fifteen on Reconstruction (H.R. 63) that was to become the Fourteenth Amendment. . . . Two days later, Bingham posed the following question in support of the resolution:

> Is it not essential to the unity of the people that the citizens of each State shall be entitled to all the privileges and immunities of citizens in the several States? Is it not essential to the unity of the Government and the unity of the people that all persons, *whether citizens or strangers, within this land,* shall have equal protection in every State in this Union in the rights of life and liberty and property?

. . . Our conclusion that the illegal aliens who are plaintiffs in these cases may claim the benefit of the Fourteenth Amendment's guarantee of equal protection only begins the inquiry. The more difficult question is whether the Equal Protection Clause has been violated by the refusal of the State of Texas to reimburse local school boards for the education of children who cannot demonstrate that their presence within the United States is lawful, or by the imposition by those school boards of the burden of tuition on those children. It is to this question that we now turn. . . .

. . . In applying the Equal Protection Clause to most forms of state action, we thus seek only the assurance that the classification at issue bears some fair relationship to a legitimate public purpose.

Of course, undocumented status is not irrelevant to any proper legislative goal. Nor is undocumented status an absolutely immutable characteristic since it is the product of conscious, indeed unlawful, action. But [this statute] is directed against children, and imposes its discriminatory burden on the basis of a legal characteristic over which children can have little control. It is thus difficult to conceive of a rational justification for penalizing these children for their presence within the United States. Yet that appears to be precisely the effect of [this statute].

Public education is not a "right" granted to individuals by the Constitution. *San Antonio Independent School Dist. v. Rodriguez* . . . (1973). But neither is it merely some governmental "benefit" indistinguishable from other forms of social welfare legislation. Both the importance of education in maintaining our basic institutions, and the lasting impact of its deprivation on the life of the child, mark the distinction. The "American people have always regarded education and [the] acquisition of knowledge as matters of supreme importance." *Meyer v. Nebraska* . . . (1923). We have recognized "the public schools as a most vital civic institution for the preservation of a democratic system of government," *Abington School District v. Schempp* . . . (1963) . . . and as the primary vehicle for transmitting "the values on which our society rests." *Ambach v. Norwick* . . . (1979). "[A]s . . . pointed out early in our history, . . . some degree of education is necessary to prepare citizens to participate effectively and intelligently in our open political system if we are to preserve freedom and independence." *Wisconsin v. Yoder* . . . (1972). And these historic "perceptions of the public schools as inculcating fundamental values necessary to the maintenance of a democratic political system have been confirmed by the observations of social scientists." *Ambach v. Norwick.* . . . In addition, education provides the basic tools by which individuals might lead economically productive lives to the benefit of us all. In sum, education has a fundamental role in maintaining the fabric of our society. We cannot ignore the significant social costs borne by our Nation when select groups are denied the means to absorb the values and skills upon which our social order rests.

In addition to the pivotal role of education in sustaining our political and cultural heritage, denial of education to some isolated group of children poses an affront to one of the goals of the Equal Protection Clause: the abolition of governmental barriers presenting unreasonable obstacles to advancement on the basis of individual merit. Paradoxically, by depriving the children of any disfavored group of an education, we foreclose the means by which that group might raise the level of esteem in which it is held by the majority. But more directly, "education prepares individuals to be self-reliant and self-sufficient participants in society." *Wisconsin v. Yoder*. . . . Illiteracy is an enduring disability. The inability to read and write will handicap the individual deprived of a basic education each and every day of his life. The inestimable toll of that deprivation on the social economic, intellectual, and psychological well-being of the individual, and the obstacle it poses to individual achievement, make it most difficult to reconcile the cost or the principle of a status-based denial of basic education with the framework of equality embodied in the Equal Protection Clause. What we said 28 years ago in *Brown v. Board of Education,* . . . (1954), still holds true:

Today, education is perhaps the most important function of state and local governments. Compulsory school attendance laws and the great expenditures for education both demonstrate our recognition of the importance of education to our democratic society. It is required in the performance of our most basic public responsibilities, even service in the armed forces. It is the very foundation of good citizenship. Today it is a principal instrument in awakening the child to cultural values, in preparing him for later professional training, and in helping him to adjust normally to his environment. In these days, it is doubtful that any child may reasonably be expected to succeed in life if he is denied the opportunity of an education. Such an opportunity, where the state has undertaken to provide it, is a right which must be made available to all on equal terms." . . .

. . . [A]ppellants appear to suggest that the State may seek to protect itself from an influx of illegal immigrants. While a State might have an interest in mitigating the potentially harsh economic effects of sudden shifts in population, [this statute] hardly offers an effective method of dealing with an urgent demographic or economic problem. There is no evidence in the record suggesting that illegal entrants impose any significant burden on the State's economy. To the contrary, the available evidence suggests that illegal aliens underutilize public services, while contributing their labor to the local economy and tax money to the state fisc. . . . The dominant incentive for illegal entry into the State of Texas is the availability of employment; few if any illegal immigrants come to this country, or presumably to the State of Texas, in order to avail themselves of a free education. Thus, even making the doubtful assumption that the net impact of illegal aliens on the economy of the State is negative, we think it clear that "[c]harging tuition to undocumented children constitutes a ludicrously ineffectual attempt to stem the tide of illegal immigration," at least when compared with the alternative of prohibiting the employment of illegal aliens. . . .

Accordingly, the judgment of the Court of Appeals in each of these cases is

Affirmed.

Justice *Marshall,* concurring.

While I join the Court's opinion, I do so without in any way retreating from my opinion in *San Antonio Independent School District v. Rodriguez.* . . . I continue to believe that an individual's interest in education is fundamental, and that this view is amply supported "by the unique status accorded public education by our society, and by the close relationship between education and some of our most basic constitutional values." . . . Fur-

thermore, I believe that the facts of these cases demonstrate the wisdom of rejecting a rigidified approach to equal protection analysis, and of employing an approach that allows for varying levels of scrutiny depending upon "the constitutional and societal importance of the interest adversely affected and the recognized invidiousness of the basis upon which the particular classification is drawn." . . . It continues to be my view that a class-based denial of public education is utterly incompatible with the Equal Protection Clause of the Fourteenth Amendment.

Justice *Blackmun,* concurring.

I join the opinion and judgment of the Court.

Like Justice Powell, I believe that the children involved in this litigation "should not be left on the streets uneducated." . . . I write separately, however, because in my view the nature of the interest at stake is crucial to the proper resolution of these cases.

The "fundamental rights" aspect of the Court's equal protection analysis—the now-familiar concept that governmental classifications bearing on certain interests must be closely scrutinized—has been the subject of some controversy. . . .

[This controversy], combined with doubts about the judiciary's ability to make fine distinctions in assessing the effects of complex social policies, led the Court in *Rodriguez* to articulate a firm rule: fundamental rights are those that "explicitly or implicitly [are] guaranteed by the Constitution." . . . It therefore squarely rejected the notion that "an ad hoc determination as to the social or economic importance" of a given interest is relevant to the level of scrutiny accorded classifications involving that interest, . . . and made clear that "[i]t is not the province of this Court to create substantive constitutional rights in the name of guaranteeing equal protection of the laws." . . .

I joined Justice Powell's opinion for the Court in *Rodriguez,* and I continue to believe that it provides the appropriate model for resolving most equal protection disputes. Classifications infringing substantive constitutional rights necessarily will be invalid, if not by force of the Equal Protection Clause, then through operation of other provisions of the Constitution. Conversely, classifications bearing on non-constitutional interests—even those involving "the most basic economic needs of impoverished human beings." . . . —generally are not subject to special treatment under the Equal Protection Clause, because they are not distinguishable in any relevant way from other regulations in "the area of economics and social welfare."

With all this said, however, I believe the Court's experience has demonstrated that the *Rodriguez* formulation does not settle every issue of "fundamental rights" arising under the Equal Protection Clause. Only a pedant would insist that there are *no* meaningful distinctions among the multitude of social and political interests regulated by the States, and *Rodriguez* does not stand for quite so absolute a proposition. To the contrary, *Rodriguez* implicitly acknowledged that certain interests, though not constitutionally guaranteed, must be accorded a special place in equal protection analysis. Thus, the Court's decisions long have accorded strict scrutiny to classifications bearing on the right to vote in state elections, and *Rodriguez* confirmed the "constitutional underpinnings of the right to equal treatment in the voting process." . . . Yet "the right to vote, *per se*, is not a constitutionally protected right." . . . Instead, regulation of the electoral process receives unusual scrutiny because "the right to exercise the franchise in a free and unimpaired manner is preservative of other basic civil and political rights." . . . In other words, the right to vote is accorded extraordinary treatment because it is, in equal protection terms, an extraordinary right: a citizen cannot hope to achieve any meaningful degree of individual political equality if granted an inferior right of participation in the political process. Those denied the vote are relegated, by state fiat, in a most basic way to second-class status. . . .

In my view, when the State provides an education to some and denies it to others, it immediately and inevitably creates class distinctions of a type fundamentally inconsistent with those purposes, mentioned above, of the Equal Protection Clause. Children denied an education are placed at a permanent and insurmountable competitive disadvantage, for an uneducated child is denied even the opportunity to achieve. And when those children are members of an identifiable group, that group—through the State's action—will have been converted into a discrete underclass. Other benefits provided by the State, such as housing and public assistance, are of course important; to an individual in immediate need, they may be more desirable than the right to be educated. But classifications involving the complete denial of education are in a sense unique, for they strike at the heart of equal protection values by involving the State in the creation of permanent class distinctions. . . . In a sense, then, denial of an education is the analogue of denial of the right to vote: the former relegates the individual to second-class social status; the latter places him at a permanent political disadvantage.

This conclusion is fully consistent with *Rodriguez*. The Court there reserved judgment on the constitutionality of a state system that "occasioned an absolute denial of educational opportunities to any of its children," noting that "no charge fairly could be made that the system . . . fails to provide each child with an opportunity to acquire . . . basic minimal skills." . . . And it cautioned that in a case "involv[ing] the most persistent and difficult questions of educational policy, . . . [the] Court's lack of specialized knowledge and experience counsels against premature interference with the informed judgments made at the state and local levels." . . . Thus *Rodriguez* held, and the Court now reaffirms, that "a State need not justify by compelling necessity every variation in the manner in which education is provided to its population." . . . Similarly, it is undeniable that education is not a "fundamental right" in the sense that it is constitutionally guaranteed. Here, however, the State has undertaken to provide an education to most of the children residing within its borders. And, in contrast to the situation in *Rodriguez*, it does not take an advanced degree to predict the effects of a complete denial of education upon those children targeted by the State's classification. In such circumstances, the voting decisions suggest that the State must offer something more than a rational basis for its classification. . . .

Chief Justice *Burger,* with whom Justice *White,* Justice *Rehnquist,* and Justice *O'Connor* join, dissenting.

Were it our business to set the Nation's social policy, I would agree without hesitation that it is senseless for an enlightened society to deprive any children—including illegal aliens—of an elementary education. I fully agree that it would be folly—and wrong—to tolerate creation of a segment of society made up of illiterate persons, many having a limited or no command of our language. However, the Constitution does not constitute us as "Platonic Guardians" nor does it vest in this Court the authority to strike down laws because they do not meet our standards of desirable social policy, "wisdom," or "common sense." . . . We trespass on the assigned function of the political branches under our structure of limited and separated powers when we assume a policymaking role as the Court does today.

The Court makes no attempt to disguise that it is acting to make up for Congress's lack of "effective leadership" in dealing with the serious national problems caused by the influx of uncountable millions of illegal aliens across our borders. . . . The failure of enforcement of the immigration laws over more than a decade and the inherent difficulty and expense of sealing our vast borders have combined to create a grave socioeconomic dilemma. It is a dilemma that has not yet even been fully assessed, let alone addressed. However, it is not the function of the Judiciary to provide "effective leadership" simply because the political branches of government fail to do so.

The Court's holding today manifests the justly criticized judicial tendency to attempt speedy and wholesale formulation of "remedies" for the failures—or simply the laggard pace—of the political processes of our system of government. The Court employs, and in my view abuses, the Fourteenth Amendment in an effort to become an omnipotent and omniscient problem solver. That the motives for doing so are noble and compassionate does not alter the fact that the Court distorts our constitutional function to make amends for the defaults of others. . . .

The Court acknowledges that, except in those cases when state classifications disadvantage a "suspect class" or impinge upon a "fundamental right," the Equal Protection Clause permits a state "substantial latitude" in distinguishing between different groups of persons. . . . Moreover, the Court expressly—and correctly—rejects any suggestion that illegal aliens are a suspect class, . . . or that education is a fundamental right. . . . Yet by patching together bits and pieces of what might be termed quasi-suspect-class and quasi-fundamental-rights analysis, the Court spins out a theory custom-tailored to the facts of these cases.

In the end, we are told little more than that the level of scrutiny employed to strike down the Texas law applies only when illegal alien children are deprived of a public education. . . . If ever a court was guilty of an unabashedly result-oriented approach, this case is a prime example. . . .

Once it is conceded—as the Court does—that illegal aliens are not a suspect class, and that education is not a fundamental right, our inquiry should focus on and be limited to whether the legislative classification at issue bears a rational relationship to a legitimate state purpose. . . .

It is significant that the Federal Government has seen fit to exclude illegal aliens from numerous social welfare programs, such as the food stamp program, . . . the old-age assistance, aid to families with dependent children, aid to the blind, aid to the permanently and totally disabled, and supplemental security income programs, . . . the Medicare hospital insurance benefits program, . . . and the Medicaid hospital insurance benefits for the aged and disabled program. . . . Although these exclusions do not conclusively demonstrate the constitutionality of the State's use of the same classification for comparable purposes, at the very least they tend to support the rationality of excluding illegal alien residents of a state from such programs so as to preserve the state's finite revenues for the benefit of lawful residents. . . .

Denying a free education to illegal alien children is not a choice I would make were I a legislator. Apart from compassionate considerations, the long-range costs of excluding any children from the public schools may well outweigh the costs of educating them. But that is not the issue; the fact that there are sound *policy* arguments against the Texas Legislature's choice does not render that choice an unconstitutional one. . . .

The Constitution does not provide a cure for every social ill, nor does it vest judges with a mandate to try to remedy every social problem. . . . Moreover, when this Court rushes in to remedy what it perceives to be the failings of the political processes, it deprives those processes of an opportunity to function. When the political institutions are not forced to exercise constitutionally allocated powers and responsibilities, those powers, like muscles not used, tend to atrophy. Today's cases, I regret to say, present yet another example of unwarranted judicial action which in the long run tends to contribute to the weakening of our political processes.

Congress, "vested by the Constitution with the responsibility of protecting our borders and legislating with respect to aliens," . . . bears primary responsibility for addressing the problems occasioned by the millions of illegal aliens flooding across our southern border. Similarly, it is for Congress, and not this Court, to assess the "social costs borne by our Nation when select groups are denied the means to absorb the values and skills upon which our social order rests." . . . While the "specter of a permanent caste" of illegal Mexican residents of the United States is indeed a disturbing one, . . . it is but one segment of a larger problem, which is for the political branches to solve. I find it difficult to believe that Congress would long tolerate such a self-destructive result—that it would fail to deport these illegal alien families or to provide for the education of their children. Yet instead of allowing the political processes to run their course—albeit with some delay—the Court seeks to do Congress's job for it, compensating for congressional inaction. It is not unreasonable to think that this encourages the political branches to pass their problems to the Judiciary.

The solution to this seemingly intractable problem is to defer to the political processes, unpalatable as that may be to some.

7. Homelessness

Peter Marin

Homelessness, in itself, is nothing more than a condition visited upon men and women (and, increasingly, children) as the final stage of a variety of problems about which the word *homelessness* tells us almost nothing. Or, to put it another way, it is a catch basin into which pour all of the people disenfranchised or marginalized or scared off by processes beyond their control, those that lie close to the heart of American life. Here are the groups packed into the single category of "the homeless":

From "Helping and Hating the Homeless," *This World* (January 25, 1987), pp. 7–9, 20. Copyright © 1987 by *Harper's Magazine*. All rights reserved. Reprinted from the January issue by special permission.

• Veterans, mainly from the war in Vietnam. In many American cities, vets make up close to 50 percent of all homeless males.

• The mentally ill. In some parts of the country, roughly a quarter of the homeless would, a couple of decades ago, have been institutionalized.

• The physically disabled or chronically ill, who do not receive any benefits or whose benefits do not enable them to afford permanent shelter.

• The elderly on fixed incomes whose funds are no longer sufficient for their needs.

• Men, women, and whole families pauperized

by the loss of a job. Some 28 percent of the homeless population is composed of families with children, and 15 percent are single women.

- Single parents, usually women, without the resources or skills to establish new lives.
- Runaway children, many of whom have been abused.
- Alcoholics and those in trouble with drugs (whose troubles often begin with one of the other conditions listed here).
- Traditional tramps, hobos and transients, who have taken to the road or the streets for a variety of reasons and who prefer to be there.

You can quickly learn two things about the homeless from this list. First, you can learn that many of the homeless, before they were homeless, were people more or less like ourselves: members of the working or middle class. And you can learn that the world of the homeless has its roots in various policies, events and ways of life for which some of us are responsible and from which some of us actually prosper.

We decide, as a people, to go to war, we ask our children to kill and to die, and the result, years later, is grown men homeless on the street.

We change, with the best intentions, the laws pertaining to the mentally ill and then, without intention, neglect to provide them with services; and the result, in our streets, drives some of us crazy with rage.

We cut taxes and prune budgets, we modernize industry and shift the balance of trade, and the result of all these actions and errors can be read, sleeping form by sleeping form, on our city streets.

The liberals cannot blame the conservatives. The conservatives cannot blame the liberals. Homelessness is the sum total of our dreams, policies, intentions, errors, omissions, cruelties, kindnesses, all of it recorded, in flesh, in the life of the streets.

The homeless can be roughly divided into two groups: those who have had homelessness forced upon them and want nothing more than to escape it; and those who have at least in part chosen it for themselves, and now accept it, or in some cases embrace it.

I understand how dangerous it is to introduce the idea of choice into a discussion of homelessness. It can all too easily be used to justify indifference or brutality toward the homeless, or to argue that they are only getting what they "deserve." And yet it seems to me that it is only by taking choice into account, in all of the intricacies of its various forms and expressions, that one can really understand certain kinds of homelessness.

The fact is, many of the homeless are not only hapless victims but voluntary exiles, "domestic refugees," people who have turned not against life itself but against us, our life, American life. Look for a moment at the vets. The price of returning to America was to forget what they had seen or learned in Vietnam, to "put it behind them." But some could not do that, and the stress of trying showed up as alcoholism, broken marriages, drug addiction, crime. And it showed up too as life on the street, which was for some vets a desperate choice made in the name of life—the best they could manage.

We must learn to accept that there may indeed be people, and not only vets, who have seen so much of our world, or seen it so clearly, that to live in it becomes impossible. Here, for example, is the story of Alice, a homeless middle-aged woman in Los Angeles, where there are perhaps 50,000 homeless people, a 50 percent increase over the previous year. It was set down last year by one of my students at the University of California at Santa Barbara, where I taught for a semester. I had encouraged them to go find the homeless and listen to their stories. And so, one day, when this student saw Alice foraging in a dumpster outside a McDonald's, he stopped and talked to her:

"She told me she had led a pretty normal life as she grew up and eventually went to college. From there she went on to Chicago to teach school. She was single and lived in a small apartment.

"One night, after she got off the train after school, a man began to follow her to her apartment building. When she got to her door she saw a knife and the man hovering behind her. She had no choice but to let him in. The man raped her.

"After that, things got steadily worse. She

had a nervous breakdown. She went to a mental institution for three months, and when she went back to her apartment she found her belongings gone. The landlord had sold them to cover the rent.

"She had no place to go and no job because the school had terminated her employment. She slipped into depression. She lived with friends until she could muster enough money for a ticket to Los Angeles. She said she no longer wanted to burden her friends, and that if she had to live outside, at least Los Angeles was warmer than Chicago.

"It is as if she began back then to take on the mentality of a street person. She resolved herself to homelessness. She's been out West since 1980, without a home or job. She seems happy, with her best friend being her cat. But the scars of memories still haunt her, and she is running from them, or should I say, him."

This is, in essence, the same story one hears over and over again on the street. You begin with an ordinary life; then an event occurs—traumatic, catastrophic; smaller events follow, each one deepening the original wound; finally, homelessness becomes inevitable, or begins to seem inevitable to the person involved—the only way out of an intolerable situation.

Every government program, almost every private project, is geared as much to the needs of those giving help as it is to the needs of the homeless.

Santa Barbara is as good an example as any. There are three main shelters in the city—all of them private. Between them they provide fewer than 100 beds a night for the homeless. Two of three shelters are religious in nature: the Rescue Mission and the Salvation Army. In the mission, as in most places in the country, there are elaborate and stringent rules. Beds go first to those who have not been there for two months, and you can stay for only two nights in any two-month period. No shelter is given to those who are not sober.

Even if you go to the mission only for a meal, you are required to listen to sermons and participate in prayer, and you are regular-

ly proselytized. There are obligatory, regimented showers. You go to bed precisely at 10: lights out, no reading, no talking. After the lights go out you will find 15 men in a room with double-decker bunks. As the night progresses the room grows stuffier and hotter. Men toss, turn, cough and moan. In the morning you are awakened precisely at 5:45. Then breakfast. At 7:30 you are back on the street.

The town's newest shelter was opened almost a year ago by a consortium of local churches. Families and those who are employed have first call on the beds—a policy that excludes the congenitally homeless. Alcohol is not simply forbidden in the shelter; those with a history of alcoholism must sign a "contract" pledging to remain sober and chemical-free. Finally, in a paroxysm of therapeutic bullying, the shelter has added a new wrinkle: If you stay more than two days you are required to fill out and then discuss with a social worker a complex form listing what you perceive as your personal failings, goals and strategies—all of this for men and women who simply want a place to lie down out of the rain.

We are moved either to "redeem" the homeless or to punish them. Perhaps there is nothing consciously hostile about. Perhaps it is simply that as the machinery of bureaucracy cranks itself up to deal with these problems, attitudes assert themselves automatically. But whatever the case, the fact remains that almost every one of our strategies for helping the homeless is simply an attempt to rearrange the world cosmetically, in terms of how it looks and smells to us. Compassion is little more than the passion for control.

The central question emerging from all this is, What does a society owe to its members in trouble, and how is that debt to be paid? It is a question that must be answered in two parts: first, in relation to the men and women who have been marginalized against their will, and then, in a slightly different way, in relation to those who have chosen (or accept or even prize) their marginality.

Suggestions for Further Reading

Anthologies

Arthur, John, and Shaw, William. *Social and Political Philosophy.* Englewood Cliffs: Prentice-Hall, 1992.

Garner, Richard T., and Oldenquist, Andrew. *Society and the Individual: Readings in Political and Social Philosophy.* Belmont: Wadsworth Publishing Co., 1990.

Sterba, James P. *Justice: Alternative Political Perspectives.* Belmont: Wadsworth Publishing Co., 2nd ed. 1992.

Basic Concepts

Plato. *The Republic.* Translated by Francis Cornford. New York: Oxford University Press, 1945.

Aristotle. *Nicomachean Ethics.* Translated by Martin Ostwald. Indianapolis: Bobbs-Merrill, 1962.

Pieper, Joseph. *Justice.* London: Faber and Faber, 1957.

Libertarianism

Hospers, John. *Libertarianism.* Los Angeles: Nash Publishing, 1971.

Nozick, Robert. *Anarchy, State and Utopia.* New York: Basic Books, 1974.

Machan, Tibor. *Individuals and Their Rights.* LaSalle: Open Court, 1989.

Welfare Liberalism

Mill, John Stuart. *On Liberty.* Indianapolis: Bobbs-Merrill Co., 1956.

Ackerman, Bruce A. *Social Justice in the Liberal State.* New Haven: Yale University Press, 1980.

Rawls, John. *A Theory of Justice.* Cambridge: Harvard University Press, 1971.

Singer, Peter. *Practical Ethics.* Cambridge: Cambridge University Press, 1979.

Sterba, James P. *How to Make People Just.* Totowa, N.J.: Rowman and Littlefield, 1988.

Socialism

Marx, Karl. *Critique of the Gotha Program.* Edited by C. P. Dutt. New York: International Publishers, 1966.

Fisk, Milton. *Ethics and Society: A Marxist Interpretation of Value.* New York: New York University Press, 1980.

Harrington, Michael. *Socialism Past and Future.* New York: Arcade Publishing, 1989.

Heilbroner, Robert L. *Marxism For and Against.* New York: W. W. Norton & Co., 1980.

Practical Applications

Friedman, David. *The Machinery of Freedom.* 2nd edition. LaSalle: Open Court, 1989.

Gorbachev, Mikhail. *Perestroika.* New York: Harper & Row, 1987.

Timmons, William. *Public Ethics and Issues.* Belmont: Wadsworth Publishing Co., 1990.

Near and Distant Peoples

Introduction

Basic Concepts

The moral problem of near and distant peoples has only recently begun to be discussed by professional philosophers. There are many reasons for this neglect, not all of them complimentary to the philosophical profession. Suffice it to say that once it became widely recognized how modern technology could significantly benefit or harm distant peoples, philosophers could no longer ignore the importance of this moral problem.

With respect to this problem, the key question that must be answered first is: Can we meaningfully speak of distant peoples as having rights against us or of our having obligations to them? Few philosophers have thought that the mere fact that people are at a distance from us precludes our having any obligations to them or their having any rights against us. Some philosophers, however, have argued that our ignorance of the specific membership of the class of distant peoples does rule out these moral relationships. Yet this cannot be right, given that in other contexts we recognize obligations to indeterminate classes of people, such as a police officer's obligation to help people in distress or the obligation of food processors not to harm those who consume their products.

What does, however, seem to be a necessary requirement before distant peoples can be said to have rights against us is that we are capable of acting across the distance that separates us. (This is simply an implication of the widely accepted philosophical principle that "ought" implies "can.") As long as this condition is met—as it typically is for people living in most technologically advanced societies—there seems to be no conceptual obstacle to claiming that distant peoples have rights against us or that we have obligations to them. Of course, showing that it is conceptually possible does not yet prove that these rights and obligations actually exist. Such proof requires a substantial moral argument.

It used to be argued that the welfare rights of distant peoples would eventually be met as a byproduct of the continued economic growth of the technologically developed societies of the world. It was believed that the transfer of investment and technology to the less developed societies of the world would eventually, if not make everyone well off, at least satisfy everyone's basic needs. Now we are not so sure. Presently more and more evidence points to the conclusion that without some substantial sacrifice on the part of the technologically developed societies of the world, many of the less developed societies will never be able to provide their members with even the basic necessities for survival. How else are we going to meet the basic needs of the 1.2 billion people who are living today in conditions of absolute poverty without some plausible policy of redistribution? Even those, like Herman Kahn, who argue that an almost utopian world situation will obtain in the distant future, still would have to admit that unless some plausible policy of redistribution is adopted, malnutrition and starvation will continue in the less developed societies for many years to come. Thus, a recognition of the welfare rights of distant peoples would appear to have significant consequences for developed and underdeveloped societies alike.

Of course, there are various senses in which distant peoples can be said to have welfare rights and various moral grounds on which those rights can be justified. First of all, the welfare rights of distant peoples can be understood to be either negative rights or positive rights. A negative right is a right not to be interfered with in some specific manner. For example, a right to liberty is usually understood to be a negative right; it guarantees each person the right not to have her liberty interfered with provided that she does not unjustifiably interfere with the liberty of any other person. On the other hand, a positive right is a right to receive some specific goods or services. Typical positive rights are the right to have a loan repaid and the right to receive one's just earnings. Second, the welfare rights of distant peoples can be understood to be either *in personam* rights or *in rem* rights. *In personam* rights are rights that hold against some specific namable person or persons while *in rem* rights hold against everyone who is in a position to abide by the rights in question. A right to liberty is usually understood to be an *in rem* right while the right to have a loan repaid or the right to receive one's just earnings are typical *in personam* rights. Finally, the rights of distant peoples can be understood to be either legal rights, that is, rights that *are enforced* by coercive sanctions, or moral rights, that is, rights that *ought to be enforced* either simply by noncoercive sanctions (for example, verbal condemnations) or by both coercive and noncoercive sanctions. Accordingly, what distinguishes the moral rights of distant peoples from the requirements of supererogation (the nonfulfillment of which is never blameworthy) is that the former but not the latter can be justifiably enforced either by noncoercive or by coercive and noncoercive sanctions.

Of the various moral grounds for justifying the welfare rights of distant peoples, quite possibly the most evident are those that appeal either to a right to life or a right to fair treatment. Libertarians interpret a person's right to life as a negative right. Welfare liberals and socialists interpret it as a positive right.

Thus, suppose we interpret a person's right to life as a positive right. So understood, the person's right to life would most plausibly be interpreted as a right to receive those goods and resources that are necessary for satisfying her basic needs. For a person's basic needs are those which must be satisfied in order not to seriously endanger her health or sanity. Thus, receiving the goods and resources that are necessary for satisfying her basic needs would preserve a person's life in the fullest sense. And if a person's positive right to life is to be universal in the sense that it is possessed by every person (as the right to life is generally understood to be) then it must be an *in rem* right. This is because an *in rem* right, unlike an *in personam* right, does not require for its possession the assumption by other persons of any special roles or contractual obligations. Interpreted as a positive *in rem* right, therefore, a person's right to life would clearly justify the welfare rights of distant peoples to have their basic needs satisfied.

Suppose, on the other hand, that we interpret a person's right to life as a negative right. Here again, if the right is to be universal in the sense that it is possessed by all persons then it must also be an *in rem* right. So un-derstood, the right would require that everyone who is in a position to do so not interfere in certain ways with a person's attempts to meet her basic needs.

But what sort of noninterference would this right to life justify? If one's basic needs have not been met, would a person's right to life require that others not interfere with her taking the goods she needs from the surplus possessions of those who already have satisfied their own basic needs? As it is standardly interpreted, a person's negative right to life would not require such noninterference. Instead, a person's negative right to life is usually understood to be limited in such circumstances by the property rights of those who have more than enough to satisfy their own basic needs. Moreover, those who claim property rights to such surplus goods and resources are usually in a position effectively to prohibit those in need from taking what they require. For surely most underdeveloped nations of the world would be able to sponsor expeditions to the American Midwest or the Australian plains for the purpose of collecting the grain necessary to satisfy the basic needs of their citizens if they were not effectively prohibited from doing so at almost every stage of the enterprise.

But are persons with such surplus goods and resources normally justified in so prohibiting others from satisfying their basic needs? Admittedly, such persons may have contributed greatly to the value of the surplus goods and resources they possess, but why should that give them power over the life and death of those less fortunate? Even though their contribution may well justify favoring their nonbasic needs over the nonbasic needs of others, how could it justify favoring their nonbasic needs over the basic needs of others? After all, a person's negative right to life, being an *in rem* right, does not depend on the assumption by other persons of any special roles or contractual obligations. By contrast, property rights that are *in personam* rights require the assumption by other persons of the relevant roles and contractual obligations that constitute a particular system of acquisition and exchange, such as the role of a neighbor and the obligations of a merchant. Consequently, with respect to such property rights, it would seem that a person could not justifiably be kept from acquiring the goods and resources necessary to satisfy her basic needs by the property rights of others to surplus possessions, unless the person herself had voluntarily agreed to be so constrained by those property rights. But obviously few people would voluntarily agree to have such constraints placed upon their ability to acquire the goods and resources necessary to satisfy their basic needs. For most people their right to acquire the goods and resources necessary to satisfy their basic needs would have priority over any other person's property rights to surplus possessions, or alternatively, they would conceive of property rights such that no one could have property rights to any surplus possessions which were required to satisfy their own basic needs.

Even if some property rights could arise, as *in rem* rights by a Lockean process of mixing one's labor with previously unowned goods and resources, there would still be a need for some sort of a restriction on such appropriations. For if these *in rem* property rights are to be *moral rights* then it must be reasonable for every affected party to accept such rights, since the requirements of morality cannot be contrary to reason. Accordingly, in order to give rise to *in rem* property rights, the appropriation of previously unowned goods and resources cannot justifiably limit anyone's ability to acquire the goods and resources necessary to satisfy her basic needs, unless it would be reasonable for the person voluntarily to agree to be so constrained. But obviously it would not be reasonable for many people, particularly those whose basic needs are not being met, voluntarily to agree to be so constrained by property rights. This means that whether property rights are *in personam* rights and arise by the assumption of the relevant roles and contractual obligations or are *in rem* rights and arise by a Lockean process of mixing one's labor with previously unowned goods and resources, such rights would rarely limit a negative right to life, interpreted as an *in rem* right to noninterference with one's attempts to acquire the goods and resources necessary to satisfy one's basic needs. So interpreted, a negative right to life would clearly justify the welfare rights of distant people.

If we turn to a consideration of a person's right to fair treatment, a similar justification of the welfare rights of distant peoples emerges. To determine the requirements of fair treatment, suppose we employ a decision procedure analogous to the one John Rawls developed in *A Theory of Justice*. Suppose, that is to say, that in deciding upon the requirements of fair treatment, we were to discount the knowledge of which particular interests happen to be our own. Since we obviously know what our particular interests are, we would just not be taking that knowledge into account when selecting the requirements for fair treatment. Rather, in selecting these requirements, we would be reasoning from our knowledge of all the particular interests of everyone who would be affected by our decision but not from our knowledge of which particular interests happen to be our own. In employing this decision procedure, therefore, we (like judges who discount prejudicial information in order to reach fair decisions) would be able to give a fair hearing to everyone's particular interests. Assuming further that we are well-informed of the particular interests that would be affected by our decision and are fully capable of rationally deliberating with respect to that information, then our deliberations would culminate in a unanimous decision. This is because each of us would be deliberating in a rationally correct manner with respect to the same information and would be using a decision procedure leading to a uniform evaluation of the alternatives. Consequently, each of us would favor the same requirements for fair treatment.

But what requirements would we select by using this decision procedure? Since by using this decision procedure we would not be using our knowledge of which particular interests happen to be our own, we would be quite concerned about the pattern according to which goods and resources would be distributed throughout the world. By using this decision procedure, we would reason as though our particular interests might be those of persons with the largest share of goods and resources as well as those of persons with the smallest share of goods and resources. Consequently, we would neither exclusively favor the interests of persons with the largest share of goods by endorsing an unlimited right to accumulate goods and resources nor exclusively favor the interests of persons with the smallest share of goods and resources by endorsing the highest possible minimum for those who are least advantaged. Rather we would compromise by endorsing a right to accumulate goods and resources that was limited by the guarantee of a minimum sufficient to provide each person with the goods and resources necessary to satisfy his or her basic needs. It seems clear, therefore, that a right to fair treatment as captured by this Rawlsian decision procedure would also justify the welfare rights of distant people.

So it would seem that the welfare rights of distant peoples can be firmly grounded either in each person's right to life or each person's right to fair treatment. As a result, it would be impossible for one to deny that distant peoples have welfare rights without also denying that each person has a right to life and a right to fair treatment, unless, that is, one drastically reinterprets the significance of a right to life and a right to fair treatment.

Alternative Views

Not surprisingly, most of the solutions to the problem of near and distant peoples that have been proposed are analogous to the solutions we discussed with regard to the problem of the distribution of income and wealth within a society. (See Section I.)

As before, there is a libertarian solution. According to this view, distant peoples have no right to receive aid from persons living in today's affluent societies, but only a right not to be harmed by them. As before, these requirements are said to be derived from a political ideal of liberty. And, as before, we can question whether such an ideal actually supports these requirements.

Garrett Hardin endorses a "no aid" view in his essay (Selection 8). However, Hardin does not support his view on libertarian grounds. Without denying that there is a general obligation to help those in need, Hardin argues that helping those who live in absolute poverty in today's world would not do any good, and *for that reason* is not required. Hardin justifies this

view on empirical grounds, claiming that the giving of aid would be ineffective and even counterproductive for controlling population growth.

Peter Singer challenges the empirical grounds on which Hardin's view rests (Selection 9). Singer claims that Hardin's view accepts the certain evil of unrelieved poverty in underdeveloped countries—for instance, Bangladesh and Somalia—so as to avoid the future possibility of still greater poverty in underdeveloped countries together with deteriorating conditions in developed and developing countries. Singer argues, however, that with a serious commitment to aid from developed countries, there is a "fair chance" that underdeveloped countries will bring their population growth under control, thus avoiding the greater evil Hardin fears. Given the likelihood of this result, Singer argues that we have no moral justification for embracing, as Hardin does, the certain evil of unrelieved poverty in underdeveloped countries by denying them aid.

The positive solution to the problem of near and distant peoples defended by Singer can be characterized as a welfare liberal solution. Singer at some point would want to defend his "pro aid" view on utilitarian grounds, but he also tries to base his view on premises of a more general appeal. The fundamental premise he relies on is this: If we can prevent something bad without sacrificing anything of comparable significance, we ought to do it. Singer notes that libertarians, like Robert Nozick, would at least initially have difficulty accepting this premise. Nozick would surely claim that the requirement this premise imposes is at best only one of charity rather than justice, and that failing to abide by it is neither blameworthy nor punishable. But if a right to life interpreted as a negative right can be shown to have the same practical implications as Singer's view, then even libertarians would have to accept a "pro aid" view. (See Section I.)

Unlike Singer, Lawrence Blum supports only a "minimal aid" view grounded not on impartiality but beneficence (Selection 10). This view, Blum claims, accounts better for the role that friendships and special relationships have in our lives. In Selection 11, however,

James Rachels questions whether the degree to which we tend to favor those special relations who are our children can really be morally justified. Although Rachels does not draw the same distinction between impartiality and beneficence that Blum does, he argues on grounds of what Blum would call beneficence that we have an obligation to provide basic necessities for needy children rather than provide luxuries for our own.

A socialist solution to the problem of near and distant peoples would place considerable stress on the responsibility of developed countries for the situation in underdeveloped countries. Socialists claim that much of the poverty and unemployment found in underdeveloped countries is the result of the disruptive and exploitative influence of developed countries. For example, it is claimed that arms supplied by developed countries enable repressive regimes in underdeveloped countries to remain in power when they would otherwise be overthrown. Under these repressive regimes, small groups of landowners and capitalists are allowed to exploit the resources in underdeveloped countries for export markets in developed countries. As a result, most people in underdeveloped countries are forced off the land that their forebears have farmed for generations and are required to compete for the few, frequently low-paying jobs that have been created to serve the export markets.

Nevertheless, even if socialists are right about the responsibility of developed countries for poverty in underdeveloped countries it is still a further question whether the socialization of the means of production and the abolition of private property are the only viable moral responses to this situation. It certainly seems possible that some form of restricted private property system that provides for the meeting of everyone's basic needs, jus-

tified either on welfare liberal grounds or on libertarian grounds, would serve as well.

Practical Application

There does not seem to be as much of a gap between the "alternative views" and the "practical applications" with respect to the problem of near and distant peoples as there is in the problem of the distribution of wealth and income. This is because most of the discussions of the alternative views have already taken up the question of practical application (e.g., Singer suggests as a practical application a 10 percent tithe on income in developed countries). The merit of Gus Speth's article, however, is that it focuses squarely on the question of practical application (Selection 12). After reviewing the world situation, Speth sketches a practical program involving conservation, sustainable growth, and equity. Because his program obviously involves substantial aid to underdeveloped and developing countries, you should not endorse such a program unless you believe that arguments such as those presented by Singer and Rachels effectively counter arguments such as those presented by Hardin and Blum.

Nevertheless, whatever solution to the problem of near and distant peoples you favor, you will still not know how goods and resources should ultimately be distributed in society unless you have a solution to the problems of abortion and euthanasia. If abortion is morally justified, perhaps we should be funding abortions so that every woman, rich or poor, can have an abortion if she wants one. And if euthanasia is morally justified, perhaps we should be reallocating resources that are now being used for the purpose of sustaining life. Appropriately, the next section of this book takes up the problem of abortion and euthanasia.

8. Lifeboat Ethics: The Case Against Helping the Poor

Garrett Hardin

Garrett Hardin argues that our first obligation is to ourselves and our posterity.
For that reason, he contends, it would be foolish for rich nations to share their
surplus with poor nations, whether through a World Food Bank, the exporting
of technology, or unrestricted immigration. In view of the growing populations
and improvident behavior of poor nations, such sharing would do no good—it
would only overload the environment and lead to demands for still greater
assistance in the future.

Environmentalists use the metaphor of the
earth as a "spaceship" in trying to persuade
countries, industries and people to stop wasting and polluting our natural resources. Since
we all share life on this planet, they argue, no
single person or institution has the right to
destroy, waste, or use more than a fair share of
its resources.

But does everyone on earth have an equal
right to an equal share of its resources? The
spaceship metaphor can be dangerous when
used by misguided idealists to justify suicidal
policies for sharing our resources through uncontrolled immigration and foreign aid. In
their enthusiastic but unrealistic generosity,
they confuse the ethics of a spaceship with
those of a lifeboat.

A true spaceship would have to be under
the control of a captain, since no ship could
possibly survive if its course were determined
by committee. Spaceship Earth certainly has
no captain; the United Nations is merely a
toothless tiger, with little power to enforce any
policy upon its bickering members.

If we divide the world crudely into rich
nations and poor nations, two thirds of them
are desperately poor, and only one third comparatively rich, with the United States the
wealthiest of all. Metaphorically each rich nation can be seen as a lifeboat full of com-

From "The Case Against Helping the Poor," *Psychology
Today* (1974), pp. 38–43, 123–126. Reprinted with permission from *Psychology Today* magazine. Copyright ©
1974 Sussex Publishers, Inc. Addendum 1989. Reprinted by permission of the author.

paratively rich people. In the ocean outside
each lifeboat swim the poor of the world, who
would like to get in, or at least to share some of
the wealth. What should the lifeboat passengers do?

First, we must recognize the limited capacity of any lifeboat. For example, a nation's land
has a limited capacity to support a population
and as the current energy crisis has shown us,
in some ways we have already exceeded the
carrying capacity of our land.

Adrift in a Moral Sea

So here we sit, say fifty people in our lifeboat.
To be generous, let us assume it has room for
ten more, making a total capacity of sixty. Suppose the fifty of us in the lifeboat see 100
others swimming in the water outside, begging
for admission to our boat or for handouts. We
have several options: we may be tempted to try
to live by the Christian ideal of being "our
brother's keeper," or by the Marxist ideal of
"to each according to his needs." Since the
needs of all in the water are the same, and
since they can all be seen as "our brothers," we
could take them all into our boat, making a
total of 150 in a boat designed for sixty. The
boat swamps, everyone drowns. Complete justice, complete catastrophe.

Since the boat has an unused excess capacity of ten more passengers, we could admit just

ten more to it. But which ten do we let in? How do we choose? Do we pick the best ten, the neediest ten, "first come, first served"? And what do we say to the ninety we exclude? If we do let an extra ten into our lifeboat, we will have lost our "safety factor," an engineering principle of critical importance. For example, if we don't leave room for excess capacity as a safety factor in our country's agriculture, a new plant disease or a bad change in the weather could have disastrous consequences.

Suppose we decide to preserve our small safety factor and admit no more to the lifeboat. Our survival is then possible, although we shall have to be constantly on guard against boarding parties.

While this last solution clearly offers the only means of our survival, it is morally abhorrent to many people. Some say they feel guilty about their good luck. My reply is simple: "Get out and yield your place to others." This may solve the problem of the guilt-ridden person's conscience, but it does not change the ethics of the lifeboat. The needy person to whom the guilt-ridden person yields his place will not himself feel guilty about his good luck. If he did, he would not climb aboard. The net result of conscience-stricken people giving up their unjustly held seats is the elimination of that sort of conscience from the lifeboat.

This is the basic metaphor within which we must work out our solutions. Let us now enrich the image, step by step, with substantive additions from the real world, a world that must solve real and pressing problems of overpopulation and hunger.

The harsh ethics of the lifeboat become even harsher when we consider the reproductive differences between the rich nations and the poor nations. The people inside the lifeboats are doubling in numbers every eighty-seven years; those swimming around outside are doubling, on the average, every thirty-five years, more than twice as fast as the rich. And since the world's resources are dwindling, the difference in prosperity between the rich and the poor can only increase.

As of 1973, the United States had a population of 210 million people, who were increasing by 0.8 percent per year. Outside our lifeboat, let us imagine another 210 million people (say the combined populations of Co-lombia, Ecuador, Venezuela, Morocco, Pakistan, Thailand, and the Philippines), who are increasing at a rate of 3.3 percent per year. Put differently, the doubling time for this aggregate population is twenty-one years, compared to eighty-seven years for the United States.

Multiplying the Rich and the Poor

Now suppose the United States agreed to pool its resources with those seven countries, with everyone receiving an equal share. Initially the ratio of Americans to non-Americans in this model would be one-to-one. But consider what the ratio would be after eighty-seven years, by which time the Americans would have doubled to a population of 420 million. By then, doubling every twenty-one years, the other group would have swollen to 354 billion. Each American would have to share the available resources with more than eight people.

But, one could argue, this discussion assumes that current population trends will continue, and they may not. Quite so. Most likely the rate of population increase will decline much faster in the United States than it will in the other countries, and there does not seem to be much we can do about it. In sharing with "each according to his needs," we must recognize that needs are determined by population size, which is determined by the rate of reproduction, which at present is regarded as a sovereign right of every nation, poor or not. This being so, the philanthropic load created by the sharing ethic of the spaceship can only increase.

The Tragedy of the Commons

The fundamental error of spaceship ethics, and the sharing it requires, is that it leads to what I call "the tragedy of the commons." Under a system of private property, the men who own property recognize their responsibility to care for it, for if they don't they will eventually suffer. A farmer, for instance, will allow no more cattle in a pasture than its carrying capacity justifies. If he overloads it, erosion sets in, weeds take over, and he loses the use of the pasture.

If a pasture becomes a commons open to all, the right of each to use it may not be matched by a corresponding responsibility to protect it. Asking everyone to use it with discretion will hardly do, for the considerate herdsman who refrains from overloading the commons suffers more than a selfish one who says his needs are greater. If everyone would restrain himself, all would be well; but it takes only one less than everyone to ruin a system of voluntary restraint. In a crowded world of less than perfect human beings, mutual ruin is inevitable if there are no controls. This is the tragedy of the commons.

One of the major tasks of education today should be the creation of such an acute awareness of the dangers of the commons that people will recognize its many varieties. For example, the air and water have become polluted because they are treated as commons. Further growth in the population or per-capita conversion of natural resources into pollutants will only make the problem worse. The same holds true for the fish of the oceans. Fishing fleets have nearly disappeared in many parts of the world; technological improvements in the art of fishing are hastening the day of complete ruin. Only the replacement of the system of the commons with a responsible system of control will save the land, air, water and oceanic fisheries.

The World Food Bank

In recent years there has been a push to create a new commons called a World Food Bank, an international depository of food reserves to which nations would contribute according to their abilities and from which they would draw according to their needs. This humanitarian proposal has received support from many liberal international groups, and from such prominent citizens as Margaret Mead, U.N. Secretary General Kurt Waldheim, and Senators Edward Kennedy and George McGovern.

A world food bank appeals powerfully to our humanitarian impulses. But before we rush ahead with such a plan, let us recognize where the greatest political push comes from, lest we be disillusioned later. Our experience with the "Food for Peace program," or Public Law 480, gives us the answer. This program moved billions of dollars worth of U.S. surplus grain to food-short, population-long countries during the past two decades. But when P.L. 480 first became law, a headline in the business magazine *Forbes* revealed the real power behind it: "Feeding the World's Hungry Millions: How It Will Mean Billions for U.S. Business."

And indeed it did. In the years 1960 to 1970, U.S. taxpayers spent a total of $7.9 billion on the Food for Peace program. Between 1948 and 1970, they also paid an additional $50 billion for other economic-aid programs, some of which went for food and food-producing machinery and technology. Though all U.S. taxpayers were forced to contribute to the cost of P.L. 480, certain special interest groups gained handsomely under the program. Farmers did not have to contribute the grain; the Government, or rather the taxpayers, bought it from them at full market prices. The increased demand raised prices of farm products generally. The manufacturers of farm machinery, fertilizers and pesticides benefited by the farmers' extra efforts to grow more food. Grain elevators profited from storing the surplus until it could be shipped. Railroads made money hauling it to ports, and shipping lines profited from carrying it overseas. The implementation of P.L. 480 required the creation of a vast Government bureaucracy, which then acquired its own vested interest in continuing the program regardless of its merits.

Extracting Dollars

Those who proposed and defended the Food for Peace program in public rarely mentioned its importance to any of these special interests.

The public emphasis was always on its humanitarian effects. The combination of silent selfish interests and highly vocal humanitarian apologists made a powerful and successful lobby for extracting money from taxpayers. We can expect the same lobby to push now for the creation of a World Food Bank.

However great the potential benefit to selfish interests, it should not be a decisive argument against a truly humanitarian program. We must ask if such a program would actually do more good than harm, not only momentarily but also in the long run. Those who propose the food bank usually refer to a current "emergency" or "crisis" in terms of world food supply. But what is an emergency? Although they may be infrequent and sudden, everyone knows that emergencies will occur from time to time. A well-run family, company, organization or country prepares for the likelihood of accidents and emergencies. It expects them, it budgets for them, it saves for them.

Learning the Hard Way

What happens if some organizations or countries budget for accidents and others do not? If each country is solely responsible for its own well-being, poorly managed ones will suffer. But they can learn from experience. They may mend their ways and learn to budget for infrequent but certain emergencies. For example, the weather varies from year to year, and periodic crop failures are certain. A wise and competent government saves out of the production of the good years in anticipation of bad years to come. Joseph taught this policy to Pharaoh in Egypt more than 2,000 years ago. Yet the great majority of the governments in the world today do not follow such a policy. They lack either the wisdom or the competence, or both. Should those nations that do manage to put something aside be forced to come to the rescue each time an emergency occurs among the poor nations?

"But it isn't their fault!" some kindhearted liberals argue. "How can we blame the poor people who are caught in an emergency? Why must they suffer for the sins of their governments?" The concept of blame is simply not relevant here. The real question is, what are the operational consequences of establishing a world food bank? If it is open to every country every time a need develops, slovenly rulers will not be motivated to take Joseph's advice. Someone will always come to their aid. Some countries will deposit food in the world food bank, and others will withdraw it. There will be almost no overlap. As a result of such solutions to food shortage emergencies, the poor countries will not learn to mend their ways and will suffer progressively greater emergencies as their populations grow.

Population Control the Crude Way

On the average, poor countries undergo a 2.5 percent increase in population each year; rich countries, about 0.8 percent. Only rich countries have anything in the way of food reserves set aside, and even they do not have as much as they should. Poor countries have none. If poor countries received no food from the outside, the rate of their population growth would be periodically checked by crop failures and famines. But if they can always draw on a world food bank in time of need, their population can continue to grow unchecked, and so will their "need" for aid. In the short run, a world food bank may diminish that need, but in the long run it actually increases the need without limit.

Without some system of worldwide food sharing, the proportion of people in the rich and poor nations might eventually stabilize. The overpopulated poor countries would decrease in numbers, while the rich countries that had room for more people would increase. But with a well-meaning system of sharing, such as a world food bank, the growth differential between the rich and the poor countries will not only persist, it will increase. Because of the higher rate of population growth in the poor countries of the world, 88 percent of today's children are born poor, and only 12 percent rich. Year by year the ratio becomes worse, as the fast-reproducing poor outnumber the slow-reproducing rich.

A world food bank is thus a commons in disguise. People will have more motivation to draw from it than to add to any common store. The less provident and less able will multiply at the expense of the abler and more provident, bringing eventual ruin upon all who share in the commons. Besides, any system of "sharing" that amounts to foreign aid from the rich nations to the poor nations will carry the taint of charity, which will contribute little to the world peace so devoutly desired by those who support the idea of a world food bank.

As past U.S. foreign-aid programs have amply and depressingly demonstrated, international charity frequently inspires mistrust and antagonism rather than gratitude on the part of the recipient nation.

Chinese Fish and Miracle Rice

The modern approach to foreign aid stresses the export of technology and advice, rather than money and food. As an ancient Chinese proverb goes: "Give a man a fish and he will eat for a day; teach him how to fish and he will eat for the rest of his days." Acting on this advice, the Rockefeller and Ford Foundations have financed a number of programs for improving agriculture in the hungry nations. Known as the "Green Revolution," these programs have led to the development of "miracle rice" and "miracle wheat," new strains that offer bigger harvests and greater resistance to crop damage. Norman Borlaug, the Nobel Prize winning agronomist who, supported by the Rockefeller Foundation, developed "miracle wheat," is one of the most prominent advocates of a world food bank.

Whether or not the Green Revolution can increase food production as much as its champions claim is a debatable but possibly irrelevant point. Those who support this well-intended humanitarian effort should first consider some of the fundamentals of human ecology. Ironically, one man who did was the late Alan Gregg, a vice president of the

Rockefeller Foundation. Two decades ago he expressed strong doubts about the wisdom of such attempts to increase food production. He likened the growth and spread of humanity over the surface of the earth to the spread of cancer in the human body, remarking that "cancerous growths demand food; but, as far as I know, they have never been cured by getting it."

Overloading the Environment

Every human born constitutes a draft on all aspects of the environment: food, air, water, forests, beaches, wildlife, scenery and solitude. Food can, perhaps, be significantly increased to meet a growing demand. But what about clean beaches, unspoiled forests, and solitude? If we satisfy a growing population's need for food, we necessarily decrease its per capita supply of the other resources needed by men.

India, for example, now has a population of 600 million, which increases by 15 million each year. This population already puts a huge load on a relatively impoverished environment. The country's forests are now only a small fraction of what they were three centuries ago, and floods and erosion continually destroy the insufficient farmland that remains. Every one of the 15 million new lives added to India's population puts an additional burden on the environment and increases the economic and social costs of crowding. However humanitarian our intent, every Indian life saved through medical or nutritional assistance from abroad diminishes the quality of life for those who remain, and for subsequent generations. If rich countries make it possible, through foreign aid, for 600 million Indians to swell to 1.2 billion in a mere twenty-eight years, as their current growth rate threatens, will future generations of Indians thank us for hastening the destruction of their environment? Will our good intentions be sufficient excuse for the consequences of our actions?

My final example of a commons in action is one for which the public has the least desire for rational discussion—immigration. Anyone who publicly questions the wisdom of current U.S. immigration policy is promptly charged with bigotry, prejudice, ethnocentrism, chauvinism, isolationism or selfishness. Rather than encounter such accusations, one would rather talk about other matters, leaving immigration policy to wallow in the crosscurrents of special interests that take no account of the good of the whole, or the interests of posterity.

Perhaps we still feel guilty about things we said in the past. Two generations ago the popular press frequently referred to Dagos, Wops, Polacks, Chinks and Krauts, in articles about how America was being "overrun" by foreigners of supposedly inferior genetic stock. But because the implied inferiority of foreigners was used then as justification for keeping them out, people now assume that restrictive policies could only be based on such misguided notions. There are other grounds.

A Nation of Immigrants

Just consider the numbers involved. Our Government acknowledges a net inflow of 400,000 immigrants a year. While we have no hard data on the extent of illegal entries, educated guesses put the figure at about 600,000 a year. Since the natural increase (excess of births over deaths) of the resident population now runs about 1.7 million per year, the yearly gain from immigration amounts to at least 19 percent of the total annual increase, and may be as much as 37 percent if we include the estimate for illegal immigrants. Considering the growing use of birth-control devices, the potential effect of educational campaigns by such organizations as Planned Parenthood Federation of America and Zero Population Growth, and the influence of inflation and the housing shortage, the fertility rate of American women may decline so much that immigration could account for all the yearly increase in population. Should we not at least ask if that is what we want?

For the sake of those who worry about whether the "quality" of the average immigrant compares favorably with the quality of the average resident, let us assume that immi-

grants and nativeborn citizens are of exactly equal quality, however one defines that term. We will focus here only on quantity; and since our conclusions will depend on nothing else, all charges of bigotry and chauvinism become irrelevant.

Immigration versus Food Supply

World food banks *move food to the people*, hastening the exhaustion of the environment of the poor countries. Unrestricted immigration, on the other hand, *moves people to the food*, thus speeding up the destruction of the environment of the rich countries. We can easily understand why poor people should want to make this latter transfer, but why should rich hosts encourage it?

As in the case of foreign-aid programs, immigration receives support from selfish interests and humanitarian impulses. The primary selfish interest in unimpeded immigration is the desire of employers for cheap labor, particularly in industries and trades that offer degrading work. In the past, one wave of foreigners after another was brought into the United States to work at wretched jobs for wretched wages. In recent years the Cubans, Puerto Ricans and Mexicans have had this dubious honor. The interests of the employers of cheap labor mesh well with the guilty silence of the country's liberal intelligentsia. White Anglo-Saxon Protestants are particularly reluctant to call for a closing of the doors to immigration for fear of being called bigots.

But not all countries have such reluctant leadership. Most educated Hawaiians, for example, are keenly aware of the limits of their environment, particularly in terms of population growth. There is only so much room on the islands, and the islanders know it. To Hawaiians, immigrants from the other forty-nine states present as great a threat as those from other nations. At a recent meeting of Hawaiian government officials in Honolulu, I had the ironic delight of hearing a speaker, who like most of his audience was of Japanese ancestry, ask how the country might practically and constitutionally close its doors to further immigration. One member of the audience countered: "How can we shut the doors now? We have many friends and relatives in Japan that we'd like to bring here some day so that they can enjoy Hawaii too." The Japanese-American speaker smiled sympathetically and answered: "Yes, but we have children now, and someday we'll have grandchildren too. We can bring more people here from Japan only by giving away some of the land that we hope to pass on to our grandchildren some day. What right do we have to do that?"

At this point, I can hear U.S. liberals asking: "How can you justify slamming the door once you're inside? You say that immigrants should be kept out. But aren't we all immigrants, or the descendants of immigrants? If we insist on staying, must we not admit all others?" Our craving for intellectual order leads us to seek and prefer symmetrical rules and morals: a single rule for me and everybody else; the same rule yesterday, today, and tomorrow. Justice, we feel, should not change with time and place.

We Americans of non-Indian ancestry can look upon ourselves as the descendants of thieves who are guilty morally, if not legally, of stealing this land from its Indian owners. Should we then give back the land to the now living American descendants of those Indians? However morally or logically sound this proposal may be, I, for one, am unwilling to live by it and I know no one else who is. Besides, the logical consequence would be absurd. Suppose that, intoxicated with a sense of pure justice, we should decide to turn our land over to the Indians. Since all our wealth has also been derived from the land, wouldn't we be morally obliged to give that back to the Indians too?

Pure Justice versus Reality

Clearly, the concept of pure justice produces an infinite regression to absurdity. Centuries ago, wise men invented statutes of limitations to justify the rejection of such pure justice, in the interest of preventing continual disorder. The law zealously defends property rights, but only relatively recent property rights. Drawing a line after an arbitrary time has elapsed may be unjust, but the alternatives are worse.

We are all the descendants of thieves, and the world's resources are inequitably distributed. But we must begin the journey to tomorrow from the point where we are today. We cannot remake the past. We cannot safely divide the wealth equitably among all peoples so long as people reproduce at different rates. To do so would guarantee that our grandchildren, and everyone else's grandchildren, would have only a ruined world to inhabit.

To be generous with one's own possessions is quite different from being generous with those of posterity. We should call this point to the attention of those who, from a commendable love of justice and equality, would institute a system of the commons, either in the form of a world food bank, or of unrestricted immigration. We must convince them if we wish to save at least some parts of the world from environmental ruin.

Without a true world government to control reproduction and the use of available resources, the sharing ethic of the spaceship is impossible. For the foreseeable future, our survival demands that we govern our actions by the ethics of a lifeboat, harsh though they may be. Posterity will be satisfied with nothing less.

Addendum 1989

Can anyone watch children starve on television without wanting to help? Naturally sympathetic, a normal human being thinks that he can imagine what it is like to be starving. We all want to do unto others as we would have them do unto us.

But wanting is not doing. Forty years of activity by the U.S. Agency for International Development, as well as episodic nongovernmental attempts to feed the world's starving, have produced mixed results. Before we respond to the next appeal we should ask, "Does what we call 'aid' really help?"

Some of the shortcomings of food aid can be dealt with briefly. Waste is unavoidable: Because most poor countries have wretched transportation systems, food may sit on a dock until it rots. Then there are the corrupt politicians who take donated food away from the poor and give it to their political supporters. In Somalia in the 1980s, fully 70 percent of the donated food went to the army.

We can school ourselves to accept such losses. Panicky projects are always inefficient: Waste and corruption are par for the course. But there is another kind of loss that we cannot—in fact, we should not—accept, and that is the loss caused by the boomerang effects of philanthropy. Before we jump onto the next "feed-the-starving" bandwagon we need to understand how well-intentioned efforts can be counterproductive.

Briefly put, it is a mistake to focus only on starving people while ignoring their surroundings. Where there is great starvation there is usually an impoverished environment: poor soil, scarce water and wildly fluctuating weather. As a result, the "carrying capacity" of the environment is low. The territory simply cannot support the population that is trying to live on it. Yet if the population were much smaller, and if it would stay smaller, the people would not need to starve.

Let us look at a particular example. Nigeria, like all the central African countries, has increased greatly in population in the last quarter-century. Over many generations, Nigerians learned that their farmlands would be most productive if crop-growing alternated with "fallow years"—years in which the land was left untilled to recover its fertility.

When modern medicine reduced the death rate, the population began to grow. More food was demanded from the same land. Responding to that need, Nigerians shortened the fallow periods. The result was counterproductive. In one carefully studied village, the average fallow period was shortened from 5.3 to 1.4 years. As a result, the yearly production (averaged over both fallow and crop years) fell by 30 percent.

Are Nigerian farmers stupid? Not at all! They know perfectly well what they are doing. But a farmer whose family has grown too large for his farm has to take care of next year's need before he can provide for the future. To fallow or not to fallow translates into this choice: zero production in a fallow year or a 30 percent shortfall over the long run. Starvation cannot wait. Long-term policies have to give way to short-term ones. So the farmer plows up his overstressed fields, thus diminishing long-term productivity.

Once the carrying capacity of a territory has been transgressed, its capacity goes down, year after year. Transgression is a one-way road to ruin. Ecologists memorialize this reality with an 11th Commandment: "Thou shalt not transgress the carrying capacity."

Transgression takes many forms. Poor people are poor in energy resources. They need energy to cook their food. Where do they get it? Typically, from animal dung or trees and bushes. Burning dung deprives the soil of nitrogen. Cutting down trees and bushes deprives the land of protection against eroding rain. Soil-poor slopes cannot support a crop of fuel-plants. Once the soil is gone, water runs off the slopes faster and floods the valleys below. First poor people deforest their land, and then deforestation makes them poorer.

When Americans send food to a starving population that has already grown beyond the environment's carrying capacity we become a partner in the devastation of their land. Food from the outside keeps more natives alive; these demand more food and fuel; greater demand causes the community to transgress the carrying capacity more, and transgression results in lowering the carrying capacity. The deficit grows exponentially. Gifts of food to an overpopulated country boomerang, increasing starvation over the long run. Our choice is really between letting some die this year and letting more die in the following years.

You may protest, "That's easy enough for a well-fed American to say, but do citizens of poor countries agree?" Well, wisdom is not restricted to the wealthy. The Somali novelist Nuruddin Farrah has courageously condemned foreign gifts as being not truly aid, but a poison, because (if continued) such gifts will make Africans permanently dependent on outside aid.

The ethicist Joseph Fletcher has given a simple directive to would-be philanthropists: "Give if it helps, but not if it hurts." We can grant that giving makes the donor feel good at first—but how will he feel later when he realizes that he has harmed the receiver?

Only one thing can really help a poor country: population control. Having accepted disease control the people must now accept population control.

What the philosopher-economist Kenneth Boulding has called "lovey-dovey charity" is not enough. "It is well to remember," he said, "that the symbol of Christian love is a cross and not a Teddy bear." A good Christian should obey the 11th Commandment, refusing to send gifts that help poor people destroy the environment that must support the next generation.

9. The Famine Relief Argument

Peter Singer

Peter Singer argues that people in rich countries, by allowing those in poor countries to suffer and die, are actually engaged in reckless homicide. This is because people in rich countries could prevent the deaths of the poor without sacrificing anything of comparable significance. Singer considers a number of objections to his argument and finds them all wanting. Against Hardin's objection that aiding the poor now will lead to disaster in the future, Singer argues that if the right sort of aid is given conditionally, a future disaster of the sort Hardin envisions can be avoided.

Some Facts

Consider these facts: by the most cautious estimates, 400 million people lack the calories, protein, vitamins and minerals needed for a normally healthy life. Millions are constantly hungry; others suffer from deficiency diseases and from infections they would be able to resist on a better diet. Children are worst affected. According to one estimate, 15 million children under five die every year from the combined effects of malnutrition and infection. In some areas, half the children born can be expected to die before their fifth birthday.

Nor is lack of food the only hardship of the poor. To give a broader picture, Robert McNamara, President of the World Bank, has suggested the term "absolute poverty." The poverty we are familiar with in industrialized nations is relative poverty—meaning that some citizens are poor, relative to the wealth enjoyed by their neighbours. People living in relative poverty in Australia might be quite comfortably off by comparison with old-age pensioners in Britain, and British old-age pensioners are not poor in comparison with the poverty that exists in Mali or Ethiopia. Absolute poverty, on the other hand, is poverty by any standard. In McNamara's words:

Poverty at the absolute level . . . is life at the very margin of existence.

The absolute poor are severely deprived human beings struggling to survive in a set of squalid and degraded circumstances almost beyond the power of our sophisticated imaginations and privileged circumstances to conceive.

Compared to those fortunate enough to live in developed countries individuals in the poorest nations have

An infant mortality rate eight times higher

From *Practical Ethics* (1979), pp. 158–181. Reprinted by permission of Cambridge University Press.

A life expectancy one-third lower

An adult literacy rate 60% less

A nutritional level, for one out of every two in the population, below acceptable standards; and for millions of infants, less protein than is sufficient to permit optimum development of the brain.

And McNamara has summed up absolute poverty as:

a condition of life so characterized by malnutrition, illiteracy, disease, squalid surroundings, high infant mortality and low life expectancy as to be beneath any reasonable definition of human decency.

Absolute poverty is, as McNamara has said, responsible for the loss of countless lives, especially among infants and young children. When absolute poverty does not cause death it still causes misery of a kind not often seen in the affluent nations. Malnutrition in young children stunts both physical and mental development. It has been estimated that the health, growth and learning capacity of nearly half the young children in developing countries are affected by malnutrition. Millions of people on poor diets suffer from deficiency diseases, like goitre, or blindness caused by a lack of vitamin A. The food value of what the poor eat is further reduced by parasites such as hookworm and ringworm, which are endemic in conditions of poor sanitation and health education.

Death and disease apart, absolute poverty remains a miserable condition of life, with inadequate food, shelter, clothing, sanitation, health services and education. According to World Bank estimates which define absolute poverty in terms of income levels insufficient to provide adequate nutrition, something like 800 million people—almost 40% of the people of developing countries—live in absolute poverty. Absolute poverty is probably the principal cause of human misery today.

This is the background situation, the situation that prevails on our planet all the time. It does not make headlines. People died from malnutrition and related diseases yesterday, and more will die tomorrow. The occasional

droughts, cyclones, earthquakes and floods that take the lives of tens of thousands in one place and at one time are more newsworthy. They add greatly to the total amount of human suffering; but it is wrong to assume that when there are no major calamities reported, all is well.

The problem is not that the world cannot produce enough to feed and shelter its people. People in the poor countries consume, on average, 400 lbs of grain a year, while North Americans average more than 2000 lbs. The difference is caused by the fact that in the rich countries we feed most of our grain to animals, converting it into meat, milk and eggs. Because this is an inefficient process, wasting up to 95% of the food value of the animal feed, people in rich countries are responsible for the consumption of far more food than those in poor countries who eat few animal products. If we stopped feeding animals on grains, soybeans and fishmeal the amount of food saved would—if distributed to those who need it—be more than enough to end hunger throughout the world.

These facts about animal food do not mean that we can easily solve the world food problem by cutting down on animal products, but they show that the problem is essentially one of distribution rather than production. The world does produce enough food. Moreover the poorer nations themselves could produce far more if they made more use of improved agricultural techniques.

So why are people hungry? Poor people cannot afford to buy grain grown by American farmers. Poor farmers cannot afford to buy improved seeds, or fertilizers, or the machinery needed for drilling wells and pumping water. Only by transferring some of the wealth of the developed nations to the poor of the underdeveloped nations can the situation be changed.

That this wealth exists is clear. Against the picture of absolute poverty that McNamara has painted, one might pose a picture of "absolute affluence." Those who are absolutely affluent are not necessarily affluent by comparison with their neighbours, but they are affluent by any reasonable definition of human needs. This means that they have more income than they need to provide themselves adequately with all the basic necessities of life. After buying food, shelter, clothing, necessary health services and education, the absolutely affluent are still able to spend money on luxuries. The absolutely affluent choose their food for the pleasures of the palate, not to stop hunger; they buy new clothes to look fashionable, not to keep warm; they move house to be in a better neighbourhood or have a play room for the children, not to keep out the rain; and after all this there is still money to spend on books and records, colour television, and overseas holidays.

At this stage I am making no ethical judgments about absolute affluence, merely pointing out that it exists. Its defining characteristic is a significant amount of income above the level necessary to provide for the basic human needs of oneself and one's dependents. By this standard Western Europe, North America, Japan, Australia, New Zealand and the oil-rich Middle Eastern states are all absolutely affluent, and so are many, if not all, of their citizens. The USSR and Eastern Europe might also be included on this list. To quote McNamara once more:

> The average citizen of a developed country enjoys wealth beyond the wildest dreams of the one billion people in countries with per capita incomes under $200. . . .

These, therefore, are the countries—and individuals—who have wealth which they could, without threatening their own basic welfare, transfer to the absolutely poor.

At present, very little is being transferred. Members of the Organization of Petroleum Exporting Countries lead the way, giving an average of 2.1% of their Gross National Product. Apart from them, only Sweden, The Netherlands and Norway have reached the modest UN target of 0.7% of GNP. Britain gives 0.38% of its GNP in official development assistance and a small additional amount in unofficial aid from voluntary organizations. The total comes to less than £1 per month per person, and compares with 5.5% of GNP spent on alcohol, and 3% on tobacco. Other, even wealthier nations, give still less: Germany gives 0.27%, the United States 0.22% and Japan 0.21%.

The Moral Equivalent of Murder?

If these are the facts, we cannot avoid concluding that by not giving more than we do, people in rich countries are allowing those in poor countries to suffer from absolute poverty, with consequent malnutrition, ill health and death. This is not a conclusion which applies only to governments. It applies to each absolutely affluent individual, for each of us has the opportunity to do something about the situation; for instance, to give our time or money to voluntary organizations like Oxfam, War on Want, Freedom From Hunger, and so on. If, then, allowing someone to die is not intrinsically different from killing someone, it would seem that we are all murderers.

Is this verdict too harsh? Many will reject it as self-evidently absurd. They would sooner take it as showing that allowing to die cannot be equivalent to killing than as showing that living in an affluent style without contributing to Oxfam is ethically equivalent to going over to India and shooting a few peasants. And no doubt, put as bluntly as that, the verdict *is* too harsh.

There are several significant differences between spending money on luxuries instead of using it to save lives, and deliberately shooting people.

First, the motivation will normally be different. Those who deliberately shoot others go out of their way to kill; they presumably want their victims dead, from malice, sadism, or some equally unpleasant motive. A person who buys a colour television set presumably wants to watch television in colour—not in itself a terrible thing. At worst, spending money on luxuries instead of giving it away indicates selfishness and indifference to the sufferings of others, characteristics which may be understandable but are not comparable with actual malice or similar motives.

Second, it is not difficult for most of us to act in accordance with a rule against killing people: it is, on the other hand, very difficult to obey a rule which commands us to save all the lives we can. To live a comfortable, or even luxurious life it is not necessary to kill anyone; but it is necessary to allow some to die whom we might have saved, for the money that we need to live comfortably could have been given away. Thus the duty to avoid killing is much easier to discharge completely than the duty to save. Saving every life we could would mean cutting our standard of living down to the bare essentials needed to keep us alive.* To discharge this duty completely would require a degree of moral heroism utterly different from what is required by mere avoidance of killing.

A third difference is the greater certainty of the outcome of shooting when compared with not giving aid. If I point a loaded gun at someone and pull the trigger, it is virtually certain that the person will be injured, if not killed; whereas the money that I could give might be spent on a project than turns out to be unsuccessful and helps no one.

Fourth, when people are shot there are identifiable individuals who have been harmed. We can point to them and to their grieving families. When I buy my colour television, I cannot know who my money would have saved if I had given it away. In a time of famine I may see dead bodies and grieving families on my new television, and I might not doubt that my money would have saved some of them; even then it is impossible to point to a body and say that had I not bought the set, that person would have survived.

Fifth, it might be said that the plight of the hungry is not my doing, and so I cannot be held responsible for it. The starving would have been starving if I had never existed. If I kill, however, I am responsible for my victims' deaths, for those people would not have died if I had not killed them. . . .

Do the five differences not only explain, but

*Strictly, we would need to cut down to the minimum level compatible with earning the income which, after providing for our needs, left us most to give away. Thus if my present position earns me, say, £10,000 a year, but requires me to spend £1,000 a year on dressing respectably and maintaining a car, I cannot save more people by giving away the car and clothes if that will mean taking a job which, although it does not involve me in these expenses, earns me only £5,000.

also justify, our attitudes? Let us consider them one by one:

1. Take the lack of an identifiable victim first. Suppose that I am a travelling salesman, selling tinned food, and I learn that a batch of tins contains a contaminant, the known effect of which when consumed is to double the risk that the consumer will die from stomach cancer. Suppose I continue to sell the tins. My decision may have no identifiable victims. Some of those who eat the food will die from cancer. The proportion of consumers dying in this way will be twice that of the community at large, but which among the consumers died because they ate what I sold, and which would have contracted the disease anyway? It is impossible to tell; but surely this impossibility makes my decision no less reprehensible than it would have been had the contaminant had more readily detectable, though equally fatal, effects.

2. The lack of certainty that by giving money I could save a life does reduce the wrongness of not giving, by comparison with deliberate killing; but it is insufficient to show that not giving is acceptable conduct. The motorist who speeds through pedestrian crossings, heedless of anyone who might be on them, is not a murderer. She may never actually hit a pedestrian; yet what she does is very wrong indeed.

3. The notion of responsibility for acts rather than omissions is more puzzling. On the one hand we feel ourselves to be under a greater obligation to help those whose misfortunes we have caused. (It is for this reason that advocates of overseas aid often argue that Western nations have created the poverty of Third World nations, through forms of economic exploitation which go back to the colonial system.) On the other hand any consequentialist would insist that we are responsible for all the consequences of our actions, and if a consequence of my spending money on a luxury item is that someone dies, I am responsible for that death. It is true that the person would have died even if I had never existed, but what is the relevance of that? The fact is that I do exist, and the consequentialist will say that our responsibilities derive from the world as it is, not as it might have been.

One way of making sense of the nonconsequentialist view of responsibility is by basing it on a theory of rights of the kind proposed by John Locke or, more recently, Robert Nozick. If everyone has a right to life, and this right is a right *against* others who might threaten my life, but not a right *to* assistance from others when my life is in danger, then we can understand the feeling that we are responsible for acting to kill but not for omitting to save. The former violates the rights of others, the latter does not.

Should we accept such a theory of rights? If we build up our theory of rights by imagining, as Locke and Nozick do, individuals living independently from each other in a "state of nature," it may seem natural to adopt a conception of rights in which as long as each leaves the other alone, no rights are violated. I might, on this view, quite properly have maintained my independent existence if I had wished to do so. So if I do not make you any worse off than you would have been if I had had nothing at all to do with you, how can I have violated your rights? But why start from such an unhistorical, abstract and ultimately inexplicable idea as an independent individual? We now know that our ancestors were social beings long before they were human beings, and could not have developed the abilities and capacities of human beings if they had not been social beings first. In any case we are not, now, isolated individuals. If we consider people living together in a community, it is less easy to assume that rights must be restricted to rights against interference. We might, instead, adopt the view that taking rights to life seriously is incompatible with standing by and watching people die when one could easily save them.

4. What of the difference in motivation? That a person does not positively wish for the death of another lessens the severity of the blame she deserves; but not by as much as our present attitudes to giving aid suggest. The behaviour of the speeding motorist is again comparable, for such motorists usually have no desire at all to kill anyone. They merely enjoy speeding and are indifferent to the consequences. Despite their lack of malice, those who kill with cars deserve not only blame but also severe punishment.

5. Finally, the fact that to avoid killing people is normally not difficult, whereas to save all one possibly could save is heroic, must make an important difference to our attitude to failure to do what the respective principles demand. Not to kill is a minimum standard of acceptable conduct we can require of everyone; to save all one possibly could is not something that can realistically be required, especially not in societies accustomed to giving as little as ours do. Given the generally accepted standards, people who give, say, £100 a year to Oxfam are more aptly praised for above average generosity than blamed for giving less than they might. The appropriateness of praise and blame is, however, a separate issue from the rightness or wrongness of actions. The former evaluates the agent: the latter evaluates the action. Perhaps people who give £100 really ought to give at least £1,000, but to blame them for not giving more could be counterproductive. It might make them feel that what is required is too demanding, and if one is going to be blamed anyway, one might as well not give anything at all.

(That an ethic which put saving all one possibly can on the same footing as not killing would be an ethic for saints or heroes should not lead us to assume that the alternative must be an ethic which makes it obligatory not to kill, but puts us under no obligation to save anyone. There are positions in between these extremes, as we shall soon see.)

To summarize our discussion of the five differences which normally exist between killing and allowing to die, in the context of absolute poverty and overseas aid: The lack of an identifiable victim is of no moral significance, though it may play an important role in explaining our attitudes. The idea that we are directly responsible for those we kill, but not for those we do not help, depends on a questionable notion of responsibility, and may need to be based on a controversial theory of rights. Differences in certainty and motivation are ethically significant, and show that not aiding the poor is not to be condemned as murdering them; it could, however, be on a par with killing someone as a result of reckless driving, which is serious enough. Finally the difficulty of completely discharging the duty of saving all one possibly can makes it inappropriate to blame those who fall short of this target as we blame those who kill; but this does not show that the act itself is less serious. Nor does it indicate anything about those who, far from saving all they possibly can, make no effort to save anyone.

These conclusions suggest a new approach. Instead of attempting to deal with the contrast between affluence and poverty by comparing not saving with deliberate killing, let us consider afresh whether we have an obligation to assist those whose lives are in danger, and if so, how this obligation applies to the present world situation.

The Obligation to Assist

The Argument for an Obligation to Assist

The path from the library at my university to the Humanities lecture theatre passes a shallow ornamental pond. Suppose that on my way to give a lecture I notice that a small child has fallen in and is in danger of drowning. Would anyone deny that I ought to wade in and pull the child out? This will mean getting my clothes muddy, and either cancelling my lecture or delaying it until I can find something dry to change into; but compared with the avoidable death of a child this is insignificant.

A plausible principle that would support the judgment that I ought to pull the child out is this: if it is in our power to prevent something very bad happening, without thereby sacrificing anything of comparable moral significance, we ought to do it. This principle seems uncontroversial. It will obviously win the assent of consequentialists; but non-consequentialists should accept it too, because the injunction to prevent what is bad applies only when nothing comparably significant is at stake. Thus the principle cannot lead to the kinds of actions of which non-consequentialists strongly disapprove—serious violations of individual rights, injustice, broken promises, and so on. If a non-consequentialist regards any of these as comparable in moral

significance to the bad thing that is to be prevented, he will automatically regard the principle as not applying in those cases in which the bad thing can only be prevented by violating rights, doing injustice, breaking promises, or whatever else is at stake. Most non-consequentialists hold that we ought to prevent what is bad and promote what is good. Their dispute with consequentialists lies in their insistence that this is not the sole ultimate ethical principle: that it is *an* ethical principle is not denied by any plausible ethical theory.

Nevertheless the uncontroversial appearance of the principle that we ought to prevent what is bad when we can do so without sacrificing anything of comparable moral significance is deceptive. If it were taken seriously and acted upon, our lives and our world would be fundamentally changed. For the principle applies, not just to rare situations in which one can save a child from a pond, but to the everyday situation in which we can assist those living in absolute poverty. In saying this I assume that absolute poverty, with its hunger and malnutrition, lack of shelter, illiteracy, disease, high infant mortality and low life expectancy, is a bad thing. And I assume that it is within the power of the affluent to reduce absolute poverty, without sacrificing anything of comparable moral significance. If these two assumptions and the principle we have been discussing are correct, we have an obligation to help those in absolute poverty which is no less strong than our obligation to rescue a drowning child from a pond. Not to help would be wrong, whether or not it is intrinsically equivalent to killing. Helping is not, as conventionally thought, a charitable act which it is praiseworthy to do, but not wrong to omit; it is something that everyone ought to do.

This is the argument for an obligation to assist. Set out more formally, it would look like this:

First premise:	If we can prevent something bad without sacrificing anything of comparable significance, we ought to do it.
Second premise:	Absolute poverty is bad.

Third premise:	There is some absolute poverty we can prevent without sacrificing anything of comparable moral significance.
Conclusion:	We ought to prevent some absolute poverty.

The first premise is the substantive moral premise on which the argument rests, and I have tried to show that it can be accepted by people who hold a variety of ethical positions.

The second premise is unlikely to be challenged. Absolute poverty is, as McNamara put it, "beneath any reasonable definition of human decency" and it would be hard to find a plausible ethical view which did not regard it as a bad thing.

The third premise is more controversial, even though it is cautiously framed. It claims only that some absolute poverty can be prevented without the sacrifice of anything of comparable moral significance. It thus avoids the objection that any aid I can give is just "drops in the ocean" for the point is not whether my personal contribution will make any noticeable impression on world poverty as a whole (of course it won't) but whether it will prevent some poverty. This is all the argument needs to sustain its conclusion, since the second premise says that any absolute poverty is bad, and not merely the total amount of absolute poverty. If without sacrificing anything of comparable moral significance we can provide just one family with the means to raise itself out of absolute poverty, the third premise is vindicated.

I have left the notion of moral significance unexamined in order to show that the argument does not depend on any specific values or ethical principles. I think the third premise is true for most people living in industrialized nations, on any defensible view of what is morally significant. Our affluence means that we have income we can dispose of without giving up the basic necessities of life, and we can use this income to reduce absolute poverty. Just how much we will think ourselves obliged to give up will depend on what we consider to be of comparable moral signifi-cance to the poverty we could prevent: colour television, stylish clothes, expensive dinners, a sophisticated stereo system, overseas holidays, a (second?) car, a larger house, private schools for our children. . . . For a utilitarian, none of these is likely to be of comparable significance to the reduction of absolute poverty; and those who are not utilitarians surely must, if they subscribe to the principle of universalizability, accept that at least *some* of these things are of far less moral significance than the absolute poverty that could be prevented by the money they cost. So the third premise seems to be true on any plausible ethical view—although the precise amount of absolute poverty that can be prevented before anything of moral significance is sacrificed will vary according to the ethical view one accepts. . . .

Objections to the Argument

Property Rights

Do people have a right to private property, a right which contradicts the view that they are under an obligation to give some of their wealth away to those in absolute poverty? According to some theories of rights (for instance, Robert Nozick's) provided one has acquired one's property without the use of unjust means like force and fraud, one may be entitled to enormous wealth while others starve. This individualistic conception of rights is in contrast to other views, like the early Christian doctrine to be found in the works of Thomas Aquinas, which holds that since property exists for the satisfaction of human needs, "whatever a man has in superabundance is owed, of natural right, to the poor for their sustenance." A socialist would also, of course, see wealth as belonging to the community rather than the individual, while utilitarians, whether socialist or not, would be prepared to override property rights to prevent great evils.

Does the argument for an obligation to assist others therefore presuppose one of these other theories of property rights, and not an individualistic theory like Nozick's? Not necessarily. A theory of property rights can insist on our *right* to retain wealth without pronouncing on whether the rich *ought* to give to the poor. Nozick, for example, rejects the use of compulsory means like taxation to redistribute income, but suggests that we can achieve the ends we deem morally desirable by voluntary means. So Nozick would reject the claim that rich people have an "obligation" to give to the poor, insofar as this implies that the poor have a right to our aid, but might accept that giving is something we ought to do and failing to give, though within one's rights, is wrong—for rights is not all there is to ethics.

The argument for an obligation to assist can survive, with only minor modifications, even if we accept an individualistic theory of property rights. In any case, however, I do not think we should accept such a theory. It leaves too much to chance to be an acceptable ethical view. For instance, those whose forefathers happened to inhabit some sandy wastes around the Persian Gulf are now fabulously wealthy, because oil lay under those sands; while those whose forefathers settled on better land south of the Sahara live in absolute poverty, because of drought and bad harvests. Can this distribution be acceptable from an impartial point of view? If we imagine ourselves about to begin life as a citizen of either Kuwait or Chad—but we do not know which—would we accept the principle that citizens of Kuwait are under no obligation to assist people living in Chad?

Population and the Ethics of Triage

Perhaps the most serious objection to the argument that we have an obligation to assist is that since the major cause of absolute poverty is overpopulation, helping those now in poverty will only ensure that yet more people are born to live in poverty in the future.

In its most extreme form, this objection is taken to show that we should adopt a policy of "triage." The term comes from medical policies adopted in wartime. With too few doctors to cope with all the casualties, the wounded were divided into three categories: those who would probably survive without medical assistance, those who might survive if they received

assistance, but otherwise probably would not, and those who even with medical assistance probably would not survive. Only those in the middle category were given medical assistance. The idea, of course, was to use limited medical resources as effectively as possible. For those in the first category, medical treatment was not strictly necessary; for those in the third category, it was likely to be useless. It has been suggested that we should apply the same policies to countries, according to their prospects of becoming self-sustaining. We would not aid countries which even without our help will soon be able to feed their populations. We would not aid countries which, even with our help, will not be able to limit their population to a level they can feed. We would aid those countries where our help might make the difference between success and failure in bringing food and population into balance.

Advocates of this theory are understandably reluctant to give a complete list of the countries they would place into the "hopeless" category; but Bangladesh is often cited as an example. Adopting the policy of triage would, then, mean cutting off assistance to Bangladesh and allowing famine, disease and natural disasters to reduce the population of that country (now around 80 million) to the level at which it can provide adequately for all.

In support of this view Garrett Hardin has offered a metaphor: we in the rich nations are like the occupants of a crowded lifeboat adrift in a sea full of drowning people. If we try to save the drowning by bringing them aboard our boat will be overloaded and we shall all drown. Since it is better that some survive than none, we should leave the others to drown. In the world today, according to Hardin, "lifeboat ethics" apply. The rich should leave the poor to starve, for otherwise the poor will drag the rich down with them.

Against this view, some writers have argued that over-population is a myth. The world produces ample food to feed its population, and could, according to some estimates, feed ten times as many. People are hungry not because there are too many but because of inequitable land distribution, the manipulation of Third World economies by the developed nations, wastage of food in the West, and so on.

Putting aside the controversial issue of the

extent to which food production might one day be increased, it is true, as we have already seen, that the world now produces enough to feed its inhabitants—the amount lost by being fed to animals itself being enough to meet existing grain shortages. Nevertheless population growth cannot be ignored. Bangladesh could, with land reform and using better techniques, feed its present population of 80 million; but by the year 2000, according to World Bank estimates, its population will be 146 million. The enormous effort that will have to go into feeding an extra 66 million people, all added to the population within a quarter of a century, means that Bangladesh must develop at full speed to stay where she is. Other low income countries are in similar situations. By the end of the century, Ethiopia's population is expected to rise from 29 to 54 million; Somalia's from 3 to 7 million, India's from 620 to 958 million, Zaire's from 25 to 47 million. What will happen then? Population cannot grow indefinitely. It will be checked by a decline in birth rates or a rise in death rates. Those who advocate triage are proposing that we allow the population growth of some countries to be checked by a rise in death rates—that is, by increased malnutrition, and related diseases; by widespread famines; by increased infant mortality; and by epidemics of infectious diseases.

The consequences of triage on this scale are so horrible that we are inclined to reject it without further argument. How could we sit by our television sets, watching millions starve while we do nothing? Would not that be the end of all notions of human equality and respect for human life? Don't people have a right to our assistance, irrespective of the consequences?

Anyone whose initial reaction to triage was not one of repugnance would be an unpleasant sort of person. Yet initial reactions based on strong feelings are not always reliable guides. Advocates of triage are rightly concerned with the long-term consequences of our actions. They say that helping the poor and starving now merely ensures more poor and starving in the future. When our capacity to help is finally unable to cope—as one day it must be—the suffering will be greater than it would be if we stopped helping now. If this is

correct, there is nothing we can do to prevent absolute starvation and poverty, in the long run, and so we have no obligation to assist. Nor does it seem reasonable to hold that under these circumstances people have a right to our assistance. If we do accept such a right, irrespective of the consequences, we are saying that, in Hardin's metaphor, we would continue to haul the drowning into our lifeboat until the boat sank and we all drowned.

If triage is to be rejected it must be tackled on its own ground, within the framework of consequentialist ethics. Here it is vulnerable. Any consequentialist ethics must take probability of outcome into account. A course of action that will certainly produce some benefit is to be preferred to an alternative course that may lead to a slightly larger benefit, but is equally likely to result in no benefit at all. Only if the greater magnitude of the uncertain benefit outweighs its uncertainty should we choose it. Better one certain unit of benefit than a 10% chance of 5 units; but better a 50% chance of 3 units than a single certain unit. The same principle applies when we are trying to avoid evils.

The policy of triage involves a certain, very great evil: population control by famine and disease. Tens of millions would die slowly. Hundreds of millions would continue to live in absolute poverty, at the very margin of existence. Against this prospect, advocates of the policy place a possible evil which is greater still: the same process of famine and disease, taking place in, say, fifty years time, when the world's population may be three times its present level, and the number who will die from famine, or struggle on in absolute poverty, will be that much greater. The question is: how probable is this forecast that continued assistance now will lead to greater disasters in the future?

Forecasts of population growth are notoriously fallible, and theories about the factors which affect it remain speculative. One theory, at least as plausible as any other, is that countries pass through a "demographic transition" as their standard of living rises. When people are very poor and have no access to modern medicine their fertility is high, but population is kept in check by high death rates. The introduction of sanitation, modern medical techniques and other improvements reduces the death rate, but initially has little effect on the birth rate. Then population grows rapidly. Most poor countries are now in this phase. If standards of living continue to rise, however, couples begin to realize that to have the same number of children surviving to maturity as in the past, they do not need to give birth to as many children as their parents did. The need for children to provide economic support in old age diminishes. Improved education and the emancipation and employment of women also reduce the birthrate, and so population growth begins to level off. Most rich nations have reached this stage, and their populations are growing only very slowly.

If this theory is right, there is an alternative to the disasters accepted as inevitable by supporters of triage. We can assist poor countries to raise the living standards of the poorest members of their population. We can encourage the governments of these countries to enact land reform measures, improve education, and liberate women from a purely childbearing role. We can also help other countries to make contraception and sterilization widely available. There is a fair chance that these measures will hasten the onset of the demographic transition and bring population growth down to a manageable level. Success cannot be guaranteed; but the evidence that improved economic security and education reduce population growth is strong enough to make triage ethically unacceptable. We cannot allow millions to die from starvation and disease when there is a reasonable probability that population can be brought under control without such horrors.

Population growth is therefore not a reason against giving overseas aid, although it should make us think about the kind of aid to give. Instead of food handouts, it may be better to give aid that hastens the demographic transition. This may mean agricultural assistance for the rural poor, or assistance with education, or the provision of contraceptive services. Whatever kind of aid proves most effective in specific circumstances, the obligation to assist is not reduced.

One awkward question remains. What should we do about a poor and already overpopulated country which, for religious or nationalistic reasons, restricts the use of contraceptives and refuses to slow its population growth? Should we nevertheless offer development assistance? Or should we make our offer conditional on effective steps being taken to reduce the birthrate? To the latter course, some would object that putting conditions on aid is an attempt to impose our own ideas on independent sovereign nations. So it is—but is this imposition unjustifiable? If the argument for an obligation to assist is sound, we have an obligation to reduce absolute poverty: but we have no obligation to make sacrifices that, to the best of our knowledge, have no prospect of reducing poverty in the long run. Hence we have no obligation to assist countries whose governments have policies which will make our aid ineffective. This could be very harsh on poor citizens of these countries—for they may have no say in the government's policies—but we will help more people in the long run by using our resources where they are most effective. (The same principles may apply, incidentally, to countries that refuse to take other steps that could make assistance effective—like refusing to reform systems of land holding that impose intolerable burdens on poor tenant farmers.) . . .

Too High a Standard?

The final objection to the argument for an obligation to assist is that it sets a standard so high that none but a saint could attain it. How many people can we really expect to give away everything not comparable in moral significance to the poverty their donation could relieve? For most of us, with commonsense views about what is of moral significance, this would mean a life of real austerity. Might it not be counter-productive to demand so much? Might not people say: "As I can't do what is morally required anyway, I won't bother to give at all." If, however, we were to set a more realistic standard, people might make a genuine effort to reach it. Thus setting a lower standard might actually result in more aid being given.

It is important to get the status of this objection clear. Its accuracy as a prediction of human behaviour is quite compatible with the argument that we are obliged to give to the point at which by giving more we sacrifice something of comparable moral significance. What would follow from the objection is that public advocacy of this standard of giving is undesirable. It would mean that in order to do the maximum to reduce absolute poverty, we should advocate a standard lower than the amount we think people really ought to give. Of course we ourselves—those of us who accept the original argument, with its higher standard—would know that we ought to do more than we publicly propose people ought to do, and we might actually give more than we urge others to give. There is no inconsistency here, since in both our private and our public behaviour we are trying to do what will most reduce absolute poverty.

For a consequentialist, this apparent conflict between public and private morality is always a possibility, and not in itself an indication that the underlying principle is wrong. The consequences of a principle are one thing, the consequences of publicly advocating it another.

Is it true that the standard set by our argument is so high as to be counterproductive? There is not much evidence to go by, but discussions of the argument, with students and others, have led me to think it might be. On the other hand the conventionally accepted standard—a few coins in a collection tin when one is waved under your nose—is obviously far too low. What level should we advocate? Any figure will be arbitrary, but there may be something to be said for a round percentage of one's income like, say, 10%—more than a token donation, yet not so high as to be beyond all but saints. (This figure has the additional advantage of being reminiscent of the ancient tithe, or tenth, which was traditionally given to the church, whose responsibilities included care of the poor in one's local community. Perhaps the idea can be revived and applied to the global community.) Some families, of course, will find 10% a considerable strain on their finances. Others may be able to give more without difficulty. No figure should be advocated as a rigid minimum or maximum; but it seems safe to advocate that those earning average or above average incomes in affluent societies, unless they have an unusually large number of dependents or other special needs, ought to give a tenth of their income to reducing absolute poverty. By any reasonable ethical standards this is the minimum we ought to do, and we do wrong if we do less.

10. Impartiality, Beneficence, and Friendship

Lawrence Blum

Lawrence Blum arges that our duty to be impartial is limited to certain institutional roles we occupy such as that of a judge, a teacher, or a doctor. Outside of those roles, Blum argues that we may have a duty of beneficence, but not impartiality, to concern ourselves with the well-being of strangers, but this duty does not rule out special treatment for our friends.

I

I will argue . . . that impartiality is a moral requirement only in certain restricted sorts of

From *Friendship, Altruism and Morality* (1980).

situations. It is not a morally incumbent perspective to take up in every situation. In particular, friendship does not typically involve us in situations in which impartiality between the interests of our friends and those of others is a moral requirement; hence in acting beneficently towards our friends we do not typically violate a duty of impartiality.

Certainly attachments to particular persons

can lead us to violate impartiality, and thus to be unfair to others. Someone in an official position to dispense jobs can use his position to get jobs for his friends and relatives, independent of their qualification for the jobs. And we may imagine a doctor who because he likes a particular patient devotes too much of his consulting time to this patient, neglecting the others who are waiting to see him.

But such situations do not point to a general conflict between helping one's friends and helping others. It is no violation of impartiality if I phone my friend to see if he is feeling better, knowing that he has been ill. Such a situation of acting from concern for a friend does not impose on me the obligation to take into account the interests of all the people whom I *might* help at that point in time, and to choose according to some impartial criterion whom to benefit. The examples so far given point to one of the primary sorts of situations in which such impartiality is demanded—namely, an official capacity within some public institution or practice.

A judge, a captain of a ship, a doctor, a nurse, a teacher, all occupy roles or positions in which a certain kind of impartiality is demanded of them regarding the interests of certain parties whom they serve or for whom they have some responsibility. This impartiality extends to persons to whom they have special attachments. The benefits or burdens dispensed by these persons are to accrue to persons not on the basis of some personal attachment of the holder of the role to them, but on the basis of some impersonal criterion, connected with need, qualification for a position, established and rational procedure, or the like.

Thus, to take the most obvious case, a judge is meant to dispense justice impartially. He is meant to make his decision on the merits of the case and not according to his attachment to one of the parties involved. A teacher is not supposed to grade a student higher because he likes him or has a special attachment to him. A nurse is supposed to help his patients according to their individual needs, not according to his own personal likings and attachments.

It is an important part of our understanding of the duties of impartiality attaching to these roles that persons who assume the roles are aware of what those duties entail; in particular, aware of how they might impinge on the interests of those to whom they are attached. Thus a doctor or nurse knows that by virtue of his position he is forbidden from attempting to secure for a friend or relative some drugs or other medical care which are properly meant for others, or which fair procedures would allot to others.

A person might refuse to (or not be allowed to) put himself in a position in which he would be required to dispense a benefit or a burden according to an impartial rule, where a friend would be one of the candidates for the benefit or burden. This could be either because he did not feel he would be capable of such impartiality, or because, if he were, he would find it too difficult or painful to be required to dispense the benefit to someone other than his friend.

For this sort of reason it is a general policy that judges not sit in cases in which they have some special connection to one of the parties (or in which they have a self-interest in the outcome). The temptations of conflict between their impersonal duties and their personal attachments would be too great and would place an extraordinary personal burden on the role-occupiers and on the friendships; so for the good of everyone such a situation is best avoided.

Institutional roles and positions are an obvious arena of life in which a certain kind of impartiality between the interests of all, including those to whom we are personally connected and attached, is demanded of us. Equally obvious is the fact that situations covered by such roles are very untypical of those in which we interact with and benefit our friends. And so the existence of such roles does not betoken a common, much less a fundamental, moral problem regarding the beneficence dispensed to our friends.

This conclusion is strengthened by the fact that even within these institutionalized roles there is a limit to the demand of impartiality, and in most cases a scope outside of that limit for benefiting those whom we choose for whatever reason (e.g., personal attachment or liking) to benefit. Thus if a doctor, having fulfilled his obligations to his patients, spends extra time on the case of a friend, this would not be a violation of impartiality, but on the contrary would be admirable behavior on his part. A teacher is permitted to give more attention to some students than to others (not merely on pedagogical grounds), as long as he gives full and adequate attention to all. The criterion here, vague though it may be, of when it is morally permissible to depart from strict impartiality, has to do with what is regarded as the duties of one's role, in contrast to what is regarded as going beyond those duties (and is in that sense supererogatory). In the latter situations, what one does for those one chooses to help is regarded as giving something of oneself, rather than as depriving others of what one owes to them by virtue of one's institutional relationship with them. The line between these is extremely difficult to draw, is not in general fixed but is subject to change (e.g., redefinition of what constitutes the responsibilities of a role), and is not applicable in all situations. But that it exists is significant for our argument. For what it shows is that even in contexts in which impartiality between the interests of one's friends and those of others is demanded, this demand is limited in its scope, and there remains an area in which we are able to express our natural care and concern for our friends, our desire to do what is good for them, outside of the constraint of impersonal considerations.

It should be noted that this argument applies not only to actual friends and personal relationships but also to people whom we like but have no substantial or developed relationship with; i.e., it applies to beneficence from personal feelings. Here too we are morally permitted to benefit them, and this benefiting is not in general required to be justified through an impartial perspective or procedure. Morality does not in most situations demand of us that we justify such beneficence with regard to the interests of others whom we could have served but did not.

II

I have claimed that institutional-role contexts are ones in which impartiality is demanded of us. What I have not yet done is to show that the demand of impartiality is limited to such institutional-role contexts. Nor, related to this, have I given a general characterization of the conditions in which such a demand is an appropriate one, from a moral point of view.

To help gain some clarity regarding the non-institutional contexts in which impartiality is incumbent upon us, it is necessary to make an important distinction. The fact that impartiality does not demand that we constantly appraise our potential beneficence to our friends by an impartial standard does not mean that we are justified in totally disregarding the interests of others when the good of our friends is at stake, even outside contexts in which strict impartiality is demanded. To take an extreme example, suppose that I am in a train crash in which many people are injured, including my best friend (but not myself). I am certainly justified in giving my first attention to my friend. But it seems also required for me to give some attention to others. Some weighting is evidently called for here. The point is that strict impartiality is not required or appropriate, but neither is ignoring the interests of others simply because the weal and woe of one's friend is at stake.

Suppose I pass two persons on the street digging their cars out of the snow, and one of them is my friend. Surely I am justified in choosing to help my friend in preference to helping the stranger, though it would also perhaps be the decent thing to do to attempt to help both of them. But if, say, the friend could very easily dig the car out by himself, and in fact had almost finished doing so (though there was still room for assistance from someone else), and the other person obviously could not do so without some assistance, then another factor will have been introduced which must be weighed against the desire to help the friend. Here it might be more appropriate that one help the other person. (One would imagine that the friend would agree that this was appropriate.)

We then have three different sorts of situations. In the first we are required to treat the interests of the relevant parties from a strictly impartial perspective, even if one of the parties is our friend. Personal attachments must be entirely overlooked (though only up to a certain point). In the second, we are required to give some attention to the interests of others, but are not required to regard those interests strictly impartially or as having equal weight to the interests of friends who are involved. In the third type of situation consideration to the interests of others is not at all appropriate or relevant. In such situations it is morally permissible to act solely for the benefit of one's friend.

The existence of the second category helps to define the limits of impartiality, while giving credence to our sense that in some situations the presence of friends does not or should not preclude attention to the interests of others. For we see that in some situations there is some moral constraint on us to attend to the weal and woe of others, even though the weal and woe of friends is also at stake; and yet the grounding of such moral constraint need not be located in a demand for impartiality. In the train crash example just described, I have claimed that one ought to give some help to injured persons who are not one's friends, though one's first concern is properly with one's own friend. Some might see this help as a strict duty (of beneficence) on the ground that great harm to others can be avoided with little sacrifice to myself (or to a person to whom I am attached). But even if one does not see this as an actual duty, it is possible to recognize some element of moral constraint in the consideration that my ability to help the injured persons ought to weigh with me in my actions.

Thus, that I ought to help the injured persons seems in many contexts to stem not from a general demand of impartiality between the interests of all concerned (including myself or my friends) but from something like a duty of beneficence. That this is so can be seen if we imagine the situation without the friend's being injured. There would still be moral constraint for us to help the other persons; yet this moral constraint cannot stem from a demand that we treat the interests of everyone, including those to whom we have a special attachment, impartially. What the presence of the friend does to the moral configuration of this situation is not so much to undercut this moral quasi-demand of attention to the weal and woe of others, but to bring into play another consideration against which it is to be balanced. It is still true that we ought to attend to the

interests of the injured strangers, but it is entirely proper for us to attend first to our friend. It would be inappropriate for us to give our entire attention to our friend, when further attention to him would produce minimal good to him compared to the much greater good which could be produced by attention to others. But, on the other side, it is also inappropriate for us at the outset to apportion our help impartially—solely according to need—ignoring the fact that one of the persons is our friend.

It could be responded here that this argument applies only to situations where the interests of others are substantially threatened— such as in a train crash—so that attention to their interests is urgent enough to be morally incumbent upon us. The same argument would not seem to hold for the case of digging the car out of the snow (above . . .), where there would seem no demand that we attend to the interests of the person who is not our friend merely because he could use some help.

Yet it seems that whatever consideration is appropriate regarding the weal and woe of the stranger is unaffected by the presence of the friend, and so is not connected to impartiality. Though there is no *duty* to help the stranger, perhaps there is some moral deficiency or inadequacy in failing to do so, if one has nothing very important to do and could help fairly readily. Yet whatever force of "oughtness" one attributes to the consideration of the man's weal and woe (regarding digging his car out) exists independently of whether the friend is present in the situation or not.

The presence of the friend merely interjects another factor which changes the overall moral configuration of the situation. We might properly not help the other, choosing instead to help the friend (assuming we cannot do both). But we do not thereby repudiate the moral consideration of helping the other.

Thus even in cases (involving friends) in which there is nothing like a duty of beneficence, a consideration to the interests of others does not stem from a requirement of impartiality; for, first, that consideration exists even when the friendship issue does not, and second, impartiality between the interests of the friend and of the other(s) is not actually required.

III

If the argument of the previous section is right, then in non-institutional contexts at least some of the morally appropriate regard to the interests of others can be accounted for without appeal to the principle of impartiality. This is a step towards defining the scope of the principle of impartiality in non-institutional contexts.

I suggest that we can learn something of that scope by asking in what the nature of impartiality, justice, and fairness consists, as virtues or traits of character exhibited in one's non-institutional (as well as institutional) life. Here the definition given by Sidgwick seems to me close to the mark:

> What then do we mean by a just man in matters where law-observance does not enter? It is natural to reply that we mean an impartial man, one who seeks with equal care to satisfy all claims which he recognizes as valid and does not let himself be unduly influenced by personal preferences.

This definition brings out that impartiality or justice has to do with overlooking personal preferences in circumstances which have to do with according burdens and benefits to persons.

For example, suppose I am helping to settle a dispute between two persons, one of whom is a friend. Both persons are looking to me for mediation in the quarrel. This is a circumstance where justice or impartiality is required, or appropriate. We are not to favor the friend simply because he is our friend. Rather we are to overlook our personal attachment and consider only the factors relevant to the dispute. Hearing the claims made on both sides, it might turn out that I feel that the non-friend's claim has more merit, and that he is more deserving of the benefit regarding which there is a dispute.

Sidgwick's definition suggests why impartiality is not always required of us, nor required in every situation in which our actions are of a potential benefit to someone. For the application of impartiality depends on the pre-existence of claims on the part of persons involved (though the claim need not actually be made, or even recognized as existing, by the person who has it). It is only when someone has a certain claim on a benefit that it is a matter of impartiality to give due regard to his interest in that benefit. If he has no claim to it then such regard is no longer a matter relevant to impartiality. (These claims can be grounded in a person's meeting the criteria relevant for relegating a certain benefit within a certain procedure—e.g., the criteria for producing the soundest argument in a dispute, or the criteria for meeting a cetain job specification.) A just person is one who can be counted on to overlook personal interest and preference, where others might tailor their views of the claims involved to their own preferences.

It is thus not impartiality regarding interest *per se* which defines impartiality, as it is impartiality regarding interests in which the parties involved have some claim, the honoring of which might require the overlooking of personal ties and preferences. This claim is not itself grounded in impartiality but is rather the grounds of it.

This is why it is not a violation of impartiality if I help my friend in preference to the other person also digging his car out of the snow. For this other person has no claim to my help. It may be good or decent of me to help him; to do so may be something which one could expect of a decent person. But it is not a claim. It is thus not a violation of impartiality if I fail to help, preferring to help my friend.

In the train-crash case the other injured persons also have no claim on my beneficence; or, rather, if one wants to argue that a duty of beneficence exists, which is thus correlative to a right or claim on the part of the injured persons, this is not the kind of claim which demands that we overlook or abstract ourselves from our personal attachments, apportioning our attention and help purely on the basis of need. (If this is so, then not every claim can be a basis for impartiality.)

Impartiality is appropriate therefore only in certain situations. It is not a perspective which defines what it is for us to act morally, to take up a moral point of view on our actions (regarding our friends). To refer to an example from Telfer, if I choose to visit a pensioner (to help decorate his flat) rather than my friend, determining that the pensioner is in greater need of my visiting, this behavior is not in accordance with the virtues of justice or fairness; for the pensioner has no claim on my visit, which requires me to overlook my relationship with my friend and make my decision purely on the basis of which one will benefit more from my visit. Depending on other factors in the situation, my visit to the pensioner can evidence a commendable concern for a particular person to whom I have no relation; and, again depending on the situation, my friend may be able to acknowledge that it was a good thing for me to visit the pensioner rather than him. But if there is some virtue here it is not the virtue of justice or impartiality. (In other circumstances the visit to the pensioner can show an insufficient regard to the friend and to the friendship.)

The same can be said of impartiality in non-institutional contexts as was said above about institutional ones, namely that in most cases in which we can act to benefit our friends, but in which it is also within our power to benefit someone else, there are no claims on our beneficence the honoring of which requires us to overlook our personal ties. Thus there is no general demand of impartiality.

In fact Sidgwick's definition could be taken to apply to institutional as well as non-institutional contexts. Institutional contexts can be seen as an application of the general definition to a certain category of situation. For we can look at institutional contexts as helping to define the claims which some persons have, with regard to their interests, on other persons. For example, the claim which a patient has to be treated in a certain way by a doctor; or the student to be graded according to certain procedures by his teacher; or an applicant to be given a certain kind of consideration by the personnel officer. Part of what characterizes such institutional contexts is that they define more precisely than is often done in ordinary life what the relevant considerations are for allocating benefits to persons. This is why institutional contexts seem so appropriate for impartiality.

Finally, it should be remembered that even

in contexts in which impartiality is demanded, there is almost always some room for the person of whom impartiality is demanded to benefit the friend in a way appropriate to friendship. For example, in the case of the quarrel mentioned above . . . , suppose I feel that the non-friend's claim to benefit is greater than that of my friend. Impartiality requires me to overlook my attachment to the friend in deciding that the benefit properly goes to the non-friend. But impartiality does not prevent me from showing special attention to my friend if he is disappointed, trying to do something to cheer him up, comforting him, etc., while not doing the same for the other person.

Thus impartiality is limited not only to certain sorts of situations. In addition, even within the situations in which it applies, it applies, so to speak only up to a point, and generally there will be room left over for extra beneficence to be shown to the friend.

To summarize the argument so far: according to one important strain of thought within the Kantian view, a principle definitive of morality is impartiality. To take up a perspective of impartiality regarding any of one's actions which impinge on the interests of others is to take up, and act from, the moral point of view. To fail to do this is to fail to act morally. A corollary is that it is contrary to morality—because contrary to impartiality—to favor the interests of oneself to one's friends simply as such, i.e., simply because they are one's own or one's friends.

Against this I have argued that it is not in general contrary to the demands of morality to prefer our friends' interests as such, i.e., to act for the sake of R's good simply because R is my friend, even if there are other persons whom it is in my power to help and who are in greater need than R. In fact it is entirely morally appropriate to do so. Such action does not typically violate the demands of impartiality; for that perspective is appropriate only in certain contexts, which do not include most friendship situations. There is no general demand of impartiality. Rather the demand of impartiality rests on prior claims to some benefit, the acknowledging of which requires the overlooking of personal preferences and attachments.

Thus acting morally is not always or fundamentally a matter of equality or impartiality towards all. For this is not what it is to act morally within friendship.

Thus in one sense it is actually misleading to say that we are necessarily or typically partial to our friends, if this is meant to imply a deviation from a morally requisite norm of impartiality. For such a norm is not typically in force in regard to our benefiting our friends. In another sense, however, we are partial to our friends, in that we benefit our friends without testing that benefiting against a norm of impartiality with respect to others; and we are not morally remiss for doing so.

If this argument is right then impartiality does not define "the moral point of view." Rather, it defines a moral viewpoint appropriate in certain circumstances but not in others. When acting from friendship it is neither required nor appropriate (normally) to look to impartial or impersonal considerations to guide our actions. Impartiality, fairness, and justice are personal virtues, but they are merely some virtues among others. They are not definitive of moral virtue altogether.

---

11. Morality, Parents, and Children

James Rachels

James Rachels argues that the idea of morality as impartiality allows for the idea of special parental obligations particularly with regard to the day-to-day care of our own children. Nevertheless, he contends that we are not justified in providing our own children with luxuries while other children lack necessities.

The Problem

At about the same time Socrates was being put to death for corrupting the youth of Athens, the great Chinese sage Mo Tzu was also antagonizing his community. Unlike the Confucianists, who were the social conservatives of the day, Mo and his followers were sharply critical of traditional institutions and practices. One of Mo's controversial teachings was that human relationships should be governed by an "all-embracing love" that makes no distinctions between friends, family, and humanity at large. "Partiality," he said, "is to be replaced by universality." To his followers, these were the words of a moral visionary. To the Confucianists, however, they were the words

From "Morality, Parents, and Children," in *Person to Person*, ed. George Grahan and Hugh LaFollette (1989).

of a man out of touch with moral reality. In particular, Mo's doctrine was said to subvert the family, for it recommended that one have as much regard for strangers as for one's own kin. Meng Tzu summed up the complaint when he wrote that "Mo Tzu, by preaching universal love, has repudiated the family." Mo did not deny it. Instead, he argued that universal love is a higher ideal than family loyalty, and that obligations within families can be properly understood only as particular instances of obligations to all mankind.

This ancient dispute has not disappeared. Do parents have special obligations to their own children? Or, to put the question a bit differently: Do they have obligations to their own children that they do not have to other children, or to children in general? Our instincts are with the Confucianists. Surely, we think, parents do have a special obligation to care for their own. Parents must love and protect their children; they must feed and clothe them; they must see to their medical needs, their education, and a hundred other things. Who could deny it? At the same time, we do not believe that we have such duties toward strangers. Perhaps we do have a general duty of beneficence toward them, but that duty is not nearly so extensive or specific as the duties we have toward our own young sons and daughters. If faced with a choice between feeding our own children and sending food to orphans in a foreign country, we would prefer our own, without hesitation.

Yet the Mohist objection is still with us. The idea that morality requires us to be impartial, clearly articulated by Mo Tzu, is a recurring theme of Western moral philosophy. Perhaps the most famous expression of this idea was Bentham's formula, "Each to count for one and none for more than one." Mill's formulation was less memorable but no less emphatic: He urged that, when weighing the interests of different people, we should be "as strictly impartial as a disinterested and benevolent spectator." Utilitarianism of the kind espoused by Bentham and Mill has, of course, often been criticized for conflicting with common-sense morality, and so it will probably come as no great surprise that utilitarian notions clash with the common-sense idea of special parental obligations. However, the idea that morality requires impartiality is by no means exclusively a utilitarian doctrine. It is common ground to a considerable range of theories and thinkers.[1]

The problem, in its most general form, is this. As moral agents, we cannot play favorites—at least, not according to the conception of morality as impartiality. But as parents, we do play favorites. Parental love is partial through and through. And we think there is nothing wrong with this; in fact, we normally think there is something wrong with the parent who is *not* deeply partial where his own children are concerned. Therefore, it would seem, one or the other of these conceptions has to be modified or abandoned.

Of course, exactly the same is true of our relations with friends, spouses, and lovers. All these relationships, and others like them, seem to include, as part of their very nature, special obligations. Friends, spouses, and lovers are not just members of the great crowd of humanity. They are all special, at least to the one who loves them. The problem is that the conception of morality as impartiality seems to conflict with *any* kind of loving personal relationship. Mo Tzu notwithstanding, it seems to conflict with love itself. In this essay I discuss only the question of parental obligations to children, but it should be kept in mind that the deeper issue has to do with personal relationships in general.

Possible Solutions

There are three obvious approaches to solving our problem: First, we might reject the idea of morality as impartiality; second, we might reject the idea of special parental obligations; or third, we might try to find some way of understanding the two notions that would make them consistent. The first approach has recently attracted some support among philosophers, who think that although the conception of morality as impartiality seems plausible when stated abstractly, it is refuted by such counter-examples as parental obligation. Their thought is that we should reject this conception and look for a new theory of morality, one that would acknowledge from the outset that personal relationships can be the source of special obligations.

Rejecting the idea of impartiality has a certain appeal, for it is always exciting to learn that some popular philosophical view is no good and that there is interesting work to be done in formulating an alternative. However, we should not be too quick here. It is no accident that the conception of morality as impartiality has been so widely accepted. It seems to express something deeply important that we should be reluctant to give up. It is useful, for example, in explaining why egoism, racism, and sexism are morally odious, and if we abandon this conception we lose our most natural and persuasive means of combating those doctrines. (The idea of morality as impartiality is closely connected to modern thoughts about human equality. That humans are in some sense equals would never have occurred to the Confucianists, which perhaps explains why they saw nothing plausible in Mo's teaching.)

Therefore, it seems desirable to retain the notion of moral impartiality in some form. The question is, can we find some way of keeping both ideas—morality as impartiality, and special parental obligations? Can we understand them in a way that makes them compatible with one another?

As it turns out, this is not a difficult task. It is fairly easy to interpret impartiality in such a way that it no longer conflicts with special parental obligations. We can say, for example, that impartiality requires us to treat people in the same way *only when there are no relevant differences between them.* This qualification is obviously needed, quite apart from any considerations about parents and children. For example, it is not a failure of impartiality to imprison a convicted criminal, while innocent citizens go free, because there is a relevant difference between them (one has committed a crime; the others have not) to which we can appeal to justify the difference in treatment. Similar examples come easily to mind. But once we have admitted the need for this qualification, we can make use of it to resolve our problem about parental obligations: We can say that there is a relevant difference between one's own children and other children that justifies treating one's own children better. The difference will have something to do with the fact that they are one's own.

We might call this the compromise view. It is appealing because it allows us to retain the plausible idea of morality as impartiality, without having to give up the equally plausible idea that we have special obligations to our own children. Having found this solution to our problem, we might be tempted to stop here. That, however, would be premature. There is a further issue that needs to be addressed, and when we do, the compromise view will begin to look less attractive.

We are not free to call just any differences between individuals relevant. Suppose a racist claimed that there is a relevant difference between blacks and whites that justifies treating whites better—the difference being that they are members of different races. We would think this mere bluster and demand to know why *that* difference should count for anything. Similarly, it is only hand-waving to say that there is a relevant difference between one's

own children and others that justifies treating one's own better—the difference being that they are one's own. We need to ask why *that* difference matters.

Why Should It Matter That a Child Is One's Own?

Why should it matter, from a moral point of view, that a child is one's own? Our natural tendency is to assume that it *does* matter and to take it as a mere philosophical puzzle to figure out why. Why should anyone want to resist this tendency? The feeling that our own children have a superior natural claim on our attention is among the deepest moral instincts we have. Can it possibly be doubted? I believe there is a powerful reason for doubting that this feeling is morally legitimate—the fact that a child is one's own may *not* matter, or at least it may not matter nearly as much as we usually assume. That reason has to do with luck.

The point about luck can be brought out like this. Suppose a parent believes that, when faced with a choice between feeding his own children and feeding starving orphans, he should give preference to his own. This is natural enough. But the orphans need the food just as much, and they are no less deserving. It is only their bad luck that they were not born to affluent parents; and why should luck count, from a moral point of view? Why should we think that a moral view is correct, if it implies that some children should be fed, while others starve, for no better reason than that some were unlucky in the circumstances of their birth? This seems to me to be an extremely important matter—important enough, perhaps, that we should take seriously the possibility that a child's being one's own does not have the moral importance that we usually assume it has.

With this in mind, let us look at some of the arguments that support the Compromise View. The idea that one's own children have a superior claim to one's care might be defended in various ways. Let us consider the three arguments that seem most important.

1. The Argument from Social Roles

The first line of reasoning begins with some observations about social roles. It is not possible for an isolated individual to have anything resembling a normal human life. For that, a social setting is required. The social setting provides roles for us to fill—thus in the context of society we are able to be citizens, friends, husbands and wives, hospital patients, construction workers, scientists, teachers, customers, sports fans, and all the rest. None of us (with rare heroic exceptions) creates the roles we play; they have evolved over many centuries of human life, and we encounter them as simply the raw materials out of which we must fashion our individual lives.

These roles define, in large measure, our relations with other people. They specify how we should behave toward others. Teachers must wisely guide their students; friends must be loyal; husbands should be faithful; and so on. To the extent that you fail in these respects, you will be an inferior teacher, a bad friend, a poor husband. You can avoid these obligations by declining to enter into these roles: Not everyone will be a teacher, not everyone will marry, and some unfortunate people will not even have friends. But you can hardly avoid *all* social roles, and you cannot fill a social role without at the same time acknowledging the special responsibilities that go with it.

Now, parenthood is a social role, and like other such roles it includes special duties as part of its very nature. You can choose not to have children, or, having had a child, you may give it up for adoption. But if you *are* a parent, you are stuck with the responsibilities that go with the role. A parent who doesn't see to his children's needs is a bad parent, just as a disloyal friend is a bad friend, and an unfaithful husband is a poor husband. And that is why (according to this argument) we have obligations to our own children that we do not have to other children.

The argument from social roles is plausible; but how far should we be persuaded by it? The argument has at least four apparent weaknesses.

(i) We need to distinguish two claims: first, that our obligations to our own children *have a different basis* from our obligations to other children; and second, that our obligations to our own children *are stronger than* (take precedence over) our obligations to other children. If successful, the argument from social roles would show only that our obligations to our own children are based on different considerations than are our obligations to other children. We have a social relationship with our own children that is the basis of our obligation to them, while our obligations to other children are based on a general duty of beneficence. The argument would not show that the former obligations are *stronger*. Thus a critic of the idea of special parental obligations could continue the dispute at another level. It could be argued that, even if one's duties to one's own children have a different basis, they nevertheless are *no stronger than* one's duties to other children.

(ii) The second point is related to the first. The argument from social roles trades on the notion of what it means to be a bad father or a bad mother. Now, suppose we admit that a man who ignores the needs of his own children is a bad father. It may also be observed that a man who ignores the cries of orphans, when he could help, is a bad *man*—a man lacking a proper regard for the needs of others. While it is undesirable to be a bad father (or mother), it is also undesirable to be a bad man (or woman). So, once again, the argument from social roles does nothing to show that our obligations to other children are weaker.

(iii) Third, there is the point about luck that I have already mentioned. The system of social roles acknowledged in our society makes special provision for children lucky enough to live in homes with parents. This system favors even more those lucky enough to have affluent parents who can provide more for them than less affluent parents are able to provide. Even granting this, we can still ask: Is it a morally decent system? The system itself can be subject to criticism.

We do not have to look far to find an obvious objection to the system. The system does well enough in providing for some children; but it does miserably where others are concerned. There is no social role comparable to the parent-child relationship that targets the interests of orphans, or the interests of children whose parents are unable or unwilling to provide for them. Thus in this system luck plays an unacceptably important part.

(iv) Finally, students of social history might find the argument from social roles rather naïve. The argument draws much of its strength from the fact that contemporary American and European ideals favor families bound together by love. Anyone who is likely to read these words will have been influenced by that ideal—consider how the reader will have passed over the second paragraph of this essay, with its easy talk of parents loving and protecting their children, without a pause. Yet the cozy nuclear family, nourished by affectionate relationships, is a relatively recent development. The norm throughout most of Western history has been very different.

In his acclaimed book *The Family, Sex and Marriage in England 1500–1800,* Lawrence Stone points out that as recently as the seventeenth century affectionate relations between husbands and wives were so rare as to be virtually nonexistent, and certainly were not expected within normal marriages. Among the upper classes, husbands and wives occupied separate stations within large households and rarely saw one another in private. Children were sent away immediately after birth to be looked after by wet-nurses for 12 to 18 months; then, returning home, they would be raised largely by nurses, governesses, and tutors. Finally they would be sent away to boarding school when they were between 7 and 13, with 10 the commonest age. The children of the poor were of course worse off: They would leave home at an equally early age, often to go and work in the houses of the rich. Stone writes,

> About all that can be said with confidence on the matter of emotional relations within the sixteenth- and early seventeenth-century family at all social levels is that there was a general psychological atmosphere of distance, manipulation, and deference. . . . Family relationships were characterized by interchangeability, so that substitution of another wife or another child was easy. . . . It was a structure held together not by affective bonds but by mutual economic interests.

And what of parental duties? Of course there has always been a recognition of *some* special parental duties, but in earlier times these were much more restricted and were not associated with bonds of affection. Until some time in the eighteenth century, it seems, the emphasis in European morals was almost entirely on the duties owed by children to parents, rather than the other way around. Children were commonly said to owe their parents absolute obedience, in gratitude for having been given life. The French historian Jean Flandrin notes that "In Brittany the son remained subject to the authority of his father until the age of sixty, but marriage contracted with the father's consent emancipated him." Pity the man whose father lived to a ripe old age and refused consent for marriage—his only emancipation would be to flee. Both Stone and Flandrin make it clear that, while parental *rights* is an old idea, the idea of extensive parental *obligations* is a notion of much more recent vintage. (The debate between Mo Tzu and the Confucians was also conducted in such terms—for them, the primary issue was whether children had special duties to their fathers, not the other way around.)

These observations about social history should be approached with care. Of course they do not refute the idea of special parental obligations. However, they do go some way toward undermining our easy confidence that present-day social arrangements only institutionalize our natural duties. That is the only moral to be drawn from them, but it is an important one. In this area, as in so many others, what seems natural just depends on the conventions of one's society.

2. The Argument from Proximity

The second argument goes like this. It is reasonable to accept a social arrangement in which parents are assigned special responsibility for their own children because parents are *better situated* to look after their own. Granted, all children need help and protection. But other children are remote, and their needs are less clear, while a parent's own children live in the same house, and the parent is (or ought to be) intimately familiar with their needs. Other things being equal, it makes sense to think that A has a greater responsibility for helping B than for helping C, if A is better situated to help B. This is true in the case of helping one's own children versus helping other children; therefore, one's obligation in the first instance is greater.

This argument is plausible if we concentrate on certain kinds of aid. Children wake up sick in the middle of the night; someone must attend to them, and that someone is usually Mother or Father. The parents are in a position to do so, and (most of the time) no one else is. The complaint that you nursed your own children, but you didn't help the other children who woke up sick elsewhere in the world is obviously misguided. The same goes for countless other ways that parents assist their children, by making them take their medicine, by stopping them from playing in the roadway, by bundling them up against the cold, and so on. These are all matters of what we might call *day-to-day care.*

Day-to-day care involves a kind of personal attention that a parent *could not* provide for many others, because it is physically impossible. The importance of physical proximity is that it makes these kinds of caring behaviors possible; the impossibility of doing the same for other children is just the impossibility of being in two places at once. So if there is partiality here, it is a partiality that we need not worry about because it cannot be avoided. There is little doubt, then, that parents are

normally in a better position to provide day-to-day care for their own children than for others.

This type of argument is less plausible, however, when we consider more general, fundamental needs, such as food. Is a parent in a better position to feed his own children than to provide for others? At one time this might have been the case. Before the advent of modern communications and transportation, and before the creation of efficient relief agencies, people might have been able to say that while they could feed their own, they were unable to do much about the plight of children elsewhere. But that is no longer true. Today, with relief agencies ready to take our assistance all over the world, needing only sufficient resources to do so, it is almost as easy to provide food for a child in Africa as to provide for one's own. The same goes for providing basic medical care: International relief agencies carry medical assistance around the world on the same basis.

Therefore, the argument from proximity is, at best, only partially successful. Some forms of assistance (such as getting up in the middle of the night to attend to sick children) do require proximity but others (such as providing food) do not. The argument might show that, where day-to-day care is concerned, parents have special duties. But the same cannot be said for the provision of fundamental needs.

3. The Argument from Personal Goods

The third argument hinges on the idea that loving relationships are personal goods of great importance: To love other people and be loved in return are part of what is involved in having a rich and satisfying human life. A loving relationship with one's children is, for many parents, a source of such happiness that they would sacrifice almost anything else to preserve it. But as we have already observed, love necessarily involves having a special concern for the well-being of the loved one, and so it is not impartial. An ethic that required absolute impartiality would therefore require forgoing a great personal good.

The intuitive idea behind this argument

may seem plain enough. Nevertheless, it is difficult to formulate the argument with any precision. Why, exactly, is a loving relationship with another person such a great good? Part of the answer may be that pacts of mutual assistance enable all of us to fare better. If A and B have this sort of relationship, then A can count on B's assistance when it is needed, and vice versa. They are both better off. Of course, deals of this kind could be made between people who are not joined by bonds of affection, but affection makes the arrangement more dependable: People who love one another are more apt to remain faithful when the going is hard. But there is more. Bonds of affection are more than just instrumentally good. To be loved is to have one's own value affirmed; thus it is a source of self-esteem. This is important for all of us, but especially for children, who are more helpless and vulnerable than adults. Moreover, there is, at a deep level, a connection between love and the meaning of life (although I cannot go into this very deeply here). We question whether our lives have meaning when we find nothing worth valuing, when it seems to us that "all is vanity." Loving relationships provide individuals with things to value, and so give their lives this kind of meaning. That is why parents who love their children, and who strive to see that they do well, can find in this meaning for their lives.

These are important points, but they do not prove as much as they are sometimes taken to prove. In the first place, there is a lot about parental love that *is* consistent with a large measure of impartiality. Loving someone is not only a matter of preferring their interests. Love involves, among other things, intimacy and the sharing of experiences. A parent shows his love by listening to the child's jokes, by talking, by being a considerate companion, by praising, and even by scolding when that is needed. It may be objected that these kinds of behavior also show partiality, since the parent does not do these things for all children. But these are only further instances of the day-to-day care that requires proximity; again, if this is partiality, it is partiality that cannot be avoided. And there is another difference between these kinds of support and such things as providing food and medical care. The companionship, the listening, the talking, and the

praising and scolding are what make personal relationships *personal*. That is why the psychic benefits that accompany such relationships are more closely associated with these matters than with such relatively impersonal things as being fed.

Moreover, it is not necessary, in order to have a loving relationship with one's children and to derive from it the benefits that the argument from personal goods envisions, to regard their interests as *always* having priority, especially when the interests in question are not comparable. One could have a loving relationship that involves all the intimacies of day-to-day care and the provision of life's necessities, while acknowledging at the same time that when it comes to choosing between luxuries for them and food for orphans, the orphans' needs should prevail. At the very least, there is nothing in the argument from personal goods that rules out such an approach.

The Moral Point of Utopian Thinking

There is another approach to our problem, favored by the Mohists, that we have not yet considered: Clinging to the ideal of impartiality, we could simply reject the idea of special parental duties. This goes against our intuitions, and it is opposed by the (partially successful) arguments we have just examined. Nevertheless, we may ask whether there is anything to be said in favor of this approach.

In fact, there is a lot that might be said in its favor. Suppose we forget, for a moment, the imperfections of actual human life, and try to imagine what it would be like if everyone behaved in a morally blameless manner. What would relations between adults and children be like in such a utopia? Here is one plausible picture of such a world. In it, children with living parents able to provide for them would be raised by their parents, who would give them all the love and care they need. Parents who through no fault of their own were unable to provide for their children would be given whatever assistance they need. Orphans would be taken in by families who would raise and love them as their own. The burdens involved in such adoptions would be shared by all.

It is fair to say that, in such a world, the ideal of impartiality is realized. In this world people do not act as if any child is more deserving than any other: One way or another, equal provision is made for the needs of all. Moreover, luck plays no part in how children will fare: The orphans' needs are satisfied too. When it is said by the Mohists that "love is universal," or by their modern counterparts, the utilitarians, that we should "promote impartially the interests of everyone alike," this might be the point: In the morally best world, we would not recognize many of the distinctions that we do recognize in the real world we inhabit.

Practical Implications

How should parents, living not in utopia but in our society, who are concerned to do what is morally best, conceive of the relation between their obligations to their own children and their obligations to other children? Here are three contrasting views; each is implausible, but for different reasons.

1. *Extreme Bias.* On this view, parents have obligations to provide for their own children, but they have *no obligations at all* to other children. Anything done for other children is at best supererogatory—good and praiseworthy if one chooses to do it, but in no way morally mandatory. On this view, parents may provide not only necessities but also luxuries for their own children, while other children starve, and yet be immune from moral criticism.

Extreme bias is not plausible, because it makes no provision whatever for a duty of general beneficence. It is hard to believe that we do not have *some* obligation to be concerned with the plight of the starving, whoever they are, even if that obligation is less extensive than our obligations to our own kin.[2] Thus it will not be surprising if this view turns out to be unacceptable.

2. *Complete Equality.* The opposite view seems to be implied by the idea of morality as impartiality—the view that all children are equal and that there is no difference at all between one's moral obligations toward one's own children and one's moral obligations toward other children. This view denies that there are any good moral grounds for preferring to feed one's own child rather than an orphan in a foreign country. In our society anyone who accepted and acted on such a view would seem to his neighbors to be morally deranged, for doing so would seem to involve a rejection of one's children—a refusal to treat them with the love that is appropriate to the parent-child relationship.

3. *The Most Common View.* What, in fact, do people in our society seem to believe? Most people seem to believe that one has an obligation to provide the necessities of life for other children only after one has already provided a great range of luxuries for one's own. On this view, it is permissible to provide one's own children with virtually everything they need in order to have a good start in life—not only food and clothing, but, if possible, a good education, opportunities for travel, opportunities for enjoyable leisure, and so forth. In the United States children of affluent families often have TV sets, stereos, and now computers, all laid out in their own rooms. They drive their own cars to high school. Few people seem to think there is anything wrong with this— parents who are unable to provide their children with such luxuries nevertheless aspire to do so.

The most common view imposes *some* duty regarding other children, but not much. In practical terms, it imposes a duty only on the very rich, who have resources left over even after they have provided ample luxuries for their own children. The rest of us, who have nothing left after doing as much as we can for our own, are off the hook. It takes only a little reflection to see that this view is also implausible. How can it be right to spend money on luxuries for some children, even one's own— buying them the latest trendy toys, for example—while others do not have enough to eat?

Perhaps, when confronted with this, many

people might come to doubt whether it is correct. But certainly most affluent people act as if it were correct.

Is there a better alternative? Is there a view that escapes the difficulties of extreme bias, complete equality, and the most common view, and is consistent with the various other points that have been made in our discussion? I suggest the following.

4. *Partial Bias.* We might say that, while we do have a substantial obligation to be concerned about the welfare of all children, our own nevertheless come first. This vague thought needs to be sharpened. One way of making it more precise is this. When considering similar needs, you may permissibly prefer to provide for the needs of your own children. For example, if you were faced with a choice between feeding your own children or contributing the money to provide food for other children, you could rightly choose to feed your own. But if the choice were between some relatively trivial thing for your own and necessities for other children, preference should be given to helping the others. Thus if the choice were between providing trendy toys for your own already well-fed children or feeding the starving, you should feed the starving.

This view will turn out to be more or less demanding, depending on what one counts as a "relatively trivial thing." We might agree that buying trendy toys for some children, even for one's own, while other children starve is indefensible. But what about buying them nice clothes? Or a college education? Am I justified in sending my children to an expensive college? Clearly, the line between the trivial and the important can be drawn at different places. (One will be pushed toward a more demanding interpretation as one takes more seriously the point about the moral irrelevance of luck.) Nevertheless, the intuitive idea is plain enough. On this view, you may provide the necessities for your own children first, but you are not justified in providing them luxuries while other children lack necessities. Even in a fairly weak form, this view would still require much greater concern for others than the view that is most common in our society.

From the point of view of the various arguments we have considered, partial bias clearly stands out as the superior view. It is closer to the utopian ideal than either extreme bias or the most common view; it is morally superior in that it makes greater provision for children who have no loving parents; it is consistent with the arguments we have considered concerning the benefits to be derived from loving relationships; and it is perhaps as much as we could expect from people in the real world. It is not, in fact, very far from the utopian ideal. If we begin with Complete Equality, and then modify it in the ways suggested in our discussion of utopia, we end up with something very much like partial bias.

What would the adoption of partial bias mean for actual families? It would mean that parents could continue to provide loving day-to-day care for their own children, with all that this involves, while giving them preferential treatment in the provision of life's necessities. But it would also mean preferring to provide the necessities for needier children, rather than luxuries for their own. Children in such families would be worse off, in an obvious sense, than the children of affluent parents who continued to live according to the dictates of extreme bias or the most common view. However, we might hope that they would not regard themselves as deprived, for they might learn the moral value of giving up their luxuries so that the other children do not starve. They might even come to see their parents as morally admirable people. That hope is itself utopian enough.

Notes

1. "The good of any one individual is of no more importance, from the point of view (if I may say so) of the Universe, than the good of any other," says Sidgwick (1907, 382). "We [must] give equal weight in our moral deliberations to the like interests of all those affected by our actions," says Singer (1971, 197). "Moral rules must be for the good of everyone alike," says Baier (1958, 200).

"A rational and impartial sympathetic spectator is a person who takes up a general perspective: he assumes a position where his own interests are not at stake and he possesses all the requisite information and powers of reasoning. So situated he is equally responsive and sympathetic to the desires and satisfactions of everyone affected by the social system. . . . Responding to the interests of each person in the same way, an impartial spectator gives free reign to his capacity for sympathetic identification by viewing each person's situation as it affects that person," says Rawls (1971, 186). In an interesting discussion, R. M. Hare argues that virtually all the major moral theories incorporate a requirement of impartiality and adds that his own "universal prescriptivism" is no exception.

2. For arguments concerning the extensiveness of our obligations toward others, see Singer (1972) and Rachels (1979).

References

Baier, Kurt. 1958. *The Moral Point of View*. Ithaca: Cornell University Press.

Fung Yu-lan. 1960. *A Short History of Chinese Philosophy*. New York: Macmillan.

Hare, R. M. 1972. "Rules of War and Moral Reasoning." *Philosophy and Public Affairs*, 1, 166–81.

Mill, John Stuart. 1957. *Utilitarianism*. Indianapolis: Bobbs-Merrill. This work, first published in 1861, is today available in many editions.

Rachels, James. 1979. "Killing and Starving to Death." *Philosophy*, 54, 159–71.

Rawls, John. 1971. *A Theory of Justice*. Cambridge: Harvard University Press.

Rubin, Vitaly A. 1976. *Individual and State in Ancient China*. New York: Columbia University Press.

Sidgwick, Henry. 1907. *The Methods of Ethics*, 7th. ed. London: Macmillan.

Singer, Peter. 1972. "Famine, Affluence, and Morality." *Philosophy and Public Affairs*, 1, 229–43.

————. 1978. "Is Racial Discrimination Arbitrary?" *Philosophia*, 8, 185–203.

Stone, Lawrence. 1979. *The Family, Sex and Marriage in England 1500–1800*. New York: Harper & Row.

12. Perspectives from the *Global 2000 Report*

Gus Speth

According to Gus Speth, the *Global 2000 Report* echoes a persistent warning sounded by many others in recent years: "Our international efforts to stem the spread of human poverty, hunger, and misery are not achieving their goals; the staggering growth of human population, coupled with ever-increasing human demands, are beginning to cause permanent damage to the planet's resource base." Speth argues that we must respond to this warning by getting serious about the conservation of resources and by pursuing a policy of sustainable economic development that is fair to the interests of the poor.

Throughout the past decade, a wide variety of disturbing studies and reports have been

From "Resources and Security: Perspectives from the *Global 2000 Report*," *World Future Society Bulletin* (1981), pp. 1–4. Reprinted by permission of *World Future Society Bulletin*.

issued by the United Nations, the Worldwatch Institute, the World Bank, the International Union for the Conservation of Nature and Natural Resources, and other organizations. These reports have sounded a persistent warning: our international efforts to stem the spread of human poverty, hunger, and misery are not achieving their goals; the staggering growth of human population, coupled with ever-increasing human demands, are beginning to cause permanent damage to the planet's resource base.

The most recent such warning—and the one with which I am most familiar—was issued in July of 1980 by the Council of Environmental Quality and the U.S. State Department. Called *Global 2000 Report to the President,* it is the result of a three-year effort by more than a dozen agencies of the U.S. Government to make long-term projections across the range of population, resource, and environmental concerns. Given the obvious limitations of such projections, the *Global 2000 Report* can best be seen as a reconnaissance of the future. And the results of that reconnaissance are disturbing.

I feel very strongly that the *Global 2000 Report*'s findings confront the United States and other nations with one of the most difficult challenges facing our planet during the next two decades—rivaling the global arms race in importance.

The Report's projections point to continued rapid population growth, with world population increasing from 4.5 billion today to more than 6 billion by 2000. More people will be added to the world's population each day in the year 2000 than were born today—about 100 million a year as compared with 75 million in 1980. Most of these additional people will live in the poorest countries, which will contain about four-fifths of the human race by the end of the century.

Unless other factors intervene, this planetary majority will see themselves growing worse off compared with those living in affluent nations. The income gap between rich and poor nations will widen, and the per capita gross national product of the less-developed countries will remain at generally low levels. In some areas—especially in parts of Latin America and East Asia—income per capita is expected to rise substantially. But gross national product in the great populous nations of South Asia—India, Bangladesh, and Pakistan—will be less than $200 per capita (in 1975 dollars) by 2000. Today, some 800 million people live in conditions of absolute poverty, their lives dominated by hunger, ill health,

and the absence of hope. By 2000, if current policies remain unchanged, their number could grow by 50 percent.

While the Report projects a 90 percent increase in overall world food production in the 30 years from 1970 to 2000, a global per capita increase of less than 15 percent is projected even for the countries that are already comparatively well-fed. In South Asia, the Middle East, and the poorer countries of Africa, per capita food consumption will increase marginally at best, and in some areas may actually decline below present inadequate levels. Real prices of food are expected to double during the same 30-year period.

The pressures of population and growing human needs and expectations will place increasing strains on the Earth's natural systems and resources. The spread of desert-like conditions due to human activities now claims an area about the size of Maine each year. Croplands are lost to production as soils deteriorate because of erosion, compaction, and waterlogging and salinization, and as rural land is converted to other uses.

The increases in world food production projected by the Report are based on improvements in crop yields per acre continuing at the same rate as the record-breaking increases of the post–World War II period. These improvements depended heavily on energy-intensive technologies like fertilizer, pesticides, fuel for tractors, and power for irrigation. But the Report's projections show no relief from the world's tight energy situation. World oil production is expected to level off by the 1990s. And for the one-quarter of humanity who depend on wood for fuel, the outlook is bleak. Projected needs for wood will exceed available supplies by about 25 percent before the turn of the century.

The conversion of forested land to agricultural use and the demand for fuelwood and forest products are projected to continue to deplete the world's forests. The Report estimates that these forests are now disappearing at rates as high as 18 to 20 million hectares—an area half the size of California—each year. As much as 40 percent of the remaining forests in poor countries may be gone by 2000. Most of the loss will occur in tropical and subtropical areas.

The loss of tropical forests, along with the

impact of pollution and other pressures on habitats, could cause massive destruction of the planet's genetic resource base. Between 500,000 and two million plant and animal species—15 to 20 percent of all species on Earth— could become extinct by the year 2000. One-half to two-thirds of the extinctions will result from the clearing or deterioration of tropical forests. This would be a massive loss of potentially valuable sources of food, pharmaceutical chemicals, building materials, fuel sources, and other irreplaceable resources.

Deforestation and other factors will worsen severe regional water shortages and contribute to the deterioration of water quality. Population growth alone will cause demands for water to at least double from 1971 levels in nearly half of the world.

Industrial growth is likely to worsen air quality. Air pollution in some cities in less-developed countries is already far above levels considered safe by the World Health Organization. Increased burning of fossil fuels, especially coal, may contribute to acid rain damage to lakes, plantlife, and the exteriors of buildings. It also contributes to the increasing concentration of carbon dioxide in the Earth's atmosphere, which could possibly lead to climatic changes with highly disruptive effects on world agriculture. Depletion of the stratospheric ozone layer, attributed partly to chlorofluorocarbon emissions from aerosol cans and refrigeration equipment, could also have an adverse effect on food crops and human health.

Disturbing as these findings are, it is important to stress that the *Global 2000 Report*'s conclusions represent not predictions of what will occur, but projections of what could occur if we do not respond. If there was any doubt before, there should be little doubt now—the nations of the world, industrialized and less developed alike, must act urgently and in concert to alter these dangerous trends before the projections of the *Global 2000 Report* become realities.

The warnings, then, are clear. Will we heed them, and will we heed them in time? For if our response is delayed, the costs could be great.

On these matters, I am cautiously optimistic. I like to think that the human race is *not*

self-destructive—that it *is* paying, or can be made to pay, attention—that as people throughout the world come to realize the full dimensions of the challenge before us, we will take the actions needed to meet it.

Our efforts to secure the future must begin with a new appreciation for, and then an application of, three fundamental concepts. They are *conservation, sustainable development, and equity*. I am convinced that each of them is essential to the development of the kind of long-term global resource strategy we need to deal with the problems I have been discussing.

Conservation

The first thing we must do is to get serious about the conservation of resources—renewable and nonrenewable alike. We can no longer take for granted the renewability of renewable resources. The natural systems— the air and water, the forests, the land—that yield food, shelter, and the other necessities of life are susceptible to disruption, contamination, and destruction.

Indeed, one of the most troubling of the findings of the *Global 2000 Report* is the effect that rapid population growth and poverty are already having on the productivity of renewable natural resource systems. In some areas, particularly in the less-developed countries, the ability of biological systems to support human populations is already being seriously damaged by efforts of present populations to meet desperate immediate needs, such as the needs for grazing land, firewood, and building materials.

And these stresses, while most acute in the developing countries, are not confined to them. In recent years, the United States has been losing annually about 3 million acres of rural land—a third of it prime agricultural land—due to the spread of housing developments, highways, shopping malls, and the like. We are also losing annually the rough equivalent—in terms of production capability—of another 3 million acres due to soil degradation—erosion and salinization. Other serious resource threats in the United States include those posed by toxic chemicals and other pollutants to groundwater supplies, which provide drinking water for half of the American public, and directly affect both commercial and sport fishing.

Achieving the necessary restraint in the use of renewable resources will require new ways of thinking by the peoples and governments of the world. It will require the widespread adoption of a "Conserver Society" ethic—an approach to resources and environment that, while attuned to the needs of each society, recognizes not only the importance of resources and environment to our own sustenance, well-being, and security, but also our obligation to pass this vital legacy along to future generations. Perhaps the most arrogant attitude of which the human spirit is capable is the notion that the riches of the Earth are ours to plunder or carelessly destroy . . . that the needs and the lives of those who will follow us on this tiny and fragile planet are of no concern to us. "Future generations," someone once said "What have they done for us?"

Fortunately, we are beginning to see signs that people in the United States and in other nations *are* becoming aware of the limits to our resources and the importance of conserving them. Energy problems, for example, are pointing the way to a future in which conservation is the password. As energy supplies go down and prices go up, we are learning that conserving—getting more and more out of each barrel of oil or ton of coal—is the cheapest and safest approach. Learning to conserve nonrenewable resources like oil and coal is the first step toward building a Conserver Society that values, nurtures, and protects all of its resources. Such a society appreciates economy in design and avoidance of waste. It realizes the limits to low-cost resources and to the environment's carrying capacity. It insists that market prices reflect all costs, social as well as private, so that consumers are fully aware in the most direct way of the real costs of consumption.

The Conserver Society prizes recycling over pollution, durability over obsolescence, quality over quantity, diversity over uniformity. It knows that beauty—whether natural or manmade—is too precious to be destroyed and that the Earth's wild creatures demand our conserving restraint not simply for utilitarian reasons but because, as part of the community of life that has evolved here with us, they too call this place home.

In this, the United States must take the lead. We cannot expect the rest of the world to adopt a Conserver Society ethic if we ourselves do not set a strong, successful example.

Sustainable Development

But the Conserver Society ethic, by itself, is not enough. It is unrealistic to expect people living at the margin of existence—people fighting desperately for their own survival—to think about the long-term survival of the planet. When people need to burn wood to keep from freezing, they will cut down trees.

We must find a way to break the cycle of poverty, population growth, and environmental deterioration. We must find ways to improve the social and economic conditions of the poor nations and poor people of the world—their incomes, their access to productive land, their educational and employment opportunities. It is only through sustainable economic development that real progress can be made in alleviating hunger and poverty and in erasing the conditions that contribute so dangerously to the destruction of our planet's carrying capacity.

One of the most important lessons of the *Global 2000 Report* is that the conflict between development and environmental protection is, in significant part, a myth. Only a concerted attack on the roots of extreme poverty—one that provides people with the opportunity to earn a decent livelihood in a nondestructive manner—will enable us to protect the world's natural systems. It is also clear that development and economic reforms will have no lasting success unless they are suffused with concern for ecological stability and wise management of resources. The key concept here, of course, is *sustainable* development. Economic development, if it is to be successful over the long term, must proceed in a way that enhances the natural resource base of all the developing nations, instead of exploiting those resources for short-term economic or political gain.

Unfortunately, the realities of the current North-South dialogue between the developed and the developing nations suggest that achieving steady, sustainable development will be a difficult process—one that will require great patience and understanding on all sides. For our part here in the United States, we must resist the strong temptation to turn inward—to tune out the rest of the world's problems and to focus exclusively on our own economic difficulties. We must remember that, relatively speaking, we Americans luxuriate in the Earth's abundance, while other nations can barely feed and clothe their people. Unless we act, this disparity between rich and poor will tend to grow, increasing the possibilities for anger and resentment from those on the short end of the wealth equation—the great majority of mankind. One does not have to be particularly farsighted to see that the trends discussed in *Global 2000* heighten the chances for global instability—for exploitation of fears, resentments, and frustrations; for incitement to violence; for conflicts based on resources.

The *Global 2000 Report* itself discusses some of the destabilizing prospects that may be in store for us if we do not act decisively:

The world will be more vulnerable both to natural disaster and to disruptions from human causes . . . Most nations are likely to be still more dependent on foreign sources of energy in 2000 than they are today. Food production will be more vulnerable to disruptions of fossil fuel energy supplies and to weather fluctuations as cultivation expands to more marginal areas. The loss of diverse germ plasm in local strains and wild progenitors of food crops, together with the increase of monoculture, could lead to greater risks of massive crop failures. Larger numbers of people will be vulnerable to higher food prices or even famine when adverse weather occurs. The world will be more vulnerable to the disruptive effects of war. The tensions that could lead to war will have multiplied. The potential for conflict over fresh water alone is underscored by the fact that out of 200

of the world's major river basins, 148 are shared by two countries and 52 are shared by three to ten countries.

The 1980 Report of the Brandt Commission on International Development Issues is eloquent in its plea for action: "War is often thought of in terms of military conflict, or even annihilation. But there is a growing awareness that an equal danger might be chaos—as a result of mass hunger, economic disaster, environmental catastrophes, and terrorism, so we should not think only of reducing the traditional threats to peace, but also of the need for change from chaos to order."

Equity

The late Barbara Ward, eminent British scholar, argued that the nations of the world can learn a valuable lesson from the experience of 19th-Century England, where the industrial revolution produced an appalling disparity in the distribution of wealth. It was a time when property owners and industrial managers reaped enormous profits while the laborers and mechanics—and their children—worked themselves into early graves.

Today, Ward observes: "The skew in world income is as great. The already developed peoples—North America, Europe, the Soviet Union, Japan—are the latter-day dukes, commanding over 70 percent of the planet's wealth for less than a quarter of the population. And in all too many developing countries the economic growth of the last two decades has been almost entirely appropriated by the wealthiest ten percent of the people. The comparisons in health, length of life, diet, literacy all work out on the old Victorian patterns of unbelievable injustice."

Ward recommends—and I heartily agree—that the developed nations of today follow the lead of men like Disraeli, who recognized the need to narrow the gap between rich and poor in 19th-Century England and to create a new social order which allowed every citizen a share of the nation's wealth. Without perceptive leaders like Disraeli and other men of conscience who saw the need for reform, Ward argues that the growing pressure for equality and social justice would have torn British society apart. The result would have been similar to that in other nations where far-thinking leadership and compassion were lacking: "social convulsion, violent revolution and an impetus to merciless worldwide war and conquest."

The situation we face in the world today is all too similar. While the humanitarian reasons for acting generously to alleviate global poverty and injustice are compelling enough in themselves, we must also recognize the extent to which global poverty and resource problems can contribute to regional and worldwide political instability—an instability that can threaten the security of nations throughout the world.

Thus, along with conservation and sustainable development, the development of global resource strategy will require a much greater emphasis on *equity*—on a fair sharing of the means to development and the products of growth—not only among nations, but within nations as well.

Suggestions for Further Reading

Anthologies

Brown, Peter, and Shue, Henry. *Boundaries*. Totowa, N.J.: Rowman and Littlefield, 1981.

Lucas, George R., Jr., and Ogletree, Thomas W. *Lifeboat Ethics*. New York: Harper & Row, 1976.

Luper-Foy, Steven. *Problems of International Justice*. Boulder, Colo.: Westview, 1988.

Partridge, Ernest. *Responsibilities to Future Generations*. Buffalo, N.Y.: Prometheus, 1981.

Sikora, R. I., and Barry, Brian. *Obligation to Future Generations*. Philadelphia: Temple University Press, 1978.

Basic Concepts

Parfit, Derek. *Reasons and Persons*. Oxford: Oxford University Press, 1985.

Alternative Views

Amur, Samir. *Unequal Development*. New York: Monthly Review Press, 1976.

Bauer, P. T. *Equality, the Third World and Economic Delusion*. Cambridge: Harvard University Press, 1981.

Bayles, Michael D. *Morality and Population Policy*. Birmingham: University of Alabama Press, 1980.

Beitz, Charles R. *Political Theory and International Relations*. Princeton: Princeton University Press, 1979.

Elfstrom, Gerald. *Ethics for a Shrinking World*. New York: St. Martin's Press, 1990.

Hardin, Garrett. *Promethean Ethics*. Seattle: University of Washington Press, 1980.

Shue, Henry. *Basic Rights*. Princeton: Princeton University Press, 1980.

Practical Applications

Lappé, Frances Moore. *World Hunger: Twelve Myths*. New York: Grove Press, 1986.

Russett, Bruce, and Starr, Harvey. *World Politics: The Menu for Choice*. San Francisco: W. H. Freeman and Co., 1981.

Schumacher, E. F. *Small Is Beautiful*. New York: Harper & Row, 1973.

Abortion and Euthanasia

Introduction

Basic Concepts

The problem of abortion and euthanasia has been as thoroughly discussed as any contemporary moral problem. As a result, the conceptual issues have been fairly well laid out, and there have been some interesting attempts to bridge the troublesome normative and practical disagreements that remain.

First of all, almost everyone agrees that the fundamental issue with respect to justifying abortion is the moral status of the fetus, although considerable disagreement exists as to what that status is.[1] Conservatives on the abortion question, like John Noonan (Selection 14), contend that from conception the fetus has full moral status and hence a serious right to life. Liberals on the abortion question, like Mary Anne Warren (Selection 15), hold that, at least until birth, the fetus has almost no moral status whatsoever and lacks a serious right to life.[2] Moderates on the abortion question adopt some position in between these two views. And still others, like Judith Jarvis Thomson (Selection 13) and Jane English (Selection 16), adopt for the sake of argument either the conservative or the liberal view on the moral status of the fetus and then try to show that such a view does not lead to the consequences its supporters assume.[3]

Second, almost everyone agrees that the position one takes on the moral status of the fetus has a bearing on whether one considers either the distinction between killing and letting die or the doctrine of double effect as relevant to the abortion question. For example, conservatives are quite interested in whether the killing and letting die distinction can be used to show that it is permissible to let the fetus die in certain contexts, even when it would be impermissible to kill it. However, liberals find the use of this distinction in such contexts to be completely unnecessary. Because liberals hold that the fetus has almost no moral status, they do not object to either killing it or letting it die. Similarly, although conservatives are quite interested in whether the doctrine of double effect can be used to permit the death of the fetus as a foreseen but unintended consequence of some legitimate course of action, liberals find no use for the doctrine of double effect in such contexts.

Third, almost everyone agrees that either the killing and letting die distinction or the doctrine of double effect could prove useful in cases of euthanasia. Agreement is possible because most of the subjects of euthanasia are human beings who, in everyone's view, have full moral status and hence a serious right to life. Accordingly, despite the disagreement as to where it is useful to apply the killing and letting die distinction and the doctrine of double effect, everyone agrees that both of these conceptual tools deserve further examination.

The distinction between killing and letting die has its advocates and its critics. Advocates maintain that, other things being equal, killing is morally worse than letting die, with the consequence that letting die is justified in cases where killing is not. The critics of this distinction maintain that, other things being equal, killing is not morally worse than letting die, with the consequence that killing is morally justified whenever letting die is. Both advocates and critics agree that other things would not be equal if the killing were justified or deserved while the letting die unwanted and undeserved. They tend to disagree, however, over whether other things would be equal if the killing were in response to a patient's request to die while the letting die involved a prolonged and excruciatingly painful death, or if the killing resulted in the death of just a few individuals while the letting die resulted in the death of many people.

Yet whatever view one adopts as to when other things are equal, it is hard to defend the moral preferability of letting die over killing when both are taken to be intentional acts. As James Rachels so graphically illustrates (Selection 18), it seems impossible to judge the act of A, who intentionally lets Z die while standing ready to finish Z off if that proves necessary, as being morally preferable to the act of B, who with similar motive and intention kills Y. But it is far from clear whether advocates of the killing and letting die distinction are claiming that the distinction holds when the killing and the letting die are both intentional acts because it is unlikely in such cases that the letting die would be morally justified when the killing is not. Rather, as Bonnie Steinbock argues (Selection 19), advocates of the distinction seem to have in mind a contrast between *intentional* killing and *unintentional* letting die, or, more fully stated, a contrast between intentional killing and unintentional letting die when the latter is the foreseen consequence of an otherwise legitimate course of action.

Steinbock maintains that there are at least two types of cases in which letting die, distinguished in this way from killing, seems justified. In the first, a doctor ceases treatment at the patient's request, foreseeing that the patient will die or die sooner than otherwise, yet not intending that result. In the second, a doctor's intention is to avoid employing treatment that is extremely painful and has little hope of benefiting the patient, even though she foresees that this may hasten the patient's death. In addition, conservatives have argued that letting die, distinguished in this way from killing, can be justified in cases of ectopic pregnancy and cancer of the uterus because in such cases the fetus's death is the foreseen but unintended consequence of medical treatment that is necessary to preserve the basic well-being of the pregnant woman.

When the killing and letting die distinction is interpreted in this way, it has much in common with the doctrine of double effect. This doctrine places four restrictions on the permissibility of acting when some of the consequences of one's action are evil. These restrictions are as follows:

1. The act is good in itself or at least indifferent.
2. Only the good consequences of the act are intended.
3. The good consequences are not the effect of the evil.
4. The good consequences are commensurate with the evil consequences.

The basic idea of the killing and letting die distinction, as we have interpreted it, is expressed by restrictions 2 and 3.

When conservatives apply the doctrine of double effect to a case in which a pregnant woman has cancer of the uterus, the doctrine is said to justify an abortion because:

1. The act of removing the cancerous uterus is good in itself.
2. Only the removal of the cancerous uterus is intended.
3. The removal of the cancerous uterus is not a consequence of the abortion.
4. Preserving the life of the mother by removing the cancerous uterus is commensurate with the death of the fetus.

The doctrine is also said to justify unintentionally letting a person die, or "passive euthanasia," at least in the two types of cases described by Steinbock.

In recent moral philosophy, the main objection to the doctrine of double effect has been to question the necessity of its restrictions. Consider the following example. Imagine that a fat person who is leading a party of spelunkers gets herself stuck in the mouth of a cave in which flood waters are rising. The trapped party of spelunkers just happens to have a stick of dynamite with which they can blast the fat person out of the mouth of the cave; either they use the dynamite or they all drown, the fat person with them. It appears that the doctrine of double effect would *not* permit the use of the dynamite in this case because the evil consequences of the act are intended as a means to securing the good consequences in violation of restrictions 2 and 3. Yet it is plausible to argue in such a case that using the dynamite would be justified on the grounds that (a) the evil to be avoided (i.e., the evil of failing to save the party of spelunkers except for the fat person) is considerably greater than the evil resulting from the means employed (i.e., the evil of intentionally causing the death of the fat person) and/or that (b) the greater part of evil resulting from the means employed (i.e., the death of the fat person) would still occur regardless of whether those means were actually employed.

Some people might want to defend the doctrine of double effect against this line of criticism by maintaining that the spelunkers need not intend the death of the fat person, but only that "she be blown into little pieces" or that "the mouth of the cave be suitably enlarged." But how is the use of dynamite expected to produce these results except by way of killing the fat person? Thus, the death of the fat person is part of the means employed by the spelunkers to secure their release from the cave, and thus would be impermissible according to the doctrine of double effect. If, however, we think that bringing about the death of the fat person could be morally justified in this case, because, for example, (a) and/or (b) obtain, we are left with a serious objection to the necessity of the restrictions imposed by the doctrine of double effect for acting morally.

Given these objections to the doctrine of double effect, Philippa Foot has suggested that we might more profitably deal with the moral questions at issue by distinguishing between negative and positive duties. *Negative duties* are said to be duties to refrain from doing certain sorts of actions. Typically, these are duties to avoid actions that inflict harm or injury on others. Thus, the duties not to kill or assault others are negative duties. By contrast, *positive duties* are duties to do certain actions, usually those that aid or benefit others. The duties to repay a debt and help others in need are positive duties. This distinction is used to resolve practical disputes by claiming that negative duties have priority over positive duties; accordingly, when negative and positive duties conflict, negative duties always take precedence over positive duties.

Applying this distinction, Foot claims that a doctor is justified in performing an abortion when nothing can be done to save the lives of both child and mother, but the life of the mother can be saved by killing the child. Obviously, this case is quite similar to the example of the fat person stuck in the mouth of the cave. But it is not clear how the distinction between positive and negative duties can help us in either situation. Since both the doctor and the group of spelunkers trapped by the fat person have a negative duty not to kill that takes precedence over any positive duty to help either themselves or others, it would seem that neither aborting the fetus nor blowing up the fat person could be justified on the basis of this distinction. Thus, the distinction between negative and positive duties no more justifies evil consequences in such cases than does the doctrine of double effect. Accordingly, if we want to provide such a justification, we

need to find some morally acceptable way of going beyond both of these requirements.

Alternative Views

As we mentioned earlier, conservatives hold that the fetus has full moral status and hence a serious right to life. As a consequence, conservatives oppose abortion in a wide range of cases. Hoping to undercut this antiabortion stance, Judith Jarvis Thomson adopts, for the sake of argument, the conservative position on the moral status of the fetus (Selection 13). She then tries to show that abortion is still justified in a wide range of cases. Thomson asks us to imagine that we are kidnapped and connected to an unconscious violinist who now shares the use of our kidneys. The situation is such that if we detach ourselves from the violinist before nine months transpire, the violinist will die. Thomson thinks it obvious that we have no obligation to share our kidneys with the violinist in such a case, and hence that, in analogous cases, abortion can be justified. Thomson's view has provoked so much discussion that the authors of each of the next four selections all feel compelled to consider her view in the course of developing their own positions.

In his selection, John Noonan objects to Thomson's use of fantasized examples (Selection 14). In place of Thomson's example of an unconscious violinist, Noonan offers a more realistic example found in the law. It is a case in which a family is found to be liable for the frostbite suffered by a dinner guest whom they refused to allow to stay overnight in their home, although it was very cold outside and the guest showed signs of being sick. But although Noonan is surely correct in pointing out the need for realistic examples, there still is an important difference between allowing a person to stay overnight in one's home and allowing a fetus to remain and develop in one's body for approximately nine months.

Mary Anne Warren also objects to Thomson's violinist example, but on grounds quite different from Noonan's (Selection 15). She claims that the example at most justifies abortion in cases of rape and hence will not provide the desired support for abortion on demand. Thomson, however, did provide additional examples and arguments in an attempt to show that abortion is justified in cases other than rape. Jane English has also argued that Thomson's case against abortion can be extended to a wider range of examples (Selection 16).

Convinced that Thomson's or anyone else's attempt to argue for abortion will prove unsuccessful if the fetus is assumed to have full moral status, Noonan wants to retain and support that assumption. His approach, however, is quite different from that usually adopted by conservatives.

Conservatives typically employ what are called "slippery slope arguments" to show that any attempt to draw a line—whether at implantation, or at quickening, or at viability, or at birth—for the purpose of separating those who do not have full moral status from those who do, fails to be nonarbitrary because of the continuity in the development of the fetus. Conservatives then contend that conception is the only point at which the line can be drawn nonarbitrarily.

By contrast, Noonan proposes to examine various models and methods employed in the debate on abortion, distinguishing those that do not work from those that do. We have already noted Noonan's objection to fantasized examples. In addition, he objects to any attempt to make exceptions for abortion when the fetus is known to be seriously defective or the result of a rape, arguing that exceptions in such cases would "eat up the rule." Surprisingly, Noonan also objects to the use of special metaphors such as direct and indirect, and in particular rejects the application of the doctrine of double effect to cases of ectopic pregnancy and the removal of a cancerous uterus containing a fetus. In such cases, Noonan claims, the doctor "necessarily intends to perform the abortion, he necessarily intends to kill." What legitimates abortion in such cases, claims Noonan, is not the doctrine of double effect, but rather the principle that whenever the fetus is a danger to the life of the mother, abortion is permissible on grounds of self-defense. But if the mother is justified on grounds of self-defense in aborting the fetus, surely some representative of the fetus would also be justified in defending the fetus against

an abortion, given that in Noonan's view the fetus has a serious right to life. Consequently, Noonan has not provided us with a moral solution to such cases. At the same time, it is difficult to see how anyone could ignore the central plea of Noonan's article that we see what otherwise might be overlooked and respond to the full range of human experience.

Like Noonan, Warren wants to build a consensus on the abortion question. To achieve this, she proposes a set of criteria for being a person with full moral status that she thinks proabortionists and antiabortionists alike could accept. The criteria are (1) consciousness; (2) developed reasoning; (3) self-motivated activity; (4) a capacity to communicate; and (5) the presence of self-concepts and self-awareness. But although most people would certainly agree that these criteria are met in paradigm cases, conservatives would still reject them as necessary requirements for being a person. As Jane English (Selection 16) argues, the concept of a person is not sharp or decisive enough to bear the weight of a solution to the abortion controversy.

English, however, agrees with Thomson that even if we endorse the conservative view that the fetus is a full-fledged person, there are still cases where abortion would be justified to prevent serious harm or death to the pregnant woman. Similarly, she contends that even if we endorse the liberal view that the fetus is not a person, there are still cases, at least in the late months of pregnancy, where abortion would not be justified, because of the fetus's resemblance to a person.

Those who find both the conservative and liberal views on abortion unattractive might be inclined toward the moderate view. This view attempts to draw a line—typically at implantation, or at quickening, or at viability—for the purpose of separating those who do not have full moral status from those who do. The United States Supreme Court in *Roe v. Wade* (1973) has frequently been understood as supporting a moderate view on abortion. In this decision, the Court by a majority of 7 to 2 decided that the constitutional right to privacy, protected by the due process clause of the Fourteenth Amendment to the Constitution, entails that (1) no law may restrict the right of a woman to be aborted by a physician during the first three months (trimester) of her pregnancy; (2) during the second trimester abortion may be regulated by law only to the extent that the regulation is reasonably related to the preservation and protection of maternal health; and (3) when the fetus becomes viable (not before the beginning of the third trimester) a law may prohibit abortion, but only subject to an exception permitting abortion whenever necessary to protect the woman's life or health (including any aspects of her physical or mental health). But regardless of whether the Court's decision was intended to support the moderate view on abortion, some have argued that in the absence of reasonable constraints, the Court's decision has led to abortion on demand.

In selection 17, Catharine MacKinnon situates the abortion debate within a feminist understanding of gender equality. She challenges the underlying assumption of the abortion debate that women significantly control sex. She argues that the limited right to abortion based on privacy recognized by the U.S. Supreme Court in *Roe v. Wade* not only accords with the restrictions on federal funding for abortion sanctioned by *Harris v. McRae*, but also fails to protect women from battery, marital rape, and exploited labor. What this shows is that a right to abortion based on a right to privacy may do little by itself to secure women's liberation. What it also suggests is that many aspects of women's liberation could be achieved without a right to abortion if men approached sex and the care and rearing of children more responsibly.

Although most of the contemporary discussion of abortion has focused on the moral status of the fetus, most of the discussion of euthanasia has focused on the killing and letting die distinction and the doctrine of double effect. As we noted before, advocates of the killing and letting die distinction and the doctrine of double effect tend to justify only passive euthanasia (i.e., letting a person die as a foreseen but unintended consequence of an otherwise legitimate course of action). In contrast, critics of the killing and letting die distinction and the doctrine of double effect tend also to justify active euthanasia (i.e., intentional killing) on the basis of its consequences.

Rachels (Selection 18) cites the case of a person suffering from cancer of the throat who has three options: (1) with continued treatment she will have a few more days of pain and then die; (2) if treatment is stopped but nothing else is done, it will be a few more hours; or (3) with a lethal injection she will die at once. In such a case, Rachels thinks, the third option—active euthanasia—is justified on the grounds that the person would be better off dying immediately.

But euthanasia is not only passive or active, it is also voluntary or involuntary. Voluntary euthanasia has the (informed) consent of the person involved. Involuntary euthanasia lacks such consent, usually but not always because the person involved is incapable of providing it. This means that at least four different types of euthanasia are possible: voluntary passive euthanasia, involuntary passive euthanasia, voluntary active euthanasia, and involuntary active euthanasia. Of the four types, voluntary passive euthanasia seems easiest to justify, involuntary active euthanasia the most difficult. But voluntary euthanasia, both passive and active, would seem more justifiable if it could be shown that there were a fundamental moral right to be assisted in bringing about one's own death if one so desired. Even if such a right could be supported, however, it would presumably only have force when one could reasonably be judged to be better off dead.

Practical Applications

It is not at all difficult to see how the various proposed solutions to the problem of abortion and euthanasia could be applied in contemporary societies. In *Planned Parenthood v. Casey* (Selection 20), the U.S. Supreme Court reaffirmed its commitment to what they took to be the essential holding of *Roe v. Wade,* which is a woman's right to terminate her pregnancy before viability, while rejecting *Roe v. Wade*'s trimester analysis in favor of an undue burden standard, which only the spousal notification requirement of Pennsylvania's Abortion Control Act violated. In Selection 21, Linda Bird Franke describes the ambivalence she felt toward her own experience of having an abortion. In *Cruzan v. Director, Missouri Department of Health* (Selection 22) the majority of the

Supreme Court held that the state of Missouri was exercising a legitimate interest in protecting and preserving human life by requiring clear and convincing evidence of an incompetent's wishes concerning the withdrawal of life-sustaining medical treatment. In Selection 23, the activities of Dr. Jack Kevorkian are described. Accordingly, if you think that different solutions to the problem of abortion and euthanasia are more morally defensible, you should favor other laws and judicial decisions.

But even as you begin to formulate the laws and social institutions, with their demands on social goods and resources, that are needed to enforce what you take to be the most morally defensible solution to the problem of abortion and euthanasia, you will still need to take into account the demands on social goods and resources that derive from solutions to other practical moral problems—such as the problem of sex equality, which is taken up in the next section.

Notes

1. The term "fetus" is understood to refer to any human organism from conception to birth.

2. Note that liberals on the abortion question need not be welfare liberals, although many of them are. Likewise, conservatives on the abortion question need not be libertarians or political conservatives.

3. Henceforth liberals, conservatives, and moderates on the abortion question are simply referred to as liberals, conservatives, and moderates.

---

13. A Defense of Abortion

Judith Jarvis Thomson

Judith Jarvis Thomson begins by assuming, for the sake of argument, that the fetus is a person. Using a series of examples, she then argues that even granting this assumption, a woman has a right to abortion in cases involving rape, in cases where the woman's life is endangered, and in cases in which the woman had taken reasonable precautions to avoid becoming pregnant. In these cases, Thomson claims, the fetus's assumed right not to be killed unjustly would not be violated by abortion. Thomson further distinguishes between cases in which it would be a good thing for a woman to forego an abortion and cases in which a woman has an obligation to do so.

Most opposition to abortion relies on the premise that the fetus is a human being, a person, from the moment of conception. The premise is argued for, but, as I think, not well. Take, for example, the most common argument. We are asked to notice that the development of a human being from conception through birth into childhood is continuous; then it is said that to draw a line, to choose a point in this development and say "before this point the thing is not a person, after this point it is a person" is to make an arbitrary choice, a choice for which in the nature of things no good reason can be given. It is concluded that the fetus is, or anyway we had better say it is, a person from the moment of conception. But this conclusion does not follow. Similar things might be said about the development of an acorn into an oak tree, and it does not follow

Abridged from Judith Jarvis Thomson, "A Defense of Abortion," *Philosophy & Public Affairs* 1, no. 1 (Fall 1971). Copyright © 1971 by Princeton University Press. Excerpts, pp. 47–62, 65–66, reprinted by permission of Princeton University Press.

that acorns are oak trees or that we had better say they are. Arguments of this form are sometimes called "slippery slope arguments"—the phrase is perhaps self-explanatory—and it is dismaying that opponents of abortion rely on them so heavily and uncritically.

I am inclined to agree, however, that the prospects for "drawing a line" in the development of the fetus look dim. I am inclined to think also that we shall probably have to agree that the fetus has already become a human person well before birth. Indeed, it comes as a surprise when one first learns how early in its life it begins to acquire human characteristics. By the tenth week, for example, it already has a face, arms and legs, fingers and toes; it has internal organs, and brain activity is detectable.[1] On the other hand, I think that the premise is false, that the fetus is not a person from the moment of conception. A newly fertilized ovum, a newly implanted clump of cells, is no more a person than an acorn is an oak tree. But I shall not discuss any of this. For it seems to me to be of great interest to ask what happens if, for the sake of argument, we allow the premise. How, precisely, are we supposed to get from there to the conclusion that abortion is morally impermissible? Opponents of abortion commonly spend most of their time establishing that the fetus is a person, and hardly any time explaining the step from there to the impermissibility of abortion. Perhaps they think the step too simple and obvious to require much comment. Or perhaps instead they are simply being economical in argument. Many of those who defend abortion rely on the premise that the fetus is not a person, but only a bit of tissue that will become a person at birth; and why pay out more arguments than you have to? Whatever the explanation, I suggest that the step they take is neither easy nor obvious, that it calls for closer examination than it is commonly given, and that when we do give it this closer examination we shall feel inclined to reject it.

I propose, then, that we grant that the fetus is a person from the moment of conception. How does the argument go from here? Something like this, I take it. Every person has a right to life. So the fetus has a right to life. No doubt the mother has a right to decide what

shall happen in and to her body; everyone would grant that. But surely a person's right to life is stronger and more stringent than the mother's right to decide what happens in and to her body, and so outweighs it. So the fetus may not be killed; an abortion may not be performed.

It sounds plausible. But now let me ask you to imagine this. You wake up in the morning and find yourself back to back in bed with an unconscious violinist. A famous unconscious violinist. He has been found to have a fatal kidney ailment, and the Society of Music Lovers has canvassed all the available medical records and found that you alone have the right blood type to help. They have therefore kidnapped you, and last night the violinist's circulatory system was plugged into yours, so that your kidneys can be used to extract poisons from his blood as well as your own. The director of the hospital now tells you, "Look, we're sorry the Society of Music Lovers did this to you—we would never have permitted it if we had known. But still, they did it, and the violinist now is plugged into you. To unplug you would be to kill him. But never mind, it's only for nine months. By then he will have recovered from his ailment, and can safely be unplugged from you." Is it morally incumbent on you to accede to this situation? No doubt it would be very nice of you if you did, a great kindness. But do you *have* to accede to it? What if it were not nine months, but nine years? Or longer still? What if the director of the hospital says, "Tough luck, I agree, but you've now got to stay in bed, with the violinist plugged into you, for the rest of your life. Because remember this. All persons have a right to life, and violinists are persons. Granted you have a right to decide what happens in and to your body, but a person's right to life outweighs your right to decide what happens in and to your body. So you cannot ever be unplugged from him." I imagine you would regard this as outrageous, which suggests that something really is wrong with that plausible-sounding argument I mentioned a moment ago.

In this case, of course, you were kidnapped; you didn't volunteer for the operation that plugged the violinist into your kidneys. Can those who oppose abortion on the ground I mentioned make an exception for a pregnancy due to rape? Certainly. They can say that persons have a right to life only if they didn't come into existence because of rape; or they can say that all persons have a right to life, but that some have less of a right to life than others, in particular, that those who came into existence because of rape have less. But these statements have a rather unpleasant sound. Surely the question of whether you have a right to life at all, or how much of it you have, shouldn't turn on the question of whether or not you are the product of a rape. And in fact the people who oppose abortion on the ground I mentioned do not make this distinction, and hence do not make an exception in case of rape.

Nor do they make an exception for a case in which the mother has to spend the nine months of her pregnancy in bed. They would agree that would be a great pity, and hard on the mother; but all the same, all persons have a right to life, the fetus is a person, and so on. I suspect, in fact, that they would not make an exception for a case in which, miraculously enough, the pregnancy went on for nine years, or even the rest of the mother's life.

Some won't even make an exception for a case in which continuation of the pregnancy is likely to shorten the mother's life; they regard abortion as impermissible even to save the mother's life. Such cases are nowadays very rare, and many opponents of abortion do not accept this extreme view. All the same, it is a good place to begin: a number of points of interest come out in respect to it.

1. Let us call the view that abortion is impermissible even to save the mother's life "the extreme view." I want to suggest first that it does not issue from the argument I mentioned earlier without the addition of some fairly powerful premises. Suppose a woman has become pregnant, and now learns that she has a cardiac condition such that she will die if she carries the baby to term. What may be done for her? The fetus, being a person, has a right to life, but as the mother is a person too, so has she a right to life. Presumably they have an equal right to life. How is it supposed to come out that an abortion may not be performed? If mother and child have an equal right to life, shouldn't we perhaps flip a coin? Or should we add to the mother's right to life her right to decide what happens in and to her body, which everybody seems to be ready to grant—the sum of her rights now outweighing the fetus' right to life?

The most familiar argument here is the following. We are told that performing the abortion would be directly killing[2] the child, whereas doing nothing would not be killing the mother, but only letting her die. Moreover, in killing the child, one would be killing an innocent person, for the child has committed no crime, and is not aiming at his mother's death. And then there are a variety of ways in which this might be continued. (1) But as directly killing an innocent person is always and absolutely impermissible, an abortion may not be performed. Or, (2) as directly killing an innocent person is murder, and murder is always and absolutely impermissible, an abortion may not be performed.[3] Or, (3) as one's duty to refrain from directly killing an innocent person is more stringent than one's duty to keep a person from dying, an abortion may not be performed. Or, (4) if one's only options are directly killing an innocent person or letting a person die, one must prefer letting the person die, and thus an abortion may not be performed.[4]

Some people seem to have thought that these are not further premises which must be added if the conclusion is to be reached, but that they follow from the very fact that an innocent person has a right to life.[5] But this seems to me to be a mistake, and perhaps the simplest way to show this is to bring out that while we must certainly grant that innocent persons have a right to life, the theses in (1) through (4) are all false. Take (2), for example. If directly killing an innocent person is murder, and thus is impermissible, then the mother's directly killing the innocent person inside her is murder, and thus is impermissible. But it cannot seriously be thought to be murder if the mother performs an abortion on herself to save her life. It cannot seriously be said that she *must* refrain, that she *must* sit passively by and wait for her death. Let us look again at the case of you and the violinist. There you are, in bed with the violinist, and the director of the hospital says to you, "It's all most distressing, and I deeply sympathize, but you see this is putting an additional strain on your kidneys, and you'll be dead within the month. But you *have* to stay where you are all the same. Because unplugging you would be directly killing an innocent violinist, and that's murder, and that's impermissible." If anything in the world is true, it is that you do not commit murder, you do not do what is impermissible, if you reach around to your back and unplug yourself from that violinist to save your life.

The main focus of attention in writings on abortion has been on what a third party may or may not do in answer to a request from a woman for an abortion. This is in a way understandable. Things being as they are, there isn't much a woman can safely do to abort herself. So the question asked is what a third party may do, and what the mother may do, if it is mentioned at all, is deduced, almost as an afterthought, from what is concluded that the third parties may do. But it seems to me that to treat the matter in this way is to refuse to grant to the mother that very status of person which is so firmly insisted on for the fetus. For we cannot simply read off what a person may do from what a third party may do. Suppose you find yourself trapped in a tiny house with a growing child. I mean a very tiny house, and a rapidly growing child—you are already up against the wall of the house and in a few minutes you'll be crushed to death. The child on the other hand won't be crushed to death; if nothing is done to stop him from growing he'll be hurt, but in the end he'll simply burst open the house and walk out a free man. Now I could well understand it if a bystander were to say, "There's nothing we can do for you. We cannot choose between your life and his, we cannot be the ones to decide who is to live, we cannot intervene." But it cannot be concluded that you too can do nothing, that you cannot attack it to save your life. However innocent the child may be, you do not have to wait passively while it crushes you to death. Perhaps a pregnant woman is vaguely felt to have the status of a house, to which we don't allow the right of self-defense. But if the woman houses the child, it should be remembered that she is a person who houses it.

I should perhaps stop to say explicitly that I am not claiming that people have a right to do anything whatever to save their lives. I think, rather, that there are drastic limits to the right of self-defense. If someone threatens you with death unless you torture someone else to death, I think you have not the right, even to save your life, to do so. But the case under consideration here is very different. In our case there are only two people involved, one whose life is threatened, and one who threatens it. Both are innocent: the one who is threatened is not threatened because of any fault, the one who threatens does not threaten because of any fault. For this reason we may feel that we bystanders cannot intervene. But the person threatened can.

In sum, a woman surely can defend her life against the threat to it posed by the unborn child, even if doing so involves its death. And this shows not merely that the theses in (1) through (4) are false; it shows also that the extreme view of abortion is false, and so we need not canvass any other possible ways of arriving at it from the argument I mentioned at the outset.

2. The extreme view could of course be weakened to say that while abortion is permissible to save the mother's life, it may not be performed by a third party, but only by the mother herself. But this cannot be right either. For what we have to keep in mind is that the mother and the unborn child are not like two tenants in a small house which has, by an unfortunate mistake, been rented to both: the mother *owns* the house. The fact that she does adds to the offensiveness of deducing that the mother can do nothing from the supposition that third parties can do nothing. But it does more than this: it casts a bright light on the supposition that third parties can do nothing. Certainly it lets us see that a third party who says "I cannot choose between you" is fooling himself if he thinks this is impartiality. If Jones has found and fastened on a certain coat, which he needs to keep him from freezing, but which Smith also needs to keep him from freezing, then it is not impartiality that says "I cannot choose between you" when Smith owns the coat. Women have said again and again "This body is *my* body!" and they have reason to feel angry, reason to feel that it has been like shouting into the wind. Smith, after all, is hardly likely to bless us if we say to him, "Of

course it's your coat, anybody would grant that it is. But no one may choose between you and Jones who is to have it. . . ."

3. Where the mother's life is not at stake, the argument I mentioned at the outset seems to have a much stronger pull. "Everyone has a right to life, so the unborn person has a right to life." And isn't the child's right to life weightier than anything other than the mother's own right to life, which she might put forward as ground for an abortion?

This argument treats the right to life as if it were unproblematic. It is not, and this seems to me to be precisely the source of the mistake.

For we should now, at long last, ask what it comes to, to have a right to life. In some views having a right to life includes having a right to be given at least the bare minimum one needs for continued life. But suppose that what in fact *is* the bare minimum a man needs for continued life is something he has no right at all to be given? If I am sick unto death, and the only thing that will save my life is the touch of Henry Fonda's cool hand on my fevered brow, then all the same, I have no right to be given the touch of Henry Fonda's cool hand on my fevered brow. It would be frightfully nice of him to fly in from the West Coast to provide it. It would be less nice, though no doubt well meant, if my friends flew out to the West Coast and carried Henry Fonda back with them. But I have no right at all against anybody that he should do this for me. Or again, to return to the story I told earlier, the fact that for continued life that violinist needs the continued use of your kidneys does not establish that he has a right to be given the continued use of your kidneys. He certainly has no right against you that *you* should give him continued use of your kidneys. For nobody has any right to use your kidneys unless you give him such a right; and nobody has the right against you that you shall give him this right—if you do allow him to go on using your kidneys, this is a kindness on your part, and not something he can claim from you as his due. Nor has he any right against anybody else that *they* should give him continued use of your kidneys. Certainly he had no right against the Society of Music Lovers that they should plug him into you in the first place. And if you now start to unplug yourself, having learned that you will other-

wise have to spend nine years in bed with him, there is nobody in the world who must try to prevent you, in order to see to it that he is given something he has a right to be given.

Some people are rather stricter about the right to life. In their view, it does not include the right to be given anything, but amounts to, and only to, the right not to be killed by anybody. But here a related difficulty arises. If everybody is to refrain from killing that violinist, then everybody must refrain from doing a great many different sorts of things. Everybody must refrain from slitting his throat, everybody must refrain from shooting him—and everybody must refrain from unplugging you from him. But does he have a right against everybody that they shall refrain from unplugging you from him? To refrain from doing this is to allow him to continue to use your kidneys. It could be argued that he has a right against us that *we* should allow him to continue to use your kidneys. That is, while he had no right against us that we should give him the use of your kidneys, it might be argued that he anyway has a right against us that we shall not now intervene and deprive him of the use of your kidneys. I shall come back to third-party interventions later. But certainly the violinist has no right against you that *you* shall allow him to continue to use your kidneys. As I said, if you do allow him to use them, it is a kindness on your part, and not something you owe him.

The difficulty I point to here is not peculiar to the right to life. It reappears in connection with all the other natural rights; and it is something which an adequate account of rights must deal with. For present purposes it is enough just to draw attention to it. But I would stress that I am not arguing that people do not have a right to life—quite to the contrary, it seems to me that the primary control we must place on the acceptability of an account of rights is that it should turn out in that account to be a truth that all persons have a right to life. I am arguing only that having a right to life does not guarantee having either a right to be given the use of or a right to be allowed continued use of another person's body—even if one needs it for life itself. So the right to life will not serve the opponents of abortion in the very simple and clear way in which they seem to have thought it would.

4. There is another way to bring out the difficulty. In the most ordinary sort of case, to deprive someone of what he has a right to is to treat him unjustly. Suppose a boy and his small brother are jointly given a box of chocolates for Christmas. If the older boy takes the box and refuses to give his brother any of the chocolates, he is unjust to him, for the brother has been given a right to half of them. But suppose that, having learned that otherwise it means nine years in bed with that violinist, you unplug yourself from him. You surely are not being unjust to him, for you gave him no right to use your kidneys, and no one else can have given him any such right. But we have to notice that in unplugging yourself, you are killing him; and violinists, like everybody else, have a right to life, and thus in the view we were considering just now, the right not to be killed.

So here you do what he supposedly has a right you shall not do, but you do not act unjustly to him in doing it.

The emendation which may be made at this point is this: the right to life consists not in the right not to be killed, but rather in the right not to be killed unjustly. This runs a risk of circularity, but never mind: it would enable us to square the fact that the violinist has a right to life with the fact that you do not act unjustly toward him in unplugging yourself, thereby killing him. For if you do not kill him unjustly, you do not violate his right to life, and so it is no wonder you do him no injustice.

But if this emendation is accepted, the gap in the argument against abortion stares us plainly in the face: it is by no means enough to show that the fetus is a person, and to remind us that all persons have a right to life—we need to be shown also that killing the fetus violates its right to life, i.e., that abortion is unjust killing. And is it?

I suppose we may take it as a datum that in a case of pregnancy due to rape the mother has not given the unborn person a right to the use of her body for food and shelter. Indeed, in what pregnancy could it be supposed that the mother has given the unborn person such a right? It is not as if there were unborn persons drifting about the world, to whom a woman who wants a child says "I invite you in."

But it might be argued that there are other ways one can have acquired a right to the use of another person's body than by having been invited to use it by that person. Suppose a woman voluntarily indulges in intercourse, knowing of the chance it will issue in pregnancy, and then she does become pregnant; is she not in part responsible for the presence, in fact the very existence, of the unborn person inside her? No doubt she did not invite it in. But doesn't her partial responsibility for its being there itself give it a right to the use of her body? If so, then her aborting it would be more like the boy's taking away the chocolates, and less like your unplugging yourself from the violinist—doing so would be depriving it of what it does have a right to, and thus would be doing it an injustice.

And then, too, it might be asked whether or not she can kill it even to save her own life: If she voluntarily called it into existence, how can she now kill it, even in self-defense?

The first thing to be said about this is that it is something new. Opponents of abortion have been so concerned to make out the independence of the fetus, in order to establish that it has a right to life, just as its mother does, that they have tended to overlook the possible support they might gain from making out that the fetus is *dependent* on the mother, in order to establish that she has a special kind of responsibility for it, a responsibility that gives it rights against her which are not possessed by any independent person—such as an ailing violinist who is a stranger to her.

On the other hand, this argument would give the unborn person a right to its mother's body only if her pregnancy resulted from a voluntary act, undertaken in full knowledge of the chance a pregnancy might result from it. It would leave out entirely the unborn person whose existence is due to rape. Pending the availability of some further argument, then, we would be left with the conclusion that unborn persons whose existence is due to rape have no right to the use of their mothers' bodies, and thus that aborting them is not depriving them of anything they have a right to and hence is not unjust killing.

And we should also notice that it is not at all plain that this argument really does go even as far as it purports to. For there are cases and cases, and the details make a difference. If the room is stuffy, and I therefore open a window to air it, and a burglar climbs in, it would be absurd to say, "Ah, now he can stay, she's given him a right to the use of her house—for she is partially responsible for his presence there, having voluntarily done what enabled him to get in, in full knowledge that there are such things as burglars, and that burglars burgle." It would be still more absurd to say this if I had had bars installed outside my windows, precisely to prevent burglars from getting in, and a burglar got in only because of a defect in the bars. It remains equally absurd if we imagine it is not a burglar who climbs in, but an innocent person who blunders or falls in. Again, suppose it were like this: people-seeds drift about in the air like pollen, and if you open your windows, one may drift in and take root in your carpets or upholstery. You don't want children, so you fix up your windows with fine mesh screens, the very best you can buy. As can happen, however, and on very, very rare occasions does happen, one of the screens is defective; and a seed drifts in and takes root. Does the person-plant who now develops have a right to the use of your house? Surely not—despite the fact that you voluntarily opened your windows, you knowingly kept carpets and upholstered furniture, and you knew that screens were sometimes defective. Someone may argue that you are responsible for its rooting, that it does have a right to your house, because after all you *could* have lived out your life with bare floors and furniture, or with sealed windows and doors. But this won't do—for by the same token anyone can avoid a pregnancy due to rape by having a hysterectomy, or anyway by never leaving home without a (reliable!) army.

It seems to me that the argument we are looking at can establish at most that there are *some* cases in which the unborn person has a right to the use of its mother's body, and therefore *some* cases in which abortion is unjust killing. There is room for much discussion and argument as to precisely which, if any. But I think we should sidestep this issue and leave it open, for at any rate the argument certainly does not establish that all abortion is unjust killing.

5. There is room for yet another argument here, however. We surely must all grant that there may be cases in which it would be moral-ly indecent to detach a person from your body at the cost of his life. Suppose you learn that what the violinist needs is not nine years of your life, but only one hour: all you need do to save his life is to spend one hour in that bed with him. Suppose also that letting him use your kidneys for that one hour would not affect your health in the slightest. Admittedly you were kidnapped. Admittedly you did not give anyone permission to plug him into you. Nevertheless it seems to me plain you *ought* to allow him to use your kidneys for that hour—it would be indecent to refuse.

Again, suppose pregnancy lasted only an hour, and constituted no threat to life or health. And suppose that a woman becomes pregnant as a result of rape. Admittedly she did not voluntarily do anything to bring about the existence of a child. Admittedly she did nothing at all which would give the unborn person a right to the use of her body. All the same it might well be said, as in the newly emended violinist story, that she *ought* to allow it to remain for that hour—that it would be indecent in her to refuse.

Now some people are inclined to use the term "right" in such a way that it follows from the fact that you ought to allow a person to use your body for the hour he needs, that he has a right to use your body for the hour he needs, even though he has not been given that right by any person or act. They may say that it follows also that if you refuse, you act unjustly toward him. This use of the term is perhaps so common that it cannot be called wrong; nevertheless it seems to me to be an unfortunate loosening of what we would do better to keep a tight rein on. Suppose that box of chocolates I mentioned earlier had not been given to both boys jointly, but was given only to the older boy. There he sits, stolidly eating his way through the box, his small brother watching enviously. Here we are likely to say "You ought not to be so mean. You ought to give your brother some of those chocolates." My own view is that it just does not follow from the truth of this that the brother has any right to any of the chocolates. If the boy refuses to give his brother any, he is greedy, stingy, callous—but not unjust. I suppose that the people I have in mind will say it does follow that the brother has a right to some of the chocolates, and thus that the boy does act unjustly if he refuses to give his brother any. But the effect of saying this is to obscure what we should keep distinct, namely the difference between the boy's refusal in this case and the boy's refusal in the earlier case, in which the box was given to both boys jointly, and in which the small brother thus had what was from any point of view clear title to half.

A further objection to so using the term "right" that from the fact that A ought to do a thing for B, it follows that B has a right against A that A do it for him, is that it is going to make the question of whether or not a man has a right to a thing turn on how easy it is to provide him with it; and this seems not merely unfortunate, but morally unacceptable. Take the case of Henry Fonda again. I said earlier that I had no right to the touch of his cool hand on my fevered brow, even though I needed it to save my life. I said it would be frightfully nice of him to fly in from the West Coast to provide me with it, but that I had no right against him that he should do so. But suppose he isn't on the West Coast. Suppose he has only to walk across the room, place a hand briefly on my brow—and lo, my life is saved. Then surely he ought to do it, it would be indecent to refuse. Is it to be said "Ah, well, it follows that in this case she has a right to the touch of his hand on her brow, and so it would be an injustice in him to refuse"? So that I have a right to it when it is easy for him to provide it, though no right when it's hard? It's rather a shocking idea that anyone's rights should fade away and disappear as it gets harder and harder to accord them to him.

So my own view is that even though you ought to let the violinist use your kidneys for the one hour he needs, we should not conclude that he has a right to do so—we should say that if you refuse, you are, like the boy who owns all the chocolates and will give none away, self-centered and callous, indecent in fact, but not unjust. And similarly, that even supposing a case in which a woman pregnant due to rape ought to allow the unborn person to use her body for the hour he needs, we should not conclude that he has a right to do so; we should conclude that she is self-centered, callous, indecent, but not unjust, if she refuses. The complaints are no less grave; they are just different. However, there is no need to insist on this point. If anyone does wish to deduce "he has a right" from "you ought," then all the same he must surely grant that there are cases in which it is not morally required of you that you allow that violinist to use your kidneys, and in which he does not have a right to use them, and in which you do not do him injustice if you refuse. And so also for mother and unborn child. Except in such cases as the unborn person has a right to demand it—and we were leaving open the possibility that there may be such cases—nobody is morally *required* to make large sacrifices, of health, of all other interests and concerns, of all other duties and commitments, for nine years, or even for nine months, in order to keep another person alive. . . .

6. My argument will be found unsatisfactory on two counts by many of those who want to regard abortion as morally permissible. First, while I do argue that abortion is not impermissible, I do not argue that it is always permissible. I am inclined to think it a merit of my account precisely that it does *not* give a general yes or a general no. It allows for and supports our sense that, for example, a sick and desperately frightened fourteen-year-old schoolgirl, pregnant due to rape, may *of course* choose abortion, and that any law which rules this out is an insane law. And it also allows for and supports our sense that in other cases resort to abortion is even positively indecent. It would be indecent in the woman to request an abortion, and indecent in a doctor to perform it, if she is in her seventh month, and wants the abortion just to avoid the nuisance of postponing a trip abroad. The very fact that the arguments I have been drawing attention to treat all cases of abortion, or even all cases of abortion in which the mother's life is not at stake, as morally on a par ought to have made them suspect at the outset.

Secondly, while I am arguing for the permissibility of abortion in some cases, I am not arguing for the right to secure the death of the unborn child. It is easy to confuse these two things in that up to a certain point in the life of the fetus it is not able to survive outside the mother's body; hence removing it from her body guarantees its death. But they are importantly different. I have argued that you are not morally required to spend nine months in bed, sustaining the life of that violinist; but to say this is by no means to say that if, when you unplug yourself, there is a miracle and he survives, you then have a right to turn round and slit his throat. You may detach yourself even if this costs him his life; you have no right to be guaranteed his death, by some other means, if unplugging yourself does not kill him. There are some people who will feel dissatisfied by this feature of my argument. A woman may be utterly devastated by the thought of a child, a bit of herself, put out for adoption and never seen or heard of again. She may therefore want not merely that the child be detached from her, but more, that it die. Some opponents of abortion are inclined to regard this as beneath contempt—thereby showing insensitivity to what is surely a powerful source of despair. All the same, I agree that the desire for the child's death is not one which anybody may gratify, should it turn out to be possible to detach the child alive.

At this place, however, it should be remembered that we have only been pretending throughout that the fetus is a human being from the moment of conception. A very early abortion is surely not the killing of a person, and so is not dealt with by anything I have said here.

Notes

---

1. Daniel Callahan, *Abortion: Law, Choice and Morality* (New York, 1970), p. 373. This book gives a fascinating survey of the available information on abortion. The Jewish tradition is surveyed in David M. Feldman, *Birth Control in Jewish Law* (New York, 1968), Part 5, the Catholic tradition in John T. Noonan, Jr., "An Almost Absolute Value in History," in *The Morality of Abortion,* ed. John T. Noonan, Jr. (Cambridge, Mass., 1970).

2. The term "direct" in the arguments I refer to is a technical one. Roughly, what is meant by "direct killing" is either killing as an end in itself, or killing as a means to some end, for example, the end of saving someone else's life. See note 5, below, for an example of its use.

3. Cf. *Encyclical Letter of Pope Pius XI on Christian Marriage,* St. Paul Editions (Boston, n.d.), p. 32: "however much we may pity the mother whose health and even life is gravely imperiled in the performance of the duty allotted to her by nature, nevertheless what could ever be a sufficient reason for excusing in any way the direct murder of the innocent? This is precisely what we are dealing with here." Noonan (*The Morality of Abortion,* p. 43) reads this as follows: "What cause can ever avail to excuse in any way the direct killing of the innocent? For it is a question of that."

4. The thesis in (4) is in an interesting way weaker than those in (1), (2), and (3): they rule out abortion even in cases in which both mother *and* child will die if the abortion is not performed. By contrast, one who held the view expressed in (4) could consistently say that one needn't prefer letting two persons die to killing one.

5. Cf. the following passage from Pius XII, *Address to the Italian Catholic Society of Midwives:* "The baby in the maternal breast has the right to life immediately from God.—Hence there is no man, no human authority, no science, no medical, eugenic, social, economic or moral 'indication' which can establish or grant a valid juridical ground for a direct deliberate disposition of an innocent human life, that is a disposition which looks to its destruction either as an end or as a means to another end perhaps in itself not illicit.—The baby, still not born, is a man in the same degree and for the same reason as the mother" (quoted in Noonan, *The Morality of Abortion,* p. 45).

14. How to Argue about Abortion

John Noonan

John Noonan examines various models and methods used in the debate on abortion, distinguishing those that do not work from those that do. According to Noonan, those that do not work involve (1) fantasized examples, such as Thomson's unconscious violinist; (2) hard cases that are resolved in ways that ignore the child's interests; and (3) spatial metaphors, such as "direct" and "indirect," which obscure the moral distinctions involved. Those that do work are (1) balancing values in a nonquantitative manner; (2) seeing what might be otherwise overlooked; and (3) responding to the full range of human experience.

At the heart of the debate about abortion is the relation of person to person in social contexts. Analogies, metaphors, and methods of debate which do not focus on persons and which do not attend to the central contexts are mischievous. Their use arises from a failure to appreciate the distinctive character of moral argument—its requirement that values be organically related and balanced, its dependence on personal vision, and its rootedness in social experience. I propose here to examine various models and methods used in the debate on abortion distinguishing those such as fantasized situations, hard cases, and linear metaphors, all of which do not work, from the balancing, seeing, and appeal to human experience which I believe to be essential. I shall move from models and metaphors which take the rule against abortion as the expression of a single value to the consideration of ways of argument intended to suggest the variety of values which have converged in the formulation of the rule. The values embodied in the rule are various because abortion is an aspect of the relation of person to person, and persons are larger than single values; and abortion is an act in a social context which cannot be reduced to a single value. I write as a critic of abortion, with no doubt a sharper eye for the weaknesses of its friends than of its foes,

From "Responding to Persons: Methods of Moral Argument in Debate over Abortion," *Theology Digest* (1973), pp. 291–307. Reprinted by permission of *Theology Digest*.

but my chief aim is to suggest what arguments count.

Artificial Cases

One way of reaching the nub of a moral issue is to construct a hypothetical situation endowed with precisely the characteristics you believe are crucial in the real issue you are seeking to resolve. Isolated from the clutter of detail in the real situation, these characteristics point to the proper solution. The risk is that the features you believe crucial you will enlarge to the point of creating a caricature. The pedagogy of your illustration will be blunted by the uneasiness caused by the lack of correspondence between the fantasized situation and the real situation to be judged. Such is the case with recent efforts by philosopher Judith Jarvis Thomson to construct arguments justifying abortion.

Suppose, says Thomson, a violinist whose continued existence depends on acquiring new kidneys. Without the violinist's knowledge—he remains innocent—a healthy person is kidnapped and connected to him so that the violinist now shares the use of healthy kidneys. May the victim of the kidnapping break the connection and thereby kill the violinist? Thomson intuits that the normal judgment will be Yes. The healthy person should not be imposed upon by a lifelong physical connection with the violinist. This construct, Thomson contends, bears upon abortion by establishing that being human does not carry with it a right to life which must be respected by another at the cost of serious inconvenience.

This ingenious attempt to make up a parallel to pregnancy imagines a kidnapping; a serious operation performed on the victim of the kidnapping; and a continuing interference with many of the activities of the victim. It supposes that violinist and victim were unrelated. It supposed nothing by which the victim's initial aversion to his yoke-mate might be mitigated or compensated. It supposes no degree of voluntariness. The similitude to pregnancy is grotesque. It is difficult to think of another age or society in which a caricature of this sort could be seriously put forward as a paradigm illustrating the moral choice to be made by a mother.

While Thomson focuses on this fantasy, she ignores a real case from which American tort law has generalized. On a January night in Minnesota, a cattle buyer, Orlando Depue, asked a family of farmers, the Flateaus, with whom he had dined, if he could remain overnight at their house. The Flateaus refused and, although Depue was sick and had fainted, put him out of the house into the cold night. Imposing liability on the Flateaus for Depue's loss of his frostbitten fingers the court said, "In the case at bar defendants were under no contract obligation to minister to plaintiff in his distress; but humanity demanded they do so, if they understood and appreciated his condition . . . The law as well as humanity required that he not be exposed in his helpless condition to the merciless elements." Depue was a guest for supper although not a guest after supper. The American Law Institute, generalizing, has said that it makes no difference whether the helpless person is a guest or a trespasser. He has the privilege of staying. His host has the duty not to injure him or put him into an environment where he becomes nonviable. The obligation arises when one person "understands and appreciates" the condition of the other. Although the analogy is not exact, the case seems closer to the mother's situation than the case imagined by Thomson; and the emotional response of the Minnesota judges seems to be a truer reflection of what humanity requires. . . .

Hard Cases and Exceptions

In the presentation of permissive abortion to the American public, major emphasis has been put on situations of great pathos—the child deformed by thalidomide, the child affected by rubella, the child known to suffer from Tay-Sachs disease or Down's syndrome, the raped adolescent, the exhausted mother of small children. These situations are not imagined, and the cases described are not analogies to those where abortion might be sought; they are themselves cases to which abortion is a solution. Who could deny the poignancy of their appeal?

Hard cases make bad law, runs the venerable legal adage, but it seems to be worse law if the distress experienced in situations such as these is not taken into account. If persons are to be given preeminence over abstract principle, should not exceptions for these cases be made in the most rigid rule against abortion? Does not the human experience of such exceptions point to a more sweeping conclusion—the necessity of abandoning any uniform prohibition of abortion, so that all the elements of a particular situation may be weighted by the woman in question and her doctor?

So far, fault can scarcely be found with this method of argumentation, this appeal to common experience. But the cases are oversimplified if focus is directed solely on the parents of a physically defective child or on the mother in the cases of rape or psychic exhaustion. The situations are very hard for the parents or the mother; they are still harder for the fetus who is threatened with death. If the fetus is a person as the opponents of abortion contend, its destruction is not the sparing of suffering by the sacrifice of a principle but by the sacrifice of a life. Emotion is a proper element in moral response, but to the extent that the emotion generated by these cases obscures the claims of the fetus, this kind of argumentation fosters erroneous judgment.

In three of the cases—the child deformed

by drugs, disease, or genetic defect—the neglect of the child's point of view seems stained by hypocrisy. Abortion is here justified as putting the child out of the misery of living a less than normal life. The child is not consulted as to the choice. Experience, which teaches that even the most seriously incapacitated prefer living to dying, is ignored. The feelings of the parents are the actual consideration, and these feelings are treated with greater tenderness than the fetal desire to live. The common unwillingness to say frankly that the abortion is sought for the parents' benefit is testimony, unwillingly given, to the intuition that such self-preference by the parents is difficult for society or for the parents themselves to accept.

The other kind of hard case does not mask preference for the parent by a pretense of concern for the fetus. The simplest situation is that of a pregnancy due to rape—in presentations to some legislatures it was usual to add a racist fillip by supposing a white woman and a black rapist—but this gratuitous pandering to bias is not essential. The fetus, unwanted in the most unequivocal way, is analogized to an invader of the mother's body—is it even appropriate to call her a mother when she did nothing to assume the special fiduciary cares of motherhood? If she is prevented from having an abortion, she is being compelled for nine months to be reminded of a traumatic assault. Do not her feelings override the right to life of her unwanted tenant?

Rape arouses fear and a desire for revenge, and reference to rape evokes emotion. The emotion has been enough for the state to take the life of the rapist. Horror of the crime is easily extended to horror of the product, so that the fetal life becomes forfeit too. If horror is overcome, adoption appears to be a more humane solution than abortion. If the rape case is not being used as a stalking horse by proponents of abortion—if there is a desire to deal with it in itself—the solution is to assure the destruction of the sperm in the one to three days elapsing between insemination and impregnation.

Generally, however, the rape case is presented as a way of suggesting a general principle, a principle which could be formulated as follows: Every unintended pregnancy may be interrupted if its continuation will cause emotional distress to the mother. Pregnancies due to bad planning or bad luck are analogized to pregnancies due to rape; they are all involuntary. Indeed many pregnancies can without great difficulty be assimilated to the hard case, for how often do persons undertake an act of sexual intercourse consciously intending that a child be the fruit of that act? Many pregnancies are unspecified by a particular intent, are unplanned, are in this sense involuntary. Many pregnancies become open to termination if only the baby consciously sought has immunity.

This result is unacceptable to those who believe that the fetus is human. It is acceptable to those who do not believe the fetus is human, but to reach it they do not need the argument based on the hard case. The result would follow immediately from the mother's dominion over a portion of her body. Opponents of abortion who out of consideration for the emotional distress caused by rape will grant the rape exception must see that the exception can be generalized to destroy the rule. If, on other grounds they believe the rule good, they must deny the exception which eats it up.

Direct and Indirect

From the paradigmatic arguments, I turn to metaphors and especially those which, based on some spatial image, are misleading. I shall begin with "direct" and "indirect" and their cousins, "affirmative" and "negative." In the abortion argument "direct" and "indirect," "affirmative" and "negative" occur more frequently in these kinds of questions: If one denies that a fetus may be killed directly, but admits that indirect abortion is permissible, is he guilty of inconsistency? If one maintains that there is a negative duty not to kill fetuses, does he thereby commit himself to an affirmative obligation of assuring safe delivery of every fetus? If one agrees that there is no affirmative duty to actualize as many spermatic, ovoid, embryonic, or fetal potentialities as possible, does one thereby concede that it is generally permissible to take steps to destroy fertilized ova? The argumentative implications of these questions can be best unravelled by looking at the force of the metaphors invoked.

"Direct" and "indirect" appeal to our experience of linedrawing and of travel. You reach a place on a piece of paper by drawing a straight or crooked line—the line is direct or indirect. You go to a place without detours or you go in a roundabout fashion—your route is direct or indirect. In each instance, whether your path is direct or indirect your destination is the same. The root experience is that you can reach the same spot in ways distinguished by their immediacy and the amount of ground covered. "Indirectly" says you proceed more circuitously and cover more ground. It does not, however, say anything of the reason why you go circuitously. You may go indirectly because you want to cover more ground or because you want to disguise your destination.

The ambiguity in the reason for indirectness—an ambiguity present in the primary usage of the term—carries over when "indirect" is applied metaphorically to human intentions. There may be a reason for doing something indirectly—you want to achieve another objective besides the indirect action. You may also act indirectly to conceal from another or from yourself what is your true destination. Because of this ambiguity in the reason for indirection, "indirect" is apt to cause confusion when applied in moral analysis.

Defenders of an absolute prohibition of abortion have excepted the removal of a fertilized ovum in an ectopic pregnancy and the removal of a cancerous uterus containing an embryo. They have characterized the abortion involved as "indirect." They have meant that the surgeon's attention is focused on correcting a pathological condition dangerous to the mother and he only performs the operation because there is no alternative way of correcting it. But the physician has to intend to achieve not only the improvement of the mother but the performance of action by which the fertilized ovum becomes nonviable. He necessarily intends to perform an abortion, he necessarily intends to kill. To say that he acts indirectly is to conceal what is being done. It is a confusing and improper use of the metaphor.

A clearer presentation of the cases of the cancerous uterus and the ectopic pregnancy would acknowledge them to be true exceptions to the absolute inviolability of the fetus. Why are they not exceptions which would eat up the rule? It depends on what the rule is considered to be. The principle that can be discerned in them is, whenever the embryo is a danger to the life of the mother, an abortion is permissible. At the level of reason nothing more can be asked of the mother. The exceptions do eat up any rule of preferring the fetus to the mother—any rule of fetus first. They do not destroy the rule that the life of the fetus has precedence over other interests of the mother. The exceptions of the ectopic pregnancy and the cancerous uterus are special cases of the general exception to the rule against killing, which permits one to kill in self-defense. Characterization of this kind of killing as "indirect" does not aid analysis.

It is a basic intuition that one is not responsible for all the consequences of one's acts. By living at all one excludes others from the air one breathes, the food one eats. One cannot foresee all the results which will flow from any given action. It is imperative for moral discourse to be able to distinguish between injury foreseeably inflicted on another, and the harm which one may unknowingly bring about. "Direct" and "indirect" are sometimes used to distinguish the foreseen consequence from the unconsidered or unknown consequence. This usage does not justify terming abortion to save a mother's life "indirect." In the case of terminating the ectopic pregnancy, the cancerous uterus, the life-threatening fetus generally, one considers precisely the consequence, the taking of the fetal life.

Just as one intuits that one is not responsible for all the consequences, so one intuits that one is not called to right all wrongs. No one is bound to the impossible. There is, therefore, an intuitive difference between the duty to refrain from doing harm to anyone and the duty to help everyone in distress. The duty to refrain is possible of fulfillment if it refers only to conscious infliction of harm. The duty to help is impossible if one is going to develop as a human being, getting educated, earning a living, marrying, raising a family, and so forth. The needs of other human beings are subordinated or postponed by everyone to the fulfillment of many of one's own needs, and rightly so. The distinction between affirmative and negative duties, another linear metaphor, rests on this universal experience. The terms do have a basis in moral life. Their usefulness in moral analysis, however, is not great. The crucial distinction is not between negative and affirmative, but between limited and unlimited duty.

It is possible to state the duty not to kill the fetus as the duty to care for the fetus. Opponents of abortion, however, do not commit thereby themselves to the position that all fertilized ova must be born. A pregnant woman may, for example, take the chance of killing the baby by going for a walk or a drive instead of staying safely in bed. She is not responsible for all the consequences of her acts. She is not called to help the fetus in every possible way. The negative duty or the convertible affirmative duty excludes acts which have a high probability of death for the fetus, but not those with a low probability of death. Similarly, one has a duty not to kill one's older children, and a duty to care for them, but no duty to keep them free from all risk of harm. No inconsistency exists in not equating a limited negative duty with an unlimited affirmative duty; no inconsistency exists in rejecting high risk acts and approving low risk acts.

Linedrawing

The prime linear metaphor is, of course, linedrawing. It is late in the history of moral thought for anyone to suppose that an effective moral retort is, "Yes, but where do you draw the line?" or to make the inference that, because any drawing of a line requires a decision, all linedrawing is arbitrary. One variant or another of these old ploys is, however, frequently used in the present controversy. From living cell to dying corpse a continuum exists. Proponents of abortion are said to be committed to murder, to euthanasia, or, at a minimum, to infanticide. Opponents are alleged to be bound to condemn contraception—after all, spermatazoa are living human cells. Even if contraception is admitted and infanticide rejected, the range of choice is still large enough for the line drawn to be challenged—is it to be

at nidation, at formation of the embryo, at quickening, at viability, at birth? Whoever adopts one point is asked why he does not move forward or backward by one stage of development. The difficulty of presenting apodictic reasons for preferring one position is made to serve as proof that the choice may be made as best suits the convenience of an individual or the state.

The metaphor of linedrawing distracts attention from the nature of the moral decision. The metaphor suggests an empty room composed of indistinguishable grey blocks. In whatever way the room is divided, there are grey blocks on either side of the line. Or if the metaphor is taken more mathematically, it suggests a series of points, which, wherever bisected, are fungible with each other. What is obscured in the spatial or mathematical model is the variety of values whose comparison enters into any moral decision. The model appeals chiefly to those novices in moral reasoning who believe that moral judgment is a matter of pursuing a principle to its logical limit. Single-mindedly looking at a single value, they ask, if this is good, why not more of it? In practice, however, no one can be so single-hearted. Insistence of this kind of logical consistency becomes the preserve of fanatics or of controversialists eager to convict their adversaries of inconsistency. If more than one good is sought by a human being, he must bring the goods he seeks into relationship with each other; he must limit one to maintain another; he must mix them.

The process of choosing multiple goods occurs in many particular contexts—in eating, in studying, in painting. No one supposes that those who take the first course must forego dessert, that the election of English means History shall not be studied, that the use of blue excludes red. Linear models for understanding choice in these matters are readily perceived as inappropriate. The commitment to values, the cutting off of values, and the mixing of values accompany each other.

Is, however, the choice of the stage of development which should not be destroyed by abortion a choice requiring the mixing of multiple goods? Is not the linear model appropriate when picking a point on the continuum of life? Are not the moral choices which require commitment and mixing made only after the selection of the stage at which a being becomes a person? To these related questions the answers must all be negative. To recognize a person is a moral decision; it depends on objective data but it also depends on the perceptions and inclinations and ends of the decision makers; it cannot be made without commitment and without consideration of alternative values. Who is a person? This is not a question asked abstractly, in the air, with no purpose in mind. To disguise the personal involvement in the response to personhood is to misconceive the issue of abortion from the start.

Those who identify the rational with the geometrical, the algebraic, the logical may insist that, if the fundamental recognition of personhood depends on the person who asks, then the arbitrariness of any position on abortion is conceded. If values must be mixed even in identifying the human, who can object to another's mixture? The issue becomes like decisions in eating, studying, and painting, a matter of discretion. A narrow rationalism of this kind uses "taste" as the ultimate epithet for the non-rational. It does not acknowledge that each art has its own rules. It claims for itself alone the honorable term "reason."

As this sort of monopoly has become unacceptable in general philosophy, so it is unnecessary to accept it here. Taste, that is perceptiveness, is basic; and if it cannot be disputed, it can be improved by experience. Enology, painting, or moral reasoning all require basic aptitude, afford wide ranges of options, have limits beyond which a choice can be counterproductive, and are better done by the experienced than by amateurs. Some persons may lack almost any capacity for undertaking one or another of them. Although all men are moral beings, not all are proficient at moral judgment, so that morality is not a democratic business. Selecting multiple goods, those who are capable of the art perceive, test, mix and judge. The process has little in common with linedrawing. In the case of abortion, it is the contention of its opponents that in such a process the right response to the data is that the fetus is a human being.

Balancing

The process of decisionmaking just described is better caught by the term "balancing." In contrast to linedrawing, balancing is a metaphor helpful in understanding moral judgment. Biologically understood, balancing is the fundamental metaphor for moral reasoning. A biological system is in balance when its parts are in the equilibrium necessary for it to live. To achieve such equilibrium, some parts—the heart, for example—must be preserved at all costs; others may be sacrificed to maintain the whole. Balance in the biological sense does not demand an egalitarian concern for every part, but an ordering and subordination which permit the whole to function. So in moral reasoning the reasoner balances values.

The mistaken common reading of this metaphor is to treat it as equivalent to weighing, so that balancing is understood as an act of quantitative comparison analogous to that performed by an assayer or a butcher. This view tacitly supposes that values are weights which are tangible and commensurate. One puts so many units on one pan of the scales and matches them with so many units on the other to reach a "balanced" judgment. To give a personal example, Daniel Callahan has questioned my position that the value of innocent life cannot be sacrificed to achieve the other values which abortion might secure. The "force of the rule," he writes, "is absolutist, displaying no 'balance' at all." He takes balancing in the sense of weighing and wonders how one value can be so heavy.

That justice often consists in the fair distribution or exchange of goods as in the familiar Aristotelian examples has no doubt worked to confirm a quantitative approach. Scales as the symbol of justice seem to suggest the antiquity of the quantitative meaning of balance. But the original sense of the scales was otherwise. In Egypt where the symbol was first used, a feather, the Egyptian hieroglyphic for truth, turned the balance. As put by David Daube in his illuminating analysis of the ancient symbolism, "The slightest turning of the scales—'but in the estimation of a hair'—will decide the issue, and the choice is between salvation and annihilation." Not a matching of weights, but a response to reality was what justice was seen to require, and what was at stake was not a slight overweighing in one direction or the other, but salvation. Moral choice, generally, has this character of a hair separating good from evil.

A fortiori then, in moral judgment, where more values are in play than in any system of strict law or commutative justice, balancing is a misleading metaphor if it suggests a matching of weights. It is an indispensable metaphor if it stands for the equilibrium of a living organism making the choices necessary for its preservation. A single value cannot be pursued to the point of excluding all other values. This is the caricature of moral argument I have already touched on in connection with the metaphor of linedrawing. But some values are more vital than others, as the heart is more vital to the body than the hand. A balanced moral judgment requires a sense of the limits, interrelations, and priority of values. It is the position of those generally opposed to abortion that a judgment preferring interests less than human life to human life is unbalanced, that a judgment denying a mother's fiduciary responsibility to her child is unbalanced, that a judgment making killing a principal part of the profession of a physician is unbalanced, that a judgment permitting agencies of the state to procure and pay for the destruction of the offspring of the poor or underprivileged is unbalanced. They contend that such judgments expand the right limits of a mother's responsibility for herself, destroy the fiduciary relation which is a central paradigm for the social bond, fail to relate to the physician's service to life and the state's care for its citizens. At stake in the acceptance of abortion is not a single value, life, against which the suffering of the mother or parents may be balanced. The values to be considered are the child's life, the mother's faithfulness to her dependent, the physician's commitment to preserving life; and in the United States today abortion cannot be discussed without awareness that if law does not prohibit it, the state will fund it, so that the value of the state's abstention from the taking of life is also at issue. The judgment which accepts abortion, it

is contended, is unbalanced in subordinating these values to the personal autonomy of the mother and the social interest in population control.

Seeing

The metaphor of balancing points to the process of combining values. But we do not combine values like watercolors. We respond to values situated in subjects. "Balancing" is an inadequate metaphor for moral thinking in leaving out of account the central moral transaction—the response of human beings to other human beings. In making moral judgments we respond to those human beings whom we see.

The metaphor of sight is a way of emphasizing the need for perception, whether by eyes or ears or touch, of those we take as subjects to whom we respond. Seeing in any case is more than the registration of a surface. It is a penetration yielding some sense of the other's structure, so that the experiencing of another is never merely visual or auditory or tactile. We see the features and comprehend the humanity at the same time. Look at the fetus, say the anti-abortionists, and you will see humanity. How long, they ask, can a man turn his head and pretend that he just doesn't see?

An accusation of blindness, however, does not seem to advance moral argument. A claim to see where others do not see is a usual claim of charlatans. "Illumination" or "enlightenment" appear to transcend experience and make moral disputation impossible. "Visionary" is often properly a term of disparagement. Is not an appeal to sight the end of rational debate?

In morals, as in epistemology, there is nonetheless no substitute for perception. Are animals within the range of beings with a right to life, and babies not, as Michael Tooley has recently suggested? Should trees be persons, as Christopher Stone has recently maintained? Questions of this kind are fundamentally frivolous for they point to the possibility of moral argument while attempting to deny the foundation of moral argument, our ability to recognize human persons. If a person could in no way perceive another person to be like himself, he would be incapable of moral response. If a person cannot perceive a cat or a tree as different from himself, he cuts off the possibility of argument. Debate should not end with pointing, but it must begin there.

Is there a contradiction in the opponents of abortion appealing to perception when fetuses are normally invisible? Should one not hold that until beings are seen they have not entered the ranks of society? Falling below the threshold of sight, do not fetuses fall below the threshold of humanity? If the central moral transaction is response to the other person, are not fetuses peculiarly weak subjects to elicit our response? These questions pinpoint the principal task of the defenders of the fetus—to make the fetus visible. The task is different only in degree from that assumed by defenders of other persons who have been or are "overlooked." For centuries, color acted as a psychological block to perception, and the blindness induced by color provided a sturdy basis for discrimination. Minorities of various kinds exist today who are "invisible" and therefore unlikely to be "heard" in the democratic process. Persons literally out of sight of society in prisons and mental institutions are often not "recognized" as fellow humans by the world with which they have "lost touch." In each of these instances those who seek to vindicate the rights of the unseen must begin by calling attention to their existence. "Look" is the exhortation they address to the callous and the negligent.

Perception of fetuses is possible with not substantially greater effort than that required to pierce the physical or psychological barriers to recognizing other human beings. The main difficulty is everyone's reluctance to accept the extra burdens of care imposed by an expansion of the numbers in whom humanity is recognized. It is generally more convenient to have to consider only one's kin, one's peers, one's country, one's race. Seeing requires personal attention and personal response. The emotion generated by identification with a human form is necessary to overcome the inertia which is protected by a vision restricted to a convenient group. If one is willing to undertake the risk that more will be required in one's action, fetuses may be seen in multiple ways—circumstantially, by the observation of a pregnant woman; photographically, by pictures of life in the womb; scientifically, in accounts written by investigators of prenatal life and child psychologists; visually, by observing a blood transfusion or an abortion while the fetus is alive or by examination of a fetal corpse after death. The proponent of abortion is invited to consider the organism kicking the mother, swimming peacefully in amniotic fluid, responding to the prick of an instrument, being extracted from the womb, sleeping in death. Is the kicker or swimmer similar to him or to her? Is the response to pain like his or hers? Will his or her own face look much different in death?

Response

Response to the fetus begins with grasp of the data which yield the fetus's structure. That structure is not merely anatomical form; it is dynamic—we apprehend the fetus's origin and end. It is this apprehension which makes response to the nameless fetus different from the conscious analogizing that goes on when we name a cat. Seeing, we are linked to the being in the womb by more than an inventory of shared physical characteristics and by more than a number of made-up psychological characteristics. The weakness of the being as potential recalls our own potential state, the helplessness of the being evokes the human condition of contingency. We meet another human subject.

Seeing is impossible apart from experience, but experience is the most imprecise of terms. What kind of experience counts, and whose? There are experiences which only women and usually only those within the ages of 14 to 46 who are fertile can have: conceiving a child, carrying a child, having an abortion, being denied an abortion, giving birth. There are experiences only a fetus can have: being carried, being aborted, being born. There is the experience of obstetricians who regularly deliver children and occasionally abort them; there is the differently textured experience of the professional abortionist. There is the experience of nurses who prepare the mother for abortion, care for her after the abortion, and dispose of the aborted fetus. There is the experience of physicians, social workers, and ministers, who advise a woman to have an abortion or not to have one. There is the experience of those who enforce a law against abortion, and those who stealthily or openly, for profit or for conscience's sake, defy it. There is the experience of those who have sexual intercourse knowing that abortion is or is not a remedy if an accidental pregnancy should result. There is the experience of society at large of a pattern of uncontrolled abortion or of its regulation.

Some arguments are unduly exclusivist in the experience they will admit. Those who suggest that abortion is peculiarly a matter for women disqualify men because the unique experience of pregnancy is beyond their achievement. Yet such champions of abortion do not regularly disqualify sterile women whose experience of pregnancy must be as vicarious as a man's. Tertullian taught that only those who have known motherhood themselves have a right to speak from experience on the choices presented by abortion. Yet even Tertullian did not go so far as to say that only mothers who had both given birth and had had abortions were qualified to speak. Efforts of this sort to restrict those who are competent rest on a confusion between the relevant and the personal. You do not have to be a judge to know that bribery is evil or a slave to know that slavery is wrong. Vicarious experience, in this as in other moral matters, is a proper basis for judgment.

Vicarious experience appears strained to the outer limit when one is asked to consider the experience of the fetus. No one remembers being born, no one knows what it is like to die. Empathy may, however, supply for memory, as it does in other instances when we refer to the experience of infants who cannot speak or to the experience of death by those who cannot speak again. The experience of the fetus is no more beyond our knowledge than the experience of the baby and the experience of dying.

Participation in an abortion is another sort of experience relevant to moral judgment.

Generals are not thought of as the best judges of the morality of war, nor is their experience thought to be unaffected by their profession, but they should be heard, when the permissibility of war is urged. Obstetricians are in an analogous position, their testimony subject to a discount. The testimony of professional abortionists is also relevant, although subject to an even greater discount. Nurses are normally more disinterested witnesses. They speak as ones who have empathized with the female patient, disposed of the fetal remains, and, like the Red Cross in wartime, have known what the action meant by seeing the immediate consequences.

The experience of individuals becomes a datum of argument through autobiography and testimony, inference and empathy. The experience of a society has to be captured by the effort of sociologists and novelists, historians and lawyers, psychologists and moralists; and it is strongly affected by the prism of the medium used. Typically the proponents of abortion have put emphasis on quantitative evidence—for example, on the number of abortions performed in the United States or in the world at large. The assumption underlying this appeal to experience is that what is done by a great many persons cannot be bad, is indeed normal. This assumption, often employed when sexual behavior is studied, is rarely favored when racial discrimination or war is considered. It is a species of natural law, identifying the usual with the natural. The experience appealed to counts as argument only for those who accept this identification and consider the usual the good.

Psychological evidence has been called upon by the opponents of abortion. Trauma and guilt have been found associated with the election of abortion. The inference is made that abortion is the cause of this unhappiness. As in many arguments based on social consequences, however, the difficulty is to isolate the cause. Do persons undergoing abortion have character predispositions which would in any event manifest themselves in psychic disturbance? Do they react as they do because of social conditioning which could be changed to encourage a positive attitude to abortion? Is the act of abortion at the root of their problems or the way in which the process is carried out? None of these questions is settled; the evidence is most likely to be convincing to those already inclined to believe that abortion is an evil.

Another kind of experience is that embedded in law. In Roman law where children generally had little status independent of their parents, the fetus was "a portion of the mother or her viscera." This view persisted in nineteenth century American tort law, Justice Holmes in a leading case describing the fetus as "a part of the body of the mother." In recent years, however, the tort cases have asked, in Justice Bok's phrase, if the fetus is a person; and many courts have replied affirmatively. The change, a striking revolution in torts law, came from the courts incorporating into their thought new biological data on the fetus as a living organism. Evidence on how the fetus is now perceived is also provided by another kind of case where abortion itself is not involved—the interpretation in wills and trusts of gifts to "children" or "issue." In these cases a basic question is, "What is the common understanding of people when they speak of children?" The answer, given repeatedly by American courts, is that "the average testator" speaking of children means to include a being who has been conceived but not born. Free from the distorting pressures of the conflict over abortion, this evidence of the common understanding suggests that social experience has found the fetus to be within the family of man.

The most powerful expression of common experience is that given by art and literature. Birth has almost everywhere been celebrated in painting. The Nativity has been a symbol of gladness not only because of its sacral significance, but because of its human meaning— "joy that a man is born into the world." Abortion, in contrast, has rarely been the subject of art. Unlike other forms of death, abortion has not been seen by painters as a release, a sacrifice, or a victory. Characteristically it has stood for sterility, futility, and absurdity. Consider, for example, Orozco's mural, "Gods of the Modern World" in the Baker Library at Dartmouth College. Academia is savagely satirized by portraying professors as impotent atten-

dants in an operating room in which truth is stillborn. Bottled fetuses in the foreground attest the professors' habitual failure. The entire force of the criticism of academic achievement comes from the painter's knowledge that everyone will recognize abortion as a grave defeat and the bottling of dead fetuses as a travesty of healthy birth. Whoever sees such a painting sees how mankind has commonly experienced abortion.

In contemporary American literature, John Updike's *Couples* comments directly upon abortion, using it at a crucial turn as both event and symbol. Piet Hanema, married to Angela, has promiscuously pursued other married women, among them Foxy Whitman, who is now pregnant by him. They have this exchange:

> All I know is what I honestly want. I want this damn thing to stop growing inside me.
> Don't cry.
> Nature is so stupid. It has all my maternal glands working, do you know what that means, Piet? You know what the great thing about being pregnant I found out was? It's something I just couldn't have imagined. You're never alone. When you have a baby inside you you are not alone. It's a person.

To procure the abortion it becomes necessary for Piet to surrender his own wife Angela to Freddy who has access to the abortionist. Embarked upon his course Piet does not stop at this act which destroys his own marriage irretrievably. Foxy's feelings at the time of the abortion are then described through Piet:

> Not until days later, after Foxy had survived the forty-eight hours alone in the house with Toby and the test of Ken's return from Chicago, did Piet learn, not from Freddy but from her as told by Freddy, that at the moment of anesthesia she had panicked; she had tried to strike the Negress pressing the sweet, sweet mask to her face and through the first waves of ether had continued to cry that she should go

home, that she was supposed to have this baby, that the child's father was coming to smash the door down with a hammer and would stop them.

Updike's only comment as an author is given as Piet then goes to Foxy's house: "Death, once invited in, leaves his muddy bootprints everywhere." The elements of the experience of abortion are here: the hatred of the depersonalized burden growing, willy-nilly, in the womb; the sense of a baby, a person, one's own child; the desperate desire to be rid of the burden extinguishing all other considerations; the ineffectual hope of delivery the moment before the child's death. A mask covers the human face of the mother. Symbolically the abortion seals a course of infidelity. Conclusively it becomes death personified. . . .

---

15. On the Moral and Legal Status of Abortion

Mary Anne Warren

Mary Anne Warren argues that if the fetus is assumed to be a person, there are a wide range of cases in which abortion cannot be defended. To provide such a defense, Warren sets out five criteria for being a person she feels should be acceptable to antiabortionists and proabortionists alike. Appealing to these criteria, she contends that fetuses, even when their potentiality is taken into account, do not sufficiently resemble persons to have a significant right to life.

In a "Postscript" to her article, she defends her view against the objection that it would justify infanticide. Although by her criteria newborn infants would not have a significant right to life, she claims that infanticide would still not be permissible, so long as there are people willing to care and provide for the well-being of such infants.

We will be concerned with both the moral status of abortion, which for our purposes we may define as the act which a woman performs in voluntarily terminating, or allowing another person to terminate, her pregnancy, and the legal status which is appropriate for this act. I will argue that, while it is not possible to produce a satisfactory defense of a woman's right to obtain an abortion without showing that a fetus is not a human being, in the morally relevant sense of that term, we ought not to conclude that the difficulties involved in determining whether or not a fetus is human

From "On the Moral and Legal Status of Abortion." Copyright 1973 The Monist, LaSalle, Illinois. Reprinted from vol. 57, no. 4, Oct. 1973 by permission; and "Postscript on Infanticide," in Today's Moral Problems, edited by Richard Wasserstrom (1979), pp. 135–136. Reprinted by permission of the author and the editor.

make it impossible to produce any satisfactory solution to the problem of the moral status of abortion. For it is possible to show that, on the basis of intuitions which we may expect even the opponents of abortion to share, a fetus is not a person, and hence not the sort of entity to which it is proper to ascribe full moral rights.

Of course, while some philosophers would deny the possibility of any such proof,[1] others will deny that there is any need for it, since the moral permissibility of abortion appears to them to be too obvious to require proof. But the inadequacy of this attitude should be evident from the fact that both the friends and the foes of abortion consider their position to be morally self-evident. Because proabortionists have never adequately come to grips with the conceptual issues surrounding abortion, most, if not all, of the arguments which they advance in opposition to laws restricting access to abortion fail to refute or even weaken the traditional antiabortion argument, i.e., that a fetus is a human being, and therefore abortion is murder.

These arguments are typically of one of two sorts. Either they point to the terrible side effects of the restrictive laws, e.g., the deaths due to illegal abortions, and the fact that it is poor women who suffer the most as a result of these laws, or else they state that to deny a woman access to abortion is to deprive her of her right to control her own body. Unfortunately, however, the fact that restricting access to abortion has tragic side effects does not, in itself, show that the restrictions are unjustified, since murder is wrong regardless of the consequences of prohibiting it; and the appeal to the right to control one's body, which is generally construed as a property right, is at best a rather feeble argument for the permissibility of abortion. Mere ownership does not give me the right to kill innocent people whom I find on my property, and indeed I am apt to be held responsible if such people injure themselves while on my property. It is equally unclear that I have any moral right to expel an innocent person from my property when I know that doing so will result in his death.

Furthermore, it is probably inappropriate to describe a woman's body as her property, since it seems natural to hold that a person is something distinct from her property, but not from her body. Even those who would object to the identification of a person with his body, or with the conjunction of his body and his mind, must admit that it would be very odd to describe, say, breaking a leg, as damaging one's property, and much more appropriate to describe it as injuring one*self*. Thus it is probably a mistake to argue that the right to obtain an abortion is in any way derived from the right to own and regulate property.

But however we wish to construe the right to abortion, we cannot hope to convince those who consider abortion a form of murder of the existence of any such right unless we are able to produce a clear and convincing refutation of the traditional antiabortion argument, and this has not, to my knowledge, been done.

With respect to the two most vital issues which that argument involves, i.e., the humanity of the fetus and its implication for the moral status of abortion, confusion has prevailed on both sides of the dispute.

Thus, both proabortionists and antiabortionists have tended to abstract the question of whether abortion is wrong to that of whether it is wrong to destroy a fetus, just as though the rights of another person were not necessarily involved. This mistaken abstraction has led to the almost universal assumption that if a fetus is a human being, with a right to life, then it follows immediately that abortion is wrong (except perhaps when necessary to save the woman's life), and that it ought to be prohibited. It has also been generally assumed that unless the question about the status of the fetus is answered, the moral status of abortion cannot possibly be determined. . . . John Noonan is correct in saying that "the fundamental question in the long history of abortion is, How do you determine the humanity of a being?"[2] He summarizes his own antiabortion argument, which is a version of the official position of the Catholic Church, as follows:

> . . . it is wrong to kill humans, however poor, weak, defenseless, and lacking in opportunity to develop their potential they may be. It is therefore morally wrong to kill Biafrans. Similarly, it is morally wrong to kill embryos.[3]

Noonan bases his claim that fetuses are human upon what he calls the theologians' criterion of humanity: that whoever is conceived of human beings is human. But although he argues at length for the appropriateness of this criterion, he never questions the assumption that if a fetus is human then abortion is wrong for exactly the same reason that murder is wrong.

Judith Thomson is, in fact, the only writer I am aware of who has seriously questioned this assumption; she has argued that, even if we grant the antiabortionist his claim that a fetus is a human being, with the same right to life as any other human being, we can still demonstrate that, in at least some and perhaps most cases, a woman is under no moral obligation to complete an unwanted pregnancy.[4] Her argument is worth examining, since if it holds up it may enable us to establish the moral permissibility of abortion without becoming involved in problems about what entitles an entity to be considered human, and accorded full moral rights. To be able to do this would be a great gain in the power and simplicity of the proabortion position, since, although I will argue that these problems can be solved at least as decisively as can any other moral problem, we should certainly be pleased to be able to avoid having to solve them as part of the justification of abortion.

On the other hand, even if Thomson's argument does not hold up, her insight, i.e., that it requires *argument* to show that if fetuses are human then abortion is properly classified as murder, is an extremely valuable one. The assumption she attacks is particularly invidious, for it amounts to the decision that it is appropriate, in deciding the moral status of abortion, to leave the rights of the pregnant woman out of consideration entirely, except possibly when her life is threatened. Obviously, this will not do; determining what moral rights, if any, a fetus possesses is only the first step in determining the moral status of abortion. Step two, which is at least equally essential, is finding a just solution to the conflict between whatever rights the fetus may have, and the rights of the woman who is unwillingly pregnant. While the historical error has been to pay far too little attention to the second step, Ms. Thomson's suggestion is that if we look at the second step first we may find that a woman has a right to obtain an abortion *regardless* of what rights the fetus has.

Our own inquiry will also have two stages. In Section I, we will consider whether or not it is possible to establish that abortion is morally permissible even on the assumption that a fetus is an entity with a full-fledged right to life. I will argue that in fact this cannot be established, at least not with the conclusiveness which is essential to our hopes of convincing those who are skeptical about the morality of abortion, and that we therefore cannot avoid dealing with the question of whether or not a fetus really does have the same right to life as a (more fully developed) human being.

In Section II, I will propose an answer to this question, namely, that a fetus cannot be considered a member of the moral community, the set of beings with full and equal moral rights, for the simple reason that it is not a person, and that it is personhood, and not genetic humanity, i.e., humanity as defined by Noonan, which is the basis for membership in this community. I will argue that a fetus, whatever its stage of development, satisfies none of the basic criteria of personhood, and is not even enough *like* a person to be accorded even some of the same rights on the basis of this resemblance. Nor, as we will see, is a fetus's *potential* personhood a threat to the morality of abortion, since, whatever the rights of potential people may be, they are invariably overridden in any conflict with the moral rights of actual people.

I

We turn now to Professor Thomson's case for the claim that even if a fetus has full moral rights, abortion is still morally permissible, at least sometimes, and for some reasons other than to save the woman's life. Her argument is based upon a clever, but I think faulty, analogy. She asks us to picture ourselves waking up one day, in bed with a famous violinist. Imagine that you have been kidnapped, and your bloodstream hooked up to that of the violinist, who happens to have an ailment which will certainly kill him unless he is permitted to share your kidneys for a period of nine months. No one else can save him, since you alone have the right type of blood. He will be unconscious all that time, and you will have to stay in bed with him, but after the nine months are over he may be unplugged, completely cured, that is, provided that you have cooperated.

Now then, she continues, what are your obligations in this situation? The antiabortionist, if he is consistent, will have to say that you are obligated to stay in bed with the violinist: for all people have a right to life, and violinists are people, and therefore it would be murder for you to disconnect yourself from him and let him die. But this is outrageous, and so there must be something wrong with the same argument when it is applied to abortion. It would certainly be commendable of you to agree to save the violinist, but it is absurd to suggest that your refusal to do so would be murder. His right to life does not obligate you to do whatever is required to keep him alive; nor does it justify anyone else in forcing you to do so. A law which required you to stay in bed with the violinist would clearly be an unjust law, since it is no proper function of the law to force unwilling people to make huge sacrifices for the sake of other people toward whom they have no such prior obligation.

Thomson concludes that, if this analogy is an apt one, then we can grant the anti-abortionist his claim that a fetus is a human being, and still hold that it is at least sometimes the case that a pregnant woman has the right to refuse to be a Good Samaritan towards the fetus, i.e., to obtain an abortion. For there is a great gap between the claim that X has a right to life, and the claim that Y is obligated to do whatever is necessary to keep X alive, let alone that he ought to be forced to do so. It is Y's duty to keep X alive only if he has somehow contracted a *special* obligation to do so; and a woman who is unwillingly pregnant, e.g., who was raped, has done nothing which obligates her to make the enormous sacrifice which is necessary to preserve the conceptus.

This argument is initially quite plausible, and in the extreme case of pregnancy due to rape is probably conclusive. Difficulties arise, however, when we try to specify more exactly the range of cases in which abortion is clearly justifiable even on the assumption that the fetus is human. Professor Thomson considers it a virtue of her argument that it does not enable us to conclude that abortion is *always* permissible. It would, she says, be "indecent" for a woman in her seventh month to obtain an abortion just to avoid having to postpone a trip to Europe. On the other hand, her argu-ment enables us to see that "a sick and desper-ately frightened schoolgirl pregnant due to rape may *of course* choose abortion, and that any law which rules this out is an insane law" (p. 65). So far, so good; but what are we to say about the woman who becomes pregnant not through rape but as a result of her own carelessness, or because of contraceptive fail-ure, or who gets pregnant intentionally and then changes her mind about wanting a child?

With respect to such cases, the violinist analo-gy is of much less use to the defender of the woman's right to obtain an abortion.

Indeed, the choice of a pregnancy due to rape, as an example of a case in which abortion is permissible even if a fetus is considered a human being, is extremely significant; for it is only in the case of pregnancy due to rape that the woman's situation is adequately analogous to the violinist case for our intuitions about the latter to transfer convincingly. The crucial difference between a pregnancy due to rape and the *normal* case of an unwanted pregnancy is that in the normal case we cannot claim that the woman is in no way responsible for her predicament; she could have remained chaste, or taken her pills more faithfully, or abstained on dangerous days, and so on. If, on the other hand, you are kidnapped by strangers, and hooked up to a strange violinist, then you are free of any shred of responsibility for the situation, on the basis of which it could be argued that you are obligated to keep the violinist alive. Only when her pregnancy is due to rape is a woman clearly just as nonrespon-sible.[5]

Consequently, there is room for the anti-abortionist to argue that in the normal case of unwanted pregnancy a woman has, by her own actions, assumed responsibility for the fetus. For if X behaves in a way which he could have avoided, and which he knows involves, let us say, a 1 percent chance of bringing into existence a human being, with a right to life, and does so knowing that if this should hap-pen then that human being will perish unless X does certain things to keep him alive, then it is by no means clear that when it does happen X is free of any obligation to what he knew in advance would be required to keep that hu-man being alive.

The plausibility of such an argument is enough to show that the Thomson analogy can provide a clear and persuasive defense of a woman's right to obtain an abortion only with respect to those cases in which the woman is in no way responsible for her pregnancy, e.g., where it is due to rape. In all other cases, we would almost certainly conclude that it was necessary to look carefully at the particular circumstances in order to determine the ex-tent of the woman's responsibility, and hence the extent of her obligation. This is an extremely unsatisfactory outcome, from the viewpoint of the opponents of restrictive abortion laws, most of whom are convinced that a woman has a right to obtain an abortion regardless of how and why she got pregnant.

Of course a supporter of the violinist analogy might point out that it is absurd to suggest that forgetting her pill one day might be sufficient to obligate a woman to complete an unwanted pregnancy. And indeed it *is* absurd to suggest this. As we will see, the moral right to obtain an abortion is not in the least dependent upon the extent to which the woman is responsible for her pregnancy. But unfortunately, once we allow the assumption that a fetus has full moral rights, we cannot avoid taking this absurd suggestion seriously. Perhaps we can make this point more clear by altering the violinist story just enough to make it more analogous to a normal unwanted pregnancy and less to a pregnancy due to rape, and then seeing whether it is still obvious that you are not obligated to stay in bed with the fellow.

Suppose, then, that violinists are peculiarly prone to the sort of illness the only cure for which is the use of someone else's bloodstream for nine months, and that because of this there has been formed a society of music lovers who agree that whenever a violinist is stricken they will draw lots and the loser will, by some means, be made the one and only person capable of saving him. Now then, would you be obligated to cooperate in curing the violinist if you had voluntarily joined this society, knowing the possible consequences, and then your name had been drawn and you had been kidnapped? Admittedly, you did not promise ahead of time that you would, but you did deliberately place yourself in a position in which it might happen that a human life would be lost if you did not. Surely this is at least a prima facie reason for supposing that you have an obligation to stay in bed with the violinist. Suppose that you had gotten your name drawn deliberately; surely *that* would be quite a strong reason for thinking that you had such an obligation.

It might be suggested that there is one important disanalogy between the modified violinist case and the case of an unwanted pregnancy, which makes the woman's responsibility significantly less, namely, the fact that the fetus *comes into existence* as the result of the woman's actions. This fact might give her a right to refuse to keep it alive, whereas she would not have had this right had it existed previously, independently, and then as a result of her actions become dependent upon her for its survival.

My own intuition, however, is that X has no more right to bring into existence, either deliberately or as a foreseeable result of actions he could have avoided, a being with full moral rights (Y), and then refuse to do what he knew beforehand would be required to keep that being alive, than he has to enter into an agreement with an existing person, whereby he may be called upon to save that person's life, and then refuse to do so when so called upon. Thus, X's responsibility for Y's existence does not seem to lessen his obligation to keep Y alive, if he is also responsible for Y's being in a situation in which only he can save him.

Whether or not this intuition is entirely correct, it brings us back once again to the conclusion that once we allow the assumption that a fetus has full moral rights it becomes an extremely complex and difficult question whether and when abortion is justifiable. Thus the Thomson analogy cannot help us produce a clear and persuasive proof of the moral permissibility of abortion. Nor will the opponents of the restrictive laws thank us for anything less; for their conviction (for the most part) is that abortion is obviously *not* a morally serious and extremely unfortunate, even though sometimes justified, act comparable to killing in self-defense or to letting the violinist die, but rather is closer to being a morally neutral act, like cutting one's hair.

The basis of this conviction, I believe, is the realization that a fetus is not a person, and thus does not have a full-fledged right to life. Perhaps the reason why this claim has been so inadequately defended is that it seems self-evident to those who accept it. And so it is, insofar as it follows from what I take to be perfectly obvious claims about the nature of personhood and about the proper grounds for ascribing moral rights, claims which ought, indeed, to be obvious to both the friends and foes of abortion. Nevertheless, it is worth examining these claims, and showing how they demonstrate the moral innocuousness of abortion, since this apparently has not been adequately done before.

II

The question which we must answer in order to produce a satisfactory solution to the problem of the moral status of abortion is this: How are we to define the moral community, the set of beings with full and equal moral rights, such that we can decide whether a human fetus is a member of this community or not? What sort of entity, exactly, has the inalienable rights to life, liberty, and the pursuit of happiness? Jefferson attributed these rights to all *men*, and it may or may not be fair to suggest that he intended to attribute them *only* to men. Perhaps he ought to have attributed them to all human beings. If so, then we arrive, first, at Noonan's problem of defining what makes a being human, and, second, at the equally vital question which Noonan does not consider, namely, What reason is there for identifying the moral community with the set of all human beings, in whatever way we have chosen to define that term?

1. On the Definition of "Human"

One reason why this vital second question is so frequently overlooked in the debate over the moral status of abortion is that the term "human" has two distinct, but not often distinguished, senses. This fact results in a slide of meaning, which serves to conceal the fallaciousness of the traditional argument that since (1) it is wrong to kill innocent human beings, and (2) fetuses are innocent human beings, then (3) it is wrong to kill fetuses. For if "human" is used in the same sense in both (1) and (2) then, whichever of the two senses is meant, one of these premises is question-begging. And if it is used in two different senses then of course the conclusion doesn't follow.

Thus, (1) is a self-evident moral truth,[6] and avoids begging the question about abortion,

only if "human being" is used to mean something like "a full-fledged member of the moral community." (It may or may not also be meant to refer exclusively to members of the species *Homo sapiens*.) *We may call this the moral* sense of "human." It is not to be confused with what we will call the *genetic* sense, i.e., the sense in which *any* member of the species is a human being, and no member of any other species could be. If (1) is acceptable only if the moral sense is intended, (2) is non-question-begging only if what is intended is the genetic sense.

In "Deciding Who Is Human," Noonan argues for the classification of fetuses with human beings by pointing to the presence of the full genetic code, and the potential capacity for rational thought (p. 135). It is clear that what he needs to show, for his version of the traditional argument to be valid, is that fetuses are human in the moral sense, the sense in which it is analytically true that all human beings have full moral rights. But, in the absence of any argument showing that whatever is genetically human is also morally human, and he gives none, nothing more than genetic humanity can be demonstrated by the presence of the human genetic code. And, as we will see, the *potential* capacity for rational thought can at most show that an entity has the potential for *becoming* human in the moral sense.

2. Defining the Moral Community

Can it be established that genetic humanity is sufficient for moral humanity? I think that there are very good reasons for not defining the moral community in this way. I would like to suggest an alternative way of defining the moral community, which I will argue for only to the extent of explaining why it is, or should be, self-evident. The suggestion is simply that the moral community consists of all and only *people*, rather than all and only human beings;[7] and probably the best way of demonstrating its self-evidence is by considering the concept of personhood, to see what sorts of entity are and are not persons, and what the decision that a being is or is not a person implies about its moral rights.

What characteristics entitle an entity to be

considered a person? This is obviously not the place to attempt a complete analysis of the concept of personhood, but we do not need such a fully adequate analysis just to determine whether and why a fetus is or isn't a person. All we need is a rough and approximate list of the most basic criteria of personhood, and some idea of which, or how many, of these an entity must satisfy in order to properly be considered a person.

In searching for such criteria, it is useful to look beyond the set of people with whom we are acquainted, and ask how we would decide whether a totally alien being was a person or not. (For we have no right to assume that genetic humanity is necessary for personhood.) Imagine a space traveler who lands on an unknown planet and encounters a race of beings utterly unlike any he has ever seen or heard of. If he wants to be sure of behaving morally toward these beings, he has to somehow decide whether they are people, and hence have full moral rights, or whether they are the sort of thing which he need not feel guilty about treating as, for example, a source of food.

How should he go about making this decision? If he has some anthropological background, he might look for such things as religion, art, and the manufacturing of tools, weapons, or shelters, since these factors have been used to distinguish our human from our prehuman ancestors, in what seems to be closer to the moral than the genetic sense of "human." And no doubt he would be right to consider the presence of such factors as good evidence that the alien beings were people, and morally human. It would, however, be overly anthropocentric of him to take the absence of these things as adequate evidence that they were not, since we can imagine people who have progressed beyond, or evolved without ever developing, these cultural characteristics.

I suggest that the traits which are most central to the concept of personhood, or humanity in the moral sense, are, very roughly, the following:

1. consciousness (of objects and events external and/or internal to the being), and in particular the capacity to feel pain;

2. reasoning (the *developed* capacity to solve new and relatively complex problems);

3. self-motivated activity (activity which is relatively independent of either genetic or direct external control);

4. the capacity to communicate, by whatever means, messages of an indefinite variety of types, that is, not just with an indefinite number of possible contents, but on indefinitely many possible topics;

5. the presence of self-concepts, and self-awareness, either individual or racial, or both.

Admittedly, there are apt to be a great many problems involved in formulating precise definitions of these criteria, let alone in developing universally valid behavioral criteria for deciding when they apply. But I will assume that both we and our explorer know approximately what (1)–(5) mean, and that he is also able to determine whether or not they apply. How, then, should he use his findings to decide whether or not the alien beings are people? We needn't suppose that an entity must have *all* of these attributes to be properly considered a person; (1) and (2) alone may well be sufficient for personhood, and quite probably (1)–(3) are sufficient. Neither do we need to insist that any one of these criteria is *necessary* for personhood, although once again (1) and (2) look like fairly good candidates for necessary conditions, as does (3), if "activity" is construed so as to include the activity of reasoning.

All we need to claim, to demonstrate that a fetus is not a person, is that any being which satisfies *none* of (1)–(5) is certainly not a person. I consider this claim to be so obvious that I think anyone who denied it, and claimed that a being which satisfied none of (1)–(5) was a person all the same, would thereby demonstrate that he had no notion at all of what a person is—perhaps because he had confused the concept of a person with that of genetic humanity. If the opponents of abortion were to deny the appropriateness of these five criteria, I do not know what further arguments would convince them. We would probably have to admit that our conceptual schemes were indeed irreconcilably different, and that our dispute could not be settled objectively.

I do not expect this to happen, however, since I think that the concept of a person is one which is very nearly universal (to people), and that it is common to both proabortionists and antiabortionists, even though neither group has fully realized the relevance of this concept to the resolution of their dispute. Furthermore, I think that on reflection even the antiabortionists ought to agree not only that (1)–(5) are central to the concept of personhood, but also that it is a part of this concept that all and only people have full moral rights. The concept of a person is in part a moral concept; once we have admitted that X is a person we have recognized, even if we have not agreed to respect, X's right to be treated as a member of the moral community. It is true that the claim that X is a *human being* is more commonly voiced as part of an appeal to treat X decently than is the claim that X is a person, but this is either because "human being" is here used in the sense which implies personhood, or because the genetic and moral senses of "human" have been confused.

Now if (1)–(5) are indeed the primary criteria of personhood, then it is clear that genetic humanity is neither necessary nor sufficient for establishing that an entity is a person. Some human beings are not people, and there may well be people who are not human beings. A man or woman whose consciousness has been permanently obliterated but who remains alive is a human being which is no longer a person; defective human beings, with no appreciable mental capacity, are not and presumably never will be people; and a fetus is a human being which is not yet a person, and which therefore cannot coherently be said to have full moral rights. Citizens of the next century should be prepared to recognize highly advanced, self-aware robots or computers, should such be developed, and intelligent inhabitants of other worlds, should such be found, as people in the fullest sense, and to respect their moral rights. But to ascribe full moral rights to an entity which is not a person is as absurd as to ascribe moral obligations and responsibilities to such an entity.

3. Fetal Development and the Right to Life

Two problems arise in the application of these suggestions for the definition of the moral community to the determination of the precise moral status of a human fetus. Given that the paradigm example of a person is a normal adult human being, then (1) How like this paradigm, in particular how far advanced since conception, does a human being need to be before it begins to have a right to life by virtue, not of being fully a person as of yet, but of being *like* a person? and (2) To what extent, if any, does the fact that a fetus has the *potential* for becoming a person endow it with some of the same rights? Each of these questions requires some comment.

In answering the first question, we need not attempt a detailed consideration of the moral rights of organisms which are not developed enough, aware enough, intelligent enough, etc., to be considered people, but which resemble people in some respects. It does seem reasonable to suggest that the more like a person, in the relevant respects, a being is, the stronger is the case for regarding it as having a right to life, and indeed the stronger its right to life is. Thus we ought to take seriously the suggestion that, insofar as "the human individual develops biologically in a continuous fashion . . . the rights of a human person might develop in the same way."[8] But we must keep in mind that the attributes which are relevant in determining whether or not an entity is enough like a person to be regarded as having some of the same moral rights are no different from those which are relevant to determining whether or not it is fully a person—i.e., are no different from (1)–(5)—and that being genetically human, or having recognizably human facial and other physical features, or detectable brain activity, or the capacity to survive outside the uterus, is simply not among these relevant attributes.

Thus it is clear that even though a seven- or eight-month fetus has features which make it apt to arouse in us almost the same powerful protective instinct as is commonly aroused by a small infant, nevertheless it is not significantly more personlike than is a very small embryo.

It is *somewhat* more personlike; it can apparently feel and respond to pain, and it may even have a rudimentary form of consciousness, insofar as its brain is quite active. Nevertheless, it seems safe to say that it is not fully conscious, in the way that an infant of a few months is, and that it cannot reason, or communicate messages of indefinitely many sorts, does not engage in self-motivated activity, and has no self-awareness. Thus, in the *relevant* respects, a fetus, even a fully developed one, is considerably less personlike than is the average mature mammal, indeed the average fish. And I think that a rational person must conclude that if the right to life of a fetus is to be based upon its resemblance to a person, then it cannot be said to have any more right to life than, let us say, a newborn guppy (which also seems to be capable of feeling pain), and that a right of that magnitude could never override a woman's right to obtain an abortion, at any stage of her pregnancy.

There may, of course, be other arguments in favor of placing legal limits upon the stage of pregnancy in which an abortion may be performed. Given the relative safety of the new techniques of artificially inducing labor during the third trimester, the danger to the woman's life or health is no longer such an argument. Neither is the fact that people tend to respond to the thought of abortion in the later stages of pregnancy with emotional repulsion, since mere emotional responses cannot take the place of moral reasoning in determining what ought to be permitted. Nor, finally, is the frequently heard argument that legalizing abortion, especially late in the pregnancy, may erode the level of respect for human life, leading, perhaps, to an increase in unjustified euthanasia and other crimes. For this threat, if it is a threat, can be better met by educating people to the kinds of moral distinctions which we are making here than by limiting access to abortion (which limitation may, in its disregard for the rights of women, be just as damaging to the level of respect for human rights).

Thus, since the fact that even a fully developed fetus is not personlike enough to have any significant right to life on the basis of its personlikeness shows that no legal restrictions upon the stage of pregnancy in which an abortion may be performed can be justified on the grounds that we should protect the rights of the older fetus; and since there is no other apparent justification for such restrictions, we may conclude that they are entirely unjustified. Whether or not it would be *indecent* (whatever that means) for a woman in her seventh month to obtain an abortion just to avoid having to postpone a trip to Europe, it would not, in itself, be *immoral*, and therefore it ought to be permitted.

4. Potential Personhood and the Right to Life

We have seen that a fetus does not resemble a person in any way which can support the claim that it has even some of the same rights. But what about its *potential*, the fact that if nurtured and allowed to develop naturally it will very probably become a person? Doesn't that alone give it at least some right to life? It is hard to deny that the fact that an entity is a potential person is a strong prima facie reason for not destroying it; but we need not conclude from this that a potential person has a right to life, by virtue of that potential. It may be that our feeling that it is better, other things being equal, not to destroy a potential person is better explained by the fact that potential people are still (felt to be) an invaluable resource, not to be lightly squandered. Surely, if every speck of dust were a potential person, we would be much less apt to conclude that every potential person has a right to become actual.

Still, we do not need to insist that a potential person has no right to life whatever. There may well be something immoral, and not just imprudent, about wantonly destroying potential people, when doing so isn't necessary to protect anyone's rights. But even if a potential person does have some prima facie right to life, such a right could not possibly outweigh the right of a woman to obtain an abortion, since the rights of any actual person invariably outweigh those of any potential person, whenever the two conflict. Since this may not be immediately obvious in the case of a human fetus, let us look at another case.

Suppose that our space explorer falls into the hands of an alien culture, whose scientists decide to create a few hundred thousand or more human beings, by breaking his body into its component cells, and using these to create fully developed human beings, with, of course, his genetic code. We may imagine that each of these newly created men will have all of the original man's abilities, skills, knowledge, and so on, and also have an individual self-concept, in short that each of them will be a bona fide (though hardly unique) person. Imagine that the whole project will take only seconds, and that its chances of success are extremely high, and that our explorer knows all of this, and also knows that these people will be treated fairly. I maintain that in such a situation he would have every right to escape if he could, and thus to deprive all of these potential people of their potential lives; for his right to life outweighs all of theirs together, in spite of the fact that they are all genetically human, all innocent, and all have a very high probability of becoming people very soon, if only he refrains from acting.

Indeed, I think he would have a right to escape even if it were not his life which the alien scientists planned to take, but only a year of his freedom, or, indeed, only a day. Nor would he be obligated to stay if he had gotten captured (thus bringing all these people-potentials into existence) because of his own carelessness, or even if he had done so deliberately, knowing the consequences. Regardless of how he got captured, he is not morally obligated to remain in captivity for *any* period of time for the sake of permitting any number of potential people to come into actuality, so great is the margin by which one actual person's right to liberty outweighs whatever right to life even a hundred thousand potential people have. And it seems reasonable to conclude that the rights of a woman will outweigh by a similar margin whatever right to life a fetus may have by virtue of its potential personhood.

Thus, neither a fetus's resemblance to a person, nor its potential for becoming a person provides any basis whatever for the claim that it has any significant right to life. Consequently, a woman's right to protect her health, happiness, freedom, and even her life,[9] by terminating an unwanted pregnancy, will always override whatever right to life it

may be appropriate to ascribe to a fetus, even a fully developed one. And thus, in the absence of any overwhelming social need for every possible child, the laws which restrict the right to obtain an abortion, or limit the period of pregnancy during which an abortion may be performed, are a wholly unjustified violation of a woman's most basic moral and constitutional rights.[10] . . .

Postscript on Infanticide

Since the publication of this article, many people have written to point out that my argument appears to justify not only abortion, but infanticide as well. For a newborn infant is not significantly more personlike than an advanced fetus, and consequently it would seem that if the destruction of the latter is permissible so too must be that of the former. Inasmuch as most people, regardless of how they feel about the morality of abortion, consider infanticide a form of murder, this might appear to represent a serious flaw in my argument.

Now, if I am right in holding that it is only people who have a full-fledged right to life, and who can be murdered, and if the criteria of personhood are as I have described them, then it obviously follows that killing a newborn infant isn't murder. It does *not* follow, however, that infanticide is permissible, for two reasons. In the first place, it would be wrong, at least in this country and in this period of history, and other things being equal, to kill a newborn infant, because even if its parents do not want it and would not suffer from its destruction, there are other people who would like to have it, and would, in all probability, be deprived of a great deal of pleasure by its destruction. Thus, infanticide is wrong for reasons analogous to those which make it wrong to wantonly destroy natural resources, or great works of art.

Second, most people, at least in this country, value infants and would much prefer that they be preserved, even if foster parents are not immediately available. Most of us would rather be taxed to support orphanages than allow unwanted infants to be destroyed. So long as there are people who want an infant preserved, and who are willing and able to provide the means of caring for it, under reasonably humane conditions, it is, *ceteris parabis,* wrong to destroy it.

But, it might be replied, if this argument shows that infanticide is wrong, at least at this time and in this country, doesn't it also show that abortion is wrong? After all, many people value fetuses, are disturbed by their destruction, and would much prefer that they be preserved, even at some cost to themselves. Furthermore, as a potential source of pleasure to some foster family, a fetus is just as valuable as an infant. There is, however, a crucial difference between the two cases: so long as the fetus is unborn, its preservation, contrary to the wishes of the pregnant woman, violates her rights to freedom, happiness, and self-determination. Her rights override the rights of those who would like the fetus preserved, just as if someone's life or limb is threatened by a wild animal, his right to protect himself by destroying the animal overrides the rights of those who would prefer that the animal not be harmed.

The minute the infant is born, however, its preservation no longer violates any of its mother's rights, even if she wants it destroyed, because she is free to put it up for adoption. Consequently, while the moment of birth does not mark any sharp discontinuity in the degree to which an infant possesses the right to life, it does mark the end of its mother's right to determine its fate. Indeed, if abortion could be performed without killing the fetus, she would never possess the right to have the fetus destroyed, for the same reasons that she has no right to have an infant destroyed.

On the other hand, it follows from my argument that when an unwanted or defective infant is born into a society which cannot afford and/or is not willing to care for it, then its destruction is permissible. This conclusion will, no doubt, strike many people as heartless and immoral; but remember that the very existence of people who feel this way, and who are willing and able to provide care for unwanted infants, is reason enough to conclude that they should be preserved.

Notes

1. For example, Roger Wertheimer, who in "Understanding the Abortion Argument" (*Philosophy and Public Affairs,* 1, no. 1 [Fall, 1971], 67–95), argues that the problem of the moral status of abortion is insoluble, in that the dispute over the status of the fetus is not a question of fact at all, but only a question of how one responds to the facts.

2. John Noonan, "Abortion and the Catholic Church: A Summary History," *Natural Law Forum,* 12 (1967), 125.

3. John Noonan, "Deciding Who Is Human," *Natural Law Forum,* 13 (1968), 134.

4. "A Defense of Abortion."

5. We may safely ignore the fact that she might have avoided getting raped, e.g., by carrying a gun, since by similar means you might likewise have avoided getting kidnapped, and in neither case does the victim's failure to take all possible precautions against a highly unlikely event (as opposed to reasonable precautions against a rather likely event) mean that he is morally responsible for what happens.

6. Of course, the principle that it is (always) wrong to kill innocent human beings is in need of many other modifications, e.g., that it may be permissible to do so to save a greater number of other innocent human beings, but we may safely ignore these complications here.

7. From here on, we will use "human" to mean genetically human, since the moral sense seems closely connected to, and perhaps derived from, the assumption that genetic humanity is sufficient for membership in the moral community.

8. Thomas L. Hayes, "A Biological View," *Commonweal,* 85 (March 17, 1967), 677–78; quoted by Daniel Callahan, in *Abortion, Law, Choice, and Morality* (London: Macmillan & Co., 1970).

9. That is, insofar as the death rate, for the woman, is higher for childbirth than for early abortion.

10. My thanks to the following people, who were kind enough to read and criticize an earlier version of this paper: Herbert Gold, Gene Glass, Anne Lauterbach, Judith Thomson, Mary Mothersill, and Timothy Binkley.

16. Abortion and the Concept of a Person

Jane English

According to Jane English, our concept of a person is not sharp or decisive enough to bear the weight of a solution to the abortion controversy. However, she argues that even if the fetus is a full-fledged person, there are still cases in which abortion would be justified to prevent harm or death to the pregnant woman. Similarly, English argues that even if the fetus is not a person, there are still cases, at least in the late months of pregnancy, in which abortion would not be justified because of the fetus's resemblance to a person.

The abortion debate rages on. Yet the two most popular positions seem to be clearly mistaken. Conservatives maintain that a human life begins at conception and that therefore abortion must be wrong because it is murder. But not all killings of humans are murders. Most notably, self-defense may justify even the killing of an innocent person.

Liberals, on the other hand, are just as mistaken in their argument that since a fetus does not become a person until birth, a woman may do whatever she pleases in and to her own body. First, you cannot do as you please with your own body if it affects other people adversely.[1] Second, if a fetus is not a person, that does not imply that you can do to it anything you wish. Animals, for example, are not persons, yet to kill or torture them for no reason at all is wrong.

At the center of the storm has been the issue of just when it is between ovulation and adulthood that a person appears on the scene. Conservatives draw the line at conception, liberals at birth. In this paper I first examine our concept of a person and conclude that no single criterion can capture the concept of a person and no sharp line can be drawn. Next I argue that if a fetus is a person, abortion is still justifiable in many cases; and if a fetus is not a person, killing it is still wrong in many cases. To a large extent, these two solutions are in agreement. I conclude that our concept of a person cannot and need not bear the weight

From the *Canadian Journal of Philosophy* 5, no. 2 (October 1975), pp. 233–243. Reprinted with permission of the publisher.

that the abortion controversy has thrust upon it.

I

The several factions in the abortion argument have drawn battle lines around various proposed criteria for determining what is and what is not a person. For example, Mary Anne Warren[2] lists five features (capacities for reasoning, self-awareness, complex communication, etc.) as her criteria for personhood and argues for the permissibility of abortion because a fetus falls outside this concept. Baruch Brody[3] uses brain waves. Michael Tooley[4] picks having-a-concept-of-self as his criterion and concludes that infanticide and abortion are justifiable, while the killing of adult animals is not. On the other side, Paul Ramsey[5] claims a certain gene structure is the defining characteristic. John Noonan[6] prefers conceived-of-humans and presents counterexamples to various other candidate criteria. For instance, he argues against viability as the criterion because the newborn and infirm would then be non-persons, since they cannot live without the aid of others. He rejects any criterion that calls upon the sorts of sentiments a being can evoke in adults on the grounds that this would allow us to exclude other races as non-persons if we could just view them sufficiently unsentimentally.

These approaches are typical: foes of abortion propose sufficient conditions for personhood which fetuses satisfy, while friends of abortion counter with necessary conditions for personhood which fetuses lack. But these both presuppose that the concept of a person can be captured in a strait jacket of necessary and/or sufficient conditions.[7] Rather, "person" is a cluster of features, of which rationality, having a self-concept and being conceived of humans are only part.

What is typical of persons? Within our concept of a person we include, first, certain biological factors: descended from humans, having a certain genetic makeup, having a head, hands, arms, eyes, capable of locomotion, breathing, eating, sleeping. There are psychological factors: sentience, perception, having a concept of self and of one's own interests and desires, the ability to use tools, the ability to use language or symbol systems, the ability to joke, to be angry, to doubt. There are rationality factors: the ability to reason and draw conclusions, the ability to generalize and to learn from past experience, the ability to sacrifice present interests for greater gains in the future. There are social factors: the ability to work in groups and respond to peer pressures, the ability to recognize and consider as valuable the interests of others, seeing oneself as one among "other minds," the ability to sympathize, encourage, love, the ability to evoke from others the responses of sympathy, encouragement, love, the ability to work with others for mutual advantage. Then there are legal factors: being subject to the law and protected by it, having the ability to sue and enter contracts, being counted in the census, having a name and citizenship, the ability to own property, inherit, and so forth.

Now the point is not that this list is incomplete, or that you can find counterinstances to each of its points. People typically exhibit rationality, for instance, but someone who was irrational would not thereby fail to qualify as a person. On the other hand, something could exhibit the majority of these features and still fail to be a person, as an advanced robot might. There is no single core of necessary and sufficient features which we can draw upon with the assurance that they constitute what really makes a person; there are only features that are more or less typical.

This is not to say that no necessary or sufficient conditions can be given. Being alive is a necessary condition for being a person, and being a U.S. Senator is sufficient. But rather than falling inside a sufficient condition or outside a necessary one, a fetus lies in the penumbra region where our concept of a person is not so simple. For this reason I think a conclusive answer to the question whether a fetus is a person is unattainable.

Here we might note a family of simple fallacies that proceed by stating a necessary condition for personhood and showing that a fetus has that characteristic. This is a form of the fallacy of affirming the consequent. For example, some have mistakenly reasoned from the premise that a fetus is human (after all, it is a human fetus rather than, say, a canine fetus), to the conclusion that it is *a* human. Adding an equivocation on "being," we get the fallacious argument that since a fetus is something both living and human, it is a human being.

Nonetheless, it does seem clear that a fetus has very few of the above family of characteristics, whereas a newborn baby exhibits a much larger proportion of them—and a two-year-old has even more. Note that one traditional anti-abortion argument has centered on pointing out the many ways in which a fetus resembles a baby. They emphasize its development ("It already has ten fingers. . . .") without mentioning its dissimilarities to adults (it still has gills and a tail). They also try to evoke the sort of sympathy on our part that we only feel toward other persons ("Never to laugh . . . or feel the sunshine?"). This all seems to be a relevant way to argue, since its purpose is to persuade us that a fetus satisfies so many of the important features on the list that it ought to be treated as a person. Also note that a fetus near the time of birth satisfies many more of these factors than a fetus in the early months of development. This could provide reason for making distinctions among the different stages of pregnancy, as the U.S. Supreme Court has done.[8]

Historically, the time at which a person has been said to come into existence has varied widely. Muslims date personhood from fourteen days after conception. Some medievals followed Aristotle in placing ensoulment at forty days after conception for a male fetus and eighty days for a female fetus.[9] In European common law since the seventeenth century, abortion was considered the killing of a person only after quickening, the time when a pregnant woman first feels the fetus move on its own. Nor is this variety of opinions surprising. Biologically, a human being develops gradually. We shouldn't expect there to be any specific time or sharp dividing point when a person appears on the scene.

For these reasons I believe our concept of a person is not sharp or decisive enough to bear the weight of a solution to the abortion controversy. To use it to solve that problem is to clarify *obscurum per obscurius*.

II

Next let us consider what follows if a fetus is a person after all. Judith Jarvis Thomson's landmark article, "A Defense of Abortion,"[10] correctly points out that some additional argumentation is needed at this point in the conservative argument to bridge the gap between the premise that a fetus is an innocent person and the conclusion that killing it is always wrong. To arrive at this conclusion, we would need the additional premise that killing an innocent person is always wrong. But killing an innocent person is sometimes permissible, most notably in self-defense. Some examples may help draw out our intuitions or ordinary judgments about self-defense.

Suppose a mad scientist, for instance, hypnotized innocent people to jump out of the bushes and attack innocent passers-by with knives. If you are so attacked, we agree you have a right to kill the attacker in self-defense, if killing him is the only way to protect your life or to save yourself from serious injury. It does not seem to matter here that the attacker is not malicious but himself an innocent pawn, for your killing of him is not done in a spirit of retribution but only in self-defense.

How severe an injury may you inflict in self-defense? In part this depends upon the severity of the injury to be avoided: you may not shoot someone merely to avoid having your clothes torn. This might lead one to the mistaken conclusion that the defense may only

equal the threatened injury in severity; that to avoid death you may kill, but to avoid a black eye you may only inflict a black eye or the equivalent. Rather, our laws and customs seem to say that you may create an injury somewhat, but not enormously, greater than the injury to be avoided. To fend off an attack whose outcome would be as serious as rape, a severe beating or the loss of a finger, you may shoot; to avoid having your clothes torn, you may blacken an eye.

Aside from this, the injury you may inflict should only be the minimum necessary to deter or incapacitate the attacker. Even if you know he intends to kill you, you are not justified in shooting him if you could equally well save yourself by the simple expedient of running away. Self-defense is for the purpose of avoiding harms rather than equalizing harms.

Some cases of pregnancy present a parallel situation. Though the fetus is itself innocent, it may pose a threat to the pregnant woman's well-being, life prospects or health, mental or physical. If the pregnancy presents a slight threat to her interests, it seems self-defense cannot justify abortion. But if the threat is on a par with a serious beating or the loss of a finger, she may kill the fetus that poses such a threat, even if it is an innocent person. If a lesser harm to the fetus could have the same defensive effect, killing it would not be justified. It is unfortunate that the only way to free the woman from the pregnancy entails the death of the fetus (except in very late stages of pregnancy). Thus a self-defense model supports Thomson's point that the woman has a right only to be freed from the fetus, not a right to demand its death.[11]

The self-defense model is most helpful when we take the pregnant woman's point of view. In the pre-Thomson literature, abortion is often framed as a question for a third party: do you, a doctor, have a right to choose between the life of the woman and that of the fetus? Some have claimed that if you were a passer-by who witnessed a struggle between the innocent hypnotized attacker and his equally innocent victim, you would have no reason to kill either in defense of the other. They have concluded that the self-defense model implies that a woman may attempt to abort herself, but that a doctor should not assist her. I think the position of the third party is somewhat more complex. We do feel some inclination to intervene on behalf of the victim rather than the attacker, other things equal. But if both parties are innocent, other factors come into consideration. You would rush to the aid of your husband whether he was attacker or attackee. If a hypnotized famous violinist were attacking a skid row bum, we would try to save the individual who is of more value to society. These considerations would tend to support abortion in some cases.

But suppose you are a frail senior citizen who wishes to avoid being knifed by one of these innocent hypnotics, so you have hired a bodyguard to accompany you. If you are attacked, it is clear we believe that the bodyguard, acting as your agent, has a right to kill the attacker to save you from a serious beating. Your rights of self-defense are transferred to your agent. I suggest that we should similarly view the doctor as the pregnant woman's agent in carrying out a defense she is physically incapable of accomplishing herself.

Thanks to modern technology, the cases are rare in which pregnancy poses as clear a threat to a woman's bodily health as an attacker brandishing a switchblade. How does self-defense fare when more subtle, complex and long-range harms are involved?

To consider a somewhat fanciful example, suppose you are a highly trained surgeon when you are kidnapped by the hypnotic attacker. He says he does not intend to harm you but to take you back to the mad scientist who, it turns out, plans to hypnotize you to have a permanent mental block against all your knowledge of medicine. This would automatically destroy your career which would in turn have a serious adverse impact on your family, your personal relationships and your happiness. It seems to me that if the only way you can avoid this outcome is to shoot the innocent attacker, you are justified in so doing. You are defending yourself from a drastic injury to your life prospects. I think it is no exaggeration to claim that unwanted pregnancies (most obviously among teenagers) often have such adverse lifelong consequences as the surgeon's loss of livelihood.

Several parallels arise between various views on abortion and the self-defense model.

Let's suppose further that these hypnotized attackers only operate at night, so that it is well known that they can be avoided completely by the considerable inconvenience of never leaving your house after dark. One view is that since you could stay home at night, therefore if you go out and are selected by one of these hypnotized people, you have no right to defend yourself. This parallels the view that abstinence is the only acceptable way to avoid pregnancy. Others might hold that you ought to take along some defense such as Mace which will deter the hypnotized person without killing him, but that if this defense fails, you are obliged to submit to the resulting injury, no matter how severe it is. This parallels the view that contraception is all right but abortion is always wrong, even in cases of contraceptive failure.

A third view is that you may kill the hypnotized person only if he will actually kill you, but not if he will only injure you. This is like the position that abortion is permissible only if it is required to save a woman's life. Finally we have the view that it is all right to kill the attacker, even if only to avoid a very slight inconvenience to yourself and even if you knowingly walked down the very street where all these incidents have been taking place without taking along any Mace or protective escort. If we assume that a fetus is a person, this is the analogue of the view that abortion is always justifiable, "on demand."

The self-defense model allows us to see an important difference that exists between abortion and infanticide, even if a fetus is a person from conception. Many have argued that the only way to justify abortion without justifying infanticide would be to find some characteristic of personhood that is acquired at birth. Michael Tooley, for one, claims infanticide is justifiable because the really significant characteristics of person are acquired some time after birth. But all such approaches look to characteristics of the developing human and ignore the relation between the fetus and the woman. What if, after birth, the presence of an infant or the need to support it posed a grave threat to the woman's sanity or life prospects? She could escape this threat by the simple expedient of running away. So a solution that does not entail the death of the infant is available. Before birth, such solutions are not available because of the biological dependence of the fetus on the woman. Birth is the crucial point not because of any characteristics the fetus gains, but because after birth the woman can defend herself by a means less drastic than killing the infant. Hence self-defense can be used to justify abortion without necessarily thereby justifying infanticide.

III

On the other hand, supposing a fetus is not after all a person, would abortion always be morally permissible? Some opponents of abortion seem worried that if a fetus is not a full-fledged person, then we are justified in treating it in any way at all. However, this does not follow. Non-persons do get some consideration in our moral code, though of course they do not have the same rights as persons have (and in general they do not have moral responsibilities), and though their interests may be overridden by the interests of persons. Still, we cannot just treat them in any way at all.

Treatment of animals is a case in point. It is wrong to torture dogs for fun or to kill wild birds for no reason at all. It is wrong Period, even though dogs and birds do not have the same rights persons do. However, few people think it is wrong to use dogs as experimental animals, causing them considerable suffering in some cases, provided that the resulting research will probably bring discoveries of great benefit to people. And most of us think it all right to kill birds for food or to protect our crops. People's rights are different from the consideration we give to animals, then, for it is wrong to experiment on people, even if others might later benefit a great deal as a result of their suffering. You might volunteer to be a subject, but this would be supererogatory; you certainly have a right to refuse to be a medical guinea pig.

But how do we decide what you may or may not do to non-persons? This is a difficult problem, one for which I believe no adequate account exists. You do not want to say, for instance, that torturing dogs is all right when-

ever the sum of its effects on people is good—when it doesn't warp the sensibilities of the torturer so much that he mistreats people. If that were the case, it would be all right to torture dogs if you did it in private, or if the torturer lived on a desert island or died soon afterward, so that his actions had no effect on people. This is an inadequate account, because whatever moral consideration animals get, it has to be indefeasible, too. It will have to be a general proscription of certain actions, not merely a weighing of the impact on people on a case-by-case basis.

Rather, we need to distinguish two levels on which consequences of actions can be taken into account in moral reasoning. The traditional objections to Utilitarianism focus on the fact that it operates solely on the first level, taking all the consequences into account in particular cases only. Thus Utilitarianism is open to "desert island" and "lifeboat" counterexamples because these cases are rigged to make the consequences of actions severely limited.

Rawls's theory could be described as a teleological sort of theory, but with teleology operating on a higher level.[12] In choosing the principles to regulate society from the original position, his hypothetical choosers make their decision on the basis of the total consequences of various systems. Furthermore, they are constrained to choose a general set of rules which people can readily learn and apply. An ethical theory must operate by generating a set of sympathies and attitudes toward others which reinforces the functioning of that set of moral principles. Our prohibition against killing people operates by means of certain moral sentiments including sympathy, compassion and guilt. But if these attitudes are to form a coherent set, they carry us further: we tend to perform supererogatory actions, and we tend to feel similar compassion toward personlike non-persons.

It is crucial that psychological facts play a role here. Our psychological constitution makes it the case that for our ethical theory to work, it must prohibit certain treatment of non-persons which are significantly personlike. If our moral rules allowed people to treat some personlike non-persons in ways we do not want people to be treated, this would undermine the system of sympathies and attitudes that makes the ethical system work. For this reason, we would choose in the original position to make mistreatment of some sorts of animals wrong in general (not just wrong in the cases with public impact), even though animals are not themselves parties in the original position. Thus it makes sense that it is those animals whose appearance and behavior are most like those of people that get the most consideration in our moral scheme.

It is because of "coherence of attitudes," I think, that the similarity of a fetus to a baby is very significant. A fetus one week before birth is so much like a newborn baby in our psychological space that we cannot allow any cavalier treatment of the former while expecting full sympathy and nurturative support for the latter. Thus, I think that antiabortion forces are indeed giving their strongest arguments when they point to the similarities between a fetus and a baby, and when they try to evoke our emotional attachment to and sympathy for the fetus. An early horror story from New York about nurses who were expected to alternate between caring for six-week premature infants and disposing of viable 24-week aborted fetuses is just that—a horror story. These beings are so much alike that no one can be asked to draw a distinction and treat them so very differently.

Remember, however, that in the early weeks after conception, a fetus is very much unlike a person. It is hard to develop these feelings for a set of genes which doesn't yet have a head, hands, beating heart, response to touch or the ability to move by itself. Thus it seems to me that the alleged "slippery slope" between conception and birth is not so very slippery. In the early stages of pregnancy, abortion can hardly be compared to murder for psychological reasons, but in the latest stages it is psychologically akin to murder.

Another source of similarity is the bodily continuity between fetus and adult. Bodies play a surprisingly central role in our attitudes toward persons. One has only to think of the philosophical literature on how far physical identity suffices for personal identity or Wittgenstein's remark that the best picture of the human soul is the human body. Even after death, when all agree the body is no longer a person, we still observe elaborate customs of respect for the human body; like people who torture dogs, necrophiliacs are not to be trusted with people.[13] So it is appropriate that we show respect to a fetus as the body continuous with the body of a person. This is a degree of resemblance to persons that animals cannot rival.

Michael Tooley also utilizes a parallel with animals. He claims that it is always permissible to drown newborn kittens and draws conclusions about infanticide.[14] But it is only permissible to drown kittens when their survival would cause some hardship. Perhaps it would be a burden to feed and house six more cats or to find other homes for them. The alternative of letting them starve produces even more suffering than the drowning. Since the kittens get their rights secondhand, so to speak, *via* the need for coherence in our attitudes, their interests are often overridden by the interests of full-fledged persons. But if their survival would be no inconvenience to people at all, then it is wrong to drown them, *contra* Tooley.

Tooley's conclusions about abortion are wrong for the same reason. Even if a fetus is not a person, abortion is not always permissible because of the resemblance of a fetus to a person. I agree with Thomson that it would be wrong for a woman who is seven months pregnant to have an abortion just to avoid having to postpone a trip to Europe. In the early months of pregnancy when the fetus hardly resembles a baby at all, then, abortion is permissible whenever it is in the interests of the pregnant woman or her family. The reasons would only need to outweigh the pain and inconvenience of the abortion itself. In the middle months, when the fetus comes to resemble a person, abortion would be justifiable only when the continuation of the pregnancy or the birth of the child would cause harms—physical, psychological, economic or social—to the woman. In the late months of pregnancy, even on our current assumption that a fetus is not a person, abortion seems to be wrong except to save a woman from significant injury or death.

The Supreme Court has recognized similar gradations in the alleged slippery slope stretching between conception and birth. To this point, the present paper has been a discussion of the moral status of abortion only, not its legal status. In view of the great physical, financial and sometimes psychological costs of abortion, perhaps the legal arrangement most compatible with the proposed moral solution would be the absence of restrictions, that is, so-called abortion "on demand."

So I conclude, first, that application of our concept of a person will not suffice to settle the abortion issue. After all, the biological development of a human being is gradual. Second, whether a fetus is a person or not, abortion is justifiable early in pregnancy to avoid modest harms and seldom justifiable late in pregnancy except to avoid significant injury or death.[15]

Notes

1. We also have paternalistic laws which keep us from harming our own bodies even when no one else is affected. Ironically, antiabortion laws were originally designed to protect pregnant women from a dangerous but tempting procedure.

2. Mary Anne Warren, "On the Moral and Legal Status of Abortion," *Monist* 57 (1973), p. 55.

3. Baruch Brody, "Fetal Humanity and the Theory of Essentialism," in Robert Baker and Frederick Elliston, eds., *Philosophy and Sex* (Buffalo, N.Y., 1975).

4. Michael Tooley, "Abortion and Infanticide," *Philosophy and Public Affairs* 2 (1971).

5. Paul Ramsey, "The Morality of Abortion," in James Rachels, ed., *Moral Problems* (New York, 1971).

6. John Noonan, "Abortion and the Catholic Church: A Summary History," *Natural Law Forum* 12 (1967), pp. 125–131.

7. Wittgenstein has argued against the possibility of so capturing the concept of a game. *Philosophical Investigations* (New York, 1958), §66–71.

8. Not because the fetus is partly a person and so has some of the rights of persons, but rather because of the rights of personlike non-persons. This I discuss in part III.

9. Aristotle himself was concerned, however, with the different question of when the soul takes form. For historical data, see Jimmye Kimmey, "How the Abortion Laws Happened," *Ms.* I (April, 1973), pp. 48ff, and John Noonan, loc. cit.

10. J. J. Thomson, "A Defense of Abortion," *Philosophy and Public Affairs* 1 (1971).

11. Ibid., p. 52.

12. John Rawls, *A Theory of Justice* (Cambridge, Mass., 1971), §3–4.

13. On the other hand, if they can be trusted with people, then our moral customs are mistaken. It all depends on the facts of psychology.

14. Op. cit., pp. 40, 60–61.

15. I am deeply indebted to Larry Crocker and Arthur Kuflik for their constructive comments.

---

17. A Feminist Perspective on the Right to Abortion

Catharine MacKinnon

Catharine MacKinnon situates the abortion debate within a feminist understanding of gender inequality. She argues that it is wrongly assumed in the abortion debate that women significantly control sex. She further contends that the liberal's proclaimed right to abortion is based on a concept of privacy that fails to protect women from battery, marital rape, and exploited labor.

Reprinted with permission from *Radical America* (vol. 17, no. 4, August 1983).

In a society where women entered sexual intercourse willingly, where adequate contraception was a genuine social priority, there would be no "abortion issue." . . . Abortion is violence. . . . It is the offspring, and will continue to be the accuser of a more pervasive and prevalent violence, the violence of rapism.

Adrienne Rich
Of Woman Born:
Motherhood as Experience
and Institution

In 1973, Roe against Wade held that a statute that made criminal all abortions except to save the mother's life violated the constitutional right to privacy.[1] In 1980, Harris against McRae decided that this privacy right did not require public funding of medically necessary abortions for women who could not afford them.[2] Here I argue that the public/private line drawn in *McRae* sustains and reveals the meaning of privacy recognized in *Roe*.

First, the experience of abortion, and the terms of the struggle for the abortion right, is situated in a context of a feminist comprehension of gender inequality, to which a critique of sexuality is central.[3] Next, the legal concept of privacy is examined in the abortion context. I argue that privacy doctrine affirms what feminism rejects: the public/private split. Once the ideological meaning of the law of privacy is connected with a feminist critique of the public/private division, the *Roe* approach looks consistent with *McRae*'s confinement of its reach. To guarantee abortions as an aspect of the private, rather than of the public, sector is to guarantee women a right to abortion subject to women's ability to provide it for ourselves. This is to guarantee access to abortion only to some women on the basis of class, not to women *as women,* and therefore, under conditions of sex inequality, to guarantee it to *all* women only on male terms. The rest of this is an attempt to unpack what I mean by that.

I will neglect two important explorations, which I bracket now. The first is: what are babies to men? Sometimes men respond to women's right to abort as if confronting the possibility of their own potential nonexistence—at *women's* hands, no less. Men's issues of potency, of continuity as a compensation

for mortality, of the thrust to embody themselves or the image of themselves in the world, seem to underlie their relation to babies, as well as to most everything else. The idea that women can undo what men have done to them on this level seems to provoke insecurity sometimes bordering on hysteria. To overlook these meanings of abortion to men as men is to overlook political and strategic as well as deep theoretical issues, is to misassess where much of the opposition to abortion is coming from, and to make a lot of mistakes. The second question I bracket is one that, unlike the first, has been discussed extensively in the abortion debate: the moral rightness of abortion itself. My view, which the rest of what I say on abortion reflects, is that the abortion choice should be available and must be *women's,* but not because the fetus is not a form of life. The more usual approach tends to make whether women should make the abortion decision somehow contingent on whether the fetus is a form of life. Why shouldn't women make life or death decisions? Which returns us to the first bracketed issue.

The issues I will discuss have largely not been discussed in the terms I will use. What has happened instead, I think, is that women's embattled need to survive in a system that is hostile to our survival, the desperation of our need to negotiate with whatever means that same system will respond to, has precluded our exploration of these issues in the way that I am about to explore them. That is, the terms on which we have addressed the issue of abortion have been shaped and constrained by the very situation that the abortion issue has put us in a position to need to address. We have not been able to risk thinking about these issues on our own terms because the terms have not been ours—either in sex, in social life in general, or in court. The attempt to grasp women's situation on our own terms, from our own point of view, defines the feminist impulse. If doing that is risky, our situation as women also makes it risky not to.

So, first feminism, then law.

Most women who seek abortions became pregnant while having sexual intercourse with men. Most did not mean or wish to conceive. In contrast to this fact of women's experience, the abortion debate has centered on the separation of control over sexuality from control over reproduction, and both from gender. Liberals have supported the availability of the abortion choice as if the woman just happened on the fetus.[4] The right recalls that intercourse precedes conception, only to urge abstinence, as if sex were up to women, while at the same time defending male authority, specifically including a wife's duty to submit to sex. Continuing this logic, many opponents of state funding of abortions, such as supporters of the Hyde Amendment, would permit funding of abortions when the pregnancy results from rape or incest.[5] These are exceptions for special occasions on which they presume women did not control sex. What I'm getting at is this convergence: many of abortion's proponents, who want to free women from reproduction in order to have sex, seem to share with abortion's opponents, who want to stick us with the consequences, the tacit assumption that women significantly *do* control sex.

Feminist investigations suggest otherwise. Sexual intercourse, the most common cause of pregnancy, cannot simply be presumed co-equally determined. Feminists have found that women feel compelled to preserve the appearance, which acted upon becomes the reality, of male direction of sexual expression, as if it is male initiative itself that we want, that turns us on. Men enforce this. It is much of what men want in a woman. It is what pornography eroticizes and prostitutes provide. Rape, by contrast, is intercourse with force that is recognized as force. The implicit standard against which rape is adjudicated, though, is not, I think, the power or even primarily the degree of force that the man wields or uses, but the degree of perceived intimacy between the parties. The more intimately acquainted you are with your accused rapist, the less likely a court is to find that what you think was rape is rape. Often indices of such intimacy include intercourse itself. If no can be taken as yes, depending on measures of familiarity rather than mutuality of desire, how free can yes be?

Under these conditions, women often do not use birth control because of its social meaning, a social meaning we did not make. Using contraception means acknowledging and planning and taking direction of intercourse, accepting one's sexual availability

and appearing nonspontaneous. It means appearing available to male incursions. A good user of contraception is a bad girl. She can be presumed sexually available, among other consequences; she can be raped with relative impunity. (If you think this isn't true, you should consider those rape cases in which the fact that a woman had a diaphragm in is taken as an indication that what happened to her was intercourse, not rape. Why did you have your diaphragm in?) Studies of abortion clinics have looked into circumstances surrounding abortions, including those of women who repeatedly seek abortions—the repeat offenders, high on the list of the right's villains, their best case for opposing abortion as female sexual irresponsibility. Ask such women why they are repeatedly pregnant, they say something like, the sex just happened. Like every night for over a year.[6] I wonder if a woman can be presumed to control access to her sexuality who feels unable to interrupt intercourse to insert a diaphragm; or worse, *cannot even want to,* aware that she risks a pregnancy she knows she doesn't want. Do you think she would stop the man for any other reason, such as, for instance—the real taboo—lack of desire? If not, how is sex, hence its consequences, meaningfully voluntary for women? Norms of sexual rhythm and romance that are felt interrupted by women's needs are constructed against women's interests. When it appears normatively less costly for women to risk an undesired, often painful, traumatic, dangerous, sometimes illegal, and potentially life-threatening procedure than it is to protect oneself in advance, sex doesn't look a whole lot like freedom. Yet the policy debate in the last twenty years has not explicitly approached abortion in the context of how women get pregnant, that is, as a consequence of sexual intercourse under conditions of gender inequality, that is, as an issue of forced sex.

Now, law. In 1973, Roe against Wade found the right to privacy "broad enough to encompass a woman's decision whether or not to terminate her pregnancy."[7] Privacy had previously been recognized as a constitutional principle in a case that decriminalized the prescription and use of contraceptives.[8] Note that courts implicitly connect contraception with abortion under the privacy rubric in a way that parallels the way I just did explicitly under the feminist rubric. In 1977, three justices observed, "In the abortion context, we have held that the right to privacy shields the woman from undue state intrusion in and external scrutiny of her very personal choice."[9] In 1980, the Supreme Court in Harris against McRae decided that this did not mean that federal Medicaid programs had to cover medically necessary abortions for poor women.[10] According to the Court, the privacy of the woman's choice was not unconstitutionally burdened by the government financing her decision to continue, but not her decision to end a conception. The Supreme Court reasoned that "although the government may not place obstacles in the path of a woman's exercise of her freedom of choice, it may not remove those not of its own creation."[11] Aside from holding the state exempt in any issue of the distribution of wealth, which is dubious, it was apparently a very short step from that which the government had a duty *not* to intervene in, as in *Roe,* and that which it has *no* duty to intervene in, as in *McRae.* That this distinction has consistent parallels in other areas of jurisprudence and social policy—such as in the distinction between negative and positive freedom[12] and in the state action requirement[13]—does not mean that the public/private line that forms their common dimension is not, there as well as here, the gender line. The result of government's stance is also the same throughout: an area of social life is cordoned off from the reach of explicitly recognized public authority. This does not mean, as they think, that government stays out really. Rather, this leaves the balance of forces where they are socially, so that government's patterns of intervention mirror and magnify, thus authorize, the existing social divisions of power.

The law of privacy, explicitly a public law *against* public intervention, is one such doctrine. Conceived as the outer edge of limited government, it embodies a tension between precluding public exposure or governmental intrusion on the one hand, and autonomy in the sense of protecting personal self-action on the other. This is a tension, not just two facets of one whole right. This tension is resolved from the liberal state's point of view—I am now moving into a critique of liberalism—by delineating the threshold of the state as its permissible extent of penetration (a term I use advisedly) into a domain that is considered free by definition: the private sphere. By this move the state secures what has been termed "an inviolable personality" by insuring what is called "autonomy or control over the intimacies of personal identity."[14] The state does this by centering its self-restraint on body and home, especially bedroom. By staying out of marriage and the family, prominently meaning sexuality, that is to say, heterosexuality, from contraception through pornography to the abortion decision, the law of privacy proposes to guarantee individual bodily integrity, personal exercise of moral intelligence, and freedom of intimacy.[15] What it actually does is translate traditional social values into the rhetoric of individual rights as a means of subordinating those rights to social imperatives.[16] In feminist terms, applied to abortion law, the logic of *Roe* consummated in *Harris* translates the ideology of the private sphere into individual women's collective needs to the imperatives of male supremacy.

This is my ten-year retrospective on Roe against Wade. Reproduction is sexual, men control sexuality, and the state supports the interest of men as a group. If *Roe* is part of this, why was abortion legalized? Why were women even imagined to have such a right as privacy? It is not an accusation of bad faith to answer that the interests of men as a social group converge here with the definition of justice embodied in law. The male point of view unites them. Taking this approach, one sees that the way the male point of view constructs a social event or legal notion is the way that event or notion is framed by state policy. For example, to the extent possession is the point of sex, illegal rape will be sex with a woman who is not yours unless the act makes her yours. If part of the kick of pornography involves eroticizing the putatively prohibited, illegal pornography—obscenity—will be prohibited enough to keep pornography desirable without ever making it truly illegitimate or unavailable. If, from the male standpoint, male is the implicit definition of human, maleness will be the implicit standard by which sex equality is measured in discrimination law. In parallel terms, the availability of abortion frames, and is framed by, the extent to which men, worked out among themselves, find it convenient to allow abortion—a reproductive consequence of intercourse—to occur. Abortion will then, to that extent, be available.

The abortion policy debate has construed the issues rather differently. The social problem posed by sexuality since Freud[17] has been seen as the problem of the repression of the innate desire for sexual pleasure by the constraints of civilization. Gender inequality arises as an issue in the Freudian context in women's repressive socialization to passivity and coolness (so-called frigidity), in women's so-called desexualization, and in the disparate consequences of biology, that is, pregnancy. Who defines what is seen as sexual, what sexuality therefore is, to whom what stimuli are erotic and why, and who defines the conditions under which sexuality is expressed—these issues are not available to be considered. "Civilization's" answer to these questions, in the Freudian context, instead fuses women's reproductivity with our attributed sexuality in its definition of what a woman is. We are, from a feminist standpoint, thus defined as women, as feminine, by the uses to which men want to put us. Seen this way, it becomes clear why the struggle for reproductive freedom, since Freud, has not included a woman's right to refuse sex. In the post-Freudian era, the notion of sexual liberation frames the sexual equality issue as a struggle for women to have sex with men on the same terms as men: "without consequences."

The abortion right, to the extent it has been admitted to have anything to do with sex, has been sought as freedom from the unequal reproductive consequences of sexual expression, with sexuality defined as centered on heterosexual genital intercourse. It has been as if it is biological organisms, rather than social relations, that have sex and reproduce the species, and sex itself is "really" a gender-neutral, hence sex-equal, activity. But if you see both sexuality and reproduction, hence gender, as socially situated, and your issue is less how more people can get more sex as it is than who, socially, defines what sexuality—hence pleasure and violation—is, the abortion right becomes situated within a very different problematic: the social and political problematic of the inequality of the sexes. As Susan Sontag said, "Sex itself is not liberating for women. Neither is more sex. . . . The question is, what sexuality shall women be liberated to enjoy?"[18] To address this for purposes of abortion policy, from a feminist perspective, requires reconceiving the problem of sexuality from the repression of drives by civilization to the oppression of women by men.

Most arguments for abortion under the rubric of feminism have rested upon the right to control one's own body, gender-neutral. I think that argument has been appealing for the same reasons it is inadequate. Women's bodies have not socially been ours; we have not controlled their meanings and destinies. So feminists have needed to assert that control while feeling unable to risk pursuing the sense that something more than our bodies singular, something closer to a net of relations, relations in which we are (so far unescapedly) gendered, might be at stake.[19] Some feminists have noticed that our "right to decide" has become merged with an overwhelmingly male professional's right not to have his professional judgment second-guessed by the government.[20] But most abortion advocates have argued in rigidly and rigorously gender-neutral terms.

Consider, for instance, Judith Jarvis Thomson's celebrated hypothetical case justifying abortion, in which a gender-neutral abducted "you" has no obligation to be a life support system for the famous violinist ("he") one is forcibly connected to. On this basis, "one" is argued to have no obligation to support a fetus.[21] Never mind that no *woman* who needs an abortion, no woman period, is valued, no potential an actual woman's life might hold would be cherished, comparable to a male famous violinist's unencumbered possibilities. In the crunch, few women look like unborn Beethovens, even to sex-blind liberals. Not to mention that the underlying parallel to rape in the hypothetical—the origin in force, in abduction, that gives it weight while confining its application to instances in which force is recognized as force—is seldom interrogated in the abortion context for its applicability to the normal case. And abortion policy has to be made for the normal case. While the hypothetical makes women's rights depend by analogy on what is not considered the normal case, Thomson finds distinguishing rape from intercourse has "a rather unpleasant sound" principally because *fetal* rights should not depend on the conditions of conception. My point is that in order to apply even something like Thomson's parallel to the usual case of need for an abortion requires establishing some relation between intercourse and rape—sexuality—and conception. This issue has been avoided in the abortion context by acting as if *assuming* women are persons sexually will make us persons reproductively, as if treating women in gender-neutral terms analytically will remove the social reality of gender from the situation. By this sentimentality, liberal feminism obscures the unequal gender basis on which it attempts to construct women's equal personhood.

Abortion without a sexual critique of gender inequality, I have said, promises women sex with men on the same terms as men. Under conditions under which women do not control access to our sexuality, this facilitates women's heterosexual availability. It promises *men* women on male terms. I mean, under conditions of gender inequality, sexual liberation in this sense does not free women, it frees male sexual aggression. Available abortion on this basis removes one substantial legitimized reason that women have had, since Freud, for refusing sex besides the headache. Analyzing the perceptions upon which initial male support for abortion was based, Andrea Dworkin says: "Getting laid was at stake."[22] The Playboy Foundation has supported abortion rights from day one; it continues to, even with shrinking disposable funds, on a level of priority comparable to its opposition to censorship. There is also evidence that men eroticize abortion itself.[23]

Privacy doctrine is an ideal legal vehicle for the process of sexual politics I have described. The democratic liberal ideal of the private holds that, so long as the public does not interfere, autonomous individuals interact freely and equally. Conceptually, this private is hermetic. It means that which is inaccessible to, unaccountable to, unconstructed by anything beyond itself. By definition, it is not part of or conditioned by anything systematic or outside itself. It is personal, intimate, autonomous, particular, individual, the original source and final outpost of the self, gender-neutral. Privacy is, in short, defined by everything that feminism reveals women have never been allowed to be or to have, as well as by everything that women have been equated with and defined in terms of *men's* ability to have. The liberal definition of the private does not envisage public complaint of social inequality within it. In the liberal view, no act of the state contributes to, hence properly should participate in, shaping its internal alignments or distributing its internal forces, including inequalities among parties in private. Its inviolability by the state, framed as an individual right, presupposes that it is not already an arm of the state. It is not even a social sphere, exactly. Intimacy is implicitly thought to guarantee symmetry of power. Injuries arise in violating the private sphere, not within and by and because of it.

In private, consent tends to be presumed. It is true that a showing of coercion voids this presumption. But the problem is getting anything private perceived as coercive. Why one would allow force in private—the "why doesn't she leave" question raised to battered women—is a question given its urgency by the social meaning of the private as a sphere of equality and choice. But for women the measure of the intimacy has been the measure of the oppression. This is why feminism has had to explode the private. This is why feminism has seen the personal as the political. In this sense, for women as such there is no private, either normatively or empirically. Feminism confronts the reality that women have no privacy to lose or to guarantee. We have no inviolability. Our sexuality is not only violable, it is, hence we are, seen in and as our violation. To confront the fact that we have no privacy is to confront the intimate degradation of women *as* the public order.

In this light, recognizing abortion under the legal right to privacy is a complicated move. Freedom *from* public intervention coexists uneasily with any right which requires social preconditions to be meaningfully delivered. If inequality, for example, is socially pervasive and enforced, meaningful equality will require intervention, not abdication. But the right to privacy is not thought to require social change to be meaningful. It is not even thought to require any social preconditions, other than nonintervention by the public. The point for the abortion cases is not only that indigency, which was the specific barrier to effective choice in *McRae,* is well within public power to remedy, nor that the state, as I said, is hardly exempt in issues of the distribution of wealth. It is rather that Roe against Wade presumes that governmental nonintervention into the private sphere in itself amounts to, or at the least promotes, woman's freedom of choice. When the alternative is jail, there is much to be said for this argument. But the *McRae* result sustains the meaning of the privacy recognized in *Roe:* women are guaranteed by the public no more than what we can secure for ourselves in private. That is, what we can extract through our intimate associations with men. Women with privileges get rights.

Women got abortion as a private privilege, not as a public right. We got control over reproduction that is controlled by "a man or The Man,"[24] an individual man or (mostly male) doctors or the government. In this sense, abortion was not simply decriminalized, it was legalized; *Roe* set the stage for state regulation of the conditions under which women can have access to this right. Much of the control that women got out of legalization of abortion went directly into the hands of men socially—husbands, doctors, fathers. Much of the rest of it women have had to fight to keep from state attempts, both legislative and administrative, to regulate it out of existence.[25]

It is not inconsistent, in this light, that a woman's decision to abort, framed as a privacy right, would have no claim on public funding and might genuinely not be seen as burdened by that deprivation. Privacy conceived as a right from public intervention and disclosure is the conceptual *opposite* of the relief *McRae* sought for welfare women. State intervention would have provided a choice these women did *not* have in private. The women in *McRae,* poor women and women of color whose sexual refusal has counted for especially little,[26] needed something to make their privacy real. The logic of the court's response to them re-

sembles that by which women are supposed to consent to sex. Preclude the alternatives, then call the sole option remaining "her choice." The point is that the women's alternatives are precluded *prior* to the reach of the chosen remedy, the legal doctrine. They are precluded by conditions of sex, race, and class— the conditions the privacy frame not only assumes, but *works to guarantee.* These women were seen, essentially, as not having lost any privacy by having public funding for abortions withheld, as having no privacy to lose. In the bourgeois sense, in which you can have all the rights you can buy, converging with that dimension of male supremacy that makes the self-disposition money can buy a prerogative of masculinity, this was true. The *McRae* result certainly *made* it true.

The way the law of privacy restricts intrusions into intimacy also bars change in control over that intimacy. The existing distribution of power and resources within the private sphere will be precisely what the law of privacy exists to protect. Just as pornography is legally protected as individual freedom of expression without questioning whose freedom and whose expression and at whose expense, abstract privacy protects abstract autonomy without inquiring into whose freedom of action is being sanctioned, at whose expense. I think it is not coincidence that the very place (the body), the very relations (heterosexual), the very activities (intercourse and reproduction), and the very feelings (intimate) that feminism has found central to the subjection of women, form the core of privacy law's coverage. In this perspective, the legal concept of privacy can and has shielded the place of battery, marital rape, and women's exploited labor, preserved the central institutions whereby women are *deprived* of identity, autonomy, control, and self-definition, and protected the primary activities through which male supremacy is expressed and enforced.

To fail to recognize the meaning of the private in the ideology and reality of women's subordination by seeking protection behind a right *to* that privacy is to cut women off from collective verification and state support in the same act. When women are segregated in private, separated from each other, one at a time, a right *to* that privacy isolates us at once from each other and from public recourse, even as it provides the only form of that recourse made available to us. So defined, the right to privacy has included a right of men "to be let alone"[27] to oppress women one at a time. It embodies and reflects the private sphere's existing definition of womanhood. As an instance of liberalism—applied to women as if we *are* persons, gender-neutral—Roe against Wade reinforces the division between public and private, a division that is not gender-neutral. It is at once an ideological division that lies about women's shared experience and mystifies the unity among the spheres of women's violation, and a very material division that *keeps* the private beyond public redress and depoliticizes women's subjection within it. It keeps some men out of the bedrooms of other men.

There seems to be a social perception that the right has the high moral ground on abortion and the liberals have the high legal ground.[28] I have tried to sketch a feminist ground, a political ground critical of the common ground under the right's morals and liberals' laws.

Notes

---

1. *Roe v. Wade*, 410 U.S. 113 (1973).

2. *Harris v. McRae*, 448 U.S. 297 (1980).

3. I talk about this in "Feminism, Marxism, Method and the State: An Agenda for Theory," *Signs: Journal of Women in Culture and Society* 7, no. 3 (Spring 1982): 515–44.

4. See D. H. Reagan, "Rewriting *Roe v. Wade*," *Michigan Law Review* 77 (August 1979): 1569–1646, in which the Good Samaritan, by analogy, happens upon the fetus.

5. As of 1973, ten states that made abortion a crime had exceptions for rape and incest; at least three had exceptions for rape only. Many of these exceptions were based on Model Penal Code Section 230.3 (Proposed Official Draft 1962), quoted in *Doe v. Bolton*, 410 U.S. 179, 205–7, app. B (1973), permitting abortion, *inter alia* in cases of "rape, incest, or other felonious intercourse." References to states with incest and rape exceptions can be found in *Roe v. Wade*, 410 U.S. 113, n. 37 (1973). Some versions of the Hyde Amendment, which prohibits use of public money to fund abortions, have contained exceptions for cases of rape or incest. Publ. L. No. 95-205, § 101, 91 Stat. 1960 (1972); Pub. L. No. 95-480, § 210, 92 Stat. 1567, 1586 (1978); Pub. L. No. 96-123, 109, 93 Stat. 923, 926 (1979); Pub. L. No. 96-536, § 109, 94 Stat. 3166, 3170 (1980). All require immediate reporting of the incident.

6. Kristin Luker, *Taking Chances: Abortion and the Decision Not to Contracept* (Berkeley: University of California Press, 1975), p. 47.

7. *Roe*, 410 U.S. at 153.

8. *Griswold v. Connecticut*, 381 U.S. 479 (1965).

9. *H. L. v. Matheson*, 450 U.S. 398, 435 (dissent) (1981); see also *Whalen v. Roe*, 429 U.S. 589, 599–600 (1977).

10. *Harris v. McRae*, 448 U.S. 297 (1980).

11. *Harris*, 448 U.S. at 316.

12. Isaiah Berlin, "Two Concepts of Liberty," in Berlin, *Four Essays on Liberty* (Oxford: Oxford University Press, 1969).

13. See Paul Brest, "State Action and Liberal Theory: A Casenote on *Flagg Brothers v. Brooks*," 130 U. Pa. L. Rev. 1296 (1982).

14. Tom Gerety, "Redefining Privacy," *Harvard Civil Rights—Civil Liberties Law Review* 12, no. 2 (Spring 1977): 236.

15. Thus the law of privacy wavers between protecting the institution of heterosexuality as such and protecting that which heterosexuality is at least theoretically only one instance of, that is, free choice in intimate behavior. For the first proposition, see, e.g., *Griswold v. Connecticut*, 381 U.S. 479 (1965) (distribution of contraceptives), *Loving v. Virginia*, 388 U.S. 1 (1967) (marriage partners), *Skinner v. Oklahoma*, 316 U.S. 535 (1942) (male fertility), as well as *Roe v. Wade, Doe v. Commonwealth's Attorney*, 403 F. Supp. 1199 (D. Va. 1975) (homosexual conduct not protected, since "no part of marriage, home or family life"). For the second, *New York v. Onofre*, 424 N.Y.S. 2d 566 (1980) (invalidating criminal sodomy statute). It is consistent with this analysis that homosexuality, when protected or found officially acceptable, would primarily be in private (i.e., in the closet) and primarily parodying rather than challenging the heterosexual model. Kenneth Karst attempts to include both approaches to privacy in his formation of "intimate association," yet implicitly retains the heterosexual mod-

el as central to his definition of the meaning of intimacy. "By 'intimate association' I mean a close and familiar personal relationship with another that is in some significant way comparable to a marriage or family relationships . . . but in principle the idea of intimate association also includes close friendship, with or without any such links." K. L. Karst, "The Freedom of Intimate Association," *Yale Law Journal* 89, no. 4 (March 1980), p. 629. On pornography, see *Stanley v. Georgia*, 394 U.S. 557 (1969) and *Lovisi v. Slayton*, 539 F.2d 349 (5th Cir. 1976). Taken together, these cases suggest that Mr. Stanley's privacy rights encompass looking at pornography regardless of the intrusiveness of its production, while the women depicted in the pornography Mr. Stanley looks at have no privacy rights, if they could not have "reasonably expect[ed]" privacy to attach when they permitted "onlookers" to take sexual pictures. For a discussion of privacy law in the pornography context see Ruth Colker, "Pornography and Privacy: Towards the Development of a Group-Based Theory for Sex-Based Intrusions of Privacy," 1, 2 *Law and Equality: A Journal of Theory and Practice* (1983).

16. This formulation learned a lot from Tom Grey, "Eros, Civilization and the Burger Court," *Law and Contemporary Problems* 43, no. 3 (Summer 1980): 83–99.

17. Nineteenth-century feminists connected the abortion right with control over access to their sexuality. See Linda Gordon, *Woman's Body, Woman's Right: A Social History of Birth Control in America* (New York: Grossman [Viking], 1976): esp. 100–115.

18. S. Sontag, "The Third World of Women," *Partisan Review* 40, no. 2 (1973), p. 188.

19. Such a relation has at least two aspects: the women/men relation; and woman/fetus relation. To the latter, see Adrienne Rich on the fetus as "neither as me nor as not-me." *Of Woman Born: Motherhood as Experience and Institution* (New York: W. W. Norton & Co., 1976), p. 64.

20. K. Glen, "Abortion in the Courts: A Lay Woman's Historical Guide to the New Disaster Area," *Feminist Studies* 4 (1978): 1.

21. Judith Jarvis Thomson, "A Defense of Abortion," *Philosophy and Public Affairs* 1, no. 1 (1971): 47–66.

22. A. Dworkin, *Right-Wing Women* (New York: Perigee, 1983). *You must read this book!* The sup-

port of men for abortion largely evaporated or became very equivocal when the women's movement produced, instead, women who refused sex with men and left men in droves. The fact that Jane Roe was pregnant from a gang rape, a fact which was not part of the litigation (" 'Jane Roe' Says She'd Fight Abortion Battle Again," *Minneapolis Star & Tribune*, Jan. 22, 1983), is emblematic of the sexual dimension of the issue. As further evidence, see Friedrich Engels arguing that removing private housekeeping into social industry would "remove all the anxiety about 'consequences,' which today is the most essential social—moral as well as economic—factor that prevents a girl from giving herself completely to the man she loves." *Origin of the Family, Private Property and the State* (New York: International Publishers, 1973, p. 139.

23. Andrea Dworkin's analysis of the Marquis de Sade's statements on abortion reveal that "Sade extolled the sexual value of murder and he saw abortion as a form of murder . . . abortion was a sexual act, an act of lust." *Pornography: Men Possessing Women* (New York: Perigee, 1981), p. 96. One woman complaining of sexual harassment said the codirector of the abortion clinic she worked at had asked to be present during her abortion: "He said he had a fantasy about having sexual intercourse with a woman on an examining table during an abortion," she reported. "Woman accuses clinic chief of sexual harassment," *Minneapolis Star & Tribune*, May 28, 1982. Ponder *Hustler's* cartoon depicting a naked man masturbating enthusiastically reading a book labeled *Fetal Positions* in the corner of an operating room where a woman lies on the operating table, knees agape in stirrups. A male doctor is holding up what he has just delivered with tongs, saying "Want a piece of ass, Earl? This one's stillborn." WAVPM Slide Show. This slide show is described in Teresa Hommel, "Images of Women in Pornography and Medicine," VIII, 2 *NYU Review of Law and Social Change* (1978–79): 207–14.

24. Johnnie Tillmon, "Welfare is a Women's Issue," *Liberation News Service*, February 26, 1972, in *America's Working Women: A Documentary History, 1600 to the Present*, ed. Baxandall, Gordon, and Reverby (New York: Vintage Books, 1976), pp. 357–58.

25. *H. L. v. Matheson*, 450 U.S. 398 (1981) (upholding statute requiring physicians to notify

parents of "dependent, unmarried minor girl" prior to performing an abortion), *Bellotti v. Baird*, 443 U.S. 672 (1977) (Bellotti II) (holding that parents may not have absolute veto power over their minor daughter's decision), *Doe v. Gerstein*, 517 F.2d 787 (5th Cir. 1975), *aff'd* 417 U.S. 281 (1974) (mandatory written consent requirements of husbands' parents unconstitutional). In *Planned Parenthood of Mo. v. Danforth*, 428 U.S. 52 (1976) the Supreme Court held that a state cannot by statute allow a man to veto a wife's abortion choice in part because the state cannot give a husband rights over the woman's reproductive choice that the state itself does not have. This leads one to wonder where the states got their power to regulate (under some circumstances preclude) abortions in the second and third trimesters, where apparently "public" considerations can weigh against the woman's "private" choice. Could states, by statutes, allow husbands to veto abortions then? Whether courts can do by injunction what states cannot do by statute is discussed if not resolved in *Hagerstown Reproductive Health Services and Bonny Ann Fritz v. Chris Allen Fritz*, 295 Md. 268, 454 A. 2d 846 (1983). See also, *City of Akron v. Akron Center for Reproductive Health*, 103 S. Ct. 2481 (1983) (invalidating five city ordinances regulating where abortions may be performed (hospitals), who needs written consent by a parent (girls younger than 15), what doctors have to tell women prior to the procedure (e.g., tactile sensitivities of a fetus), when an abortion can be performed (24 hours after consent), and how the "fetal remains" must be disposed of).

26. The following statistics were reported in 1970: 79 percent of New York City's abortion deaths occurred among black and Puerto Rican women; the abortion death rate was 4.7 times as high for Puerto Rican women, and 8 times as high for black women as for white women. Lucinda Cisler, "Unfinished Business: Birth Control and Women's Liberation," in *Sisterhood Is Powerful: An Anthology of Writings from the Women's Liberation Movement*, ed. Robin Morgan (New York: Vintage, 1970), p. 291.

27. The classic article formulating privacy as "the right to be let alone" is S. D. Warren and L. D. Brandeis, "The Right to Privacy," *Harvard Law Review* 4 (1890), p. 205. But note that *state* constitutional privacy provisions are sometimes interpreted to require funding for abortions. *Committee to Defend Reproductive Rights v. Meyers*, 29 C. 3d 252, 172 Cal. Rptr. 866, 625 P. 2d 779 (1981), *Moe v. Society of Administration and Finance*, 417 N.E. 2d 387 (Mass. 1981).

28. I owe this conception of public debate to Jay Garfield, Hampshire College, Amherst, Massachusetts.

18. Euthanasia, Killing, and Letting Die

James Rachels

James Rachels criticizes a policy statement of the American Medical Association on the grounds that it endorses the doctrine that there is an important moral difference between active and passive euthanasia. Rachels denies that there is any moral difference between the two. He argues that once we judge a patient would be better off dead, it should not matter much whether that patient is killed or let die. He points out that both killing and letting die can be intentional and deliberate and can proceed from the same motives; further, that when killing and letting die are similar in these and other relevant respects, our moral assessment of these acts is also similar. Rachels concludes by considering a number of counterarguments to his view and finds them all wanting. In particular, Rachels rejects the idea that the killing and letting die distinction can be supported on the grounds that our duty to refrain from harming people is much stronger than our duty to help people in need. Rather, he contends that when conditions are similar our duty to refrain from harming people and our duty to help people in need have a similar moral force.

Dr. F. J. Ingelfinger, former editor of *The New England Journal of Medicine,* observes that

> this is the heyday of the ethicist in medicine. He delineates the rights of patients, of experimental subjects, of fetuses, of mothers, of animals, and even of doctors. (And what a far cry it is from the days when medical "ethics" consisted of condemning economic improprieties such as fee splitting and advertising!) With impeccable logic—once certain basic assumptions are granted—and with graceful prose, the ethicist develops his arguments. . . . Yet his precepts are essentially the products of armchair exercise and remain abstract and idealistic until they have been tested in the laboratory of experience.[1]

One problem with such armchair exercises, he complains, is that in spite of the impeccable logic and the graceful prose, the result is often an absolutist ethic which is unsatisfactory when applied to particular cases, and which is

From *Ethical Issues Relating to Life and Death,* edited by John Ladd, pp. 146–161. Copyright © 1979 Oxford University Press, Inc. Reprinted by permission.

therefore of little use to the practicing physician. Unlike some absolutist philosophers, "the practitioner appears to prefer the principles of individualism. As there are few atheists in fox holes, there tend to be few absolutists at the bedside."[2]

I must concede at the outset that this chapter is another exercise in "armchair ethics" in the sense that I am not a physician but a philosopher. Yet I am no absolutist; and my purpose is to examine a doctrine that *is* held in an absolute form by many doctors. The doctrine is that there is an important moral difference between active and passive euthanasia, such that even though the latter is sometimes permissible, the former is always forbidden. This is an absolute which doctors hold "at the bedside" as well as in the seminar room, and the "principles of individualism" make little headway against it. But I will argue that this is an irrational dogma, and that there is no sound moral basis for it.

I will not argue, simply, that active euthanasia is all right. Rather, I will be concerned with the *relation* between active euthanasia and passive euthanasia: I will argue that there is no moral difference between them. By this I mean that there is no reason to prefer one over the other as a matter of principle—the fact that one case of euthanasia is active, while another is passive, is not *itself* a reason to think one morally better than the other. If you already think that passive euthanasia is all right, and you are convinced by my arguments, then you may conclude that active euthanasia must be all right, too. On the other hand, if you believe that active euthanasia is immoral, you may want to conclude that passive euthanasia must be immoral, too. Although I prefer the former alternative, I will not argue for it here. I will only argue that the two forms of euthanasia are morally equivalent—either both are acceptable or both are unacceptable.

I am aware that this will at first seem incredible to many readers, but I hope that this impression will be dispelled as the discussion proceeds. The discussion will be guided by two methodological considerations, both of which are touched on in the editorial quoted above. The first has to do with my "basic assumptions." My arguments are intended to appeal to all reasonable people, and not merely to those who already share my philosophical preconceptions. Therefore, I will try not to rely on any assumptions that cannot be accepted by any reasonable person. None of my arguments will depend on morally eccentric premises. Second, Dr. Ingelfinger is surely correct when he says that we must be as concerned with the realities of medical practice as with the more abstract issues of moral theory. As he notes, the philosopher's precepts "remain abstract and idealistic until they are tested in the laboratory of experience." Part of my argument will be precisely that, when "tested in the laboratory of experience," the doctrine in question has terrible results. I believe that if this doctrine were to be recognized as irrational, and rejected by the medical profession, the benefit to both doctors and patients would be enormous. In this sense, my paper is not intended as an "armchair exercise" at all.

The American Medical Association Policy Statement

"Active euthanasia," as the term is used, means taking some positive action designed to kill the patient; for example, giving him a lethal injection of potassium chloride. "Passive euthanasia," on the other hand, means simply refraining from doing anything to keep the patient alive. In passive euthanasia we withhold medication or other life-sustaining therapy, or we refuse to perform surgery, etc., and let the patient die "naturally" of whatever ills already afflict him.

Many doctors and theologians prefer to use the term "euthanasia" only in connection with active euthanasia, and they use other words to refer to what I am calling "passive euthanasia"—for example, instead of "passive euthanasia" they may speak of "the right to death with dignity." One reason for this choice of terms is the emotional impact of the words: it *sounds* so much better to defend "death with dignity" than to advocate "euthanasia" of any sort. And of course if one believes that there is a great moral difference between active and passive euthanasia—as most doctors and religious writers do—then one may prefer a terminology which puts as much psychological distance as possible between them. However, I do not want to become involved in a pointless dispute about terminology, because nothing of substance depends on which label is used. I will stay with the terms "active euthanasia" and "passive euthanasia" because they are the most convenient; but if the reader prefers a different terminology he may substitute his own throughout, and my arguments will be unaffected.

The belief that there is an important moral difference between active and passive euthanasia obviously has important consequences for medical practice. It makes a difference to what doctors are willing to do. Consider, for example, the following familiar situation. A patient who is dying from incurable cancer of the throat is in terrible pain that we can no longer satisfactorily alleviate. He is certain to die within a few days, but he decides that he does not want to go on living for those days since the pain is unbearable. So he asks the doctor to end his life now; and his family joins in the request. One way that the doctor might comply with this request is simply by killing the patient with a lethal injection. Most doctors would not do that, not only because of the possible legal consequences, but because they think such a course would be immoral. And this is understandable: the idea of killing someone goes against very deep moral feelings; and besides, as we are often reminded, it is the special business of doctors to save and protect life, not to destroy it. Yet, even so, the physician may sympathize with the dying patient's request and feel that it is entirely reasonable for him to prefer death now rather than after a few more days of agony. The doctrine that we are considering tells the doctor what to do: it says that although he may not administer the lethal injection— that would be "active euthanasia," which is forbidden—he *may* withhold treatment and let the patient die sooner than he otherwise would.

It is no wonder that this simple idea is so widely accepted, for it seems to give the doctor a way out of his dilemma without having to kill the patient, and without having to prolong the patient's agony. The idea is not a new one. What *is* new is that the idea is now being incorporated into official documents of medical ethics. What was once unofficially done is now becoming official policy. The idea is expressed, for example, in a 1973 policy statement of the American Medical Association, which says (in its entirety):

> The intentional termination of the life of one human being by another—mercy killing—is contrary to that for which the medical profession stands and is contrary to the policy of the American Medical Association.
>
>   The cessation of the employment of extraordinary means to prolong the life of the body when there is irrefutable evidence that biological death is imminent is the decision of the patient and/or his immediate family. The advice and judgment of the physician should be freely available to the patient and/or his immediate family.[3]

This is a cautiously worded statement, and it is not clear *exactly* what is being affirmed. I take it, however, that at least these three propositions are intended:

1. Killing patients is absolutely forbidden; however, it is sometimes permissible to allow patients to die.

2. It is permissible to allow a patient to die if
   a. there is irrefutable evidence that he will die soon anyway;
   b. "extraordinary" measures would be required to keep him alive; and
   c. the patient and/or his immediate family requests it.

3. Doctors should make their own advice and judgments available to the patient and/or his immediate family when the latter are deciding whether to request that the patient be allowed to die.

The first proposition expresses the doctrine which is the main subject of this paper. As for the third, it seems obvious enough, provided that 1 and 2 are accepted, so I shall say nothing further about it.

I do want to say a few things about 2. Physicians often allow patients to die; however, they do *not* always keep to the guidelines set out in 2. For example, a doctor may leave instructions that if a hopeless, comatose patient suffers cardiac arrest, nothing be done to start his heart beating again. "No-coding" is the name given to this practice, and the consent of the patient and/or his immediate family is not commonly sought. This is thought to be a medical decision (in reality, of course, it is a moral one) which is the doctor's affair. To take a different sort of example, when a Down's infant (a mongoloid) is born with an intestinal blockage, the doctor and parents may agree that there will be no operation to remove the blockage, so that the baby will die.[4] (If the same infant were born without the obstruction, it certainly would not be killed. This is a clear application of the idea that "letting die" is all right even though killing is forbidden.) But in such cases it is clear that the baby is *not* going to die soon anyway. If the surgery were performed, the baby would proceed to a "normal" infancy—normal, that is, for a mongoloid. Moreover, the treatment required to save the baby—abdominal surgery—can hardly be called "extraordinary" by today's medical standards.

Therefore, all three conditions which the AMA statement places on the decision to let die are commonly violated. It is beyond the scope of this paper to determine whether doctors are right to violate those conditions. But I firmly believe that the second requirement—

2b—is not acceptable. Only a little reflection is needed to show that the distinction between ordinary and extraordinary means is not important. Even a very conservative, religiously oriented writer such as Paul Ramsey stresses this. Ramsey gives these examples:

> Suppose that a diabetic patient long accustomed to self-administration of insulin falls victim to terminal cancer, or suppose that a terminal cancer patient suddenly develops diabetes. Is he in the first case obliged to continue, and in the second case obliged to begin, insulin treatment and die painfully of cancer, or in either or both cases may the patient choose rather to pass into diabetic coma and an earlier death? . . . Or an old man slowly deteriorating who from simply being inactive and recumbent gets pneumonia: are we to use antibiotics in a likely successful attack upon this disease which from time immemorial has been called "the old man's friend"?[5]

I agree with Ramsey, and with many other writers, that in such cases treatment may be withheld even though it is not "extraordinary" by any reasonable standard. Contrary to what is implied by the AMA statement, the distinction between heroic and nonheroic means of treatment can *not* be used to determine when treatment is or is not mandatory.

Killing and Letting Die

I return now to the distinction between active and passive euthanasia. Of course, not every doctor believes that this distinction is morally important. Over twenty years ago Dr. D. C. S. Cameron of the American Cancer Society said that "Actually the difference between euthanasia [i.e., killing] and letting the patient die by omitting life-sustaining treatment is a moral quibble."[6] I argue that Cameron was right.

The initial thought can be expressed quite simply. In any case in which euthanasia seems desirable, it is because we think that the patient would literally be better off dead—or at least, no worse off dead—than continuing the kind of life available to him. (Without this

assumption, even *passive* euthanasia would be unthinkable.) But, as far as the main question of ending the patient's life is concerned, it does not matter whether the euthanasia is active or passive: *in either case*, he ends up dead sooner than he otherwise would. And if the results are the same, why should it matter so much which method is used?

Moreover, we need to remember that, in cases such as that of the terminal cancer patient, the justification for allowing him to die, rather than prolonging his life for a few more hopeless days, is that he is in horrible pain. But if we simply withhold treatment, it may take him *longer* to die, and so he will suffer *more* than he would if we were to administer the lethal injection. This fact provides strong reason for thinking that, once we have made the initial decision not to prolong his agony, active euthanasia is actually preferable to passive euthanasia rather than the reverse. It also shows a kind of incoherence in the conventional view: to say that passive euthanasia is preferable is to endorse the option which leads to more suffering rather than less, and is contrary to the humanitarian impulse which prompts the decision not to prolong his life in the first place.

But many people are convinced that there is an important moral difference between active and passive euthanasia because they think that, in passive euthanasia, the doctor does not really *do* anything. No action whatever is taken; the doctor simply does nothing, and the patient dies of whatever ills already afflict him. In active euthanasia, however, we *do something* to bring about the patient's death. We kill him. Thus, the difference between active and passive euthanasia is thought to be the difference between doing something to bring about someone's death, and not doing anything to bring about anyone's death. And of course if we conceive the matter in *this* way, passive euthanasia seems preferable. Ramsey, who denounces the view I am defending as "extremist" and who regards the active/passive distinction as one of the "flexibly wise categories of traditional medical ethics," takes just this view of the matter. He says that the choice between active and passive euthanasia "is not a choice between directly and indirectly willing and doing something. *It is rather the important choice between doing something and doing nothing,* or (better said) ceasing to do something that was begun in order to do something that is better because now more fitting."[7]

This is a very misleading way of thinking, for it ignores the fact that in passive euthanasia the doctor *does* do one thing which is very important: namely, he lets the patient die. We may overlook this obvious fact—or at least, we may put it out of our minds—if we concentrate only on a very restricted way of describing what happens: "The doctor does not administer medication or any other therapy; he does not instruct the nurses to administer any such medication; he does not perform any surgery"; and so on. And of course this description of what happens is correct, as far as it goes—these are all things that the doctor does not do. But the point is that the doctor *does* let the patient die when he could save him, and this must be included in the description, too.

There is another reason why we might fall into this error. We might confuse *not saving* someone with *letting him die.* Suppose a patient is dying, and Dr. X could prolong his life. But he decides not to do so and the patient dies. Now it is true of everyone on earth that he did not save the patient. Dr. X did not save him, and neither did you, and neither did I. So we might be tempted to think that all of us are in the same moral position, reasoning that since neither you nor I are responsible for the patient's death, neither is Dr. X. None of us did anything. This, however, is a mistake, for even though it is true that none of us saved the patient, it is *not* true that we all let him die. In order to let someone die, one must be *in a position* to save him. You and I were not in a position to save the patient, so we did not let him die. Dr. X, on the other hand, was in a position to save him, and did let him die. Thus the doctor is in a special moral position which not just everyone is in.

Here we must remember some elementary points, which are so obvious that they would not be worth mentioning except for the fact that overlooking them is a source of so much confusion in this area. The act of letting someone die may be intentional and deliberate, just as the act of killing someone may be intentional and deliberate. Moreover, the doctor is *responsible* for his decision to let the patient die,

just as he would be responsible for giving the patient a lethal injection. The decision to let a patient die is subject to moral appraisal in the same way that a decision to kill is subject to moral appraisal: it may be assessed as wise or unwise, compassionate or sadistic, right or wrong. If a doctor deliberately let a patient die who was suffering from a routinely curable illness, then he would be to blame for what he did, just as he would be to blame if he had needlessly killed the patient. It would be no defense at all for him to insist that, *really,* he didn't "do anything" but just stand there. We would all know that he did do something very serious indeed, for he let the patient die.

These considerations show how misleading it is to characterize the difference between active and passive euthanasia as a difference between doing something (killing), for which the doctor may be morally culpable; and doing nothing (just standing there while the patient dies), for which the doctor is not culpable. The real difference between them is, rather, the difference between *killing* and letting die, both of which are actions for which a doctor, or anyone else, will be morally responsible.

Now we can formulate our problem more precisely. If there is an important moral difference between active and passive euthanasia, it must be because *killing someone is morally worse than letting someone die.* But is it? Is killing, in itself, worse than letting die? In order to investigate this issue, we may consider two cases which are exactly alike except that one involves killing where the other involves letting someone die. Then we can ask whether this difference makes any difference to our moral assessments. It is important that the cases be *exactly* alike except for this one difference, since otherwise we cannot be confident that it is *this* difference which accounts for any variation in our assessments.

1. Smith stands to gain a large inheritance if anything should happen to his six-year-old cousin. One evening while the child is taking his bath, Smith sneaks into the bathroom and drowns the child, and then arranges things so that it will look like an accident.

2. Jones also stands to gain if anything should happen to his six-year-old cousin. Like Smith, Jones sneaks in planning to drown the child in his bath. However, just as he enters the bathroom Jones sees the child slip, hit his head, and fall face down in the water. Jones is delighted; he stands by, ready to push the child's head back under if it is necessary, but it is not necessary. With only a little thrashing about, the child drowns all by himself, "accidentally," as Jones watches and does nothing.

Now Smith killed the child, while Jones "merely" let the child die. That is the only difference between them. Did either man behave better, from a moral point of view? Is there a moral difference between them? *If the difference between killing and letting die were itself a morally important matter, then we should say that Jones's behavior was less reprehensible than Smith's.* But do we actually want to say that? I think not, for several reasons. In the first place, both men acted from the same motive, personal gain, and both had exactly the same end in view when they acted. We may infer from Smith's conduct that he is a bad man, although we may withdraw or modify that judgment if we learn certain further facts about him; for example, that he is mentally deranged. But would we not also infer the very same thing about Jones from his conduct? And would not the same further considerations also be relevant to any modification of that judgment? Moreover, suppose Jones pleaded in his defense, "After all, I didn't kill the child. I only stood there and let him die." Again, if letting die were in itself less bad than killing, this defense should have some weight. But—morally, at least—it does not. Such a "defense" can only be regarded as a grotesque perversion of moral reasoning.

Thus, it seems that when we are careful not to smuggle in any further differences which prejudice the issue, the mere difference between killing and letting die does not itself make any difference to the morality of actions concerning life and death.[8]

Now it may be pointed out, quite properly, that the cases of euthanasia with which doctors are concerned are not like this at all. They do not involve personal gain or the destruction of normal, healthy children. Doctors are concerned only with cases in which the patient's life is of no further use to him, or in which the patient's life has become or soon will become a positive burden. However, the point is the same in those cases: the difference between killing or letting die does not, *in itself*, make a difference, from the point of view of morality. If a doctor lets a patient die, for humane reasons, he is in the same moral position as if he had given the patient a lethal injection for humane reasons. If his decision was wrong—if, for example, the patient's illness was in fact curable—then the decision would be equally regrettable no matter which method was used to carry it out. And if the doctor's decision was the right one, then the method he used is not itself important.

The AMA statement isolates the crucial issue very well: "the intentional termination of the life of one human being by another." But then the statement goes on to deny that the cessation of treatment *is* the intentional termination of a life. This is where the mistake comes in, for what is the cessation of treatment, in those circumstances, if it is not "the intentional termination of the life of one human being by another"? Of course it is exactly that; if it were not, there would be no point to it.

Counterarguments

Our argument has now brought us to this point: we cannot draw any moral distinction between active and passive euthanasia on the grounds that one involves killing while the other only involves letting someone die, because that is a difference that does not make a difference, from a moral point of view. Some people will find this hard to accept. One reason, I think, is that they fail to distinguish the question of whether killing is, in itself, worse than letting die, from the very different question of whether most actual cases of killing are more reprehensible than most actual cases of letting die. Most actual cases of killing are clearly terrible—think of the murders reported in the newspapers—and we hear of such cases almost every day. On the other hand, we hardly ever hear of a case of letting die, except for the actions of doctors who are motivated by humanitarian reasons. So we learn to think of killing in a much worse light than letting die; and we conclude, invalidly, that there must be something about killing which makes it *in itself* worse than letting die. But this does not follow for it is not the bare difference between killing and letting die that makes the difference in these cases. Rather, it is the other factors—the murderer's motive of personal gain, for example, contrasted with the doctor's humanitarian motivation, or the fact that the murderer kills a healthy person while the doctor lets die a terminal patient racked with disease—that account for our different reactions to the different cases.

There are, however, some substantial arguments that may be advanced to oppose my conclusion. Here are two of them:

The first counterargument focuses specifically on the concept of *being the cause of someone's death*. If we kill someone, then we are the cause of his death. But if we merely let someone die, we are not the cause; rather, he dies of whatever condition he already has. The doctor who gives the cancer patient a lethal injection will have caused his patient's death, and will have this on his conscience; whereas if he merely ceases treatment, the cancer and not the doctor is the cause of death. This is supposed to make a moral difference. This argument has been advanced many times. Ramsey, for example, urges us to remember that "In omission no human agent causes the patient's death, directly or indirectly."[9] And, writing in the *Villanova Law Review* for 1968, Dr. J. Russell Elkinton said that what makes the active/passive distinction important is that in passive euthanasia, "the patient does not die from the act [e.g. the act of turning off the respirator] but from the underlying disease or injury."[10]

This argument will not do, for two reasons. First, just as there is a distinction to be drawn between being and not being the cause of someone's death, there is also a distinction to be drawn between letting someone die and not letting anyone die. It is certainly desirable, in

general, not to be the cause of anyone's death; but it is also desirable, in general, not to let anyone die when we can save them. (Doctors act on this precept every day.) Therefore, we cannot draw any special conclusion about the relative desirability of passive euthanasia just on these grounds. Second, the reason why we think it is bad to be the cause of someone's death is that we think that death is a great evil—and so it is. However, if we have decided that euthanasia, even passive euthanasia, is desirable in a given case, then we have decided that in *this* instance death is no greater an evil than the patient's continued existence. And if this is true, then the usual reason for not wanting to be the cause of someone's death simply does not apply. To put the point just a bit differently: There is nothing wrong with being the cause of someone's death if his death is, all things considered, a good thing. And if his death is *not* a good thing, then *no* form of euthanasia, active or passive, is justified. So once again we see that the two kinds of euthanasia stand or fall together.

The second counterargument appeals to a favorite idea of philosophers, namely that our duty not to harm people is generally more stringent than our duty to help them. The law affirms this when it forbids us to kill people, or steal their goods, but does not require us in general to save people's lives or give them charity. And this is said to be not merely a point about the law, but about morality as well. We do not have a strict moral duty to help some poor man in Ethiopia—although it might be kind and generous of us if we did—but we *do* have a strict moral duty to refrain from doing anything to harm him. Killing someone is a violation of our duty not to harm, whereas letting someone die is merely a failure to give help. Therefore, the former is a more serious breach of morality than the latter; and so, contrary to what was said above, there is a morally significant difference between killing and letting die.

This argument has a certain superficial plausibility, but it cannot be used to show that there is a morally important difference between active and passive euthanasia. For one thing, it only seems that our duty to help people is less stringent than our duty not to harm them when we concentrate on certain sorts of cases: cases in which the people we could help are very far away, and are strangers to us; or cases in which it would be very difficult for us to help them, or in which helping would require a substantial sacrifice on our part. Many people feel that, in *these* types of cases, it may be kind and generous of us to give help, but we are not morally required to do so. Thus it is felt that when we give money for famine relief we are being especially big-hearted, and we deserve special praise—even if it would be immodest of us to seek such praise—because we are doing more than, strictly speaking, we are required to do.[11]

However, if we think of cases in which it would be very easy for us to help someone who is close at hand and in which no great personal sacrifice is required, things look very different. Think again of the child drowning in the bathtub: *of course* a man standing next to the tub would have a strict moral duty to help the child. Here the alleged asymmetry between the duty to help and the duty not to do harm vanishes. Since most of the cases of euthanasia with which we are concerned are of this latter type—the patient is close at hand, it is well within the professional skills of the physician to keep him alive—the alleged asymmetry has little relevance.

It should also be remembered, in considering this argument, that the duty of doctors toward their patients *is* precisely to help them; that is what doctors are supposed to do. Therefore, even if there were a general asymmetry between the duty to help and the duty not to harm—which I deny—it would not apply in the special case of the relation between doctors and their patients. Finally, it is not clear that killing such a patient *is* harming him, even though in other cases it certainly is a great harm to someone to kill him, for as I said before, we are going under the assumption that the patient would be no worse off dead than he is now; if this is so, then killing him is not harming him. For the same reason we should not classify letting such a patient die as failing to help him. Therefore, even if we grant that our duty to help people is less stringent than our duty not to harm them, nothing follows about our duties with respect to kill-

ing and letting die in the special case of euthanasia.

Practical Consequences

This is enough, I think, to show that the doctrine underlying the AMA statement is false. There is no general moral difference between active and passive euthanasia; if one is permissible, so is the other. Now if this were merely an intellectual mistake, having no significant consequences for medical practice, the whole matter would not be very important. But the opposite is true: the doctrine has terrible consequences for, as I have already mentioned—and as doctors know very well—the process of being "allowed to die" can be relatively slow and painful, while being given a lethal injection is relatively quick and painless. Dr. Anthony Shaw describes what happens when the decision has been made not to perform the surgery necessary to "save" a mongoloid infant:

> When surgery is denied [the doctor] must try to keep the infant from suffering while natural forces sap the baby's life away. As a surgeon whose natural inclination is to use the scalpel to fight off death, standing by and watching a salvageable baby die is the most emotionally exhausting experience I know. It is easy at a conference, in a theoretical discussion, to decide that such infants should be allowed to die. It is altogether different to stand by in the nursery and watch as dehydration and infection wither a tiny being over hours and days. This is a terrible ordeal for me and the hospital staff—much more so than for the parents who never set foot in the nursery.[12]

Why must the hospital staff "stand by in the nursery and watch as dehydration and infection wither a tiny being over hours and days"? Why must they merely "try" to reduce the infant's suffering? The doctrine which says that the baby may be allowed to dehydrate and wither, but not be given an injection which would end its life without suffering, is not only irrational but cruel.

The same goes for the case of the man with cancer of the throat. Here there are three options: with continued treatment, he will have a few more days of pain, and then die; if treatment is stopped, but nothing else is done, it will be a few more hours; and with a lethal injection, he will die at once. Those who oppose euthanasia in all its forms say that we must take the first option, and keep the patient alive for as long as possible. This view is so patently inhumane that few defend it; nevertheless, it does have a certain kind of integrity. It is at least consistent. The third option is the one I think best. But the *middle* position—that, although the patient need not suffer for days before dying, he must nevertheless suffer for a few more hours—is a "moderate" view which incorporates the worst, and not the best, features of both extremes.

Let me mention one other practice that we would be well rid of if we stopped thinking that the distinction between active and passive euthanasia is important. About one in six hundred babies born in the United States is mongoloid. Most of these babies are otherwise healthy—that is, with only the usual pediatric care, they will proceed to a "normal" infancy. Some, however, are born with other congenital defects such as intestinal obstructions which require surgery if the baby is to live. As I have already mentioned, sometimes the surgery is withheld and the baby dies. But when there is no defect requiring surgery, the baby lives on.[13] Now surgery to remove an intestinal obstruction is not difficult; the reason why it is not performed in such cases is, clearly, that the child is mongoloid and the parents and doctor judge that because of *this* it is better for the child to die.

But notice that this situation is absurd, no matter what view one takes of the lives and potentials of such babies. If you think that the life of such an infant is worth preserving, then what does it matter if it needs a simple operation? Or, if you think it better that such a baby not live on, then what difference does it make if its intestinal tract is *not* blocked? In either case, the matter of life or death is being decided on irrelevant grounds. It is the mongolism, and not the intestine, that is the issue. The matter should be decided, if at all, on *that* basis, and not be allowed to depend on the essentially irrelevant question of whether the intestinal tract is blocked.

What makes this situation possible, of course, is the idea that when there is an intestinal obstruction we can "let the baby die," but when there is no such defect there is nothing we can do, for we must not "kill" it. The fact that this idea leads to such results as deciding life or death on irrelevant grounds is another good reason why it should be rejected.

Doctors may think that all of this is only of academic interest, the sort of thing which philosophers may worry about but which has no practical bearing on their own work. After all, doctors must be concerned about the legal consequences of what they do, and active euthanasia is clearly forbidden by the law. They are right to be concerned about this. There have not been many prosecutions of doctors in the United States for active euthanasia, but there have been some. Prosecutions for passive euthanasia, on the other hand, are virtually nonexistent, even though there are laws under which charges could be brought, and even though this practice is much more widespread. Passive euthanasia, unlike active euthanasia, is by and large tolerated by the law. The law may sometimes compel a doctor to take action which he might not otherwise take to keep a patient alive,[14] but of course this is very different from bringing criminal charges against him after the patient is dead.

Even so, doctors should be concerned with the fact that the law and public opinion are forcing upon them an indefensible moral position, which has a considerable effect on their practices. Of course, most doctors are not now in the position of being coerced in this matter, for they do not regard themselves as merely going along with what the law requires. Rather, in statements such as the AMA statement that I quoted, they are endorsing the doctrine as a central point of medical ethics. In that statement, active euthanasia is condemned not merely as illegal but as "contrary to that for which the medical profession stands," while passive euthanasia is approved. However, if my arguments have been sound, there really is no intrinsic moral difference between them (although there may be morally important differences in their consequences, varying from case to case); so while doctors may have to discriminate between them to satisfy the law, they should not do any *more* than that. In particular, they should not give the distinction any added authority and weight by writing it into official statements of medical ethics.

Notes

1. F. J. Ingelfinger, "Bedside Ethics for the Hopeless Case," The *New England Journal of Medicine* 289 (25 October 1973), p. 914.

2. Ibid.

3. This statement was approved by the House of Delegates of the AMA on December 4, 1973. It is worth noting that some state medical societies have advised *patients* to take a similar attitude toward the termination of their lives. In 1973 the Connecticut State Medical Society approved a "background statement" to be signed by terminal patients which includes this sentence: "I value life and the dignity of life, so that I am not asking that my life be directly taken, but that my life not be unreasonably prolonged or the dignity of life be destroyed." Other state medical societies have followed suit.

4. A discussion of this type of case can be found in Anthony Shaw, " 'Doctor, Do We Have a Choice?' " The *New York Times Magazine*, 30 January 1972, pp. 44–54. Also see Shaw's "Dilemmas of 'Informed Consent' in Children," The *New England Journal of Medicine* 289 (25 October 1973), pp. 885–90.

5. Paul Ramsey, *The Patient as Person* (New Haven, Conn.: Yale University Press, 1970), pp. 115–16.

6. D. C. S. Cameron, *The Truth About Cancer* (Englewood Cliffs, N.J.: Prentice-Hall, 1956), p. 116.

7. Ramsey, *The Patient as Person*, p. 151.

8. Judith Jarvis Thomson has argued that this line of reasoning is unsound. Consider, she says, this argument which is parallel to the one involving Smith and Jones:

Alfrieda knows that if she cuts off Alfred's head he will die, and wanting him to die, cuts it off; Bertha knows that if she punches Bert in the nose he will die—Bert is in peculiar physical condition—and, wanting him to die, punches him in the nose. But what Bertha does is surely every bit as bad as what Alfrieda does. So cutting off a man's head isn't worse than punching a man in the nose. ("Killing, Letting Die, and the Trolley Problem," The *Monist* 59 [1976], p. 204.)

She concludes that, since this absurd argument doesn't prove anything, the Smith/Jones argument doesn't prove anything either.

However, I think that the Alfrieda/Bertha argument is not absurd, as strange as it is. A little analysis shows that it is a sound argument and that its conclusion is true. We need to notice first that the reason why it is wrong to chop someone's head off is, obviously, that this causes death. The act is objectionable because of its consequences. Thus, a different act with the same consequences may be equally objectionable. In Thomson's example, punching Bert in the nose has the same consequences as chopping off Alfred's head; and, indeed, the two actions are equally bad.

Now the Alfrieda/Bertha argument presupposes a distinction between the act of chopping off someone's head, and the results of this act, the victim's death. (It is stipulated that, except for the fact that Alfrieda chops off someone's head, while Bertha punches someone in the nose, the two acts are "in all other respects alike." The "*other* respects" include the act's consequence, the victim's death.) This is not a distinction we would normally think to make, since we cannot in fact cut off someone's head without killing him. Yet in thought the distinction can be drawn. The question raised in the argument, then, is whether, *considered apart from their consequences*, head-chopping is worse than nose-punching. And the answer to *this* strange question is No, just as the argument says it should be.

The conclusion of the argument should be construed like this: The bare fact that one act is an act of head-chopping, while another act is an act of nose-punching, is not a reason for judging the former to be worse than the latter. At the same time—and this is perfectly compatible with the argument—the fact that one act causes death, while another does not, *is* a reason for judging the former to be worse. The parallel construal of my conclusion is: The bare fact that one act is an act of killing, while another act is an act of letting die, is not a reason for judging the former to be worse than the latter. At the same time—and this is perfectly compatible with my argument—the fact that an act (of killing, for example) prevents suffering, while another act (of letting die, for example) does not, *is* a reason for preferring one over the other. So once we see exactly how the Alfrieda/Bertha argument *is* parallel to the Smith/Jones argument, we find that Thomson's argument is, surprisingly, quite all right.

9. Ramsey, *The Patient as Person*, p. 151.

10. J. Russell Elkinton, "The Dying Patient, the Doctor, and the Law," *Villanova Law Review* 13 (Summer 1968), p. 743.

11. For the purposes of this essay we do not need to consider whether this way of thinking about "charity" is justified. There are, however, strong arguments that it is morally indefensible: see Peter Singer, "Famine, Affluence, and Morality,"

Philosophy and Public Affairs 1 (Spring 1972), pp. 229–43. Also see James Rachels, "Killing and Letting People Die of Starvation," *Philosophy* 54 (1979), pp. 159–71, for a discussion of the killing/letting die distinction in the context of world hunger, as well as further arguments that the distinction is morally unimportant.

12. Shaw, " 'Doctor, Do We Have a Choice?' " p. 54.

13. See the articles by Shaw cited in note 4.

14. For example, in February 1974 a Superior Court judge in Maine ordered a doctor to proceed with an operation to repair a hole in the esophagus of a baby with multiple deformities. Otherwise the operation would not have been performed. The baby died anyway a few days later. "Deformed Baby Dies Amid Controversy," The *Miami Herald*, 25 February 1974, p. 4-B.

---

19. The Intentional Termination of Life

Bonnie Steinbock

Bonnie Steinbock defends the policy statement of the American Medical Association on euthanasia against James Rachels's critique. She argues that the statement does not rest on the belief that there is a moral difference between active and passive euthanasia. Rather, she contends that the statement rejects both active and passive euthanasia but permits "the cessation of the employment of extraordinary means," which she claims is not the same as passive euthanasia. She points out that doctors can cease to employ extraordinary means to respect the wishes of the patient or because continued treatment is painful and has little chance of success, without intending to let the patient die. She allows, however, that in some cases, ceasing to employ extraordinary means does amount to intending to let the patient die and also that in other cases, killing may even be morally preferable to letting die.

According to James Rachels[1] a common mistake in medical ethics is the belief that there is a moral difference between active and passive euthanasia. This is a mistake, [he] argues, because the rationale underlying the distinction

Reprinted with permission from *Ethics in Science and Medicine*, pp. 59–64, Bonnie Steinbock, "The Intentional Termination of Life." Copyright 1979, Pergamon Press, Ltd.

between active and passive euthanasia is the idea that there is a significant moral difference between intentionally killing and letting die. . . . Whether the belief that there is a significant moral difference (between intentionally killing and intentionally letting die) is mistaken is not my concern here. For it is far from clear that this distinction *is* the basis of the doctrine of the American Medical Association which Rachels attacks. And if the killing/letting die distinction is not the basis of the AMA doctrine, then arguments showing that the distinction has no moral force do not, in themselves, reveal in the doctrine's adherents either "confused thinking" or "a moral point of view unrelated to the interests of individuals." Indeed, as we examine the AMA doctrine, I think it will become clear that it appeals to and makes use of a number of overlapping distinctions, which may have moral significance in particular cases, such as the distinction between intending and foreseeing, or between ordinary and extraordinary care. Let us then turn to the statement, from the House of Delegates of the American Medical Association, which Rachels cites:

> The intentional termination of the life of one human being by another—mercy-killing—is contrary to that for which the medical profession stands and is contrary to the policy of the American Medical Association.
>
>   The cessation of the employment of extraordinary means to prolong the life of the body when there is irrefutable evidence that biological death is imminent is the decision of the patient and/or his immediate family. The advice and judgment of the physician should be freely available to the patient and/or his immediate family.[2]

Rachels attacks this statement because he believes that it contains a moral distinction between active and passive euthanasia. . . .

I intend to show that the AMA statement does not imply support of the active/passive euthanasia distinction. In forbidding the intentional termination of life, the statement rejects both active and passive euthanasia. It does allow for ". . . the cessation of the employment of extraordinary means . . ." to prolong life. The mistake Rachels makes is in identifying the cessation of life-prolonging treatment with passive euthanasia, or intentionally letting die. If it were right to equate the two, then the AMA statement would be self-contradictory, for it would begin by condemning, and end by allowing, the intentional termination of life. But if the cessation of life-prolonging treatment is not always or necessarily passive

euthanasia, then there is no confusion and no contradiction.

Why does Rachels think that the cessation of life-prolonging treatment is the intentional termination of life? He says:

> The AMA policy statement isolates the crucial issue very well: the crucial issue is "the intentional termination of the life of one human being by another." But after identifying this issue, and forbidding "mercy-killing," the statement goes on to deny that the cessation of treatment is the intentional termination of a life. This is where the mistake comes in, for what is the cessation of treatment, in these circumstances, if it is not "the intentional termination of the life of one human being by another"? Of course it is exactly that, and if it were not, there would be no point to it.[3]

However, there *can* be a point (to the cessation of life-prolonging treatment) other than an endeavor to bring about the patient's death, and so the blanket identification of cessation of treatment with the intentional termination of a life is inaccurate. There are at least two situations in which the termination of life-prolonging treatment cannot be identified with the intentional termination of the life of one human being by another.

The first situation concerns the patient's right to refuse treatment. Rachels gives the example of a patient dying of an incurable disease, accompanied by unrelievable pain, who wants to end the treatment which cannot cure him but can only prolong his miserable existence. Why, they ask, may a doctor accede to the patient's request to stop treatment, but not provide a patient in a similar situation with a lethal dose? The answer lies in the patient's right to refuse treatment. In general, a competent adult has the right to refuse treatment, even where such treatment is necessary to prolong life. Indeed, the right to refuse treatment has been upheld even when the patient's reason for refusing treatment is generally agreed to be inadequate.[4] This right can be overridden (if, for example, the patient has dependent children) but, in general, no one may legally compel you to undergo treatment to which you have not consented. "Historically, surgical intrusion has always been considered a technical battery upon the person and one to be excused or justified by consent of the patient or justified by necessity created by the circumstances of the moment. . . ."[5]

At this point, it might be objected that if one has the right to refuse life-prolonging treatment, then consistency demands that one have the right to decide to end his life, and to obtain help in doing so. The idea is that the right to refuse treatment somehow implies a right to voluntary euthanasia, and we need to see why someone might think this. The right to refuse treatment has been considered by legal writers as an example of the right to privacy or, better, the right to bodily self-determination. You have the right to decide what happens to your own body, and the right to refuse treatment is an instance of that more general right. But if you have the right to determine what happens to your body, then should you not have the right to choose to end your life, and even a right to get help in doing so?

However, it is important to see that the right to refuse treatment is not the same as, nor does it entail, a right to voluntary euthanasia, even if both can be derived from the right to bodily self-determination. The right to refuse treatment is not itself a "right to die"; that one may choose to exercise this right even at the risk of death, or even *in order to die*, is irrelevant. The purpose of the right to refuse medical treatment is not to give persons a right to decide whether to live or die, but to protect them from the unwanted interferences of others. Perhaps we ought to interpret the right to bodily self-determination more broadly so as to include a right to die: but this would be a substantial extension of our present understanding of the right to bodily self-determination, and not a consequence of it. Should we recognize a right to voluntary euthanasia, we would have to agree that people have the right not merely to be left alone, but also the right to be killed. I leave to one side that substantive moral issue. My claim is simply that there can be a reason for terminating life-prolonging treatment other than "to bring about the patient's death."

The second case in which termination of treatment cannot be identified with intentional termination of life is where continued treatment has little chance of improving the patient's condition and brings greater discomfort than relief.

The question here is what treatment is appropriate to the particular case. A cancer specialist describes it in this way:

> My general rule is to administer therapy as long as a patient responds well and has the potential for a reasonably good quality of life. But when all feasible therapies have been administered and a patient shows signs of rapid deterioration, the continuation of therapy can cause more discomfort than the cancer. From that time I recommend surgery, radiotherapy, or chemotherapy only as a means of relieving pain. But if a patient's condition should once again stabilize after the withdrawal of active therapy and if it should appear that he could still gain some good time, I would immediately reinstitute active therapy. The decision to cease anticancer treatment is never irrevocable, and often the desire to live will push a patient to try for another remission, or even a few more days of life.[6]

The decision here to cease anticancer treatment cannot be construed as a decision that the patient die, or as the intentional termination of life. It is a decision to provide the most appropriate treatment for that patient at that time. Rachels suggests that the point of the cessation of treatment is the intentional termination of life. But here the point of discontinuing treatment is not to bring about the patient's death but to avoid treatment that will cause more discomfort than the cancer and has little hope of benefiting the patient. Treatment that meets this description is often called "extraordinary."[7] The concept is flexible, and what might be considered "extraordinary" in one situation might be ordinary in another. The use of a respirator to sustain a patient through a severe bout with a respiratory disease would be considered ordinary; its use to sustain the life of a severely brain damaged person in an irreversible coma would be considered extraordinary.

Contrasted with extraordinary treatment is ordinary treatment, the care a doctor would normally be expected to provide. Failure to provide ordinary care constitutes neglect, and can even be construed as the intentional infliction of harm, where there is a legal obligation to provide care. The importance of the ordinary/extraordinary care distinction lies partly in its connection to the doctor's intention. The withholding of extraordinary care should be seen as a decision not to inflict painful treatment on a patient without reasonable hope of success. The withholding of ordinary care, by contrast, must be seen as neglect. Thus, one doctor says, "We have to draw a distinction between ordinary and extraordinary means. We never withdraw what's needed to make a baby comfortable, we would never withdraw the care a parent would provide. We never kill a baby. . . . But we may decide certain heroic intervention is not worthwhile."[8]

We should keep in mind the ordinary/extraordinary care distinction when considering an example given by Rachels to show the irrationality of the active/passive distinction with regard to infanticide. The example is this: a child is born with Down's syndrome and also has an intestinal obstruction which requires corrective surgery. If the surgery is not performed, the infant will starve to death, since it cannot take food orally. This may take days or even weeks, as dehydration and infection set in. Commenting on this situation, Rachels says:

> I can understand why some people are opposed to all euthanasia, and insist that such infants must be allowed to live. I think I can also understand why other people favor destroying these babies quickly and painlessly. But why should anyone favor letting "dehydration and infection wither a tiny being over hours and days"? The doctrine that says that a baby may be allowed to dehydrate and wither, but may not be given an injection that would end its life without suffering, seems so patently cruel as to require no further refutation.[9]

Such a doctrine perhaps does not need further refutation; but this is not the AMA doctrine.

For the AMA statement criticized by Rachels allows only for the cessation of extraordinary means to prolong life when death is imminent. Neither of these conditions is satisfied in this example. Death is not imminent in this situation, any more than it would be if a normal child had an attack of appendicitis. Neither the corrective surgery to remove the intestinal obstruction, nor the intravenous feeding required to keep the infant alive until such surgery is performed, can be regarded as extraordinary means, for neither is particularly expensive, nor does either place an overwhelming burden on the patient or others. (The continued existence of the child might be thought to place an overwhelming burden on its parents, but that has nothing to do with the characterization of the means to prolong its life as extraordinary. If it had, then *feeding* a severely defective child who required a great deal of care could be regarded as extraordinary.) The chances of success if the operation is undertaken are quite good, though there is always a risk in operating on infants. Though the Down's syndrome will not be alleviated, the child will proceed to an otherwise normal infancy.

It cannot be argued that the treatment is withheld for the infant's sake, unless one is prepared to argue that all mentally retarded babies are better off dead. This is particularly implausible in the case of Down's syndrome babies who generally do not suffer and are capable of giving and receiving love, of learning and playing, to varying degrees.

In a film on this subject entitled, "Who Should Survive?," a doctor defended a decision not to operate, saying that since the parents did not consent to the operation, the doctor's hands were tied. As we have seen, surgical intrusion requires consent, and in the case of infants, consent would normally come from the parents. But, as their legal guardians, parents are required to provide medical care for their children, and failure to do so can constitute criminal neglect or even homicide. In general, courts have been understandably reluctant to recognize a parental right to terminate life-prolonging treatment.[10] Although prosecution is unlikely, physicians who comply with invalid instructions from the parents and permit the infant's death could be liable for aiding and abetting, failure to report child neglect, or even homicide. So it is not true that, in this situation, doctors are legally bound to do as the parents wish.

To sum up, I think that Rachels is right to regard the decision not to operate in the Down's syndrome example as the intentional termination of life. But there is no reason to believe that either the law or the AMA would regard it otherwise. Certainly the decision to withhold treatment is not justified by the AMA statement. That such infants have been allowed to die cannot be denied; but this, I think, is the result of doctors misunderstanding the law and the AMA position.

Withholding treatment in this case is the intentional termination of life because the infant is deliberately allowed to die; that is the point of not operating. But there are other cases in which that is not the point. If the point is to avoid inflicting painful treatment on a patient with little or no reasonable hope of success, this is not the intentional termination of life. The permissibility of such withholding of treatment, then, would have no implications for the permissibility of euthanasia, active or passive.

The decision whether or not to operate, or to institute vigorous treatment, is particularly agonizing in the case of children born with spina bifida, an opening in the base of the spine usually accompanied by hydrocephalus and mental retardation. If left unoperated, these children usually die of meningitis or kidney failure within the first few years of life. Even if they survive, all affected children face a lifetime of illness, operations and varying degrees of disability. The policy used to be to save as many as possible, but the trend now is toward selective treatment, based on the physician's estimate of the chances of success. If operating is not likely to improve significantly the child's condition, parents and doctors may agree not to operate. This is not the intentional termination of life, for again the purpose is not the termination of the child's life but the avoidance of painful and pointless treatment. Thus, the fact that withholding treatment is justified does not imply that killing the child would be equally justified.

Throughout the discussion, I have claimed that intentionally ceasing life-prolonging treatment is not the intentional termination of life unless the doctor has, as his or her purpose in stopping treatment, the patient's death.

It may be objected that I have incorrectly characterized the conditions for the intentional termination of life. Perhaps it is enough that the doctor intentionally ceases treatment, foreseeing that the patient will die; perhaps the reason for ceasing treatment is irrelevant to its characterization as the intentional termination of life. I find this suggestion implausible, but am willing to consider arguments for it. Rachels has provided no such arguments: indeed, he apparently shares my view about the intentional termination of life. For when he claims that the cessation of life-prolonging treatment *is* the intentional termination of life, his reason for making the claim is that "if it were not, there would be no point to it." Rachels believes that the point of ceasing treatment, "in these cases," is to bring about the patient's death. If that were not the point, he suggests, why would the doctor cease treatment? I have shown, however, that there can be a point to ceasing treatment which is not the death of the patient. In showing this, I have refuted Rachels's reason for identifying the cessation of life-prolonging treatment with the intentional termination of life, and thus his argument against the AMA doctrine.

Here someone might say: Even if the withholding of treatment is not the intentional termination of life, does that make a difference, morally speaking? If life-prolonging treatment may be withheld, for the sake of the child, may not an easy death be provided, for the sake of the child, as well? The unoperated child with spina bifida may take months or even years to die. Distressed by the spectacle of children "lying around waiting to die," one doctor has written, "It is time that society and medicine stopped perpetuating the fiction that withholding treatment is ethically different from terminating a life. It is time that society began to discuss mechanisms by which we can alleviate the pain and suffering for those individuals whom we cannot help."[11]

I do not deny that there may be cases in which death is in the best interests of the patient. In such cases, a quick and painless death may be the best thing. However, I do not think that, once active or vigorous treatment is stopped, a quick death is always preferable to a lingering one. We must be cautious about attributing to defective children *our* distress at seeing them linger. Waiting for them to die may be tough on parents, doctors and nurses—it isn't necessarily tough on the child. The decision not to operate need not mean a decision to neglect, and it may be possible to make the remaining months of the child's life comfortable, pleasant and filled with love. If this alternative is possible, surely it is more decent and humane than killing the child. In such a situation, withholding treatment, foreseeing the child's death, is not ethically equivalent to killing the child, and we cannot move from the permissibility of the former to that of the latter. I am worried that there will be a tendency to do precisely that if active euthanasia is regarded as morally equivalent to the withholding of life-prolonging treatment.

Conclusion

The AMA statement does not make the distinction Rachels wishes to attack, i.e., that between active and passive euthanasia. Instead, the statement draws a distinction between the intentional termination of life, on the one hand, and the cessation of the employment of extraordinary means to prolong life, on the other. Nothing said by Rachels shows that this distinction is confused. It may be that doctors have misinterpreted the AMA statement, and that this had led, for example, to decisions to allow defective infants slowly to starve to death. I quite agree with Rachels that the decisions to which they allude were cruel and made on irrelevant grounds. Certainly it is worth pointing out that allowing someone to die can be the intentional termination of life, and that it can be just as bad as, or worse than, killing someone. However, the withholding of life-prolonging treatment is not necessarily the intentional termination of life, so that if it is permissible to withhold life-prolonging treatment, it does not follow that, other things being equal, it is permissible to kill. Furthermore, most of the time, other things are not equal. In many of the cases in which it would be right to cease treatment, I do not think that it would also be right to kill.

Notes

1. James Rachels, Active and passive euthanasia. *New Engl. J. Med.,* **292**, 78–80, 1975.

2. Rachels, p. 78.

3. Rachels, p. 79–80.

4. For example, *In re Yetter,* 62 Pa. D. & C. 2d 619, C.P., Northampton County Ct., 1974.

5. David W. Meyers, Legal aspects of voluntary euthanasia, *Dilemmas of Euthanasia* (Edited by John Behnke and Sissela Bok), p. 56. Anchor Books, New York, 1975.

6. Ernest H. Rosenbaum, MD., *Living with Cancer,* p. 27. Praeger, New York, 1975.

7. Cf. Tristam Engelhardt, Jr., Ethical issues in aiding the death of young children, *Beneficent Euthanasia* (Edited by Marvin Kohl), Prometheus Books, Buffalo, N.Y., 1975.

8. B. D. Colen, *Karen Ann Quinlan: Living and Dying in the Age of Eternal Life,* p. 115. Nash, 1976.

9. Rachels, p. 79.

10. Cf. Norman L. Cantor, Law and the termination of an incompetent patient's life-preserving care. *Dilemmas of Euthanasia,* op. cit., pp. 69–105.

11. John Freeman, Is there a right to die— quickly?, *J. Pediat.* **80**, p. 905.

20. *Planned Parenthood v. Casey*

Supreme Court of the United States

The issue before the Supreme Court was whether the Pennsylvania Abortion Control Act as amended in 1988 and 1989 violated the due process clause of the U.S. Constitution by requiring informed consent, a twenty-four-hour waiting period, parental consent in the case of a minor, spousal notification, and certain reporting and recordkeeping by facilities that provide abortion services. While reaffirming its commitment to the essential holding of *Roe v. Wade*, the Court allowed that the state had a legitimate interest in imposing all of the above requirements except spousal notification.

Justices *O'Connor, Kennedy,* and *Souter* announcing the judgment of the Court in which Justices *Blackmun* and *Stevens* concurred in part:

Liberty finds no refuge in a jurisprudence of doubt. Yet 19 years after our holding that the Constitution protects a woman's right to terminate her pregnancy in its early stages, *Roe v. Wade* . . . (1973), that definition of liberty is still questioned. . . .

At issue in these cases are five provisions of the Pennsylvania Abortion Control Act of 1982 as amended in 1988 and 1989. . . . The Act requires that a woman seeking an abortion give her informed consent prior to the abortion procedure, and specifies that she be provided with certain information at least 24 hours before the abortion is performed. . . . For a minor to obtain an abortion, the Act requires the informed consent of one of her parents, but provides for a judicial bypass option if the minor does not wish to or cannot obtain a parent's consent. . . . Another provision of the Act requires that, unless certain exceptions apply, a married woman seeking an abortion must sign a statement indicating that she has notified her husband of her intended abortion. . . . The Act exempts compliance with these three requirements in the event of a "medical emergency." . . . In addition to the above provisions regulating the performance of abortions, the Act imposes certain reporting requirements on facilities that provide abortion services. . . .

It must be stated at the outset and with clarity that *Roe*'s essential holding, the holding we reaffirm, has three parts. First is a recognition of the right of the woman to choose to have an abortion before viability and to obtain it without undue interference from the State. Before viability, the State's interests are not strong enough to support a prohibition of abortion or the imposition of a substantial obstacle to the woman's effective right to elect the procedure. Second is a confirmation of the State's power to restrict abortions after fetal viability, if the law contains exceptions for pregnancies which endanger a woman's life or health. And third is the principle that the State has legitimate interests from the outset of the pregnancy in protecting the health of the woman and the life of the fetus that may become a child. These principles do not contradict one another; and we adhere to each.

Constitutional protection of the woman's decision to terminate her pregnancy derives from the Due Process Clause of the Fourteenth Amendment. It declares that no State shall "deprive any person of life, liberty, or property, without due process of law." The controlling word in the case before us is "liberty." . . .

Men and women of good conscience can disagree, and we suppose some always shall disagree, about the profound moral and spiritual implications of terminating a pregnancy, even in its earliest stage. Some of us as individuals find abortion offensive to our most basic principles of morality, but that cannot control our decision. Our obligation is to define the liberty of all, not to mandate our own moral code. The underlying constitutional issue is whether the State can resolve these philosophic questions in such a definitive way that a woman lacks all choice in the matter, except perhaps in those rare circumstances in which the pregnancy is itself a danger to her own life or health, or is the result of rape or incest.

It is conventional constitutional doctrine that where reasonable people disagree the government can adopt one position or the other. . . . That theorem, however, assumes a state of affairs in which the choice does not intrude upon a protected liberty. Thus, while some people might disagree about whether or not the flag should be saluted, or disagree about the proposition that it may not be defiled, we have ruled that a State may not compel or enforce one view or the other. . . .

Our law affords constitutional protection to personal decisions relating to marriage, procreation, contraception, family relationships, child rearing, and education. . . . Our cases recognize "the right of the *individual,* married or single, to be free from unwarranted governmental intrusion into matters so fundamentally affecting a person as the decision whether to bear or beget a child." . . . Our precedents "have respected the private realm of family life which the state cannot enter." . . . These matters, involving the most intimate and personal choices a person may make in a lifetime, choices central to personal dignity and autonomy, are central to the liberty protected by the Fourteenth Amendment. At the heart of liberty is the right to define one's own concept of existence, of meaning, of the universe, and of the mystery of human life. Beliefs about these matters could not define the attributes of personhood were they formed under compulsion of the State.

These considerations begin our analysis of the woman's interest in terminating her pregnancy but cannot end it, for this reason: though the abortion decision may originate within the zone of conscience and belief, it is more than a philosophic exercise. Abortion is a unique act. It is an act fraught with consequences for others: for the woman who must live with the implications of her decision; for the persons who perform and assist in the

procedure; for the spouse, family, and society which must confront the knowledge that these procedures exist, procedures some deem nothing short of an act of violence against innocent human life; and, depending on one's beliefs, for the life or potential life that is aborted. Though abortion is conduct, it does not follow that the State is entitled to proscribe it in all instances. That is because the liberty of the woman is at stake in a sense unique to the human condition and so unique to the law. The mother who carries a child to full term is subject to anxieties, to physical constraints, to pain that only she must bear. That these sacrifices have from the beginning of the human race been endured by woman with a pride that ennobles her in the eyes of others and gives to the infant a bond of love cannot alone be grounds for the State to insist she make the sacrifice. Her suffering is too intimate and personal for the State to insist, without more, upon its own vision of the woman's role, however dominant that vision has been in the coure of our history and our culture. The destiny of the woman must be shaped to a large extent on her own conception of her spiritual imperatives and her place in society.

It should be recognized, moreover, that in some critical respects the abortion decision is of the same character as the decision to use contraception, to which *Griswold v. Connecticut, Eisenstadt v. Baird,* and *Carey v. Population Services International,* afford constitutional protection. We have no doubt as to the correctness of those decisions. They support the reasoning in *Roe* relating to the woman's liberty because they involve personal decisions concerning not only the meaning of procreation but also human responsibility and respect for it. As with abortion, reasonable people will have differences of opinion about these matters. One view is based on such reverence for the wonder of creation that any pregnancy ought to be welcomed and carried to full term no matter how difficult it will be to provide for the child and ensure its well-being. Another is that the inability to provide for the nurture and care of the infant is a cruelty to the child and an anguish to the parent. These are intimate views with infinite variations, and their deep, personal character underlay our decisions in *Griswold, Eisenstadt,* and *Carey.* The same concerns are present when the woman confronts the reality that, perhaps despite her attempts to avoid it, she has become pregnant.

It was this dimension of personal liberty that *Roe* sought to protect, and its holding invoked the reasoning and the tradition of the precedents we have discussed, granting protection to substantive liberties of the person. *Roe* was, of course, an extension of those cases and, as the decision itself indicated, the separate States could act in some degree to further their own legitimate interests in protecting pre-natal life. The extent to which the legislatures of the States might act to outweigh the interests of the woman in choosing to terminate her pregnancy was a subject of debate both in *Roe* itself and in decisions following it.

While we appreciate the weight of the arguments made on behalf of the State in the case before us, arguments which in their ultimate formulation conclude that *Roe* should be overruled, the reservations any of us may have in reaffirming the central holding of *Roe* are outweighed by the explication of individual liberty we have given combined with the force of *stare decisis*. We turn now to that doctrine.

The obligation to follow precedent begins with necessity, and a contrary necessity marks its outer limit. With Cardozo, we recognize that no judicial system could do society's work if it eyed each issue afresh in every case that raised it. . . . Indeed, the very concept of the rule of law underlying our own Constitution requires such continuity over time that a respect for precedent is, by definition, indispensable. . . . At the other extreme, a different necessity would make itself felt if a prior judicial ruling should come to be seen so clearly as error that its enforcement was for that very reason doomed. . . .

So in this case we may inquire whether *Roe*'s central . . . rule's limitation on state power could be removed without serious inequity to those who have relied upon it or significant damage to the stability of the society governed by the rule in question. . . .

Abortion is customarily chosen as an unplanned response to the consequence of unplanned activity or to the failure of conventional birth control, and except on the assumption that no intercourse would have occurred but for *Roe*'s holding, such behavior may appear to justify no reliance claim. Even if reliance could be claimed on that unrealistic assumption, the argument might run, any reliance interest would be *de minimis*. This argument would be premised on the hypothesis that reproductive planning could take virtually immediate account of any sudden restoration of state authority to ban abortions.

To eliminate the issue of reliance that easily, however, one would need to limit cognizable reliance to specific instances of sexual activity. But to do this would be simply to refuse to face the fact that for two decades of economic and social developments, people have organized intimate relationships and made choices that define their views of themselves and their places in society, in reliance on the availability of abortion in the event that contraception should fail. The ability of women to participate equally in the economic and social life of the Nation has been facilitated by their ability to control their reproductive lives. . . .

We have seen how time has overtaken some of *Roe*'s factual assumptions: advances in maternal health care allow for abortions safe to the mother later in pregnancy than was true in 1973. . . . But these facts go only to the scheme of time limits on the realization of competing interests, and the divergences from the factual premises of 1973 have no bearing on the validity of *Roe*'s central holding, that viability marks the earliest point at which the State's interest in fetal life is constitutionally adequate to justify a legislative ban on nontherapeutic abortions. The soundness or unsoundness of that constitutional judgment in no sense turns on whether viability occurs at approximately 28 weeks, as was usual at the time of *Roe*, at 23 to 24 weeks, as it sometimes does today, or at some moment even slightly earlier in pregnancy, as it may if fetal respiratory capacity can somehow be enhanced in the future. Whenever it may occur, the attainment of viability may continue to serve as the critical fact, just as it has done since *Roe* was decided; which is to say that no change in *Roe*'s factual underpinning has left its central holding obsolete, and none supports an argument for overruling it.

The sum of the precedential inquiry to this

point shows *Roe*'s underpinnings unweakened in any way affecting its central holding. While it has engendered disapproval, it has not been unworkable. An entire generation has come of age free to assume *Roe*'s concept of liberty in defining the capacity of women to act in society, and to make reproductive decisions; no erosion of principle going to liberty or personal autonomy has left *Roe*'s central holding a doctrinal remnant; *Roe* portends no developments at odds with other precedent for the analysis of personal liberty; and no changes of fact have rendered viability more or less appropriate as the point at which the balance of interests tips. Within the bounds of normal *stare decisis* analysis, then, and subject to the considerations on which it customarily turns, the stronger argument is for affirming *Roe*'s central holding, with whatever degree of personal reluctance any of us may have, not for overruling it. . . .

From what we have said so far it follows that it is a constitutional liberty of the woman to have some freedom to terminate her pregnancy. We conclude that the basic decision in *Roe* was based on a constitutional analysis which we cannot now repudiate. The woman's liberty is not so unlimited, however, that from the outset the State cannot show its concern for the life of the unborn, and at a later point in fetal development the State's interest in life has sufficient force so that the right of the woman to terminate the pregnancy can be restricted.

That brings us, of course, to the point where much criticism has been directed at *Roe*, a criticism that always inheres when the Court draws a specific rule from what in the Constitution is but a general standard. We conclude, however, that the urgent claims of the woman to retain the ultimate control over her destiny and her body, claims implicit in the meaning of liberty, require us to perform that function. Liberty must not be extinguished for want of a line that is clear. And it falls to us to give some real substance to the woman's liberty to determine whether to carry her pregnancy to full term.

We conclude the line should be drawn at viability, so that before that time the woman has a right to choose to terminate her pregnancy. Any judicial act of line-drawing may seem somewhat arbitrary, but *Roe* was a reasoned statement, elaborated with great care. We have twice reaffirmed it in the face of great opposition. . . .

The woman's right to terminate her pregnancy before viability is the most central principle of *Roe v. Wade*. It is a rule of law and a component of liberty we cannot renounce.

On the other side of the equation is the interest of the State in the protection of potential life. The *Roe* Court recognized the State's "important and legitimate interest in protecting the potentiality of human life." . . . The weight to be given this state interest, not the strength of the woman's interest, was the difficult question faced in *Roe*. We do not need to say whether each of us, had we been Members of the Court when the valuation of the State interest came before it as an original matter, would have concluded, as the *Roe* Court did, that its weight is insufficient to justify a ban on abortions prior to viability even when it is subject to certain exceptions. The matter is not before us in the first instance, and coming as it does after nearly 20 years of litigation in *Roe*'s wake we are satisfied that the immediate question is not the soundness of *Roe*'s resolution of the issue, but the precedential force that must be accorded to its holding. And we have concluded that the essential holding of *Roe* should be reaffirmed.

Yet it must be remembered that *Roe v. Wade* speaks with clarity in establishing not only the woman's liberty but also the State's "important and legitimate interest in potential life." . . . That portion of the decision in *Roe* has been given too little acknowledgement and implementation by the Court in its subsequent cases. Those cases decided that any regulation touching upon the abortion decision must survive strict scrutiny, to be sustained only if drawn in narrow terms to further a compelling state interest. . . . Not all of the cases decided under that formulation can be reconciled with the holding in *Roe* itself that the State has legitimate interests in the health of the woman and in protecting the potential life within her. In resolving this tension, we choose to rely upon *Roe*, as against the later cases.

Roe established a trimester framework to govern abortion regulations. Under this elaborate but rigid construct, almost no regulation at all is permitted during the first trimester of pregnancy; regulations designed to protect the woman's health, but not to further the State's interest in potential life, are permitted during the second trimester; and during the third trimester, when the fetus is viable, prohibitions are permitted provided the life or health of the mother is not at stake. . . . Most of our cases since *Roe* have involved the application of rules derived from the trimester framework. . . .

The trimester framework no doubt was erected to ensure that the woman's right to choose not become so subordinate to the State's interest in promoting fetal life that her choice exists in theory but not in fact. We do not agree, however, that the trimester approach is necessary to accomplish this objective. A framework of this rigidity was unnecessary and in its later interpretation sometimes contradicted the State's permissible exercise of its powers.

Though the woman has a right to choose to terminate or continue her pregnancy before viability, it does not at all follow that the State is prohibited from taking steps to ensure that this choice is thoughtful and informed. Even in the earliest stages of pregnancy, the State may enact rules and regulations designed to encourage her to know that there are philosophic and social arguments of great weight that can be brought to bear in favor of continuing the pregnancy to full term and that there are procedures and institutions to allow adoption of unwanted children as well as a certain degree of state assistance if the mother chooses to raise the child herself. " '[T]he Constitution does not forbid a State or city, pursuant to democratic processes, from expressing a preference for normal childbirth.' " . . . It follows that States are free to enact laws to provide a reasonable framework for a woman to make a decision that has such profound and lasting meaning. This, too, we find consistent with *Roe*'s central premises, and indeed the inevitable consequence of our holding that the State has an interest in protecting the life of the unborn.

We reject the trimester framework, which we do not consider to be part of the essential holding of *Roe*. . . . Measures aimed at ensuring that a woman's choice contemplates the consequences for the fetus do not necessarily interfere with the right recognized in *Roe*, although those measures have been found to be inconsistent with the rigid trimester framework announced in that case. A logical reading of the central holding in *Roe* itself, and a necessary reconciliation of the liberty of the woman and the interest of the State in promoting prenatal life, require, in our view, that we abandon the trimester framework as a rigid prohibition on all previability regulation aimed at the protection of fetal life. The trimester framework suffers from these basic flaws: in its formulation it misconceives the nature of the pregnant woman's interest; and in practice it undervalues the State's interest in potential life, as recognized in *Roe*. . . .

The very notion that the State has a substantial interest in potential life leads to the conclusion that not all regulations must be deemed unwarranted. Not all burdens on the right to decide whether to terminate a pregnancy will be undue. In our view, the undue burden standard is the appropriate means of reconciling the State's interest with the woman's constitutionally protected liberty. . . .

An undue burden exists, and therefore a provision of law is invalid, if its purpose or effect is to place a substantial obstacle in the path of a woman seeking an abortion before the fetus attains viability. . . .

The Court of Appeals applied what it believed to be the undue burden standard and upheld each of the provisions except for the husband notification requirement. We agree generally with this conclusion. . . .

Studies reveal that family violence occurs in two million families in the United States. This figure, however, is a conservative one that substantially understates (because battering is usually not reported until it reaches life-threatening proportions) the actual number of families affected by domestic violence. In fact, researchers estimate that one of every two women will be battered at some time in their life. . . .

In well-functioning marriages, spouses discuss important intimate decisions such as whether to bear a child. But there are millions of women in this country who are the victims of regular physical and psychological abuse at the hands of their husbands. Should these women become pregnant, they may have very good reasons for not wishing to inform their husbands of their decision to obtain an abortion. Many may have justifiable fears of physical abuse, but may be no less fearful of the consequences of reporting prior abuse to the Commonwealth of Pennsylvania. Many may have a reasonable fear that notifying their husbands will provoke further instances of child abuse. . . . Many may fear devastating forms of psychological abuse from their husbands, including verbal harassment, threats of future violence, the destruction of possessions, physical confinement to the home, the withdrawal of financial support, or the disclosure of the abortion to family and friends. . . . And many women who are pregnant as a result of sexual assaults by their husbands will be unable to avail themselves of the exception for spousal sexual assault . . . because the exception requires that the woman have notified law enforcement authorities within 90 days of the assault, and her husband will be notified of her report once an investigation begins. . . . If anything in this field is certain, it is that victims of spousal sexual assault are extremely reluctant to report the abuse to the government; hence, a great many spousal rape victims will not be exempt from the notification requirement. . . .

The spousal notification requirement is thus likely to prevent a significant number of women from obtaining an abortion. It does not merely make abortions a little more difficult or expensive to obtain; for many women, it will impose a substantial obstacle. We must not blind ourselves to the fact that the significant number of women who fear for their safety and the safety of their children are likely to be deterred from procuring an abortion as surely as if the Commonwealth had outlawed abortion in all cases. . . .

We recognize that a husband has a "deep and proper concern and interest . . . in his wife's pregnancy and in the growth and development of the fetus she is carrying." . . . With regard to the children he has fathered and raised, the Court has recognized his "cognizable and substantial" interest in their custody. . . . If this case concerned a State's ability to require the mother to notify the father before taking some action with respect to a living child raised by both, therefore, it would be reasonable to conclude as a general matter that the father's interest in the welfare of the child and the mother's interest are equal.

Before birth, however, the issue takes on a very different cast. It is an inescapable biological fact that state regulation with respect to the child a woman is carrying will have a far greater impact on the mother's liberty than on the father's. The effect of state regulation on a woman's protected liberty is doubly deserving of scrutiny in such a case, as the State has touched not only upon the private sphere of the family but upon the very bodily integrity of the pregnant woman. . . . The Court has held that "when the wife and the husband disagree on this decision, the view of only one of the two marriage partners can prevail. Inasmuch as it is the woman who physically bears the child and who is the more directly and immediately affected by the pregnancy, as between the two, the balance weighs in her favor." . . . This conclusion rests upon the basic nature of marriage and the nature of our Constitution: "[T]he marital couple is not an independent entity with a mind and heart of its own, but an association of two individuals each with a separate intellectual and emotional makeup. If the right of privacy means anything, it is the right of the *individual,* married or single, to be free from unwarranted governmental intrusion into matters so fundamentally affecting a person as the decision whether to bear or beget a child." . . . The Constitution protects individuals, men and women alike, from unjustified state interference, even when that interference is enacted into law for the benefit of their spouses. . . .

The husband's interest in the life of the child his wife is carrying does not permit the State to empower him with this troubling degree of authority over his wife. The contrary view leads to consequences reminiscent of the common law. A husband has no enforceable right to require a wife to advise him before she exercises her personal choices. If a husband's interest in the potential life of the child outweighs a wife's liberty, the State could require a married woman to notify her husband before she uses a postfertilization contraceptive. Perhaps next in line would be a statute requiring pregnant married women to notify their husbands before engaging in conduct causing risks to the fetus. After all, if the husband's interest in the fetus's safety is a sufficient predicate for state regulation, the State could reasonably conclude that pregnant wives should notify their husbands before drinking alcohol or smoking. Perhaps married women should notify their husbands before using contraceptives or before undergoing any type of surgery that may have complications affecting the husband's interest in his wife's reproductive organs. And if a husband's interest justifies notice in any of these cases, one might reasonably argue that it justifies exactly what the *Danforth* Court held it did not justify—a requirement of the husband's consent as well. A State may not give to a man the kind of dominion over his wife that parents exercise over their children. . . .

Our Constitution is a convenant running from the first generation of Americans to us and then to future generations. It is a coherent succession. Each generation must learn anew that the Constitution's written terms embody ideas and aspirations that must survive more ages than one. We accept our responsibility not to retreat from interpreting the full meaning of the covenant in light of all of our precedents. We invoke it once again to define the freedom guaranteed by the Constitution's own promise, the promise of liberty.

---

21. Abortion: A Personal Moral Dilemma

Linda Bird Francke

Linda Bird Francke describes her own experience of having an abortion, the reasons why she had the abortion, and the ambivalence she felt before and after.

"Jane Doe," thirty-eight, had an abortion in New York City in 1973. The mother of three children, then three, five, and eleven, Jane had just started a full-time job in publishing. She and her husband, an investment banker, decided together that another baby would add an almost unbearable strain to their lives, which were already overfull. What Jane had not anticipated was the guilt and sadness that followed the abortion. She wrote about the experience shortly thereafter and filed the story away. Three years later she reread it and decided it might be helpful to other women who experience the ambivalence of abortion. The *New York Times* ran it on their Op-Ed page in May 1976. This is what she wrote:

We were sitting in a bar on Lexington Avenue when I told my husband I was pregnant. It is not a memory I like to dwell on. Instead of the champagne and hope

which had heralded the impending births of the first, second and third child, the news of this one was greeted with shocked silence and Scotch. "Jesus," my husband kept saying to himself, stirring the ice cubes around and around. "Oh, Jesus."

Oh, how we tried to rationalize it that night as the starting time for the movie came and went. My husband talked about his plans for a career change in the next year, to stem the staleness that fourteen years with the same investment-banking firm had brought him. A new baby would preclude that option.

The timing wasn't right for me either. Having juggled pregnancies and child care with what freelance jobs I could fit in between feedings, I had just taken on a full-time job. A new baby would put me right back in the nursery just when our youngest child was finally school age. It was time for *us*, we tried to rationalize. There just wasn't room in our lives now for another baby. We both agreed. And agreed. And agreed.

How very considerate they are at the Women's Services, known formally as the Center for Reproductive and Sexual Health. Yes, indeed, I could have an abortion that very Saturday morning and be out in time to drive to the country that afternoon. Bring a first morning urine specimen, a sanitary belt and napkins, a money order or $125 cash—and a friend.

My friend turned out to be my husband, standing awkwardly and ill at ease as men always do in places that are exclusively for women, as I checked in at nine A.M. Other men hovered around just as anxiously, knowing that they had to be there, wishing they weren't. No one spoke to each other. When I would be cycled out of there four hours later, the same men would be slumped in their same seats, locked downcast in their cells of embarrassment.

The Saturday morning women's group was more dispirited than the men in the waiting room. There were around fifteen of us, a mixture of races, ages and backgrounds. Three didn't speak English at all and a fourth, a pregnant Puerto Rican girl around eighteen, translated for them.

There were six black women and a hodge-podge of whites, among them a T-shirted teenager who kept leaving the room to throw up and a puzzled middle-aged woman from Queens with three grown children.

"What form of birth control were you using?" the volunteer asked each of us. The answer was inevitably "none." She then went on to describe the various forms of birth control available at the clinic, and offered them to each of us.

The youngest Puerto Rican girl was asked through the interpreter which she'd like to use, the loop, diaphragm, or pill. She shook her head "no" three times. "You don't want to come back here again, do you?" the volunteer pressed. The girl's head was so low her chin rested on her breastbone. "*Si*," she whispered.

We had been there two hours by that time, filling out endless forms, giving blood and urine, receiving lectures. But unlike any other group of women I've been in, we didn't talk. Our common denominator, the

one which usually floods language and economic barriers into familiarity, today was one of shame. We were losing life that day, not giving it.

The group kept getting cut back to smaller, more workable units, and finally I was put in a small waiting room with just two other women. We changed into paper bathrobes and paper slippers, and we rustled whenever we moved. One of the women in my room was shivering and an aide brought her a blanket.

"What's the matter?" the aide asked her. "I'm scared," the woman said. "How much will it hurt?" The aide smiled. "Oh, nothing worse than a couple of bad cramps," she said. "This afternoon you'll be dancing a jig."

I began to panic. Suddenly the rhetoric, the abortion marches I'd walked in, the telegrams sent to Albany to counteract the Friends of the Fetus, the Zero Population Growth buttons I'd worn, peeled away, and I was all alone with my microscopic baby. There were just the two of us there, and soon, because it was more convenient for me and my husband, there would be one again.

How could it be that I, who am so neurotic about life that I step over bugs rather than on them, who spend hours planting flowers and vegetables in the spring even though we rent out the house and never see them, who make sure the children are vaccinated and inoculated and filled with vitamin C, could so arbitrarily decide that this life shouldn't be?

"It's not a life," my husband had argued, more to convince himself than me. "It's a bunch of cells smaller than my fingernail."

But any woman who has had children knows that certain feeling in her taut, swollen breasts, and the slight but constant ache in her uterus that signals the arrival of life. Though I would march myself into blisters for a woman's right to exercise the option of motherhood, I discovered there in the waiting room that I was not the modern woman I thought I was.

When my name was called, my body felt so heavy the nurse had to help me into the examining room. I waited for my husband to burst through the door and yell "stop," but of course he didn't. I concentrated on three black spots in the acoustic ceiling until they grew in size to the shape of saucers, while the doctor swabbed my insides with antiseptic.

"You're going to feel a burning sensation now," he said, injecting the Novocaine into the neck of the womb. The pain was swift and severe, and I twisted to get away from him. He was hurting my baby, I reasoned, and the black saucers quivered in the air. "Stop," I cried. "Please stop." He shook his head, busy with his equipment. "It's too late to stop now," he said. "It'll just take a few more seconds."

What good sports we women are. And how obedient. Physically the pain passed even before the hum of the machine signaled that the vacuuming of my uterus was completed, my baby sucked up like ashes after a cocktail party. Ten minutes from start to finish. And I was back on the arm of the nurse.

There were twelve beds in the recovery room. Each one had a gaily flowered draw sheet and a soft green or blue thermal blanket. It was all very feminine. Lying on these beds for an hour or more were the shocked victims of their sex, their full wombs now stripped clean, their futures less encumbered.

It was a very quiet room. The only voice was that of the nurse, locating the new women who had just come in so she could monitor their blood pressure, and checking out the recovered women who were free to leave.

Juice was being passed about, and I found myself sipping a Dixie cup of Hawaiian Punch. An older woman with tightly curled bleached hair was just getting up from the next bed, "That was no goddamn snap," she said, resting before putting on her miniskirt and high white boots. Other women came and went, some walking out as dazed as they had entered, others with a bounce that signaled they were going right back to Bloomingdales.

Finally then, it was time for me to leave. I checked out, making an appointment to return in two weeks for an IUD insertion. My husband was slumped in the waiting room, clutching a single yellow rose wrapped in a wet paper towel and stuffed into a baggie.

We didn't talk the whole way home, but just held hands very tightly. At home there were more yellow roses and a tray in bed for me and the children's curiosity to divert.

It had certainly been a successful operation. I didn't bleed at all for two days just as they had predicted, and then I bled only moderately for another four days. Within a week my breasts had subsided and the tenderness vanished, and my body felt mine again instead of the eggshell it becomes when it's protecting someone else.

My husband and I are back to planning our summer vacation and his career switch.

And it certainly does make more sense not to be having a baby right now—we say that to each other all the time. But I have this ghost now. A very little ghost that only appears when I'm seeing something beautiful, like the full moon on the ocean last weekend. And the baby waves at me. And I wave at the baby. "Of course, we have room," I cry to the ghost. "Of course, we do."

I am "Jane Doe." Using a pseudonym was not the act of cowardice some have said it was, but rather an act of sympathy for the feelings of my family. My daughters were too young then to understand what an abortion was, and my twelve-year-old son (my husband's stepson) reacted angrily when I even broached the subject of abortion to him. Andrew was deeply moralistic, as many children are at that age, and still young enough to feel threatened by the actions of adults; his replies to my "suppose I had an abortion" queries were devastating. "I think abortion is okay if the boy and girl aren't married, and they just made a mistake," he said. "But if you had an abortion, that would be different. You're married, and there is no reason for you not to have another baby. How could you just kill something—no matter how little it is—that's going to grow and have legs and wiggle its fingers?"

"I would be furious with you if you had an abortion. I'd lose all respect for you for being so selfish. I'd make you suffer and remind you of it all the time. I would think of ways to be mean. Maybe I'd give you the silent treatment or something."

"If God had meant women to have abortions, He would have put buttons on their stomachs."

I decided to wait until he was older before we discussed it again.

There were other considerations as well. My husband and I had chosen not to tell our parents about the abortion. My mother was very ill at the time and not up to a barrage of phone calls from her friends about "what Linda had written in the newspaper." And there were my parents-in-law, who had always hoped for a male grandchild to carry on the family name. So I avoided the confessional and simply wrote what I thought would be a helpful piece for other women who might have shared my experience.

The result was almost great enough to be recorded on a seismograph. Interpreting the piece as an antiabortion grist, the Right-to-Lifers reproduced it by the thousands and sent it to everyone on their mailing lists. In one Catholic mailing, two sentences were deleted from the article: one that said I was planning to return to the clinic for an IUD insertion, and the other the quote from a middle-aged woman, "That was no goddamn snap." Papers around the country and in Canada ran it, culminating in its appearance in the Canadian edition of the *Reader's Digest,* whose staff took it upon their editorial selves to delete the last paragraph about the "little ghost" because they considered it "mawkish." They also changed the title from "There Just Wasn't Room in Our Lives for Another Baby" to "A Successful Operation" in the hopes that it would change their magazine's pro-abortion image.

Hundreds of letters poured into the *New York Times,* some from Right-to-Lifers, who predictably called me a "murderer," and others from pro-choice zealots who had decided the article was a "plant" and might even have been written by a man. Women wrote about their own abortions, some of which had been positive experiences and some disastrous. One woman even wrote that she wished her own mother had had an abortion instead of subjecting her to a childhood that was "brutal and

crushing." Many of the respondents criticized me, quite rightly, for not using birth control in the first place. I was stunned, and so was the *New York Times.* A few weeks later they ran a sampling of the letters and my reply, which follows:

The varied reactions to my abortion article do not surprise me at all. They are all right. And they are all wrong. There is no issue so fundamental as the giving of life, or the cessation of it. These decisions are the most personal one can ever make and each person facing them reacts in her own way. It is not black-and-white as the laws governing abortion are forced to be. Rather it is the gray area whose core touches our definition of ourselves that produces "little ghosts" in some, and a sense of relief in others.

I admire the woman who chose not to bear her fourth child because she and her husband could not afford to give that child the future they felt necessary. I admire the women who were outraged that I had failed to use any form of contraception. And I ache for the woman whose mother had given birth to her even though she was not wanted, and thus spent an empty, lonely childhood. It takes courage to take the life of someone else in your own hands, and even more courage to assume responsibility for your own.

I had my abortion over two years ago. And I wrote about it shortly thereafter. It was only recently, however, that I decided to publish it. I felt it was important to share how one person's abortion had affected her, rather than just sit by while the pro and con groups haggled over legislation.

The effect has indeed been profound. Though my husband was very supportive of me, and I, I think, of him, our relationship slowly faltered. As our children are girls, my husband anguished at the possibility that I had been carrying a son. Just a case of male macho, many would argue. But still, that's the way he feels, and it is important. I hope we can get back on a loving track again.

Needless to say, I have an IUD now, instead of the diaphragm that is too easily forgotten. I do not begrudge my husband his lack of contraception. Condoms are awkward. Neither do I feel he should have a vasectomy. It is profoundly difficult for him to face the possibility that he might never have that son. Nor do I regret having the abortion. I am just as much an avid supporter of children by choice as I ever was.

My only regret is the sheer irresponsibility on my part to become pregnant in the first place. I pray to God that it will never happen again. But if it does, I will be equally thankful that the law provides women the dignity to choose whether to bring a new life into the world or not.

I had obviously and unintentionally touched a national nerve. With abortion becoming an everyday occurrence since the Supreme Court ruling in 1973, which overturned the right of individual states to intervene in a woman's decision to abort in the first trimester (twelve weeks) of pregnancy and to intervene in the second trimester (twenty-four weeks) only to ensure medical practices "reasonably related to maternal health," American women of all ages, races, and backgrounds were facing the same sort of dilemma I had. . . .

. . . So much has happened in the short time since abortion was legalized that only now is there an opportunity to draw breath and begin to evaluate what the 1973 Supreme Court decision has wrought, and what repercussions the 1977 Supreme Court decision upholding states' rights to withhold abortion funding for the poor will have. Abortion is not new by any means. But confronting the fact of it without furtiveness and danger is. The quantum leap from women's age-old need and desire to control their reproductive lives to their sanctioned ability finally to do so has raised questions of ethics and morality that have yet to be answered. Perhaps they never will be.

---

22. *Cruzan v. Director, Missouri Department of Health*

Supreme Court of the United States

The issue before the Supreme Court was whether the state of Missouri's requirement of clear and convincing evidence of an incompetent's wishes concerning the withdrawal of life-sustaining medical treatment conflicts with the U.S. Constitution. Justice Rehnquist speaking for the majority of the Court held that the state of Missouri had a legitimate interest in protecting and preserving human life in imposing its clear and convincing evidence requirement. He further held that in imposing this requirement the state of Missouri need not make any judgment about the quality of human life.

Justice *Rehnquist* delivered the majority opinion:

Petitioner Nancy Beth Cruzan was rendered incompetent as a result of severe injuries sustained during an automobile accident. Co-petitioners Lester and Joyce Cruzan, Nancy's parents and co-guardians, sought a court order directing the withdrawal of their daughter's artificial feeding and hydration equipment after it became apparent that she had virtually no chance of recovering her cognitive faculties. The Supreme Court of Missouri held that because there was no clear and convincing evidence of Nancy's desire to have life-sustaining treatment withdrawn under such circumstances, her parents lacked authority to effectuate such a request. We . . . now affirm.

On the night of January 11, 1983, Nancy Cruzan lost control of her car as she traveled down Elm Road in Jasper County, Missouri. The vehicle overturned, and Cruzan was discovered lying face down in a ditch without detectable respiratory or cardiac function. Paramedics were able to restore her breathing and heartbeat at the accident site, and she was transported to a hospital in an unconscious state. An attending neurosurgeon diagnosed her as having sustained probable cerebral contusions compounded by significant anoxia (lack of oxygen). The Missouri trial court in this case found that permanent brain damage generally results after 6 minutes in an anoxic state; it was estimated that Cruzan was deprived of oxygen from 12 to 14 minutes. She remained in a coma for approximately three weeks and then progressed to an unconscious state in which she was able to orally ingest some nutrition. In order to ease feeding and further the recovery, surgeons implanted a gastrostomy feeding and hydration tube in Cruzan with the consent of her then husband. Subsequent rehabilitative efforts proved unavailing. She now lies in a Missouri state hospital in what is commonly referred to as a persistent vegetative state: generally, a condition in which a person exhibits motor reflexes but evinces no indications of significant cognitive function.[1] The State of Missouri is bearing the cost of her care.

After it had become apparent that Nancy Cruzan had virtually no chance of regaining her mental faculties her parents asked hospital employees to terminate the artificial nutrition and hydration procedures. All agree that such a removal would cause her death. The employees refused to honor the request without court approval. The parents then sought and received authorization from the state trial court for termination. The court found that a person in Nancy's condition had a fundamental right under the State and Federal Constitutions to refuse or direct the withdrawal of "death prolonging procedures." The court also found that Nancy's "expressed thoughts at age twenty-five in somewhat serious conversation with a housemate friend that if sick or injured she would not wish to continue her life unless she could live at least halfway normally suggests that given her

present condition she would not wish to continue on with her nutrition and hydration."

The Supreme Court of Missouri reversed by a divided vote. The court recognized a right to refuse treatment embodied in the common-law doctrine of informed consent, but expressed skepticism about the application of that doctrine in the circumstances of this case. The court also declined to read a broad right of privacy into the State Constitution which would "support the right of a person to refuse medical treatment in every circumstance," and expressed doubt as to whether such a right existed under the United States Constitution. It then decided that the Missouri Living Will statute (1986) embodied a state policy strongly favoring the preservation of life. The court found that Cruzan's statements to her roommate regarding her desire to live or die under certain conditions were "unreliable for the purpose of determining her intent," "and thus insufficient to support the co-guardians' claim to exercise substituted judgment on Nancy's behalf." It rejected the argument that Cruzan's parents were entitled to order the termination of her medical treatment, concluding that "no person can assume that choice for an incompetent in the absence of the formalities required under Missouri's Living Will statutes or the clear and convincing, inherently reliable evidence absent here." . . .

We granted certiorari to consider the question of whether Cruzan has a right under the United States Constitution which would require the hospital to withdraw life-sustaining treatment from her under these circumstances.

At common law, even the touching of one person by another without consent and without legal justification was a battery. Before the turn of the century, this Court observed that "[n]o right is held more sacred, or is more carefully guarded, by the common law, than the right of every individual to the possession and control of his own person, free from all restraint or interference of others, unless by clear and unquestionable authority of law." This notion of bodily integrity has been embodied in the requirement that informed consent is generally required for medical treatment. Justice Cardozo, while on the Court of Appeals of New York, aptly described this doctrine: "Every human being of adult years and sound mind has a right to determine what shall be done with his own body; and a surgeon who performs an operation without his patient's consent commits an assault, for which he is liable in damage." The informed consent doctrine has become firmly entrenched in American tort law.

The logical corollary of the doctrine of informed consent is that the patient generally possesses the right not to consent, that is, to refuse treatment. Until about 15 years ago and the seminal decision [of the New Jersey Supreme Court] in *In re Quinlan* (1976), the number of right-to-refuse-treatment decisions were relatively few. Most of the earlier cases involved patients who refused medical treatment forbidden by their religious beliefs, thus implicating First Amendment rights as well as common law rights of self-determination. More recently, however, with the advance of medical technology capable of sustaining life well past the point where natural forces would have brought certain death in earlier times, cases involving the right to refuse life-sustaining treatment have burgeoned.

In the *Quinlan* case, young Karen Quinlan suffered severe brain damage as the result of anoxia, and entered a persistent vegetative state. Karen's father sought judicial approval to disconnect his daughter's respirator. The New Jersey Supreme Court granted the relief, holding that Karen had a right of privacy grounded in the Federal Constitution to terminate treatment. Recognizing that this right was not absolute, however, the court balanced it against asserted state interests. Noting that the State's interest "weakens and the individual's right to privacy grows as the degree of bodily invasion increases and the prognosis dims," the court concluded that the state interests had to give way in that case. The court also concluded that the "only practical way" to prevent the loss of Karen's privacy right due to her incompetence was to allow her guardian and family to decide "whether she would exercise it in these circumstances."

After *Quinlan,* however, most courts have based a right to refuse treatment either solely on the common law right to informed consent or on both the common law right and a constitutional privacy right. . . .

. . . State courts have available to them for decision a number of sources—state constitutions, statutes, and common law—which are not available to us. In this Court, the question is simply and starkly whether the United States Constitution prohibits Missouri from choosing the rule of decision which it did. This is the first case in which we have been squarely presented with the issue of whether the United States Constitution grants what is in common parlance referred to as a "right to die." We follow the judicious counsel . . . that in deciding "a question of such magnitude and importance . . . it is the [better] part of wisdom not to attempt, by any general statement, to cover every possible phase of the subject."

The Fourteenth Amendment provides that no State shall "deprive any person of life, liberty, or property, without due process of law." The principle that a competent person has a constitutionally protected liberty interest in refusing unwanted medical treatment may be inferred from our prior decisions. In *Jacobson v. Massachusetts* (1905), for instance, the Court balanced an individual's liberty interest in declining an unwanted smallpox vaccine against the State's interest in preventing disease. . . .

Just this Term, in the course of holding that a State's procedures for administering antipsychotic medication to prisoners were sufficient to satisfy due process concerns, we recognized that prisoners possess "a significant liberty interest in avoiding the unwanted administration of antipsychotic drugs under the Due Process Clause of the Fourteenth Amendment." Still other cases support the recognition of a general liberty interest in refusing medical treatment.

But determining that a person has a "liberty interest" under the Due Process Clause does not end the inquiry;[2] "whether respondent's constitutional rights have been violated must be determined by balancing his liberty interests against the relevant state interests."

Petitioners insist that under the general holdings of our cases, the forced administration of life-sustaining medical treatment, and even of artificially delivered food and water essential to life, would implicate a competent person's liberty interest. Although we think the logic of the cases [referred to] above would embrace such a liberty interest, the dramatic consequences involved in refusal of such treatment would inform the inquiry as to whether the deprivation of that interest is constitutionally permissible. But for purposes of this case, we assume that the United States Constitution would grant a competent person a constitutionally protected right to refuse life-saving hydration and nutrition.

Petitioners go on to assert that an incompetent person should possess the same right in this respect as is possessed by a competent person. . . .

The difficulty with petitioners' claim is that in a sense it begs the question: an incompetent person is not able to make an informed and voluntary choice to exercise a hypothetical right to refuse treatment or any other right. Such a "right" must be exercised for her, if at all, by some sort of surrogate. Here, Missouri has in effect recognized that under certain circumstances a surrogate may act for the patient in electing to have hydration and nutrition withdrawn in such a way as to cause death, but it has established a procedural safeguard to assure that the action of the surrogate conforms as best it may to the wishes expressed by the patient while competent. Missouri requires that evidence of the incompetent's wishes as to the withdrawal of treatment be proved by clear and convincing evidence. The question, then, is whether the United States Constitution forbids the establishment of this procedural requirement by the State. We hold that it does not.

Whether or not Missouri's clear and convincing evidence requirement comports with the United States Constitution depends in part on what interests the State may properly seek to protect in this situation. Missouri relies on its interest in the protection and preservation of human life, and there can be no gainsaying this interest. As a general matter, the States—indeed, all civilized nations—demonstrate their commitment to life by treating homicide as serious crime. Moreover, the majority of States in this country have laws imposing criminal penalties on one who assists another to commit suicide. We do not think a State is required to remain neutral in the face of an informed and voluntary decision by a physically able adult to starve to death.

But in the context presented here, a State has more particular interests at stake. The choice between life and death is a deeply personal decision of obvious and overwhelming finality. We believe Missouri may legitimately seek to safeguard the personal element of this choice through the imposition of heightened evidentiary requirements. It cannot be disputed that the Due Process Clause protects an interest in life as well as an interest in refusing life-sustaining medical treatment. Not all incompetent patients will have loved ones available to serve as surrogate decisionmakers. And even where family members are present, "[t]here will, of course, be some unfortunate situations in which family members will not act to protect a patient." A State is entitled to guard against potential abuses in such situations. Similarly, a State is entitled to consider that a judicial proceeding to make a determination regarding an incompetent's wishes may very well not be an adversarial one, with the added guarantee of accurate factfinding that the adversary process brings with it. Finally, we think a State may properly decline to make judgments about the "quality" of life that a particular individual may enjoy, and simply assert an unqualified interest in the preservation of human life to be weighed against the constitutionally protected interests of the individual.

In our view, Missouri has permissibly sought to advance these interests through the adoption of a "clear and convincing" standard of proof to govern such proceedings. "The function of a standard of proof, as that concept is embodied in the Due Process Clause and in the realm of factfinding, is to 'instruct the factfinder concerning the degree of confidence our society thinks he should have in the correctness of factual conclusions for a particular type of adjudication.' " . . .

We think it self-evident that the interests at stake in the instant proceedings are more substantial, both on an individual and societal level, than those involved in a run-of-the-mill civil dispute. But not only does the standard of proof reflect the importance of a particular adjudication, it also serves as "a societal judgment about how the risk of error should be distributed between the litigants." The more stringent the burden of proof a party must bear, the more that party bears the risk of an erroneous decision. We believe that Missouri may permissibly place an increased risk of an erroneous decision on those seeking to terminate an incompetent individual's life-sustaining treatment. An erroneous decision not to terminate results in a maintenance of the status quo; the possibility of subsequent developments such as advancements in medical science, the discovery of new evidence regarding the patient's intent, changes in the law, or simply the unexpected death of the patient despite the administration of life-sustaining treatment, at least create the potential that a wrong decision will eventually be corrected or its impact mitigated. An erroneous decision to withdraw life-sustaining treatment, however, is not susceptible of correction. . . .

In sum, we conclude that a State may apply a clear and convincing evidence standard in proceedings where a guardian seeks to discontinue nutrition and hydration of a person diagnosed to be in a persistent vegetative state. . . .

The Supreme Court of Missouri held that in this case the testimony adduced at trial did not amount to clear and convincing proof of the patient's desire to have hydration and nutrition withdrawn. In so doing, it reversed a decision of the Missouri trial court which had found that the evidence "suggest[ed]" Nancy Cruzan would not have desired to continue such measures, but which had not adopted the standard of "clear and convincing evidence" enunciated by the Supreme Court. The testimony adduced at trial consisted primarily of Nancy Cruzan's statements made to a housemate about a year before her accident that she would not want to live should she face life as a "vegetable," and other observations to the same effect. The observations did not deal in terms with withdrawal of medical treatment or of hydration and nutrition. We cannot say that the Supreme Court of Missouri committed constitutional error in reaching the conclusion that it did.[3]

Petitioners alternatively contend that Missouri must accept the "substituted judgment" of close family members even in the absence of substantial proof that their views reflect the views of the patient. . . .

No doubt is engendered by anything in this record but that Nancy Cruzan's mother and father are loving and caring parents. If the State were required by the United States Constitution to repose a right of "substituted judgment" with anyone, the Cruzans would surely qualify. But we do not think the Due Process Clause requires the State to repose judgment on these matters with anyone but the patient herself. Close family members may have a strong feeling—a feeling not at all ignoble or unworthy, but not entirely disinterested, either—that they do not wish to witness the continuation of the life of a loved one which they regard as hopeless, meaningless, and even degrading. But there is no automatic assurance that the view of close family members will necessarily be the same as the patient's would have been had she been confronted with the prospect of her situation while competent. All of the reasons previously discussed for allowing Missouri to require clear and convincing evidence of the patient's wishes lead us to conclude that the State may choose to defer only to those wishes, rather than confide the decision to close family members.

The judgment of the Supreme Court of Missouri is *Affirmed*.

Notes

1. The State Supreme Court, adopting much of the trial court's findings, described Nancy Cruzan's medical condition as follows: ". . . In sum, Nancy is diagnosed as in a persistent vegetative state. She is not dead. She is not terminally ill. Medical experts testified that she could live another thirty years." . . .

2. Although many state courts have held that a right to refuse treatment is encompassed by a generalized constitutional right of privacy, we have never so held. We believe this issue is more properly analyzed in terms of a Fourteenth Amendment liberty interest. See *Bowers vs. Hardwick* (1986).

3. The clear and convincing standard of proof has been variously defined in this context as "proof sufficient to persuade the trier of fact that the patient held a firm and settled commitment to the termination of life supports under the

circumstances like those presented," and as evidence which "produces in the mind of the trier of fact a firm belief or conviction as to the truth of the allegations sought to be established, evidence so clear, direct and weighty and convincing as to enable [the factfinder] to come to a clear conviction, without hesitancy, of the truth of the precise facts in issue." . . .

---

23. The Case of Dr. Kevorkian

In a campaign to allow physician-assisted suicide, Dr. Jack Kevorkian has helped a number of nonterminally ill but seriously impaired people in the state of Michigan to take their own lives. Responding to Kevorkian's actions, the state of Michigan recently outlawed assisted suicide for fifteen months to allow the issue to be studied.

A California man paralyzed from the neck down says he plans to come to Michigan in early 1993 to commit suicide with the help of Dr. Jack Kevorkian, according to a published report due out Monday.

The man, identified only as Gary, tells *Time* magazine he doesn't want to die but finds life as a quadriplegic unacceptable. He plans to end his life in Michigan before a temporary state law banning assisted suicide takes effect March 31.

"They're going to shut him down April 1, and I'm going to be one of the lifeboats off the Titanic," Gary told the magazine for its Dec. 28 issue.

"I'm thinking somewhere between January and March," he said. "It could be sooner. The luxury of having more time is gone."

There was no answer late Saturday afternoon at Kevorkian's apartment in the Detroit suburb of Royal Oak. His attorney, Geoffrey Fieger, said there were no plans for the man to come to Michigan.

"I don't know if Jack will help him," Fieger said Saturday. "If he's announced that he's been counseling with Jack, I suppose that's true. I think Jack has been counseling him to continue to live, not to end his life."

Kevorkian has been present at the suicides of eight people, all women, since June 1990.

He was present at the suicides of two suburban Detroit women last week, just hours before Gov. John Engler signed a bill outlawing assisted suicide for 15 months while the issue is studied.

Fieger said the California man's wife wrote Kevorkian several weeks ago, saying his spirits had improved.

"The last I heard was that she for the first time had seen some glimmer of hope and . . . if that's true, and I certainly hope it is, then he should consider not coming."

Gary, 34, was left paralyzed from the neck down after being shot in the spine five years ago. "Realistically, there is no cure and this type of life is not acceptable to me," he told the magazine.

Gary said he first contacted the retired pathologist in April. Last month, Kevorkian called to ask how soon he would be ready because of impending legislative action, Gary said.

"I think his words were something to the effect, 'We have to wrap this up. How soon can you be here?' I thought for about 10 or 15 seconds and I said, 'One week,'" he said.

Gary said Kevorkian told him he could change his mind at any time.

"I look at my situation like a war," Gary said. ". . . In the final analysis I may not win this war. But I fought back hard. I don't want to die, but I don't want to live like this."

Reprinted from the *South Bend Tribune*, December 20, 1992 by permission of Associated Press.

Suggestions for Further Reading

Anthologies

Brody, Baruch, and Engelhardt, Tristan. *Bioethics*. Englewood Cliffs, N.J.: Prentice-Hall, 1987.

Cohen, Marshall, and others. *The Rights and Wrongs of Abortion*. Princeton: Princeton University Press, 1974.

Feinberg, Joel. *The Problem of Abortion*. Belmont, Calif.: Wadsworth Publishing Co., 1973.

Kohl, Marvin. *Beneficent Euthanasia*. Buffalo, N.Y.: Prometheus, 1975.

Ladd, John. *Ethical Issues Relating to Life and Death*. New York: Oxford University Press, 1979.

Munson, Ronald. *Interventions and Reflections*. Belmont, Calif.: Wadsworth Publishing Co., 1979.

Basic Concepts

Devine, Philip. *The Ethics of Homicide*. Ithaca, N.Y.: Cornell University Press, 1978.

Glover, Jonathan. *Causing Death and Saving Lives*. New York: Penguin Books, 1977.

Steinbock, Bonnie, ed. *Killing and Letting Die*. Englewood Cliffs, N.J.: Prentice-Hall, 1980.

Alternative Views

Callahan, Daniel. *Abortion: Law, Choice and Morality*. New York: Macmillan, 1970.

Grisez, Germain, and Boyle, Joseph. *Life and Death with Liberty and Justice*. Notre Dame: University of Notre Dame Press, 1979.

Kluge, Eike-Henner. *The Practice of Death*. New Haven: Yale University Press, 1975.

Luker, Kristin. *Abortion and the Politics of Motherhood*. Berkeley: University of California Press, 1984.

Nicholson, Susan. *Abortion and the Roman Catholic Church*. Knoxville: Religious Ethics, 1978.

Pojman, Louis P. *Life and Death*. Boston: Jones and Bartlett Publishers, 1992.

Rachels, James. *The End of Life*. New York: Oxford University Press, 1986.

Ramsey, Paul. *The Patient as Person*. New Haven: Yale University Press, 1970.

Summer, L. W. *Abortion and Moral Theory*. Princeton: Princeton University Press, 1981.

Practical Applications

Denes, Magda. *In Necessity and Sorrow: Life and Death in an Abortion Hospital*. New York: Penguin Books, 1977.

Law Reform Commission of Canada. *Euthanasia, Aiding Suicide and Cessation of Treatment*. Working Paper 28, 1982.

Manier, Edward, and others, eds. *Abortion: New Directions for Policy Studies*. Notre Dame: University of Notre Dame Press, 1977.

Sex Equality

Introduction

Basic Concepts

The problem of sex equality concerns the question of whether the sexes should be treated equally, and, if so, what constitutes equal treatment. This question was at the heart of the decade-long public debate on the Equal Rights Amendment to the Constitution (the ERA), which began in March 1972, when the Senate passed the amendment with a vote of 84 to 8, and ended in June 1982, when the extended deadline for the ERA expired—three states short of the 38 required for ratification.

The complete text of the ERA was as follows:

1. Equality of rights under the law shall not be denied or abridged by the United States or by any state on account of sex.
2. The Congress shall have the power to enforce by appropriate legislation the provisions of this article.
3. This amendment shall take effect two years after the date of ratification.

Public support for the ERA over this period, judging from opinion polls, hovered between 55 and 60 percent, but in key states anti-ERA forces were able to mount sufficient resistance to prevent its passage. In the end, Alabama, Arizona, Arkansas, Florida, Georgia, Illinois, Louisiana, Mississippi, Missouri, Nevada, North Carolina, Oklahoma, Utah, and Virginia failed to ratify the amendment.

Anti-ERA forces were able to block ratification because they successfully shifted the debate from equal rights to the substantive changes the ERA might bring about. This strategy was effective because support for the amendment generally came from individuals sympathetic to the notion of "equal rights" but not necessarily committed to substantive changes in women's roles.[1] For example, in one national survey, 67 percent of the people who claimed to have heard or read about the ERA favored it, 25 percent were opposed to it,

and 8 percent had no opinion. Many people in the sample, however, had quite traditional views about women's roles. Two-thirds of the respondents thought that preschool children would suffer if their mothers worked, 62 percent thought married women should not hold jobs when jobs were scarce and their husbands could support them, and 55 percent thought it was more important for a woman to advance her husband's career than to have one of her own.

But what substantive changes would the ERA have brought about if it had been ratified in 1982? The surprising answer is not many, at least in the short run.[2] In 1970, when the ERA first reached the floor of Congress, a significant number of laws and official practices denied women "equality of rights under the law." For example, in 1970, eight states treated all property that a couple bought with their earnings during marriage as "community property," and these states normally gave the husband managerial control over such property. By 1976, most of these laws had been voluntarily changed or struck down by the Supreme Court's interpretation of the equal protection clause of the Fourteenth Amendment. Of course, supporters of the ERA did attempt to argue for the amendment on the grounds that it would bring about equal pay for equal work. Lobbyists for the ERA in state capitols wore buttons that said "59¢" to remind legislators that women who worked full time outside the home still typically earned only 59 cents for every dollar men earned—a ratio that has changed little since the federal government first began publishing such statistics in the 1950s. But the passage of the ERA would have had little immediate impact on that inequality. The ERA would have kept the federal or state governments from legally denying or abridging "equality of rights under the law." However, to help workers, the ERA would have had to do more than just make the law gender blind. It would have had to forbid wage discrimination by *private* organizations and individuals. And this it did not do.

Moreover, the ERA would have had few of the effects its opponents predicted. For example, Phyllis Schlafly frequently claimed that the ERA would require unisex public toilets and combat duty for women, but the Supreme

Court would have found the first requirement an infringement of the right to privacy and the second would have run afoul of the war powers clause of the Constitution, which gives military commanders the freedom to decide how best to use their forces. Yet despite the fact that the immediate impact of the passage of the ERA would have been largely symbolic, neither proponents nor opponents sufficiently recognized this or, if they did, were not willing to surrender their exaggerated claims about the effects the amendment would have. Leaders on both sides of this debate may have feared the difficulty of motivating their followers if these exaggerated claims were abandoned.

Alternative Views

Susan Okin argues (Selection 24) that women have not achieved equality in society. Most of the unpaid labor in the family is done by women. Most jobs assume that workers have wives at home, and traditional gender-structured families make women vulnerable in ways that men are not vulnerable. Okin points out that contemporary political philosophers have ignored all this. They have assumed without argument the justice of traditional gender-structured families. Okin contends that this is a morally unacceptable state of affairs. Families are the first school of justice, and they must be shown to be just if we are to have a just society.

In Selection 25, James P. Sterba argues that if family structures are to be just they must meet the requirements of feminist justice, which he identifies with an ideal of androgyny. This ideal of androgyny requires that traits that are truly desirable in society be equally available to both women and men, or in the case of virtues, equally expected of both women and men. He considers attempts to derive the ideal of androgyny either from a right to equal opportunity that is a central requirement of a welfare liberal conception of justice or from an equal right of self-development that is a central requirement of a socialist conception of justice. He argues that although the ideal of androgyny is compatible with the requirements of both of these two conceptions of justice, it also transcends them

by requiring that all virtues be equally expected of both women and men.

Sterba further argues that the ideal of androgyny would require (1) that all children irrespective of their sex must be given the same type of upbringing consistent with their native capabilities and (2) that mothers and fathers must also have the same opportunities for education and employment consistent with their native capabilities. He then goes on to consider how achieving equal opportunity for women and men requires vastly improved day care facilities and flexible (usually part-time) work schedules for both women and men.

In Selection 26, Christina Sommers criticizes the attack by feminist philosophers, like Okin and Sterba, on the traditional family structures. She distinguishes liberal feminists from radical feminists. She contends that liberal feminists, like herself, want equal opportunity in the workplace and politics, but would leave marriage and motherhood "untouched and unimpugned." By contrast, Sommers contends that radical feminists are committed to an assimilationist or androgynous ideal that would destroy the (traditional) family and deny most women what they want. Sommers, however, never explains how it is possible to secure for women equal opportunity in the workplace and politics while rejecting androgyny in favor of traditional gender roles. For example, how could women be passive, submissive, dependent, indecisive, and weak and still enjoy the same opportunities in the workplace and politics that are enjoyed by men who are aggressive, dominant, independent, decisive, and strong?

Marilyn Friedman (Selection 27) does not challenge Sommers's contention that radical feminists are committed to an assimilationist or androgynous ideal. There is, however, an important distinction between these two ideals. According to an assimilationist ideal, "one's sex should be no more noticeable than one's eye color," but according to an androgynous ideal, this need not be the case, as long as all desirable traits are equally open to both women and men, and all virtues equally expected of both women and men.

Friedman does, however, question whether what Sommers supports is really what most women want. She quotes a 1983 survey which indicated that 63 percent of women preferred nontraditional family relationships, and points out that in 1977 only 16 percent of American households were traditional families in the sense of families consisting of a legally married heterosexual couple and their children, in which the man is the sole breadwinner and "head" of the household, and the woman does the domestic work and childcare. In responding to Friedman, Sommers explains that what she means by a traditional family is one that consists of two heterosexual parents and one or more children in which the mother plays a distinctive gender role in caring for the children.[3] This definition obviously broadens the class of families to which Sommers is referring. But in her response, Sommers goes on to renounce any attempt to be promoting even the traditional family—even as she defines it. What she claims to be promoting is simply "the right and liberty to live under the arrangement of one's choice." According to Sommers, if people want to live in nontraditional families, they should be free to do so.

Friedman further disagrees with Sommers contending that no woman should "swoon at the sight of Rhett Butler carrying Scarlett O'Hara up the stairs to a fate undreamt of in feminist philosophy." According to Friedman, what Rhett Butler is doing in *Gone With the Wind* is raping Scarlett O'Hara. In a subsequent response to Sommers, Friedman, noting that Scarlett O'Hara, although initially unwilling, later appears to be a willing sexual partner, defines "rape" as "any very intimate sexual contact which is *initiated* forcefully or against the will of the recipient."[4] Friedman allows that others might want to define such activity as sexual domination rather than rape, but under either definition, Friedman condemns it, whereas Sommers does not. In her response, Sommers cites approvingly the following passage from *Scarlett's Women: Gone With the Wind and Its Female Fans.*

> The majority of my correspondents (and I agree) recognize the ambiguous nature of the encounter and interpret it as a scene of mutually pleasurable rough sex. . . . By far the majority of women who responded to me saw the episode as erotically exciting,

emotionally stirring and profoundly memorable. Few of them referred to it as "rape."[5]

Practical Applications

Turning to practical applications, we can see that, at least in the statement of the National Organization for Women (NOW) Bill of Rights (Selection 28), there was never any confusion that the ERA would achieve all the goals of the organization. In this Bill of Rights, the ERA is one of eight goals to be achieved.

Recently, maternity leave rights in employment, another of NOW's goals, was at stake in California Federal Savings and Loan versus the Department of Fair Employment and Housing (Selection 29). Here the issue before the Supreme Court was whether Title VII of the Civil Rights Act of 1964 as amended by the Pregnancy Discrimination Act of 1978 (PDA) nullifies a California law that requires employers to provide leave and reinstatement to employees disabled by pregnancy. The majority of the court ruled that it did not nullify the law for two reasons. First, in passing PDA, Congress simply wanted to prohibit discrimination against pregnant women; there was no discussion of preferential treatment for pregnant women. In addition, by allowing both men and women to have families without losing their jobs, the California law did share with Title VII and PDA the goal of equal opportunity. Second, even if PDA did prohibit preferential treatment for pregnant women, an employer could avoid violating both PDA and the California statute by giving comparable benefits to all similarly disabled employees.

What is interesting is that NOW opposed the Court's decision in this case. Apparently, NOW's leaders were concerned that such preferential treatment might lead to a resurgence of nineteenth-century protective legislation that encouraged sexual stereotypes and restrained women from taking their rightful place in the workplace. Although this is a legitimate concern, it can be addressed by determining whether each particular piece of relevant legislation advances the goal of equal opportunity. If it does, as the California law seems to do, there shouldn't be any objection to it, at least from a welfare liberal or socialist point of view.

Notes

---

1. Jane J. Mansbridge, *Why We Lost the ERA* (Chicago: University of Chicago Press, 1986), Chapter 3.

2. Ibid., Chapters 5–7.

3. Christina Sommers, "Do These Feminists Like Women?" *Journal of Social Philosophy* (1991), pp. 66–74.

4. Marilyn Friedman, "Does Sommers Like Women?" *Journal of Social Philosophy* (1991), pp. 75–90.

5. Ibid., p. 72.

---

24. Justice and Gender

Susan Okin

Susan Okin points out that in the face of the radical inequality that exists between women and men in our society there is still a widespread failure of political philosophers to address gender issues in their political theories. She claims that this is true even among those philosophers who have seen the need to adopt gender-neutral language. Okin argues that no theory of justice can be adequate until it addresses these issues.

We as a society pride ourselves on our democratic values. We don't believe people should be constrained by innate differences from being able to achieve desired positions of influence to improve their well-being; equality of opportunity is our professed aim. The Preamble to our Constitution stresses the importance of justice, as well as the general welfare and the blessings of liberty. The Pledge of Allegiance asserts that our republic preserves "liberty and justice for all."

Yet substantial inequalities between the sexes still exist in our society. In economic terms, full-time working women (after some very recent improvement) earn on average 71 percent of the earnings of full-time working men. One-half of poor and three-fifths of chronically poor households with dependent children are maintained by a single female parent. The poverty rate for elderly women is nearly twice that for elderly men. On the political front, two out of a hundred U.S. senators are women, one out of nine justices seems to be considered sufficient female representation on the Supreme Court, and the number of men chosen in each congressional election far exceeds the number of women elected in the entire history of the country. Underlying and intertwined with all these inequalities is the unequal distribution of the unpaid labor of the family.

An equal sharing between the sexes of family responsibilities, especially child care, is "the great revolution that has not happened." Women, including mothers of young children, are, of course, working outside the household far more than their mothers did. And the small proportion of women who reach high-level positions in politics, business, and the professions command a vastly disproportionate amount of space in the media, compared with the millions of women who work at low-paying, dead-end jobs, the millions who do part-time work with its lack of benefits, and the millions of others who stay home performing for no pay what is frequently not even acknowledged as work. Certainly, the fact that women are doing more paid work does not imply that they are more equal. It is often said that we are living in a postfeminist era. This claim, due in part to the distorted emphasis on women who have "made it," is false, no matter which of its meanings is intended. It is certainly not true that feminism has been vanquished, and equally untrue that it is no longer needed because its aims have been fulfilled. Until there is justice within the family, women will not be able to gain equality in politics, at work, or in any other sphere.

. . . The typical current practices of family life, structured to a large extent by gender, are not just. Both the expectation and the experience of the division of labor by sex make women vulnerable. As I shall show, a cycle of power relations and decisions pervades both family and workplace, each reinforcing the inequalities between the sexes that already exist within the other. Not only women, but children of both sexes, too, are often made vulnerable by gender-structured marriage. One-quarter of children in the United States now live in families with only one parent—in almost 90 percent of cases, the mother. Contrary to common perceptions—in which the situation of never-married mothers looms largest—65 percent of single-parent families are a result of marital separation or divorce. Recent research in a number of states has shown that, in the average case, the standard of living of divorced women and the children who live with them plummets after divorce, whereas the economic situation of divorced men tends to be better than when they were married.

A central source of injustice for women these days is that the law, most noticeably in the event of divorce, treats more or less as equals those whom custom, workplace discrimination, and the still conventional division of labor within the family have made very unequal. Central to this socially created inequality are two commonly made but inconsistent presumptions: that women are primarily responsible for the rearing of children; and that serious and committed members of the work force (regardless of class) do not have primary responsibility, or even shared responsibility, for the rearing of children. The old assumption of the workplace, still implicit, is that workers have wives at home. It is built not only into the structure and expectations of the workplace but into other crucial social institutions, such as schools, which make no attempt to take account, in their scheduled hours or vacations, of the fact that parents are likely to hold jobs.

Now, of course, many wage workers do not have wives at home. Often, they *are* wives and mothers, or single, separated, or divorced mothers of small children. But neither the family nor the workplace has taken much account of this fact. Employed wives still do by far the greatest proportion of unpaid family work, such as child care and housework. Women are far more likely to take time out of the workplace or to work part-time because of family responsibilities than are their husbands or male partners. And they are much more likely to move because of their husbands' employment needs or opportunities than their own. All these tendencies, which are due to a number of factors, including the sex segregation and discrimination of the workplace itself, tend to be cyclical in their effects: wives advance more slowly than their husbands at work and thus gain less seniority, and the discrepancy between their wages increases over time. Then, because both the power structure of the family and what is regarded as consensual "rational" family decision-making reflect the fact that the husband usually earns more, it will become even less likely as time goes on that the unpaid work of the family will be shared between the spouses. Thus the cycle of inequality is perpetuated. Often hidden from view within a marriage, it is in the increasingly likely event of marital breakdown that the socially constructed inequality of married women is at its most visible.

This is what I mean when I say that gender-structured marriage *makes* women vulnerable. These are not matters of natural necessity, as some people would believe. Surely nothing in our natures dictates that men should not be equal participants in the rearing of their children. Nothing in the nature of work makes it impossible to adjust it to the fact that people are parents as well as workers. That these things have not happened is part of the historically, socially constructed differentiation between the sexes that feminists have come to call *gender*. We live in a society that has over the years regarded the innate characteristic of sex as one of the clearest legitimizers of different rights and restrictions, both formal and informal. While the legal sanctions that uphold male dominance have begun to be eroded in the past century, and more rapidly in the last twenty years, the heavy weight of tradition, combined with the effects of socialization, still works powerfully to reinforce sex roles that are commonly regarded as of unequal prestige and worth. The sexual division of labor has not only been a fundamental part of the marriage contract, but so deeply influences us in our formative years that feminists of both sexes who try to reject it can find themselves struggling against it with varying degrees of ambivalence. Based on this linchpin, "gender"—by which I mean *the deeply entrenched institutionalization of sexual difference*—still permeates our society.

The Construction of Gender

Due to feminism and feminist theory, gender is coming to be recognized as a social factor of major importance. Indeed, the new meaning of the word reflects the fact that so much of what has traditionally been thought of as sexual difference is now considered by many to be largely socially produced. Feminist scholars from many disciplines and with radically different points of view have contributed to the enterprise of making gender fully visible and comprehensible. At one end of the spectrum are those whose explanations of the subordination of women focus primarily on biological difference as causal in the construction of gender, and at the other end are those who argue that biological difference may not even lie at the core of the social construction that is gender; the views of the vast majority of feminists fall between these extremes. The rejection of biological determinism and the corresponding emphasis on gender as a social construction characterize most current feminist scholarship. Of particular relevance is work in psychology, where scholars have in-

vestigated the importance of female primary parenting in the formation of our gendered identities, and in history and anthropology, where emphasis has been placed on the historical and cultural variability of gender. Some feminists have been criticized for developing theories of gender that do not take sufficient account of differences *among* women, especially race, class, religion, and ethnicity. While such critiques should always inform our research and improve our arguments, it would be a mistake to allow them to detract our attention from gender itself as a factor of significance. Many injustices are experienced by women *as women*, whatever the differences among them and whatever other injustices they also suffer from. The past and present gendered nature of the family, and the ideology that surrounds it, affects virtually all women, whether or not they live or ever lived in traditional families. Recognizing this is not to deny or de-emphasize the fact that gender may affect different subgroups of women to a different extent and in different ways.

The potential significance of feminist discoveries and conclusions about gender for issues of social justice cannot be over-emphasized. They undermine centuries of argument that started with the notion that not only the distinct differentiation of women and men but the domination of women by men, being natural, was therefore inevitable and not even to be considered in discussions of justice. As I shall make clear in later chapters, despite the fact that such notions cannot stand up to rational scrutiny, they not only still survive but flourish in influential places.

During the same two decades in which feminists have been intensely thinking, researching, analyzing, disagreeing about, and rethinking the subject of gender, our political and legal institutions have been increasingly faced with issues concerning the injustices of gender and their effects. These issues are being decided within a fundamentally patriarchal system, founded in a tradition in which "individuals" were assumed to be male heads of households. Not surprisingly, the system has demonstrated a limited capacity for determining what is just, in many cases involving gender. Sex discrimination, sexual harassment, abortion, pregnancy in the workplace, parental leave, child care, and surrogate mothering have all become major and well-publicized issues of public policy, engaging both courts and legislatures. Issues of family justice, in particular—from child custody and terms of divorce to physical and sexual abuse of wives and children—have become increasingly visible and pressing, and are commanding increasing attention from the police and court systems. There is clearly a major "justice crisis" in contemporary society arising from issues of gender.

Theories of Justice and the Neglect of Gender

During these same two decades, there has been a great resurgence of theories of social justice. Political theory, which had been sparse for a period before the late 1960s except as an important branch of intellectual history, has become a flourishing field, with social justice as its central concern. Yet, remarkably, major contemporary theorists of justice have almost without exception ignored the situation I have just described. They have displayed little interest in or knowledge of the findings of feminism. They have largely bypassed the fact that the society to which their theories are supposed to pertain is heavily and deeply affected by gender, and faces difficult issues of justice stemming from its gendered past and present assumptions. Since theories of justice are centrally concerned with whether, how, and why persons should be treated differently from one another, this neglect seems inexplicable. These theories are *about* which initial or acquired characteristics or positions in society legitimize differential treatment of persons by social institutions, laws, and customs. They are *about* how and whether and to what extent beginnings should affect outcomes. The division of humanity into two sexes seems to provide an obvious subject for such inquiries. But, as we shall see, this does not strike most contemporary theorists of justice, and their theories suffer in both coherence and relevance because of it. This book is about this remarkable case of neglect. It is also an attempt to

rectify it, to point the way toward a more fully humanist theory of justice by confronting the question, "How just is gender?"

Why is it that when we turn to contemporary theories of justice, we do not find illuminating and positive contributions to this question? How can theories of justice that are ostensibly about people in general neglect women, gender, and all the inequalities between the sexes? One reason is that most theorists *assume*, though they do not discuss, the traditional, gender-structured family. Another is that they often employ gender-neutral language in a false, hollow way. Let us examine these two points.

The Hidden Gender-Structured Family

In the past, political theorists often used to distinguish clearly between "private" domestic life and the "public" life of politics and the marketplace, claiming explicitly that the two spheres operated in accordance with different principles. They separated out the family from what they deemed the subject matter of politics, and they made closely related, explicit claims about the nature of women and the appropriateness of excluding them from civil and political life. Men, the subjects of the theories, were able to make the transition back and forth from domestic to public life with ease, largely because of the functions performed by women in the family. When we turn to contemporary theories of justice, superficial appearances can easily lead to the impression that they are inclusive of women. In fact, they continue the same "separate spheres" tradition, by ignoring the family, its division of labor, and the related economic dependency and restricted opportunities of most women. The judgment that the family is "nonpolitical" is implicit in the fact that it is simply not discussed in most works of political theory today. In one way or another, . . . almost all current theorists continue to assume that the "individual" who is the basic subject of their theories is the male head of a fairly traditional household. Thus the application of principles of justice to relations between the sexes, or within the household, is frequently, though tacitly, ruled out from the start. In the most influential of all twentieth-century theories of justice, that of John Rawls, family life is not only assumed, but is assumed to be just—and yet the prevalent gendered division of labor within the family is neglected, along with the associated distribution of power, responsibility, and privilege. . . .

Moreover, this stance is typical of contemporary theories of justice. They persist, despite the wealth of feminist challenges to their assumptions, in their refusal even to discuss the family and its gender structure, much less to recognize the family as a political institution of primary importance. Recent theories that pay even less attention to issues of family justice than Rawls's include Bruce Ackerman's *Social Justice in the Liberal State*, Ronald Dworkin's *Taking Rights Seriously*, William Galston's *Justice and the Human Good*, Alasdair MacIntyre's *After Virtue* and *Whose Justice? Whose Rationality?*, Robert Nozick's *Anarchy, State, and Utopia*, and Roberto Unger's *Knowledge and Politics* and *The Critical Legal Studies Movement*. Philip Green's *Retrieving Democracy* is a welcome exception. Michael Walzer's *Spheres of Justice*, too, is exceptional in this regard, but . . . the conclusion that can be inferred from his discussion of the family—that its gender structure is unjust—does not sit at all easily with his emphasis on the shared understandings of a culture as the foundation of justice. For gender is one aspect of social life about which clearly, in the United States in the latter part of the twentieth century, there are no shared understandings.

What is the basis of my claim that the family, while neglected, is *assumed* by theorists of justice? One obvious indication is that they take mature, independent human beings as the subjects of their theories without any mention of how they got to be that way. We know, of course, that human beings develop and mature only as a result of a great deal of attention and hard work, by far the greater part of it done by women. But when theorists of justice talk about "work," they mean paid work performed in the marketplace. They must be assuming that women, in the gender-structured family, continue to do their unpaid work of nurturing and socializing the young and providing a haven of intimate relations—otherwise there would be no moral subjects for

them to theorize about. But these activities apparently take place outside the scope of their theories. Typically, the family itself is not examined in the light of whatever standard of justice the theorist arrives at.

The continued neglect of the family by theorists of justice flies in the face of a great deal of persuasive feminist argument. . . . Scholars have clearly revealed the interconnections between the gender structure inside and outside the family and the extent to which the personal is political. They have shown that the assignment of primary parenting to women is crucial, both in forming the gendered identities of men and women and in influencing their respective choices and opportunities in life. Yet, so far, the simultaneous assumption and neglect of the family has allowed the impact of these arguments to go unnoticed in major theories of justice.

False Gender Neutrality

Many academics in recent years have become aware of the objectionable nature of using the supposedly generic male forms of nouns and pronouns. As feminist scholars have demonstrated, these words have most often *not* been used, throughout history and the history of philosophy in particular, with the intent to include women. *Man, mankind*, and *he* are going out of style as universal representations, though they have by no means disappeared. But the gender-neutral alternatives that most contemporary theorists employ are often even more misleading than the blatantly sexist use of male terms of reference. For they serve to disguise the real and continuing failure of theorists to confront the fact that the human race consists of persons of two sexes. They are by this means able to ignore the fact that there are *some* socially relevant physical differences between women and men, and the even more important fact that the sexes have had very different histories, very different assigned social roles and "natures," and very different degrees of access to power and opportunity in all human societies up to and including the present.

False gender neutrality is not a new phenomenon. Aristotle, for example, used *anthropos*—"human being"—in discussions of "the human good" that turn out not only to exclude women but to depend on their subordination. Kant even wrote of "all rational beings as such" in making arguments that he did not mean to apply to women. But it was more readily apparent that such arguments or conceptions of the good were not about all of us, but only about male heads of families. For their authors usually gave at some point an explanation, no matter how inadequate, of why what they were saying did not apply to women and of the different characteristics and virtues, rights, and responsibilities they thought women ought to have. Nevertheless, their theories have often been read as though they pertain (or can easily be applied) to all of us. Feminist interpretations of the last fifteen years or so have revealed the falsity of this "add women and stir" method of reading the history of political thought.

The falseness of the gender-neutral language of contemporary political theorists is less readily apparent. Most, though not all, contemporary moral and political philosophers use "men and women," "he or she," "persons," or the increasingly ubiquitous "self." Sometimes they even get their computers to distribute masculine and feminine terms of reference randomly. Since they do not explicitly exclude or differentiate women, as most theorists in the past did, we may be tempted to read their theories as inclusive of all of us. But we cannot. Their merely terminological responses to feminist challenges, in spite of giving a superficial impression of tolerance and inclusiveness, often strain credulity and sometimes result in nonsense. They do this in two ways: by ignoring the irreducible biological differences between the sexes, and/or by ignoring their different assigned social roles and consequent power differentials, and the ideologies that have supported them. Thus gender-neutral terms frequently obscure the fact that so much of the real experience of "persons," so long as they live in gender-structured societies, *does* in fact depend on what sex they are.

False gender neutrality is by no means confined to the realm of theory. Its harmful effects can be seen in public policies that have directly affected large numbers of women adversely. It was used, for example, in the Supreme Court's 1976 decision that the exclusion of pregnancy-related disabilities from employers' disability insurance plans was "not a gender-based discrimination at all." In a now infamous phrase of its majority opinion, the Court explained that such plans did not discriminate against women because the distinction drawn by such plans was between pregnant women and "non-pregnant *persons*."

. . . I will illustrate the concept [of false gender neutrality in contemporary political theory] by citing just two examples. Ackerman's *Social Justice in the Liberal State* is a book containing scrupulously gender-neutral language. He breaks with this neutrality only, it seems, to *defy* existing sex roles; he refers to the "Commander," who plays the lead role in the theory, as "she." However, the argument of the book does not address the existing inequality or role differentiation between the sexes, though it has the potential for doing so. The full impact of Ackerman's gender-neutral language without attention to gender is revealed in his section on abortion: a two-page discussion written, with the exception of a single "she," in the completely gender-neutral language of fetuses and their "parents." The impression given is that there is no relevant respect in which the relationship of the two parents to the fetus differs. Now it is, of course, possible to imagine (and in the view of many feminists, would be desirable to achieve) a society in which differences in the relation of women and men to fetuses would be so slight as to reasonably play only a minor role in the discussion of abortion. But this would have to be a society without gender—one in which sexual difference carried no social significance, the sexes were equal in power and interdependence, and "mothering" and "fathering" a child meant the same thing, so that parenting and earning responsibilities were equally shared. We certainly do not live in such a society. Neither is there any discussion of one in Ackerman's theory, in which the division of labor between the sexes is not considered a matter of social (in)justice. In such a context, a "gender-neutral" discussion of abortion is almost as misleading as the Supreme Court's "gender-neutral" discussion of pregnancy.

A second illustration of false gender neutrality comes from Derek Phillips's *Toward a Just Social Order*. Largely because of the extent of his concern—rare among theorists of justice—with how we are to *achieve and maintain* a just social order, Phillips pays an unusual amount of attention to the family. He writes about the family as the locus for the development of a sense of justice and self-esteem, of an appreciation of the meaning of reciprocity, of the ability to exercise unforced choice, and of an awareness of alternative ways of life. The problem with this otherwise admirable discussion is that, apart from a couple of brief exceptions, the family itself is presented in gender-neutral terms that bear little resemblance to actual, gender-structured life.* It is because of "parental affection," "parental nurturance," and "child rearing" that children in Phillips's families become the autonomous moral agents that his just society requires its citizens to be. The child's development of a sense of identity is very much dependent upon being raised by "parental figures who themselves have coherent and well-integrated personal identities," and we are told that such a coherent identity is "ideally one built around commitments to work and love." This all sounds very plausible. But it does not take into account the multiple inequalities of gender. In gender-structured societies—in which the child rearers are women, "parental nurturance" is largely mothering, and those who do what society regards as "meaningful work" are assumed *not* to be primary parents—women in even the best of circumstances face considerable conflicts between love (a fulfilling family life) and "meaningful work." Women in less fortunate circumstances face even greater conflicts between love (even basic care of their children) and any kind of paid work at all.

It follows from Phillips's own premises that these conflicts are very likely to affect the strength and coherence in women of that

---

*He points out the shortcomings of the "earlier ethic of sacrifice," especially for women. He also welcomes the recent lessening of women's dependence on their husbands, but at the same time blames it for tending to weaken family stability. The falseness of Phillips's gender neutrality in discussing parenting is clearly confirmed later in the book (chaps. 8 and 9), where paid work is "men's" and it is "fathers" who bequeath wealth or poverty on their children.

sense of identity and self-esteem, coming from love and meaningful work, that he regards as essential for being an autonomous moral agent. In turn, if they are mothers, it is also likely to affect their daughters' and sons' developing senses of their identity. Gender is clearly a major obstacle to the attainment of a social order remotely comparable to the just one Phillips aspires to—but his false gender-neutral language allows him to ignore this fact. Although he is clearly aware of how distant in some other respects his vision of a just social order is from contemporary societies, his use of falsely gender-neutral language leaves him quite unaware of the distance between the type of family that might be able to socialize just citizens and typical families today.

The combined effect of the omission of the family and the falsely gender-neutral language in recent political thought is that most theorists are continuing to ignore the highly political issue of gender. The language they use makes little difference to what they actually do, which is to write about men and about only those women who manage, in spite of the gendered structures and practices of the society in which they live, to adopt patterns of life that have been developed to suit the needs of men. The fact that human beings are born as helpless infants—not as the purportedly autonomous actors who populate political theories—is obscured by the implicit assumption of gendered families, operating outside the range of the theories. To a large extent, contemporary theories of justice, like those of the past, are about men with wives at home.

Gender as an Issue of Justice

For three major reasons, this state of affairs is unacceptable. The first is the obvious point that women must be fully included in any satisfactory theory of justice. The second is that equality of opportunity, not only for women but for children of both sexes, is seriously undermined by the current gender injustices of our society. And the third reason is that, as has already been suggested, the family—currently the linchpin of the gender structure—must be just if we are to have a just society, since it is within the family that we first come to have that sense of ourselves and our relations with others that is at the root of moral development.

Counting Women In

When we turn to the great tradition of Western political thought with questions about the justice of the treatment of the sexes in mind, it is to little avail. Bold feminists like Mary Astell, Mary Wollstonecraft, William Thompson, Harriet Taylor, and George Bernard Shaw have occasionally challenged the tradition, often using its own premises and arguments to overturn its explicit or implicit justification of the inequality of women. But John Stuart Mill is a rare exception to the rule that those who hold central positions in the tradition almost never question the justice of the subordination of women. This phenomenon is undoubtedly due in part to the fact that Aristotle, whose theory of justice has been so influential, relegated women to a sphere of "household justice"—populated by persons who are not fundamentally equal to the free men who participate in political justice, but inferiors whose natural function is to serve those who are more fully human. The liberal tradition, despite its supposed foundation of individual rights and human equality, is more Aristotelian in this respect than is generally acknowledged. In one way or another, almost all liberal theorists have assumed that the "individual" who is the basic subject of the theories is the male head of a patriarchal household. Thus they have not usually considered applying the principles of justice to women or to relations between the sexes.

When we turn to contemporary theories of justice, however, we expect to find more illuminating and positive contributions to the subject of gender and justice. As the omission of the family and the falseness of their gender-neutral language suggest, however, mainstream contemporary theories of justice do not address the subject any better than those of the past. Theories of justice that apply to only half of us simply won't do; the inclusiveness falsely implied by the current use of gender-neutral terms must become real. Theories of justice must apply to all of us, and to all of human life, instead of *assuming* silently that half of us take care of whole areas of life that are considered outside the scope of social justice. In a just society, the structure and practices of families must afford women the same opportunities as men to develop their capacities, to participate in political power, to influence social choices, and to be economically as well as physically secure.

Unfortunately, much feminist intellectual energy in the 1980s has gone into the claim that "justice" and "rights" are masculinist ways of thinking about morality that feminists should eschew or radically revise, advocating a morality of care. The emphasis is misplaced, I think, for several reasons. First, what is by now a vast literature on the subject shows that the evidence for differences in women's and men's ways of thinking about moral issues is not (at least yet) very clear; neither is the evidence about the source of whatever differences there might be. It may well turn out that any differences can be readily explained in terms of roles, including female primary parenting, that are socially determined and therefore alterable. There is certainly no evidence—nor could there be, in such a gender-structured society—for concluding that women are somehow naturally more inclined toward contextuality and away from universalism in their moral thinking, a false concept that unfortunately reinforces the old stereotypes that justify separate spheres. The capacity of reactionary forces to capitalize on the "different moralities" strain in feminism is particularly evident in Pope John Paul II's recent Apostolic Letter, "On the Dignity of Women," in which he refers to women's special capacity to care for others in arguing for confining them to motherhood or celibacy.

Second, . . . I think the distinction between an ethic of justice and an ethic of care has been overdrawn. The best theorizing about justice, I argue, has integral to it the notions of care and empathy, of thinking of the interests and well-being of others who may be very different from ourselves. It is, therefore, misleading to draw a dichotomy as though they were two contrasting ethics. The best theorizing about justice is not some abstract "view from nowhere," but results from the carefully attentive consideration of *everyone's* point of view. This means, of course, that the best theorizing about justice is not good enough if it does not, or cannot readily be adapted to, include women and their points of view as fully as men and their points of view.

Gender and Equality of Opportunity

The family is a crucial determinant of our opportunities in life, of what we "become." It has frequently been acknowledged by those concerned with real equality of opportunity that the family presents a problem. But though they have discerned a serious problem, these theorists have underestimated it because they have seen only half of it. They have seen that the disparity among families in terms of the physical and emotional environment, motivation, and material advantages they can give their children has a tremendous effect upon children's opportunities in life. We are not born as isolated, equal individuals in our society, but into family situations: some in the social middle, some poor and homeless, and some superaffluent; some to a single or soon-to-be-separated parent, some to parents whose marriage is fraught with conflict, some to parents who will stay together in love and happiness. Any claims that equal opportunity exists are therefore completely unfounded. Decades of neglect of the poor, especially of poor black and Hispanic households, accentuated by the policies of the Reagan years, have brought us farther from the principles of equal opportunity. To come close to them would require, for example, a high and uniform standard of public education and the provision of equal social services—including health care, employment training, job opportunities, drug rehabilitation, and decent housing—for all who need them. In addition to redistributive taxation, only massive reallocations of resources from the military to social services could make these things possible.

But even if all these disparities were somehow eliminated, we would still not attain equal opportunity for all. This is because what has not been recognized as an equal opportunity problem, except in feminist literature and circles, is the disparity *within* the family, the fact that its gender structure is itself a major obstacle to equality of opportunity. This is very important in itself, since one of the factors with most influence on our opportunities in life is the social significance attributed to our sex. The opportunities of girls and women are centrally affected by the structure and practices of family life, particularly by the fact that women are almost invariably primary parents. What nonfeminists who see in the family an obstacle to equal opportunity have *not* seen is that the extent to which a family is gender-structured can make the sex we belong to a relatively insignificant aspect of our identity and our life prospects or an all-pervading one. This is because so much of the social construction of gender takes place in the family, and particularly in the institution of female parenting.

Moreover, especially in recent years, with the increased rates of single motherhood, separation, and divorce, the inequalities between the sexes have *compounded* the first part of the problem. The disparity among families has grown largely because of the impoverishment of many women and children after separation or divorce. The division of labor in the typical family leaves most women far less capable than men of supporting themselves, and this disparity is accentuated by the fact that children of separated or divorced parents usually live with their mothers. The inadequacy—and frequent nonpayment—of child support has become recognized as a major social problem. Thus the inequalities of gender are now directly harming many children of both sexes as well as women themselves. Enhancing equal opportunity for women, important as it is in itself, is also a crucial way of improving the opportunities of many of the most disadvantaged children.

As there is a connection among the parts of this problem, so is there a connection among some of the solutions: much of what needs to be done to end the inequalities of gender, and to work in the direction of ending gender itself, will also help to equalize opportunity from one family to another. Subsidized, high-quality day care is obviously one such thing; another is the adaptation of the workplace to the needs of parents. . . .

The Family as a School of Justice

One of the things that theorists who have argued that families need not or cannot be just, or who have simply neglected them, have failed to explain is how, within a formative social environment that is *not* founded upon principles of justice, children can learn to develop that sense of justice they will require as citizens of a just society. Rather than being one among many co-equal institutions of a just society, a just family is its essential foundation.

It may seem uncontroversial, even obvious, that families must be just because of the vast influence they have on the moral development of children. But this is clearly not the case. I shall argue that unless the first and most formative example of adult interaction usually experienced by children is one of justice and reciprocity, rather than one of domination and manipulation or of unequal altruism and one-sided self-sacrifice, and unless they themselves are treated with concern and respect, they are likely to be considerably hindered in becoming people who are guided by principles of justice. Moreover, I claim, the sharing of roles by men and women, rather than the division of roles between them, would have a further positive impact because the experience of *being* a physical and psychological nurturer—whether of a child or of another adult—would increase that capacity to identify with and fully comprehend the viewpoints of others that is important to a sense of justice. In a society that minimized gender this would be more likely to be the experience of all of us.

Almost every person in our society starts life in a family of some sort or other. Fewer of these families now fit the usual, though by no means universal, standard of previous generations, that is, wage-working father, homemaking mother, and children. More families these days are headed by a single parent; lesbian and gay parenting is no longer so rare; many children have two wage-working parents, and receive at least some of their early care outside the home. While its forms are varied, the family in which a child is raised, especially in the earliest years, is clearly a crucial place for early moral development and for the formation of our basic attitudes to others. It is, potentially, a place where we can *learn to be just*. It is especially important for the development of a sense of justice that grows from sharing the experiences of others and becoming aware of the points of view of others who are different in some respects from ourselves, but with whom we clearly have some interests in common.

The importance of the family for the moral development of individuals was far more often recognized by political theorists of the past than it is by those of the present. Hegel, Rousseau, Tocqueville, Mill, and Dewey are obvious examples that come to mind. Rousseau, for example, shocked by Plato's proposal to abolish the family, says that it is

> as though there were no need for a natural base on which to form conventional ties; as though the love of one's nearest were not the principle of the love one owes the state; as though it were not by means of the small fatherland which is the family that the heart attaches itself to the large one.

Defenders of both autocratic and democratic regimes have recognized the political importance of different family forms for the formation of citizens. On the one hand, the nineteenth-century monarchist Louis de Bonald argued against the divorce reforms of the French Revolution, which he claimed had weakened the patriarchal family, on the grounds that "in order to keep the state out of the hands of the people, it is necessary to keep the family out of the hands of women and children." Taking this same line of thought in the opposite direction, the U.S. Supreme Court decided in 1879 in *Reynolds v. Nebraska* that familial patriarchy fostered despotism and was therefore intolerable. Denying Mormon men the freedom to practice polygamy, the Court asserted that it was an offense "subversive of good order" that "leads to the patriarchal principle, . . . [and] when applied to large communities, fetters the people in stationary despotism, while that principle cannot long exist in connection with monogamy." However, while de Bonald was consistent in his adherence to an hierarchical family structure as necessary for an undemocratic political system, the Supreme Court was by no means consistent in promoting an egalitarian family as an essential underpinning for political democracy. For in other decisions of the same period—such as *Bradwell v. Illinois*, the famous 1872 case that upheld the exclusion of women from the practice of law—the Court rejected women's claims to legal equality, in the name of a thoroughly patriarchal, though monogamous, family that was held to require the dependence of women and their exclusion from civil and political life. While bigamy was considered patriarchal, and as such a threat to republican, democratic government, the refusal to allow a married woman to employ her talents and to make use of her qualifications to earn an independent living was not considered patriarchal. It was so far from being a threat to the civil order, in fact, that it was deemed necessary for it, and as such was ordained by both God and nature. Clearly in both *Reynolds* and *Bradwell*, "state authorities enforced family forms preferred by those in power and justified as necessary to stability and order." The Court noticed the despotic potential of polygamy, but was blind to the despotic potential of patriarchal monogamy. This was perfectly acceptable to them as a training ground for citizens.

Most theorists of the past who stressed the importance of the family and its practices for the wider world of moral and political life by no means insisted on congruence between the structures or practices of the family and those of the outside world. Though concerned with moral development, they bifurcated public from private life to such an extent that they had no trouble reconciling inegalitarian, sometimes admittedly unjust, relations founded upon sentiment within the family with a more just, even egalitarian, social structure outside the family. Rousseau, Hegel, Tocqueville—all thought the family was centrally important for the development of morality in citizens, but all defended the hierarchy of the marital structure while spurning such a degree of hierarchy in institutions and practices outside the household. Preferring instead to rely on love, altruism, and generosity as the basis for family relations, none of these theorists argued for *just* family structures as necessary for socializing children into citizenship in a just society.

The position that justice within the family is irrelevant to the development of just citizens was not plausible even when only men were citizens. John Stuart Mill, in *The Subjection of Women,* takes an impassioned stand against it. He argues that the inequality of women within the family is deeply subversive of justice in general in the wider social world, because it subverts the moral potential of men. Mill's first answer to the question, "For whose good are all these changes in women's rights to be undertaken?" is: "the advantage of having the most universal and pervading of all human relations regulated by justice instead of injustice." Making marriage a relationship of equals, he argues, would transform this central part of daily life from "a school of despotism" into "a school of moral cultivation." He goes on to discuss, in the strongest of terms, the noxious effect of growing up in a family not regulated by justice. Consider, he says, "the self-worship, the unjust self-preference," nourished in a boy growing up in a household in which "by the mere fact of being born a male he is by right the superior of all and every one of an entire half of the human race." Mill concludes that the example set by perpetuating a marital structure "contradictory to the first principles of social justice" must have such "a perverting influence" that it is hard even to imagine the good effects of changing it. All other attempts to educate people to respect and practice justice, Mill claims, will be superficial "as long as the citadel of the enemy is not attacked." Mill felt as much hope for what the family might be as he felt despair at what it was not. "The family, justly constituted, would be the real school of the virtues of freedom," primary among which was "justice, . . . grounded as before on equal, but now also on sympathetic association." Mill both saw clearly and had the courage to address what so many other political philosophers either could not see, or saw and turned away from.

Despite the strength and fervor of his advocacy of women's rights, however, Mill's idea of a just family structure falls far short of that of many feminists even of his own time, including his wife, Harriet Taylor. In spite of the fact that Mill recognized both the empowering effect of earnings on one's position in the family and the limiting effect of domestic responsibility on women's opportunities, he balked at questioning the traditional division of labor between the sexes. For him, a woman's choice of marrige was parallel to a man's choice of a profession: unless and until she had fulfilled her obligations to her husband and children, she should not undertake anything else. But clearly, however equal the legal rights of husbands and wives, this position largely undermines Mill's own insistence upon the importance of marital equality for a just society. His acceptance of the traditional division of labor, without making any provision for wives who were thereby made economically dependent upon their husbands, largely undermines his insistence upon family justice as the necessary foundation for social justice.

Thus even those political theorists of the past who have perceived the family as an important school of moral development have rarely acknowledged the need for congruence between the family and the wider social order, which suggests that families themselves need to be just. Even when they have, as with Mill, they have been unwilling to push hard on the traditional division of labor within the family in the name of justice or equality.

Contemporary theorists of justice, with few exceptions, have paid little or no attention to the question of moral development—of how we are to *become* just. Most of them seem to think, to adapt slightly Hobbes's notable phrase, that just men spring like mushrooms from the earth. Not surprisingly, then, it is far less often acknowledged in recent than in past theories that the family is important for moral development, and especially for instilling a sense of justice. As I have already noted, many theorists pay no attention at all to either the family or gender. In the rare case that the issue of justice within the family is given any sustained attention, the family is not viewed as a potential school of social justice. In the rare case that a theorist pays any sustained attention to the development of a sense of justice or morality, little if any attention is likely to be paid to the family. Even in the rare event that theorists pay considerable attention to the family *as* the first major locus of moral socialization, they do not refer to the fact that

families are almost all still thoroughly gender-structured institutions.

Among major contemporary theorists of justice, John Rawls alone treats the family seriously as the earliest school of moral development. He argues that a just, well-ordered society will be stable only if its members continue to develop a sense of justice. And he argues that families play a fundamental role in the stages by which this sense of justice is acquired. From the parents' love for their child, which comes to be reciprocated, comes the child's "sense of his own value and the desire to become the sort of person that they are." The family, too, is the first of that series of "associations" in which we participate, from which we acquire the capacity, crucial for a sense of justice, to see things from the perspectives of others. . . . This capacity—the capacity for empathy—is essential for maintaining a sense of justice of the Rawlsian kind. For the perspective that is necessary for maintaining a sense of justice is not that of the egoistic or disembodied self, or of the dominant few who overdetermine "our" traditions or "shared understandings," or (to use Nagel's term) of "the view from nowhere," but rather the perspective of every person in the society for whom the principles of justice are being arrived at. . . . The problem with Rawls's rare and interesting discussion of moral development is that it rests on the unexplained *assumption* that family institutions are just. If gendered family institutions are *not* just, but are, rather, a relic of caste or feudal societies in which responsibilities, roles, and resources are distributed, not in accordance with the principles of justice he arrives at or with any other commonly respected values, but in accordance with innate differences that are imbued with enormous social significance, then Rawls's theory of moral development would seem to be built on uncertain ground. This problem is exacerbated by suggestions in some of Rawls's most recent work that families are "private institutions," to which it is not appropriate to apply standards of justice. But if families are to help form just individuals and citizens, surely they must be *just families*.

In a just society, the structure and practices of families must give women the same opportunities as men to develop their capacities, to participate in political power and influence social choices, and to be economically secure. But in addition to this, families must be just because of the vast influence that they have on the moral development of children. The family is the primary institution of formative moral development. And the structure and practices of the family must parallel those of the larger society if the sense of justice is to be fostered and maintained. While many theorists of justice, both past and present, appear to have denied the importance of at least one of these factors, my own view is that both are absolutely crucial. A society that is committed to equal respect for all of its members, and to justice in social distributions of benefits and responsibilities, can neither neglect the family nor accept family structures and practices that violate these norms, as do current gender-based structures and practices. It is essential that children who are to develop into adults with a strong sense of justice and commitment to just institutions spend their earliest and most formative years in an environment in which they are loved and nurtured, *and* in which principles of justice are abided by and respected. What is a child of either sex to learn about fairness in the average household with two full-time working parents, where the mother does, at the very least, twice as much family work as the father? What is a child to learn about the value of nurturing and domestic work in a home with a traditional division of labor in which the father either subtly or not so subtly uses the fact that he is the wage earner to "pull rank" on or to abuse his wife? What is a child to learn about responsibility for others in a family in which, after many years of arranging her life around the needs of her husband and children, a woman is faced with having to provide for herself and her children but is totally ill-equipped for the task by the life she agreed to lead, has led, and expected to go on leading?

---

25. Feminist Justice and the Family

James P. Sterba

James P. Sterba sets out and defends an ideal of androgyny that he identifies with feminist justice. This ideal requires that traits that are truly desirable in society be equally available to both women and men, or in the case of virtues, equally expected in both women and men. He considers attempts to derive the ideal of androgyny either from a right to equal opportunity that is a central requirement of a welfare liberal conception of justice or from an equal right of self-development that is a central requirement of a socialist conception of justice. Sterba further argues that the ideal of androgyny would require (1) that all children irrespective of their sex must be given the same type of upbringing consistent with their native capabilities and (2) that mothers and fathers must also have the same opportunities for education and employment consistent with their native capabilities.

From *Perspectives on the Family* (1990), edited by Robert Moffat, Joseph Grcic, and Michael Bayles. Reprinted with revisions by permission.

Contemporary feminists almost by definition seek to put an end to male domination and to secure women's liberation. To achieve these goals, many feminists support the political ideal of androgyny.* According to these feminists, all assignments of rights and duties are ultimately to be justified in terms of the ideal of androgyny. Since a conception of justice is usually thought to provide the ultimate grounds for the assignment of rights and duties in a society, I shall refer to this ideal of androgyny as "feminist justice."

The Ideal of Androgyny

But how is this ideal of androgyny to be interpreted? In a well-known article, Joyce Trebilcot distinguishes two forms of androgyny. The first form postulates the same ideal for everyone. According to this form of androgyny, the ideal person "combines characteristics usually attributed to men with characteristics usually attributed to women." Thus, we should expect both nurturance and mastery, openness and objectivity, compassion and competitiveness from each and every person who has the capacities for these traits.

By contrast, the second form of androgyny does not advocate the same ideal for everyone but rather a variety of options from "pure" femininity to "pure" masculinity. As Trebilcot points out, this form of androgyny shares with the first the view that biological sex should not be the basis for determining the appropriateness of gender characterization. It differs in that it holds that "all alternatives with respect to gender should be equally available to and equally approved for everyone, regardless of sex."

*Someone might object that if feminist justice is worth considering, why not racial justice? In principle I have no objection to a separate consideration of racial justice although the main issues that are relevant to such a discussion have standardly been taken up in discussions of the other conceptions of justice. By contrast, feminist justice raises new issues that have usually been ignored in discussions of the other conceptions of justice (e.g., equal opportunity within the family), and for that reason, I think, this conception of justice deserves separate consideration.

It would be a mistake, however, to sharply distinguish between these two forms of androgyny. Properly understood, they are simply two different facets of a single ideal. For, as Mary Ann Warren has argued, the second form of androgyny is appropriate *only* "with respect to feminine and masculine traits which are largely matters of personal style and preference and which have little direct moral significance." However, when we consider so-called feminine and masculine *virtues,* it is the first form of androgyny that is required because, then, other things being equal, the same virtues are appropriate for everyone.

We can even formulate the ideal of androgyny more abstractly so that it is no longer specified in terms of so-called feminine and masculine traits. We can, for example, specify the ideal as requiring no more than that the traits that are truly desirable in society be equally available to both women and men, or in the case of virtues, equally expected of both women and men.

There is a problem, of course, in determining which traits of character are virtues and which traits are largely matters of personal style and preference. To make this determination, Trebilcot has suggested that we seek to bring about the second form of androgyny, where people have the option of acquiring the full range of so-called feminine and masculine traits. But surely when we already have good grounds for thinking that certain traits are virtues, such as courage and compassion, fairness and openness, there is no reason to adopt such a laissez-faire approach to moral education. Although, as Trebilcot rightly points out, proscribing certain options will involve a loss of freedom, nevertheless, we should be able to determine at least with respect to some character traits when a gain in virtue is worth the loss of freedom. It may even be the case that the loss of freedom suffered by an individual now will be compensated for by a gain of freedom to that same individual in the future once the relevant virtue or virtues have been acquired.

So understood, the class of virtues will turn out to be those desirable traits that can be reasonably expected of both women and men. Admittedly, this is a restrictive use of the term virtue. In normal usage, "virtue" is almost synonymous with "desirable trait." But there is good reason to focus on those desirable traits that can be justifiably inculcated in both women and men, and, for present purposes, I will refer to this class of desirable traits as virtues.

Unfortunately, many of the challenges to the ideal of androgyny fail to appreciate how the ideal can be interpreted to combine a required set of virtues with equal choice from among other desirable traits. For example, some challenges interpret the ideal as attempting to achieve "a proper balance of moderation" among opposing feminine and masculine traits and then question whether traits like feminine gullibility or masculine brutality could ever be combined with opposing gender traits to achieve such a balance. Other challenges interpret the ideal as permitting unrestricted choice of personal traits and then regard the possibility of Total Women and Hells Angels androgynes as a *reductio ad absurdum* of the ideal. But once it is recognized that the ideal of androgyny can not only be interpreted to expect of everyone a set of virtues (which need not be a mean between opposing extreme traits), but can also be interpreted to limit everyone's choice to desirable traits, then such challenges to the ideal clearly lose their force.

Actually the main challenge raised by feminists to the ideal of androgyny is that the ideal is self-defeating in that it seeks to eliminate sexual stereotyping of human beings at the same time that it is formulated in terms of the very same stereotypical concepts it seeks to eliminate. Or as Warren has put it, "Is it not at least mildly paradoxical to urge people to cultivate both 'feminine' and 'masculine' virtues, while at the same time holding that virtues ought not to be sexually stereotyped?"

But in response to this challenge, it can be argued that to build a better society we must begin where we are now, and where we are now people still speak of feminine and masculine character traits. Consequently, if we want to easily refer to such traits and to formulate an ideal with respect to how they should be distributed in society it is plausible to refer to them in the way that people presently refer to them, that is, as feminine or masculine traits.

Alternatively, to avoid misunderstanding altogether, the ideal could be formulated in the more abstract way I suggested earlier so that it no longer specifically refers to so-called feminine or masculine traits. So formulated, the ideal requires that the traits that are truly desirable in society be equally available to both women and men or in the case of virtues equally expected of women and men. So formulated the ideal would, in effect, require that men and women have in the fullest sense an equal right of self-development. The ideal would require this because an equal right to self-development can only be effectively guaranteed by expecting the same virtues of both women and men and by making other desirable traits equally available to both women and men.

So characterized the ideal of androgyny represents neither a revolt against so-called feminine virtues and traits nor their exaltation over so-called masculine virtues and traits. Accordingly, the ideal of androgyny does not view women's liberation as *simply* the freeing of women from the confines of traditional roles thus making it possible for them to develop in ways heretofore reserved for men. Nor does the ideal view women's liberation as *simply* the revaluation and glorification of so-called feminine activities like housekeeping or mothering or so-called feminine modes of thinking as reflected in an ethic of caring. The first perspective ignores or devalues genuine virtues and desirable traits traditionally associated with women while the second ignores or devalues genuine virtues and desirable traits traditionally associated with men. By contrast, the ideal of androgyny seeks a broader-based ideal for both women and men that combines virtues and desirable traits traditionally associated with women with virtues and desirable traits traditionally associated with men. Nevertheless, the ideal of androgyny will clearly reject any so-called virtues or desirable traits traditionally associated with women or men that have been supportive of discrimination or oppression against women or men.

Defenses of Androgyny

Now there are various contemporary defenses of the ideal of androgyny. Some feminists have attempted to derive the ideal from a Welfare Liberal Conception of Justice. Others have attempted to derive the ideal from a Socialist Conception of Justice. Let us briefly consider each of these defenses in turn.

In attempting to derive the ideal of androgyny from a Welfare Liberal Conception of Justice, feminists have tended to focus on the right to equal opportunity which is a central requirement of a Welfare Liberal Conception of Justice. Of course, equal opportunity could be interpreted minimally as providing people only with the same legal rights of access to all advantaged positions in society for which they are qualified. But this is not the interpretation given the right by welfare liberals. In a Welfare Liberal Conception of Justice, equal opportunity is interpreted to require in addition the same prospects for success for all those who are relevantly similar, where relevant similarity involves more than simply present qualifications. For example, Rawls claims that persons in his original position would favor a right to "fair equality of opportunity," which means that persons who have the same natural assets and the same willingness to use them would have the necessary resources to achieve similar life prospects. The point feminists have been making is simply that failure to achieve the ideal of androgyny translates into a failure to guarantee equal opportunity to both women and men. The present evidence for this failure to provide equal opportunity is the discrimination that exists against women in education, employment, and personal relations. Discrimination in education begins early in a child's formal educational experience as teachers and school books support different and less desirable roles for girls than for boys. Discrimination in employment has been well documented. Women continue to earn only a fraction of what men earn for the same or comparable jobs and although women make up almost half of the paid labor force in the U.S., 70 percent of them are concentrated in just twenty different job categories, only five more than in 1905. Finally, discrimination in personal relations is the most entrenched of all forms of discrimination against women. It primarily manifests itself in traditional family structures in which the woman is responsible for domestic work and childcare and the man's task is "to protect against the outside world and to show how to meet this world successfully." In none of these areas, therefore, do women have the same prospects for success as compared with men with similar natural talents and similar desires to succeed.

Now the support for the ideal of androgyny provided by a Socialist Conception of Justice appears to be much more direct than that provided by a Welfare Liberal Conception of Justice. This is because the Socialist Conception of Justice and the ideal of androgyny can be interpreted as requiring the very same equal right of self-development. What a Socialist Conception of Justice purports to add to this interpretation of the ideal of androgyny is an understanding of how the ideal is best to be realized in contemporary capitalist societies. For according to advocates of this defense of androgyny, the ideal is best achieved by socializing the means of production and satisfying people's nonbasic as well as their basic needs. Thus, the general idea behind this approach to realizing the ideal of androgyny is that a cure for capitalist exploitation will also be a cure for women's oppression.

Yet despite attempts to identify the feminist ideal of androgyny with a right to equal opportunity endorsed by a Welfare Liberal Conception of Justice or an equal right of self-development endorsed by a Socialist Conception of Justice, the ideal still transcends both of these rights by requiring not only that desirable traits be equally available to both women and men but also that the same virtues be equally expected of both women and men. Of course, part of the rationale for expecting the same virtues in both women and men is to support such rights. And if support for such rights is to be fairly allocated, the virtues needed to support such rights must be equally expected of both women and men. Nevertheless, to hold that the virtues required to support a right to equal opportunity or an equal right to self-development must be equally expected of both women and men is different from claiming, as the ideal of androgyny does, that human virtues, sans phrase, should be equally expected of both women and men. Thus, the ideal of androgyny clearly requires an inculcation of virtues beyond what is necessary to support a right to equal opportunity or an equal right to self-development. What additional virtues are required by the ideal obviously depends upon what other rights should be recognized. In this regard, the ideal of androgyny is somewhat open-ended. Feminists who endorse the ideal would simply have to go along with the best arguments for additional rights and corresponding virtues. In particular, I would claim that they would have to support a right to welfare that is necessary for meeting the basic needs of all legitimate claimants given the strong case that can be made for such a right from welfare liberal, socialist and even libertarian perspectives.

Now, in order to provide all legitimate claimants with the resources necessary for meeting their basic needs, there obviously has to be a limit on the resources that will be available for each individual's self-development, and this limit will definitely have an effect upon the implementation of the ideal of androgyny. Of course, some feminists would want to pursue various possible technological transformations of human biology in order to implement their ideal. For example, they would like to make it possible for women to inseminate other women and for men to lactate and even to bring fertilized ova to term. But bringing about such possibilities would be very costly indeed. Consequently, since the means selected for meeting basic needs must be provided to all legitimate claimants including distant peoples and future generations, it is unlikely that such costly means could ever be morally justified. Rather it seems preferable radically to equalize the opportunities that are conventionally provided to women and men and wait for such changes to ultimately have their effect on human biology as well. Of course, if any "technological fixes" for achieving androgyny should prove to be cost efficient as a means for meeting people's basic needs, then obviously there would be every reason to utilize them.

Unfortunately, the commitment of a Feminist Conception of Justice to a right of equal opportunity raises still another problem for the view. For some philosophers have contended that equal opportunity is ultimately an incoherent goal. As Lloyd Thomas has put the charge, "We have a problem for those who

advocate competitive equality of opportunity: the prizes won in the competitions of the first generation will tend to defeat the requirements of equality of opportunity for the next." The only way to avoid this result, Thomas claims, "is by not permitting persons to be dependent for their self-development on others at all," which obviously is a completely unacceptable solution.

But this is a problem, as Thomas points out, that exists for competitive opportunities. They are opportunities for which, even when each person does her best, there are considerably more losers than winners. With respect to such opportunities, the winners may well be able to place themselves and their children in an advantageous position with respect to subsequent competitions. But under a Welfare Liberal Conception of Justice, and presumably a Feminist Conception of Justice as well, most of the opportunities people have are not competitive opportunities at all, but rather noncompetitive opportunities to acquire the resources necessary for meeting their basic needs. These are opportunities with respect to which virtually everyone who does her best can be a winner. Of course, some people who do not do their best may fail to satisfy their basic needs, and this failure may have negative consequences for their children's prospects. But under a Welfare Liberal Conception of Justice, and presumably a Feminist Conception of Justice as well, every effort is required to insure that each generation has the same opportunities to meet their basic needs, and as long as most of the opportunities that are available are of the noncompetitive sort, this goal should not be that difficult to achieve.

Now it might be objected that if all that will be accomplished under the proposed system of equal opportunity is, for the most part, the satisfaction of people's basic needs, then that would not bring about the revolutionary change in the relationship between women and men that feminists are demanding. For don't most women in technologically advanced societies already have their basic needs satisfied, despite the fact that they are not yet fully liberated?

In response, it should be emphasized that the concern of defenders of the ideal of androgyny is not just with women in technologically advanced societies. The ideal of androgyny is also applicable to women in Third World and developing societies, and in such societies it is clear that the basic needs of many women are not being met. Furthermore, it is just not the case that all the basic needs of most women in technologically advanced societies are being met. Most obviously, their basic needs for self-development are still not being met. This is because they are being denied an equal right to education, training, jobs, and a variety of social roles for which they have the native capabilities. In effect, women in technologically advanced societies are still being treated as second-class persons, no matter how well-fed, well-clothed, well-housed they happen to be. This is why there must be a radical restructuring of social institutions even in technologically advanced societies if women's basic needs for self-development are to be met.

Androgyny and the Family

Now the primary locus for the radical restructuring required by the ideal of androgyny is the family. Here two fundamental changes are needed. First, all children irrespective of their sex must be given the same type of upbringing consistent with their native capabilities. Second, mothers and fathers must also have the same opportunities for education and employment consistent with their native capabilities.

Surprisingly, however, some welfare liberals have viewed the existence of the family as imposing an acceptable limit on the right to equal opportunity. Rawls, for example, claims the principle of fair opportunity can be only imperfectly carried out, at least as long as the institution of the family exists. The extent to which natural capacities develop and reach fruition is affected by all kinds of social conditions and class attitudes. Even the willingness to make an effort, to try, and so to be deserving in the ordinary sense is itself dependent upon happy family and social circumstances. It is impossible in practice to secure equal chances of achievement and culture for those similarly endowed, and therefore we may want to adopt a principle which recog-

nizes this fact and also mitigates the arbitrary effects of the natural lottery itself.

Thus, according to Rawls, since different families will provide different opportunities for their children, the only way to fully achieve "fair equality of opportunity" would require us to go too far and abolish or radically modify traditional family structures.

Yet others have argued that the full attainment of equal opportunity requires that we go even further and equalize people's native as well as their social assets. For only when everyone's natural and social assets have been equalized would everyone have exactly the same chance as everyone else to attain the desirable social positions in society. Of course, feminists have no difficulty recognizing that there are moral limits to the pursuit of equal opportunity. Accordingly, feminists could grant that other than the possibility of special cases, such as sharing a surplus organ like a second kidney, it would be too much to ask people to sacrifice their native assets to achieve equal opportunity.

Rawls, however, proposes to limit the pursuit of equal opportunity still further by accepting the inequalities generated by families in any given sector of society, provided that there is still equal opportunity between the sectors or that the existing inequality of opportunity can be justified in terms of its benefit to those in the least-advantaged position. Nevertheless, what Rawls is concerned with here is simply the inequality of opportunity that exists between individuals owing to the fact that they come from different families. He fails to consider the inequality of opportunity that exists in traditional family structures, especially between adult members, in virtue of the different roles expected of women and men. When viewed from the original position, it seems clear that this latter inequality of opportunity is sufficient to require a radical modification of traditional family structures, even if the former inequality, for the reasons Rawls suggests, does not require any such modifications.

Yet at least in the United States this need radically to modify traditional family structures to guarantee equal opportunity confronts a serious problem. Given that a significant proportion of the available jobs are at least 9 to 5, families with preschool children require day care facilities if their adult members are to pursue their careers. Unfortunately, for many families such facilities are simply unavailable. In New York City, for example, more than 144,000 children under the age of six are competing for 46,000 full-time slots in day care centers. In Seattle, there is licensed day care space for 8,800 of the 23,000 children who need it. In Miami, two children, 3 and 4 years old, were left unattended at home while their mother worked. They climbed into a clothes dryer while the timer was on, closed the door and burned to death.

Moreover, even the available day care facilities are frequently inadequate either because their staffs are poorly trained or because the child/adult ratio in such facilities is too high. At best, such facilities provide little more than custodial care; at worst, they actually retard the development of those under their care. What this suggests is that at least under present conditions if preschool children are to be adequately cared for, frequently, one of the adult members of the family will have to remain at home to provide that care. But since most jobs are at least 9 to 5, this will require that the adult members who stay at home temporarily give up pursuing a career. However, such sacrifice appears to conflict with the equal opportunity requirement of Feminist Justice.

Now families might try to meet this equal opportunity requirement by having one parent give up pursuing a career for a certain period of time and the other give up pursuing a career for a subsequent (equal) period of time. But there are problems here too. Some careers are difficult to interrupt for any significant period of time, while others never adequately reward latecomers. In addition, given the high rate of divorce and the inadequacies of most legally mandated child support, those who first sacrifice their careers may find themselves later faced with the impossible task of beginning or reviving their careers while continuing to be the primary caretaker of their children. Furthermore, there is considerable evidence that children will benefit more from equal rearing from both parents. So the option of having just one parent doing the child-rearing for any length of time is, other things being equal, not optimal.

It would seem, therefore, that to truly share child-rearing within the family what is needed is flexible (typically part-time) work schedules that also allow both parents to be together with their children for a significant period every day. Now some flexible job schedules have already been tried by various corporations. But if equal opportunity is to be a reality in our society, the option of flexible job schedules must be guaranteed to all those with preschool children. Of course, to require employers to guarantee flexible job schedules to all those with preschool children would place a significant restriction upon the rights of employers, and it may appear to move the practical requirements of Feminist Justice closer to those of Socialist Justice. But if the case for flexible job schedules is grounded on a right to equal opportunity then at least defenders of Welfare Liberal Justice will have no reason to object. This is clearly one place where Feminist Justice with its focus on equal opportunity within the family tends to drive Welfare Liberal Justice and Socialist Justice closer together in their practical requirements.

Recently, however, Christina Hoff Sommers has criticized feminist philosophers for being "against the family." Sommers's main objection is that feminist philosophers have criticized traditional family structures without adequately justifying what they would put in its place. In this paper, I have tried to avoid any criticism of this sort by first articulating a defensible version of the feminist ideal of androgyny which can draw upon support from both Welfare Liberal and Socialist Conceptions of Justice and then by showing what demands this ideal would impose upon family structures. Since Sommers and other critics of the feminist ideal of androgyny also support a strong requirement of equal opportunity, it is difficult to see how they can consistently do so while denying the radical implications of that requirement (and the ideal of androgyny that underlies it) for traditional family structures.

26. Philosophers against the Family

Christina Sommers

Christina Sommers distinguishes liberal feminists from radical feminists. She contends that liberal feminists, like herself, want equal opportunity in the workplace and politics, but would leave marriage and motherhood "untouched and unimpugned." By contrast, Sommers contends that radical feminists are committed to an assimilationist or androgynous ideal that would destroy the (traditional) family and deny most women what they want.

Much of what commonly counts as personal morality is measured by how well we behave within family relationships. We live our moral lives as son or daughter to this mother and that father, as brother or sister to that sister or brother, as father or mother, grandfather, granddaughter to that boy or girl or that man or woman. These relationships and the moral duties defined by them were once popular topics of moral casuistry; but when we turn to the literature of recent moral philosophy, we find little discussion on what it means to be a good son or daughter, a good mother or father, a good husband or wife, a good brother or sister.

Modern ethical theory concentrates on more general topics. Perhaps the majority of us who do ethics accept some version of Kantianism or utilitarianism, and these mainstream doctrines are better designed for telling us about what we should do as persons in general than about our special duties as parents or children or siblings. We believe, perhaps, that these universal theories can fully account for the morality of special relations. In any case, modern ethics is singularly silent on the bread and butter issues of personal morality in daily life. But silence is only part of it. With the exception of marriage itself, the relationships in the family are biologically given. The contemporary philosopher is, on the whole, actively unsympathetic to the idea that we have *any* duties defined by relationships that we have not voluntarily entered into. We do not, after all, choose our parents or sib-

From "Philosophers against the Family," in *Person to Person*, George Graham and Hugh LaFollette, eds. (1989).

lings, and even if we do choose to have children, this is not the same as choosing, say, our friends. Because the special relationships that constitute the family as a social arrangement are, in this sense, not voluntarily assumed, many moralists feel bound in principle to dismiss them altogether. The practical result is that philosophers are to be found among those who are contributing to an ongoing disintegration of the traditional family. In what follows I expose some of the philosophical roots of the current hostility to family morality. My own view that the ethical theses underlying this hostility are bad philosophy is made evident throughout the discussion.

The Moral Vantage

Social criticism is a heady pastime to which philosophers are professionally addicted. One approach is Aristotelian in method and temperament. It is antiradical, though it may be liberal, and it approaches the task of needed reform with a prima facie respect for the norms of established morality. It is conservationist and cautious in its recommendations for change. It is therefore not given to such proposals as abolishing the family or abolishing private property and, indeed, does not look kindly on such proposals from other philosophers. The antiradicals I am concerned about are not those who would be called Burkean. I call them liberal but this use of the term is somewhat perverse since, in my stipulative use, a liberal is a philosopher who advocates social reform but always in a conservative spirit. My liberals share with Aristotle the conviction that the traditional arrangements have great moral weight and that common opinion is a primary source of moral truth. A good modern example is Henry Sidgwick with his constant appeal to common sense. But philosophers like John Stuart Mill, William James, and Bertrand Russell can also be cited. On the other hand, since no radical can be called a liberal in my sense, many so-called liberals could be perversely excluded. Thus when John Rawls toys with the possibility of abolishing the family because kinship bias is a force inimical to equality of opportunity, he is no liberal.

The more exciting genre of social criticism is not liberal-Aristotelian but radical and Platonist in spirit. Its vantage is external or even supernal to the social institutions it has placed under moral scrutiny. Plato was as aware as anyone could be that what he called the cave was social reality. One reason for calling it a cave was to emphasize the need, as he saw it, for an external, objective perspective on established morality. Another point in so calling it was his conviction that common opinion was benighted, and that reform could not be accomplished except by a great deal of consciousness raising and enlightened social engineering. Plato's supernal vantage made it possible for him to look on social reality in somewhat the way the Army Corps of Engineers looks upon a river that needs to have its course changed and its waywardness tamed. In our own day much social criticism of a Marxist variety has taken this radical approach to social change. And of course much of contemporary feminist philosophy is radical. . . .

Feminism and the Family

I have said that the morality of the family has been relatively neglected. The glaring exception to this is of course the feminist movement. This movement is complex, but I am primarily confined to its moral philosophers, of whom the most influential is Simone de Beauvoir. For de Beauvoir, a social arrangement that does not allow all its participants the scope and liberty of a human subjectivity is to be condemned. De Beauvoir criticizes the family as an unacceptable arrangement since, for women, marriage and childbearing are essentially incompatible with their subjectivity and freedom:

> The tragedy of marriage is not that it fails to assure woman the promised happiness . . . but that it mutilates her: it dooms her to repetition and routine. . . . At twenty or thereabouts mistress of a home, bound permanently to a man, a child in her arms, she stands with her life virtually finished forever (1952, 534).

For de Beauvoir the tragedy goes deeper than marriage. The loss of subjectivity is unavoidable as long as human reproduction requires the woman's womb. De Beauvoir starkly describes the pregnant woman who ought to be a "free individual" as a "stockpile of colloids, an incubator of an egg" (p. 553). And as recently as 1977 she compared childbearing and nurturing to slavery (p. 2).

It would be a mistake to say that de Beauvoir's criticism of the family is outside the mainstream of Anglo-American philosophy. Her criterion of moral adequacy may be formulated in continental existentialist terms, but its central contention is generally accepted: Who would deny that an arrangement that systematically thwarts the freedom and autonomy of the individual is *eo ipso* defective? What is perhaps a bit odd to Anglo-American ears is that de Beauvoir makes so little appeal to ideals of fairness and equality. For her, it is the loss of autonomy that is decisive.

De Beauvoir is more pessimistic than most feminists she has influenced about the prospects for technological and social solutions. But implicit in her critique is the ideal of a society in which sexual differences are minimal or nonexistent. This ideal is shared by many contemporary feminist philosophers. The views of Richard Wasserstrom (1980), Ann Ferguson (1977), and Allison Jagger (1977; 1983; 1986) are representative.

Wasserstrom's approach to social criticism is Platonist in its use of a hypothetical good society. The ideal society is nonsexist and "assimilationist": "In the assimilationist society in respect to sex, persons would not be socialized so as to see or understand themselves or others as essentially or significantly who they were or what their lives would be like because they were either male or female" (1980, 26). Social reality is scrutinized for its approximation to this ideal, and criticism is directed against all existing norms. Take the custom of having sexually segregated bathrooms: Whether this is right or wrong "depends on what the good society would look like in respect to sexual differentiation." The key question in evaluating any law or arrangement in which sex difference figures is: "What would the good or just society make of [it]?" (p. 23).

Thus the supernal light shines on the cave revealing its moral defects. *There*, in the ideal society, gender in the choice of lover or spouse would be of no more significance than eye color. *There* the family would consist of adults but not necessarily of different sexes and not necessarily in pairs. *There* we find equality ensured by a kind of affirmative action which compensates for disabilities. If women are somewhat weaker than men, or if they are subject to lunar disabilities, then this must be compensated for. (Wasserstrom compares women to persons with congenital defects for whom the good society makes special arrangements.) Male-dominated sports such as wrestling and football will there be eliminated, and marriage as we know it will not exist.

Other feminist philosophers are equally confident about the need for sweeping change. Ann Ferguson (1977) wants a "radical reorganization of child rearing" (p. 51). She recommends communal living and a de-emphasis on biological parenting. In the ideal society "love relationships would be based on the meshing together of androgynous human beings" (p. 66). Carol Gould (1983) argues for androgyny and for abolishing legal marriage. She favors single parenting, co-parenting, and communal parenting. The only arrangement she emphatically opposes is the traditional one where the mother provides primary care for the children. Janice Raymond (1975, 61) is an assimilationist who objects to the ideal of androgyny, preferring instead to speak of a genderless ideal free of male or female stereotypes. Allison Jagger's ideal is described in a science-fiction story depicting a society in which "neither sex bears children, but both sexes, through hormone treatments, suckle them . . . thus [the author] envisions a society where every baby has three social 'mothers,' who may be male or female, and at least two of

whom agree to breast-feed it" (1983, 41). To those of us who find this bizarre, Jagger replies that this shows the depth of our prejudice in favor of the natural family.

Though they differ in detail, these feminists hold to a common social ideal that is broadly assimilationist in character and inimical to the traditional family. Sometimes it seems as if the radical feminist simply takes the classical Marxist eschatology of the *Communist Manifesto* and substitutes "gender" for "class." Indeed, the feminist and the old-fashioned Marxist do have much in common. Both see their caves as politically divided into two warring factions: one oppressing, the other oppressed. Both see the need of raising the consciousness of the oppressed group to its predicament and to the possibility of removing its shackles. Both look forward to the day of a classless or genderless society. And both are zealots, paying little attention to the tragic personal costs to be paid for the revolution they wish to bring about. The feminists tell us little about that side of things. To begin with, how can the benighted myriads in the cave who do not wish to mesh together with other androgynous beings be reeducated? And how are children to be brought up in the genderless society? Plato took great pains to explain his methods. Would the new methods be as thoroughgoing? Unless these questions can be given plausible answers, the supernal attack on the family must always be irresponsible. The appeal to the just society justifies nothing until it can be shown that the radical proposals do not have monstrous consequences. That has not been shown. Indeed, given the perennially dubious state of the social sciences, it is precisely what *cannot* be shown.

Any social arrangement that falls short of the assimilationist ideal is labeled sexist. It should be noted that this characteristically feminist use of the term differs significantly from the popular or literal sense. Literally, and popularly, sexism connotes unfair discrimination. But in its extended philosophical use it connotes discrimination, period. Wasserstrom and many feminists trade on the popular pejorative connotations of sexism when they invite us to be antisexist. Most liberals are antisexist in the popular sense. But to be antisexist in the technical, radical philosophical sense is not merely to be opposed to discrimination against women; it is to be *for* what Wasserstrom calls the assimilationist ideal. The philosopher antisexist opposes any social policy that is nonandrogynous, objecting, for example, to legislation that allows for maternity leave. As Allison Jagger remarks: "We do not, after all, elevate 'prostate leave' into a special right of men" (1977, 102). From being liberally opposed to sexism, one may in this way insensibly be led to a radical critique of the family whose ideal is assimilationist and androgynous. For it is very clear that the realization of the androgynous ideal is incompatible with the survival of the family as we know it.

The neological extension of labels such as "sexism," "slavery," and "prostitution" is a feature of radical discourse. The liberal too will sometimes call for radical solutions to social problems. Some institutions are essentially unjust. To reform slavery or totalitarian systems of government is to eliminate them. The radical trades on these extreme practices in characterizing other practices—for example, characterizing low wages as "slave" wages and the worker who is paid them as a "slave" laborer. Taking these descriptions seriously may put one on the way to treating a system of a free labor market as a "slave system," which, in simple justice, must be overthrown and replaced by an alternative system of production.

Comparing mothers and wives to slaves is a common radical criticism of the family. Presumably most slaves do not want to be slaves. In fact, the majority of wives and mothers want to be wives and mothers. Calling these women slaves is therefore a pejorative extension of the term. To be slaves in the literal sense these women would have to be too dispirited and oppressed or too corrupt even to want freedom from slavery. Yet that is how some feminist philosophers look upon women who opt for the traditional family. It does seem fanciful and not a little condescending to see them so, but let us suppose that it is in fact a correct and profound description of the plight of married women and mothers. Would it now follow that the term "slave" literally applies to them? Not quite yet. Before we could call these women slaves, we should have to have made a further assumption. Even timorous slaves too fearful of taking any step to freedom are under no illusion that they are not slaves. Yet it is a fact that most women and

mothers do not *think* of themselves as slaves, so we must assume that the majority of women have been systematically deluded into thinking they are free. And that assumption, too, is often explicitly made. Here the radical feminist will typically explain that, existentially, women, being treated by men as sex objects, are especially prone to bad faith and false consciousness. Marxist feminists will see them as part of an unawakened and oppressed economic class. Clearly we cannot call on a deluded woman to cast off her bonds before we have made her *aware* of her bondage. So the first task of freeing the slave woman is dispelling the thrall of a false and deceptive consciousness. One must raise her consciousness to the reality of her situation. (Some feminists acknowledge that it may in fact be too late for many of the women who have fallen too far into the delusions of marriage and motherhood. But the educative process can save many from falling into the marriage and baby trap.)

In this sort of rhetorical climate nothing is what it seems. Prostitution is another term that has been subjected to a radical enlargement. Allison Jagger believes that a feminist interpretation of the term "prostitution" is badly needed and asks for a "philosophical theory of prostitution" (1986). Observing that the average woman dresses for men, marries a man for protection and so on, she says: "For contemporary radical feminists, prostitution is the archetypal relationship of women to men" (1986, 115).

Of course, the housewife Jagger has in mind might be offended at the suggestion that she herself is a prostitute, albeit less well paid and less aware of it than the professional street prostitute. To this the radical feminist reply is, to quote Jagger:

> Individuals' intentions do not necessarily indicate the true nature of what is going on. Both man and woman might be outraged at the description of their candlelit dinner as prostitution, but the radical feminist argues this outrage is due simply to the participants' failure or refusal to perceive the social context in which the dinner occurs (1986, 117).

Apparently, this failure or refusal to perceive affects most women. Thus we may even suppose that the majority of women who have been treated by a man to a candlelit dinner prefer it to other dining alternatives they have experienced. To say that these preferences are misguided is a hard and condescending doctrine. It would appear that most feminist philosophers are not overly impressed with Mill's principle that there can be no appeal from a majority verdict of those who have experienced two alternatives.

The dismissive feminist attitude to the widespread preferences of women takes its human toll. Most women, for example, prefer to have children, and few of those who have them regret having them. It is no more than sensible, from a utilitarian standpoint, to take note of the widespread preference and to take it seriously in planning one's own life. But a significant number of women discount this general verdict as benighted, taking more seriously the idea that the reported joys of motherhood are exaggerated and fleeting, if not altogether illusory. These women tell themselves and others that having babies is a trap to be avoided. But for many women childlessness has become a trap of its own, somewhat lonelier than the more conventional traps of marriage and babies. Some come to find their childlessness regrettable; this sort of regret is common to those who flout Mill's reasonable maxim by putting the verdict of ideology over the verdict of human experience.

It is a serious defect of American feminism that it concentrates its zeal on impugning femininity and feminine culture at the expense of the grass root fight against economic and social injustices to which women are subjected. As we have seen, the radical feminist attitude to the woman who enjoys her femininity is condescending or even contemptuous. Indeed, the contempt for femininity reminds one of misogynist biases in philosophers such as Kant, Rousseau, and Schopenhauer, who believed that femininity was charming but incompatible with full personhood and reasonableness. The feminists deny the charm, but they too accept the verdict that femininity is weakness. It goes without saying that an essential connection between femininity and powerlessness has not been established by *either* party.

By denigrating conventional feminine roles and holding to an assimilationist ideal in social policy, the feminist movement has lost its natural constituency. The actual concerns, beliefs, and aspirations of the majority of women are not taken seriously *except* as illustrations of bad faith, false consciousness, and successful brainwashing. What women actually want is discounted and reinterpreted as to what they have been led to *think* they want (a man, children). What most women *enjoy* (male gallantry, candlelit dinners, sexy clothes, makeup) is treated as an obscenity (prostitution).

As the British feminist Jennifer Radcliffe Richards says:

> Most women still dream about beauty, dress, weddings, dashing lovers, domesticity and babies . . . but if feminists seem (as they do) to want to eliminate nearly all of these things—beauty, sex conventions, families and all—for most people that simply means the removal of everything in life which is worth living for (1980, 341–342).

Radical feminism creates a false dichotomy between sexism and assimilation, as if there were nothing in between. This is to ignore completely the middle ground in which it could be recognized that a woman can be free of oppression and nevertheless feminine in the sense abhorred by many feminists. For women are simply not waiting to be freed from the particular chains the radical feminists are trying to sunder. The average woman enjoys her femininity. She wants a man, not a roommate. She wants fair economic opportunities, and she wants children and the time to care for them. These are the goals that women actually have, and they are not easily attainable. But they will never be furthered by an elitist radical movement that views the actual aspirations of women as the product of a false consciousness. There is room for a liberal feminism that would work for reforms that would give women equal opportunity in the workplace and in politics, but would leave untouched and unimpugned the basic institutions that women want and support: marriage and motherhood. Such a feminism is already in operation in some European countries. But it has been obstructed here in the United States by the ideologues who now hold the seat of power in the feminist movement (Hewlett, 1986).

In characterizing and criticizing American feminism, I have not taken into account the latest revisions and qualifications of a lively and variegated movement. There is a kind of feminism-of-the-week that one cannot hope to keep abreast of, short of giving up all other concerns. The best one can do for the present purposes is attend to central theses and arguments that bear on the feminist treatment of the family. Nevertheless, even for this limited purpose, it would be wrong to omit discussion of an important turn taken by feminism in the past few years. I have in mind the recent literature on the idea that there is a specific female ethic that is more concrete, less rule-oriented, more empathetic and caring, and more attentive to the demands of a particular context. The kind of feminism that accepts the idea that women differ from men in approaching ethical dilemmas and social problems from a care perspective is not oriented to androgyny as an ideal. Rather it seeks to develop this special female ethic and to give it greater practical scope.

The stress on context might lead one to think these feminists are more sympathetic to the family as the social arrangement that shapes the moral development of women and is the context for many of the moral dilemmas that women actually face. However, one sees as yet no attention being paid to the fact that feminism itself is a force working against the preservation of the family. Psychologists like Carol Gilligan and philosophers like Lawrence Blum concentrate their attention on the moral quality of the caring relationships, but these relationships are themselves not viewed in their concrete embeddedness in any formal social arrangement.

It should also be said that some feminists are moving away from the earlier hostility to motherhood (Trebilcot, 1984). Here, too, one sees the weakening of the assimilationist ideal in the acknowledgment of a primary gender role. However, childrearing is not primarily seen within the context of the family but as a special relationship between mother and daughter or—more awkwardly—between mother and son, a relationship that effectively excludes the male parent. And the often cultist celebration of motherhood remains largely hostile to traditional familial arrangements.

It is too early to say whether a new style of nonassimilationist feminism will lead to a mitigation of the assault on the family or even

on femininity. In any case, the recognition of a female ethic of care and responsibility is hardly inconsistent with a social ethic that values the family as a vital, perhaps indispensable, institution. And the recognition that women have their own moral style may well be followed by a more accepting attitude to the kind of femininity that the more assimilationist feminists reject.

References

De Beauvoir, Simone. 1952. *The Second Sex*. H. M. Parshley, trans. New York: Random House.

———. 1977. "Talking to De Beauvoir." In *Spare Rib*.

Ferguson, Ann. 1977. "Androgyny as an Ideal for Human Development." In M. Vetterling-Braggin, F. Elliston, and J. English, eds. *Feminism and Philosophy*, pp. 45–69. Totowa, N.J.: Rowman and Littlefield.

Gould, Carol. 1983. "Private Rights and Public Virtues: Woman, the Family and Democracy." In Carol Gould, ed. *Beyond Domination*, pp. 3–18. Totowa, N.J.: Rowman and Allanheld.

Hewlett, Sylvia Ann. 1986. *A Lesser Life: The Myth of Woman's Liberation in America*. New York: Morrow.

Jagger, Allison. 1977. "On Sex Equality." In Jane English, ed. *Sex Equality*, Englewood Cliffs, N.J.: Prentice-Hall.

———. 1983. "Human Biology in Feminist Theory: Sexual Equality Reconsidered." In Gould, ed. *Beyond Domination*.

———. 1986. "Prostitution." In Marilyn Pearsell, ed. *Women and Values: Readings in Recent Feminist Philosophy*, pp. 108–21. Belmont, Calif.: Wadsworth.

Raymond, Janice. 1975. "The Illusion of Androgyny." *Quest: A Feminist Quarterly*, 2.

Richards, Jennifer Radcliffe. 1980. *The Skeptical Feminist*. Harmondsworth: Penguin.

Trebilcot, Joyce, ed. 1984. *Mothering: Essays in Feminist Theory*. Totowa, N.J.: Rowman and Allanheld.

Wasserstrom, Richard. 1980. *Philosophy and Social Issues*. Notre Dame, Ind.: University of Notre Dame Press.

27. They Lived Happily Ever After: Sommers on Women and Marriage

Marilyn Friedman

Marilyn Friedman questions whether what Christina Sommers supports is really what most women want. She quotes a 1983 survey which indicated that 63 percent of women preferred nontraditional family relationships. She points out that in 1977 only 16 percent of American households were traditional families. She argues that femininity as slavishly deferring to men is not good for women, and contends that no woman should "swoon at the sight of Rhett Butler carrying Scarlett O'Hara up the stairs to a fate undreamt of in feminist philosophy."

1. In a series of papers which has recently appeared in several philosophical and general academic publications,[1] Christina Sommers mounts a campaign against feminist philosophers (1989a, 85; 1989b, B2) and "American feminism" in general (1989a, 90–91). Sommers blames feminists for contributing to the current divorce rate and the breakdown of the traditional family, and she repudiates feminist critiques of traditional forms of marriage, family, and femininity. In this paper, I explore Sommers's views in some detail. My aim is not primarily to defend her feminist targets, but to ferret out Sommers's own views of traditional marriage, family, and femininity, and to see whether or not they have any philosophical merit.

2. In her writings, Sommers generally defends what she claims that feminists have challenged. Whether or not she is actually discussing the same things is often open to question since she fails to define the key terms behind which she rallies. Sommers, for example, endorses "the family," the "traditional family," and "the family as we know it" (1989a, 87–88). These are not equivalent expressions. The so-called "traditional family"—a nuclear family consisting of a legally married heterosexual couple and their children, in which the man is the sole breadwinner and "head" of the household, and the woman does the domestic work and childcare—comprised only 16% of all U.S.

From "They Lived Happily Ever After: Sommers on Women and Marriage," *Journal of Social Philosophy* (1990).

households in 1977, according to the U.S. Census Bureau.[2] Hence, the "traditional family" is no longer "*the* family" or "*the* family as we know it" (italics mine) but is only one sort of family that we know.

Sommers also rallies behind "femininity," "feminine culture," "conventional feminine roles," and "a primary gender role" (1989a, 90, 92). These expressions, as well, call for clarification; they do not necessarily refer to the same practices. In recent years, many feminists have defended various aspects of what might also be called "feminine culture." Sommers notes a few of these authors and works (Carol Gilligan, for example), but finds one reason or another for repudiating each one that she cites.[3]

3. To see what Sommers is promoting under the banner of "feminine culture," we should look to Sommers's claims about what women value, want, and enjoy.[4] First, there are wants, values, and enjoyments pertaining to men.[5] Sommers claims that women want "a man," "marriage," and "to marry good providers."[6] She asserts that "most women" enjoy "male gallantry," that the "majority of women" enjoy being "treated by a man to a candlelit dinner," and that "many women . . . swoon at the sight of Rhett Butler carrying Scarlett O'Hara up the stairs to a fate undreamt of in feminist philosophy."[7]

Second, there are wants, values, and enjoyments having to do with children. Women, Sommers tells us, want children, motherhood, "*conventional* motherhood," "family," and "the time to care for children."[8] In a revealing turn of phrase, Sommers also asserts that women are "willing to pay the price" for family and motherhood (1989b, B2). Sommers does not say, however, what she thinks the price is.

Third, there are wants, values, and enjoyments having to do with femininity. Women are said to enjoy their "femininity," makeup, "sexy clothes," and, even more specifically, "clothes that render them 'sex objects.' "[9] On the topic of femininity, Sommers also quotes approvingly (1989a, 90–91) the words of Janet Radcliffe Richards who wrote that, "Most women still dream about beauty, dress, weddings, dashing lovers," and "domesticity," and that, for "most people," "beauty, sex conventions, families and all" comprise "everything in life which is worth living for."[10]

4. A very few of the wants which Sommers attributes to women do not fit into my three-part classification scheme (men, children femininity). Sommers claims that women want "fair economic opportunities" (1989a, 91), and that they are "generally receptive to liberal feminist reforms that enhance their political and economic powers" (1989b, B2). Sommers, ironically, does not recognize that the enhanced economic and political power of women makes them less needful of traditional marriage to a "good provider," and when they are married, makes them less afraid to resort to divorce to solve marital and family problems. The economic concerns of liberal feminism directly threaten one colossal support for the "traditional family," namely, the extreme economic vulnerability of the non-income-earning woman and her concomitant material dependence on a "good provider."

Under traditional arrangements, most women did not merely *want* marriage; they *needed* it. It was by far a woman's most socially legitimated option for economic survival. Take away the need, as liberal feminism seeks to do, and at least some of the want also disappears. One otherwise very traditional aunt of mine became a wealthy widow in her late fifties when my rich uncle died. She never remarried. Now a dynamic woman of 82 who travels widely and lives well, she confesses that no man has interested her enough to make it worthwhile to give up her freedom a second time. "I'm lucky," she confides, "I don't need a meal-ticket." Even a nonfeminist can understand what she is getting at.

5. Before assessing Sommers's overall views, let us rescue Scarlett O'Hara. Sommers's remark that Scarlett O'Hara's rape by Rhett Butler is a fate undreamt of in feminist philosophy is . . . simply stunning. (Note that Sommers does not use the word "rape" here—one of many omissions in her writings.) Even a passing knowledge of feminist philosophy reveals that rape is hardly undreamt of in it.[11] Rape, of course, is not a dream; it is a nightmare. Any form of sexual aggression can involve coercion, intimidation, degradation, physical abuse, battering, and, in extreme cases, death.

The reality of rape is rendered invisible by the many novels and films, such as *Gone with the Wind*, which romanticize and mystify it. They portray the rapist as a handsome man whose domination is pleasurable in bed, and portray women as happy to have their own sexual choices and refusals crushed by such men. In a culture in which these sorts of portrayals are routine, it is no surprise that this scene arouses the sexual desire of some women. However, the name of Richard Speck,[12] to take one example, can remind us that real rape is not the pleasurable fantasy intimated in *Gone with the Wind*. To put the point graphically: would "many women" still swoon over Butler's rape of O'Hara if they knew that he urinated on her? When you're the victim of rape, you don't have much choice over what goes on.

6. Let us move on to femininity. Sommers never spells out exactly what she means by femininity. For guidance on this topic, we could turn to literature in social psychology which identifies the important traits of femininity and which explores the social devaluation of the feminine (Eagly, 1987). However, it might be more revealing to turn to a different sort of "expert." By a lucky coincidence, I recently acquired a gem of a cultural artifact, a 1965 book entitled, *Always Ask a Man: Arlene Dahl's Key to Femininity*, written by a rather well-known actress and model of the 1960s, Arlene Dahl. I have learned a great deal from this femininity manifesto.

As you might guess from the title, one guiding theme of the book, and of the femininity it aims to promote, is utter deference to the opinions of men. Dahl instructs the female reader: "Look at Yourself Objectively (try to see yourself through a man's eyes)" (p. 2). In Dahl's view, the "truly feminine" woman works "instinctively" at pleasing men and making men feel important. "When [a man] speaks to her, she listens with rapt attention to every word" (p. 5). Dahl believes that every woman has the capacity to measure up to men's ideals of femininity. This is because "Every woman is an actress. (Admit it!) Her first role is that of a coquette. (If you have any doubts just watch a baby girl with her father)" (p. 6).

Dahl's book is laced with quotations from male celebrities who are treated as incontrovertible authorities on what women should be like. Yul Brynner, for example, wants women to be good listeners who are not particularly logical (p. 3). Richard Burton likes women who are "faintly giggly" (p. 3). Tony Perkins thinks that a "girl should act like a girl and not like the head of a corporation—even if she is" (p. 8). The most revealing observation comes from George Hamilton: "A woman is often like a strip of film—obliterated, insignificant— until a man puts a light behind her" (pp. 5–6).

Surprisingly, some of the traits advocated for women by these male celebrities are actually valuable traits: honesty, straightforwardness, maturity, ingenuity, understanding, dignity, generosity, and humor. These traits are not distinctively feminine, however, and that may be the reason why they quickly disappear from Dahl's discussion. The twin themes that resound throughout this femininity manual are that of cultivating one's physical attractiveness and slavishly deferring to men. Instead of a chapter on honesty, a chapter on dignity, and so on, the book features chapters on every aspect of bodily grooming and adornment, including a separate chapter on each of the four basic categories of Caucasian hair color: blonde, redhead, "brownette," and brunette.

The slavish deference to men is crucial, since the whole point of the enterprise is to get a man. Thus, Dahl explains in the introduction that this book is written to counteract a tendency for women to dress to please other women, and it is also not for "women who want to be beautiful for beauty's sake. Such

beauty serves no purpose, other than self-satisfaction, if that can be considered a purpose" (pp. x–xi).

The quintessential prohibition involved in femininity seems to be this: "NEVER upstage a man. Don't try to top his joke, even if you have to bite your tongue to keep from doing it. Never launch loudly into your own opinion on a subject—whether it's petunias or politics. Instead, draw out his ideas to which you can gracefully add your footnotes from time to time" (p. 12). Dahl is less sanguine than Sommers that the role of motherhood fits comfortably into a feminine life; she advises, ". . . don't get so involved with your role of MOTHER that you forget to play WIFE" (p. 9). Once married, your own interests should never override your husband's interests, job, and even hobbies, and, "There should be nothing that takes precedence in your day's schedule over making yourself attractive and appealing for the man in your life," not even your "children's activities" (p. 175)!

Voila, femininity. Such servility shows the dubiousness of Sommers's claim that "a woman can be free of oppression and nevertheless feminine in the sense abhorred by many feminists" (1989a, 91).

7. Let us turn now to Sommers's overall philosophical defense of traditional marriage, family, and femininity. Having asserted that most women value or want all of these traditions, Sommers charges feminist views with a serious defect: they either dismiss or disparage these popular feminine wants and values.[13] Sommers herself defers to these alleged views of most women as if they were as such authoritative: because "most women" (as she alleges) want traditional marriage and family, therefore these practices must be better than any alternatives. It is important to note that Sommers does not argue that traditional marriage and so on, on balance, promote important moral values better than any feminist alternatives.[14] No comprehensive moral comparisons appear in her writings. Her argument begins (and ends, as I will argue) with an appeal to popular opinion.

8. Is Sommers right about what "most women" think? She refers to no studies, no representative samples whatsoever to support her generalizations. Whole categories of

women are patently excluded from her reference group and are invisible in her writings. This is a fitting moment to mention the "L" word—and I don't mean "liberal." Obviously, no lesbians, unless seriously closeted, are among Sommers's alleged majority of women who want "a man," conventional marriage, or a traditional family.

Even among nonlesbians, a goodly number of women these days do not want a *traditional* marriage or a *traditional* family. Some heterosexual women simply do not want to marry or to have children at all, and many others want *non*-traditional marriages and *non*-traditional families. Surveys show that *this* attitude, and not the preference for tradition alleged by Sommers, is actually in the majority. In one 1983 study, 63% of women surveyed expressed preferences for non-traditional family arrangements (Sapiro, 1990, 355). Sommers's factual claims are, thus, debatable.

Even apart from questions of popularity, the wants, values, and enjoyments which Sommers attributes to "most women" are frankly suspicious as an ensemble. Candlelit dinners do not combine easily with babies. Dashing lovers (extra-marital!) can be disastrous for a marriage. This list of wants and values seems to show a failure to separate what is idealized and mythic from what is (to put it very advisedly) authentic and genuinely possible in the daily reality of marital and family relationships over the long haul. To hear Sommers tell it, women are blandly unconcerned about wife-battering, incest, marital rape, or the profound economic vulnerability of the traditional non-income-earning wife. This is hard to believe. What is more likely is that, for many women, ". . . they got married and lived happily ever after," is only a fairy tale—especially for those who have been married for awhile. Even the most traditional of women, I am convinced, has some sense of the risks involved in traditional heterosexual relationships. As an old saying goes, "When two hearts beat as one, someone is dead."[15]

Sommers's list of women's wants and values is also woefully short. It suggests that this is *all* that "most women" want, that women's aspirations extend no farther than to being "feminine," getting a man—any man—and having babies. On the contrary, many women want meaningful and fulfilling work apart from childcare and domestic labor. Many women aspire to making a social contribution, or they have artistic impulses seeking expresson, spiritual callings, deep friendships with other women, and abiding concerns for moral value and their own integrity.[16] One foundational motivation for feminism has always been the aim to overcome the *constraints* on women's genuinely wide-ranging aspirations posed by traditional marital and family arrangements.

9. What philosophical difference would it make if Sommers were right about women's wants and values in general? The popularity of an opinion is hardly an infallible measure of its empirical or moral credibility. Even popular opinions may be based on misinformation, unfounded rumor, and so on. Sommers ignores these possibilities and recommends that we defer to popular opinion on the basis of ". . . Mill's principle that there can be no appeal from a majority verdict of those who have experienced two alternatives" (1989a, 89–90). Sommers is evidently suggesting that feminist critiques of traditional family, marriage, and femininity should be judged by whether or not they conform to the "majority verdict of those who have experienced" the relevant alternatives. Now, carefully understood, this is actually not such a bad idea. However, rather than supporting Sommers's deference to popular opinion, this principle repudiates it.

First, there are more than just "two" feminist alternatives to any of the traditions in question. Consider, for example, the traditionally married, heterosexual couple comprised of dominant, breadwinning male and domestic, childrearing female. Feminists have recommended various alternative family arrangements, including egalitarian heterosexual marriage, communal living, lesbian relationships, and single parenting when economic circumstances are favorable.[17] To decide the value of traditional marriage and family, one would have to try all the relevant alternatives—or at least *some* of them. And on Mill's view, merely experiencing alternatives is not enough; one must also be capable of "appreciating and enjoying" them (Mill, 1979, 9). If Sommers is right, however, most women want and choose traditional family, traditional marriage, and traditional femininity, and, thus, do not either experience or enjoy living according to any feminist alternatives. Women such as these are not what Mill calls "competent judges" of the value of those traditions since "they know only their own side of the question" (p. 10). And it is only from the verdict of *competent judges* that Mill believes that "there can be no appeal" (p. 11).

Second, of the "competent judges," in Mill's sense, that is, of the women who *have* experienced and enjoyed feminist alternatives to traditional marriage and family, most (I would wager) *prefer the feminist alternatives*. I am referring, among others, to women in lesbian relationships, and women in genuinely egalitarian heterosexual relationships. If I am right about this, then by Mill's principle, we must reject "popular opinion" along with traditional marriage and the rest.

10. The truth of the matter is that, in the end, Sommers does not rest her case on Mill's principle. Apparently without realizing that she changes her argument, she ends by appealing to something less vaunted than the majority verdict of those who have experienced and enjoyed *both* traditional family, etc., and various feminist alternatives. Her final court of appeal is simply to "what most people think," to so-called "commonsense," and to "tradition" itself (1989a, 95, 97). Sommers urges that "A moral philosophy that does not give proper weight to the customs and opinions of the community is presumptuous in its attitude and pernicious in its consequences" (1989a, 103). She speaks warmly of the Aristotelian conviction that "traditional arrangements have great moral weight and that common opinion is a primary source of moral truth" (1989a, 83). When it comes to tradition, Sommers would do well to consider Mill again. Mill often deferred to tradition, but it was not a deference from which he thought there was "no appeal," as he amply demonstrated in the important *indictment* of nineteenth century marital traditions on which he collaborated with Harriet Taylor (Mill & Taylor, 1970). (It would be interesting to know what "pernicious . . . consequences," to use Sommers's phrase, flowed from Mill's and Taylor's critique.)

Tradition is a fickle husband. He is constantly changing his mind. On the grounds of tradition, eighty years ago, Sommers would have opposed women's suffrage. One hundred and fifty years ago, she would have opposed women speaking in public (She would have had to do so in private!), opposed the rights of married women to property in their own names, opposed the abolition of slavery, and so on. She would have supported wife-battering since it was permitted by legal tradition—so long as the rod was no bigger around than the size of the husband's thumb.

Not only is tradition ever-changing, it is also plural, both within our own society and globally. Which tradition shall we follow when there is more than one from which to choose? Islam is the world's most widely practiced religion. Shall we non-Islamic women heed the most globally numerous of our sisters' voices and don the veil, retire from public life, and allow husbands to marry up to four wives? Within our own society, marital traditions also vary. Shall we follow the traditions of orthodox Jewish and orthodox Catholic women and avoid all contraceptives? My maternal grandmother did so; she had fourteen births. At nine months per gestation, she spent ten and a half years of her life being pregnant. Although she lingered on to the age of eighty-seven, she seemed even older than her age for the final sixteen, worn-out years of her life in which I knew her. Doubtless, that, too, was part of her tradition.

Why suppose that there is special merit to any of the alternative traditions that we happen to have at this historical moment in this particular geopolitical location? Why suppose that any of our current traditions are better or more deserving of loyalty and support than the traditions toward which we are evolving? And how will we ever evolve if we remain deadlocked in loyalty to all of the traditions we happen to have today?

11. Sommers allows that our traditions may need reform and even recommends "piecemeal social engineering" to deal with "imperfections" in the family (1989a, 97)—although it is noteworthy that she never specifies what these imperfections are, and, in a different passage, she inconsistently calls upon American feminism to leave marriage and motherhood simply "untouched and unimpugned" (1989a, 91).[18] Nevertheless, she insists that her arguments are directed only against those radical feminists who seek the

abolition of the family and the "radical reform of preferences, values, aspirations, and prejudices" (1990, 151, 148).

A serious concern to reform imperfections in the family should lead someone to consider the views of non-radical feminist reformers who also criticize marital and family traditions. Many feminists would be content with piecemeal family reform—so long as it was genuine reform (Thorne & Yalom, 1982; Okin, 1987; 1989). At any rate, this issue is a red herring. A dispute over the pace of reform does not show that radical feminist critiques of family traditions are wrong in substance. Most important, by allowing that change is *needed* in family traditions, Sommers effectively concedes that we should not automatically defer to tradition. To admit that reform of tradition is morally permissible is to reject tradition *per se* as an incontestable moral authority. The controversy can only be decided by directly evaluating the conditions of life established by marital and family traditions—and their alternatives.

12. Sommers has one final twist to her argument which we should consider. She notes briefly—all too briefly—that traditions "have prima facie moral force" so long as they are not "essentially unjust" (1989a, 97). Sommers does not explain what she means by "essential injustice." Just how much injustice makes a traditional practice "essentially unjust?"

Despite its vagueness, this concession to injustice is critically important. It makes the merit of Sommers's own appeal to tradition contingent on the essential non-injustice of the particular traditions in question. Sommers, however, provides no argument to establish that traditional marriage practices and so forth are not essentially unjust. Nor does she respond substantively to those feminist arguments which claim to locate important injustices in these traditional practices. She rejects all feminist criticisms of the traditional family because they do not coincide with "popular opinion," "commonsense," or tradition. Traditional marriage and family are not essentially unjust, in Sommers's view, simply because most people allegedly do not *think* they are.

We seem to have come full circle. Sommers rejects feminist critiques of traditional marriage and so on because they are inconsistent with popular opinion, commonsense, and tradition. Tradition is to be relied on, in turn, so long as it is not essentially unjust. But Sommers rejects feminist arguments to show injustices in marital and family traditions simply on the grounds that those arguments are inconsistent with popular opinion, commonsense, and tradition itself. Sommers's defense of traditional marriage and family is, in the final analysis, circular and amounts to nothing more than simple *deference to tradition*—indeed, to particular traditions which are no longer so pervasive or popular as Sommers thinks.

13. One final concern: Sommers blames feminists for contributing to the growing divorce rate and the "disintegration of the traditional family."[19] However, feminism could only contribute to the divorce rate if married women ended their marriages as a result of adopting feminist ideas. If Sommers is right, however, in thinking that "most women" reject non-liberal feminist values, then non-liberal feminists could not be having a significant impact on the divorce rate. Sommers cannot have it both ways. Either feminism *is* significantly contributing to the growing divorce rate, in which case it must be in virtue of the wide appeal of feminist ideas about marriage and family, or feminist ideas do *not* have wide appeal, in which case they cannot be significantly contributing to the growing divorce rate.

14. To conclude: My overall assessment of Sommers's views on marriage, family, and femininity is grim.[20] Most important, Sommers rejects feminist views of marriage, family, and femininity ultimately on the basis of her own simple deference to (allegedly) popular opinion, commonsense, and tradition. This deference is defensible only if feminist views about injustices in those traditions can be shown, on *independent* grounds, to be misguided—and Sommers never provides this independent argument.

Notes

1. Sommers: 1988, 1989a, 1989b, and 1990.
2. Cited in Thorne & Yalom, 1982, 5.
3. Sommers repudiates the feminist literature

which explores the value of mothering (e.g., Trebilcot, 1984) on the grounds that it "remains largely hostile to traditional familial arrangements." She also claims that this literature focuses only on an abstracted mother-child relationship, especially the mother-daughter relationship—a focus that "effectively excludes the male parent." (1989a, 92) Aside from inaccurately summarizing a body of literature, this latter comment, ironically, ignores the fact that under "traditional familial arrangements," the male parent plays a *negligible role* in day-to-day, primary childcare, especially in a child's early years.

The comment also ignores the work of Dorothy Dinnerstein (1977) and, especially, of Nancy Chodorow (1978), which precisely urges *shared parenting* and a prominent role for the male parent. This work has been extremely influential and widely cited among feminists. I suspect, however, that shared parenting is not the way in which Sommers wants to include the male parent, since this arrangement is not "traditional" and it challenges the idea of a "primary gender role" that Sommers appears to support (1989a, 92). Sommers, herself, thus fails to clarify the role of the male parent in her account.

4. Sommers complains that feminist philosophers have not been entrusted by ordinary women with a mission of speaking on behalf of those ordinary women (1989b, B3). Sommers, however, appears to think that she *is* thus entrusted, since she does not hesitate to make claims about what "most women . . . prefer," what "women actually want," and what "most women *enjoy*" (1989a, 90).

5. The following classification scheme is my own. The categories are not meant to be mutually exclusive.

6. Quotations are, respectively, from: 1989a, 90; 1989a, 91; and 1990, 150.

7. Quotations are, respectively, from: 1989a, 90; 1989a, 89; and 1989b, B3.

8. Quotations are, respectively, from: 1989a, 90; 1989a, 91; 1990, 150, italics mine; 1989b, B2; and 1989a, 91.

9. Quotations are, respectively, from: 1989a, 90; 1989a, 90; 1989a, 90; and 1990, 150.

10. Richards, 1980, 341–42. Quoted in Sommers, 1989a, 90–91.

11. Some important early papers are anthologized in: Vetterling-Braggin et al., 1977, Part VI. Another important, relatively early study is Brownmiller, 1976.

12. In 1966, Richard Speck stunned the city of Chicago and the nation by raping, killing, and, in some cases, mutilating the bodies of eight out of nine nursing students who shared a house together on Chicago's South Side. The nurse who survived did so by hiding under a bed until Speck left the house after having apparently lost count. That woman might well swoon over Scarlett O'Hara's rape, but it would not be a swoon of ecstasy.

13. 1989a, 88–91. Sommers writes: "It is a serious defect of American feminism that it concentrates its zeal on impugning femininity and feminine culture at the expense of the grass root fight against economic and social injustices to which women are subjected" (p. 90). American feminism has hardly neglected the fight against economic or social injustice against women. Apart from that, the *Philosopher's Index* back to 1970 contains no citations of writings by Sommers herself on "the economic and social injustices to which women are subjected." In the essays reviewed here, she does not even identify the injustices she has in mind.

14. Sommers does warn that "many women" who avoid motherhood find themselves lonely (1989a, 90), and she suggests that those who avoid or divorce themselves from the patriarchal family "often" suffer harm and "might" feel "betrayed by the ideology" which led them to this state (1989b, B3). These faintly threatening suggestions are left unexplained and unsupported.

15. I was reminded of this old saying by an article by Janyce Katz (1990, 88) in which Dagmar Celeste, then the "First Lady of Ohio," is quoted as mentioning it.

16. Raising children involves awesome moral responsibilities, as Sommers herself emphasizes when lamenting the increasing divorce rate. These profound moral responsibilities entail that we should not casually reinforce the cultural ideology which declares that the only hope of women's fulfillment in life depends on their *having* children. Sommers complains about divorce because of the harm it inflicts on children (1989a, 98–102), but she never cautions women to consider these moral obligations before marrying or having children in the first place.

17. Cf. Hunter College Women's Studies Collective, 1983, Ch. 9.

18. My worry is that Sommers's occasional, reasonable call for piecemeal family reform disguises a hidden agenda which aims to deadlock us in certain family traditions as we know them now (or knew them three decades ago). This appearance might be dispelled if she were to identify the imperfections that she recognizes in the family.

19. 1989a, 82–83, 99–102. Sommers admits that "no reliable study has yet been made comparing children of divorced parents to children from intact families who [sic] parents do not get on well together." She claims cavalierly that "any such study would be compromised by some arbitrary measures of parental incompatibility and one could probably place little reliance on them" (1989a, 101). However, she ignores her own claims of limited evidence on this issue and argues as if it were simply established that children of divorced parents are invariably worse off than if their parents had remained married.

When Sommers discusses the problem of divorce, she tends to assimilate the philosophical culprits onto one model: They are all wrong for disregarding "special duties" to family members, especially to children. This latter accusation is simply irrelevant in regard to feminists; no serious feminist literature suggests that responsibilities toward children should be disregarded.

20. Overall, her presentations are marred by ambiguities, inconsistencies, dubious factual claims, misrepresentations of feminist literature, and faulty arguments.

References

Brownmiller, Susan. 1976. *Against Our Will: Men, Women and Rape.* New York: Bantam.

Chodorow, Nancy. 1978. *The Reproduction of Mothering.* Berkeley: University of California Press.

Dahl, Arlene. 1965. *Always Ask a Man: Arlene Dahl's Key to Femininity.* Englewood Cliffs, N.J.: Prentice-Hall.

Dinnerstein, Dorothy. 1977. *The Mermaid and the Minotaur: Sexual Arrangements and Human Malaise.* New York: Harper & Row.

Eagly, Alice. 1987. *Sex Differences in Social Behavior.* Hillsdale, N.J.: Erlbaum.

Hunter College Women's Studies Collective. 1983. *Women's Realities, Women's Choices.* New York: Oxford University Press.

Katz, Janyce. 1990. "Celestial Reasoning: Ohio's First Lady Talks About Love and Feminism." *Ms: The World of Women,* 1, 2 (September/October), p. 88.

Mill, John Stuart. 1979. *Utilitarianism.* George Sher, ed. Indianapolis: Hackett.

Mill, John Stuart and Harriet Taylor. 1970. *Essays on Sex Equality.* Alice S. Rossi, ed. Chicago: University of Chicago Press.

Okin, Susan Moller. 1987. "Justice and Gender." *Philosophy & Public Affairs,* 16 (Winter), pp. 42–72.

———. 1989. *Justice, Gender, and the Family.* New York: Basic Books.

Richards, Janet Radcliffe. 1980. *The Sceptical Feminist.* Harmondsworth: Penguin.

Sapiro, Virginia. 1990. *Women in American Society.* Mountain View, Calif.: Mayfield Publishing Co.

Sommers, Christina. 1988. "Should the Academy Support Academic Feminism?" *Public Affairs Quarterly,* 2, 3 (July), 97–120.

———. 1989a. "Philosophers Against the Family." In: George Graham and Hugh LaFollette, eds. *Person to Person.* Philadelphia: Temple University Press, 82–105.

———. 1989b. "Feminist Philosophers Are Oddly Unsympathetic to the Women They Claim to Represent." *Chronicle of Higher Education,* October 11, pp. B2–B3.

———. 1990. "The Feminist Revelation," *Social Philosophy and Policy Center,* 8, 1 (Autumn), 141–158.

Thorne, Barrie with Marilyn Yalom, eds. 1982. *Rethinking the Family.* New York: Longman.

Trebilcot, Joyce, ed. 1984. *Mothering: Essays in Feminist Theory.* Totowa, N.J.: Rowman and Allanheld.

Vetterling-Braggin, Mary, Frederick A. Elliston, and Jane English, eds. 1977. *Feminism and Philosophy.* Totowa, N.J.: Littlefield, Adams & Co.

28. National Organization for Women (NOW) Bill of Rights

  I Equal Rights Constitutional Amendment
 II Enforce Law Banning Sex Discrimination in Employment
III Maternity Leave Rights in Employment and in Social Security Benefits
 IV Tax Deduction for Home and Child Care Expenses for Working Parents
  V Child Care Centers
 VI Equal and Unsegregated Education
VII Equal Job Training Opportunities and Allowances for Women in Poverty
VIII The Right of Women to Control Their Reproductive Lives

We Demand:

I That the United States Congress immediately pass the Equal Rights Amendment to the Constitution to provide that "Equality of rights under the law shall not be denied or abridged by the United States or by any State on account of sex," and that such then be immediately ratified by the several States.

II That equal employment opportunity be guaranteed to all women, as well as men, by insisting that the Equal Employment Opportunity Commission enforce the prohibitions against sex discrimination in employment under Title VII of the Civil Rights Act of 1964 with the same vigor as it enforces the prohibitions against racial discrimination.

III That women be protected by law to ensure their rights to return to their jobs within a reasonable time after childbirth without loss of seniority or other accrued benefits, and be paid maternity leave as a form of social security and/or employee benefit.

IV Immediate revision of tax laws to permit the deduction of home and child care expenses for working parents.

V That child care facilities be established by law on the same basis as parks, libraries, and public schools, adequate to the needs of children from the preschool years through adolescence, as a community resource to be used by all citizens from all income levels.

VI That the right of women to be educated to their full potential equally with men be secured by Federal and State Legislation, eliminating all discrimination and segregation by sex, written and unwritten, at all levels of education, including colleges, graduate and professional schools, loans and fellowships, and Federal and State training programs such as the Job Corps.

VII The right of women in poverty to secure job training, housing, and family allowances on equal terms with men, but without prejudice to a parent's right to remain at home to care for his or her children; revision of welfare legislation and poverty programs which deny women dignity, privacy and self-respect.

VIII The right of women to control their own reproductive lives by removing from penal codes laws limiting access to contraceptive information and devices and laws governing abortion.

29. *California Federal Savings and Loan v. Department of Fair Employment and Housing*

Supreme Court of the United States

The issue before the Supreme Court was whether Title VII of the Civil Rights Act of 1964 as amended by the Pregnancy Discrimination Act of 1978 (PDA) nullified a California law requiring employers to provide leave and reinstatement to employees disabled by pregnancy. The majority of the Court ruled that it did not for two reasons. First, in passing PDA, Congress was concerned with prohibiting discrimination against pregnancy; preferential treatment, as found in the California law, was not discussed. Second, even if PDA did prohibit preferential treatment of pregnancy, an employer could avoid violating PDA and the California law by giving comparable benefits to all similarly disabled employees. In dissent, Justices White, Burger, and Powell argued that even though Congress did not explicitly consider the possibility of preferential treatment of pregnancy, the language of PDA ruled it out. In addition, they argued that if such preferential treatment were ruled out, those who wrote the California law could not have intended requiring comparable benefits for all similarly disabled employees.

Justice *Marshall* delivered the opinion of the Court.

The question presented is whether Title VII of the Civil Rights Act of 1964, as amended by the Pregnancy Discrimination Act of 1978, pre-empts a state statute that requires employers to provide leave and reinstatement to employees disabled by pregnancy.

California's Fair Employment and Housing Act (FEHA), Cal. Gov't Code Ann. § 12900 *et seq.* . . . is a comprehensive statute that prohibits discrimination in employment and housing. In September 1978, California amended the FEHA to proscribe certain forms of employment discrimination on the basis of pregnancy. . . . Subdivision (b)(2)—the provision at issue here—is the only portion of the statute that applies to employers subject to Title VII. . . . It requires these employers to provide female employees an unpaid pregnancy disability leave of up to four months. Respondent Fair Employment and Housing Commission, the state agency authorized to interpret the FEHA, has construed § 12945(b)(2) to require California employers to reinstate an employee returning from such pregnancy leave to the job she previously held, unless it is no longer

available due to business necessity. In the latter case, the employer must make a reasonable, good faith effort to place the employee in a substantially similar job. The statute does not compel employers to provide *paid* leave to pregnant employees. Accordingly, the only benefit pregnant workers actually derive from § 12945(b)(2) is a qualified right to reinstatement.

Title VII of the Civil Rights Act of 1964 . . . also prohibits various forms of employment discrimination, including discrimination on the basis of sex. However, in *General Electric Co. v. Gilbert,* . . . this Court ruled that discrimination on the basis of pregnancy was not sex discrimination under Title VII. In response to the *Gilbert* decision, Congress passed the Pregnancy Discrimination Act of 1978 (PDA). . . . The PDA specifies that sex discrimination includes discrimination on the basis of pregnancy.

Petitioner California Federal Savings and Loan Association (Cal Fed) is a federally chartered savings and loan association based in Los Angeles; it is an employer covered by both Title VII and § 12945(b)(2). Cal Fed has a facially neutral leave policy that permits employees who have completed three months of service to take unpaid leaves of absence for a variety of reasons, including disability and pregnancy. Although it is Cal Fed's policy to try to provide an employee taking unpaid leave with a similar position upon returning, Cal Fed expressly reserves the right to terminate an employee who has taken a leave of absence if a similar position is not available.

Lillian Garland was employed by Cal Fed as a receptionist for several years. In January 1982, she took a pregnancy disability leave. When she was able to return to work in April of that year, Garland notified Cal Fed, but was informed that her job had been filled and that there were no receptionist or similar positions available. Garland filed a complaint with respondent Department of Fair Employment and Housing, which issued an administrative accusation against Cal Fed on her behalf. Respondent charged Cal Fed with violating § 12945(b)(2) of the FEHA. Prior to the scheduled hearing before respondent Fair Housing and Employment Commission, Cal Fed, joined by petitioners . . . , brought this action in the United States District Court for the Central District of California. They sought a declaration that § 12945(b)(2) is inconsistent with and pre-empted by Title VII and an injunction against enforcement of the section. . . .

. . . In order to decide whether the California statute requires or permits employers to violate Title VII, as amended by the PDA, or is inconsistent with the purposes of the statute, we must determine whether the PDA prohibits the States from requiring employers to provide reinstatement to pregnant workers, regardless of their policy for disabled workers generally. . . .

Petitioners argue that the language of the federal statute itself unambiguously rejects California's "special treatment" approach to pregnancy discrimination, thus rendering any resort to the legislative history unnecessary. They contend that the second clause of the PDA forbids an employer to treat pregnant employees any differently than other disabled employees. . . .

The context in which Congress considered the issue of pregnancy discrimination sup-

ports this view of the PDA. Congress had before it extensive evidence of discrimination *against* pregnancy, particularly in disability and health insurance programs like those challenged in *Gilbert* and *Nashville Gas Co. v. Satty.* . . . The reports, debates, and hearings make abundantly clear that Congress intended the PDA to provide relief for working women and to end discrimination against pregnant workers. In contrast to the thorough account of discrimination against pregnant workers, the legislative history is devoid of any discussion of preferential treatment of pregnancy, beyond acknowledgments of the existence of state statutes providing for such preferential treatment. . . .

In support of their argument that the PDA prohibits employment practices that favor pregnant women, petitioners and several *amici* cite statements in the legislative history to the effect that the PDA does not *require* employers to extend any benefits to pregnant women that they do not already provide to other disabled employees. For example, the House Report explained that the proposed legislation "does not require employers to treat pregnant employees in any particular manner. . . ." We do not interpret these references to support petitioners' construction of the statute. On the contrary, if Congress had intended to *prohibit* preferential treatment, it would have been the height of understatement to say only that the legislation would not *require* such conduct. It is hardly conceivable that Congress would have extensively discussed only its intent not to require preferential treatment if in fact it had intended to prohibit such treatment.

We also find it significant that Congress was aware of state laws similar to California's but apparently did not consider them inconsistent with the PDA. In the debates and reports on the bill, Congress repeatedly acknowledged the existence of state antidiscrimination laws that prohibit sex discrimination on the basis of pregnancy. Two of the States mentioned then required employers to provide reasonable leave to pregnant workers. After citing these state laws, Congress failed to evince the requisite "clear and manifest purpose" to supersede them. . . . To the contrary, both the House and Senate Reports suggest that these laws would continue to have effect under the PDA.

Title VII, as amended by the PDA, and California's pregnancy disability leave statute share a common goal. The purpose of Title VII is "to achieve equality of employment opportunities and remove barriers that have operated in the past to favor an identifiable group of . . . employees over other employees." . . . Rather than limiting existing Title VII principles and objectives, the PDA extends them to cover pregnancy. As Senator Williams, a sponsor of the Act, stated: "The entire thrust . . . behind this legislation is to guarantee women the basic right to participate fully and equally in the workforce, without denying them the fundamental right to full participation in family life." . . .

Section 12945(b)(2) also promotes equal employment opportunity. By requiring employers to reinstate women after a reasonable pregnancy disability leave, § 12945(b)(2) ensures that they will not lose their jobs on account of pregnancy disability. . . . By "taking pregnancy into account," California's pregnancy disability leave statute allows women, as well as men, to have families without losing their jobs.

We emphasize the limited nature of the benefits § 12945(b)(2) provides. The statute is narrowly drawn to cover only the period of *actual physical disability* on account of pregnancy, childbirth, or related medical conditions. Accordingly, unlike the protective labor legislation prevalent earlier in this century, § 12945(b)(2) does not reflect archaic or stereotypical notions about pregnancy and the abilities of pregnant workers. A statute based on such stereotypical assumptions would, of course, be inconsistent with Title VII's goal of equal employment opportunity. . . .

Moreover, even if we agreed with petitioners' construction of the PDA, we would nonetheless reject their argument that the California statute requires employers to violate Title VII. . . . Section 12945(b)(2) does not compel California employers to treat pregnant workers *better* than other disabled employees; it merely establishes benefits that employers must, at a minimum, provide to pregnant workers. Employers are free to give comparable benefits to other disabled employees, thereby treating "women affected by pregnancy" no better

than "other persons not so affected but similar in their ability or inability to work." Indeed, at oral argument, petitioners conceded that compliance with both statutes "is theoretically possible." . . .

Thus, petitioners' facial challenge to § 12945(b)(2) fails. The statute is not preempted by Title VII, as amended by the PDA, because it is not inconsistent with the purposes of the federal statute, nor does it require the doing of an act which is unlawful under Title VII.

The judgment of the Court of Appeals is *Affirmed*

. . . Justice *White*, with whom The *Chief Justice* and Justice *Powell* join, dissenting.

I disagree with the Court that Cal. Gov't Code Ann. § 12945(b)(2) . . . is not pre-empted by the Pregnancy Discrimination Act of 1978 (PDA). . . . Section 703(a) of Title VII . . . forbids discrimination in the terms of employment on the basis of race, color, religion, sex, or national origin. The PDA gave added meaning to discrimination on the basis of sex:

> The terms "because of sex" or "on the basis of sex" [in section 703(a) of this title] include, but are not limited to, because of or on the basis of pregnancy, childbirth or related medical conditions; and women affected by pregnancy, childbirth, or related medical conditions shall be treated the same for all employment-related purposes, including receipt of benefits under fringe benefit programs, as other persons not so affected but similar in their ability or inability to work. . . .

The second clause quoted above could not be clearer: it mandates that pregnant employees "Shall be treated the same for all employment-related purposes" as nonpregnant employees similarly situated with respect to their ability or inability to work. . . .

Contrary to the mandate of the PDA, California law requires every employer to have a disability leave policy for pregnancy even if it has none for any other disability. An employer complies with California law if it has a leave policy for pregnancy but denies it for every other disability. On its face, § 12945(b)(2) is in square conflict with the PDA and is therefore pre-empted. . . .

The majority nevertheless would save the California law on two grounds. First, it holds that the PDA does not require disability from pregnancy to be treated the same as other disabilities; instead, it forbids less favorable, but permits more favorable, benefits for pregnancy disability. . . .

. . . Given the evidence before Congress of the widespread discrimination against pregnant workers, it is probable that most Congresspersons did not seriously consider the possibility that someone would want to afford preferential treatment to pregnant workers. The parties and their *amici* argued vigorously to this Court the policy implications of preferential treatment of pregnant workers. In favor of preferential treatment it was urged with conviction that preferential treatment merely enables women, like men, to have children without losing their jobs. In opposition to preferential treatment it was urged with equal conviction that preferential treatment represents a resurgence of the 19th century protective legislation which perpetuated sex-role stereotypes and which impeded women in their efforts to take their rightful place in the workplace. . . . It is not the place of this Court, however, to resolve this policy dispute. . . .

Congress's acknowledgment of state antidiscrimination laws does not support a contrary inference. The most extensive discussion of state laws governing pregnancy discrimination is found in the House Report. . . . The Report did not in any way set apart the Connecticut and Montana statutes, on which the majority relies, from the other state statutes. The House Report gave no indication that these statutes required anything more than equal treatment. . . .

The Court's second, and equally strange, ground is that even if the PDA does prohibit special benefits for pregnant women, an employer may still comply with both the California law and the PDA: it can adopt the specified leave policies for pregnancy and at the same time afford similar benefits for all other disabilities. This is untenable. California surely had no intent to require employers to provide general disability leave benefits. It intended to prefer pregnancy and went no farther. . . .

In sum, preferential treatment of pregnant workers is prohibited by Title VII, as amended by the PDA. Section 12945(b)(2) of the California Gov't Code, which extends preferential benefits for pregnancy, is therefore pre-empted. . . .

Suggestions for Further Reading

Anthologies

Bishop, Sharon, and Weinzweig, Marjorie. *Philosophy and Women*. Belmont, Calif.: Wadsworth Publishing Co., 1979.

Freeman, Jo. *Women: A Feminist Perspective*. 4th ed. Palo Alto: Mayfield Publishing Co., 1989.

Gould, Carol C., and Wartofsky, Marx W. *Women and Philosophy*. New York: G. P. Putnam & Sons, 1976.

Jaggar, Alison, and Struhl, Paula Rothenberg. *Feminist Frameworks*. New York: McGraw-Hill Co., 1981.

Kourany, Janet, Sterba, James, and Tong, Rosemarie. *Feminist Frameworks*. Englewood Cliffs N.J.: Prentice-Hall, 1992.

Basic Concepts

Jaggar, Alison M. *Feminist Politics and Human Nature*. Totowa, N.J.: Rowman & Allanheld, 1983.

Tong, Rosemarie. *Feminist Thought*. Boulder: Westview Press, 1989.

Alternative Views

DeCrow, Karen. *Sexist Justice*. New York: Vintage, 1975.

Eisenstein, Zellah. *Feminism and Sexual Equality.* New York: Monthly Review, 1984.

Friedan, Betty. *The Feminine Mystique.* New York: W. W. Norton & Co., 1963.

Frye, Marilyn. *The Politics of Reality.* New York: The Crossing Press, 1983.

Okin, Susan. *Justice, Gender and the Family.* New York: Basic Books, 1989.

Pateman, Carole. *The Sexual Contract.* Stanford: Stanford University Press, 1988.

Young, Iris. *Justice and the Politics of Difference.* Princeton: Princeton University Press, 1990.

Practical Applications

Irving, John. *The World According to Garp.* New York: Dutton, 1978.

United States Commission on Civil Rights. *Statement on the Equal Rights Amendment.* Washington, D.C.: U.S. Government Printing Office, 1978.

Affirmative Action and Comparable Worth

Introduction

Basic Concepts

Solutions to the problem of discrimination and prejudice tend to be either backward-looking or forward-looking. Backward-looking solutions seek to rectify and compensate for past injustices caused by discrimination or prejudice. Forward-looking solutions seek to realize an ideal of a society free from discrimination and prejudice. To justify a backward-looking solution to the problem of discrimination and prejudice, it is necessary to determine (1) who has committed or benefited from a wrongful act of discrimination or prejudice and (2) who deserves compensation for that act. To justify a forward-looking solution to the problem, it is necessary to determine (1) what a society free from discrimination and prejudice would be like and (2) how such a society might be realized. Solutions of both types have been proposed to deal with racism and sexism, the dominant forms of discrimination and prejudice in our times.

One useful way of approaching the topic of discrimination and prejudice is to note what particular solutions to the problem are favored by the political ideals of libertarianism, welfare liberalism, and socialism. (See Section I.)

Libertarians, for whom liberty is the ultimate political ideal, are not likely to recognize any need to rectify acts of discrimination and prejudice. Bad as these acts may be, they usually do not—according to libertarians—violate anyone's rights, and hence do not demand rectification. In particular, because no one can demand a right to equal basic educational opportunities (a person's educational opportunities being simply a function of the property he or she controls), no one can justify affirmative action or comparable worth on the basis that such a right was previously denied.

Socialists, for whom equality is the ultimate political ideal, recognize a need to correct for discrimination and prejudice. However, the corrective measures they favor are not limited to affirmative action or comparable worth; socialists ultimately want to socialize the means

of production and do away with private property.

Finally, affirmative action and comparable worth are central requirements of the political program of welfare liberals, whose ultimate political ideal is contractual fairness.

Proposed solutions to the problem of discrimination and prejudice usually involve favoring or compensating certain qualified individuals when there has been a wrongful denial of opportunities or benefits in the past. This practice is called affirmative action, preferential treatment, or reverse discrimination when what is provided are jobs or other desirable positions. It is called comparable worth when what is provided is equal pay for equal or comparable work. "Affirmative action" and "preferential treatment" are basically forward-looking designations employed by proponents of the practice. "Reverse discrimination" is basically a backward-looking designation employed by opponents of the practice. "Comparable worth" is a forward-looking designation employed by both proponents and opponents of the practice.

Alternative Views

In Selection 30, Barry R. Gross raises four objections to reverse discrimination:

1. Those who have suffered discrimination cannot be identified on the grounds that they are underrepresented in certain good jobs.
2. The practice of reverse discrimination is undesirable, for example, because it may involve hiring the incompetent.
3. Reverse discrimination does not fit the legal models of compensation, reparation, or restitution.
4. Reverse discrimination is unfair to those it discriminates against.

Objections 1 and 4 are taken up by Bernard Boxill in Selection 31.

Boxill argues that what shows that blacks have suffered discrimination is not just that they are underrepresented in certain job areas, because as Gross shows even groups who have not suffered discrimination might be underrepresented in certain job areas. What shows that blacks have been discriminated against, according to Boxill, is that they are underrepresented in *all* attractive fields. Boxill also denies that affirmative action or reverse discrimination is unfair to whites who are passed over for affirmative action candidates. After all, although these whites may not have actually discriminated against blacks themselves, Boxill argues that they did benefit from the discrimination of others, for example, through unequal educational opportunities. Hence, blacks do deserve compensation for this discrimination, according to Boxill, and he contends that affirmative action is an appropriate form of compensation. Of course, Gross would deny that affirmative action or reverse discrimination is ever the appropriate corrective for discrimination. Unfortunately, Gross never provides any account of what sort of correctives for discrimination would be appropriate.

Irrespective of whether affirmative action is fair or not, Charles Murray (Selection 32) argues that it has actually worked against the interests of blacks by encouraging a new form of racism. The old racism openly held that blacks are permanently less competent than whites. The new racism holds that blacks are temporarily less competent than whites. The main problem with the new racism, according to Murray, is that it tends to perpetuate the racial inequalities it purports to remedy. However, the examples of this new racism that Murray discusses are all composites drawn from personal observations and, hence, as even he seems to realize, do not by themselves support any generalizations. At the same time, Murray wants to conclude from his discussion that there is no such thing as good racial discrimination.

Murray looks to the qualifications of blacks to explain their poor performance. In contrast, Claude M. Steele (Selection 33) argues that the reason blacks do poorly in school is racial stigma, which is "the endemic devaluation many blacks face in our society and schools." Steele points out that this devaluation affects well-prepared and less well-prepared blacks equally, which, of course, is not what one would expect if the poor performance were due to lack of qualifications. Steele contends that if blacks are made less racially vulnerable in school, they can overcome even substantial obstacles. He cites an example of a Mathematics Workshop Program in Berkeley that took black students from the bottom of their class and inspired them to outperform their white and Asian counterparts. Steele suggests that if we want to, we can do much to remove racial stigma from our schools.

While admitting that some of the pay disparity between women and men in the job market is unfair, Clifford Hackett in Selection 34 objects to using a program of comparable worth to correct for that disparity because he thinks that such a program would undermine a free market. Instead, he recommends that women either seek employment in the better-paying job categories where men now predominate or engage in various forms of job actions, like strikes, to gain higher pay. In contrast, Elaine Sorensen argues in Selection 35 that a program of comparable worth is needed because a free market does not eliminate discrimination. Historically, she points out, it took new laws and court rulings to eliminate some of the most blatant discriminatory practices that prevailed in the labor market.

But even if we were to agree with Sorensen that free markets don't always correct for discrimination, couldn't Hackett still be right that comparable worth would seriously undermine free markets? For example, suppose we raise the wages of secretaries, judging what they do is comparable to what truck drivers do. Won't that increase the supply of secretaries and decrease the supply of truck drivers, with the consequence that the wages of truck drivers will rise, leading to a new round of comparable worth wage adjustments? Not at all. Because even if more people would compete for secretarial positions if secretaries were paid more, it doesn't follow either that more secretaries would be hired or that the pool of would-be truck drivers would decrease as long as these jobs remained as sex segregated as they presently are. Of course, if the sex segregation were to end, there would no longer appear to be grounds for comparable worth.

Practical Applications

Assuming that we accept the need for affirmative action programs to compensate for past injustices, there remains the question of what form such programs should take. In a recent decision, *Sheet Metal Workers v. The Equal Opportunity Commission,* the majority of the U.S. Supreme Court ruled that in appropriate circumstances it was legitimate to order affirmative action that would benefit individuals who are not the actual victims of past discrimination. In this decision, the majority of the court attempted to eliminate the confusion and uncertainty caused by its ruling in *Firefighters v. Stotts,* where the court seemed to hold that remedies could be ordered only to people who had been the actual victims of illegal discrimination. In the Sheet Metal Workers case, the majority of the court ruled against this interpretation, claiming that when discrimination has been persistent and egregious, it is appropriate to employ remedies that benefit members of the relevant group even when they are not the identified victims of the past discrimination.

However, in *City of Richmond v. Croson* (Selection 36), the Supreme Court struck down an affirmative action plan of the city of Richmond that required that prime contractors awarded city construction contracts to subcontract at least 30 percent of the dollar amount of each contract to one or more "Minority Business Enterprises." Justice O'Connor in delivering the opinion of the court argued that the City of Richmond's plan was not supported by the type of evidence of past discrimination in the city's construction industry that would authorize a race-based relief under the equal protection clause of the Fourteenth Amendment. Justice Marshall,

with Justices Brennan and Blackmun concurring, argued that the national evidence of discrimination against minority contractors and the local evidence that only .67 percent of the dollar value of local construction contracts went to minority contractors, together with the Supreme Court's own *Fullilove v. Klutznick* decision, which allowed a 10 percent set-aside of federal contracts for minority contractors, justified the city's adoption of the plan.

Although the case for past discrimination presented by the dissenting justices does seem strong, the City of Richmond clearly erred in defining minority business members to include groups who most likely have not been discriminated against by the Richmond community. The city also erred in not determining the number of minority business enterprises in the Richmond area and whether they would be capable of handling the 30 percent set-aside.

But surely it is possible to fashion affirmative action programs that lack the negative features of the Richmond program but possess all its positive features. And surely welfare liberals along with socialists would regard such programs as justified. Libertarians, of course, would strongly object to this application on the grounds that people lack a right to the relevant equal opportunity needed to justify any affirmative action program. Hence, our evaluation of the Supreme Court's decision depends on our evaluations of these alternative political ideals.

30. The Case against Reverse Discrimination

Barry R. Gross

Barry R. Gross argues that there are four objections to reverse discrimination:

1. Those who have suffered discrimination cannot be identified on the grounds that they are underrepresented in certain good jobs.
2. The practice of reverse discrimination is undesirable, for example, because it may involve hiring the incompetent.
3. Reverse discrimination does not fit the legal models of compensation, reparation, or restitution.
4. Reverse discrimination is unfair to those it discriminates against.

The balance of argument weighs against reverse discrimination for four interrelated sets of reasons. First, the procedures designed to isolate the discriminated are flawed. Second, the practice has undesirable and dangerous consequences. Third, it fails to fit any of the models of compensation or reparations. Fourth, it falls unjustly upon both those it favors and those it disfavors. I conclude that if to eliminate discrimination against the members of one group we find ourselves discriminating against another, we have gone too far.

Sociologically, groups are simply not represented in various jobs and at various levels in percentages closely approximating their percentage of the population. When universities in general and medical schools in particular discriminated heavily against them, Jews were represented in the medical profession in far greater percentages than their percentage of the population. At the same time, they were represented in far lower percentages in banking, finance, construction, and engineering than their percentage in the population, especially the population of New York City. A similar analysis by crudely drawn group traits—Jew, Roman Catholic, WASP, Irish, and so forth—of almost any trade, business or profession would yield similar results.

But the argument from population per-

"Is Turn About Fair Play?" *Journal of Critical Analysis* 5, no. 4 (January/April 1975). Reprinted by permission of the publisher.

centages may be meant not as an analysis of what is the case, but as an analysis of what ought to be the case. A proponent might put it this way: It is true that groups are not usually represented in the work force by their percentage in the population at large, but minority C has been systematically excluded from the good places. Therefore, in order to make sure that they get some of them, we should now systematically include them in the good places, and a clear way of doing it is by their percentage in the population. Or we might conclude instead: therefore, in order to make up for past exclusion, they should be included in the good places as reparation, and an easy way to do it is by their percentage in the population.

If the definition of a minority discriminated against is ipso facto their representation in certain jobs in percentages less than their percentage in the general population, then one has to remark that the reasoning is circular. For we are trying to prove: (1) that minority C is discriminated against.

We use as a premise (3) that minority C is underrepresented in good jobs. Since (1) does not follow from (3) (mere underrepresentation not being even prima facie evidence of discrimination), it is necessary to insert (2) that their underrepresentation is due to discrimination. But this completes the circle.

A critic might reply that we know perfectly well what is meant. The groups discriminated against are blacks, Puerto Ricans, Mexican-Americans, American Indians, and women.

He is correct, though his answer does not tell us *how to find out* who is discriminated against. This critic, for example, left out Jews and Orientals. If he should reply that Jews and Orientals do well enough, we point out that the question was not "Who fails to do well?" but rather, "Who is discriminated against?" This argument shows that the mechanisms for identifying the victims of discrimination and for remedying it are seriously deficient.

Even if we allow that the percentage of the group in the work force versus its percentage in the population is the criterion of discrimination, who is discriminated against will vary depending upon how we divide the groups. We may discover that Republicans are discriminated against by our literary or intellectual journals—*New York Review, Dissent, Commentary*. We may also discover that wealthy Boston residents are discriminated against by the Los Angeles Dodgers, that women are discriminated against by the Army, and that idiots (we hope) are discriminated against by universities.

What employment or profession a person chooses depends upon a number of variables—background, wealth, parents' employment, schooling, intelligence, drive, ambition, skill, and not least, luck. Moreover, the analysis will differ depending upon what group identification or stratification you choose. None seems to have priority over the others. Every person can be typed according to many of these classifications. It seems, therefore, that the relevant analysis cannot even be made, much less justified.

In addition, some proponents of the population-percentage argument seem to hold: (4) From the contingent fact that members of the group C were discriminated against, it follows necessarily that they are underrepresented in the good positions. They then go on to assert (5) if members of group C were not discriminated against they would not be underrepresented, or (6) if they are underrepresented, then they are discriminated against.

But clearly (4) is itself a contingent, not a necessary truth. Clearly also neither (5) nor (6) follows from it, (5) being the fallacy of denying the antecedent and (6) the fallacy of affirming the consequent. Last, neither (5) nor (6) is necessarily true. The members of a group might simply lack interest in certain jobs (for example, Italians in the public school system are in short supply). Could one argue that, even though neither (4), (5), nor (6) is *necessarily* true, the mere fact of underrepresentation in certain occupations does provide evidence of discrimination? The answer is no—no more than the fact of "overrepresentation" in certain occupations is evidence of favoritism.

At most, underrepresentation can be used to support the contention of discrimination when there is *other* evidence as well.

Fair Play: Ought We to Discriminate in Reverse?

There are at least three difficulties with reverse discrimination: first, it is inconsistent; second, it licenses discrimination; third, it is unfair.

If we believe the principle that equal opportunity is a right of everyone, then if members of group C are excluded from enjoying certain opportunities merely because they are members of group C, their right is being abrogated. They are entitled to this right, but so is everybody else, even those persons who presently deny it to them. If both are made to enjoy equal opportunity, then both are enjoying their right. To give either oppressors or oppressed more than equal opportunity is equally to deny the rights of one or the other in violation of the principle of equal opportunity.

Proponents of reverse discrimination seem to be caught on the horns of a dilemma: either discrimination is illegitimate or it is not. If it is illegitimate, then it ought not to be practiced against anyone. If it is not, then there exists no reason for *now* favoring blacks, Puerto Ricans, Chicanos, Indians, women, and so forth over whites.

Two strategies present themselves. Either we can analyze one disjunct with a view to showing that distinctions can be made which require compensation or reparations in the form of reverse discrimination to be made to wronged individuals or groups; or we can try to soften one of the disjuncts so as to make a case for exceptions in favor of the wronged. The first appeals both to our reason and our sense of justice. The second appeals to our emotions. I shall argue that neither strategy works.

Now reverse discrimination can take several forms, but I think that what many of its proponents have in mind is a strong form of compensation—a form which requires us to discriminate against non-C members and favor C members even if less qualified. One may well wonder whether there is not a little retribution hidden in this form of compensation.

The "Softened" General Principle

The argument for construing reverse discrimination as compensation or reparation has a great appeal which can be brought out by contrasting it with another approach. One might agree that as a general rule reverse discrimination is illegitimate but that it need not be seen as universally illegitimate. In particular, in the case where people have been so heavily discriminated against as to make it impossible for them now to gain a good life, there is no possibility of their having a fair chance, no possibility of their starting out on anything like equal terms, then and only then is it legitimate to discriminate in their favor and hence against anyone else.

Against this "softened" general principle I shall urge two sorts of objections which I call respectively "practical" and "pragmatic." Against the reparations type of argument, I shall urge first that there is some reason to think the conditions for exacting and accepting them are lacking, and second that, owing to the peculiar nature of the reparations to be exacted (reverse discrimination), the very exaction of them is unreasonable and unfair to both parties—exactors and exactees.

I mention briefly two sorts of practical objections to the "softened" general principle. First, it is simply the case that when discrimination is made in favor of someone regardless of his qualifications, there is the greatest possible danger that the person get-

ting the position will not be competent to fill it. Second, when a person is placed in a position because of discrimination in his favor, he may come to feel himself inferior. This may easily lead to the permanent conferral of inferior status on the group, an inferiority which is all the stronger because self-induced. Its psychological effects should not be underestimated.

The pragmatic objection to the "softened" general principle is much stronger. Discrimination in any form is invidious. Once licensed, its licenses rebound upon its perpetrators as well as others. Principles tend to be generalized without consideration of restrictions or the circumstances to which they were intended to apply. Students of the Nazi movement will have noticed that in licensing the discrimination, isolation, persecution, and "final solution" of the Jews, the Nazis (foreign and German) licensed their own. (Hitler's plans for extermination included political groups, for example, the Rohm faction of the SA, as well as other racial groups, for example, Slavs and Balts who fought on the German side.) It is necessary to be quite careful what principles one adopts. In view of the long and bloody history of discrimination, one ought to be very chary of sanctioning it.

Compensation, Reparations, and Restitution

Because it escapes most of these objections, the reparations argument becomes very attractive. What is more obvious than the principle that people ought to be compensated for monetary loss, pain and suffering inflicted by others acting either as agents of government or as individuals? From the negligence suit to reparations for war damage, the principle is comfortable, familiar, and best of all, legal. For victims of broken sidewalks, open wells, ignored stop signs, the conditions under which damages are awarded are quite clear. (1) There is specific injury, specific victim, specific time and place. (2) A specific individual or set of individuals must be found responsible either (a) by actually having done the injury, or (b) by failing to act in such a way (for example, repairing the sidewalk, sealing the well) so as to remove a particular potential source of injury on their property. (3) A reasonable assessment of the monetary value of the claim can be made. In such cases no moral blame is attached to the person forced to pay compensation.

But reparations are somewhat less clear. How much does Germany owe France for causing (losing?) World War I? Can we say that *Germany* caused the war? Can we say that Germany *caused* the war? Germany did pay, at least in part, based upon rough calculations of the cost of the Allied armies, including pensions, the loss of allied GNP, indemnities for death and for the destruction of property.

Besides the ability to calculate the indemnities, reparations between countries require at least three other conditions to be met: (1) Responsibility for the events must be able to be assigned and accepted. (2) There must be governments or government-like agencies between which the transfer of goods and services and money takes place. (3) There must be a *modus agendi* worked out. The transfer of vast amounts of goods, money, and services is immensely complicated. In the end Germany could refuse to pay and the Allies to accept large parts of the reparations. Part of the Allied refusal is instructive. Britain, for example, simply could not absorb the payments without extreme economic dislocation.

The meaning of *reparations* was extended to cover payments to Israel and payments to individuals both in and out of Germany who suffered losses through the actions of the Third Reich. The payments to Israel, which did not exist during the war, were to reimburse that state, as the representative of the Jewish people, for the expenses incurred by Jewish organizations during the war in resettling persons uprooted by persecutions and made victims of "unspeakable Nazi crimes."

German payments to individuals were called *Wiedergutmachung* (restitution). *Wiedergutmachung* was awarded not merely for damages or injuries but in order to restore a person to his former position in life. It was calculated on a precise basis. You could be indemnified for: (1) loss of property; (2) loss of income; (3) loss of family; (4) length and type of imprisonment; (5) what you would have earned based upon a reasonable calcula-

tion, if you were young and had not yet begun a career. To qualify for indemnities, one had to produce, respectively, proof of ownership and value of property, a calculation of the difference between what one earned as a refugee and would have earned, proof of loss of family, proof of imprisonment.

Inapplicability of These Paradigms

Can reverse discrimination be construed to fit any of these paradigms? Can favoring blacks, Chicanos, Indians, women, and so forth over whites or males be seen as compensation, reparations, or restitution? The answer is no for two general reasons and for several which are specific to the various paradigms. The general reasons are, first, that responsibility for discrimination past and present and for its deleterious consequences is neither clearly assigned nor accepted. Some seem to think that the mere fact of its existence makes all whites (or males in the case of antifeminism) responsible. But I do not know an analysis of responsibility which bears out this claim. Second, there is a great difficulty, if not an impossibility, in assigning a monetary value to the damage done and the compensation allegedly owed—that is to say, reverse discrimination.

If we turn to the negligence paradigm, all the conditions seem to fail. *Specific* injury is lacking, *specific* individual responsibility is lacking, and there is no way to assess the monetary value of the "loss." Indeed, in the case of reverse discrimination it is not monetary value which is claimed but preferential treatment. Under the large-scale reparations paradigm two conditions beyond responsibility are lacking. There are no governments or government-like agencies between which the transfer could take place, and there is no *modus agendi* for the transfer to take place.

Where the transfer is to be of preferential treatment, it is unclear how it is even to be begun. So we come to the third paradigm: individual restitution. This is much closer, for it deals with compensating individual victims of persecution. Again, however, it fails to provide a model, first, because reverse discrimination cannot be looked at in monetary terms, and second, even if it could, the restitution is designed to bring a person back to where he was before the deprivation. In the case of the minorities in question, there can be no question of restoring them to former positions or property. Precisely, the point of the reparation is to pay them for what they, because of immoral social practices, never had in the first place.

But doesn't Condition 5 under *Wiedergutmachung* seem ready-made for the purpose here? Does it not require calculation of what the person would have earned had his life not been blighted? If A was a doctor, lawyer, office manager, beginning a career, or even a mere student, you could get a rough estimate of what he might earn based upon his family position, the average earnings for that occupation, and so forth. But suppose A is young, uneducated, unskilled, unemployed, from a broken home; what might he have been had circumstances been different? Anything. And that is the tragedy. But how can you calculate his earnings on that basis, and how can you translate them into reverse discrimination?

Justice

Finally, if we ignore all that has been said and simply go ahead and discriminate in reverse, calling it reparation, it remains to ask whether it would be either reasonable or just? I think the answer is no. It is possible to hold that in some set of cases, other things being equal, compensation is required and yet to argue either that since other things are not equal compensation is not required, or that even if some compensation is required it ought not to take the form of reverse discrimination. Certainly, from the fact that some form of compensation or reparation must be made it does not follow that any *specific* form of compensation is in order. If X is discriminated against in awarding professorships because he is a member of C group, it scarcely follows that if compensation is in order it *must* take the form of

his being discriminated in favor of for another professorship, at least not without adopting the principle of "an eye for an eye" (and only an *eye* for an eye?). Consider X being turned down for an apartment because he is a C member. Must compensation consist just in his being offered another ahead of anybody else? Even if he has one already? To go from the relatively innocuous principle that where *possible* we ought to compensate for damages, to sanction reverse discrimination as the proper or preferred form of redress, requires us to go beyond mere compensation to some principle very much like "let the punishment mirror the crime." But here the person "punished," the person from whom the compensation is exacted, is often not the "criminal." Nor will it help to say that the person deprived of a job or advancement by reverse discrimination is not really being punished or deprived, since the job did not belong to him in the first place. Of course it didn't; nor did it belong to the successful candidate. What belonged to both is equal consideration, and that is what one of them is being deprived of.

There is an element of injustice or unfairness in all reparations. The money derived from taxes paid by all citizens is used for reparations regardless of whether they were responsible for, did nothing about, opposed, or actually fought the policies or government in question. Yet we say that this is the only way it can be done, that the element of unfairness is not great, and that on the whole it is better that this relatively painless way of appropriating money from Jones, who is innocent, be used than that the victims of persecution or crime go uncompensated. But the consequences of reverse discrimination are quite different, especially when it is based upon group membership rather than individual desert. It is possible and is sometimes the case that though most C members are discriminated against, Y is a C member who has met with no discrimination at all. Under the principle that all C members should be discriminated in favor of, we would offer "compensation" to Y. But what are we compensating him *for*? By hypothesis he was no victim of discrimination. Do we compensate him for what happened to others? Do we pay Jones for what we buy from Smith? We seem to be compensating him for being a C member, but why? Do we secretly hold C members inferior? Some claim that society as a whole must bear the burden of reparation. But then reverse discrimination will hardly do the trick. It does not exact redress from the government, or even from all white (responsible?) citizens equally, but falls solely against those who apply for admissions, or jobs *for which blacks or other minorities are applying at the same time.* By the same token, it does not compensate or "reparate" all minority persons equally but merely those applying for admission, jobs, promo-

tions, and so forth. Those whose positions are secure would not be made to pay, and those who do not apply for anything would not be paid. A white person who fought for civil rights for blacks may be passed over for promotion or displaced, a victim of reverse discrimination, while a Ku Klux Klan man at the top of the job ladder pays nothing. This would be a laughably flawed system if it were not seriously advocated by responsible people, and partly implemented by the government. Surely, it violates the principles of both compensatory and distributive justice.

31. The Case for Affirmative Action

Bernard Boxill

Bernard Boxill argues that affirmative action is right because blacks as individuals and as a group have been discriminated against in the past and, therefore, deserve compensation. Affirmative action, Boxill contends, is an appropriate form of compensation. He responds to various objections to this argument for affirmative action and finds them all wanting.

Liberals into Former Liberals

As Michael Kinsley has observed in *Harper's,* "No single development of the past fifteen years has turned more liberals into former liberals than affirmative action." This metamorphosis, if it is not merely an unmasking, is ostensibly due to the belief that affirmative action perverts the just goal of civil rights. That goal, protest the disillusioned liberals, is to guarantee that persons be treated as individuals and judged on their merits; but affirmative action, they complain, guarantees that individuals are treated as mere members of racial groups, and their merits disparaged and ignored.

These liberals were not appeased by Allan

Reprinted from *Blacks and Social Justice* (1991, Rowman and Littlefield). Reprinted by permission.

Bakke's victory in the Supreme Court in 1978. For although the court ruled that Bakke was wrongly denied admission to the medical school at the University of California at Davis, it allowed that race could be used as a factor in considering applicants. As *Time* announced on its cover: "What Bakke Means. Race: Yes. Quotas: No."

As with busing, the arguments for preferential treatment fell into two classes, backward-looking and forward-looking. Backward-looking arguments justify preferential treatment considered as compensation for past and present wrongs done to blacks and their effects. Forward-looking arguments justify preferential treatment considered as a means to present or future goods, particularly equality. Both the assumptions and the aims of these two kinds of argument must be carefully distinguished.

Backward-looking arguments assume that blacks have been, or are being, wronged.

Forward-looking arguments assume that blacks are generally inferior to whites in status, education, and income. Backward-looking arguments aim at compensating blacks. Forward-looking arguments aim at improving the status, education, and income of blacks.

The Backward-looking Argument

The fundamental backward-looking argument is simply stated: Black people have been and are being harmed by racist attitudes and practices. Those wronged deserve compensation. Therefore, black people deserve compensation. Preferential treatment is an appropriate form of compensation for black people. Therefore black people deserve preferential treatment.

Criticism of this argument falls into two main classes: on the one hand, critics charge that the claims to compensation of the black beneficiaries of preferential treatment are unfounded or vacuously satisfied; on the other hand, they charge that these claims are outweighed by other considerations.

The most common version of the first type always uttered by the critic with an air of having played a trump, is that, since those members of groups that have been discriminated against who benefit from preferential hiring must be minimally qualified, they are not the members of the group who deserve compensation. The philosopher Alan Goldman, for example, argues this way: "Since hiring within the preferred group still depends upon relative qualifications and hence upon past opportunities for acquiring qualifications, there is in fact a reverse ratio established between past discriminations and present benefits, so that those who most benefit from the program, those who actually get jobs, are those who least deserve to." But surely a conclusion that preferential hiring is unjustified based on the argument above is a non sequitur. Let us grant that qualified blacks are less deserving of compensation than unqualified blacks, that those who most deserve compensation should be compensated first, and finally that preferen-

tial hiring is a form of compensation. How does it follow that preferential hiring of qualified blacks is unjustified? Surely the assumption that unqualified blacks are more deserving of compensation than qualified blacks does not require us to conclude that qualified blacks deserve no compensation. Because I have lost only one leg, I may be less deserving of compensation than another who has lost two legs, but it does not follow that I deserve no compensation at all.

Even Thomas Nagel, one of the country's leading philosophers and a strong defender of preferential treatment on the basis of the forward-looking argument, resorts to this criticism of the backward-looking argument. Thus he labels a "bad" argument, one that maintains that the "beneficiaries of affirmative action deserve it as compensation for past discrimination," because, he says, "no effort is made to give preference to those who have suffered most from discrimination." Indeed, Nagel makes exactly the same point as Goldman: Because the blacks who benefit from preferential treatment are qualified, "they are not necessarily, or even probably the ones who especially deserve it. Women or blacks who don't have the qualifications even to be considered are likely to have been handicapped more by the effects of discrimination than those who receive preference." But for the reasons given, this criticism is bogus. Furthermore, since Nagel defends preferential treatment on forward-looking, egalitarian grounds, this puts him into deeper trouble than it does those who reject preferential treatment altogether.

For, if preferential treatment makes no effort to give preference to those who have suffered most, neither does it make an effort to give preference to those who are most unequal to whites. In other words, if the qualified have suffered least, they are also least unequal, and it seems a bad strategy, if one is aiming for equality, to prefer them. Nagel could object that preferring the qualified is a good egalitarian strategy because it will lead indirectly to equality. But a variant of the idea is open to the advocate of the backward-looking argument. He could argue that preferential treatment of the qualified also helps to compensate the unqualified insofar as it shows them that if one is qualified, being black is no longer a bar to promotion.

One claim which would make the objection to compensating qualified blacks stick, and which the critics appear not to have made, is that compensation can be made to only one section of a group—either the qualified or the unqualified—but not to both. If this were true, and if the unqualified are most deserving of compensation, then a case could be mounted for claiming that, under the circumstances, a policy of preferential hiring should not be instituted because it takes from those who are most deserving of compensation (the unqualified) to give to those who are less deserving (the qualified). But if the critics are making this assumption, they have not stated it.

But perhaps the critics mean that qualified blacks are not simply less deserving of compensation than unqualified blacks, but that they deserve no compensation at all, precisely because they are qualified.

Why should this be so? I am not questioning the possibility that, on practical grounds, we may be unable to compensate the qualified members of a group generally discriminated against. I am questioning the assumption that, just because a person has overcome his injury, he no longer has a right to compensation. If I am swindled and through time and effort retrieve my money, shouldn't I be compensated for my time and effort? And if I have plenty of money and hire a good lawyer, shouldn't I also claim from my swindlers the money I paid the lawyer?

But in their eagerness to demolish the case for preferential treatment the critics have become extraordinarily careless, and *have* moved from the claim that qualified blacks are the least harmed and wronged blacks to the unsubstantiated claim that qualified blacks are not harmed or wronged at all. Thus Goldman first made the claim in his essay, "Reparations to Individuals or Groups" that in preferential hiring of qualified minority candidates, there is "an inverse ratio established between past discrimination and present benefits." But then, almost immediately, he makes the very much stronger claim—which does not at all proceed logically from the first—that preferential hiring "singles out for benefits within a generally unjustly treated minority just that

minority that has not been unjustly treated." And he makes a similar error in his book, *Justice and Reverse Discrimination*. First he says that "those who are not most qualified will tend to be those who have been discriminated against least," then follows this observation with the assertion that blacks "who have altogether escaped harm from previous injustice . . . will be the ones benefitting from preference." These transitions from one argument to another and others like them, embody several confusions. Most obviously, there is the submerged conflation of those least harmed or wronged, slightly harmed or wronged, and not at all harmed or wronged. Less obviously, the distinction between being harmed, and being wronged or treated unjustly, is not taken seriously enough.

The argument I am proposing in support of preferential treatment should be distinguished from another argument which, I admit, has a certain superficial attractiveness. My argument is that qualified blacks deserve compensation for discrimination because even they have been wronged and probably harmed by it, and that preferential treatment is appropriate compensation for them because it suits their objectives and abilities. The other, superficially attractive, argument is that qualified blacks deserve compensation because they are probably the very blacks who would, in the absence of discrimination, have qualified without preferential treatment. But only a moment's reflection is needed to see that this argument is flawed. As James S. Fishkin points out in *Justice, Equal Opportunity and the Family,* "There is no reason to believe that those blacks who are presently 'best prepared' offer even a remote approximation to those blacks 'who in the absence of discrimination probably would have qualified.' "

But this eminently sound observation does not imply that the "best prepared" are not wronged or harmed by discrimination. That is an altogether distinct claim. The best prepared need not be the ones who would have qualified in the absence of discrimination, but they may nevertheless be disadvantaged by discrimination. Thus, I reject Fishkin's concomitant, completely unsupported, claim that, "it is far from clear that the more advantaged members of a racial minority generally are worse off than they would otherwise have been, were it not for discrimination practiced against their forebears in previous generations." This assumes that discrimination does not generally disadvantage those who are discriminated against, and that is an outrageous and gratuitous conclusion.

But suppose I am wrong and many blacks have in fact escaped the effects of discrimination? This is the fundamental objection to preferential treatment, for, if so many blacks have escaped discrimination and its effects that it results in "compensation" being given large numbers of people who did not deserve it, then it would be unfair. However, even if some blacks escape discrimination altogether, it must be admitted that there is a pervasive prejudice against blacks as a group and a tendency to discriminate against them. Consequently, if . . . the realistic threat of transgression is itself transgression, even those who escape discrimination are wronged and possibly harmed by the discrimination against other blacks. This leads us to the argument proposed by Judith Jarvis Thomson that "even those who were not themselves down-graded for being black or female have suffered the consequences of the down-grading of other blacks and women: lack of self-confidence and lack of self-respect." Goldman has taken this argument as the basis for belief in the concept of a kind of "indirect," "vicarious" wrong. Thus he objects that we should reserve "vicarious compensation"—and what he means by this I do not know—"to those who suffer psychologically or vicariously from injustice toward others, and that we should draw the line [past which compensation is no longer called for] at indirect psychological pressures." But his objection misses the point about the harmfulness of discrimination.

Consider, for example, how Goldman illustrates his point: "A traumatized witness," he writes, "does not suffer the harm of the real victim. Similarly, a Jewish millionaire in Scarsdale, no matter how much he suffered vicariously or psychologically from hearing of the German concentration camps, is not owed the reparations due a former inmate." But Goldman fails to distinguish two kinds of witness to injustice. There is the witness who identifies with the victim, and there is the witness who

the transgressors identify with the victim. The first suffers vicariously. The second may not suffer vicariously. However, it does not follow that the latter does not suffer at all. He certainly might suffer at the realization that he too was under sentence and could be next. Therefore there are two completely different kinds of suffering that a witness to the persecution of others might endure. The first stems from sympathy for the victims; it is vicarious and could be called indirect. The second stems from the witness's self-interested realization that he may be under sentence too and could be the next to be harmed. But, though this suffering may be "psychological," it is not vicarious, and there is nothing indirect about it. The example of the Scarsdale Jew— the stipulation that he is a millionaire is irrelevant—obscures this. Safely ensconced in Scarsdale, any Jew, millionaire or not, was safe from Hitler. Goldman's example insinuates that the Jew who was not himself victimized could feel only vicarious suffering. To make the argument more balanced, I suggest pondering the plight of a Jewish multi-millionaire in Berlin.

Failure to distinguish these two kinds of suffering is responsible for the idea that vicarious suffering is relevant to a consideration of the undermining of self-confidence and self-respect to which Judith Jarvis Thomson was presumably referring. For while the realization that, like the actual victim, the witness to discrimination is also under sentence and could be next, has everything to do with the undermining of his self-confidence and self-respect, vicarious suffering has nothing to do with it. Consequently, the vicarious suffering of middle-class blacks for lower-class blacks, if it exists to any appreciable degree, is completely irrelevant to the question of what undermines their self-confidence and self-respect. What does is the uncertainty and ambiguity of their own lives.

But the red herring of vicarious suffering is misleading in yet another way: It suggests that the undermining of self-confidence and self-respect is a consequence of "injustice toward others." Of course, one's vicarious suffering is no indication of injustice to oneself. Though a white person may suffer vicariously at the thought of discrimination against lower-class blacks, the injustice is to them and not to him. However, when black people feel threatened and insulted when other black people are discriminated against because of their color, the injustice is both to those actually discriminated against and to those who are spared. Because the blacks discriminated against are discriminated against because they are black, all black people receive a warning that they too may experience the same treatment. They are wronged, and liable to be wrongfully harmed, in two ways. First, they are wronged because the realistic threat under which they live transgresses their right to equal security. Second, they are wronged by the judgmental injustice that assumes that because they are black they deserve less consideration than others. Justice Thurgood Marshall's comment in *Bakke* is apropos: "It is unnecessary in twentieth century America to have individual Negroes demonstrate that they have been victims of racial discrimination. [It] has been so pervasive that none, regardless of wealth or position, has managed to escape its impact."

To sum up to this point: The criticism of the backward-looking argument for preferential treatment under consideration is unsound in one of its forms, and irrelevant in the other. Insofar as it assumes that many blacks have escaped wrongful harm as a result of discrimination it is unsound. Even if some blacks have escaped harm this would not be sufficient to make preferential treatment unjustified, because the overwhelming majority it benefited would deserve compensation. Insofar as the criticism assumes the blacks preferred are less wronged or harmed than other blacks it is irrelevant. The backward-looking argument does not exclude compensating unqualified blacks, or deny that they are more deserving of compensation. Neither does it say that qualified blacks must be compensated first. It asserts only that blacks deserve compensation for the wrongful harms of discrimination. Thus, it is unaffected by the claim that qualified blacks may be the least wronged and harmed of blacks. The fact that qualified blacks are wrongfully harmed at all, and that preferential treatment is appropriate compensation, is sufficient justification for it.

Now, I have admitted that it is a weak argument which tries to justify preferential treatment of qualified blacks applying for desirable places and positions on the grounds that, had there been no discrimination, these blacks would probably have qualified for such places and positions without preferential treatment. The key assumption in this argument is simply not plausible. But if we assume that compensation is owed to blacks as a group, then a stronger version of that argument can be advanced, which goes as follows: Blacks as a group have been wronged, and are disadvantaged, by slavery and discrimination. Consequently, blacks as a group deserve compensation. Furthermore, had it not been for slavery and discrimination, blacks as a group would be more nearly equal in income, education, and well-being to other groups who did not suffer from slavery or the extent and kind of discrimination from which blacks have suffered. Consequently, assuming that compensating a group for wrongful disadvantages requires bringing it to the condition it would have been in had it not been wrongfully disadvantaged, compensating blacks as a group requires making them, as a group, more nearly equal to those other groups. But if blacks as a group were more nearly equal in income, education, and well-being to such groups, some blacks would then fill desirable positions. Accordingly, compensating blacks as a group requires putting some blacks in desirable positions. However, only the blacks who are now most qualified can, fittingly, be placed in desirable positions. Hence, even if those blacks are *not* the very ones who would have filled such places and positions had there been no slavery and discrimination, compensating blacks as a group may specifically require preferential treatment of qualified blacks.

Many objections can be raised to this argument. Perhaps the most obvious is that its conception of compensation differs from the conception of compensation used in the argument that blacks, as individuals, deserve compensation. In that argument, I did not contend that compensating blacks requires placing then in positions they would have occupied had there been no slavery and discrimination. I contended that blacks deserve compensation because they are wronged by discrimination, and that places in universities and professional schools are appropriate compensation for qualified blacks because of their interests and objectives. However, in outlining the group compensation argument I am saying that compensating blacks as a group requires placing them in positions they would have occupied had there been no slavery and discrimination. Is this inconsistent? I think I can demonstrate that it isn't.

I endorse the view that, ideally, compensating either individuals or groups for wrongs requires placing them in positions they would have occupied had they not been wronged. The problem is that this ideal conception of compensation cannot be applied in the case of compensation for individual blacks for the wrongs of slavery and discrimination. To place a wronged individual in a position he would have occupied had he not been wronged depends on an estimate of how much the wrong has detracted from his assets, which in turn depends on an estimate of his assets. For an individual's assets—his capacities, abilities, goals, interests, and enjoyments—determine in large part the position he will come to occupy if he is not wronged. For example, if thugs break the basketball player Dr. J's legs, he will receive more compensation than I would if they broke my legs, because it is known that his legs are a greater asset to him than are my legs to me. Similarly, some years ago the newspapers reported that a certain screen star had insured her legs with Lloyd's of London for several million pounds. Whether or not the story was true, it seemed good sense to many people because they thought the star's legs were such an enormous asset that it would take several million pounds to compensate her for them if they were flawed or lost. It should now be clear why the ideal conception of compensation cannot be used to support an argument in favor of compensating black individuals for the wrongs of slavery and discrimination. In most cases, it simply makes no sense to even try to estimate what any black individual's assets might have been before he was wronged by slavery and discrimination. For, from the very start of their lives—while they are yet in the womb—and of their parents' lives, and of the lives of their ancestors, all the way back to the first black slaves born in the New World, blacks have been wronged by slavery and discrimina-tion. Yet the fact remains that because they have been wronged they deserve compensa-tion. Accordingly, under the circumstances the ideal conception of compensation must be discarded. By way of compensating blacks all that can practically be done is to adopt my proposal and award them some benefit—such as preferential treatment—appropriate to their interests and objectives.

The argument for group compensation does not run into this sort of difficulty. We can form some estimate of the assets blacks as a group had before slavery and discrimination. Consequently, we can apply the ideal concep-tion of compensation, and reasonably propose to place blacks as a group in the position they would have occupied had there been no slav-ery and discrimination.

It may be objected, however, that placing blacks in the position they would have occu-pied had there been no slavery and dis-crimination would not make blacks equal or nearly equal to other groups because blacks are inferior to other groups, especially white groups, in native talent. But this objection begs the question. The claim that blacks are inferior to whites in native talent is an inference based largely on the fact that the average black I.Q. is lower than the average white I.Q. But that inference is highly controversial. Another, possibly sounder inference, is that black I.Q.s have been lowered as a result of slavery and discrimination. If this assumption is sound, and if I.Q.s are as important for determining people's lives as they are said to be, then blacks' lower average I.Q., far from support-ing the case against compensation, very much supports the case for it.

A somewhat less radical objection is that the estimate we can form of the assets of blacks as a group before slavery and discrimination sug-gests that even without slavery and discrimina-tion they would not have been nearly equal to other groups. Thomas Sowell, for example, suggests this. ". . . the wide diversity among American ethnic groups," he argues, "pre-cludes any assumptions that any group—especially from a non-urban, non-industrial background—would earn the national average in income." But this is not only a weak argu-ment in itself, it is also inconsistent with many other points Sowell himself has stressed as important and decisive in relation to the issue of discrimination.

It is a weak argument, first, because some groups from a "non-urban, non-industrial background," for example, the Irish Catholics, earn *above* the national average income. If Irish Catholics can, why not blacks? Sowell's assertion that such groups tend to earn considerably less than the national average income may be true if we look only at relatively recent immigrants such as the Puerto Ricans. But blacks have been in America for three hundred years. It is invidious to assume that, unlike other groups from non-urban, non-industrial backgrounds, they would not have bettered themselves had it not been for slavery and its aftermath. Finally, although blacks originally came from a non-urban, non-industrial background, it does not follow that they lacked economically valuable assets. Sowell's master, Booker T. Washington boasted that the policy of importing black slaves proved that blacks had economically valuable skills, and given the importance Sowell attributes to motives of economic self-interest, he is in no position to confound Washington's argument. Given that blacks did have economically valuable skills, surely, in the absence of slavery and discrimination, they would have realized their assets, parlayed their earnings in order to further improve their skills, and, with three hundred years in which to do it, would today be as urbanized and industrialized as anybody else.

Sowell's argument that because of their non-urban, non-industrial origins, blacks, even if there had been no slavery, would be unlikely to be earning near the national average income, is also inconsistent with certain other theories he holds dear. Recall, for example, his view that middle-class blacks are almost always descended from blacks who were freed before emancipation, a view which he uses in support of the theory that progress is an "intergenerational race." . . . If this view and theory are correct, it is difficult to advance any reason why most blacks would not be earning much nearer the national average income if there had been no slavery and discrimination. And there is an even more striking inconsistency in Sowell's argument. The fact he most prizes in support of his contention that it

is American blacks' culture, not racial discrimination, which holds them back, is that West Indian blacks, who are physically indistinguishable from American blacks, earn just a little less than white Americans. But the West Indies hardly constitute an industrialized region of the world. Consequently, the fact that a group has a non-industrialized background cannot be the basis of an argument that they are unlikely to earn near the national average income. And so it is with much of Sowell's reasoning. He says one thing to support one point, and the opposite to support another point, and never notices anything amiss.

But what if Sowell is right, and "culture—not discrimination—decides who gets ahead"? Assuming that a group's culture is what determines the jobs and positions its members are interested in, certain philosophers seem to agree with him. Thus, Barry Gross implies that blacks may simply not be interested in desirable positions, and argues that black underrepresentation in desirable positions is no clear indication of discrimination: "The members of a group might simply lack interest in certain jobs (for example, Italians in the public school system are in short supply)." But this analogy fails, though Gross does not appear to notice it, when applied to the case of blacks. For it isn't as if blacks are underrepresented in the public school system, or in law, or in banking, or in the professions. They are underrepresented in all of these fields. Consequently, though Gross may be right and that sociologically, certain groups are simply not represented in various jobs and at various levels in percentages closely approximating their percentage of the population, he fails to see that the case of blacks presents a matter of an altogether different order. Lack of interest—presumably culturally determined—in this or in that area may explain away the underrepresentation of a cultural group in one or two specific areas. However, unless we assume that some cultural groups have no interest in *any* of the traditional professional areas, we cannot explain a group's underrepresentation in all desirable positions by citing cultural differences.

The deeper and more serious implication of the claim that blacks are disadvantaged by their culture, not by discrimination, is that blacks, because of their culture, lack the discipline necessary for becoming qualified for desirable positions. But whether or not this is true, it cannot weigh against the argument for group compensation for blacks. For even if the traits which inhibit the success of blacks—supposedly a lack of appropriate work habits and discipline—are cultural traits it does not follow that they are not the result of wrongful harm. In order to survive and retain their sanity and equilibrium in impossibly unjust situations, people may have to resort to patterns of behavior, and consequently may develop habits or traits, which are debilitating and unproductive in a more humane environment. I see no reason why these cultural traits—which may be deeply ingrained and extremely difficult to eradicate—should not be classed as unjust injuries. This being the case, we have discovered another inconsistency in Sowell's argument. The cultural characteristics he blames for holding back blacks he considers to be the result of slavery and its aftermath. The "legacy of slavery," he declares, is "foot-dragging, work avoiding patterns," "duplicity and theft," and a "tragic hostility to menial jobs." Consequently, if it is blacks' culture which holds them back, then blacks deserve compensation for the culture which slavery imposed on them. Yet Sowell affirms the premise and denies the conclusion.

It is admittedly unusual to think of cultural traits as wrongful harms because we think of culture as, in an important sense, self-imposed. This is true of most cultures in the traditional sense of ethnic and national cultures. Such cultures come with built-in philosophical self-justifications. In the sense that participants in them therefore have elaborate resources with which to justify themselves, they may be viewed as self-imposed. Consequently, though such cultures may encourage development of traits which inhibit advancement in modern society, it would be philosophically hazardous to call such traits wrongful harms. At most, they might be considered self-imposed harms. But not all cultures are self-imposed, and certain cultures contain no mechanism of philosophical self-justification and self-definition. Thus, in describing what he calls the "culture of poverty,"

Oscar Lewis notes that though it is a genuine culture in the traditional anthropological sense, in that it provides human beings with a "design for living," it "does not provide much support. . . . Poverty of culture is one of the crucial traits of the culture of poverty." Consequently, if we assume that the cultural legacy of slavery is of this nature and is harmful, inasmuch as it tends to block self-development, self-realization, and autonomy, as well as undermine self-respect and self-esteem, it follows that blacks have been wrongfully harmed, and therefore, according to the terms of the backward-looking argument, deserve compensation.

Moreover, there are other grounds on which the claim that blacks constitute a cultural group is not notably advantageous for the critics of preferential treatment. For, if it is true, it confounds the objection of some critics that blacks do not comprise a group in the sense required by the group compensation argument. For example, Goldman objects to treating blacks as a legitimate group eligible for compensatory treatment because they "do not qualify as genuine groups or social organizations in the sense in which sociologists generally use these terms." He goes on to point out that in genuine groups there is "actual interaction among members, each of whom occupies a certain position or plays a certain role in the group reciprocal to other roles, roles being reciprocal when their performances are mutually dependent. But by that very account cultural groups do qualify as genuine groups. There is "actual interaction" among the members of a cultural group. That interaction is, of course, not specifically economic or political. Members of a cultural group do not, for example, necessarily buy from each other or employ each other or rule each other. Still, they do interact and that interaction is just as important as economic or political interaction.

Members of a cultural group share basic values and ideals—that is what we mean by culture—and they interact intellectually by exchanging ideas about these values and ideals; by clarifying, criticizing, and extending them; and by severing and drawing connections between them. In this way they come better to understand themselves. All prosperous and progressive peoples engage in this bustling process of self-clarification. W. E. B. Dubois thought that it was a condition of progress, and it was the basis of his theory of "the talented tenth." If a group is to progress, he argued, it must pay special attention to the cultural education of its talented tenth. If we make "technical skill the object of education," he observed, "we may possess artisans but not, in nature, men." Other writers, Booker T. Washington particularly, have believed that cultural activity is the reward of progress. In either case, it is obviously a great good. If, then, it is argued that blacks are under-represented in positions of wealth and prestige because of culturally induced differences, then they have been wronged as a group, and preferential hiring of qualified blacks is justified as a way of compensating the group. For, it needs no argument to show that the intellectually most active and advanced members of a cultural group play a crucial role in the process of self-clarification. If, then, as seems likely, they will be among those qualified, and preferential hiring will give them the opportunity to play this crucial role, then preferential hiring is a way of compensating the group.

I am not, myself, altogether comfortable with the claim that blacks are a cultural group, or that they interact enough, and are sufficiently interdependent, to support the group compensation argument. These claims ultimately depend on empirical investigation, and even if the contention I made earlier is correct, and all blacks, whatever their class, are wronged, and have good reason to feel threatened by racial discrimination, the often cited disparity between the black middle class and the black underclass still undermines the force of the group compensation argument. That point conceded, I must however reject certain other criticisms of the group compensation argument. For example, according to Fishkin the objection to compensating present-day blacks for slavery and past discrimination—that were it not for these injustices, these individuals would not exist—can also be offered when the argument for compensating blacks is reformulated to rest on the premise that blacks deserve compensation as a group. For, says Fishkin, just as it is impossible

to return black individuals to the positions they would have held had there been no slavery and discrimination, because without these injustices present-day blacks would not exist, so also it is impossible to return the black group to the position it would have held had there been no slavery and discrimination, because had it not been for these injustices the group would not have the kind of interdependence among its members required by the group compensation argument. In support of this Fishkin reasons as follows: "had injustices to blacks not been committed, it is arguable that we might have a society in which race functioned the way eye color does now. In a racially neutral society, blacks would not constitute a social group or natural class. Their status, identity, and welfare would not be tied to their group membership." But if Fishkin's thesis is "arguable," it is, at best, barely so. Its gratuitous premise is that racial persecution is the only factor which binds blacks together as a social group. The slaves did not all share an identical culture and language, but their cultures and languages certainly had a family resemblance which, together with their common African origins, could well have operated to bind them together. Indeed, without slavery these factors would have operated more strongly than they did with slavery, since, as is well known, slave masters did their very best to destroy the slaves' cultures, languages, and traditions. Why does Fishkin write as if he believes blacks are different from other people? Many European minorities, without the benefit of slavery, manage to retain their identities. Why suppose that blacks would be so anxious to lose theirs? And, if Fishkin's observations are in any way correct, is it not likely that this is because of the very persecution which has served to bind them together in another way? . . .

. . . It has seemed to many critics that preferential treatment, insofar as it involves preferential admissions and hiring, is unfair to young white males. For example, according to Robert K. Fullinwider, a research associate at the Center for Philosophy and Public Policy at the University of Maryland, the compensation argument for preferential treatment confuses the sound compensation principle—"he who wrongs another shall pay for the wrong"—

with the "suspect" principle—"he who benefits from a wrong shall pay for the wrong." To clinch the point, Fullinwider asks us to consider the following ingenious example: A neighbor pays a construction company to pave his driveway, but someone maliciously directs the workmen to pave Fullinwider's driveway instead. Fullinwider admits that his neighbor has been "wronged and damaged" and that he himself has "benefited from the wrong." However, since he is not responsible for the wrong, he denies that he is "morally required to compensate" his neighbor by "paying" him for it.

This example makes us see that not all cases where compensation may be due are straightforward, though one kind of case clearly is. If John steals Jeff's bicycle and "gives" it to me, however innocent I may be, I have no right to it and must return it to Jeff as soon as I discover the theft. Given that this example is unproblematic, in what way does it differ from Fullinwider's, which is problematic?

One difference is that, whereas I can simply hand over Jeff's bicycle to him, Fullinwider cannot simply hand over the pavement in his driveway. It will be objected that the proposal was not that Fullinwider should hand over the pavement, but that he should pay his neighbor for it. But this is a different case. I did not say that I had a duty to pay Jeff for his bicycle. I said that I had a duty to return the bicycle to Jeff. If Jeff told me to keep the bicycle but pay him for it, I do not admit that I would have a duty to do so. I could object fairly that when I accepted the bicycle I did not believe that I would have to pay for it, and if I had thought that I would have to, I might have not accepted it. Paying for the bicycle now would impose on me, because I might have preferred to spend my money in a different way and, being innocent of any wrongdoing, I see no reason why I should be penalized. The point is that though the beneficiary of an injustice has no right to his advantage, if he is innocent of the injustice, he does not deserve to be penalized. Thus, where compensation is concerned, the obligations of the innocent beneficiary of injustice and of the person responsible for the injustice are quite different. Though the former has no right to his benefits, the process

of compensation cannot impose any losses on him over and above the loss of his unfair benefits. If compensation is impossible without such loss, it is unjustified. On the other hand, in the case of the person responsible for injustice, even if compensation requires him to give up more than he has unfairly gained, it is still justified.

But, though Fullinwider's example is cogent as far as it goes, it is irrelevant as an argument against preferential hiring. It is cogent as far as it goes because, as the above analysis shows, requiring young white males to pay women and minorities for all the unfair advantages they have enjoyed would indeed be unfair. The advantages cannot, as in my example of the bicycle, simply be transferred from their hands into those of the preferred group. Compensation of this kind would impose on young white males time and effort over and above the cost of the unfair advantages they are required to return. They could justly protest that they are being penalized, because they might not have accepted the advantages had they known what they would cost them—now they are "out" both the advantages and their time and effort. But preferential hiring does not require young white males to pay, at an additional cost to themselves, the price of their advantages. It proposes instead to compensate the injured with goods no one has yet established a right to and therefore in a way that imposes no unfair losses on anyone. And these goods are, of course, jobs.

It may be objected that, although a white male applicant may not have established a right to this or that job, he has a right to fair competition for it, and preferential hiring violates that right. But, on the contrary, by refusing to allow him to get the job because of an unfair advantage, preferential hiring makes the competition fairer. The white male applicant can still complain, of course, that, had he known that preferential hiring would be instituted, he would not have accepted his advantages in the first place. Since, if he knew that preferential hiring would be instituted, he would necessarily also have known that his advantages were unfair, his complaint would amount to his saying that, had he known his advantages were unfair, he would not have accepted them. But then, if he is concerned with fairness, and if preferential hiring makes the competition fairer, he should have no objections to it. Or to state the proposition somewhat less contentiously, preferential hiring imposes no unfair losses on him.

Thus, a fairer application of Fullinwider's example about the driveway to the case of preferential hiring would be as follows: Suppose an "improve-your-neighborhood group" offered a valuable prize for the best driveway on the block. Would Fullinwider be justified in insisting that he deserves to get the prize over his neighbor who has, at further cost to himself, built another somewhat inferior driveway?

To sum up my discussion of forms of the backward-looking argument for preferential treatment, while I have insisted that all, or nearly all, blacks are victims of racial injustice, I have conceded that it has handicapped some blacks more than others. . . . Consequently, although the backward-looking argument is the bedrock of the case for preferential treatment, to complete that case we must look forward.

The Forward-looking Argument

Whereas the backward-looking argument tried to justify preferential treatment as compensation for past wrongful harms, the forward-looking argument tries to justify preferential treatment on the grounds that it may secure greater equality or increase total social utility. Moreover, the fact that blacks were slaves and the victims of discrimination is irrelevant to the forward-looking argument, which its proponents imply, would not lose force even if blacks had never been slaves and never discriminated against. All that is relevant to the argument is that blacks are often poor, generally less than equal to whites in education, influence, and income, and preferentially treating them will alleviate their poverty, reduce their inequality, and generally increase total utility.

The forward-looking argument has one very clear advantage over the backward-looking argument. As we have seen, a persistent criticism of the backward-looking argument is that, although some blacks deserve no compensation for discrimination because they have not been harmed by discrimination, they are precisely the ones benefiting from preferential treatment. I have tried to rebut this criticism, but this is unnecessary if the forward-looking argument is adopted. For that argument does not require the assumption that the beneficiaries of preferential treatment have been harmed by discrimination, or even that they have been harmed at all. Indeed, it does not require that they be less than equal to whites, and is consistent with their being relatively privileged. For it endorses a strategy of increasing the incomes and education even of blacks superior in those respects to most whites if, however indirectly, this will, in the long run, effectively increase blacks' equality and increase total social utility.

Now whether or not preferential treatment has such consequences is in the end an empirical question, but some critics, as I will show, insist on concocting specious a priori arguments to show that preferential treatment necessarily causes a loss in social utility.

Thus it has been argued that since, by definition, preferential treatment awards positions to the less qualified over the more qualified, and since the more qualified perform more efficiently than the less qualified, therefore preferential treatment causes a loss of utility. But suppose that less qualified blacks are admitted to medical school in preference to more qualified whites, and suppose the resulting black doctors practice in poor black neighborhoods treating serious illnesses, while if the whites they were preferred to had been admitted they would have practiced in affluent white neighborhoods, treating minor illnesses. In that sort of case, it is not at all necessarily true that preferential treatment causes a loss in utility. Some authors try to avoid the force of this argument by switching the basis of their criticism from the fact that preferential treatment may reward the less qualified to the false assertion that preferential treatment may reward the "unqualified." Thus, Goldman reminds us that "all will suffer when unqualified persons occupy many positions." This is criticism of a straw man.

It has also been claimed that the forward-looking argument that preferential treatment increases utility is open to a serious philosophical objection. Thus philosopher George Sher writes that the utilitarian, or forward-looking, defense of preferential treatment is "vulnerable" to the "simple but serious" objection that "if it is acceptable to discriminate in favor of minorities and women when doing so maximises utility then it is hard to see why it should not also be acceptable to discriminate against minorities and women when that policy maximises welfare." And against Thomas Nagel who argues that racial discrimination, unlike reverse discrimination, "has no social advantages . . . and attaches a sense of reduced worth to a feature with which people are born," Sher makes a similar objection. He says that Nagel gives us no reason to believe that "there could never be alternative circumstances in which racial, ethnic, or sexual discrimination had social advantages which did outweigh the sense of reduced worth it produced," and maintains that Nagel still has not shown us that such discrimination is illegitimate under "any circumstances at all."

The serious utilitarian is likely to dismiss Sher's criticisms with the same impatience with which he dismisses the stock criticism that utilitarianism allows slavery. As R. M. Hare notes, it is the "strength" of the utilitarian doctrine that "the utilitarian cannot reason a priori that whatever the facts about the world and human nature, slavery is wrong. He has to show it is wrong by showing, through a study of history and other factual observation, that slavery does have the effects (namely the pro-duction of misery) that make it wrong." In particular, he is not undone by the arguments of the intuitionist who thinks up "fantastic" examples which show slavery to be right according to the principles of utilitarianism, because these show only that the intuitionist has "lost contact with the actual world." Much the same thing can be said about Sher's notion that there are circumstances in which racial discrimination would be legitimate according to utilitarian principles. . . .

I have used more space in rebutting criticisms than in arguing positively for conclusions. This is because the main arguments for affirmative action are straightforward, and yet philosophers persist in concocting ever more desperately ingenious objections to it. Not that I believe that any one of the various backward- and forward-looking arguments is by itself sufficient to justify affirmative action. Affirmative action is justified by the combined force of these arguments and by the way they complement and support each other. The weaknesses in some are made up by the strengths of others. For example, the weakness in the case for compensation on an individual basis is made up for by the case for compensation on a group basis, and the weaknesses of both these cases are strengthened by considerations stemming from the forward-looking argument. A society which tries to be just tries to compensate the victims of its injustice, and when these victims are easily identified, either as individuals or as a group less than equal to others, the case for treating them preferentially is overwhelming.

32. Affirmative Racism

Charles Murray

Charles Murray argues that preferential treatment for blacks has actually worked
against their interest by encouraging a new form of racism that tacitly accepts
the view that blacks are temporarily less competent than whites. The problem
with this new form of racism, Murray claims, is that it perpetuates the race-
based inequality it seeks to eliminate.

A few years ago, I got into an argument with a lawyer friend who is a partner in a New York firm. I was being the conservative, arguing that preferential treatment of blacks was immoral; he was being the liberal, urging that it was the only way to bring blacks to full equality. In the middle of all this he abruptly said, "But you know, let's face it. We must have hired at least ten blacks in the last few years, and none of them has really worked out." He then returned to his case for still stronger affirmative action, while I wondered what it had been like for those ten blacks. And if he could make a remark like that so casually, what remarks would he be able to make some years down the road, if by that time it had been fifty blacks who hadn't "really worked out"?

My friend's comment was an outcropping of a new racism that is emerging to take its place alongside the old. It grows out of preferential treatment for blacks, and it is not just the much-publicized reactions, for example, of the white policemen or firemen who are passed over for promotion because of an affirmative action court order. The new racism that is potentially most damaging is located among the white elites—educated, affluent, and occupying the positions in education, business, and government from which this country is run. It currently focuses on blacks; whether it will eventually extend to include Hispanics and other minorities remains to be seen.

The new racists do not think blacks are inferior. They are typically longtime support-

ers of civil rights. But they exhibit the classic behavioral symptom of racism: they treat blacks differently from whites, because of their race. The results can be as concretely bad and unjust as any that the old racism produces. Sometimes the effect is that blacks are refused an education they otherwise could have gotten. Sometimes blacks are shunted into dead-end jobs. Always, blacks are denied the right to compete as equals.

The new racists also exhibit another characteristic of racism: they *think* about blacks differently from the way they think about whites. Their global view of blacks and civil rights is impeccable. Blacks must be enabled to achieve full equality. They are still unequal, through no fault of their own (it is the fault of racism, it is the fault of inadequate opportunity, it is the legacy of history). But the new racists' local view is that the blacks they run across professionally are not, on the average, up to the white standard. Among the new racists, lawyers have gotten used to the idea that the brief a black colleague turns in will be a little less well-rehearsed and argued than the one they would have done. Businessmen expect that a black colleague will not read a balance sheet as subtly as they do. Teachers expect black students to wind up toward the bottom of the class.

The new racists also tend to think of blacks as a commodity. The office must have a sufficient supply of blacks, who must be treated with special delicacy. The personnel problems this creates are more difficult than most because whites barely admit to themselves what's going on.

What follows is a foray into very poorly

From the *New Republic* (December 31, 1984). Reprinted
by permission of The *New Republic* © 1984, The New
Republic, Inc.

mapped territory. I will present a few numbers that explain much about how the process gets started. But the ways that the numbers get translated into behavior are even more important. The cases I present are composites constructed from my own observations and taken from firsthand accounts. All are based on real events and real people, stripped of their particularities. But the individual cases are not intended as evidence, because I cannot tell you how often they happen. They have not been the kind of thing that social scientists or journalists have wanted to count. I am writing this because so many people, both white and black, to whom I tell such stories know immediately what I am talking about. It is apparent that a problem exists. How significant is it? What follows is as much an attempt to elicit evidence as to present it.

As in so many of the crusades of the 1960s, the nation began with a good idea. It was called "affirmative action," initiated by Lyndon Johnson through Executive Order 11246 in September 1965. It was an attractive label and a natural corrective to past racism: actively seek out black candidates for jobs, college, or promotions, without treating them differently in the actual decision to hire, admit, or promote. The term originally evoked both the letter and the spirit of the order.

Then, gradually, affirmative action came to mean something quite different. In 1970 a federal court established the legitimacy of quotas as a means of implementing Johnson's executive order. In 1971 the Supreme Court ruled that an employer could not use minimum credentials as a prerequisite for hiring if the credentials acted as a "built-in headwind" for minority groups—even when there was no discriminatory intent and even when the hiring procedures were "fair in form." In 1972 the Equal Employment Opportunity Commission acquired broad, independent enforcement powers.

Thus by the early 1970s it had become generally recognized that a good-faith effort to recruit qualified blacks was not enough—especially if one's school depended on federal grants or one's business depended on federal contracts. Even for businesses and schools not directly dependent on the government, the simplest way to withstand an accusation of violating Title VII of the Civil Rights Act of 1964 was to make sure not that they had not just interviewed enough minority candidates, but that they had actually hired or admitted enough of them. Employers and admissions committees arrived at a rule of thumb: if the blacks who are available happen to be the best candidates, fine; if not, the best available black candidates will be given some sort of edge in the selection process. Sometimes the edge will be small; sometimes it will be predetermined that a black candidate is essential, and the edge will be very large.

Perhaps the first crucial place where the edge applies is in admission to college. Consider the cases of the following three students: John, William, and Carol, 17 years old and applying to college, are all equal on paper. Each has a score of 520 in the mathematics section of the Scholastic Aptitude Test, which puts them in the top third—at the 67th percentile—of all students who took the test. (Figures are based on 1983 data.)

John is white. A score of 520 gets him into the state university. Against the advice of his high school counselor, he applies to a prestigious school, Ivy U., where his application is rejected in the first cut—its average white applicant has math scores in the high 600s.

William is black, from a middle-class family who sent him to good schools. His score of 520 puts him at the 95th percentile of all blacks who took the test. William's high school counselor points out that he could probably get into Ivy U. William applies and is admitted—Ivy U. uses separate standards for admission of whites and blacks, and William is among the top blacks who applied.

Carol is black, educated at an inner city school, and her score of 520 represents an extraordinary achievement in the face of terrible schooling. An alumnus of Ivy U. who regularly looks for promising inner city candidates finds her, recruits her, and sends her off with a full scholarship to Ivy U.

When American universities embarked on policies of preferential admissions by race, they had the Carols in mind. They had good reason to be optimistic that preferential treatment would work—for many years, the best universities had been weighting the test scores of applicants from small-town public schools when they were compared against those of applicants from the top private schools, and had been giving special breaks to students from distant states to ensure geographic distribution. The differences in preparation tended to even out after the first year or so. Blacks were being brought into a long-standing and successful tradition of preferential treatment.

In the case of blacks, however, preferential treatment ran up against a large black-white gap in academic performance combined with ambitious goals for proportional representation. This gap has been the hardest for whites to confront. But though it is not necessary or even plausible to believe that such differences are innate, it is necessary to recognize openly that the differences exist. By pretending they don't, we begin the process whereby both the real differences and the racial factor are exaggerated.

The black-white gap that applies most directly to this discussion is the one that separates blacks and whites who go to college. In 1983, for example, the mean Scholastic Aptitude Test score for all blacks who took the examination was more than 100 points below the white score on both the verbal and the math sections. Statistically, it is an extremely wide gap. To convert the gap into more concrete terms, think of it this way: in 1983, the same Scholastic Aptitude Test math score that put a black at the 50th percentile of all blacks who took the test put him at the 16th percentile of all whites who took the test.

These results clearly mean we ought to be making an all-out effort to improve elementary and secondary education for blacks. But that doesn't help much now, when an academic discrepancy of this magnitude is fed into a preferential admissions process. As universities scramble to make sure they are admitting enough blacks, the results feed the new racism. Here's how it works:

In 1983, only 66 black students nationwide scored above 700 in the verbal section of the Scholastic Aptitude Test, and only 205 scored above 700 in the mathematics section. This handful of students cannot begin to meet the demand for blacks with such scores. For example, Harvard, Yale, and Princeton have in recent years been bringing an aggregate of about 270 blacks into each entering class. If the black students entering these schools had the same distribution of scores as that of the freshman class as a whole, then every black student in the nation with a verbal score in the 700s, and roughly 70 percent of the ones with a math score in the 700s, would be in their freshman classes.

The main problem is not that a few schools monopolize the very top black applicants, but that these same schools have much larger implicit quotas than they can fill with those applicants. They fill out the rest with the next students in line—students who would not have gotten into these schools if they were not black, who otherwise would have been showing up in the classrooms of the nation's less glamorous colleges and universities. But the size of the black pool does not expand appreciably at the next levels. The number of blacks scoring in the 600s on the math section in 1983, for example, was 1,531. Meanwhile, 31,704 nonblack students in 1983 scored in the 700s on the math section and 121,640 scored in the 600s. The prestige schools cannot begin to absorb these numbers of other highly qualified freshmen, and they are perforce spread widely throughout the system.

At schools that draw most broadly from the student population, such as the large state universities, the effects of this skimming produce a situation that confirms the old racists in everything they want most to believe. There are plenty of outstanding students in such student bodies (at the University of Colorado, for example, 6 percent of the freshmen in 1981 had math scores in the 700s and 28 percent had scores in the 600s), but the skimming process combined with the very small raw numbers means that almost none of them are black. What students and instructors see in their day-to-day experience in the classroom is a disproportionate number of blacks who are below the white average, relatively few blacks who are at the first rank. The image that the white student carries away is that blacks are less able than whites.

I am not exalting the SAT as an infallible measure of academic ability, or pointing to test scores to try to convince anyone that blacks are performing below the level of whites. I am simply using them to explain what instructors and students already notice, and talk about, among themselves.

They do not talk openly about such matters. One characteristic of the new racism is that whites deny in public but acknowledge in private that there are significant differences in black and white academic performance. Another is that they dismiss the importance of tests when black scores are at issue, blaming cultural bias and saying that test scores are not good predictors of college performance. At the same time, they watch anxiously over their own children's test scores.

The differences in academic performance do not disappear by the end of college. Far from narrowing, the gap separating black and white academic achievement appears to get larger. Various studies, most recently at Harvard, have found that during the 1970s blacks did worse in college (as measured by grade point average) than their test scores would have predicted. Moreover, the black-white gap in the Graduate Record Examination is larger than the gap in the Scholastic Aptitude Test. The gap between black and white freshmen is a bit less than one standard deviation (the technical measure for comparing scores). Black and white seniors who take the Graduate Record Examination reveal a gap of about one and a quarter standard deviations.

Why should the gap grow wider? Perhaps it is an illusion—for example, perhaps a disproportionate number of the best black students never take the examination. But there are also reasons for suspecting that in fact blacks get a worse education in college than whites do. Here are a few of the hypotheses that deserve full exploration.

Take the situation of William—a slightly above-average student who, because he is black, gets into a highly competitive school. William studies very hard during the first year. He nonetheless gets mediocre grades. He has a choice. He can continue to study hard and continue to get mediocre grades, and be seen by his classmates as a black who cannot do very well. Or he can explicitly refuse to engage in the academic game. He decides to opt out, and his performance gets worse as time goes on. He emerges from college with a poor education and is further behind the whites than he was as a freshman.

If large numbers of other black students at the institution are in the same situation as William, the result can be group pressure not to compete academically. (At Harvard, it is said, the current term among black students for a black who studies like a white is "incognegro.") The response is not hard to understand. If one subpopulation of students is conspicuously behind another population and is visibly identifiable, then the population that is behind must come up with a good excuse for doing poorly. "Not wanting to do better" is as good as any.

But there is another crucial reason why blacks might not close the gap with whites during college: they are not taught as well as whites are. Racist teachers impeding the progress of students? Perhaps, but most college faculty members I know tend to bend over backward to be "fair" to black students— and that may be the problem. I suggest that inferior instruction is more likely to be a manifestation of the new racism than the old.

Consider the case of Carol, with outstanding abilities but deprived of decent prior schooling: she struggles the first year, but she gets by. Her academic skills still show the aftereffects of her inferior preparation. Her instructors diplomatically point out the more flagrant mistakes, but they ignore minor lapses, and never push her in the aggressive way they push white students who have her intellectual capacity. Some of them are being patronizing (she is doing quite well, considering). Others are being prudent: teachers who criticize black students can find themselves being called racists in the classroom, in the campus newspaper, or in complaints to the administration.

The same process continues in graduate school. Indeed, because there are even fewer blacks in graduate schools than in undergraduate schools, the pressure to get black students through to the degree, no matter what, can be still greater. But apart from differences in preparation and ability that have accumulated by the end of schooling, the process whereby we foster the appearance of black inferiority continues. Let's assume that William did not give up during college. He goes to business school, where he gets his Masters degree. He signs up for interviews with the corporate recruiters. There are 100 persons in his class, and William is ranked near the middle. But of the 5 blacks in his class, he ranks first (remember that he was at the 95th percentile of blacks taking the Scholastic Aptitude Test). He is hired on his first interview by his first-choice company, which also attracted the very best of the white students. He is hired alongside 5 of the top-ranking white members of the class.

William's situation as one of 5 blacks in a class of 100 illustrates the proportions that prevail in business schools, and business schools are by no means one of the more extreme examples. The pool of black candidates for any given profession is a small fraction of the white pool. This works out to a 20-to-1 edge in business; it is even greater in most of the other professions. The result, when many hiring institutions are competing, is that a major gap between the abilities of new black and white employees in any given workplace is highly likely. Everyone needs to hire a few blacks, and the edge that "being black" confers in the hiring decision warps the sequence of hiring in such a way that a scarce resource (the blacks with a given set of qualifications) is exhausted at an artificially high rate, producing a widening gap in comparison with the remaining whites from which an employer can choose.

The more aggressively affirmative action is enforced, the greater the imbalance. In general, the first companies to hire can pursue strategies that minimize or even eliminate the difference in ability between the new black and white employees. IBM and Park Avenue law firms can do very well, just as Harvard does quite well in attracting the top black students. But the more effectively they pursue these strategies, the more quickly they strip the population of the best black candidates.

To this point I have been discussing problems that are more or less driven by realities we have very little hope of manipulating in the short term except by discarding the laws regarding preferential treatment. People do differ in acquiring abilities. Currently, acquired abilities in the white and black populations are distributed differently. Schools and firms do form a rough hierarchy when

they draw from these distributions. The results follow ineluctably. The dangers they represent are not a matter of statistical probabilities, but of day-to-day human reactions we see around us.

The damage caused by these mechanistic forces should be much less in the world of work than in the schools, however. Schools deal in a relatively narrow domain of skills, and "talent" tends to be assigned specific meanings and specific measures. Workplaces deal in highly complex sets of skills, and "talent" consists of all sorts of combinations of qualities. A successful career depends in large part upon finding jobs that elicit and develop one's strengths.

At this point the young black professional must sidestep a new series of traps laid by whites who need to be ostentatiously nonracist. Let's say that William goes to work for the XYZ Corporation, where he is assigned with another management trainee (white) to a department where much of the time is spent preparing proposals for government contracts. The white trainee is assigned a variety of scut work—proofreading drafts, calculating the costs of minor items in the bid, making photocopies, taking notes at conferences. William gets more dignified work. He is assigned portions of the draft to write (which are later rewritten by more experienced staff), sits in on planning sessions, and even goes to Washington as a highly visible part of the team to present the bid. As time goes on, the white trainee learns a great deal about how the company operates, and is seen as a go-getting young member of the team. William is perceived to be a bright enough fellow, but not much of a detail man and not really much of a self-starter.

Even if a black is hired under terms that put him on a par with his white peers, the subtler forms of differential treatment work against him. Particularly for any corporation that does business with the government, the new employee has a specific, immediate value purely because he is black. There are a variety of requirements to be met and rituals to be observed for which a black face is helpful. These have very little to do with the long-term career interests of the new employee; on the contrary, they often lead to a dead end as head of the minority-relations section of the personnel department.

Added to this is another problem that has nothing to do with the government. When the old racism was at fault (as it often still is), the newly hired black employee was excluded from the socialization process because the whites did not want him to become part of the group. When the new racism is at fault, it is because many whites are embarrassed to treat black employees as badly as they are willing to treat whites. Hence another reason that whites get on-the-job training that blacks do not: much of the early training of an employee is intertwined with menial assignments and mild hazing. Blacks who are put through these routines often see themselves as racially abused (and when a black is involved, old-racist responses may well have crept in). But even if the black is not unhappy about the process, the whites are afraid that he is, and so protect him from it. There are many variations, all having the same effect: the black is denied an apprenticeship that the white has no way of escaping. Without serving the apprenticeship, there is no way of becoming part of the team.

Carol suffers a slightly different fate. She and a white woman are hired as reporters by a major newspaper. They both work hard, but after a few months there is no denying it: neither one of them can write. The white woman is let go. Carol is kept on, because the paper cannot afford to have any fewer blacks than it already has. She is kept busy with reportorial work, even though they have to work around the writing problem. She is told not to worry—there's lots more to being a journalist than writing.

It is the mascot syndrome. A white performing at a comparable level would be fired. The black is kept on, perhaps to avoid complications with the Equal Employment Opportunity Commission (it can be very expensive to fire a black), perhaps out of a more diffuse wish not to appear discriminatory. Everybody pretends that nothing is wrong—but the black's career is at a dead end. The irony, of course, is that the white who gets fired and has to try something else has been forced into accepting a chance of making a success in some other line of work whereas the black is seduced into *not* taking the same chance.

Sometimes differential treatment takes an even more pernicious form: the conspiracy to promote a problem out of existence. As part of keeping Carol busy, the newspaper gives her some administrative responsibilities. They do not amount to much. But she has an impressive title on a prominent newspaper and she is black—a potent combination. She gets an offer from a lesser paper in another part of the country to take a senior editorial post. Her current employer is happy to be rid of an awkward situation and sends along glowing references. She gets a job that she is unequipped to handle—only this time, she is in a highly visible position, and within a few weeks the deficiencies that were covered up at the old job have become the subject of jokes all over the office. Most of the jokes are openly racist.

It is important to pause and remember who Carol is: an extremely bright young woman, not (in other circumstances) a likely object of condescension. But being bright is no protection. Whites can usually count on the market to help us recognize egregious career mistakes and to prevent us from being promoted too far from a career line that fits our strengths, and too far above our level of readiness. One of the most prevalent characteristics of white differential treatment of blacks has been to exempt blacks from these market considerations, substituting for them a market premium attached to race.

The most obvious consequence of preferential treatment is that every black professional, no matter how able, is tainted. Every black who is hired by a white-run organization that hires blacks preferentially has to put up with the knowledge that many of his coworkers believe he was hired because of his race; and he has to put up with the suspicion in his own mind that they might be right.

Whites are curiously reluctant to consider this a real problem—it is an abstraction, I am told, much less important than the problem that blacks face in getting a job in the first place. But black professionals talk about it, and they tell stories of mental breakdowns; of people who had to leave the job altogether; of long-term professional paralysis. What white would want to be put in such a situation? Of course it would be a constant humiliation to be resented by some of your coworkers and condescended to by others. Of course it would affect your perceptions of yourself and your self-confidence. No system that produces such side effects—as preferential treatment *must* do—can be defended unless it is producing some extremely important benefits.

And that brings us to the decisive question. If the alternative were no job at all, as it was for so many blacks for so long, the resentment and condescension are part of the price of getting blacks into the positions they deserve. But is that the alternative today? If the institutions of this country were left to their own devices now, to what extent would they refuse to admit, hire, and promote people because they were black? To what extent are American institutions kept from being racist by the government's intervention?

It is another one of those questions that are seldom investigated aggressively, and I have no evidence. Let me suggest a hypothesis that bears looking into: that the signal event in the struggle for black equality during the last thirty years, the one with real impact, was not the Civil Rights Act of 1964 or Executive Order 11246 or any other governmental act. It was the civil rights movement itself. It raised to a pitch of acute and lasting discomfort the racial consciousness of the generations of white Americans who are now running the country. I will not argue that the old racism is dead at any level of society. I will argue, however, that in the typical corporation or in the typical admissions office, there is an abiding desire to be not-racist. This need not be construed as brotherly love. Guilt will do as well. But the civil rights movement did its job. I suggest that the laws and the court decisions and the continuing intellectual respectability behind preferential treatment are not holding many doors open to qualified blacks that would otherwise be closed.

Suppose for a moment that I am right. Suppose that, for practical purposes, racism would not get in the way of blacks if preferential treatment were abandoned. How, in my most optimistic view, would the world look different?

There would be fewer blacks at Harvard and Yale; but they would all be fully competitive with the whites who were there. White students at the state university would encounter a cross-section of blacks who span the full range of ability, including the top levels, just as whites do. College remedial courses would no longer be disproportionately black. Whites rejected by the school they wanted would quit assuming they were kept out because a less-qualified black was admitted in their place. Blacks in big corporations would no longer be shunted off to personnel-relations positions, but would be left on the mainline tracks toward becoming comptrollers and sales managers and chief executive officers. Whites would quit assuming that black colleagues had been hired because they were black. Blacks would quit worrying that they had been hired because they were black.

Would blacks still lag behind? As a population, yes, for a time, and the nation should be mounting a far more effective program to improve elementary and secondary education for blacks than it has mounted in the last few decades. But in years past virtually every ethnic group in America has at one time or another lagged behind as a population, and has eventually caught up. In the process of catching up, the ones who breached the barriers were evidence of the success of that group. Now blacks who breach the barriers tend to be seen as evidence of the inferiority of that group.

And that is the evil of preferential treatment. It perpetuates an impression of inferiority. The system segments whites and blacks who come in contact with each other so as to maximize the likelihood that whites have the advantage in experience and ability. The system then encourages both whites and blacks to behave in ways that create self-fulfilling prophecies even when no real differences exist.

It is here that the new racism links up with the old. The old racism has always openly held that blacks are permanently less competent than whites. The new racism tacitly accepts that, in the course of overcoming the legacy of the old racism, blacks are temporarily less competent than whites. It is an extremely fine distinction. As time goes on, fine distinctions tend to be lost. Preferential treatment is providing persuasive evidence for the old racists, and we can already hear it *sotto voce:* "We gave you your chance, we let you educate them and push them into jobs they couldn't have gotten on their own and coddle them every way you could. And see: they still aren't as good as whites, and you are beginning to admit it yourselves." Sooner or later this message is going to be heard by a white elite that needs to excuse its failure to achieve black equality.

The only happy aspect of the new racism is that the corrective—to get rid of the policies encouraging preferential treatment—is so natural. Deliberate preferential treatment by race has sat as uneasily with America's equal-opportunity ideal during the post-1965 period as it did during the days of legalized segregation. We had to construct tortuous rationalizations when we permitted blacks to be kept on the back of the bus—and the rationalizations to justify sending blacks to the head of the line have been just as tortuous. Both kinds of rationalization say that sometimes it is all right to treat people of different races in different ways. For years, we have instinctively sensed this was wrong in principle but intellectualized our support for it as an expedient. I submit that our instincts were right. There is no such thing as good racial discrimination.

---

33. Race and the Schooling of Black Americans

Claude M. Steele

Claude M. Steele argues that the reason why blacks do poorly in school is racial stigma, which is "the endemic devaluation many blacks face in our society and schools." Steele points out that this devaluation equally affects well-prepared and less prepared blacks. He contends that if blacks are made less racially vulnerable in school, they can overcome even substantial obstacles, and he suggests various ways this might be done.

My former university offered minority students a faculty mentor to help shepherd them into college life. As soon as I learned of the program, I volunteered to be a mentor, but by then the school year was nearly over. Undaunted, the program's eager staff matched me with a student on their waiting list—an appealing nineteen-year-old black woman from Detroit, the same age as my daughter. We met finally in a campus lunch spot just about two weeks before the close of her freshman year. I realized quickly that I was too late. I have heard that the best way to diagnose someone's depression is to note how depressed you feel when you leave the person. When our lunch was over, I felt as gray as the snowbanks that often lined the path back to my office. My lunchtime companion was a statistic brought to life, a living example of one of the most disturbing facts of racial life in America today: the failure of so many black Americans to thrive in school. Before I could lift a hand to help this student, she had decided to do what 70 percent of all black Americans at four-year colleges do at some point in their academic careers—drop out.

I sense a certain caving-in of hope in America that problems of race can be solved. Since the sixties, when race relations held promise for the dawning of a new era, the issue has become one whose persistence causes "problem fatigue"—resignation to an unwanted condition of life.

This fatigue, I suspect, deadens us to the deepening crisis in the education of black Americans. One can enter any desegregated school in America, from grammar school to high school to graduate or professional school, and meet a persistent reality: blacks and whites in largely separate worlds. And if one asks a few questions or looks at a few records, an-

From "Race and the Schooling of Black Americans," *Atlantic Monthly* (1992). Reprinted by permission.

other reality emerges: these worlds are not equal, either in the education taking place there or in the achievement of the students who occupy them.

As a social scientist, I know that the crisis has enough possible causes to give anyone problem fatigue. But at a personal level, perhaps because of my experience as a black in American schools, or perhaps just as the hunch of a myopic psychologist, I have long suspected a particular culprit—a culprit that can undermine black achievement as effectively as a lock on a schoolhouse door. The culprit I see is *stigma*, the endemic devaluation many blacks face in our society and schools. This status is its own condition of life, different from class, money, culture. It is capable, in the words of the late sociologist Erving Goffman, of "breaking the claim" that one's human attributes have on people. I believe that its connection to school achievement among black Americans has been vastly underappreciated.

This is a troublesome argument, touching as it does on a still unhealed part of American race relations. But it leads us to a heartening principle: if blacks are made less racially vulnerable in school, they can overcome even substantial obstacles. Before the good news, though, I must at least sketch in the bad: the worsening crisis in the education of black Americans.

Despite their socioeconomic disadvantages as a group, blacks begin school with test scores that are fairly close to the test scores of whites their age. The longer they stay in school, however, the more they fall behind; for example, by the sixth grade blacks in many school districts are two full grade levels behind whites in achievement. This pattern holds true in the middle class nearly as much as in the lower class. The record does not improve in high school. In 1980, for example, 25,500 minority students, largely black and Hispanic, entered high school in Chicago. Four years later only 9,500 graduated, and of those only 2,000 could read at grade level. The situation in other cities is comparable.

Even for blacks who make it to college, the problem doesn't go away. As I noted, 70 percent of all black students who enroll in four-year colleges drop out at some point, as compared with 45 percent of whites. At any given time nearly as many black males are incarcerated as are in college in this country. And the grades of black college students average half a letter below those of their white classmates. At one prestigious university I recently studied, only 18 percent of the graduating black students had grade averages of B or above, as compared with 64 percent of the whites. This pattern is the rule, not the exception, in even the most elite American colleges. Tragically, low grades can render a degree essentially "terminal" in the sense that they preclude further schooling.

Blacks in graduate and professional schools face a similarly worsening or stagnating fate. For example, from 1977 to 1990, though the number of Ph.D.s awarded to other minorities increased and the number awarded to whites stayed roughly the same, the number awarded to American blacks dropped from 1,116 to 828. And blacks needed more time to get those degrees.

Standing ready is a familiar set of explanations. First is societal disadvantage. Black Americans have had, and continue to have, more than their share: a history of slavery, segregation, and job ceilings; continued lack of economic opportunity; poor schools; and the related problems of broken families, drug-infested communities, and social isolation. Any of these factors—alone, in combination, or through accumulated effects—can undermine school achievement. Some analysts point also to black American culture, suggesting that, hampered by disadvantage, it doesn't sustain the values and expectations critical to education, or that it fosters learning orientations ill suited to school achievement, or that it even "opposes" mainstream achievement. These are the chestnuts, and I had always thought them adequate. Then several facts emerged that just didn't seem to fit.

For one thing, the achievement deficits occur even when black students suffer no major financial disadvantage—among middle-class students on wealthy college campuses and in graduate school among black students receiving substantial financial aid. For another thing, survey after survey shows that even poor black Americans value education highly, often more than whites. Also, as I will demonstrate, several programs have improved black school achievement without addressing culturally specific learning orientations or doing anything to remedy socioeconomic disadvantage.

Neither is the problem fully explained, as one might assume, by deficits in skill or preparation which blacks might suffer because of background disadvantages. I first doubted that such a connection existed when I saw flunk-out rates for black and white students at a large, prestigious university. Two observations surprised me. First, for both blacks and whites the level of preparation, as measured by Scholastic Aptitude Test scores, didn't make much difference in who flunked out; low scorers (with combined verbal and quantitative SATs of 800) were no more likely to flunk out than high scorers (with combined SATs of 1,200 to 1,500). The second observation was racial: whereas only two percent to 11 percent of the whites flunked out, 18 percent to 33 percent of the blacks flunked out, even at the highest levels of preparation (combined SATs of 1,400). Dinesh D'Souza has argued recently that college affirmative-action programs cause failure and high dropout rates among black students by recruiting them to levels of college work for which they are inadequately prepared. That was clearly not the case at this school; black students flunked out in large numbers even with preparation well above average.

And, sadly, this proved the rule, not the exception. From elementary school to graduate school, something depresses black achievement *at every level of preparation, even the highest.* Generally, of course, the better prepared achieve better than the less prepared, and this is about as true for blacks as for whites. But given any level of school preparation (as measured by tests and earlier grades), blacks somehow achieve less in subsequent schooling than whites (that is, have poorer grades, have lower graduation rates, and take longer to graduate), no matter how strong that preparation is. Put differently, the same achievement level requires better preparation for blacks than for whites—far better: among students with a C+ average at the university I just described, the mean American College Testing Program (ACT) score for blacks was at the 98th percentile, while for whites it was at only the 34th percentile. This pattern has been documented so broadly across so many regions of the country, and by so many investigations (literally hundreds), that it is virtually a social law in this society—as well as a racial tragedy.

Clearly, something is missing from our understanding of black underachievement. Disadvantage contributes, yet blacks underachieve even when they have ample resources, strongly value education, and are prepared better than adequately in terms of knowledge and skills. Something else has to be involved. That something else could be of just modest importance—a barrier that simply adds its effect to that of other disadvantages—or it could be pivotal, such that were it corrected, other disadvantages would lose their effect.

That something else, I believe, has to do with the process of identifying with school. I offer a personal example:

I remember conducting experiments with my research adviser early in graduate school and awaiting the results with only modest interest. I struggled to meet deadlines. The research enterprise—the core of what one does as a social psychologist—just wasn't *me* yet. I was in school for other reasons—I wanted an advanced degree, I was vaguely ambitious for intellectual work, and being in graduate school made my parents proud of me. But as time passed, I began to like the work. I also began to grasp the value system that gave it meaning, and the faculty treated me as if they thought I might even be able to do it. Gradually I began to think of myself as a social psychologist. With this change in self-concept came a new accountability; my self-esteem was affected now by what I did as a social psychologist, something that hadn't been true before. This added a new motivation to my work; self-respect, not just parental respect, was on the line. I noticed changes in myself. I worked without deadlines. I bored friends with applications of arcane theory to their daily lives. I went to conventions. I lived and died over how experiments came out.

Before this transition one might have said that I was handicapped by my black working-class background and lack of motivation. After the transition the same observer might say that even though my background was working class, I had special advantages: achievement-oriented parents, a small and attentive college. But these facts alone would miss the importance of the identification process I had experienced: the change in self-definition and in the activities on which I based my self-esteem. They would also miss a simple condition necessary for me to make this identification: treatment as a valued person with good prospects.

I believe that the "something else" at the root of black achievement problems is the failure of American schooling to meet this simple condition for many of its black students. Doing well in school requires a belief that school achievement can be a promising basis of self-esteem, and that belief needs constant reaffirmation even for advantaged students. Tragically, I believe, the lives of black Americans are still haunted by a specter that threatens this belief and the identification that derives from it at every level of schooling.

The Specter of Stigma and Racial Vulnerability

I have a good friend, the mother of three, who spends considerable time in the public school classrooms of Seattle, where she lives. In her son's third-grade room, managed by a teacher of unimpeachable good will and competence, she noticed over many visits that the extraordinary art work of a small black boy named Jerome was ignored—or, more accurately perhaps, its significance was ignored. As genuine art talent has a way of doing—even in the third grade—his stood out. Yet the teacher seemed hardly to notice. Moreover, Jerome's reputation, as it was passed along from one grade to the next, included only the slightest mention of his talent. Now, of course, being ignored like this could happen to anyone—such is the overload in our public schools. But my friend couldn't help wondering how the school would have responded to this talent had the artist been one of her own, middle-class white children.

Terms like "prejudice" and "racism" often miss the full scope of racial devaluation in our society, implying as they do that racial devaluation comes primarily from the strongly prejudiced, not from "good people" like Jerome's teacher. But the prevalence of racists—deplorable though racism is—misses the full extent of Jerome's burden, perhaps even the most profound part.

He faces a devaluation that grows out of our images of society and the way those images catalogue people. The catalogue need never be taught. It is implied by all we see around us: the kinds of people revered in advertising (consider the unrelenting racial advocacy of Ralph Lauren ads) and movies (black women are rarely seen as romantic partners, for example); media discussions of whether a black can be President; invitation lists to junior high school birthday parties; school curricula; literary and musical canons. These details create an image of society in which black Americans simply do not fare well. When I was a kid, we captured it with the saying "If you're white you're right, if you're yellow you're mellow, if you're brown stick around, but if you're black get back."

In ways that require no fueling from strong prejudice or stereotypes, these images expand the devaluation of black Americans. They act as mental standards against which information about blacks is evaluated: that which fits these images we accept; that which contradicts them we suspect. Had Jerome had a reading problem, which fits these images, it might have been accepted as characteristic more readily than his extraordinary art work, which contradicts them.

These images do something else as well, something especially pernicious in the classroom. They set up a jeopardy of double devaluation for blacks, a jeopardy that does not apply to whites. Like anyone, blacks risk devaluation for a particular incompetence, such as a failed test or a flubbed pronunciation. But they further risk that such performances will confirm the broader, racial inferiority they are suspected of. Thus, from the first grade through graduate school, blacks have the extra fear that in the eyes of those around them their full humanity could fall with a poor answer or a mistaken stroke of the pen.

Moreover, because these images are conditioned in all of us, collectively held, they can spawn racial devaluation in all of us, not just in the strongly prejudiced. They can do this even in blacks themselves: a majority of black children recently tested said they like and prefer to play with white rather than black dolls—almost fifty years after Kenneth and Mamie Clark, conducting similar experiments, documented identical findings and so paved the way for *Brown v. Topeka Board of Education*. Thus Jerome's devaluation can come from a circle of people in his world far greater than the expressly prejudiced—a circle that apparently includes his teacher.

In ways often too subtle to be conscious but sometimes overt, I believe, blacks remain devalued in American schools, where, for example, a recent national survey shows that through high school they are still more than twice as likely as white children to receive corporal punishment, be suspended from school, or be labeled mentally retarded.

Tragically, such devaluation can seem inescapable. Sooner or later it forces on its victims two painful realizations. The first is that society is preconditioned to see the worst in them. Black students quickly learn that acceptance, if it is to be won at all, will be hard won. The second is that even if a black student achieves exoneration in one setting—with the teacher and fellow students in one classroom, or at one level of schooling, for example—this approval will have to be rewon in the next classroom, at the next level of schooling. Of course, individual characteristics that enhance one's value in society—skills, class status, appearance, and success—can diminish the racial devaluation one faces. And sometimes the effort to prove oneself fuels achievement. But few from any group could hope to sustain so daunting and everlasting a struggle. Thus, I am afraid, too many black students are left hopeless and deeply vulnerable in America's classrooms.

"Disidentifying" with School

I believe that in significant part the crisis in black Americans' education stems from the power of this vulnerability to undercut identification with schooling, either before it happens or after it has bloomed.

Jerome is an example of the first kind. At precisely the time when he would need to see school as a viable source of self-esteem, his teachers fail to appreciate his best work. The devalued status of his race devalues him and his work in the classroom. Unable to entrust his sense of himself to this place, he resists measuring himself against its values and goals. He languishes there, held by the law, perhaps even by his parents, but not allowing achievement to affect his view of himself. This psychic alienation—the act of not caring—makes him less vulnerable to the specter of devaluation that haunts him. Bruce Hare, an educational researcher, has documented this process among fifth-grade boys in several schools in Champaign, Illinois. He found that although the black boys had considerably lower achievement-test scores than their white classmates, their overall self-esteem was just as high. This stunning imperviousness to poor academic performance was accomplished, he found, by their deemphasizing school achievement as a basis of self-esteem and giving preference to peer-group relations—a domain in which their esteem prospects were better. They went where they had to go to feel good about themselves.

But recall the young student whose mentor I was. She had already identified with school, and wanted to be a doctor. How can racial vulnerability break so developed an achievement identity? To see, let us follow her steps onto campus: Her recruitment and admission stress her minority status perhaps more strongly than it has been stressed at any other time in her life. She is offered academic and social support services, further implying that she is "at risk" (even though, contrary to common belief, the vast majority of black college students are admitted with qualifications well above the threshold for whites). Once on campus, she enters a socially circumscribed world in which blacks—still largely separate from whites—have lower status; this is reinforced by a sidelining of minority material and interests in the curriculum and in university life. And she can sense that everywhere in this new world her skin color places her under suspicion of intellectual inferiority. All of this gives her the double vulnerability I spoke of: she risks confirming a particular incompetence, at chemistry or a foreign language, for example; but she also risks confirming the racial inferiority she is suspected of—a judgment that can feel as close at hand as a mispronounced word or an ungrammatical sentence. In reaction, usually to some modest setback, she withdraws, hiding her troubles from instructors, counselors, even other students. Quickly, I believe, a psychic defense takes over. She *disidentifies* with achievement; she changes her self-conception, her outlook and values, so that achievement is no longer so important to her self-esteem. She may continue to feel pressure to stay in school—from her parents, even from the potential advantages of a college degree. But now she is psychologically insulated from her academic life, like a disinterested visitor. Cool, unperturbed. But, like a painkilling drug, disidentification undoes her future as it relieves her vulnerability.

The prevalence of this syndrome among black college students has been documented extensively, especially on predominantly white campuses. Summarizing this work, Jacqueline Fleming, a psychologist, writes, "The fact that black students must matriculate in an atmosphere that feels hostile arouses defensive reactions that interfere with intellectual performance. . . . They display academic demotivation and think less of their abilities. They profess losses of energy." Among a sample of blacks on one predominantly white campus, Richard Nisbett and Andrew Reaves, both psychologists, and I found that attitudes related to disidentification were more strongly predictive of grades than even academic preparation (that is, SATs and high school grades).

To make matters worse, once disidentification occurs in a school, it can spread like the common cold. Blacks who identify and try to achieve embarrass the strategy by valuing the very thing the strategy denies the value of. Thus pressure to make it a group norm can evolve quickly and become fierce. Defectors are called "oreos" or "incognegroes." One's identity as an authentic black is held hostage, made incompatible with school identification. For black students, then, pressure to disidentify with school can come from the already

demoralized as well as from racial vulnerability in the setting.

Stigmatization of the sort suffered by black Americans is probably also a barrier to the school achievement of other groups in our society, such as lower-class whites, Hispanics, and women in male-dominated fields. For example, at a large midwestern university I studied, women match men's achievement in the liberal arts, where they suffer no marked stigma, but underachieve compared with men (get lower grades than men with the same ACT scores) in engineering and premedical programs, where they, like blacks across the board, are more vulnerable to suspicions of inferiority.

"Wise" Schooling

Erving Goffman, borrowing from gays of the 1950s, used the term "wise" to describe people who don't themselves bear the stigma of a given group but who are accepted by the group. These are people in whose eyes the full humanity of the stigmatized is visible, people in whose eyes they feel less vulnerable. If racial vulnerability undermines black school achievement, as I have argued, then this achievement should improve significantly if schooling is made "wise"—that is, made to see value and promise in black students and to act accordingly.

And yet, although racial vulnerability at school may undermine black achievement, so many other factors seem to contribute—from the debilitations of poverty to the alleged dysfunctions of black American culture—that one might expect "wiseness" in the classroom to be of little help. Fortunately, we have considerable evidence to the contrary. Wise schooling may indeed be the missing key to the schoolhouse door.

In the mid-seventies black students in Philip Uri Treisman's early calculus courses at the University of California at Berkeley consistently fell to the bottom of every class. To help, Treisman developed the Mathematics Workshop Program, which, in a surprisingly short time, reversed their fortunes, causing them to outperform their white and Asian counterparts. And although it is only a freshman program, black students who take it graduate at a rate comparable to the Berkeley average. Its central technique is group study of calculus concepts. But it is also wise; it does things that allay the racial vulnerabilities of these students. Stressing their potential to learn, it recruits them to a challenging "honors" workshop tied to their first calculus course. Building on their skills, the workshop gives difficult work, often beyond course content, to students with even modest preparation (some of their math SATs dip to the 300s). Working together, students soon understand that everyone knows something and nobody knows everything, and learning is speeded through shared understanding. The wisdom of these tactics is their subtext message: "You are valued in this program because of your academic potential—regardless of your current skill level. You have no more to fear than the next person, and since the work is difficult, success is a credit to your ability, and a setback is a reflection only of the challenge." The black students' double vulnerability around failure—the fear that they lack ability, and the dread that they will be devalued—is thus reduced. They can relax and achieve. The movie *Stand and Deliver* depicts Jaime Escalante using the same techniques of assurance and challenge to inspire advanced calculus performance in East Los Angeles Chicano high schoolers. And, explaining Xavier University's extraordinary success in producing black medical students, a spokesman said recently, "What doesn't work is saying, 'You need remedial work.' What does work is saying, 'You may be somewhat behind at this time but you're a talented person. We're going to help you advance at an accelerated rate.'"

The work of James Comer, a child psychiatrist at Yale, suggests that wiseness can minimize even the barriers of poverty. Over a fifteen-year period he transformed the two worst elementary schools in New Haven, Connecticut, into the third and fifth best in the city's thirty-three-school system without any change in the type of students—largely poor and black. His guiding belief is that learning requires a strongly accepting relationship between teacher and student. "After all," he

notes, "what is the difference between scribble and a letter of the alphabet to a child? The only reason the letter is meaningful, and worth learning and remembering, is because a *meaningful* other wants him or her to learn and remember it." To build these relationships Comer focuses on the overall school climate, shaping it not so much to transmit specific skills, or to achieve order per se, or even to improve achievement, as to establish a valuing and optimistic atmosphere in which a child can—to use his term—"identify" with learning. Responsibility for this lies with a team of ten to fifteen members, headed by the principal and made up of teachers, parents, school staff, and child-development experts (for example, psychologists or special-education teachers). The team develops a plan of specifics: teacher training, parent workshops, coordination of information about students. But at base I believe it tries to ensure that the students—vulnerable on so many counts—get treated essentially like middle-class students, with conviction about their value and promise. As this happens, their vulnerability diminishes, and with it the companion defenses of disidentification and misconduct. They achieve, and apparently identify, as their achievement gains persist into high school. Comer's genius, I believe, is to have recognized the importance of these vulnerabilities as barriers to *intellectual* development, and the corollary that schools hoping to educate such students must learn first how to make them feel valued.

These are not isolated successes. Comparable results were observed, for example, in a Comer-type program in Maryland's Prince Georges County, in the Stanford economist Henry Levin's accelerated-schools program, and in Harlem's Central Park East Elementary School, under the principalship of Deborah Meier. And research involving hundreds of programs and schools points to the same conclusion: black achievement is consistently linked to conditions of schooling that reduce racial vulnerability. These include relatively harmonious race relations among students; a commitment by teachers and schools to seeing minority-group members achieve; the instructional goal that students at all levels of preparation achieve; desegregation at the classroom as well as the school level; and a de-emphasis on ability tracking.

That erasing stigma improves black achievement is perhaps the strongest evidence that stigma is what depresses it in the first place. This is no happy realization. But it lets in a ray of hope: whatever other factors also depress black achievement—poverty, social isolation, poor preparation—they may be substantially overcome in a schooling atmosphere that reduces racial and other vulnerabilities, not through unrelenting niceness or ferocious regimentation but by wiseness, by *seeing* value and acting on it.

What Makes Schooling Unwise

But if wise schooling is so attainable, why is racial vulnerability the rule, not the exception, in American schooling?

One factor is the basic assimilationist offer that schools make to blacks: You can be valued and rewarded in school (and society), the schools say to these students, but you must first master the culture and ways of the American mainstream, and since that mainstream (as it is represented) is essentially white, this means you must give up many particulars of being black—styles of speech and appearance, value priorities, preferences—at least in mainstream settings. This is asking a lot. But it has been the "color-blind" offer to every immigrant and minority group in our nation's history, the core of the melting-pot ideal, and so I think it strikes most of us as fair. Yet nonimmigrant minorities like blacks and Native Americans have always been here, and thus are entitled, more than new immigrants, to participate in the defining images of the society projected in school. More important, their exclusion from these images denies their contributive history and presence in society. Thus, whereas immigrants can tilt toward assimilation in pursuit of the opportunities for which they came, American blacks may find it harder to assimilate. For them, the offer of acceptance in return for assimilation carries a primal insult: it asks them to join in something that has made them invisible.

Now, I must be clear. This is not a criticism of Western civilization. My concern is an omission of image-work. In his incisive essay "What America Would Be Like Without Blacks," Ralph Ellison showed black influence on American speech and language, the themes of our finest literature, and our most defining ideals of personal freedom and democracy. In *The World They Made Together*, Mechal Sobel described how African and European influences shaped the early American South in everything from housing design and land use to religious expression. The fact is that blacks are not outside the American mainstream but, in Ellison's words, have always been "one of its major tributaries." Yet if one relied on what is taught in America's schools, one would never know this. There blacks have fallen victim to a collective self-deception, a society's allowing itself to assimilate like mad from its constituent groups while representing itself to itself as if the assimilation had never happened, as if progress and good were almost exclusively Western and white. A prime influence of American society on world culture is the music of black Americans, shaping art forms from rock-and-roll to modern dance. Yet in American schools, from kindergarten through graduate school, these essentially black influences have barely peripheral status, are largely outside the canon. Thus it is not what is taught but what is *not* taught, what teachers and professors have never learned the value of, that reinforces a fundamental unwiseness in American schooling, and keeps black disidentification on full boil.

Deep in the psyche of American educators is a presumption that black students need academic remediation, or extra time with elemental curricula to overcome background deficits. This orientation guides many efforts to close the achievement gap—from grammar school tutoring to college academic-support programs—but I fear it can be unwise. Bruno Bettelheim and Karen Zelan's article "Why Children Don't Like to Read" comes to mind: apparently to satisfy the changing sensibilities of local school boards over this century, many books that children like were dropped from school reading lists; when children's reading scores also dropped, the approved texts were replaced by simpler books; and when reading scores dropped again, these were replaced by even simpler books, until eventually the children could hardly read at all, not because the material was too difficult but because they were bored stiff. So it goes, I suspect, with a great many of these remediation efforts. Moreover, because so many such programs target blacks primarily, they virtually equate black identity with substandard intellectual status, amplifying racial vulnerability. They can even undermine students' ability to gain confidence from their achievement, by sharing credit for their successes while implying that their failures stem from inadequacies beyond the reach of remediation.

The psychologist Lisa Brown and I recently uncovered evidence of just how damaging this orientation may be. At a large, prestigious university we found that whereas the grades of black graduates of the 1950s improved during the students' college years until they virtually matched the school average, those of blacks who graduated in the 1980s (we chose only those with above-average entry credentials, to correct for more-liberal admissions policies in that decade) worsened, ending up considerably below the school average. The 1950s graduates faced outward discrimination in everything from housing to the classroom, whereas the 1980s graduates were supported by a phalanx of help programs. Many things may contribute to this pattern. The Jackie Robinson, "pioneer" spirit of the 1950s blacks surely helped them endure. And in a pre-affirmative-action era, they may have been seen as intellectually more deserving. But one cannot ignore the distinctive fate of 1980s blacks: a remedial orientation put their abilities under suspicion, deflected their ambitions, distanced them from their successes, and painted them with their failures. Black students on today's campuses may experience far less overt prejudice than their 1950s counterparts but, ironically, may be more racially vulnerable.

The Elements of Wiseness

For too many black students school is simply the place where, more concertedly, persistently, and authoritatively than anywhere else in society, they learn how little valued they are.

Clearly, no simple recipe can fix this, but I believe we now understand the basics of a corrective approach. Schooling must focus more on reducing the vulnerabilities that block identification with achievement. I believe that four conditions, like the legs of a stool, are fundamental.

▪ If what is meaningful and important to a teacher is to become meaningful and important to a student, the student must feel valued by the teacher for his or her potential and as a person. Among the more fortunate in society, this relationship is often taken for granted. But it is precisely the relationship that race can still undermine in American society. As Comer, Escalante, and Treisman have shown, when one's students bear race and class vulnerabilities, building this relationship is the first order of business—at all levels of schooling. No tactic of instruction, no matter how ingenious, can succeed without it.

▪ The challenge and the promise of personal fulfillment, not remediation (under whatever guise), should guide the education of these students. Their present skills should be taken into account, and they should be moved along at a pace that is demanding but doesn't defeat them. Their ambitions should never be scaled down but should instead be guided to inspiring goals even when extraordinary dedication is called for. Frustration will be less crippling than alienation. Here psychology is everything: remediation defeats, challenge strengthens—affirming their potential, crediting them with their achievements, inspiring them.

But the first condition, I believe, cannot work without the second, and vice versa. A valuing teacher-student relationship goes nowhere without challenge, and challenge will always be resisted outside a valuing relationship. (Again, I must be careful about something: in criticizing remediation I am not opposing affirmative-action recruitment in the schools. The success of this policy, like that of school integration before it, depends, I believe, on the tactics of implementation. Where students are valued and challenged, they generally succeed.)

• Racial integration is a generally useful element in this design, if not a necessity. Segregation, whatever its purpose, draws out group differences and makes people feel more vulnerable when they inevitably cross group lines to compete in the larger society. This vulnerability, I fear, can override confidence gained in segregated schooling unless that confidence is based on strongly competitive skills and knowledge—something that segregated schooling, plagued by shortages of resources and access, has difficulty producing.

• The particulars of black life and culture—art, literature, political and social perspective, music—must be presented in the mainstream curriculum of American schooling, not consigned to special days, weeks, or even months of the year, or to special-topic courses and programs aimed essentially at blacks. Such channeling carries the disturbing message that the material is not of general value. And this does two terrible things: it wastes the power of this material to alter our images of the American mainstream—continuing to frustrate black identification with it—and it excuses in whites and others a huge ignorance of their own society. The true test of democracy, Ralph Ellison has said, "is . . . the inclusion—not assimilation—of the black man."

Finally, if I might be allowed a word specifically to black parents, one issue is even more immediate: our children may drop out of school before the first committee meets to accelerate the curriculum. Thus, although we, along with all Americans, must strive constantly for wise schooling, I believe we cannot wait for it. We cannot yet forget our essentially heroic challenge: to foster in our children a sense of hope and entitlement to mainstream American life and schooling, even when it devalues them.

---

34. Comparable Worth: Better from a Distance

Clifford Hackett

While admitting that some of the pay disparity between women and men in the job market is unfair, Clifford Hackett objects to using a program of comparable worth to correct that disparity. Rather than seek some "objective criteria" for evaluating the jobs people have and then attempt to readjust their salaries according to these criteria, Hackett recommends either that women seek employment in the better-paying job categories where men now predominate or that women engage in various forms of job actions, like strikes, to gain higher pay. Hackett further argues that it is not possible, over the longer term, to have pockets of comparable worth in an otherwise competitive economy without creating serious problems.

Should women be paid for jobs on the basis of what men earn in entirely different jobs? The answer would seem to be yes following the federal equal-pay-for-equal-work law of 1963 which laid the ground for improved work opportunities for women. . . .

The appeal of comparable worth is con-

Reprinted from *Commonweal* (May 31, 1985) with permission from the Commonweal Foundation.

siderable—especially from a distance. It seems to address a basic economic injustice: men earn more than women whether the measure is annual income, average hourly wages, starting salaries, or concentration in top-paying jobs. This differential also exists within jobs and professions, and persists even as women are moving into new job fields and upward in career tracks. Clearly, comparable worth defenders say, these discrepancies are unfair, perhaps illegal, and should be ended by law.

There is another broad appeal to justice related to the issue: the seeming inability of the free market economy to provide reasonable pay scales crossing vocational lines. Some of us are appalled by plumbers who get $40 for a house call; others are repelled by lawyers who earn $200 an hour. Johnny Carson and NFL football players prompt many to say, "No one can be worth that much!" An unstated comparison in our minds pits these "overpaid" exemplars against those of us who perform the hum-drum jobs which keep the economy going or who (and these are mostly women) undertake the most humane, compassionate, and bedeviling jobs in all societies: nursing, child care, and primary education—all low-paying labors. Is this pay disparity fair? Clearly not.

But the closer one looks at comparable worth, the more doubtful its real value appears. Instead of helping move women into new jobs as the equal-pay law did, comparable worth seems to give up that fight. It pleads for higher pay for women on two quite different, but equally dubious, bases: first, it argues that jobs women actually perform are undervalued and should be upgraded by law; second, it maintains that women's abilities, education, and experience are undervalued and they should get more money no matter *what* jobs they do.

Whatever happened to the premise of equal pay for women, that if women earned the same as men in a particular job category they would more surely compete for those jobs? For many reasons, women still do not always seek the same jobs men do. Comparable worth advocates conclude society must reevaluate the work women do choose. But this revaluing without regard to the job market is at the heart of the comparable worth dispute, the cause of dismay among almost everyone except those who think women would gain from a radical remaking of the economy.

Comparable worth entails assigning numbers to every important aspect of every paying job. Some incredible mechanism of government would then insure that everyone with the same numbers would get the same pay. Who assigns the numbers and weighs job skills against education, experience versus risks, and so on? A committee of personnel experts! But doesn't the open market already perform its own kind of valuation when people put their skills out for examination and competition? Yes, but unfairness results because women's work or women themselves are undervalued.

Let's be clear about what comparable worth is and isn't. It is not about the fact that football players and movie stars earn too much money, but that women make less money than men. Comparable worth is not concerned with the kinds of jobs women do, only how much they earn. Finally, comparable worth is not about job opportunity, job mobility, or job advancement, but about whether the open marketplace for jobs, with its flaws, should be abolished.

What is wrong with this new approach? First, it ignores the source of the problem: the labor pool has an oversupply of women who are available for too limited a number of entry-level jobs. Second, even admitting that economic life is not always fair, who is wise enough to evaluate continuously the varying worths which society applies to jobs? Who will decide, for instance, the worth of four years studying elementary education at a first-class university compared to four years studying engineering at a community college? Who will weigh the relative worth of a super-salesman who actually spends much of his time preparing for a few million-dollar sales a month and a senior secretary whose long hours and mental strain are usually endured under someone else's direct control?

The answer of comparable worth advocates is that these factors be judged by a committee of personnel experts who regularly analyze job content and make comparisons of skills and experience in large firms and within government. Yet such experts as Norman D. Willis, head of a personnel advisory firm which the state of Washington employed in one of the most famous comparable-worth cases, says he recoils at the possibility that his classifications, or anyone else's, should become law.

Even if large numbers of employers were persuaded to apply comparable worth, the concept could not be limited to women alone. It would have to apply to men's jobs as well. Would not church workers and writers, to take just two obvious examples of underpaid professions, have claims on higher pay based on the comparable worth of their education, skills, and contributions to society? It's not hard to see why private employers cannot take seriously the idea of actually setting pay by comparable worth rules.

Private employers pay the lowest possible wages needed to stay in competition. As long as the competition remains relatively open, workers benefit by maintaining the mobility and skills to move into better paying or more interesting jobs. The two are not always the same, but moving up usually means more demanding work. It may include not only greater skills but longer or irregular hours, and sometimes higher risks. Firefighters are paid for risking their lives in a pattern which alternates boredom with real danger. Most workers do not desire such a life, and those who do are thus able to demand higher wages and earlier retirements. Often the demands consist of entrance hurdles, like bar exams, advanced degrees and other qualifiers. Comparable worth proponents are sometimes accused of "credentialism" for seeking more pay for those women, like nurses and librarians, who also face educational hurdles for qualifications. But the pay which women, as well as men, receive is based not only on the credentials but also on market competition. If women want higher wages, they soon learn to avoid jobs with many qualified competitors, whether men or women. Why should employers pay librarians as much as electricians when the supply of the former will produce ample numbers at little more than the minimum white collar wage, while electricians are almost always scarce and, therefore, expensive?

Facing great hostility in the private sector, comparable worth has moved with some success into closed markets like state and local government where worker and union pressures combine with trendy political constituencies. Minnesota, a progressive state by most standards, recently passed laws requiring a study of job characteristics of all government jobs, state and local, and set aside money to start applying the program. In San Jose, California, a similar plan was initiated with $1.5 million for pay equity adjustments. What is

wrong, then, with these plans, especially if they have public support?

The long-term problem is that comparable worth destroys the link between work and its marketplace evaluation. In the private sector, this linkage is vital to keep a company competitive. In government, paying secretaries without regard to their cost in the local job market destroys confidence in government's ability to match the efficiency of business. Eventually, elected officials will have to account for the pay of their secretaries and their plumbers. If the secretary earns premium pay in order to match the plumber's wage, private sector workers who pay the taxes will object. It is not possible, over the longer term, to have pockets of comparable worth in an otherwise competitive economy without problems.

Take the case of San Jose. It conducted a jobs study as the result of a strike over comparable worth. The study concluded that both librarians and electricians were worth $3,000 a month. In the local, competitive economy, however, librarians could be hired for much less while electricians in the area were paid more. The city must now pay electricians more than the study said they were "worth," while librarians are being paid above-market salaries. With victories like that, comparable worth will eventually fall of its own weight.

Behind all the arguments and the tactics of the comparable worth debate is the strong conviction that discrimination against women is a major factor in the labor market. But a careful look at female employment proves inconclusive on this point. Labor economists start by identifying known differentials on jobs and pay by sex, race, age, and occupational group. They weigh factors like intermittent and part-time work, interruptions for pregnancies, and other causes for lower pay for women. But because of the complexities in the job market there are always too many "other" or "unknown" factors of such analyses to explain the residual differential of lower pay for women. Yet, this inconclusive method of reductional analysis is at present the only "proof" of discrimination against women.

A recent article in a U.S. Labor Department journal by Janice Shack-Marquez, a federal economist, says, "Most of the studies of the pay disparity between men and women have been motivated by a desire to quantify the effects of discrimination in the labor market on women's earnings." Labor market discrimination, she notes, may be only one answer, of undetermined importance, in assessing women's lower pay. The pay difference, she says, is much smaller when narrowly defined white collar jobs are compared for men and women than in broader studies. Ms. Shack-Marquez says "not enough is known" about individual earnings "to be confident that all the labor market variables in which men and women differ have been isolated."

No such caution animates the comparable worth advocates. Editors of a recent book *Comparable Worth and Wage Discrimination* . . . note that the authors, mostly women, represent a "broad spectrum" of views on the issue. Yet they agree that salary disparities between male- and female-dominated jobs "are based in large part on discrimination."

For the women's movement itself, comparable worth seems a very depressing course to take. To back the principle that women must be paid more because they are women implies a pessimism about the chances of full integration of women in the job market. If women can compete, this argument goes, they will; otherwise, they want to doctor the system so that the work they do gets more pay through government or judicial fiat.

Comparable worth advocates answer this argument in several ways, none fully cogent. First, they say, this competition of women in a men's job market will be enhanced if women in lower-paying jobs get the same pay as comparable men. Employers would then choose workers by merit, not gender. Second, the predominance of women in some low-paying jobs—retail clerking, secretarial and clerical work, child care and domestic work—has patterned so many women for so long that many are now too old to be retrained. Third, pay equity advocates say, these jobs are undervalued simply because women hold them. Why should women, who like to nurse or teach school, change jobs just to earn as much as men with comparable skills, education, and experience? Society is, in fact, subtly undervaluing jobs only because women perform

them. And that, advocates say, is discrimination.

Correcting this discrimination will not bankrupt the country, proponents of comparable worth say, pointing to several cases where the system has been applied to government and private organizations. But these instances provide thin gruel to nourish the cause. While the only large-scale case, involving the state of Washington, is still in the courts, state taxpayers may have to pay over $1 billion if the suit prevails. The Washington state legislature's study of state jobs, which used the Willis scale, concluded that women's work was underpaid. Yet the governor's request for funds to implement the study was rejected in a budget crisis. The federal judge who heard the case decided that the state acted in bad faith by commissioning a study whose findings of pay discrimination were then not implemented. The state is certain to appeal the decision to the Supreme Court.

Even if the Washington state decision is sustained and the state government gets a huge bill for back wages, the case's impact on comparable worth remains unclear. Failure to pay, not the principles of comparable worth, are at issue here. Federal courts have, in several other cases, specifically excluded comparable worth from decisions about pay differences between men and women.

In a major decision in 1977 (*Christensen v. Iowa*), the Supreme Court cited the attempt to use the Civil Rights Act of 1964 as a basis for comparable worth. It rejected this approach saying: "We find nothing in the text and history of Title VII (of the Act) suggesting that Congress intended to abrogate the laws of supply and demand or other economic principles that determine wage rates for different kinds of work." Even in the 1981 *Gunther* case, cited most often by women as holding the door open for comparable worth actions, the Supreme Court said that the women prison guards' claim of lower pay because they were women "is not based on the controversial concept of 'comparable worth.'"

In order to make progress and to avoid another stalemate like the ERA, comparable worth advocates will have to either change the law or convince judges that existing laws require comparable worth interpretations. Neither the mood of the present Supreme Court, nor the explicit scorn of the Reagan administration is promising in this regard.

Over a dozen states have passed laws which refer to comparable worth, pay equity, or similar goals in their civil service systems, but most of these laws are too new or too vague to have established comparable worth up to now. Minnesota's 1982–83 laws on the subject were backed with an initial appropriation of $27 million to adjust state salaries. Until further studies are done, no one knows what the total cost to the state and its local governments, also covered, will be.

Comparable worth is like the parable of the golden egg. If its advocates insist on using political pressures to pay women in government more than wages in the private sector, cities and states will eventually react to increased costs by contracting much of "women's work" to the private sector.

In conclusion, if comparable worth seems such a mistaken solution for misconceived problems, here are several principles with which to insure that maximum benefits accrue to women in their search for true pay and job equity:

Not every difference between men and women in the job market comes from malevolent causes. Even if we reach the most perfect system of job access and pay for women, there may still be important differences in both the jobs they hold and what they earn. The values that women share may always be different from those of men. Anticipation of motherhood, its arrival, and its consequences will always affect women in the job market. Women's values, and the jobs they embody, are important for society and for the women who perform them, even when the pay is not high.

Economic rewards are not the only measure of job value for women or men. Many male-dominated jobs also pay less than others with lower investments of skills, education, and experience. The churches, the universities, art, and the government often pay less than business and industry. But pay, for these lesser-paid workers, is fortunately not the only consideration in their jobs.

Choosing motherhood may not be fully compatible

with other career choices. This is such an old truth that it may *have* to be completely forgotten so we can learn it again. Yet many women know this before motherhood or shortly after. This fact of maternal life is not, in itself, unfair or a matter for the courts to handle. But motherhood should not bar the maximum participation a woman wants in the job marketplace. A genuine problem, worth some of the attention given to comparable worth, is how mothers of all ages can gain and hold such participation without sacrificing, jeopardizing, or postponing motherhood.

Comparable worth may have some benefits as an ideal if it leads toward better job integration. Even if most plumbers will always be men and most day-care workers women, society benefits when rigid job segregation by sex is softened. First, most women do not want to be shunted away, by gender, from certain jobs even if they choose other work. Second, men and women complement each other in social values, temperaments, and sensitivities. This relation may help and almost certainly does not hinder any workplace, even if not all jobs are interchangeable.

Women should consider more selective and specific approaches to better pay and job integration. In Colorado, nurses sought better wages through comparable worth action but lost in court. When they went on strike, however, they won. Job actions—whether in a single job, in one business or industry at a time, or nationwide—will probably command more attention and get more results in the long term than the murky concepts of comparable worth.

There will be no revolution in the workplace no matter what the strategy. There have been important changes this century in women's wages which have risen faster than men's since 1900, according to a recent Rand Corporation study. The sixty cents a woman earns today, on average, to a man's dollar, will rise to seventy-four cents by the end of the next decade. But the competing interests of blacks, Hispanics, and others who want to change the job market according to their legitimate grievances will prevent a clear field for women. Black women, for example, have now closed the wage gap with white women. Black men, however, hold many of the male-dominated blue collar jobs which comparable worth proponents cite as examples of unfairly high pay. Further, the private sector has so far largely ignored the comparable worth approach as a frothy concoction of no import. If state or court actions move toward serious implementation of the concept, a fierce reaction to the perceived threat against the free market will come. This assault against comparable worth could make the ERA debacle look mild by comparison. To avoid this course, more measured, more confident, and more reasonable goals are needed for women.

One unspoken premise of the comparable worth fight is resentment against the male domination of the political, social, and economic life of our society. However, the appropriate response to this male dominance is a realistic demand for fairness to women in the job market, not a casually conceived and marginally tenable idea like comparable worth.

35. The Comparable Worth Debate

Elaine Sorensen

In defense of comparable worth, Elaine Sorensen argues that the free market does not eliminate discrimination. Historically, it took new laws and court rulings to eliminate some of the most blatant discriminatory practices that prevailed in the labor market. She further argues that less than half of the sex- and race-based earning disparity between women and minorities and white men can be accounted for by differences in productivity-related characteristics such as the level of education or the willingness to choose a lower-paying job if it provides more flexible working hours. Responding to the objection that different jobs cannot be compared, Sorensen argues that all that comparable worth requires is the same job evaluation procedures currently used by management for different purposes.

Introduction

The U.S. Civil Rights Commission Chairman, Clarence Pendleton, denounced the concept as "the looniest idea since 'Looney Tunes.'" President Reagan called it "a cockamamie idea . . . [that] would destroy the basis of free enterprise." These men were referring to a strategy for rectifying economic inequities confronting women and minorities known as equal pay for comparable worth. Despite this opposition, comparable worth has gained considerable momentum during the past few years. Nearly every state government has taken initiative on

From *The Imperiled Economy Book II*, edited by Robert Cherry. Reprinted by permission.

this issue and at least fifteen have increased salaries for workers in occupations that have an over-representation of women or minorities. Numerous labor unions, feminist organizations, and the Democratic Party have also endorsed the idea.

As popular support for comparable worth policies has grown, so has its opposition. Conservative opponents of comparable worth argue that a comparable worth policy would undermine the "free market" system of wage determination, a system which they believe is above reproach both logically and legally. On the other hand, some progressive persons argue against a comparable worth strategy. They contend that it is divisive, pitting blue-collar and minority workers against their female co-workers. Furthermore, it is argued that comparable worth proposals do not reduce inequality and may even exacerbate it by increasing the salaries of skilled workers more than unskilled workers.

This essay will first introduce the concept of comparable worth. It will then survey the general objections to the concept and analyze their shortcomings.

Comparable Worth and Wage Discrimination

Comparable worth policies seek to counteract the persistent wage inequities that women and minorities experience in the labor market. White women's earnings relative to white men's earnings have remained disturbingly rigid during the past thirty years. In 1986, white women employed full time still earned $.63 for every dollar that white men earned, the same ratio as in 1956 (U.S. Census, 1987). Although the earnings gap has improved slightly during this period for people of color, the earnings gap is greater for minority women than it is for white women (black women earn $.57 and Hispanic women earn $.53) and minority men still earn substantially less than white men (black men earn $.71 and Hispanic men earn $.65). Earnings increase with education for all workers, but women and minorities earn less than white men at every level of education. For example, women with four years of college education earn less on average than men who have not completed high school (black men with four years of college education earn about the same as white men who have completed high school).

Severe occupational segregation by sex and race also characterize the U.S. labor force. Nearly one out of three white women and one out of four women of color are employed as clerical workers. Another one-fourth of the white female work force is employed in service work and two professional classifications: teaching and nursing. Minority women are also heavily concentrated in service work (21 percent) and many work as machine operators (14 percent). Men of color are highly concentrated in different occupations than

women and white men. For example, two out of three black men are employed in blue-collar and service work, and only one out of six are employed as managers or professionals. Within blue-collar work, 70 percent work as laborers and operators. One-fourth of white men, on the other hand, are employed as managers and professionals, and another one-fifth are employed as craft workers.

Proponents of comparable worth policies argue that extensive occupational segregation in the labor force contributes to the sex- and race-based earnings disparities that persist in the U.S. labor market. It allows firms to pay lower wages to workers in jobs with an over-representation of women and minorities. These jobs become identified as "women's work" or "minority men's work," and simply because of these labels firms pay workers less than they would if these jobs employed white men. For example, in the state of Washington a comparable worth study found that the job of licensed practical nurse was held primarily by women and that the job of correctional officer was dominated by men. It also found that these two jobs were equivalent with respect to the amount of knowledge, mental demands, accountability, and working conditions associated with the two jobs. However, in 1983, the state of Washington paid an entry level licensed practical nurse $985 per month while paying the correctional officer $1358 per month.

Proponents of comparable worth posit that if a single employer pays jobs with an over-representation of women or minorities less than jobs with an over-representation of white men, one that cannot be supported by corresponding differences in the requirements of the job, then the employer is guilty of sex- and race-based wage discrimination. The purpose of a comparable worth policy is to eliminate this type of discrimination. After it is implemented, wages for jobs with an over-representation of women or minorities will reflect job responsibilities, unencumbered by sexually or racially biased notions. Thus, in the state of Washington a comparable worth strategy would increase the salary of the licensed practical nurse to that received by comparable male dominated occupations such as that of correctional officer.

The Comparable Worth Debate

Conservative Arguments

Conservative opponents of comparable worth espouse three arguments against comparable worth policies all of which assume that the labor market is free and competitive: discrimination is not a major problem in today's labor market; the sex- and race-based earnings disparities are due to productivity differences between women (minorities) and men (whites); and jobs do not have intrinsic worth to a firm, their value is determined by supply and demand.

1. The Free Market Eliminates Discrimination

Conservative opponents of comparable worth argue that discrimination is not a principal factor contributing to the sex- and race-based earnings gaps. According to this view, a free market provides sufficient incentive to eliminate discrimination. In such a market, employers can not afford to discriminate against minority and female workers. If they did, an incentive would exist for some employer to hire them since discrimination would depress their market wage compared to that received by white men. With this cost advantage, the non-discriminating employer would outperform those who discriminate. Eventually, competitive forces would compel discriminating employers to discontinue such practices or lose their business, thus eliminating discrimination from the market.

Although in theory the free market ensures that employers do not discriminate, in fact, until the passage of the anti-discrimination laws of the early 1960s, the U.S. labor market was characterized by blatant discriminatory practices and institutions. Employers could pay women less than men for exactly the same work and they could refuse to hire blacks and other minorities, simply because of their race. These types of blatant discriminatory practices did not wither away under competitive pressures. Instead, legal prohibition was necessary

to eliminate them. Thus, federal policies and court rulings have clearly reduced the discriminatory practices that are deeply imbedded in American labor markets. Unfortunately, however, these changes have not eliminated all types of discrimination. Proponents of comparable worth have identified yet another pervasive discriminatory pattern that causes workers in female or minority dominated jobs to receive less than they would if these jobs were dominated by white men. This form of discrimination deserves judicial and legislative attention, just as other forms have received.

2. Pay Gaps Are Caused by Productivity and Labor Supply Differences

Conservative opponents of comparable worth argue that women and minorities have different supply characteristics than white men and these differences explain their low relative earnings. They claim that women expect to drop out of the labor force while raising their children, and thus choose low paying occupations that do not impose severe wage penalties for discontinuous labor market behavior. They also select occupations that are close to home, have convenient hours, and do not require overtime, to accommodate their family responsibilities. These choices limit women's labor supply and reduce their earnings potential. Conservative opponents of comparable worth also claim that minorities receive less education and poorer quality education, on average, than whites. This limits the types of occupations available to minorities and thus reduces their relative earnings.

Empirical research, however, has repeatedly shown that less than half of the sex- and race-based earnings disparities can be accounted for by differences in productivity-related characteristics between women and minorities and white men. In other words, differences in labor force attachment between women and men and differences in education between minorities and whites do not explain most of the earnings gaps. Consequently, existing research shows that even if women and minority men had identical labor market behavior as white men, they would still earn considerably less than white men. Comparable worth proposals attempt to eliminate that portion of the pay gaps which is unaccounted for by productivity-related differences, and which would remain even if women and minority men had identical labor force behavior to white men's.

In addition, an explanation of the earnings gap between women (minorities) and men (whites) that focuses upon productivity differences ignores the dramatic changes that have taken place in the productivity characteristics of women and minorities over the past thirty years. Between 1955 and 1977, the work life expectancy of a 20-year-old woman increased from 14.5 to 26 years. In contrast, the work life expectancy of a 20-year-old man drifted down from 41 to 37 years (Smith 1982). Thus, the number of years that women work in the labor force has clearly increased relative to men. Women are also marrying later, having fewer children and heading more of their own households than 30 years ago. All of these changes suggest an increased attachment to the labor force among women and yet their relative earnings have not improved.

The educational attainment of black men has also dramatically increased during the past 25 years. In 1962, white men in the civilian labor force had completed an average of 12.1 years of education; black men had completed an average of 9.0 years. By 1980, this education gap had almost disappeared: white men's average educational attainment increased to 12.7 years and black men's increased to 12.3 years (U.S. Department of Labor, 1982). Yet, black men working full-time still earn 71 percent as much as white men. Thus, the productivity characteristics of women and minorities have changed, yet their pay persistently lags behind that of white men.

3. Different Jobs Can Not Be Compared

Opponents of comparable worth have expressed concern over the comparisons of dissimilar jobs that are made by comparable worth proposals. Can the job of nurse be compared to that of a tree trimmer to assess the relative worth of these jobs? They contend that job evaluations, the method used by comparable worth proposals to compare different jobs, are not an objective measure of a job's worth; the only objective measure is the salary that an employer must pay to attract workers to the job. Such a salary is determined by competitive market forces of supply and demand, forces external to an individual firm.

Advocates of comparable worth argue that wages are not exclusively determined by market forces; other factors, such as discrimination, also play a role. Furthermore, market forces themselves reflect and reproduce discrimination. This allows employers to pay workers in jobs with an over-representation of women and minorities less than if those jobs were held by white men. Advocates of comparable worth need a technique to measure the extent to which salaries are discriminatorily depressed in jobs with an over-representation of women and minorities.

Most comparable worth proposals have used an a priori factor-point job evaluation plan to assess jobs, the most commonly used plan in the United States. It consists of a set of factors and weights which are expected to reflect the requirements of a job. The factors generally fall into four broad categories: skill, effort, responsibility, and working conditions. Weights are applied to each factor and indicate their relative importance. Once the weights and factors are chosen, a basic set of procedures are followed to evaluate jobs. First, questionnaires specifically designed for the factor-point plan are completed. Based upon this information, jobs are evaluated on each factor. Jobs are assigned a level of points that is commensurate with the amount of each factor required to perform the job. These factor scores are summed for each job to produce a total score, which are used to establish an internal ranking of jobs according to their worth to the firm.

Comparable worth proposals do not alter the basic procedures of a job evaluation plan; they use the same techniques that management has traditionally used to evaluate jobs. The differences between comparable worth proposals and management's traditional practices do not take place during the evaluation of jobs, but during the determination of wages.

Management uses job evaluation plans as an instrument in wage determination, but they typically limit its use to comparisons within so-called job families. Job families consist of jobs that have similar skill requirements or are performed in the same division of the firm. Wages from the external labor market are pegged to a few occupations within each job family. Management determines the occupational salaries of other jobs within each job family by comparing job evaluation scores to those of the few occupations with external wages. For example, suppose the prevailing wage for a clerk/typist is $1000 per month, then all jobs within the clerk/typist job family would be adjusted around that salary according to their job evaluation score in comparison to that of the clerk/typist. Thus, the prevailing wages of other occupations outside of the clerk/typist job family, such as janitor or truck driver, would not enter into the determination of wages for this job family.

Comparable worth studies use the results of a job evaluation to examine a firm's existing salary practices for all jobs, regardless of their job family. Rather than using external wages for certain occupations, they use the salaries received by jobs dominated by white men as their set of comparison occupations. Salary comparisons are made between jobs with an over-representation of women or minorities and jobs that are dominated by white men. If the former salaries are less than the latter and the jobs are deemed comparable according to the criteria established by the job evaluation plan, then a comparable worth policy would increase the salaries of jobs with an over-representation of women or minorities.

Opponents of comparable worth argue that job evaluations can not be used in this way. Yet, numerous jurisdictions have already conducted such studies. Unfortunately, opponents of comparable worth tend to think that job evaluations are only capable of fulfilling their original purpose, which was to justify and perpetuate the existing wage structure. Clearly, comparable worth proposals alter the existing wage structure, by eliminating sex- and race-based wage discrimination. However, they do so by applying the basic procedures used by management to evaluate jobs.

Progressive Arguments

The progressive concerns regarding comparable worth legislation have focused upon its possible divisive nature and its reinforcement of existing salary practices.

Comparable Worth Would Lower Male Wages

Some have feared that comparable worth will benefit women at the expense of men, hindering attempts to unify male and female workers. Yet, in no instance has comparable worth been introduced in a form which has resulted in wage cuts for male workers. It is generally accepted by the courts and Congress that the elimination of wage discrimination is best accomplished by increasing the wages of those discriminated against, not by decreasing the wages of those unaffected by discrimination. Federal legislation mandating a comparable worth study of federal pay practices (H.R. 5680-Oakar, 1984) specifically prohibited reducing anyone's pay because of this legislation. Similar prohibitions have been included in many state and local comparable worth proposals as well.

Employers may suggest lowering male salaries in particular jobs considered "over-valued" or they may suggest lower across-the-board increases for all workers in order to pay for higher wages in female dominated jobs. Advocates of comparable worth have consistently fought against these employer suggestions. For example, in May 1984, Donald Devine, then director of the federal Office of Personnel Management, held a private meeting of union officials representing federal employees and attempted to convince them that the wages of blue-collar workers would be lowered if a comparable worth bill before the House was enacted. The union officials were not convinced by Devine's arguments. They later testified before the Subcommittee on Compensation and Employee Benefits that unions were long familiar with employer "divide and conquer" tactics.

A policy of equal pay for comparable worth can be seen as a threat to those who are trying to maintain their *relative* wage or it can be seen as an egalitarian policy, one that can increase the likelihood that all workers receive a fair wage. As an egalitarian policy comparable worth can unite workers in their struggle with employers for decent wages for all workers. Advocates of comparable worth will most likely continue to fight against suggestions of lowering male wages to pay for comparable worth since this approach could undermine a general consensus for the policy.

Comparable Worth Will Decrease the Earnings of Minority Males

Some progressive and conservative opponents of comparable worth have argued that its implementation will decrease the earnings of men of color. This position was stated quite forcefully by Michael J. Horowitz, counsel to the director of the Office of Management and Budget, when he remarked that: "There is nothing that the Reagan Administration has done that holds as much long-term threat to the black community as comparable worth. The maintenance man will be paid less so the librarian can be paid more" (*New York Times*, 22 January 1984).

This position ignores the wage discrimination that minority males experience due to race- and sex-based occupational segregation. Many public sector comparable worth studies have shown that a disproportionate number of minority males work in female or minority dominated jobs. Furthermore, they earn less than workers in comparable white male dominated jobs (NCPE, 1987). A number of states, including New Jersey, New York, and Wisconsin, have already begun increasing the salaries of workers who are employed in minority or female dominated jobs. Clearly, additional research is needed in this area, but it would be rather surprising to find that occupational segregation by race does not contribute to the earnings disparities that minority workers face.

Comparable Worth Justifies Existing Wage Inequities

It is sometimes argued that comparable worth does not sufficiently challenge the present hierarchical wage structure. According to one opponent of comparable worth, "advocates of comparable worth don't want to achieve equality" (Cowley, 1984, 57). Instead, comparable worth will "enshrine" the existing earnings inequalities "by giving them the force of law" (Cowley, 1984, 57). Similar sentiments were echoed by a more sympathetic author when she stated that comparable worth "can have only a modest effect on the overall degree of inequality because it does not attack all forms of inequality" (Feldberg, 1984, 323). She later added that comparable worth "does not directly challenge the concept of a [wage] hierarchy; in fact, its insistence that jobs be evaluated implies a hierarchy" (Feldberg, 1984, 323).

Comparable worth proposals attack the existing hierarchical wage structure by arguing that it reflects wage discrimination against workers in female and minority dominated jobs and that this source of wage inequality should be eliminated. They do, however, accept a wage hierarchy as long as that hierarchy reflects job requirements and not the predominant sex or race of the worker in the occupation. In fact, job requirements are the criteria used to measure the extent to which female or minority dominated jobs are underpaid relative to comparable white male dominated jobs.

Some analysts argue that job requirements are the traditional criteria used by firms to justify wage inequity and thus its use by comparable worth proposals reinforces existing wage inequities. However, one of the most important findings of comparable worth studies is that employers have *not* applied this criteria uniformly to all occupations. Instead, they have applied a different set of standards for occupations with a disproportionate number of women or minorities than that used for occupations with a disproportionate number of white men.

Using job requirements to determine the extent of wage inequities does not imply that so-called unskilled female or minority dominated jobs will be unaffected by comparable worth proposals, in fact, quite the contrary. The largest disparities between current salaries and proposed comparable worth salaries typically occur among the lowest paid and supposedly unskilled female dominated occupations. For example, the occupational categories with the largest comparable worth pay disparities in the state of Washington were: telephone operator, laundry worker, nurse's assistant, general clerk, and secretary, three of which were the least skilled female dominated occupations examined.

It is true that comparable worth proposals would not cure all forms of inequality in U.S. society. However, they would reduce a serious source of earnings inequality in the United States, namely sex- and race-based wage discrimination against women and minorities. It would accomplish this by increasing the salaries of jobs with an over-representation of women or minorities, all of which tend to earn *less* than the average white male. For example, the highest paid female dominated job in the United States is the job of registered nurse and it pays less than the average salary received by white men. Thus, if the ideal is greater income equality, a comparable worth policy would certainly move the United States towards that goal.

Conclusion

The demand for comparable worth has emerged at an opportune moment. Many people have become increasingly aware of a disturbing trend towards greater inequality in the distribution of income in the United States. It is argued that the tax and budgets cuts under the Reagan Administration, as well as the relative decline of the smoke stack industries and the absolute rise in the service sector, have contributed to this trend. An increase in the poverty rate has also been noted. By 1986,

13.6 percent of the population lived in poverty, up from 11.4 percent in 1978. Women represent two-thirds of the poor adult population, while half of the families living in poverty are headed by women, the fastest growing type in the country. A comparable worth policy would increase the salaries of low paying traditionally female and minority dominated occupations within the service sector. Thus a comparable worth policy could alleviate the unfortunate trend toward greater income inequality.

References

Cowley, Geoffrey. 1984. Comparable Worth: Another Terrible Idea. *Washington Monthly* 15:52–57.

Feldberg, Roslyn L. 1984. Comparable Worth: Toward Theory and Practice in the United States. *Signs: Journal of Women in Culture and Society* 10(2):311–328.

National Committee on Pay Equity (NCPE). 1987. *Pay Equity: An Issue of Race, Ethnicity, and Sex.* Washington, D.C.: NCPE.

U.S. Bureau of the Census. 1987. Money Income and Poverty Status of Families and Persons in the United States: 1986. *Current Population Reports.* P-60 Series, No. 157. Washington, D.C.: U.S. Government Printing Office.

U.S. Department of Labor. 1982. *Employment and Training Report of the President.* Washington, D.C.: U.S. Government Printing Office.

36. *City of Richmond v. Croson*

Supreme Court of the United States

The issue before the Supreme Court is whether the City of Richmond's plan requiring prime contractors awarded city construction contracts to subcontract at least 30 percent of the dollar amount of each contract to one or more "Minority Business Enterprises" was in violation of the equal protection clause of the Fourteenth Amendment. Justice O'Connor in delivering the opinion of the Court argued that the City of Richmond's plan was not supported by the type of evidence of past discrimination in the city's construction industry that would authorize a race-based relief under the equal protection clause of the Fourteenth Amendment. Justice Marshall, with Justices Brennan and Blackmun concurring, argued that the national evidence of discrimination against minority contractors and the local evidence that only .67 percent of the dollar value of local construction contracts went to minority contractors, together with the Supreme Court's own *Fullilove v. Klutznick* decision, which allowed a 10 percent set-aside of federal contracts for minority contractors, justified the city's adoption of the plan.

Justice *O'Connor* announced the judgment of the Court. . . .

On April 11, 1983, the Richmond City Council adopted the Minority Business Utilization Plan (the Plan). The Plan required prime contractors to whom the city awarded construction contracts to subcontract at least 30% of the dollar amount of the contract to one or more Minority Business Enterprises (MBEs). . . . The 30% set-aside did not apply to city contracts awarded to minority-owned prime contractors. . . .

The Plan defined an MBE as "[a] business at least fifty-one (51) percent of which is owned and controlled . . . by minority group members." . . . "Minority group members" were defined as "[c]itizens of the United States who are Blacks, Spanish-speaking, Orientals, Indians, Eskimos, or Aleuts." . . . There was no geographic limit to the Plan; an otherwise qualified MBE from anywhere in the United States could avail itself of the 30% set-aside. The Plan declared that it was "remedial" in nature, and enacted "for the purpose of promoting wider participation by minority business enterprises in the construction of public projects." . . . The Plan expired on June 30,

1988, and was in effect for approximately five years. . . .

The Plan authorized the Director of the Department of General Services to promulgate rules which "shall allow waivers in those individual situations where a contractor can prove to the satisfaction of the director that the requirements herein cannot be achieved." . . . To this end, the Director promulgated Contract Clauses, Minority Business Utilization Plan. . . . Section D of these rules provided:

> No partial or complete waiver of the foregoing [30% set-aside] requirement shall be granted by the city other than in exceptional circumstances. To justify a waiver, it must be shown that every feasible attempt has been made to comply, and it must be demonstrated that sufficient, relevant, qualified Minority Business Enterprises . . . are unavailable or unwilling to participate in the contract to enable meeting the 30% MBE goal. . . .

The Director also promulgated "purchasing procedures" to be followed in the letting of city contracts in accordance with the Plan. . . . Bidders on city construction contracts were provided with a "Minority Business Utilization Plan Commitment Form." . . . Within 10 days of the opening of the bids, the lowest otherwise responsive bidder was required to submit a commitment form naming the MBEs to be used on the contract and the percentage of the total contract price awarded to the minority firm or firms. The prime contractor's commitment form or request for a waiver of the 30% set-aside was then referred to the city Human Relations Commission (HRC). The HRC verified that the MBEs named in the commitment form were in fact minority owned, and then either approved the commitment form or made a recommendation regarding the prime contractor's request for a partial or complete waiver of the 30% set-aside. . . . The Director of General Services made the final determination on compliance with the set-aside provisions or the propriety of granting a waiver. . . . His discretion in this regard appears to have been plenary. There was no direct administrative appeal from the Director's denial of a waiver. Once a contract had been awarded to another firm a bidder denied an award for failure to comply with the MBE requirements had a general right of protest under Richmond procurement policies. . . .

The Plan was adopted by the Richmond City Council after a public hearing. . . . Seven members of the public spoke to the merits of the ordinance: five were in opposition, two in favor. Proponents of the set-aside provision relied on a study which indicated that, while the general population of Richmond was 50% black, only .67% of the city's prime construction contracts had been awarded to minority businesses in the 5-year period from 1978 to 1983. It was also established that a variety of contractors' associations, whose representatives appeared in opposition to the ordinance, had virtually no minority businesses within their membership. . . . The city's legal counsel indicated his view that the ordinance was constitutional under this Court's decision in *Fullilove v. Klutznick,* . . . Councilperson Marsh, a proponent of the ordinance, made the following statement:

There is some information, however, that I want to make sure that we put in the record. I have been practicing law in this community since 1961, and I am familiar with the practices in the construction industry in this area, in the State, and around the nation. And I can say without equivocation, that the general conduct of the construction industry in this area, and the State, and around the nation, is one in which race discrimination and exclusion on the basis of race is widespread. . . .

There was no direct evidence of race discrimination on the part of the city in letting contracts or any evidence that the city's prime contractors had discriminated against minority-owned subcontractors. . . . ("[The public witnesses] indicated that the minority contractors were just not available. There wasn't a one that gave any indication that a minority contractor would not have an opportunity, if he were available").

Opponents of the ordinance questioned both its wisdom and its legality. They argued that a disparity between minorities in the population of Richmond and the number of prime contracts awarded to MBEs had little probative value in establishing discrimination in the construction industry. . . . Representatives of various contractors' associations questioned whether there were enough MBEs in the Richmond area to satisfy the 30% set-aside requirement. . . . Mr. Murphy noted that only 4.7% of all construction firms in the United States were minority owned and that 41% of these were located in California, New York, Illinois, Florida, and Hawaii. He predicted that the ordinance would thus lead to a windfall for the few minority firms in Richmond. . . . Councilperson Gillespie indicated his concern that many local labor jobs, held by both blacks and whites, would be lost because the ordinance put no geographic limit on the MBEs eligible for the 30% set-aside. . . . Some of the representatives of the local contractors' organizations indicated that they did not discriminate on the basis of race and were in fact actively seeking out minority members. . . . ("The company I work for belonged to all these [contractors'] organizations. Nobody that I know of, black, Puerto Rican or any minority, has ever been turned down. They're actually sought after to join, to become part of us"). . . .

Councilperson Gillespie expressed his concern about the legality of the Plan, and asked that a vote be delayed pending consultation with outside counsel. His suggestion was rejected, and the ordinance was enacted by a vote of six to two, with councilmember Gillespie abstaining. . . .

We think it clear that the factual predicate offered in support of the Richmond Plan suffers from the same two defects identified as fatal in *Wygant*. The District Court found the city council's "findings sufficient to ensure that, in adopting the Plan, it was remedying the present effects of past discrimination in the *construction industry*." . . . Like the "role model" theory employed in *Wygant*, a generalized assertion that there has been past discrimination in an entire industry provides no guidance for a legislative body to determine the precise scope of the injury it seeks to remedy. It "has no logical stopping point." . . . "Relief" for such an ill-defined wrong could extend until the percentage of public contracts awarded to MBEs in Richmond mirrored the percentage of minorities in the population as a whole.

Appellant argues that it is attempting to remedy various forms of past discrimination that are alleged to be responsible for the small number of minority businesses in the local contracting industry. Among these the city cites the exclusion of blacks from skilled construction trade unions and training programs. This past discrimination has prevented them "from following the traditional path from laborer to entrepreneur." . . . The city also lists a host of nonracial factors which would seem to face a member of any racial group attempting to establish a new business enterprise, such as deficiencies in working capital, inability to meet bonding requirements, unfamiliarity with bidding procedures, and disability caused by an inadequate track record. . . .

While there is no doubt that the sorry history of both private and public discrimination in this country has contributed to a lack of opportunities for black entrepreneurs, this observation, standing alone, cannot justify a rigid racial quota in the awarding of public contracts in Richmond, Virginia. Like the claim that discrimination in primary and secondary schooling justifies a rigid racial preference in medical school admissions, an amorphous claim that there has been past discrimination in a particular industry cannot justify the use of an unyielding racial quota.

It is sheer speculation how many minority firms there would be in Richmond absent past societal discrimination, just as it was sheer speculation how many minority medical students would have been admitted to the medical school at Davis absent past discrimination in educational opportunities. Defining these sorts of injuries as "identified discrimination" would give local governments license to create a patchwork of racial preferences based on statistical generalizations about any particular field of endeavor.

These defects are readily apparent in this case. The 30% quota cannot in any realistic sense be tied to any injury suffered by anyone. The District Court relied upon five predicate "facts" in reaching its conclusion that there was an adequate basis for the 30% quota: (1) the ordinance declares itself to be remedial; (2) several proponents of the measure stated their views that there had been past discrimination in the construction industry; (3) minority businesses received .67% of prime contracts from the city while minorities constituted 50% of the city's population; (4) there were very few minority contractors in local and state contractors' associations; and (5) in 1977, Congress made a determination that the effects of past discrimination had stifled minority participation in the construction industry nationally. . . .

None of these "findings," singly or together, provide the city of Richmond with a "strong basis in evidence for its conclusion that remedial action was necessary." . . . There is nothing approaching a prima facie case of a constitutional or statutory violation by *anyone* in the Richmond construction industry. . . .

The District Court accorded great weight to the fact that the city council designated the Plan as "remedial." But the mere recitation of a "benign" or legitimate purpose for a racial classification, is entitled to little or no weight. . . . Racial classifications are suspect, and that means that simple legislative assurances of good intention cannot suffice.

The District Court also relied on the highly

conclusionary statement of a proponent of the Plan that there was racial discrimination in the construction industry "in this area, and the State, and around the nation." . . . It also noted that the city manager had related his view that racial discrimination still plagued the construction industry in his home city of Pittsburgh. . . . These statements are of little probative value in establishing identified discrimination in the Richmond construction industry. The fact-finding process of legislative bodies is generally entitled to a presumption of regularity and deferential review by the judiciary. . . . But when a legislative body chooses to employ a suspect classification, it cannot rest upon a generalized assertion as to the classification's relevance to its goals. . . . A governmental actor cannot render race a legitimate proxy for a particular condition merely by declaring that the condition exists. . . . The history of racial classifications in this country suggests that blind judicial deference to legislative or executive pronouncements of necessity has no place in equal protection analysis. . . .

Reliance on the disparity between the number of prime contracts awarded to minority firms and the minority population of the city of Richmond is similarly misplaced. There is no doubt that "[w]here gross statistical disparities can be shown, they alone in a proper case may constitute prima facie proof of a pattern or practice of discrimination" under Title VII. . . . But it is equally clear that "[w]hen special qualifications are required to fill particular jobs, comparisons to the general population (rather than to the smaller group of individuals who possess the necessary qualifications) may have little probative value." . . .

In the employment context, we have recognized that for certain entry level positions or positions requiring minimal training, statistical comparisons of the racial composition of an employer's workforce to the racial composition of the relevant population may be probative of a pattern of discrimination. . . . But where special qualifications are necessary, the relevant statistical pool for purposes of demonstrating discriminatory exclusion must be the number of minorities qualified to undertake the particular task. . . .

In this case, the city does not even know how many MBEs in the relevant market are qualified to undertake prime or subcontracting work in public construction projects. . . . Nor does the city know what percentage of total city construction dollars minority firms now receive as subcontractors on prime contracts let by the city.

To a large extent, the set-aside of subcontracting dollars seems to rest on the unsupported assumption that white prime contractors simply will not hire minority firms. . . . Indeed, there is evidence in this record that overall minority participation in city contracts in Richmond is seven to eight percent, and that minority contractor participation in Community Block Development Grant *construction* projects is 17% to 22%. . . . Without any information on minority participation in subcontracting, it is quite simply impossible to evaluate overall minority representation in the city's construction expenditures.

The city and the District Court also relied on evidence that MBE membership in local contractors' associations was extremely low. Again, standing alone this evidence is not probative of any discrimination in the local construction industry. There are numerous explanations for this dearth of minority participation, including past societal discrimination in education and economic opportunities as well as both black and white career and entrepreneurial choices. Blacks may be disproportionately attracted to industries other than construction. See The State of Small Business: A Report of the President Transmitted to the Congress 201 (1986) ("Relative to the distribution of all businesses, black-owned businesses are more than proportionally represented in the transportation industry, but considerably less than proportionally represented in the wholesale trade, manufacturing, and finance industries"). The mere fact that black membership in these trade organizations is low, standing alone, cannot establish a prima facie case of discrimination. . . .

For low minority membership in these associations to be relevant, the city would have to link it to the number of local MBEs eligible for membership. If the statistical disparity between eligible MBEs and MBE membership were great enough, an inference of discriminatory exclusion could arise. In such a case, the city would have a compelling interest in preventing its tax dollars from assisting these organizations in maintaining a racially segregated construction market. . . .

Finally, the city and the District Court relied on Congress's finding in connection with the set-aside approved in *Fullilove* that there had been nationwide discrimination in the construction industry. The probative value of these findings for demonstrating the existence of discrimination in Richmond is extremely limited. By its inclusion of a waiver procedure in the national program addressed in *Fullilove*, Congress explicitly recognized that the scope of the problem would vary from market area to market area. . . .

Moreover, as noted above, Congress was exercising its powers under § 5 of the Fourteenth Amendment in making a finding that past discrimination would cause federal funds to be distributed in a manner which reinforced prior patterns of discrimination. While the States and their subdivisions may take remedial action when they possess evidence that their own spending practices are exacerbating a pattern of prior discrimination, they must identify that discrimination, public or private, with some specificity before they may use race-conscious relief. Congress has made national findings that there has been societal discrimination in a host of fields. If all a state or local government need do is find a congressional report on the subject to enact a set-aside program, the constraints of the Equal Protection Clause will, in effect, have been rendered a nullity. . . .

Justice Marshall apparently views the requirement that Richmond identify the discrimination it seeks to remedy in its own jurisdiction as a mere administrative headache, an "onerous documentary obligatio[n]." . . . We cannot agree. In this regard, we are in accord with Justice Stevens' observation in *Fullilove,* that "[b]ecause racial characteristics so seldom provide a relevant basis for disparate treatment, and because classifications based on race are potentially so harmful to the entire body politic, it is especially important that the reasons for any such classification be clearly

identified and unquestionably legitimate." . . . The "evidence" relied upon by the dissent, the history of school desegregation in Richmond and numerous congressional reports, does little to define the scope of any injury to minority contractors in Richmond or the necessary remedy. The factors relied upon by the dissent could justify a preference of any size or duration.

Moreover, Justice Marshall's suggestion that findings of discrimination may be "shared" from jurisdiction to jurisdiction in the same manner as information concerning zoning and property values is unprecedented. . . . We have never approved the extrapolation of discrimination in one jurisdiction from the experience of another. . . . ("Disparate treatment of white and Negro students occurred within the Detroit school system, and not elsewhere, and on this record the remedy must be limited to that system.")

In sum, none of the evidence presented by the city points to any identified discrimination in the Richmond construction industry. We, therefore, hold that the city has failed to demonstrate a compelling interest in apportioning public contracting opportunities on the basis of race. To accept Richmond's claim that past societal discrimination alone can serve as the basis for rigid racial preferences would be to open the door to competing claims for "remedial relief" for every disadvantaged group. The dream of a Nation of equal citizens in a society where race is irrelevant to personal opportunity and achievement would be lost in a mosaic of shifting preferences based on inherently unmeasurable claims of past wrongs. "Courts would be asked to evaluate the extent of the prejudice and consequent harm suffered by various minority groups. Those whose societal injury is thought to exceed some arbitrary level of tolerability then would be entitled to preferential classifications. . . ." . . . We think such a result would be contrary to both the letter and spirit of a constitutional provision whose central command is equality. . . .

Justice *Marshall,* with whom Justice *Brennan* and Justice *Blackmun* join, dissenting.

It is a welcome symbol of racial progress when the former capital of the Confederacy acts forthrightly to confront the effects of racial discrimination in its midst. In my view, nothing in the Constitution can be construed to prevent Richmond, Virginia, from allocating a portion of its contracting dollars for businesses owned or controlled by members of minority groups. Indeed, Richmond's set-aside program is indistinguishable in all meaningful respects from—and in fact was patterned upon—the federal set-aside plan which this Court upheld in *Fullilove v. Klutznick*, . . .

A majority of this Court holds today, however, that the Equal Protection Clause of the Fourteenth Amendment blocks Richmond's initiative. The essence of the majority's position is that Richmond has failed to catalogue adequate findings to prove that past discrimination has impeded minorities from joining or participating fully in Richmond's construction contracting industry. I find deep irony in second-guessing Richmond's judgment on this point. As much as any municipality in the United States, Richmond knows what racial discrimination is; a century of decisions by this and other federal courts has richly documented the city's disgraceful history of public and private racial discrimination. In any event, the Richmond City Council *has* supported its determination that minorities have been wrongly excluded from local construction contracting. Its proof includes statistics showing that minority-owned businesses have received virtually no city contracting dollars and rarely if ever belonged to area trade associations; testimony by municipal officials that discrimination has been widespread in the local construction industry; and the same exhaustive and widely publicized federal studies relied on in *Fullilove,* studies which showed that pervasive discrimination in the Nation's tight-knit construction industry had operated to exclude minorities from public contracting. These are precisely the types of statistical and testimonial evidence which, until today, this Court had credited in cases approving of race-conscious measures designed to remedy past discrimination.

More fundamentally, today's decision marks a deliberate and giant step backward in

this Court's affirmative action jurisprudence. Cynical of one municipality's attempt to redress the effects of past racial discrimination in a particular industry, the majority launches a grapeshot attack on race-conscious remedies in general. The majority's unnecessary pronouncements will inevitably discourage or prevent governmental entities, particularly States and localities, from acting to rectify the scourge of past discrimination. This is the harsh reality of the majority's decision, but it is not the Constitution's command.

As an initial matter, the majority takes an exceedingly myopic view of the factual predicate on which the Richmond City Council relied when it passed the Minority Business Utilization Plan. The majority analyzes Richmond's initiative as if it were based solely upon the facts about local construction and contracting practices adduced during the City Council session at which the measure was enacted. . . . In so doing, the majority downplays the fact that the City Council had before it a rich trove of evidence that discrimination in the Nation's construction industry had seriously impaired the competitive position of businesses owned or controlled by members of minority groups. It is only against this backdrop of documented national discrimination, however, that the local evidence adduced by Richmond can be properly understood. The majority's refusal to recognize that Richmond has proven itself no exception to the dismaying pattern of national exclusion which Congress so painstakingly identified infects its entire analysis of this case.

Six years before Richmond acted, Congress passed, and the President signed, the Public Works Employment Act of 1977, . . . a measure which appropriated $4 billion in federal grants to state and local governments for use in public works projects. Section 103(f)(2) of the Act was a minority business set-aside provision. It required state or local grantees to use 10% of their federal grants to procure services or supplies from businesses owned or controlled by members of statutorily identified minority groups, absent an administrative waiver. In 1980, in *Fullilove,* . . . this Court upheld the validity of this federal set-aside. Chief Justice Burger's opinion noted the importance of overcoming those "criteria, methods, or practices thought by Congress to have the effect of defeating, or substantially impairing, access by the minority business community to public funds made available by congressional appropriations." . . . Finding the set-aside provision properly tailored to this goal, the plurality concluded that the program was valid under either strict or intermediate scrutiny. . . .

The congressional program upheld in *Fulli-love* was based upon an array of congressional and agency studies which documented the powerful influence of racially exclusionary practices in the business world. A 1975 report by the House Committee on Small Business concluded:

> The effects of past inequities stemming from racial prejudice have not remained in the past. The Congress has recognized the reality that past discriminatory practices have, to some degree, adversely affected our present economic system.
>
> While minority persons comprise about 16 percent of the Nation's population, of the 13 million businesses in the United States, only 382,000, or approximately 3.0 percent, are owned by minority individuals. The most recent data from the Department of Commerce also indicates that the gross receipts of all businesses in this country totals about $2,540.8 billion, and of this amount only $16.6 billion, or about 0.65 percent was realized by minority business concerns.
>
> These statistics are not the result of random chance. *The presumption must be made that past discriminatory systems have resulted in present economic inequities.* . . .

A 1977 Report by the same Committee concluded:

> [O]ver the years, there has developed a business system which has traditionally excluded measurable minority participation. In the past more than the present, this system of conducting business transactions overtly precluded minority input. Currently, we more often encounter a business system which is racially neutral on

its face, but because of past overt social and economic discrimination is presently operating, in effect, to perpetuate these past inequities. Minorities, until recently, have not participated to any measurable extent, in our total business system generally, or in the construction industry in particular. . . .

Congress further found that minorities seeking initial public contracting assignments often faced immense entry barriers which did not confront experienced nonminority contractors. A report submitted to Congress in 1975 by the United States Commission on Civil Rights, for example, described the way in which fledgling minority-owned businesses were hampered by "deficiencies in working capital, inability to meet bonding requirements, disabilities caused by an inadequate 'track record,' lack of awareness of bidding opportunities, unfamiliarity with bidding procedures, preselection before the formal advertising process, and the exercise of discretion by government procurement officers to disfavor minority businesses." . . .

Thus, as of 1977, there was "abundant evidence" in the public domain "that minority businesses ha[d] been denied effective participation in public contracting opportunities by procurement practices that perpetuated the effects of prior discrimination." . . . Significantly, this evidence demonstrated that discrimination had prevented existing or nascent minority-owned businesses from obtaining not only federal contracting assignments, but state and local ones as well. . . .

The members of the Richmond City Council were well aware of these exhaustive congressional findings, a point the majority, tellingly, elides. The transcript of the session at which the Council enacted the local set-aside initiative contains numerous references to the 6-year-old congressional set-aside program, to the evidence of nationwide discrimination barriers described above, and to the *Fullilove* decision itself. . . .

The City Council's members also heard testimony that, although minority groups made up half of the city's population, only .67% of the $24.6 million which Richmond had dispensed in construction contracts during the five years ending in March 1983 had gone to minority-owned prime contractors. . . . They heard testimony that the major Richmond area construction trade associations had virtually no minorities among their hundreds of members. Finally, they heard testimony from city officials as to the exclusionary history of the local construction industry. As the District Court noted, not a single person who testified before the City Council denied that discrimination in Richmond's construction industry had been widespread. . . . So long as one views Richmond's local evidence of discrimination against the backdrop of systematic nationwide racial discrimination which Congress had so painstakingly identified in this very industry, this case is readily resolved.

The majority is wrong to trivialize the continuing impact of government acceptance or use of private institutions or structures once wrought by discrimination. When government channels all its contracting funds to a white-dominated community of established contractors whose racial homogeneity is the product of private discrimination, it does more than place its imprimatur on the practices which forged and which continue to define that community. It also provides a measurable boost to those economic entities that have thrived within it, while denying important economic benefits to those entities which, but for prior discrimination, might well be better qualified to receive valuable government contracts. In my view, the interest in ensuring that the government does not reflect and reinforce prior private discrimination in dispensing public contracts is every bit as strong as the interest in eliminating private discrimination—an interest which this Court has repeatedly deemed compelling. . . . The more government bestows its rewards on those persons or businesses that were positioned to thrive during a period of private racial discrimination, the tighter the dead-hand grip of prior discrimination becomes on the present and future. Cities like Richmond may not be constitutionally required to adopt set-aside plans. . . . But there can be no doubt that when Richmond acted affirmatively to stem the perpetuation of patterns of discrimination

through its own decision making, it served an interest of the highest order.

Had the majority paused for a moment on the facts of the Richmond experience, it would have discovered that the city's leadership is deeply familiar with what racial discrimination is. The members of the Richmond City Council have spent long years witnessing multifarious acts of discrimination, including, but not limited to, the deliberate diminution of black residents' voting rights, resistance to school desegregation, and publicly sanctioned housing discrimination. Numerous decisions of federal courts chronicle this disgraceful recent history. . . . [F]or example, this Court denounced Richmond's decision to annex part of an adjacent county at a time when the city's black population was nearing 50% because it was "infected by the impermissible purpose of denying the right to vote based on race through perpetuating white majority power to exclude Negroes from office." . . .

In *Bradley v. School Board of City of Richmond, Virginia,* . . . the Court of Appeals for the Fourth Circuit, sitting en banc, reviewed in the context of a school desegregation case Richmond's long history of inadequate compliance with *Brown v. Board of Education,* . . . and the cases implementing its holding. The dissenting judge elaborated:

> The sordid history of Virginia's, and Richmond's attempts to circumvent, defeat, and nullify the holding of *Brown I* has been recorded in the opinions of this and other courts, and need not be repeated in detail here. It suffices to say that there was massive resistance and every state resource, including the services of the legal officers of the state, the services of private counsel (costing the State hundreds of thousands of dollars), the State police, and the power and prestige of the Governor, was employed to defeat *Brown I.* In Richmond, as has been mentioned, not even freedom of choice became actually effective until 1966, *twelve years after the decision of Brown I.* . . .

The Court of Appeals majority in *Bradley* used equally pungent words in describing public

and private housing discrimination in Richmond. Though rejecting the black plaintiffs' request that it consolidate Richmond's school district with those of two neighboring counties, the majority nonetheless agreed with the plaintiffs' assertion that "within the City of Richmond there has been state (also federal) action tending to perpetuate apartheid of the races in ghetto patterns throughout the city."
. . .

When the legislatures and leaders of cities with histories of pervasive discrimination testify that past discrimination has infected one of their industries, armchair cynicism like that exercised by the majority has no place. . . .

Finally, I vehemently disagree with the majority's dismissal of the congressional and Executive Branch findings noted in *Fullilove* as having "extremely limited" probative value in this case. . . . The majority concedes that Congress established nothing less than a "presumption" that minority contracting firms have been disadvantaged by prior discrimination. . . . The majority, inexplicably, would forbid Richmond to "share" in this information, and permit only Congress to take note of these ample findings. . . . In thus requiring that Richmond's local evidence be severed from the context in which it was prepared, the majority would require cities seeking to eradicate the effects of past discrimination within their borders to reinvent the evidentiary wheel and engage in unnecessarily duplicative, costly, and time-consuming factfinding. . . .

As for Richmond's 30% target, the majority states that this figure "cannot be said to be narrowly tailored to any goal, except perhaps outright racial balancing." . . . The majority ignores two important facts. First, the set-aside measure affects only 3% of overall city contracting; thus, any imprecision in tailoring has far less impact than the majority suggests. But more important, the majority ignores the fact that Richmond's 30% figure was patterned directly on the *Fullilove* precedent. Congress's 10% figure fell "roughly halfway between the present percentage of minority contractors and the percentage of minority group members in the Nation." . . . The Richmond City Council's 30% figure similarly falls roughly halfway between the present percentage of

Richmond-based minority contractors (almost zero) and the percentage of minorities in Richmond (50%). In faulting Richmond for not presenting a different explanation for its choice of a set-aside figure, the majority honors *Fullilove* only in the breach.

The majority today sounds a full-scale retreat from the Court's longstanding solicitude to race-conscious remedial efforts "directed toward deliverance of the century-old promise of equality of economic opportunity." . . . The new and restrictive tests it applies scuttle one city's effort to surmount its discriminatory past, and imperil those of dozens more localities. I, however, profoundly disagree with the cramped vision of the Equal Protection Clause which the majority offers today and with its application of that vision to Richmond, Virginia's, laudable set-aside plan. The battle against pernicious racial discrimination or its effects is nowhere near won. I must dissent.

Justice *Blackmun,* with whom
Justice *Brennan* joins, dissenting.

I join Justice Marshall's perceptive and incisive opinion revealing great sensitivity toward those who have suffered the pains of economic discrimination in the construction trades for so long.

I never thought that I would live to see the day when the city of Richmond, Virginia, the cradle of the Old Confederacy, sought on its own, within a narrow confine, to lessen the stark impact of persistent discrimination. But Richmond, to its great credit, acted. Yet this Court, the supposed bastion of equality, strikes down Richmond's efforts as though discrimination had never existed or was not demonstrated in this particular litigation. Justice Marshall convincingly discloses the fallacy and the shallowness of that approach. History is irrefutable, even though one might sympathize with those who—though possibly innocent in themselves—benefit from the wrongs of past decades.

So the Court today regresses. I am confident, however, that, given time, it one day again will do its best to fulfill the great promises of the Constitution's Preamble and of the guarantees embodied in the Bill of Rights—a fulfillment that would make this Nation very special.

Suggestions for Further Reading

Anthologies

Cohen, M., Nagel, T., and Scanlon, T. *Equality and Preferential Treatment*. Princeton, N.J.: Princeton University Press, 1977.

Gould, C. C., and Wartofsky, M. W. *Women and Philosophy*. New York: G. P. Putnam & Sons, 1976.

Gross, B. *Reverse Discrimination*. Buffalo, N.Y.: Prometheus, 1976.

Remick, H. *Comparable Worth and Wage Discrimination*. Philadelphia: Temple University Press, 1985.

Statham, Anne. *The Worth of Woman's Work*. Albany: State University of New York Press, 1988.

Alternative Views

Aaron, H., and Cameran, L. *The Comparable Worth Controversy*. Washington, D.C.: Brookings, 1986.

Bergman, Barbara. *The Economic Emergence of Women*. New York: Basic Books, 1986.

England, Paula. *Comparable Worth: Theories and Evidence*. Hawthorne: Aldine de Gruyter, 1993.

Fullinwider, R. *The Reverse Discrimination Controversy*. Totowa, N.J.: Rowman and Littlefield, 1980.

Goldman, A. *Justice and Reverse Discrimination*. Princeton, N.J.: Princeton University Press, 1979.

Paul, Ellen Frankel. *Equity and Gender: The Comparable Worth Debate*. New Brunswick, N.J.: Transaction Publishers, 1989.

Rosenfeld, Michel. *Affirmative Action and Justice*. New Haven, Conn.: Yale University Press, 1991.

Sowell, T. *Markets and Minorities*. New York: Basic Books, 1981.

United States Commission on Civil Rights. *Comparable Worth: Issue for the 80's*. Washington, D.C.: U.S. Government Printing Office, 1984.

Practical Applications

United States Commission on Civil Rights. *Toward an Understanding of Bakke*. Washington, D.C.: U.S. Government Printing Office, 1979.

Pornography

Introduction

Basic Concepts

The problem of pornography, as Catharine MacKinnon formulates it in Selection 37, is whether pornography should be prohibited for promoting discrimination and violence against women. But this has not been how the problem has been traditionally understood. In the Anglo-American legal tradition, pornography has always been identified with obscenity.[1] The test for obscenity set forth by the U.S. Supreme Court in *Roth v. United States* (1957) is "whether to the average person, applying contemporary community standards, the dominant theme of the material taken as a whole appeals to prurient interest." This test itself was an attempt to improve upon an 1868 test of obscenity that was taken over from English law. According to this earlier test, obscene materials are such that they have the tendency "to deprave and corrupt those whose minds are open to such immoral influences, and into whose hands a publication of this sort may fall." In *Roth v. United States,* the U.S. Supreme Court sought to remedy three defects in this 1868 test. First, the 1868 test permitted books to be judged obscene on the basis of isolated passages read out of context. In contrast, the Roth test requires that material be judged as obscene only if "the dominant theme of the material taken as a whole" is so judged. Second, the 1868 test allowed the obscenity of a work to be determined by its likely effects on unusually susceptible persons. By contrast, the Roth test judges material to be obscene on the basis of its likely effect on the "average person." Third, the 1868 test posited standards of obscenity fixed for all time. By contrast, the Roth test only appeals to "contemporary community standards."

Yet despite these advantages of the Roth test, problems remained. First, who was the average person to whose prurience the obscene materials has to appeal? In *Miskin v. New York* (1966), the Supreme Court needed to apply its Roth test to books that described sadomasochistic sexual acts, fetishism, lesbian-

ism, and male homosexuality. Since these works did not appeal to the prurient interest of the average person in the population at large, the Supreme Court reformulated its Roth test so that when "material is designed for and primarily disseminated to a clearly defined deviant sexual group, . . . the prurient-appeal requirement of the Roth test is satisfied if the dominant theme of the material taken as a whole appeals to the prurient interest in sex of the members of that group." Second, how was the Supreme Court to avoid the task of having to determine what are community standards for an endless number of obscenity cases? In *Miller v. California* (1973), the Supreme Court dealt with the problem by delegating and relativizing the task of determining contemporary community standards to local communities. Henceforth, the application of local community standards determines whether material appeals to prurient interest. Obviously, this puts a severe burden on national publishers who now have to take into account local community standards for any work they distribute. For example, when Larry C. Flynt routinely mailed a copy of his publication *Hustler* to a person who had ordered it by mail from a town in Ohio, he was subsequently tried for a violation of the Ohio obscenity statutes and sentenced to 7 to 25 years in prison. So even with these improvements in the Supreme Court's test for obscenity, problems still remain.

Alternative Views

In Selection 37, Catharine MacKinnon takes an entirely new approach to pornography and obscenity. She sees pornography as a practice of sex discrimination, a violation of women's civil rights. She defines pornography "as the graphic sexually explicit subordination of women through pictures or words that also includes women dehumanized as sexual objects, things or commodities; enjoying pain or humiliation or rape; being tied up, cut up, mutilated, bruised, or physically hurt; in postures of sexual submission or servility or display; reduced to body parts, penetrated by objects or animals, or presented in scenarios of degradation, injury, torture; shown as filthy or inferior; bleeding, bruised or hurt in a context that makes these conditions sexual." By contrast, she defines erotica "as sexually explicit materials premised on equality." She argues that pornography is a harmful form of gender inequality that outweighs any social interest in its protection by recognized First Amendment standards. She points to recent experimental research that shows that pornography causes harm to women through increasing men's attitudes and behavior of discrimination in both violent and nonviolent forms.

In Selection 38, Lisa Duggan, Nan Hunter, and Carole Vance oppose MacKinnon's antipornography position. They argue that although the legislation she proposes claims to prohibit only material that is sexually explicit, violent, and sexist, it actually prohibits anything that is merely sexually explicit. They further argue that because of the diverse interests of those behind the antipornography movement, it is unlikely that these interests will unite behind a more limited notion of pornography. This latter objection, however, does not seem to touch the moral defensibility of a view modeled after MacKinnon's, which would aim at prohibiting only material that is sexually explicit, violent, and sexist, but would also employ better legal criteria for specifying material of this sort.

Duggan, Hunter, and Vance also question whether pornography harms women, but here they seem to have in mind a broader notion of pornography than the one we are considering. Yet even assuming that pornography more narrowly defined does harm women, Duggan, Hunter, and Vance further question whether it causes more harm than some other aspects of our sexist society that are not prohibited. But suppose that Duggan, Hunter, and Vance are right that pornography causes no more harm than some other aspects of our sexist society. What would that show? It may simply show that pornography as well as those other aspects of our sexist society should be prohibited.

Some opponents of any legal prohibition on pornography point to the Danish experience, where the legalization of pornography has not led to any increase in reported incidents of sexual assault against women. But even here the evidence is mixed because, for example, although the number of rapes reported to the authorities has decreased over the years, it is estimated that the number of actual rapes has increased.

Practical Application

In *American Booksellers v. Hudnutt* (Selection 39), the federal judiciary ruled against an Indianapolis ordinance contending that pornography which qualified as constitutionally protected speech could not be prohibited on the grounds that it caused harm to women. At the same time, the Court seemed to regard the issue of harm to women to be relevant when it argued that pornography did not harm those women who cooperated in the production of pornography because they "generally have the capacity to protect themselves from participating in and being personally victimized by pornography." By contrast, the Supreme Court of Canada judged that preventing harm to women is an acceptable grounds for restricting pornography, and that, moreover, restricting pornography would in fact prevent harm to women.

One explanation for the difference between the rules of the U.S. and Canadian Courts is that, as MacKinnon points out, in sexist societies, it is difficult to recognize the harm that pornography causes women. Yet if MacKinnon is right, treating women equally in this regard will require a radical transformation of our society that will also affect the solutions to the other moral problems discussed in this anthology. Moreover, this radical transformation would be the kind that libertarians would be expected to champion since they are so concerned with preventing harm to others.

Note

1. In ordinary usage, to call something obscene is to condemn that thing as blatantly disgusting, whereas to call something pornographic is simply to characterize it as sexually explicit. So in ordinary usage, unlike the law, it is an open question whether the pornographic is also obscene.

37. Pornography, Civil Rights and Speech

Catharine MacKinnon

Catharine MacKinnon argues that pornography is a practice of sex discrimination and, hence, a violation of women's civil rights. According to MacKinnon,
pornography celebrates and legitimizes rape, battery, sexual harassment, and the
sexual abuse of children. More generally, it eroticizes the dominance and submission that is the dynamic common to them all. She argues for the constitutionality
of city ordinances, which she has helped design, that prohibit pornography.

. . . There is a belief that this is a society in which women and men are basically equals. Room for marginal corrections is conceded, flaws are known to exist, attempts are made to correct what are conceived as occasional lapses from the basic condition of sex equality. Sex discrimination law has concentrated most of its focus on these occasional lapses. It is difficult to overestimate the extent to which this belief in equality is an article of faith for most people, including most women, who wish to live in self-respect in an internal universe, even (per-haps especially) if not in the world. It is also partly an expression of natural law thinking: if we are inalienably equal, we can't "really" be degraded.

This is a world in which it is worth trying. In this world of presumptive equality, people make money based on their training or abili-ties or diligence or qualifications. They are employed and advanced on the basis of merit. In this world of just deserts, if someone is abused, it is thought to violate the basic rules of the community. If it doesn't, victims are seen to have done something they could have chosen to do differently, by exercise of will or better judgment. Maybe such people have placed themselves in a situation of vulnerabil-ity to physical abuse. Maybe they have done something provocative. Or maybe they were just unusually unlucky. In such a world, if such a person has an experience, there are words for it. When they speak and say it, they are listened to. If they write about it, they will be published. If certain experiences are never spoken about, if certain people or issues are seldom heard from, it is supposed that silence has been chosen. The law, including much of the law of sex discrimination and the First Amendment, operates largely within the realm of these beliefs.

Feminism is the discovery that women do not live in this world, that the person occupy-ing this realm is a man, so much more a man if he is white and wealthy. This world of poten-tial credibility, authority, security, and just re-wards, recognition of one's identity and capac-ity, is a world that some people do inhabit as a condition of birth, with variations among them. It is not a basic condition accorded humanity in this society, but a prerogative of status, a privilege, among other things, of gender.

I call this a discovery because it has not been an assumption. Feminism is the first theory, the first practice, the first movement, to take seriously the situation of all women from the point of view of all women, both on our situa-tion and on social life as a whole. The discov-ery has therefore been made that the implicit social content of humanism, as well as the standpoint from which legal method has been designed and injuries have been defined, has not been women's standpoint. Defining femi-nism in a way that connects epistemology with power as the politics of women's point of view, this discovery can be summed up by saying that women live in another world: specifically, a world of *not* equality, a world of inequality.

Looking at the world from this point of view, a whole shadow world of previously invisible silent abuse has been discerned. Rape, battery, sexual harassment, forced prostitution, and the sexual abuse of children emerge as common and systematic. We find that rape happens to women in all contexts, from the family, including rape of girls and babies, to students and women in the workplace, on the streets, at home, in their own bedrooms by men they do not know and by men they do know, by men they are married to, men they have had a social conversation with, and, least often, men they have never seen before. Overwhelmingly, rape is something that men do or attempt to do to women (44 percent of American women according to a recent study) at some point in our lives. Sexual harassment of women by men is common in workplaces and educational institutions. Based on reports in one study of the federal workforce, up to 85 percent of women will experience it, many in physical forms. Between a quarter and a third of women are battered in their homes by men. Thirty-eight percent of little girls are sexually molested inside or outside the family. Until women listened to women, this world of sexual abuse was *not spoken* of. It was the unspeakable. What I am saying is, if you *are* the tree falling in the epistemological forest, your demise doesn't make a sound if no one is listening. Women did not "report" these events, and overwhelmingly do not today, because no one is listening, because no one believes us. This silence does not mean nothing happened, and it does not mean consent. It is the silence of women of which Adrienne Rich has written, "Do not confuse it with any kind of absence."

Believing women who say we are sexually violated has been a radical departure, both methodologically and legally. The extent and nature of rape, marital rape, and sexual harassment itself, were discovered in this way. Domestic battery as a syndrome, almost a habit, was discovered through refusing to believe that when a woman is assaulted by a man to whom she is connected, that it is not an assault. The sexual abuse of children was uncovered, Freud notwithstanding, by believing that children were not making up all this sexual abuse. Now what is striking is that when each discovery is made, and somehow made real in the world, the response has been: it happens to men too. If women are hurt, men

are hurt. If women are raped, men are raped. If women are sexually harassed, men are sexually harassed. If women are battered, men are battered. Symmetry must be reasserted. Neutrality must be reclaimed. Equality must be reestablished.

The only areas where the available evidence supports this, where anything like what happens to women also happens to men, involve children—little boys are sexually abused—and prison. The liberty of prisoners is restricted, their freedom restrained, their humanity systematically diminished, their bodies and emotions confined, defined, and regulated. If paid at all, they are paid starvation wages. They can be tortured at will, and it is passed off as discipline or as means to a just end. They become compliant. They can be raped at will, at any moment, and nothing will be done about it. When they scream, nobody hears. To be a prisoner means to be defined as a member of a group for whom the rules of what can be done to you, of what is seen as abuse of you, are reduced as part of the definition of your status. To be a woman is that kind of definition and has that kind of meaning.

Men *are* damaged by sexism. (By men I mean the status of masculinity that is accorded to males on the basis of their biology but is not itself biological.) But whatever the damage of sexism to men, the condition of being a man is not defined as subordinate to women by force. Looking at the facts of the abuses of women all at once, you see that a woman is socially defined as a person who, whether or not she is or has been, can be treated in these ways by men at any time, and little, if anything, will be done about it. This is what it means when feminists say that maleness is a form of power and femaleness is a form of powerlessness.

In this context, all of this "men too" stuff means that people don't really believe that the things I have just said are true, though there really is little question about their empirical accuracy. The data are extremely simple, like women's pay figure of fifty-nine cents on the dollar. People don't really seem to believe that either. Yet there is no question of its empirical validity. This is the workplace story: what women do is seen as not worth much, or what is not worth much is seen as something for women to do. *Women* are seen as not worth much, is the thing. Now why are these basic realities of the subordination of women to men, for example, that only 7.8 percent of women have never been sexually assaulted, not effectively believed, not perceived as real in the face of all this evidence? Why don't *women* believe our own experiences? In the face of all this evidence, especially of systematic sexual abuse—subjection to violence with impunity is one extreme expression, although not the only expression, of a degraded status—the view that basically the sexes are equal in this society remains unchallenged and unchanged. The day I got this was the day I understood its real message, its real coherence: *This is equality for us.*

I could describe this, but I couldn't explain it until I started studying a lot of pornography. In pornography, there it is, in one place, all of the abuses that women had to struggle so long even to begin to articulate, all the *unspeakable* abuse: the rape, the battery, the sexual harassment, the prostitution, and the sexual abuse of children. Only in the pornography it is called something else: sex, sex, sex, sex, and sex, respectively. Pornography sexualizes rape, battery, sexual harassment, prostitution, and child sexual abuse; it thereby celebrates, promotes, authorizes, and legitimizes them. More generally, it eroticizes the dominance and submission that is the dynamic common to them all. It makes hierarchy sexy and calls that "the truth about sex" or just a mirror of reality. Through this process pornography constructs what a woman is as what men want from sex. This is what the pornography means.

Pornography constructs what a woman is in terms of its view of what men want sexually, such that acts of rape, battery, sexual harassment, prostitution, and sexual abuse of children become acts of sexual equality. Pornography's world of equality is a harmonious and balanced place. Men and women are perfectly complementary and perfectly bipolar. Women's desire to be fucked by men is equal to men's desire to fuck women. All the ways men love to take and violate women, women love to be taken and violated. The women who most love this are most men's equals, the most liberated; the most participatory child is the most grown-up, the most equal to an adult.

Their consent merely expresses or ratifies these preexisting facts.

The content of pornography is one thing. There, women substantively desire dispossession and cruelty. We desperately want to be bound, battered, tortured, humiliated, and killed. Or, to be fair to the soft core, merely taken and used. This is erotic to the male point of view. Subjection itself, with self-determination ecstatically relinquished, is the content of women's sexual desire and desirability. Women are there to be violated and possessed, men to violate and possess us, either on screen or by camera or pen on behalf of the consumer. On a simple descriptive level, the inequality of hierarchy, of which gender is the primary one, seems necessary for sexual arousal to work. Other added inequalities identify various pornographic genres or subthemes, although they are always added through gender: age, disability, homosexuality, animals, objects, race (including anti-Semitism), and so on. Gender is never irrelevant.

What pornography *does* goes beyond its content: it eroticizes hierarchy, it sexualizes inequality. It makes dominance and submission into sex. Inequality is its central dynamic; the illusion of freedom coming together with the reality of force is central to its working. Perhaps because this is a bourgeois culture, the victim must look free, appear to be freely acting. Choice is how she got there. Willing is what she is when she is being equal. It seems equally important that then and there she actually be forced and that forcing be communicated on some level, even if only through still photos of her in postures of receptivity and access, available for penetration. Pornography in this view is a form of forced sex, a practice of sexual politics, an institution of gender inequality.

From this perspective, pornography is neither harmless fantasy nor a corrupt and confused misrepresentation of an otherwise natural and healthy sexual situation. It institutionalizes the sexuality of male supremacy, fusing the erotization of dominance and submission with the social construction of male and female. To the extent that gender is sexual, pornography is part of constituting the meaning of that sexuality. Men treat women as who they see women as being. Pornography constructs who that is. Men's power over women means that the way men see women defines who women can be. Pornography is that way. Pornography is not imagery in some relation to a reality elsewhere constructed. It is not a distortion, reflection, projection, expression, fantasy, representation, or symbol either. It is a sexual reality.

In Andrea Dworkin's definitive work, *Pornography: Men Possessing Women*, sexuality itself is a social construct gendered to the ground. Male dominance here is not an artificial overlay upon an underlying inalterable substratum of uncorrupted essential sexual being. Dworkin presents a sexual theory of gender inequality of which pornography is a constitutive practice. The way pornography produces its meaning constructs and defines men and women as such. Gender has no basis in anything other than the social reality its hegemony constructs. Gender is what gender means. The process that gives sexuality its male supremacist meaning is the same process through which gender inequality becomes socially real.

In this approach, the experience of the (overwhelmingly) male audiences who consume pornography is therefore not fantasy or simulation or catharsis but sexual reality, the level of reality on which sex itself largely operates. Understanding this dimension of the problem does not require noticing that pornography models are real women to whom, in most cases, something real is being done; nor does it even require inquiring into the systematic infliction of pornography and its sexuality upon women, although it helps. What matters is the way in which the pornography itself provides what those who consume it want. Pornography *participates* in its audience's eroticism through creating an accessible sexual object, the possession and consumption of which *is* male sexuality, as socially constructed; to be consumed and possessed as which, *is* female sexuality, as socially constructed; pornography is a process that constructs it that way.

The object world is constructed according to how it looks with respect to its possible uses. Pornography defines women by how we look according to how we can be sexually used.

Pornography codes how to look at women, so you know what you can do with one when you see one. Gender is an assignment made visually, both originally and in everyday life. A sex object is defined on the basis of its looks, in terms of its usability for sexual pleasure, such that both the looking—the quality of the gaze, including its point of view—and the definition according to use become eroticized as part of the sex itself. This is what the feminist concept "sex object" means. In this sense, sex in life is no less mediated than it is in art. Men have sex with their image of a woman. It is not that life and art imitate each other; in this sexuality, they *are* each other.

To give a set of rough epistemological translations, to defend pornography as consistent with the equality of the sexes is to defend the subordination of women to men as sexual equality. What in the pornographic view is love and romance looks a great deal like hatred and torture to the feminist. Pleasure and eroticism become violation. Desire appears as lust for dominance and submission. The vulnerability of women's projected sexual availability, that acting we are allowed (that is, asking to be acted upon), is victimization. Play conforms to scripted roles. Fantasy expresses ideology, is not exempt from it. Admiration of natural physical beauty becomes objectification. Harmlessness becomes harm. Pornography is a harm of male supremacy made difficult to see because of its pervasiveness, potency, and, principally, because of its success in making the world a pornographic place. Specifically, its harm cannot be discerned, and will not be addressed, if viewed and approached neutrally, because it *is* so much of "what is." In other words, to the extent pornography succeeds in constructing social reality, it becomes invisible as harm. If we live in a world that pornography creates through the power of men in a male-dominated situation, the issue is not what the harm of pornography is, but how that harm is to become visible.

Obscenity law provides a very different analysis and conception of the problem of pornography. In 1973 the legal definition of obscenity became that which the average person, applying contemporary community standards, would find that, taken as a whole, appeals to the prurient interest; that which depicts or describes in a patently offensive way—you feel like you're a cop reading someone's *Miranda* rights—sexual conduct specifically defined by the applicable state law; and that which, taken as a whole, lacks serious literary, artistic, political or scientific value. Feminism doubts whether the average person gender-neutral exists; has more questions about the content and process of defining what community standards are than it does about deviations from them; wonders why prurience counts but powerlessness does not and why sensibilities are better protected from offense than women are from exploitation; defines sexuality, and thus its violation and expropriation, more broadly than does state law; and questions why a body of law that has not in practice been able to tell rape from intercourse should, without further guidance, be entrusted with telling pornography from anything less. Taking the work "as a whole" ignores that which the victims of pornography have long known: legitimate settings diminish the perception of injury done to those whose trivialization and objectification they contextualize. Besides, and this is a heavy one, if a woman is subjected, why should it matter that the work has other value? Maybe what redeems the work's value is what enhances its injury to women, not to mention that existing standards of literature, art, science, and politics, examined in a feminist light, are remarkably consonant with pornography's mode, meaning, and message. And finally—first and foremost, actually—although the subject of these materials is overwhelmingly women, their contents almost entirely made up of women's bodies, our invisibility has been such, our equation as a sex *with* sex has been such, that the law of obscenity has never even considered pornography a women's issue.

Obscenity, in this light, is a moral idea, an idea about judgments of good and bad. Pornography, by contrast, is a political practice, a practice of power and powerlessness. Obscenity is ideational and abstract; pornography is concrete and substantive. The two concepts represent two entirely different things. Nudity, excess of candor, arousal or excitement, prurient appeal, illegality of the acts depicted,

and unnaturalness or perversion are all qualities that bother obscenity law when sex is depicted or portrayed. Sex forced on real women so that it can be sold at a profit and forced on other real women; women's bodies trussed and maimed and raped and made into things to be hurt and obtained and accessed, and this presented as the nature of women in a way that is acted on and acted out, over and over; the coercion that is visible and the coercion that has become invisible—this and more bothers feminists about pornography. Obscenity as such probably does little harm. Pornography is integral to attitudes and behaviors of violence and discrimination that define the treatment and status of half the population.

At the request of the city of Minneapolis, Andrea Dworkin and I conceived and designed a local human rights ordinance in accordance with our approach to the pornography issue. We define pornography as a practice of sex discrimination, a violation of women's civil rights, the opposite of sexual equality. Its point is to hold those who profit from and benefit from that injury accountable to those who are injured. It means that women's injury—our damage, our pain, our enforced inferiority—should outweigh their pleasure and their profits, or sex equality is meaningless.

We define pornography as the graphic sexually explicit subordination of women through pictures or words that also includes women dehumanized as sexual objects, things, or commodities; enjoying pain or humiliation or rape; being tied up, cut up, mutilated, bruised, or physically hurt; in postures of sexual submission or servility or display; reduced to body parts, penetrated by objects or animals, or presented in scenarios of degradation, injury, torture; shown as filthy or inferior; bleeding, bruised, or hurt in a context that makes these conditions sexual. Erotica, defined by distinction as not this, might be sexually explicit materials premised on equality. We also provide that the use of men, children, or transsexuals in the place of women is pornography. The definition is substantive in that it is sex-specific, but it covers everyone in a sex-specific way, so is gender neutral in overall design. . . .

This law aspires to guarantee women's

rights consistent with the First Amendment by making visible a conflict of rights between the equality guaranteed to all women and what, in some legal sense, is now the freedom of the pornographers to make and sell, and their consumers to have access to, the materials this ordinance defines. Judicial resolution of this conflict, if the judges do for women what they have done for others, is likely to entail a balancing of the rights of women arguing that our lives and opportunities, including our freedom of speech and action, are constrained by—and in many cases flatly precluded by, in, and through—pornography, against those who argue that the pornography is harmless, or harmful only in part but not in the whole of the definition; or that it is more important to preserve the pornography than it is to prevent or remedy whatever harm it does.

In predicting how a court would balance these interests, it is important to understand that this ordinance cannot now be said to be either conclusively legal or illegal under existing law or precedent, although I think the weight of authority is on our side. This ordinance enunciates a new form of the previously recognized governmental interest in sex equality. Many laws make sex equality a governmental interest. Our law is designed to further the equality of the sexes, to help make sex equality real. Pornography is a practice of discrimination on the basis of sex, on one level because of its role in creating and maintaining sex as a basis for discrimination. It harms many women one at a time and helps keep all women in an inferior status by defining our subordination as our sexuality and equating that with our gender. It is also sex discrimination because its victims, including men, are selected for victimization on the basis of their gender. But for their sex, they would not be so treated.

The harm of pornography, broadly speaking, is the harm of the civil inequality of the sexes made invisible as harm because it has become accepted as the sex difference. Consider this analogy with race: if you see Black people as different, there is no harm to segregation; it is merely a recognition of that difference. To neutral principles, separate but equal was equal. The injury of racial separation to Blacks arises "solely because [they] choose to put that construction upon it." Epistemologically translated: how you see it is not the way it is. Similarly, if you see women as just different, even or especially if you don't know that you do, subordination will not look like subordination at all, much less like harm. It will merely look like an appropriate recognition of the sex difference.

Pornography does treat the sexes differently, so the case for sex differentiation can be made here. But men as a group do not tend to be (although some individuals may be) treated the way women are treated in pornography. As a social group, men are not hurt by pornography the way women as a social group are. Their social status is not defined as *less* by it. So the major argument does not turn on mistaken differentiation, particularly since the treatment of women according to pornography's dictates makes it all too often accurate. The salient quality of a distinction between the top and the bottom in a hierarchy is not difference, although top is certainly different from bottom; it is power. So the major argument is: subordinate but equal is not equal.

Particularly since this is a new legal theory, a new law, and "new" facts, perhaps the situation of women it newly exposes deserves to be considered on its own terms. Why do the problems of 53 percent of the population have to look like somebody else's problems before they can be recognized as existing? Then, too, they can't be addressed if they do look like other people's problems, about which something might be done if something is done about these. This construction of the situation truly deserves inquiry. Limiting the justification for this law to the situation of the sexes would serve to limit the precedential value of a favorable ruling.

Its particularity to one side, the *approach* to the injury is supported by a whole array of prior decisions that have justified exceptions to First Amendment guarantees when something that matters is seen to be directly at stake. What unites many cases in which speech interests are raised and implicated but not, on balance, protected, is harm, harm that counts. In some existing exceptions, the definitions are much more open-ended than ours. In some the sanctions are more severe, or potentially more so. For instance, ours is a civil law;

most others, although not all, are criminal. Almost no other exceptions show as many people directly affected. Evidence of harm in other cases tends to be vastly less concrete and more conjectural, which is not to say that there is necessarily less of it. None of the previous cases addresses a problem of this scope or magnitude—for instance, an eight-billion-dollar-a-year industry. Nor do other cases address an abuse that has such widespread legitimacy. Courts have seen harm in other cases. The question is, will they see it here, especially given that the pornographers got there first. I will confine myself here to arguing from cases on harm to people, on the supposition that, the pornographers notwithstanding, women are not flags. . . .

To reach the magnitude of this problem on the scale it exists, our law makes trafficking in pornography—production, sale, exhibition, or distribution—actionable. Under the obscenity rubric, much legal and psychological scholarship has centered on a search for the elusive link between harm and pornography defined as obscenity. Although they were not very clear on what obscenity was, it was its harm they truly could not find. They looked high and low—in the mind of the male consumer, in society or in its "moral fabric," in correlations between variations in levels of antisocial acts and liberalization of obscenity laws. The only harm they have found has been harm to "the social interest in order and morality." Until recently, no one looked very persistently for harm to women, particularly harm to women through men. The rather obvious fact that the sexes *relate* has been overlooked in the inquiry into the male consumer and his mind. The pornography doesn't just drop out of the sky, go into his head, and stop there. Specifically, men rape, batter, prostitute, molest, and sexually harass women. Under conditions of inequality, they also hire, fire, promote, and grade women, decide how much or whether we are worth paying and for what, define and approve and disapprove of women in ways that count, that determine our lives.

If women are not just born to be sexually used, the fact that we are seen and treated as though that is what we are born for becomes something in need of explanation. If we see

that men relate to women in a pattern of who they see women as being, and that forms a pattern of inequality, it becomes important to ask where that view came from or, minimally, how it is perpetuated or escalated. Asking this requires asking different questions about pornography than the ones obscenity law made salient.

Now I'm going to talk about causality in its narrowest sense. Recent experimental research on pornography shows that the materials covered by our definition cause measurable harm to women through increasing men's attitudes and behaviors of discrimination in both violent and nonviolent forms. Exposure to some of the pornography in our definition increases the immediately subsequent willingness of normal men to aggress against women under laboratory conditions. It makes normal men more closely resemble convicted rapists attitudinally, although as a group they don't look all that different from them to start with. Exposure to pornography also significantly increases attitudinal measures known to correlate with rape and self-reports of aggressive acts, measures such as hostility toward women, propensity to rape, condoning rape, and predicting that one would rape or force sex on a woman if one knew one would not get caught. On this latter measure, by the way, about a third of all men predict that they would rape, and half would force sex on a woman.

As to that pornography covered by our definition in which normal research subjects seldom perceive violence, long-term exposure still makes them see women as more worthless, trivial, nonhuman, and objectlike, that is, the way those who are discriminated against are seen by those who discriminate against them. Crucially, all pornography by our definition acts dynamically over time to diminish the consumer's ability to distinguish sex from violence. The materials work behaviorally to diminish the capacity of men (but not women) to perceive that an account of a rape is an account of a rape. The so-called sex-only materials, those in which subjects perceive no force, also increase perceptions that a rape victim is worthless and decrease the perception that she was harmed. The overall direction of current research suggests that the more expressly violent materials accomplish with less exposure what the less overtly violent—that is, the so-called sex-only materials—accomplish over the longer term. Women are rendered fit for use and targeted for abuse. The only thing that the research cannot document is which individual women will be next on the list. (This cannot be documented experimentally because of ethics constraints on the researchers—constraints that do not operate in life.) Although the targeting is systematic on the basis of sex, for individuals it is random. They are selected on a roulette basis. Pornography can no longer be said to be just a mirror. It does not just reflect the world or some people's perceptions. It *moves* them. It increases attitudes that are lived out, circumscribing the status of half the population.

What the experimental data predict will happen actually does happen in women's real lives. You know, it's fairly frustrating that women have known for some time that these things do happen. As Ed Donnerstein, an experimental researcher in this area, often puts it, "We just quantify the obvious." It is women, primarily, to whom the research results have been the obvious, because we live them. But not until a laboratory study predicts that these things *will* happen do people begin to believe you when you say they *did* happen to you. There is no—*not any*—inconsistency between the patterns the laboratory studies predict and the data on what actually happens to real women. Show me an abuse of women in society, I'll show it to you made sex in the pornography. If you want to know who is being hurt in this society, go see what is being done and to whom in pornography and then go look for them other places in the world. You will find them being hurt in just that way. We did in our hearings.

In our hearings women spoke, to my knowledge for the first time in history in public, about the damage pornography does to them. We learned that pornography is used to break women, to train women to sexual submission, to season women, to terrorize women, and to silence their dissent. It is this that has previously been termed "having no effect." The way men inflict on women the sex they experience through the pornography gives women no choice about seeing the pornography or doing the sex. Asked if anyone ever tried to inflict unwanted sex acts on them that they knew came from pornography, 10 percent of women in a recent random study said yes. Among married women, 24 percent said yes. That is a lot of women. A lot more don't know. Some of those who do testified in Minneapolis. One wife said of her ex-husband, "He would read from the pornography like a textbook, like a journal. In fact when he asked me to be bound, when he finally convinced me to do it, he read in the magazine how to tie the knots." Another woman said of her boyfriend, "[H]e went to this party, saw pornography, got an erection, got me . . . to inflict his erection on . . . There is a direct causal relationship there." One woman, who said her husband had rape and bondage magazines all over the house, discovered two suitcases full of Barbie dolls with rope tied on their arms and legs and with tape across their mouths. Now think about the silence of women. She said, "He used to tie me up and he tried those things on me." A therapist in private practice reported:

> Presently or recently I have worked with clients who have been sodomized by broom handles, forced to have sex with over 20 dogs in the back seat of their car, tied up and then electrocuted on their genitals. These are children, [all] in the ages of 14 to 18, all of whom [have been directly affected by pornography,] [e]ither where the perpetrator has read the manuals and manuscripts at night and used these as recipe books by day or had the pornography present at the time of the sexual violence.

One woman, testifying that all the women in a group of ex-prostitutes were brought into prostitution as children through pornography, characterized their collective experience: "[I]n my experience there was not one situation where a client was not using pornography while he was using me or that he had not just watched pornography or that it was verbally referred to and directed me to pornography." "Men," she continued, "witness the abuse of women in pornography constantly and if they can't engage in that behavior with their wives, girl friends or children, they force a whore to do it."

Men also testified about how pornography hurts them. One young gay man who had seen *Playboy* and *Penthouse* as a child said of such heterosexual pornography: "It was one of the places I learned about sex and it showed me that sex was violence. What I saw there was a specific relationship between men and women. . . . [T]he woman was to be used, objectified, humiliated and hurt; the man was in a superior position, a position to be violent. In pornography I learned that what it meant to be sexual with a man or to be loved by a man was to accept his violence." For this reason, when he was battered by his first lover, which he described as "one of the most profoundly destructive experiences of my life," he accepted it.

Pornography also hurts men's capacity to relate to women. One young man spoke about this in a way that connects pornography—not the prohibition on pornography—with fascism. He spoke of his struggle to repudiate the thrill of dominance, of his difficulty finding connection with a woman to whom he is close. He said: "My point is that if women in a society filled by pornography must be wary for their physical selves, a man, even a man of good intentions, must be wary for his mind. . . . I do not want to be a mechanical, goose-stepping follower of the Playboy bunny, because that is what I think it is. . . . [T]hese are the experiments a master race perpetuates on those slated for extinction." The woman he lives with is Jewish. There was a very brutal rape near their house. She was afraid; she tried to joke. It didn't work. "She was still afraid. And just as a well-meaning German was afraid in 1933, I am also very much afraid."

Pornography stimulates and reinforces, it does not cathect or mirror, the connection between one-sided freely available sexual access to women and masculine sexual excitement and sexual satisfaction. The catharsis hypothesis is fantasy. The fantasy theory is fantasy. Reality is: pornography conditions male orgasm to female subordination. It tells men what sex means, what a real woman is, and codes them together in a way that is behaviorally reinforcing. This is a real five-dollar sentence, but I'm going to say it anyway: pornography is a set of hermeneutical equivalences that work on the epistemological level.

Substantively, pornography defines the meaning of what a woman is seen to be by connecting access to her sexuality with masculinity through orgasm. What pornography means *is* what it does.

So far, opposition to our ordinance centers on the trafficking provision. This means not only that it is difficult to comprehend a group injury in a liberal culture—that what it *means* to be a woman is defined by this and that it is an injury for all women, even if not for all women equally. It is not only that the pornography has got to be accessible, which is the bottom line of virtually every objection to this law. It is also that power, as I said, is when you say something, it is taken for reality. If you talk about rape, it will be agreed that rape is awful. But rape is a conclusion. If a victim describes the facts of a rape, maybe she was asking for it or enjoyed it or at least consented to it, or the man might have thought she did, or maybe she had had sex before. It is now agreed that there is something wrong with sexual harassment. But describe what happened to you, and it may be trivial or personal or paranoid, or maybe you should have worn a bra that day. People are against discrimination. But describe the situation of a real woman, and they are not so sure she wasn't just unqualified. In law, all these disjunctions between women's perspective on our injuries and the standards we have to meet go under dignified legal rubrics like burden of proof, credibility, defenses, elements of the crime, and so on. These standards all contain a definition of what a woman is in terms of what sex is and the low value placed on us through it. They reduce injuries done to us to authentic expressions of who we are. Our silence is written all over them. So is the pornography.

We have as yet encountered comparatively little objection to the coercion, force, or assault provisions of our ordinance. I think that's partly because the people who make and approve laws may not yet see what they do as that. They *know* they use the pornography as we have described it in this law, and our law defines that, the reality of pornography, as a harm to women. If they suspect that they might on occasion engage in or benefit from coercion or force or assault, they may think that the victims won't be able to prove it—and they're right. Women who charge men with sexual abuse are not believed. The pornographic view of them is: they want it; they all want it. When women bring charges of sexual assault, motives such as veniality or sexual repression must be invented, because we cannot really have been hurt. Under the trafficking provision, women's lack of credibility cannot be relied upon to negate the harm. There's no woman's story to destroy, no credibility-based decision on what happened. The hearings establish the harm. The definition sets the standard. The grounds of reality definition are authoritatively shifted. Pornography is bigotry, *period*. We are now—*in* the world pornography has decisively defined—having to meet the burden of proving, once and for all, for all of the rape and torture and battery, all of the sexual harassment, all of the child sexual abuse, all of the forced prostitution, *all* of it that the pornography is part of and that is part of the pornography, that the harm *does happen* and that when it happens it looks like this. Which may be why all this evidence never seems to be enough.

It is worth considering what evidence has been enough when other harms involving other purported speech interests have been allowed to be legislated against. By comparison to our trafficking provision, analytically similar restrictions have been allowed under the First Amendment, with a legislative basis far less massive, detailed, concrete, and conclusive. Our statutory language is more ordinary, objective, and precise and covers a harm far narrower than the legislative record substantiates. Under *Miller*, obscenity was allowed to be made criminal in the name of the "danger of offending the sensibilities of unwilling recipients, or exposure to juveniles." Under our law, we have direct evidence of harm, not just a conjectural danger, that unwilling women in considerable numbers are not simply offended in their sensibilities, but are violated in their persons and restricted in their options. Obscenity law also suggests that the applicable standard for legal adequacy in measuring such connections may not be statistical certainty. The Supreme Court has said that it is not their job to resolve empirical uncertainties that underlie state obscenity legisla-

tion. Rather, it is for them to determine whether a legislature could reasonably have determined that a connection might exist between the prohibited material and harm of a kind in which the state has legitimate interest. Equality should be such an area. The Supreme Court recently recognized that prevention of sexual exploitation and abuse of children is, in their words, "a governmental objective of surpassing importance." This might also be the case for sexual exploitation and abuse of women, although I think a civil remedy is initially more appropriate to the goal of empowering adult women than a criminal prohibition would be.

Other rubrics provide further support for the argument that this law is narrowly tailored to further a legitimate governmental interest consistent with the goals underlying the First Amendment. Exceptions to the First Amendment—you may have gathered from this—exist. The reason they exist is that the harm done by some speech outweighs its expressive value, if any. In our law a legislature recognizes that pornography, as defined and made actionable, undermines sex equality. One can say—and I have—that pornography is a causal factor in violations of women; one can also say that women will be violated so long as pornography exists; but one can also say simply that pornography violates women. Perhaps this is what the woman had in mind who testified at our hearings that for her the question is not just whether pornography causes violent acts to be perpetrated against some women. "Porn is already a violent act against women. It is our mothers, our daughters, our sisters, and our wives that are for sale for pocket change at the newsstands in this country." *Chaplinsky v. New Hampshire* recognized the ability to restrict as "fighting words" speech which, "by [its] very utterance inflicts injury." Perhaps the only reason that pornography has not been "fighting words"—in the sense of words that by their utterance tend to incite immediate breach of the peace—is that women have seldom fought back, yet.

Some concerns that are close to those of this ordinance underlie group libel laws, although the differences are equally important. In group libel law, as Justice Frankfurter's opinion in *Beauharnais* illustrates, it has been understood that an individual's treatment and alternatives in life may depend as much on the reputation of the group to which that person belongs as on their own merit. Not even a partial analogy can be made to group libel doctrine without examining the point made by Justice Brandeis and recently underlined by Larry Tribe: would more speech, rather than less, remedy the harm? In the end, the answer may be yes, but not under the abstract system of free speech, which only enhances the power of the pornographers while doing nothing substantively to guarantee the free speech of women, for which we need civil equality. The situation in which women presently find ourselves with respect to the pornography is one in which more *pornography* is inconsistent with rectifying or even counterbalancing its damage through speech, because so long as the pornography exists in the way it does there *will not be more speech by women*. Pornography strips and devastates women of credibility, from our accounts of sexual assault to our everyday reality of sexual subordination. We are stripped of authority and reduced and devalidated and silenced. Silenced here means that the purposes of the First Amendment, premised upon conditions presumed and promoted by protecting free speech, do not pertain to women because they are not our conditions. Consider them: individual self-fulfillment—how does pornography promote our individual self-fulfillment? How does sexual inequality even permit it? Even if she can form words, who listens to a woman with a penis in her mouth? Facilitating consensus—to the extent pornography does so, it does so one-sidedly by silencing protest over the injustice of sexual subordination. Participation in civic life—central to Professor Meiklejohn's theory—how does pornography enhance women's participation in civic life? Anyone who cannot walk down the street or even lie down in her own bed without keeping her eyes cast down and her body clenched against assault is unlikely to have much to say about the issues of the day, still less will she become Tolstoy. Facilitating change—*this law* facilitates the change that existing First Amendment theory had been used to throttle. Any system of freedom of expression that does not address a problem where the free speech of men silences the free speech

of women, a real conflict between speech interests as well as between people, is not serious about securing freedom of expression in this country.

For those of you who still think pornography is only an idea, consider the possibility that obscenity law got one thing right. Pornography is more actlike than thoughtlike. The fact that pornography, in a feminist view, furthers the idea of the sexual inferiority of women, which is a political idea, doesn't make the pornography itself into a political idea. One can express the idea a practice embodies. That does not make that practice into an idea. Segregation expresses the idea of the inferiority of one group to another on the basis of race. That does not make segregation an idea. A sign that says "Whites Only" is only words. Is it therefore protected by the First Amendment? Is it not an act, a practice, of segregation because what it means is inseparable from what it does? *Law* is only words.

The issue here is whether the fact that words and pictures are the central link in the cycle of abuse will immunize that entire cycle, about which we cannot do anything without doing something about the pornography. As Justice Stewart said in *Ginsburg*, "When expression occurs in a setting where the capacity to make a choice is absent, government regulation of that expression may coexist with and *even implement* First Amendment guarantees." I would even go so far as to say that the pattern of evidence we have closely approaches Justice Douglas's requirement that "freedom of expression can be suppressed if, and to the extent that, it is so closely brigaded with illegal action as to be an inseparable part of it." Those of you who have been trying to separate the acts from the speech—that's an act, that's an act, there's a law against that act, regulate that act, don't touch the speech—notice here that the illegality of the acts involved doesn't mean that the speech that is "brigaded with" it *cannot* be regulated. This is when it *can* be.

I take one of two penultimate points from Andrea Dworkin, who has often said that pornography is not speech for women, it is the silence of women. Remember the mouth taped, the woman gagged, "Smile, I can get a lot of money for that." The smile is not her expression, it is her silence. It is not her expression not because it didn't happen, but because it *did* happen. The screams of the women in pornography are silence, like the screams of Kitty Genovese, whose plight was misinterpreted by some onlookers as a lovers' quarrel. The flat expressionless voice of the woman in the New Bedford gang rape, testifying, is silence. She was raped as men cheered and watched, as they do in and with the pornography. When women resist and men say, "Like this, you stupid bitch, here is how to do it" and shove their faces into the pornography, this "truth of sex" is the silence of women. When they say, "If you love me, you'll try," the enjoyment we fake, the enjoyment we learn is silence. Women who submit because there is more dignity in it than in losing the fight over and over live in silence. Having to sleep with your publisher or director to get access to what men call speech is silence. Being humiliated on the basis of your appearance, whether by approval or disapproval, because you have to look a certain way for a certain job, whether you get the job or not, is silence. The absence of a woman's voice, everywhere that it cannot be heard, is silence. And anyone who thinks that what women say in pornography is women's speech—the "Fuck me, do it to me, harder," all of that—has never heard the sound of a woman's voice.

The most basic assumption underlying First Amendment adjudication is that, socially, speech is free. The First Amendment says Congress shall not abridge the freedom of speech. Free speech, get it, *exists*. Those who wrote the First Amendment *had* speech—they wrote the Constitution. *Their* problem was to keep it free from the only power that realistically threatened it: the federal government. They designed the First Amendment to prevent government from constraining that which, if unconstrained by government, was free, meaning *accessible to them*. At the same time, we can't tell much about the intent of the framers with regard to the question of women's speech, because I don't think we crossed their minds. It is consistent with this analysis that their posture toward freedom of speech tends to presuppose that whole segments of the population are not systematically silenced socially, prior to government action. If everyone's power were equal to theirs, if this were a nonhierarchical society, that might make sense. But the place of pornography in the inequality of the sexes makes the assumption of equal power untrue.

This is a hard question. It involves risks. Classically, opposition to censorship has involved keeping government off the backs of people. Our law is about getting some people off the backs of other people. The risks that it will be misused have to be measured against the risks of the status quo. Women will never have that dignity, security, compensation that is the promise of equality so long as the pornography exists as it does now. The situation of women suggests that the urgent issue of our freedom of speech is not primarily the avoidance of state intervention as such, but getting affirmative access to speech for those to whom it has been denied.

38. Feminist Antipornography Legislation

Lisa Duggan, Nan Hunter, and Carole Vance

Lisa Duggan, Nan Hunter, and Carole Vance challenge the recent legal attempt to prohibit pornography as a form of sex discrimination. They claim that although such legislation aims at prohibiting only material that is sexually explicit, violent, and sexist, in fact, it prohibits anything that is merely sexually explicit and, hence, it could contribute to an antifeminist crusade. Duggan, Hunter, and Vance also question whether pornography causes any more harm to women than other aspects of our sexist society that are not prohibited.

In the United States, after two decades of increasing community tolerance for dissenting or disturbing sexual or political materials, there is now growing momentum for retrenchment. In an atmosphere of increased conservatism, evidenced by a wave of book banning and anti-gay harassment, support for new repressive legislation of various kinds—from an Oklahoma law forbidding schoolteachers from advocating homosexuality to new antipornography laws passed in Minneapolis and Indianapolis—is growing.

The antipornography laws have mixed roots of support, however. Though they are popular with the conservative constituencies that traditionally favor legal restrictions on sexual expression of all kinds, they were drafted and are endorsed by antipornography feminists who oppose traditional obscenity and censorship laws. The model law of this type, which is now being widely copied, was drawn up in the politically progressive city of Minneapolis by two radical feminists, author Andrea Dworkin and attorney Catharine MacKinnon. It was passed by the city council there, but vetoed by the mayor. A similar law was also passed in Indianapolis, but later declared unconstitutional in federal court, a ruling that the city will appeal. Other versions of the legislation are being considered in numerous cities, and Pennsylvania senator Arlen

From *Women Against Censorship,* edited by Varda Burstyn (Vancouver: Groundwood Books/Douglas & McIntyre, 1985). Reprinted by permission of the publisher.

Specter has introduced legislation modeled on parts of the Dworkin-MacKinnon bill in the U.S. Congress.

Dworkin, MacKinnon and their feminist supporters believe that the new antipornography laws are not censorship laws. They also claim that the legislative effort behind them is based on feminist support. Both of these claims are dubious at best. Though the new laws are civil laws that allow individuals to sue the makers, sellers, distributors or exhibitors of pornography, and not criminal laws leading to arrest and imprisonment, their censoring impact would be substantially as severe as criminal obscenity laws. Materials could be removed from public availability by court injunction, and publishers and booksellers could be subject to potentially endless legal harassment. Passage of the laws was therefore achieved with the support of right-wing elements who expect the new laws to accomplish what censorship efforts are meant to accomplish. Ironically, many antifeminist conservatives backed these laws, while many feminists opposed them. In Indianapolis, the law was supported by extreme right-wing religious fundamentalists, including members of the Moral Majority, while there was *no* local feminist support. In other cities, traditional procensorship forces have expressed interest in the new approach to banning sexually explicit materials. Meanwhile, anticensorship feminists have become alarmed at these new developments and are seeking to galvanize feminist opposition to the new antipornography legislative strategy pioneered in Minneapolis.

One is tempted to ask in astonishment, how can this be happening? How can feminists be entrusting the patriarchal state with the task of legally distinguishing between permissible and impermissible sexual images? But in fact this new development is not as surprising as it at first seems. . . . [P]ornography has come to be seen as a central cause of women's oppression by a significant number of feminists. Some even argue that pornography is the root of virtually all forms of exploitation and discrimination against women. It is a short step from such a belief to the conviction that laws against pornography can end the inequality of the sexes. But this analysis takes feminists very close—indeed far too close—to measures that will ultimately support conservative, anti-sex, procensorship forces in American society, for it is with these forces that women have forged alliances in passing such legislation.

The first feminist-inspired antipornography law was passed in Minneapolis in 1983. Local legislators had been frustrated when their zoning restrictions on porn shops were struck down in the courts. Public hearings were held to discuss a new zoning ordinance. The Neighborhood Pornography Task Force of South and South Central Minneapolis invited Andrea Dworkin and Catharine MacKinnon, who were teaching a course on pornography at the University of Minnesota, to testify. They proposed an alternative that, they claimed, would completely eliminate, rather than merely regulate, pornography. They suggested that pornography be defined as a form of sex discrimination, and that an amendment to the city's civil rights law be passed to proscribe it. City officials hired Dworkin and MacKinnon to develop their new approach and to organize another series of public hearings.

The initial debate over the legislation in Minneapolis was intense, and opinion was divided within nearly every political grouping. In contrast, the public hearings held before the city council were tightly controlled and carefully orchestrated; speakers invited by Dworkin and MacKinnon—sexual abuse victims, counselors, educators and social scientists—testified about the harm pornography does women. (Dworkin and MacKinnon's agenda was the compilation of a legislative rec-

ord that would help the law stand up to its inevitable court challenges.) The legislation passed, supported by antipornography feminists, neighborhood groups concerned about the effects of porn shops on residential areas, and conservatives opposed to the availability of sexually explicit materials for "moral" reasons.

In Indianapolis, the alignment of forces was different. For the previous two years, conservative antipornography groups had grown in strength and public visibility, but they had been frustrated in their efforts. The police department could not convert its obscenity arrests into convictions; the city's zoning law was also tied up in court challenges. Then Mayor William Hudnutt III, a Republican and a Presbyterian minister, learned of the Minneapolis law. Mayor Hudnutt thought Minneapolis's approach to restricting pornography might be the solution to the Indianapolis problems. Beulah Coughenour, a conservative Republican stop-ERA activist, was recruited to sponsor the legislation in the city-county council.

Coughenour engaged MacKinnon as consultant to the city—Dworkin was not hired, but then, Dworkin's passionate radical feminist rhetoric would not have gone over well in Indianapolis. MacKinnon worked with the Indianapolis city prosecutor (a well-known anti-vice zealot), the city's legal department and Coughenour on the legislation. The law received the support of neighborhood groups, the Citizens for Decency and the Coalition for a Clean Community. There were no crowds of feminist supporters—in fact, there were no feminist supporters at all. The only feminists to make public statements opposed the legislation, which was nevertheless passed in a council meeting packed with 300 religious fundamentalists. All 24 Republicans voted for its passage; all five Democrats opposed it to no avail.

A group of publishers and booksellers challenged the law in Federal District Court, where they won the first round. This legal setback for the ordinance may cause some other cities considering similar legislation to hold off until the final resolution of the appeal of the Indianapolis decision; meanwhile, however, mutated versions of the Dworkin-

MacKinnon bill have begun to appear. A version of the law introduced in Suffolk County on Long Island in New York emphasized its conservative potential—pornography was said to cause "sodomy" and "disruption" of the family unit, in addition to rape, incest, exploitation and other acts "inimical to the public good." In Suffolk, the law was put forward by a conservative, anti-ERA male legislator who wishes to "restore ladies to what they used to be." The Suffolk County bill clearly illustrates the repressive, antifeminist potential of the new antipornography legislation. The appearance of a federal bill, together with the possibility of a new, Reagan-appointed commission to study new antipornography legislation, indicates how widespread the repressive effects of the ordinances may become.

Yet it is true that some of the U.S. laws have been proposed and supported by antipornography feminists. This is therefore a critical moment in the feminist debate over sexual politics. As anticensorship feminists work to develop alternatives to antipornography campaigns, we also need to examine carefully the new laws and expose their underlying assumptions. We need to know why these laws, for all their apparent feminist rhetoric, actually appeal to conservative antifeminist forces, and why feminists should be preparing to move in a different direction.

Definitions: The Central Flaw

The antipornography ordinances passed in Minneapolis and Indianapolis were framed as amendments to municipal civil rights laws. They provide for complaints to be filed against pornography in the same manner that complaints are filed against employment discrimination. If enforced, the laws would make illegal public or private availability (except in libraries) of any materials deemed pornographic.

Such material could be the object of a lawsuit on several grounds. The ordinance would penalize four kinds of behavior associated with pornography: its production, sale, exhibition or distribution ("trafficking"); coercion into pornographic performance; forcing pornography on a person; and assault or physical attack due to pornography. . . .

Although proponents claim that the Minneapolis and Indianapolis ordinances represent a new way to regulate pornography, the strategy is still laden with our culture's old, repressive approach to sexuality. The implementation of such laws hinges on the definition of pornography as interpreted by the court. The definition provided in the Minneapolis legislation is vague, leaving critical phrases such as "the sexually explicit subordination of women," "postures of sexual submission" and "whores by nature" to the interpretation of the citizen who files a complaint and to the civil court judge who hears the case. The legislation does not prohibit just the images of gross sexual violence that most supporters claim to be its target, but instead drifts toward covering an increasingly wide range of sexually explicit material.

The most problematic feature of this approach, then, is a conceptual flaw embedded in the law itself. Supporters of this type of legislation say that the target of their efforts is misogynist, sexually explicit and violent representation, whether in pictures or words. Indeed, the feminist antipornography movement is fueled by women's anger at the most repugnant examples of pornography. But a close examination of the wording of the model legislative text, and examples of purportedly actionable material offered by proponents of the legislation in court briefs suggest that the law is actually aimed at a range of material considerably broader than what proponents claim is their target. The discrepancies between the law's explicit and implicit aims have been almost invisible to us, because these distortions are very similar to distortions about sexuality in the culture as a whole. The legislation and supporting texts deserve close reading. Hidden beneath illogical transformations, nonsequiturs, and highly permeable definitions are familiar sexual scripts drawn from mainstream, sexist culture that potentially could have very negative consequences for women.

The Venn diagram [on the next page] illustrates the three areas targeted by the law, and represents a scheme that classifies words or images that have any of three characteristics: violence, sexual explicitness or sexism.

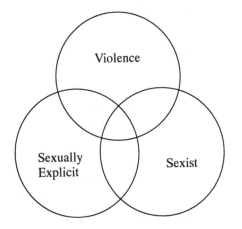

Clearly, a text or an image might have only one characteristic. Material can be violent but not sexually explicit or sexist: for example, a war movie in which both men and women suffer injury or death without regard to or because of their gender. Material can be sexist but not sexually explicit and violent. A vast number of materials from mainstream media—television, popular novels, magazines, newspapers—come to mind, all of which depict either distraught housewives or the "happy sexism" of the idealized family, with mom self-sacrificing, other-directed and content. Finally, material can be sexually explicit but not violent or sexist: for example, the freely chosen sexual behavior depicted in sex education films or women's own explicit writing about sexuality.

As the diagram illustrates, areas can also intersect, reflecting a range of combinations of the three characteristics. Images can be violent and sexually explicit without being sexist—for example, a narrative about a rape in a men's prison, or a documentary about the effect of a rape on a woman. The latter example illustrates the importance of context in evaluating whether material that is sexually explicit and violent is also sexist. The intent of the maker, the context of the film and the perception of the viewer together render a depiction of a rape sympathetic, harrowing, even educational, rather than sensational, victim-blaming and laudatory.

Another possible overlap is between material that is violent and sexist but not sexually explicit. Films or books that describe violence directed against women by men in a way that clearly shows gender antagonism and inequality, and sometimes strong sexual tension, but no sexual explicitness fall into this category— for example, the popular genre of slasher films in which women are stalked, terrified and killed by men, or accounts of mass murder of women, fueled by male rage. Finally, a third point of overlap arises when material is sexually explicit and sexist without being violent— that is, when sex is consensual but still reflects themes of male superiority and female abjectness. Some sex education materials could be included in this category, as well as a great deal of regular pornography.

The remaining domain, the inner core, is one in which the material is simultaneously violent, sexually explicit and sexist—for example, an image of a naked woman being slashed by a knife-wielding rapist. The Minneapolis law, however, does not by any means confine itself to this material.

To be actionable under the law as pornography, material must be judged by the courts to be "the sexually explicit subordination of women, graphically depicted whether in pictures or in words that also includes at least one or more" of nine criteria. Of these, only four involve the intersection of violence, sexual explicitness and sexism, and then only arguably. . . . Even in these cases, many questions remain about whether images with all three characteristics do in fact cause violence against women. . . . And the task of evaluating material that is ostensibly the target of these criteria becomes complicated—indeed, hopeless—because most of the clauses that contain these criteria mix actions or qualities of violence with those that are not particularly associated with violence.

The section that comes closest to the stated purpose of the legislation is clause (iii): "women are presented as sexual objects who experience sexual pleasure in being raped." This clause is intended to cover depictions of rape that are sexually explicit and sexist; the act of rape itself signifies the violence. But other clauses are not so clearcut, because the list of characteristics often mixes signs or byproducts of violence with phenomena that are unrelated or irrelevant to judging violence. We might be willing to agree that clause (ii)— "women are presented as sexual objects who enjoy pain"—signifies the conjunction of all three characteristics, with violence the presumed cause of pain, but the presence of the words "and humiliation" at the end of the clause is problematic. Humiliation may be offensive or disagreeable, but it does not necessarily imply violence.

A similar problem occurs with clause (iv): "women are presented as sexual objects tied up or cut up or mutilated or bruised or physically hurt." All these except the first, "tied up," generally occur as a result of violence. "Tied up," if part of consensual sex, is not violent and, for some practitioners, not particularly sexist. Women who are tied up may be participants in nonviolent sex play involving bondage, a theme in both heterosexual and lesbian pornography. (See, for example, *The Joy of Sex* and *Coming to Power*.) Clause (ix) contains another mixed list, in which "injury," "torture," "bleeding," "bruised" and "hurt" are combined with words such as "degradation" and "shown as filthy and inferior," neither of which is violent. Depending on the presentation, "filthy" and "inferior" may constitute sexually explicit sexism, although not violence. "Degradation" is a sufficiently inclusive term to cover most acts of which a viewer disapproves.

Several other clauses have little to do with violence at all; they refer to material that is sexually explicit and sexist, thus falling outside the triad of characteristics at which the legislation is supposedly aimed. For example, movies in which "women are presented as dehumanized sexual objects, things, or commodities" may be infuriating and offensive to feminists, but they are not violent.

Finally, some clauses describe material that is neither violent nor necessarily sexist. Clause (v), "women . . . in postures of sexual submission or sexual servility, including by inviting penetration," and clause (viii), "women . . . being penetrated by objects or animals," are sexually explicit, but not violent and not obviously sexist unless one believes that penetration—whether heterosexual, lesbian, or autoerotic masturbation—is indicative of gender inequality and female oppression. Sim-

ilarly problematic are clauses that invoke representations of "women . . . as whores by nature" and "women's body parts . . . such that women are reduced to those parts."

Texts filed in support of the Indianapolis law show how broadly it could be applied. In the amicus brief filed on behalf of Linda Marchiano ("Linda Lovelace," the female lead in *Deep Throat*) in Indianapolis, Catharine MacKinnon offered *Deep Throat* as an example of the kind of pornography covered by the law. *Deep Throat* served a complicated function in this brief, because the movie, supporters of the ordinance argue, would be actionable on two counts: coercion into pornographic performance, because Marchiano alleges that she was coerced into making the movie; and trafficking in pornography, because the content of the film falls within one of the categories in the Indianapolis ordinance's definition—that which prohibits presenting women as sexual objects "through postures or positions of servility or submission or display." Proponents of the law have counted on women's repugnance at allegations of coerced sexual acts to spill over and discredit the sexual acts themselves in this movie.

The aspects of *Deep Throat* that MacKinnon considered to be indicative of "sexual subordination" are of particular interest, since any movie that depicted similar acts could be banned under the law. MacKinnon explained in her brief that the film "subordinates women by using women . . . sexually, specifically as eager servicing receptacles for male genitalia and ejaculate. The majority of the film represents 'Linda Lovelace' in, minimally, postures of sexual submission and/or servility." In its brief, the City of Indianapolis concurred: "In the film *Deep Throat* a woman is being shown as being ever eager for oral penetration by a series of men's penises, often on her hands and knees. There are repeated scenes in which her genitalia are graphically displayed and she is shown as enjoying men ejaculating on her face."

These descriptions are very revealing, since they suggest that multiple partners, group sex and oral sex subordinate women and hence are sexist. The notion that the female character is "used" by men suggests that it is improbable that a woman would engage in fellatio of her own accord. *Deep Throat* does draw on several sexist conventions common in advertising and the entire visual culture—the woman as object of the male gaze, and the assumption of heterosexuality, for example. But it is hardly an unending paean to male dominance, since the movie contains many contrary themes. In it, the main female character is shown as both actively seeking her own pleasure and as trying to please men; a secondary female character is shown as actually directing encounters with multiple male partners. Both briefs described a movie quite different from the one viewers see.

At its heart, this analysis implies that heterosexual sex itself is sexist; that women do not engage in it of their own volition; and that behavior pleasurable to men is repugnant to women. In some contexts, for example, the representation of fellatio and multiple partners can be sexist, but are we willing to concede that they always are? If not, then what is proposed as actionable under the Indianapolis law includes merely sexually explicit representation (the traditional target of obscenity laws), which proponents of the legislation vociferously insist they are not interested in attacking.

Some other examples offered through exhibits submitted with the City of Indianapolis brief and also introduced in the public hearing further illustrate this point. Many of the exhibits are depictions of sadomasochism. The court briefs treat SM material as depicting violence and aggression, not consensual sex, in spite of avowals to the contrary by many SM practitioners. With this legislation, then, a major question for feminists that has only begun to develop would be closed for discussion. Instead, a simplistic reduction has been advanced as the definitive feminist position. The description of the material in the briefs focused on submissive women and implied male domination, highlighting the similarity proponents would like to find between all SM narratives and male/female inequality. The actual exhibits, however, illustrated plots and power relations far more diverse than the descriptions provided by MacKinnon and the City of Indianapolis would suggest, including SM between women and female dominant/male submissive SM. For example, the In-

dianapolis brief stated that in the magazine *The Bitch Goddesses,* "women are shown in torture chambers with their nude body parts being tortured by their 'master' for 'even the slightest offense'. . . . The magazine shows a woman in a scenario of torture." But the brief failed to mention that the dominants in this magazine are all female, with one exception. This kind of discrepancy characterized many examples offered in the briefs.

This is not to say that such representations do not raise questions for feminists. The current lively discussion about lesbian SM clearly demonstrates that this issue is still unresolved. But in the Indianapolis briefs all SM material was assumed to be male dominant/female submissive, thereby squeezing a nonconforming reality into prepackaged, inadequate—and therefore dangerous—categories. This legislation would virtually eliminate all SM pornography by recasting it as violent, thereby attacking a sexual minority while masquerading as an attempt to end violence against women.

Analysis of clauses in the Minneapolis ordinance and several examples offered in court briefs filed in connection with the Indianapolis ordinance show that the law targets material that is sexually explicit and sexist, but ignores material that is violent and sexist, violent and sexually explicit, only violent or only sexist.

Certain troubling questions arise here, for if one claims, as some antipornography activists do, that there is a direct relationship between images and behavior, why should images of violence against women or scenarios of sexism in general not be similarly proscribed? Why is sexual explicitness singled out as the cause of women's oppression? For proponents to exempt violent and sexist images, or even sexist images, from regulation is inconsistent, especially since they are so pervasive.

Even more difficulties arise from the vagueness of certain terms crucial in interpreting the ordinances. The term "subordination" is especially important, since pornography is defined as the "sexually explicit subordination of women." The authors of this legislation intend it to modify each of the clauses, and they appear to believe that it provides a definition of sexism that each example must meet. The term is never defined in the legislation, yet the Indianapolis brief, for example, suggests that the average viewer, on the basis of "his or her common understanding of what it means for one person to subordinate another" should be able to decide what is pornographic. But what kind of sexually explicit acts place a woman in an inferior status? To some, *any* graphic sexual act violates women's dignity and therefore subordinates them. To others, consensual heterosexual lovemaking within the boundaries of procreation and marriage is acceptable, but heterosexual acts that do not have reproduction as their aim lower women's status and hence subordinate them. Still others accept a wide range of nonprocreative, perhaps even nonmarital, heterosexuality but draw the line at lesbian sex, which they view as degrading.

The term "sex object" is also problematic. The City of Indianapolis's brief maintains that "the term sexual object, often shortened to sex object, has enjoyed a wide popularity in mainstream American culture in the past fifteen years, and is used to denote the objectification of a person on the basis of their sex or sex appeal. . . . People know what it means to disregard all aspects of personhood but sex, to reduce a person to a thing used for sex." But, indeed, people do not agree on this point. The definition of "sex object" is far from clear or uniform. For example, some feminist and liberal cultural critics have used the term to mean sex that occurs without strong emotional ties and experience. More conservative critics maintain that any detachment of women's sexuality from procreation, marriage and family objectifies it, removing it from its "natural" web of associations and context. Unredeemed and unprotected by domesticity and family, women—and their sexuality—become things used by men. In both these views, women are never sexually autonomous agents who direct and enjoy their sexuality for their own purposes, but rather are victims. In the same vein, other problematic terms include "inviting penetration," "whores by nature" and "positions of display."

Through close analysis of the proposed legislation one sees how vague the boundaries of the definitions that contain the inner core of the Venn diagram really are. Their dissolution does not happen equally at all points, but only at some: the inner core begins to include sexually explicit and sexist material, and finally expands to include purely sexually explicit

material. Thus "sexually explicit" becomes identified and equated with "violent" with no further definition or explanation.

It is also striking that so many feminists have failed to notice that the laws (as well as examples of actionable material) cover so much diverse work, not just that small and symbolic epicentre where many forms of opposition to women converge. It suggests that for us, as well as for others, sexuality remains a difficult area. We have no clearly developed framework in which to think about sex equivalent to the frameworks that are available for thinking about race, gender and class issues. Consequently, in sex, as in few other areas of human behavior, unexamined and unjustifiable prejudice passes itself off as considered opinion about what is desirable and normal. And finally, sex arouses considerable anxiety, stemming from both the meeting with individual difference and from the prospect—suggested by feminists themselves—that sexual behavior is constructed socially and is not simply natural.

The law takes advantage of everyone's relative ignorance and anxious ambivalence about sex, distorting and oversimplifying what confronts us in building a sexual politic. For example, antipornography feminists draw on several feminist theories about the role of violent, aggressive or sexist representations. The first is relatively straightforward: that these images trigger men into action. The second suggests that violent images act more subtly, to socialize men to act in sexist or violent ways by making this behavior seem commonplace and more acceptable, if not expected. The third assumption is that violent, sexually explicit or even sexist images are offensive to women, assaulting their sensibilities and sense of self. Although we have all used metaphor to exhort women to action or illustrate a point, antipornography proponents have frequently used these conventions of speech as if they were literal statements of fact. But these metaphors have gotten out of hand, as Julie Abraham has noted, for they fail to recognize that the assault committed by a wife beater is quite different from the visual "assault" of a sexist ad on TV. The nature of that difference is still being clarified in a complex debate within feminism that must continue; this law cuts off speculation, settling on a causal relationship between image and action that is starkly simple, if unpersuasive.

This metaphor also paves the way for reclassifying images that are merely sexist as also violent and aggressive. Thus, it is no accident that the briefs supporting the legislation first invoke violent images and rapidly move to include sexist and sexually explicit images without noting that they are different. The equation is made more easy by the constant shifts back to examples of depictions of real violence, almost to draw attention away from the sexually explicit or sexist material that in fact would be affected by the laws.

Most important, what underlies this legislation and the success of its analysis in blurring and exceeding boundaries is an appeal to a very traditional view of sex: sex is degrading to women. By this logic, any illustrations or descriptions of explicit sexual acts that involve women are in themselves affronts to women's dignity. In its brief, the City of Indianapolis was quite specific about this point: "The harms caused by pornography are by no means limited to acts of physical aggression. The mere existence of pornography in society degrades and demeans all women." Embedded in this view are several other familiar themes: that sex is degrading to women, but not to men; that men are raving beasts; that sex is dangerous for women; that sexuality is male, not female; that women are victims, not sexual actors; that men inflict "it" on women; that penetration is submission; that heterosexual sexuality, rather than the institution of heterosexuality, is sexist.

These assumptions, in part intended, in part unintended, lead us back to the traditional target of obscenity law: sexually explicit material. What initially appeared novel, then, is really the reappearance of a traditional theme. It's ironic that a feminist position on pornography incorporates most of the myths about sexuality that feminism has struggled to displace.

The Dangers of Application

The Minneapolis and Indianapolis ordinances embody a political view that holds pornography to be a central force in "creating and maintaining" the oppression of women. This view appears in summary form in the legislative findings section at the beginning of the Minneapolis bill, which describes a chain reaction of misogynistic acts generated by pornography. The legislation is based on the interweaving of several themes: that pornography constructs the meaning of sexuality for women and, as well, leads to discrete acts of violence against women; that sexuality is the primary cause of women's oppression; that explicitly sexual images, even if not violent or coerced, have the power to subordinate women; and that women's own accounts of force have been silenced because, as a universal and timeless rule, society credits pornographic constructions rather than women's experiences. Taking the silencing contention a step further, advocates of the ordinance effectively assume that women have been so conditioned by the pornographic world view that if their own experiences of the sexual acts identified in the definition are not subordinating, then they must simply be victims of false consciousness.

The heart of the ordinance is the "trafficking" section, which would allow almost anyone to seek the removal of any materials falling within the law's definition of pornography. Ordinance defenders strenuously protest that the issue is not censorship because the state, as such, is not authorized to initiate criminal prosecutions. But the prospect of having to defend a potentially infinite number of privately filed complaints creates at least as much of a chilling effect against pornographic or sexual speech as does a criminal law. And as long as representatives of the state—in this case, judges—have ultimate say over the interpretation, the distinction between this ordinance and "real" censorship will not hold.

In addition, three major problems should dissuade feminists from supporting this kind of law: first, the sexual images in question do not cause more harm than other aspects of misogynist culture; second, sexually explicit speech, even in male-dominated society, serves positive social functions for women; and third, the passage and enforcement of antipornography laws such as those supported in Minneapolis and Indianapolis are more likely to impede, rather than advance, feminist goals.

Ordinance proponents contend that pornography does cause violence because it conditions male sexual response to images of violence and thus provokes violence against women. The strongest research they offer is based on psychology experiments that employ films depicting a rape scene, toward the end of which the woman is shown to be enjoying the attack. The ordinances, by contrast, cover a much broader range of materials than this one specific heterosexual rape scenario. Further, the studies ordinance supporters cite do not support the theory that pornography causes violence against women. . . .

In addition, the argument that pornography itself plays a major role in the general oppression of women contradicts the evidence of history. It need hardly be said that pornography did not lead to the burning of witches or the English common law treatment of women as chattel property. If anything functioned then as the prime communication medium for woman-hating, it was probably religion. Nor can pornography be blamed for the enactment of laws from at least the eighteenth century that allowed a husband to rape or beat his wife with impunity. In any period, the causes of women's oppression have been many and complex, drawing on the fundamental social and economic structures of society. Ordinance proponents offer little evidence to explain how the mass production of pornography—a relatively recent phenomenon—could have become so potent a causative agent so quickly.

The silencing of women is another example of the harm attributed to pornography. Yet if this argument were correct, one would expect that as the social visibility of pornography has increased, the tendency to credit women's accounts of rape would have decreased. In fact, although the treatment of women complainants in rape cases is far from perfect, the last 15 years of work by the women's movement has resulted in marked improvements. In many places, the corroboration requirement has now been abolished; cross-examination of victims as to past sexual experiences has been prohibited; and a number of police forces have developed specially trained units and procedures to improve the handling of sexual assault cases. The presence of rape fantasies in pornography may in part reflect a backlash against these women's movement

advances, but to argue that most people routinely disbelieve women who file charges of rape belittles the real improvements made in social consciousness and law.

The third type of harm suggested by the ordinance backers is a kind of libel: the maliciously false characterization of women as a group of sexual masochists. Like libel, the City of Indianapolis brief argues, pornography is "a lie [which] once loosed" cannot be effectively rebutted by debate and further speech.

To claim that all pornography as defined by the ordinance is a lie is a false analogy. If truth is a defence to charges of libel, then surely depictions of consensual sex cannot be thought of as equivalent to a falsehood. For example, some women (and men) do enjoy being tied up or displaying themselves. The declaration by fiat that even sadomasochism is a "lie" about sexuality reflects an arrogance and moralism that feminists should combat, not engage in. When mutually desired sexual experiences are depicted, pornography is not "libelous." . . .

These laws, which would increase the state's regulation of sexual images, present many dangers for women. Although the ordinances draw much of their feminist support from women's anger at the market for images of sexual violence, they are aimed not at violence, but at sexual explicitness. Far-right elements recognize the possibility of using the full potential of the ordinances to enforce their sexually conservative world view, and have supported them for that reason. Feminists should therefore look carefully at the text of these "model" laws in order to understand why many believe them to be a useful tool in antifeminist moral crusades.

The proposed ordinances are also dangerous because they seek to embody in law an analysis of the role of sexuality and sexual images in the oppression of women with which even all feminists do not agree. Underlying virtually every section of the proposed laws there is an assumption that sexuality is a realm of unremitting, unequaled victimization for women. Pornography appears as the monster that made this so. The ordinances' authors seek to impose their analysis by putting state power behind it. But this analysis is not the only feminist perspective on sexuality. Feminist theorists have also argued that the sexual terrain, however power laden, is actively contested. Women are agents, and not merely victims, who make decisions and act on them, and who desire, seek out and enjoy sexuality.

Acknowledgments

For stimulating discussion and political comradeship, thanks to FACT (Feminist Anti-Censorship Task Force), New York, and to members of the Scholar and the Feminist IX study group (Julie Abraham, Hannah Alderfer, Meryl Altman, Jan Boney, Frances Doughty, Kate Ellis, Faye Ginsburg, Diane Harriford, Beth Jaker, Barbara Kerr, Mary Clare Lennon, Marybeth Nelson, Ann Snitow, Paula Webster and Ellen Willis). Special thanks to Rayna Rapp and Janice Irvine for comments and criticisms, to Lawrence Krasnoff for graphics and to Ann Snitow for aid above and beyond the call of duty. We are grateful to Varda Burstyn for her helpful suggestions and patience. We remain responsible for the opinions expressed here.

39. *American Booksellers v. Hudnutt*

United States District Court and Court of Appeals

The issue before the federal judiciary was whether the Indianapolis ordinance that sought to prohibit pornography as a practice that discriminated against women was restricting speech rather than conduct, and if it was restricting speech whether it was restricting speech that was protected by the First Amendment to the United States Constitution. The federal judiciary ruled that the ordinance was restricting speech rather than conduct and that the speech it was restricting was in fact protected by the First Amendment.

Indianapolis enacted an ordinance defining "pornography" as a practice that discriminates against women. "Pornography" is to be redressed through the administrative and judicial methods used for other discrimination. . . .

"Pornography" under the ordinance is "the graphic sexually explicit subordination of women, whether in pictures or in words, that also includes one or more of the following:

1. Women are presented as sexual objects who enjoy pain or humiliation; or

2. Women are presented as sexual objects who experience sexual pleasure in being raped; or

3. Women are presented as sexual objects tied up or cut up or mutilated or bruised or physically hurt, or as dismembered or truncated or fragmented or severed into body parts; or

4. Women are presented as being penetrated by objects or animals; or

5. Women are presented in scenarios of degradation, injury, abasement, torture, shown as filthy or inferior, bleeding, bruised, or hurt in a context that makes these conditions sexual; or

6. Women are presented as sexual objects for domination, conquest, violation, exploitation, possession, or use, or through postures or positions of servility or submission or display." . . .

First Amendment Requirements

This Ordinance cannot be analyzed adequately without first recognizing this: the drafters of the Ordinance have used what appears to be a legal term of art, "pornography," but have in fact given the term a specialized meaning which differs from the meanings ordinarily assigned to that word in both legal and common parlance. In Section 16-3(v) (page 6), the Ordinance states:

Pornography shall mean the sexually explicit subordination of women, graphically depicted, whether in pictures or in words, that includes one or more of the following:
. . .

There follows at that point a listing of five specific presentations of women in various settings which serve as examples of "pornography" and as such further define and describe that term under the Ordinance.

As is generally recognized, the word "pornography" is usually associated, and sometimes synonymous, with the word, "obscenity." "Obscenity" not only has its own separate and specialized meaning in the law, but in laymen's use also, and it is a much broader meaning than the definition given the word "pornography" in the Ordinance which is at issue in this action. There is thus a considerable risk of confusion in analyzing this ordinance unless care and precision are used in that process.

The Constitutional analysis of this Ordinance requires a determination of several underlying issues: first, the Court must determine whether the Ordinance imposes restraints on speech or behavior (content versus conduct); if the Ordinance is found to regulate speech, the Court must next determine whether the subject speech is protected or not protected under the First Amendment; if the speech which is regulated by this Ordinance is protected speech under the Constitution, the Court must then decide whether the regulation is constitutionally permissible as being based on a compelling state interest justifying the removal of such speech from First Amendment protections.

Do the Ordinances Regulate Speech or Behavior (Content or Conduct)?

It appears to be central to the defense of the Ordinance by defendants that the Court accept their premise that the City-County Council has not attempted to regulate speech, let alone protected speech. Defendants repeat throughout their briefs the incantation that their Ordinance regulates conduct, not speech. They contend (one senses with a certain sleight of hand) that the production, dissemination, and use of sexually explicit words and pictures is the actual subordination of women and not an expression of ideas deserving of First Amendment protection. . . .

Defendants claim support for their theory by analogy, arguing that it is an accepted and established legal distinction that has allowed other courts to find that advocacy of a racially "separate but equal" doctrine in a civil rights context is protected speech under the First Amendment though "segregation" is not constitutionally protected behavior. Accordingly, defendants characterize their Ordinance here as a civil rights measure, through which they seek to prevent the distribution, sale, and exhibition of "pornography," as defined in the Ordinance, in order to regulate and control the underlying unacceptable conduct.

The content-versus-conduct approach espoused by defendants is not persuasive, however, and is contrary to accepted First Amendment principles. Accepting as true the City-County Council's finding that pornography conditions society to subordinate women, the means by which the Ordinance attempts to combat this sex discrimination is nonetheless through the regulation of speech.

For instance, the definition of pornography, the control of which is the whole thrust of the Ordinance, states that it is "the sexually explicit subordination of women, graphically *depicted,* whether in *pictures* or in *words,* that includes one or more of the following:" (emphasis supplied) and the following five descriptive subparagraphs begin with the words, "Women are *presented* . . . ." . . .

The unlawful acts and discriminatory practices under the Ordinance are set out in Section 16-3(g):

(4) Trafficking in pornography: the production, sale, exhibition, or distribution of pornography. . . .

(5) Coercion into pornographic performance: coercing, intimidating or fraudulently inducing any person . . . into performing for pornography.
   . . .

(6) Forcing pornography on a person:
   . . . .

(7) Assault or physical attack due to pornography: the assault, physical attack, or injury of any woman, man, child or transsexual in a way that is directly caused by specific pornography. . . .

Section (7), *supra,* goes on to provide a cause of action in damages against the perpetrators, makers, distributors, sellers and exhibitors of pornography and injunctive relief against the further exhibition, distribution or sale of pornography.

In summary, therefore, the Ordinance establishes through the legislative findings that pornography causes a tendency to commit these various harmful acts, and outlaws the pornography (that is, the "depictions"), the activities involved in the production of pornography, and the behavior caused by or resulting from pornography.

Thus, though the purpose of the Ordinance is cast in civil rights terminology—"to prevent and prohibit all discriminatory practices of sexual subordination or inequality through pornography" . . .—it is clearly aimed at controlling the content of the speech and ideas which the City-County Council has found harmful and offensive. Those words and pictures which depict women in sexually subordinate roles are banned by the Ordinance. Despite defendants' attempt to redefine offensive speech as harmful action, the clear wording of the Ordinance discloses that they seek to control speech, and those restrictions must be analyzed in light of applicable constitutional requirements and standards.

Is the Speech Regulated by the Ordinance Protected or Unprotected Speech Under the First Amendment?

The First Amendment provides that government shall make no law abridging the freedom of speech. However, "the First and Fourteenth Amendments have never been thought to give absolute protection to every individual to speak whenever or wherever he pleases or to use any form of address in any circumstances that he chooses." *Cohen v. California,* . . . (1971). Courts have recognized only a "relatively few categories of instances," . . . where the government may regulate certain forms of individual expression. The traditional categories of speech subject to permissible government regulation include "the lewd and obscene, the profane, the libelous, and the insulting or 'fighting' words—those which by their very utterance inflict injury or tend to incite an immediate breach of the peace." *Chaplinsky v. State of New Hampshire,* . . . (1942). In addition, the Supreme Court has recently upheld legislation prohibiting the dissemination of material depicting children engaged in sexual conduct. *New York v. Ferber,* . . . (1982).

Having found that the Ordinance at issue here seeks to regulate speech (and not conduct), the next question before the Court is whether the Ordinance, which seeks to restrict the distribution, sale, and exhibition of "pornography" as a form of sex discrimination against women, falls within one of the established categories of speech subject to permissible government regulation, that is, speech deemed to be unprotected by the First Amendment.

It is clear that this case does not present issues relating to profanity, libel, or "fighting words." In searching for an analytical "peg," the plaintiffs argue that the Ordinance most closely resembles obscenity, and is, therefore, subject to the requirements set forth in *Miller v. California,* . . . (1973). . . . But the defendants admit that the scope of the Ordinance is not limited to the regulation of legally obscene material as defined in *Miller.* . . . In fact, defendants concede that the "pornography" they seek to control goes beyond obscenity, as defined by the Supreme Court and excepted from First Amendment protections. Accordingly, the parties agree that the materials encompassed in the restrictions set out in the Ordinance include to some extent what have traditionally been protected materials.

The test under *Miller* for determining whether material is legal obscenity is:

> (a) whether "the average person, applying contemporary community standards" would find that the work, taken as a whole, appeals to the prurient interest, . . . ; (b) whether the work depicts or describes, in a patently offensive way, sexual conduct specifically defined by the applicable state law; and (c) whether the work, taken as a whole, lacks serious literary, artistic, political, or scientific value. . . .

It is obvious that this three-step test is not directly applicable to the present case, because, as has been noted, the Ordinance goes beyond legally obscene material in imposing its controls. The restrictions in the Indianapolis ordinance reach what has otherwise traditionally been regarded as protected speech under the *Miller* test. Beyond that, the Ordinance does not speak in terms of a "community standard" or attempt to restrict the dissemination of material that appeals to the "prurient interest." Nor has the Ordinance been drafted in a way to limit only distributions of "patently offensive" materials. Neither does it provide for the dissemination of works which, though "pornographic," may have "serious literary, artistic, political or scientific value." Finally, the Ordinance does not limit its reach to "hard core sexual conduct," though conceivably "hard core" materials may be included in its proscriptions.

Because the Ordinance spans so much more broadly in its regulatory scope than merely "hard core" obscenity by limiting the distribution of "pornography," the proscriptions in the Ordinance intrude with defendants' explicit approval into areas of otherwise protected speech. Under ordinary constitutional analysis, that would be sufficient grounds to overturn the Ordinance, but defendants argue that this case is not governed by any direct precedent, that it raises a new

issue for the Court and even though the Ordinance regulates protected speech, it does so in a constitutionally permissible fashion.

Does Established First Amendment Law Permit the Regulation Provided for in the Ordinance of Otherwise Protected Speech?

In conceding that the scope of this Ordinance extends beyond constitutional limits, it becomes clear that what defendants actually seek by enacting this legislation is a newly defined class of constitutionally unprotected speech, labeled "pornography" and characterized as sexually discriminatory.

Defendants vigorously argue that *Miller* is not the " 'constitutional divide' separating protected from unprotected expression in this area." . . . Defendants point to three cases which allegedly support their proposition that *Miller* is not the exclusive guideline for disposing of pornography/obscenity cases, and that the traditional obscenity test should not be applied in the present case. . . .

Defendants first argue that the Court must use the same reasoning applied by the Supreme Court in *New York v. Ferber*, . . . which upheld a New York statute prohibiting persons from promoting child pornography by distributing material which depicted such activity, and carve out another similar exception to protected speech under the First Amendment.

Defendants can properly claim some support for their position in *Ferber*. There the Supreme Court allowed the states "greater leeway" in their regulation of pornographic depictions of children in light of the State's compelling interest in protecting children who, without such protections, are extraordinarily vulnerable to exploitation and harm. The court stated in upholding the New York statute:

> The prevention of sexual exploitation and abuse of children constitutes a government objective of surpassing importance. The legislative findings accompanying passage of the New York laws reflect this concern: . . . .

. . . The Supreme Court continued in *Ferber* by noting that the *Miller* standard for legal obscenity does not satisfy the unique concerns and issues posed by child pornography where children are involved; it is irrelevant, for instance, that the materials sought to be regulated contain serious literary, artistic, political or scientific value. In finding that some speech, such as that represented in depictions of child pornography, is outside First Amendment protections, the *Ferber* court stated:

> When a definable class of material, . . . , bears so heavily and pervasively on the welfare of children engaged in its production, we think the balance of competing interests is clearly struck and that it is permissible to consider these materials as without the protection of the First Amendment.

Defendants, in the case at bar, argue that the interests of protecting women from sex-based discrimination are analogous to and every bit as compelling and fundamental as those which the Supreme Court upheld in *Ferber* for the benefit of children. But *Ferber* appears clearly distinguishable from the instant case on both the facts and law.

As has already been shown, the rationale applied by the Supreme Court in *Ferber* appears intended to apply solely to child pornography cases. In *Ferber,* the court recognized "that a state's interest in 'safeguarding the physical and psychological well-being of a minor' is 'compelling.' " . . . Also, the obscenity standard in *Miller* is appropriately abandoned in child pornography cases because it "[does] not reflect the State's particular and more compelling interest in prosecuting those who promote the sexual exploitations of children." . . . Since a state's compelling interest in preventing child pornography outweighs an individual's First Amendment rights, the Supreme Court held that "the states are entitled to greater leeway in the regulation of pornographic depictions of children." . . .

In contrast, the case at bar presents issues more far reaching than those in *Ferber.* Here, the City-County Council found that the distribution, sale, and exhibition of words and pictures depicting the subordination of women is a form of sex discrimination and as such is appropriate for governmental regulation. The state has a well-recognized interest in preventing sex discrimination, and, defendants argue, it can regulate speech to accomplish that end.

But the First Amendment gives primacy to free speech and any other state interest (such as the interest of sex-based equality under law) must be so compelling as to be fundamental; only then can it be deemed to outweigh the interest of free speech. This Court finds no legal authority or public policy argument which justifies so broad an incursion into First Amendment freedoms as to allow that which defendants attempt to advance here. *Ferber* does not open the door to allow the regulation contained in the Ordinance for the reason that adult women as a group do not, as a matter of public policy or applicable law, stand in need of the same type of protection which has long been afforded children. This is true even of women who are subject to the sort of inhuman treatment defendants have described and documented to the Court in support of this Ordinance. The Supreme Court's finding in *Ferber* of the uncontroverted state interest in "safeguarding the physical and psychological well being of a minor" and its resultant characterization of that interest as "compelling," . . . is an interest which inheres to children and is not an interest which is readily transferrable to adult women as a class. Adult women generally have the capacity to protect themselves from participating in and being personally victimized by pornography, which makes the State's interest in safeguarding the physical and psychological well-being of women by prohibiting "the sexually explicit subordination of women, graphically depicted, whether in pictures or in words" not so compelling as to sacrifice the guarantees of the First Amendment. In any case, whether a state interest is so compelling as to be a fundamental interest sufficient to warrant an exception from constitutional protections, therefore, surely must turn on something other than mere legislative dictate, which issue is discussed more fully further on in this Opinion. . . .

The second case relied upon by defendants to support their contention that *Miller* is not controlling in the present case is *FCC v. Pacifica Foundation,* . . . (1978). According to defendants, *Pacifica* exemplifies the Supreme Court's refusal to make obscenity the sole legal basis for regulating sexually explicit conduct.

In *Pacifica,* the Supreme Court was faced with the question of whether a broadcast of patently offensive words dealing with sex and excretion may be regulated on the basis of their content. . . . The Court held that this type of speech was not entitled to absolute constitutional protection in every context. . . . Since the context of the speech in *Pacifica* was broadcasting, it was determined only to be due "the most limited First Amendment protection." . . . The reason for such treatment was two-fold:

> First, the broadcast media have established a uniquely pervasive presence in all the lives of all Americans. Patently offensive, indecent material presented over the airwaves confronts the citizen, not only in public, but also in the privacy of the home, where the individual's right to be left alone plainly outweighs the First Amendment rights of an intruder.

> Second, broadcasting is uniquely accessible to children, even those too young to read. . . .

Although the defendants correctly point out that the Supreme Court did not use the traditional obscenity test in *Pacifica,* this Court is not persuaded that the rule enunciated there is applicable to the facts of the present case. The Ordinance does not attempt to regulate the airwaves; in terms of its restrictions, it is not even remotely concerned with the broadcast media. The reasons for the rule in *Pacifica,* that speech in certain contexts should be afforded minimal First Amendment protection, are not present here, since we are not dealing with a medium that "invades" the privacy of the home. In contrast, if an individual is offended by "pornography," as defined in the Ordinance, the logical thing to do is avoid it, an option frequently not available to the public with material disseminated through broadcasting.

In addition, the Ordinance is not written to protect children from the distribution of pornography, in contrast to the challenged FCC regulation in *Pacifica.* Therefore, the peculiar state interest in protecting the "well-being of its youth," . . . does not underlie this Ordinance and cannot be called upon to justify a decision by this Court to uphold the Ordinance.

The third case cited by defendants in support of their proposition that the traditional obscenity standard in *Miller* should not be used to overrule the Ordinance is *Young v. American Mini Theatres, Inc.,* . . . (1976). In *Young* the Supreme Court upheld a city ordinance that restricted the location of movie theatres featuring erotic films. The Court, in a plurality opinion, stated that "[e]ven though the First Amendment protects communication in this area from total suppression, we hold that the State may legitimately use the content of these materials as the basis for placing them in a different classification from other motion pictures." . . . The Court concluded that the city's interest in preserving the character of its neighborhoods justified the ordinance which required that adult theatres be separated, rather than concentrated, in the same areas as it is permissible for other theaters to do without limitation. . . .

Young is distinguishable from the present case because we are not here dealing with an attempt by the City-County Council to restrict the time, place, and manner in which "pornography" may be distributed. Instead, the Ordinance prohibits completely the sale, distribution, or exhibition of material depicting women in a sexually subordinate role, at all times, in all places and in every manner.

The Ordinance's attempt to regulate speech beyond one of the well-defined exceptions to protected speech under the First Amendment is not supported by other Supreme Court precedents. The Court must, therefore, examine the underlying premise of the Ordinance: that the State has so compelling an interest in regulating the sort of sex discrimination imposed and perpetuated through "pornography" that it warrants an exception to free speech.

Is Sex Discrimination a Compelling State Interest Justifying an Exception to First Amendment Protections?

It is significant to note that the premise of the Ordinance is the sociological harm, *i.e.,* the discrimination, which results from "pornography" to degrade women as a class. The Ordinance does not presume or require specifically defined, identifiable victims for most of its proscriptions. The Ordinance seeks to protect adult women, as a group, from the diminution of their legal and sociological status as women, that is, from the discriminatory stigma which befalls women *as women* as a result of "pornography." On page one of the introduction to defendants' *Amicus Brief,* counsel explicitly argues that the harm which underlies this legislation is the "harm to the treatment and *status* of women . . . on the basis of sex." . . .

This is a novel theory advanced by the defendants, an issue of first impression in the courts. If this Court were to accept defendants' argument—that the State's interest in protecting women from the humiliation and degradation which comes from being depicted in a sexually subordinate context is so compelling as to warrant the regulation of otherwise free speech to accomplish that end—one wonders what would prevent the City-County Council (or any other legislative body) from enacting protections for other equally compelling claims against exploitation and discrimination as are presented here. Legislative bodies, finding support here, could also enact legislation prohibiting other unfair expression—the publication and distribution of racist material, for instance, on the grounds that it causes racial discrimination,* or legislation prohibiting ethnic or religious slurs on the grounds that they cause discrimination against particular ethnic or religious groups, or legislation barring literary depictions which are uncomplimentary or oppressive to handicapped persons on the grounds that they cause discrimination against that group of people, and so on. If this Court were to extend to this case the rationale in *Ferber* to uphold the Amendment, it would signal so great a potential encroachment upon First Amendment freedoms that the precious liberties reposed within those guarantees would not survive. The compelling state interest, which defendants claim gives constitutional life to their Ordinance, though important and valid as that interest may be in other contexts, is not so fundamental an interest as to warrant a broad intrusion into otherwise free expression.

Defendants contend that pornography is not deserving of constitutional protection because its harms victimize all women. It is argued that "pornography" not only negatively affects women who risk and suffer the direct abuse of its production, but also, those on whom violent pornography is forced through such acts as compelled performances of "dangerous acts such as being hoisted upside down by ropes, bound by ropes and chains, hung from trees and scaffolds or having sex with animals. . . ." It is also alleged that exposure to pornography produces a negative impact on its viewers, causing in them an increased willingness to aggress toward women, *ibid.* . . . , and experience self-generated rape fantasies, increases in sexual arousal and a rise in the self-reported possibility of raping. . . . In addition, it causes discriminatory attitudes and behavior toward all women. . . . The City-County Council, after considering testimony and social research studies, enacted the Ordi-

---

*In *Beauharnais v. Illinois,* . . . (1952), the Supreme Court upheld an Illinois libel statute prohibiting the dissemination of materials promoting racial or religious hatred and which tended to produce a breach of the peace and riots. It has been recognized that "the rationale of that decision turns quite plainly on the strong tendency of the prohibited utterances to cause violence and disorder." *Collin v. Smith,* . . . (7th Cir. 1978). The Supreme Court has recognized breach of the peace as the traditional justification for upholding a criminal libel statute. *Beauharnais,* . . . Therefore, a law preventing the distribution of material that causes racial discrimination, an attitude, would be upheld under this analysis. Further, the underlying reasoning of the *Beauharnais* opinion, that the punishment of libel raises no constitutional problems, has been questioned in many recent cases. . . .

nance in order to "combat" pornography's "concrete and tangible harms to women." . . .

Defendants rely on *Paris Adult Theatre I v. Slaton,* . . . (1973), to justify their regulation of "pornography." In that case the Supreme Court held "that there are legitimate state interests at stake in stemming the tide of commercialized obscenity . . . [which] include the interest of the public in the quality of life and the total community environment, the tone of commerce in the great city centers, and, possibly, the public safety itself." . . .

The Georgia Legislature had determined that in that case exposure to obscene material adversely affected men and women, that is to say, society as a whole. Although the petitioners argued in that case that there was no scientific data to conclusively prove that proposition, the Court said, "[i]t is not for us to resolve empirical uncertainties underlying state legislation, save in the exceptional case where that legislation plainly impinges upon rights protected by the constitution itself." . . .

Based on this reasoning, defendants argue that there is more than enough "empirical" evidence in the case at bar to support the City-County Council's conclusion that "pornography" harms women in the same way obscenity harms people, and, therefore, this Court should not question the legislative finding. As has already been acknowledged, it is not the Court's function to question the City-County Council's legislative finding. The Court's solitary duty is to ensure that the Ordinance accomplishes its purpose without violating constitutional standards or impinging upon constitutionally protected rights. In applying those tests, the Court finds that the Ordinance cannot withstand constitutional scrutiny.

It has already been noted that the Ordi-

nance does not purport to regulate legal obscenity, as defined in *Miller*. Thus, although the City-County Council determined that "pornography" harms women, this Court must and does declare the Ordinance invalid without being bound by the legislative findings because "pornography," as defined and regulated in the Ordinance, is constitutionally protected speech under the First Amendment and such an exception to the First Amendment protections is constitutionally unwarranted. This Court cannot legitimately embark on judicial policy making, carving out a new exception to the First Amendment simply to uphold the Ordinance, even when there may be many good reasons to support legislative action. To permit every interest group, especially those who claim to be victimized by unfair expression, their own legislative exceptions to the First Amendment so long as they succeed in obtaining a majority of legislative votes in their favor demonstrates the potentially predatory nature of what defendants seek through this Ordinance and defend in this lawsuit.

It ought to be remembered by defendants and all others who would support such a legislative initiative that, in terms of altering sociological patterns, much as alteration may be necessary and desirable, free speech, rather than being the enemy, is a long-tested and worthy ally. To deny free speech in order to engineer social change in the name of accomplishing a greater good for one sector of our society erodes the freedoms of all and, as such, threatens tyranny and injustice for those subjected to the rule of such laws. The First Amendment protections presuppose the evil of such tyranny and prevent a finding by this Court upholding the Ordinance. . . .

40. *Donald Victor Butler v. Her Majesty the Queen*

The Supreme Court of Canada

The issue before the Supreme Court of Canada was that of determining whether and to what extent Parliament may legitimately criminalize obscenity. The Court ruled that the criminalization of obscenity accorded with *Canadian Charter of Rights and Freedom*. In particular, the material to be suppressed depicted women "as sexual playthings, hysterically and instantly responsive to male sexual demands" and was produced simply for economic profit. The Court ruled that just as in the case of hate propaganda, it need not require conclusive social science evidence of harm to women before justifying prohibition. The Court judged that "a reasonable apprehension of harm" sufficed. The Court further judged that less intrusive legislation would not be as effective in preventing harm to women.

This appeal calls into question the constitutionality of the obscenity provisions of the *Criminal Code*, . . . s. 163. They are attacked on the ground that they contravene . . . the *Canadian Charter of Rights and Freedoms*. The case requires the Court to address one of the most difficult and controversial of contemporary issues, that of determining whether, and to what extent, Parliament may legitimately criminalize obscenity. I propose to begin with a review of the facts which gave rise to this appeal, as well as of the proceedings in the lower courts.

Facts and Proceedings

In August 1987, the appellant, Donald Victor Butler, opened the Avenue Video Boutique located in Winnipeg, Manitoba. The shop sells and rents "hard core" videotapes and magazines as well as sexual paraphernalia. Outside the store is a sign which reads:

"Avenue Video Boutique; a private members only adult video/visual club. Notice: if sex oriented material offends you, please do not enter. No admittance to persons under 18 years.

On August 21, 1987, the City of Winnipeg Police entered the appellant's store with a search warrant and seized all the inventory. The appellant was charged with 173 counts in the first indictment: three counts of selling obscene material, . . . 41 counts of possessing obscene material for the purpose of distribution, . . . 128 counts of possessing obscene material for the purpose of sale . . . and one count of exposing obscene material to public view. . . .

On October 19, 1987, the appellant re-opened the store at the same location. As a result of a police operation a search warrant was executed on October 29, 1987, resulting in the arrest of an employee, Norma McCord. The appellant was arrested at a later date.

A joint indictment was laid against the appellant doing business as Avenue Video Boutique and Norma McCord. The joint indictment contains 77 counts: . . . two counts of selling obscene material, . . . 73 counts of possessing obscene material for the purpose of distribution, . . . one count of possessing obscene material for the purpose of sale . . . and one count of exposing obscene material to public view. . . .

The trial judge convicted the appellant on eight counts relating to eight films. Convictions were entered against the co-accused McCord with respect to two counts relating to two of the films. Fines of $1,000 per offence were imposed on the appellant. Acquittals were entered on the remaining charges.

The Crown appealed the 242 acquittals with respect to the appellant and the appellant cross-appealed the convictions. The majority of the Manitoba Court of Appeal allowed the appeal of the Crown and entered convictions for the appellant with respect to all of the counts, Twaddle and Helper J. J. A. dissenting. . . .

In reaching the conclusion that legislation proscribing obscenity is a valid objective which justifies some encroachment of the right to freedom of expression, I am persuaded in part that such legislation may be found in most free and democratic societies. As Nemetz C. J. B. C. aptly pointed out in *R. v. Red Hot Video,* . . . for centuries democratic societies have set certain limits to freedom of expression. He cited . . . the following passage of Dickson J. A. . . . in *R. v. Great West News Ltd.:*

All organized societies have sought in one manner or another to suppress obscenity. The right of the state to legislate to protect its moral fibre and well-being has long been recognized, with roots deep in history. It is within this frame that the Courts and Judges must work.

The advent of the *Charter* did not have the effect of dramatically depriving Parliament of a power which it has historically enjoyed. It is also noteworthy that the criminalization of obscenity was considered to be compatible with the *Canadian Bill of Rights.* As Dickson J. A. stated in *R. v. Prairie Schooner News Ltd.* . . . :

Freedom of speech is not unfettered either in criminal law or civil law. The *Canadian Bill of Rights* was intended to protect, and does protect, basic freedoms of vital importance to all Canadians. It does not serve as a shield behind which obscene matter may be disseminated without concern for criminal consequences. The interdiction of the publications which are the subject of the present charges in no way trenches upon the freedom of expression which the *Canadian Bill of Rights* assures.

. . . Finally, it should be noted that the burgeoning pornography industry renders the concern even more pressing and substantial than when the impugned provisions were first enacted. I would therefore conclude that the objective of avoiding the harm associated with the dissemination of pornography in this case is sufficiently pressing and substantial to warrant some restriction on full exercise of the right to freedom of expression. The analysis of whether the measure is proportional to the objective must, in my view, be undertaken in light of the conclusion that the objective of the impugned section is valid only insofar as it relates to the harm to society associated with obscene materials. Indeed, the section as interpreted in previous decisions and in these reasons is fully consistent with that objective. The objective of maintaining conventional standards of propriety, independently of any harm to society, is no longer justified in light of the values of individual liberty which underlie the *Charter.* This, then, being the objective of s. 163, which I have found to be pressing and substantial, I must now determine whether the section is rationally connected and proportional to this objective. As outlined above, s. 163 criminalizes the exploitation of sex and sex and violence, when, on the basis of the community test, it is undue. The determination of when such exploitation is undue is directly related to the immediacy of a risk of harm to society which is reasonably perceived as arising from its dissemination. . . .

The proportionality requirement has three aspects:

1. the existence of a rational connection between the impugned measures and the objective;

2. minimal impairment of the right or freedom; and

3. a proper balance between the effects of the limiting measures and the legislative objective.

In assessing whether the proportionality test is met, it is important to keep in mind the nature of expression which has been infringed. In the *Prostitution Reference,* . . . Dickson C. J. wrote:

When a *Charter* freedom has been infringed by state action that takes the form of criminalization, the Crown bears the heavy burden of justifying that infringement. Yet, the expressive activity, as with any infringed *Charter* right, should also be analysed in the particular context of the case. Here, the activity to which the impugned legislation is directed is expression with an economic purpose. It can hardly be said that communications regarding an economic transaction of sex for money lie at, or even near, the core of the guarantee of freedom of expression.

The values which underlie the protection of freedom of expression relate to the search for truth, participation in the political process, and individual self-fulfilment. The Attorney General for Ontario argues that of these, only "individual self-fulfilment," and only in its most base aspect, that of physical arousal, is engaged by pornography. On the other hand, the civil liberties groups argue that pornography forces us to question conventional notions of sexuality and thereby launches us into an inherently political discourse. In their factum, the B. C. Civil Liberties Association adopts a passage from R. West, "The Feminist-Conservative Anti-Pornography Alliance and the 1986 Attorney General's Commission on Pornography Report." . . . :

> Good pornography has value because it validates women's will to pleasure. It celebrates female nature. It validates a range of female sexuality that is wider and truer than that legitimated by the non-pornographic culture. Pornography when it is good celebrates both female pleasure and male rationality.

A proper application of the test should not suppress what West refers to as "good pornography." The objective of the impugned provision is not to inhibit the celebration of human sexuality. However, it cannot be ignored that the realities of the pornography industry are far from the picture which the B. C. Civil Liberties Association would have us paint.

Shannon J., in *R. v. Wagner* . . . , describes the materials more accurately when he observed:

> Women, particularly, are deprived of unique human character or identity and are depicted as sexual playthings, hysterically and instantly responsive to male sexual demands. They worship male genitals and their own value depends upon the quality of their genitals and breasts.

In my view, the kind of expression which is sought to be advanced does not stand on equal footing with other kinds of expression which directly engage the "core" of the freedom of expression values.

This conclusion is further buttressed by the fact that the targeted material is expression which is motivated, in the overwhelming majority of cases, by economic profit. This Court held in *Rocket v. Royal College of Dental Surgeons of Ontario* . . . that an economic motive for expression means that restrictions on the expression might "be easier to justify than other infringements."

I will now turn to an examination of the three basic aspects of the proportionality test.

Rational Connection

The message of obscenity which degrades and dehumanizes is analogous to that of hate propaganda. As the Attorney General of Ontario has argued in its factum, obscenity wields the power to wreak social damage in that a significant portion of the population is humiliated by its gross misrepresentations.

Accordingly, the rational link between s. 163 and the objective of Parliament relates to the actual causal relationship between obscenity and the risk of harm to society at large. On this point, it is clear that the literature of the social sciences remains subject to controversy. In *Fringe Product Inc.,* . . . Charron Dist. Ct. J. considered numerous written reports and works and heard six days of testimony from experts who endeavoured to describe the status of the social sciences with respect to the study of the effects of pornography. Charron Dist. Ct. J. reached the conclusion that the relationship between pornography and harm was sufficient to justify Parliament's intervention. This conclusion is not supported unanimously.

The recent conclusions of the Fraser Report . . . could not postulate any causal relationship between pornography and the commission of violent crimes, the sexual abuse of children, or the disintegration of communities and society. . . .

While a direct link between obscenity and harm to society may be difficult, if not impossible, to establish, it is reasonable to presume that exposure to images bears a causal relationship to changes in attitudes and beliefs. The Meese Commission Report . . . concluded in respect of sexually violent material:

> The available evidence strongly supports the hypothesis that substantial exposure to sexually violent materials as described here bears a causal relationship to antisocial acts of sexual violence and, for some subgroups, possibly to unlawful acts of sexual violence.
>
> Although we rely for this conclusion on significant scientific empirical evidence, we feel it worthwhile to note the underlying logic of the conclusion. The evidence says simply that the images that people are exposed to bears a causal relationship to their behavior. This is hardly surprising. What would be surprising would be to find otherwise, and we have not so found. We have not, of course, found that the images people are exposed to are a greater cause of sexual violence than all or even many other possible causes the investigation of which has been beyond our mandate. Nevertheless, it would be strange indeed if graphic representations of a form of behavior, especially in a form that almost exclusively portrays such behavior as desirable, did not have at least some effect on patterns of behavior.

In the face of inconclusive social science evidence, the approach adopted by our Court in *Irwin Toy* is instructive. In that case, the basis for the legislation was that television advertising directed at young children is *per se* manipulative. The Court made it clear that in choosing its mode of intervention, it is sufficient that Parliament had a *reasonable basis*:

> In the instant case, the Court is called upon to assess competing social science evidence respecting the appropriate means for addressing the problem of children's advertising. The question is whether the government had a reasonable basis, on the evidence tendered, for concluding that the ban on all advertising directed at children impaired freedom of expression as little as possible given the government's pressing and substantial objective.

> . . . the Court also recognized that the government was afforded a margin of appreciation to form legitimate objectives based on somewhat inconclusive social science evidence.

Similarly, . . . the absence of proof of a causative link between hate propaganda and hatred of an identifiable group was discounted as a determinative factor in assessing the constitutionality of the hate literature provisions of the *Criminal Code*. Dickson C. J. stated:

> First, to predicate the limitation of free expression upon proof of actual hatred gives insufficient attention to the severe psychological trauma suffered by members of those identifiable groups targeted by hate propaganda. Second, it is clearly difficult to prove a causative link between a specific statement and hatred of an identifiable group.

McLachlin J. (dissenting) expressed it as follows:

> To view hate propaganda as "victimless" in the absence of any proof that it moved its listeners to hatred is to discount the wrenching impact that it may have on members of the target group themselves. . . . Moreover, it is simply not possible to assess with any precision the effects that

expression of a particular message will have on all those who are ultimately exposed to it.

The American approach on the necessity of a causal link between obscenity and harm to society was set out by Burger C. J. in *Paris Adult Theatre* . . . :

Although there is no conclusive proof of a connection between antisocial behavior and obscene material, the legislature . . . could quite reasonably determine that such a connection does or might exist. . . .

I am in agreement with Twaddle J. A. who expressed the view that Parliament was entitled to have a "reasoned apprehension of harm" resulting from the desensitization of individuals exposed to materials which depict violence, cruelty, and dehumanization in sexual relations.

Accordingly, I am of the view that there is a sufficiently rational link between the criminal sanction, which demonstrates our community's disapproval of the dissemination of materials which potentially victimize women and which restricts the negative influence which such materials have on changes in attitudes and behaviour, and the objective. . . .

Minimal Impairment

In determining whether less intrusive legislation may be imagined, this Court stressed in the *Prostitution Reference* . . . that it is not necessary that the legislative scheme be the "perfect" scheme, but that it be appropriately tailored *in the context of the infringed right.* . . . Furthermore, in *Irwin Toy*, Dickson C. J., Lamer and Wilson J. J. stated:

While evidence exists that other less intrusive options reflecting more modest objectives were available to the government, there is evidence establishing the necessity of a ban to meet the objectives the government had reasonably set. This Court will

not, in the name of minimal impairment, take a restrictive approach to social science evidence and require legislatures to choose the least ambitious means to protect vulnerable groups. . . .

There are several factors which contribute to the finding that the provision minimally impairs the freedom which is infringed.

First, the impugned provision does not proscribe sexually explicit erotica without violence that is not degrading or dehumanizing. It is designed to catch material that creates a risk of harm to society. It might be suggested that proof of actual harm should be required. It is apparent from what I have said above that it is sufficient in this regard for Parliament to have a reasonable basis for concluding that harm will result and this requirement does not demand actual proof of harm.

Second, materials which have scientific, artistic or literary merit are not captured by the provision. As discussed above, the court must be generous in its application of the "artistic defence." For example, in certain cases, materials such as photographs, prints, books and films which may undoubtedly be produced with some motive for economic profit, may nonetheless claim the protection of the *Charter* insofar as their defining characteristic is that of aesthetic expression, and thus represent the artist's attempt at individual fulfilment. The existence of an accompanying economic motive does not, of itself, deprive a work of significance as an example of individual artistic or self-fulfilment.

Third, in considering whether the provision minimally impairs the freedom in question, it is legitimate for the court to take into account Parliament's past abortive attempts to replace the definition with one that is more explicit. In *Irwin Toy*, our Court recognized that it is legitimate to take into account the fact that earlier laws and proposed alternatives were thought to be less effective than the legislation that is presently being challenged. The attempt to provide exhaustive instances of obscenity has been shown to be destined to fail. . . . It seems that the only practicable alternative is to strive towards a more abstract definition of obscenity which is contextually sensitive and responsive to progress in the knowledge and understanding of the phenomenon to which the legislation is directed. In my view, the standard of "undue exploitation" is therefore appropriate. The intractable nature of the problem and the impossibility of precisely defining a notion which is inherently elusive makes the possibility of a more explicit provision remote. In this light, it is appropriate to question whether, and at what cost, greater legislative precision can be demanded.

Fourth, while the discussion in this appeal has been limited to the definition portion of s. 163, I would note that the impugned section, . . . has been held by this Court not to extend its reach to the private use or viewing of obscene materials. *R. v. Rioux* . . . unanimously upheld the finding of the Quebec Court of Appeal that s. 163 . . . does not include the private viewing of obscene materials. Hall J. affirmed the finding of Pratte J.:

> . . . I would therefore say that showing obscene pictures to a friend or projecting an obscene film in one's own home is not in itself a crime nor is it enough to establish intention of circulating them nor help to prove such an intention. . . .

This Court also cited with approval the words of Hyde J.:

> Before I am prepared to hold that private use of written matter or pictures within an individual's residence may constitute a criminal offence, I require a much more specific text of law than we are now dealing with. It would have been very simple for Parliament to have included the word "exhibit" in this section if it had wished to cover this situation. . . .

Accordingly, it is only the public distribution and exhibition of obscene materials which is in issue here.

Finally, I wish to address the arguments of the interveners, Canadian Civil Liberties Association and Manitoba Association for Rights and Liberties, that the objectives of this kind of legislation may be met by alternative, less intrusive measures. First, it is submitted that reasonable time, manner and place restrictions would be preferable to outright prohibition. I am of the view that this argument should be rejected. Once it has been established that the objective is the avoidance of harm caused by the degradation which many women feel as "victims" of the message of obscenity, and of the negative impact exposure to such material has on perceptions and attitudes towards women, it is untenable to argue that these harms could be avoided by placing restrictions on access to such material. Making the materials more difficult to obtain by increasing their cost and reducing their availability does not achieve the same objective. Once Parliament has reasonably concluded that certain acts are harmful to certain groups in society and to society in general, it would be inconsistent, if not hypocritical, to argue that such acts could be committed in more restrictive conditions. The harm sought to be avoided would remain the same in either case.

It is also submitted that there are more effective techniques to promote the objectives of Parliament. For example, if pornography is seen as encouraging violence against women, there are certain activities which discourage it—counselling rape victims to charge their assailants, provision of shelter and assistance for battered women, campaigns for laws against discrimination on the grounds of sex, education to increase the sensitivity of law enforcement agencies and other governmental authorities. In addition, it is submitted that education is an under-used response.

It is noteworthy that many of the above suggested alternatives are in the form of *responses* to the harm engendered by negative attitudes against women. The role of the impugned provision is to control the dissemination of the very images that contribute to such attitudes. Moreover, it is true that there are additional measures which could alleviate the problem of violence against women. However, given the gravity of the harm, and the threat to the values at stake, I do not believe that the measure chosen by Parliament is equalled by the alternatives which have been suggested. Education, too, may offer a means of combating negative attitudes to women, just as it is currently used as a means of addressing other problems dealt with in the *Code*. However, there is no reason to rely on education alone. It should be emphasized that this is in no way intended to deny the value of other educational and counselling measures to deal with the roots and effects of negative attitudes. Rather, it is only to stress the arbitrariness and unacceptability of the claim that such measures represent the sole legitimate means of addressing the phenomenon. Serious social problems such as violence against women require multi-pronged approaches by government. Education and legislation are not alternatives but complements in addressing such problems. There is nothing in the *Charter* which requires Parliament to choose between such complementary measures.

Balance Between Effects of Limiting Measures and Legislative Objective

The final question to be answered in the proportionality test is whether the effects of the law so severely trench on a protected right that the legislative objective is outweighed by the infringement. The infringement on freedom of expression is confined to a measure designed to prohibit the distribution of sexually explicit materials accompanied by violence, and those without violence that are degrading or dehumanizing. As I have already concluded, this kind of expression lies far from the core of the guarantee of freedom of expression. It appeals only to the most base aspect of individual fulfilment, and it is primarily economically motivated.

The objective of the legislation, on the other hand, is of fundamental importance in a free and democratic society. It is aimed at avoiding harm, which Parliament has reasonably concluded will be caused directly or indirectly, to individuals, groups such as women and children, and consequently to society as a whole, by the distribution of these materials. It thus seeks to enhance respect for all members of society, and non-violence and equality in their relations with each other.

I therefore conclude that the restriction on freedom of expression does not outweigh the importance of the legislative objective.

Suggestions for Further Reading

Anthologies

Copp, D., and Wendell, S. *Pornography and Censorship*. Buffalo: Prometheus Press, 1983.

Donnerstein, E., Linz, D., and Pernod S. *The Question of Pornography*. New York: Free Press, 1987.

Alternative Views

Dworkin, A. *Pornography: Men Possessing Women*. New York: Perigee, 1981.

Griffin, S. *Pornography and Silence*. New York: Harper & Row, 1981.

Lovelace, L., and McGrady, M. *Ordeal*. New York: Berkeley Books, 1980.

Soble, A. *Pornography*. New Haven: Yale University Press, 1986.

Practical Applications

Report of the Attorney General's Commission on Pornography. Washington, D.C.: Government Printing Office, 1986.

Sexual Harassment

Introduction

Basic Concepts

The moral problem of sexual harassment is the problem of determining the nature of sexual harassment and how to avoid it. Actually, sexual harassment was not recognized by U.S. trial courts as an offense until the late 1970s, and it was only affirmed by the U.S. Supreme Court as an offense in the 1980s. The term "sexual harassment" itself was not even coined until the 1970s. So the moral problem of sexual harassment is one that many people have only recently come to recognize. Obviously, the Senate Judiciary Committee hearings on Anita Hill's charge that Clarence Thomas had sexually harassed her has helped heighten people's awareness of this problem.

In 1980, the Equal Employment Opportunity Commission issued guidelines finding harassment on the basis of sex to be a violation of Title VII of the Civil Rights Act of 1964, labeling sexual harassment "unwelcome sexual advances, requests for sexual favors, and other verbal or physical conduct of a sexual nature" when such behavior occurred in any of three circumstances:

1. Where submission to such conduct is made either explicitly or implicitly a term or condition of an individual's employment.
2. Where submission to or rejection of such conduct by an individual is used as the basis for employment decisions affecting such individual.
3. Where such conduct has the purpose or effect of unreasonably interfering with an individual's work performance or creating an intimidating, hostile, or offensive working environment.

In 1986, the U.S. Supreme Court in *Meritor Savings Bank v. Vinson* agreed with the EEOC, ruling that there could be two types of sexual harassment: harassment that conditions concrete employment benefits on granting sexual favors (often called the quid pro quo type) and harassment that creates a hostile or offensive work environment without affecting economic benefits (the hostile environment type). Nevertheless, the court made it quite difficult for a plaintiff to establish that either of these types of sexual harassment had occurred. For example, a polite verbal no does not suffice to show that sexual advances are unwelcome; a woman's entire conduct both in and outside the workplace is subject to appraisal determining whether or not she welcomed the advances. But isn't it odd that a woman should have to prove that an offer "If you don't sleep with me you will be fired" is unwelcomed? Moreover, if a woman rejects such an offer and is fired, unless she is a perfect employee, she will have difficulty proving that she was fired because she rejected the offer. Actually, in such a case, what the Supreme Court should have required is that the employer be able to show that a woman who rejects a sexual advance would still have been fired even if she had said yes.

U.S. courts have also made it difficult to classify work environments as hostile to women. In *Christoforou v. Ryder Truck Rental, Inc.*, a supervisor's actions of fondling a plaintiff's rear end and breasts, propositioning her and trying to force a kiss at a Christmas party were considered "too sporadic and innocuous" to support a finding of a hostile work environment. In *Rabidue v. Osceola Refining Co.*, a workplace where pictures of nude and scantily clad women abounded, including one, which hung on a wall for eight years, of a woman with a golf ball on her breasts and a man with his golf club, standing over her and yelling "fore," and where a co-worker, never disciplined despite repeated complaints, routinely referred to women as "whores," "cunts," and "pussy" was judged not sufficiently hostile an environment to constitute sexual harassment. At times, the courts seem to be appealing to the pervasiveness of certain forms of harassment as grounds for tolerating them. As though we should only prohibit wrongful acts if most people aren't doing them. At other times, the courts appear to be judging sexual harassment to be what men, but not women, say it is. What this shows is that the problem of avoiding sexual harassment is intimately tied to its definition, and women and men seem to disagree radically about what constitutes sexual harassment.

Alternative Views

In Selection 41, Barbara A. Gutek surveys the research that has been done on defining sexual harassment and determining how frequently it occurs. Gutek notes that a number of factors influence whether some behavior is classified as sexual harassment:

1. How intrusive and persistent the behavior is. (The more physically intrusive and persistent the behavior is, the more likely that it will be defined as sexual harassment.)
2. The nature of the relationship between the actors. (The better the actors know each other, the less likely the behavior will be labeled sexual harassment.)
3. The characteristics of the observer. (Men and people in authority are less likely to label behavior as sexual harassment.)
4. The inequality in the relationship. (The greater the inequality, the more likely the behavior will be labeled sexual harassment.)

Gutek contends that the frequency of sexual harassment in the workplace is relatively high. For example, the U.S. Merit System Protection Board found that 42 percent of the women responding to its study reported experiencing sexual harassment on the job within the previous two years. She seeks to explain this frequency as due to the fact that women are stereotypically identified as sexual objects in ways that men are not. She notes that women are stereotypically characterized as sexy, affectionate, and attractive, whereas men are stereotypically characterized as competent and active. These stereotypes, Gutek claims, spill over into the workplace, making it difficult for women to be perceived as fellow workers rather than sex objects, and these perceptions foster sexual harassment. It would seem, therefore, that eliminating the problem of sexual harassment from our society will require breaking down these stereotypes.

Unlike Gutek, Ellen Frankel Paul (Selection 42) argues that the problem of sexual harassment is overblown. She thinks sexual harassment has been exaggerated to include everything from rape to "looks." Paul argues that the extortion of sexual favors by a supervisor from a subordinate by threatening to penalize, fire, or fail to reward is sexual harassment, but she argues that a hostile working environment should be regarded as sexual harassment only when the "reasonable man" of tort law would find the working environment offensive. However, as one of Gutek's studies shows, reasonable men and reasonable women can disagree over what constitutes sexual harassment in the workplace. In this study, 67.2 percent of men as compared to 16.8 percent of women would be flattered if asked to have sex, while 15 percent of the men and 62.8 percent of the women said they would be insulted by such an offer. So the crucial question is: Whose perspective should be determinative?

Practical Application

In Selection 43, Nancy Fraser analyzes the Senate Judiciary Committee hearings on Anita Hill's claim that Clarence Thomas had sexually harassed her by creating a hostile working environment. Fraser sees the hearings as a struggle with three phases. In the first gender-dominated phase, she claims that Anita Hill was not able to prevent intensive examination of her private life whereas Clarence Thomas was able to declare key areas of his private life as off-limits, for example, his practice of viewing and discussing pornographic films. In the second race-dominated phase, Fraser claims that Thomas was able to characterize the attack on him as motivated by the stereotypes of black men as male studs and rapists, whereas Hill became functionally white. In this phase of the struggle, Fraser claims that the black woman's perspective was never taken into account, the sexist abuse that black women suffer from black men was never discussed. In the third class-dominated phase of the struggle, Fraser claims that class resentment was mobilized in favor of Thomas through his "working class" supporter J. C. Alvarez whereas Hill, despite her lower class origins and the fact that Thomas had been her boss, was associated with her "upper class" supporter Susan Hoerchner.

In a struggle with so many phases, the fact

that the actions Hill claimed that Thomas had performed were sexual harassment was sometimes lost sight of. Yet even Thomas agreed that if he had performed the actions that Hill claimed he had performed, he would be guilty of sexual harassment. The crucial question, then, is why did most people support Thomas rather than Hill? Did they not believe her charges against Thomas or did they just not think that what she claimed Thomas had done to her was really sexual harassment? Obviously, to the extent that people disagree over what constitutes sexual harassment, the problem of avoiding it will become all that more difficult.

41. Understanding Sexual Harassment at Work

Barbara A. Gutek

Barbara A. Gutek surveys the research that has been done on defining sexual harassment and determining how frequently it occurs. Gutek notes that a number of factors influence whether some behavior is classified as sexual harassment:

1. How intrusive and persistent the behavior is.
2. The nature of relationship between the actors.
3. The characteristics of the observer.
4. The inequality in the relationship.

Gutek contends that the frequency of sexual harassment in the workplace is relatively high. For example, the U.S. Merit System Protection Board found that 42 percent of the women responding to its study reported experiencing sexual harassment on the job within the previous two years. Gutek seeks to explain this frequency as due to the fact that women are stereotypically identified as sexual objects in ways that men are not.

I. Introduction

The topic of sexual harassment at work was virtually unstudied until the concern of feminists brought the issue to the attention of the public and researchers. Much of the research on sexual harassment addresses two complementary questions. (1) How do people define sexual harassment? (2) How common is it? Research on these two issues provides useful background information for lawyers and policy makers interested in seeking legal redress for harassment victims, and ultimately in eradicating sexual harassment. . . .

From "Understanding Sexual Harassment at Work," *Notre Dame Journal of Law, Ethics and Public Policy* (1992). Reprinted by permission.

The first issue, people's definitions of sexual harassment, shows the extent to which laws and regulations reflect broad public consensus. Knowing the frequency of sexual harassment—a workplace problem that had no name until the mid-1970s—is important for those seeking to establish laws and procedures to remedy the problem. Further, frequency or prevalence deserves study because sexual harassment has negative consequences for women workers and organizations. These two areas—definition and prevalence—are often studied independently, using different research subjects, research designs, and methods of data collection.

This article traces the development of research on sexual behavior in the workplace from its early emphasis on defining and documenting sexual harassment through other findings concerning sexual nonharassment. In order to understand sex at work, several frameworks or theories are discussed, with special emphasis on the concept of sex-role spillover.

The term "sexual behavior" will be used throughout this article to encompass the range of sexual behaviors, such as non-work related behavior with sexual content or overtones, found within the workplace and included in many research studies. Few studies attempt to limit themselves to legally liable sexual harassment. Thus, the term "sexual behavior" consists of behavior that is legally considered sexual harassment as well as nonharassing sexual behavior.

Finally, it should be noted that this article is not a review of the status of sexual harassment laws or legal practices. It is limited to the social science research which addresses issues relevant to sexual harassment policy and lawsuits.

II. The Discovery of Sexual Harassment

In the mid-1970s, sexuality in the workplace suddenly received considerable attention through the discovery of sexual harassment, which appeared to be relatively widespread and to have long-lasting, harmful effects on a significant number of working women. This "discovery" was somewhat counterintuitive, since some women were believed to benefit from seductive behavior and sexual behaviors at work, gaining unfair advantage and acquiring perks and privileges from their flirtatious and seductive behavior. The first accounts of sexual harassment were journalistic reports and case studies. Soon the topic was catapulted into public awareness through the publication of two important books. Lin Farley's book, *Sexual Shakedown: The Sexual Harassment of Women on the Job*, aimed to bring sexual harassment to public attention, create a household word, and make people aware of harassment as a social problem. Catharine MacKinnon's book, *Sexual Harassment of Working Women*, sought a legal mechanism for handling sexual harassment

and compensating its victims. In a strong and compelling argument, MacKinnon contended that sexual harassment was primarily a problem for women, that it rarely happened to men, and therefore that it should be viewed as a form of sex discrimination. Viewing sexual harassment as a form of sex discrimination would make available to victims the same legal protection available to victims of sex discrimination. In 1980, the Equal Employment Opportunity Commission (EEOC) established guidelines consistent with MacKinnon's position and defined sexual harassment under Title VII of the 1964 Civil Rights Act as a form of unlawful sex-based discrimination. Several states have passed their own increasingly strong laws aimed at eliminating sexual harassment and legal scholars have sought additional avenues to recover damages incurred from sexual harassment. Various public and private agencies as well as the courts have seen a steady if uneven increase in sexual harassment complaints since the early 1980s.

The various guidelines and regulations define sexual harassment broadly. For example, the updated EEOC guidelines state that

> [u]nwelcome sexual advances, requests for sexual favors, and other verbal or physical conduct of a sexual nature constitute sexual harassment when (1) submission to such conduct is made either explicitly or implicitly a term or condition of an individual's employment or academic advancement, (2) submission to or rejection of such conduct by an individual is used as the basis for employment decisions or academic decisions affecting such individual, or (3) such conduct has the purpose or effect of reasonably interfering with an individual's work or academic performance or creating an intimidating, hostile, or offensive working or academic environment.

Researchers began serious study of sex at work only after Farley's and MacKinnon's books and two compendia of information on sexual harassment were in progress and generally after the EEOC had established guidelines in 1980. Not surprisingly, researchers were heavily influenced by these important developments in policy and law. These developments focused the concerns of researchers on the two specific issues mentioned above: definition of harassment and frequency of occurrence.

III. Defining Sexual Harassment

The first issue can be succinctly stated: "What constitutes sexual harassment?" For lawyers, the courts, personnel managers, ombudspersons, and others, this is perhaps the most important issue that they must face. If "it" is harassment, it is illegal; otherwise it is not. Researchers, aware of the problems in defining harassment and perhaps eager to contribute to the developments in law and policy, began to supply a spate of studies.

Studies concerned with the definition of sexual harassment come in two types. First are surveys of various populations of people who are asked to tell whether various acts constitute sexual harassment. Second are experimental studies in which students, employees, or managers are asked to rate one or more hypothetical situations in which aspects of the situation are varied along important dimensions. These experimental studies using a hypothetical situation, also known as the "paper people paradigm," come in two variants. In the first variant, subjects are asked to determine whether a particular scenario depicts an instance of sexual harassment. In the second variant, researchers examine the attributions of subjects to understand how subjects' interpretations of a scenario affect their use of the label, sexual harassment.

The strengths of the experimental research design—random assignment to conditions and manipulation of causal variables—allow researchers to make causal statements about what affects how people define sexual harassment. The weakness of the design is that the situation is invariably insufficiently "real": subjects who have limited information and little appreciation of, or experience with, the subject matter may not respond the way people would in a real (rather than hypothetical) situation.

The survey studies show that sexual activity as a requirement of the job is defined as sexual harassment by about eighty-one percent to ninety-eight percent of working adults, and similar results have been reported with students as subjects. Lesser forms of harassment such as sexual touching are not as consistently viewed as sexual harassment. For example, I found that fifty-nine percent of men but eighty-four percent of women asserted that sexual touching at work is sexual harassment. A sizable minority (twenty-two percent of men and thirty-three percent of women) considered sexual comments at work meant to be complimentary to be sexual harassment.

In contrast to the survey studies which often ask respondents to specify which of a set of actions constitutes harassment, in experimental studies, subjects are usually asked to rate how harassing some incident is, on a five-point or seven-point scale. Such a method makes it impossible to say what percentage of people consider any particular act or event harassment and results are usually reported as mean scores (on, say, a three-, five-, or seven-point scale). It should be noted that experimental studies are generally not concerned with the percentage of their subjects, usually students, who consider behavior X to be harassment, but instead address the factors or variables which affect whether or not some specified incident or act is labeled harassment.

The experimental studies show that except for the most outrageous and clearly inappropriate behavior, whether or not an incident is labeled harassment varies with several characteristics of the incident and the people involved. In these studies, the following variables make a difference: (1) the behavior in question, (2) the relationship between harasser and victim, (3) the sex of the harasser, (4) the sex and age of the victim, (5) the sex of the rater, and (6) the occupation of the person doing the rating. Another way of categorizing these factors is shown below: characteristics of the behavior, nature of the relationship between the actors, characteristics of the observer/rater, and context factors all affect whether or not a particular act or event is considered sexual harassment.

Factors Affecting the Definition of Sexual Harassment

1. *Characteristics of the behavior.* The more physically intrusive and persistent the behavior, the more likely it is to be defined as sexual harassment by an observer.

2. *The nature of the relationship between actors.* The better the two actors know each other (friends, spouses, long-time co-workers) the less likely the behavior will be labeled sexual harassment by an observer.

3. *Characteristics of the observer.* Men and people in authority (e.g., senior faculty, senior managers) are less likely than others to label a behavior sexual harassment.

4. *Context factors.* The greater the inequality (in position, occupation, age), the more likely the behavior will be labeled sexual harassment by an observer. When the "recipient" of the behavior is low status or relatively powerless (female, young, poor), the behavior is more likely to be judged harassment than when the "recipient" is high status or relatively powerful.

The most important factor determining judgment of sexual harassment is the behavior involved. The experimental studies and survey studies yield the same pattern of findings: explicitly sexual behavior and behavior involving implied or explicit threats are more likely to be perceived as harassment than other, less threatening or potentially complimentary behavior. Touching is also more likely to be rated as sexual harassment than comments, looks, or gestures. In addition, Weber-Burdin and Rossi concluded that the initiator's behavior is much more important than the recipient's behavior, although if a female recipient behaved seductively, college student raters may reduce the ratings of harassment.

The relationship between the two people is also important. The situation is considered more serious harassment when the initiator is a supervisor of the recipient rather than an equal or a subordinate or more serious if the person previously declined to date the harasser than if the two people had a prior dating relationship. The incident is more likely to be viewed as sexual harassment when a man is the harasser, a woman is the victim and when the female victim is young.

The person doing the rating makes a difference. The most important characteristic of the rater is gender. When women are doing the rating, they define a wide variety of sexual behavior at work as sexual harassment, while men tend to rate only the more extreme behaviors as harassment. Similarly, on a scale of Tolerance for Sexual Harassment (TSHI), college men reported more tolerance than women, that is, men objected less than women to sexual harassing behavior. In short, the finding that women apply a broader definition of sexual harassment than men is pervasive and widely replicated although not universally found. It is worth noting that at least one factor strongly associated with gender, sex role identity, did not make much of a difference in people's judgments of sexual harassment. Powell, using a student sample, found that sex-role identity generally did not affect definition of sexual harassment although highly feminine subjects were somewhat more likely than others to label some behaviors sexual harassment and highly masculine male students were somewhat less likely than others to label insulting sexual remarks sexual harassment. In addition, organizational status seems to have an effect. Higher-level managers rating an incident are less likely to see it as serious harassment than middle-level or lower-level managers. In one study, faculty tended to view an incident as less serious than students whereas in another, there were no substantial differences in the ratings of faculty and students.

The experimental studies using an attribution analysis probe an evaluator's thought processes as he or she makes a determination whether or not a particular scenario constitutes harassment. Pryor suggested that people are more likely to judge a man's behavior sexual harassment if his behavior is attributed to his enduring negative intentions toward the target woman. Such negative intentions can either reflect hostility or insensitivity to women. Pryor and Day found that the perspective people take in interpreting a social-sexual encounter affects their judgments of sexual harassment. This may help explain why men and women tend to differ in their judgments of sexual harassment, that is, men may take the man's (usually the initiator's) point of view whereas women are more likely to take the woman's (the victim in many experimental studies) point of view. In support of this view, Konrad and Gutek found that women's greater experience with sexual harassment helps to explain the sex differences in defining sexual harassment. In a similar vein, Kenig and Ryan came to the conclusion that men's and women's perceptions of sexual harassment reflect their own self-interest. It is in men's self-interest to see relatively little sexual harassment because men are most often the offenders whereas it is in women's self-interest to see relatively more sexual harassment because women tend to be the victims in sexual harassment encounters.

Cohen and Gutek's analyses suggest that people may make different attributions depending on whether or not they view the initiator and recipient as friends. More specifically, they found that when student subjects were asked to evaluate an ambiguous, potentially mildly sexually harassing encounter, they tended to assume that the two participants were friends, perhaps dating partners, and that the behavior was welcome and complimentary rather than harassing. Similarly, student subjects were less likely to rate a behavior harassment if they knew that the parties formerly dated and were more likely to rate a behavior harassment if the woman recipient had formerly refused to date the male initiator. In the latter case, subjects may attribute the man's overture to his "enduring negative intentions" toward the woman since her prior refusal of a date presumably eliminates the explanation that he was unsure how she felt about him.

IV. Frequency of Sexual Harassment at Work

The other area of research that developed in response to legal and policy development was a documentation of the forms and prevalence of harassment experienced by people. In 1979, MacKinnon wrote: "The unnamed should not be taken for the nonexistent." Thus, providing a label and then a definition for sexual harassment was an important step in developing ways to measure the prevalence of sexual harassment.

The research on frequency of harassment focuses heavily but not exclusively on heterosexual encounters. It is often studied separate from the research on definition and employs a different research design and different subjects. Research aiming to establish rates of harassment in a population must be concerned with drawing a representative sample from a known population in order to generalize results in that population.

The research on prevalence shows a broad range of rates, depending in part on the time frame used. The U.S. Merit Systems Protection Board's study found that forty-two percent of the women respondents reported experiencing sexual harassment on the job within the previous two years. When the study was repeated several years later, the figure remained the same. In a Seattle, Washington study of city employees, more than one-third of all respondents reported sexual harassment in the previous twenty-four months of city employment. Dunwoody-Miller and Gutek found that twenty percent of California state civil service employees reported being sexually harassed at work in the previous five years. Reviewing the results from several different measures of prevalence she used, Gutek suggested that up to fifty-three percent of women had been harassed sometime in their working life. The figures are higher in the military; two-thirds of women surveyed in a 1990 study said they have been sexually harassed.

Other studies using purposive or convenience samples generally show higher rates of harassment. In a study by the Working Women's Institute, seventy percent of the employed women respondents said they had experienced sexual harassment on their jobs. An early study of the readers of *Redbook* magazine found that eighty-eight percent of those mailing in questionnaires had experienced sexual harassment. Schneider reported that more than two-thirds of her matched sample of lesbian and heterosexual working women had experienced unwelcome sexual advances within in the previous year.

Because respondents in purposive or convenience samples can choose whether or not to respond, and participating in the study may require some expenditure of effort, researchers assume that people who have been harassed may be more motivated to participate. Thus, the incidence rates are likely to be somewhat inflated.

Although women of all ages, races, occupations, income levels, and marital statuses experience harassment, research suggests that young and unmarried women are especially vulnerable. Not surprisingly, most women are harassed by men, not by women. In addition, women in nontraditional jobs (e.g., truck driver, neurosurgeon, engineer, roofer) and in nontraditional industries such as the military and mining are more likely to experience harassment than other women. These higher rates are over and above what is expected by their high amount of work contact with men. On the basis of the set of studies done so far, it seems likely that overall, from one-third to one-half of all women have been sexually harassed at some time in their working lives, although frequency rates in some types of work may be higher.

Sexual harassment at work has also been reported by men in several studies. The U.S. Merit Systems Protection Board's study found fifteen percent of the men to be harassed by males or females at work. On the basis of men's reports of specific behavior, Gutek suggested that up to nine percent of men could have been harassed by women sometime in their working lives. After a careful analysis of men's accounts of harassment, however, Gutek concluded that very few of the reported incidents were sexual harassment as it is legally defined, and some of the incidents may not have even been considered sexual if the same behavior had been initiated by a man or by another woman who was considered a less desirable sexual partner by the man.

V. Frequency of Sexual Nonharassment

Several studies have also examined other kinds of sexual behavior at work, behavior that most people do not consider harassment, including comments or whistles intended to be compliments, quasi-sexual touching such as hugging or an arm around the shoulder, requests for a date or sexual activity often in a joking manner, and sexual jokes or comments that are not directed to a particular person. These other "nonharassing," less serious, and presumably nonproblematic behaviors are considerably more common than harassment. For example, Gutek found that sixty-one percent of men and sixty-eight percent of women said that they had received at least one sexual comment that was meant to be complimentary sometime in their working lives. In addition, fifty-six percent of men and sixty-seven percent of women reported that they had been the recipient of at least one sexual look or gesture that was intended to be complimentary. About eight out of every ten workers have been recipients of some kind of sexual overture that was intended to be a compliment. Schneider found that fifty-five percent of a sample of heterosexual working women and sixty-seven percent of a sample of lesbian working women reported that within the last year at work, someone had joked with them about their body or appearance. Other studies show similar findings. Dunwoody-Miller and Gutek reported that seventy-six percent of women and fifty-five percent of men indicated that as California state civil service employees, they had received complimentary comments of a sexual nature. Looks and gestures of a sexual nature that were meant as compliments were also common (reported by sixty-seven percent of women and forty-seven percent of men).

Although men seem rarely to be harassed, the amount of sexual behavior reported by them at work remains substantial. For example, Gutek found that men were more likely than women to say that they were sexually touched by an opposite-sex person on their job. According to Abbey, Davies, and Gottfried and Fasenfest, men are more likely than women to perceive the world in sexual terms. Also, men are more likely than women to mistake friendliness for seduction and find the office is a little too exciting with women around. This seems consistent with the common stimulus-response view that women's presence elicits sexual behavior from men. Reports from men, however, suggest that sex is present in male-dominated workplaces, whether or not women are actually present. This "floating sex" takes the form of posters, jokes, sexual metaphors for work, comments, obscene language, and the like. The relationship seems to be quite straightforward: the more men, the more sexualized the workplace. The fact that much of this sexualization of work is degrading to women as well as sexual is what creates the "hostile" environment that government regulations aim to eliminate.

Taken together, the research on harassment and "nonharassment" shows that sexual behavior is so common at work that one might say that sex permeates work. An equally important conclusion of this body of research is that the legal behavior is considerably more common than the illegal sexual harassment. This finding is not surprising, but it is important; when some people first hear about sexual harassment, they may confuse it with the more common legal behavior at work which they, themselves, have seen and experienced. This confusion of non-threatening legal behavior with sexual harassment can lead some to incorrectly denigrate women's complaints as prudish or overly sensitive.

VI. Impacts of Sexual Behavior at Work

Any behavior that is as common as sexual harassment and nonharassment at work is likely to have a wide variety of ramifications, for the individuals involved. So far researchers have concentrated on identifying negative effects of sexual harassment, in order to call attention to harassment as a social and workplace problem. Only scattered attempts, however, have been made toward studying the impacts of other types of sexual behavior at work.

Sexual harassment has a variety of negative consequences for women workers. In addition to the discomfort associated with the sexually harassing experiences and violation of physical privacy, women often find that their careers are interrupted. Up to ten percent of women have quit a job because of sexual harassment. Others fear becoming victims of retaliation if they complain about the harassment, and some are asked to leave. For example, Coles found that among eighty-one cases filed with the California Department of Fair Employment and Housing between 1979 and 1983, almost half of the complainants were fired and another quarter quit out of fear or frustration.

Women may also experience lower productivity, less job satisfaction, reduced self-confidence, and a loss of motivation and commitment to their work and their employer. They may avoid men who are known harassers, even though contact with those men is important for their work. Thus, harassment constrains the potential for forming friendships or work alliances with male workers. Furthermore, women are likely to feel anger and resentment and even exhibit self-blame, which leads to additional stress. Crull and Cohen also stated that, while the implicit/overt types of harassment may not have the same direct repercussions as those of the explicit/overt types, all types of sexual harassment at work create high stress levels and serve as a hidden occupational hazard. Finally, sexual harassment helps to maintain the sex segregation of work when it is used to coerce women out of nontraditional jobs.

Besides affecting their work, sexual harassment affects women's personal lives in the form of physical and emotional illness and disruption of marriage or other relationships with men. For example, Tangri, Burt, and Johnson reported that thirty-three percent of women said their emotional or physical condition became worse, and Gutek found that fifteen percent of women victims of harassment said their health was affected and another fifteen percent said it damaged their relationships with men.

What is even more intriguing is that nonharassing sexual behavior also has negative work-related consequences for women workers, although even they are not always aware of them. For example, Gutek found that the experience of all kinds of sexual behavior, including remarks intended to be complimentary, was associated with lower job satisfaction among women workers. In addition, women reported that they are not flattered, and in fact are insulted, by sexual overtures of all kinds from men. In one study, sixty-two percent of women said they would be insulted by a sexual proposition from a man at work. Another example, the office "affair," can have serious detrimental effects on a woman's credibility as well as her career, especially if the relationship is with a supervisor.

Men seem to suffer virtually no work-related consequences of sexual behavior at work. Less than one percent of men reported that they quit a job because of sexual harassment, and, in the course of discussing sexual incidents, not one man said he lost a job as a consequence of a sexual overture or request from a woman at work. In the same study, sixty-seven percent of men said they would be flattered by sexual overtures from women. In addition, many men view a certain amount of sexual behavior as appropriate to the work setting, and, as noted above, they are less likely to consider any given behavior as sexual harassment. In one study, fifty-one percent of the men who received overtures from women said they themselves were at least somewhat responsible for the incident. That men experience so few work-related consequences of sex at work is especially odd, since they report so much sexual behavior both that is directed at them by women and that seems to float throughout the workplace.

When men do report "consequences," they are personal rather than work-related, and again, they are viewed in a positive manner. Most often, they report dating relationships or affairs that they find enjoyable; for instance, "There was this little blond who had the hots for me" or "I think she liked me. I was young and she was married. She wasn't very happy with her husband."

VII. Understanding Sexual Behavior at Work

As mentioned earlier, most studies of sexual behavior at work have been in response to the discovery of sexual harassment and policies developed to address harassment. Much of the research is descriptive and diverse, providing interesting information about sexual behavior at work, and useful information for policymakers and lawyers. Some researchers have begun to develop frameworks for studying sexual behavior at work.

One framework sometimes used to study harassment is the power perspective; that is, sexual harassment is an expression of power relationships, and women constitute a threat to men's economic and social standing. Within that perspective, Lipman-Blumen viewed the women's "seductive" behavior as micromanipulation, as a response to male control of social institutions—including the workplace and the academy—which she labeled macromanipulation. Other researchers explicitly borrowed from the literature on rape. They contend that sexual harassment is analogous to rape in that power, not sexual drive, is the dominant motivation. They further contend that victims of rape and harassment experience similar effects.

In an attempt to explain their own findings on sexual harassment, Tangri, Burt, and Johnson developed three models: the natural/biological model, the organizational model, and the sociocultural model. The natural/biological model assumes that sexual harassment and other forms of sexual expression at work are simply manifestations of natural attraction between two people. According to Tangri, Burt, and Johnson, one version of this model suggests that because men have a stronger sex drive, they more often initiate sexual overtures at work as well as in other settings. The organizational model assumes that sexual harassment is the result of certain opportunity structures within organizations such as hierarchies. People in higher positions can use their authority (their legitimate power) and their status to coerce lower-status people into accepting a role of sex object or engaging in sexual interactions. The third model, the sociocultural model, "argues that sexual harassment reflects the larger society's differential distribution of power and status between the sexes." Harassment is viewed as a mechanism for maintaining male dominance over women, in work and in society more generally. Male dominance is maintained by patterns of male-female interaction as well as by male domination of economic and political matters. Tangri, Burt, and Johnson's analysis revealed that none of the three models could by itself offer an adequate explanation of their data on sexual harassment. Another model, emphasizing the effects of sex-role expectations in an organizational context, is called sex-role spillover. The following analysis builds on earlier research on this concept.

VIII. Sex-Role Spillover

Sex-role spillover denotes the carryover of gender-based expectations into the workplace. Among the characteristics assumed by many to be associated with femaleness (such as passivity, loyalty, emotionality, nurturance) is being a sex object. Women are assumed to be sexual and to elicit sexual overtures from men rather naturally. In a thirty-nation study of sex stereotypes, the characteristics of sexy, affectionate, and attractive were associated with femaleness. This aspect of sex-role spillover, the sex-object aspect, is most relevant to the study of sex at work.

Sex-role spillover occurs when women, more than men in the same work roles, are expected to be sex objects or are expected to project sexuality through their behavior, appearance, or dress. What is equally important is the fact that there is no strongly held comparable belief about men. For example, of the forty-nine items that were associated with maleness in at least nineteen of the twenty-five countries studied by Williams and Best, none was directly or indirectly related to sexuality. While it is generally assumed that men are more sexually active than women and men are the initiators in sexual encounters, the cluster of characteristics that are usually associated with the male personality do not include a sexual component. Rather the stereotype of men revolves around the dimension of competence and activity. It includes the belief that men are rational, analytic, assertive, tough, good at math and science, competitive, and make good leaders. The stereotype of men—the common view of the male personality—is the perfect picture of asexuality. Sex-role spillover, thus, introduces the view of women as sexual beings in the workplace, but it simply reinforces the view of men as organizational beings—"active, work-oriented." It should also be noted that these stereotypes of female characteristics and male characteristics have remained quite stable through the 1970s and into the 1980s.

The spillover of the female sex-role, including the sexual aspect, occurs at work for at least four reasons. First, gender is the most noticeable social characteristic, that is, people immediately notice whether a person is a man or a woman. Second, men may feel more comfortable reacting to women at work in the same manner that they react to other women in their lives, and unless a woman is too young, too old, or too unattractive, that includes viewing her as a potential sexual partner. Third, women may feel comfortable reacting to men in a manner expected by the men, that is, conforming to the men's stereotype. Fourth, characteristics of work and sex roles may facilitate the carryover of sex role into work role. Sex roles remain relatively stable throughout our lives and permeate all domains of life. On the other hand, the work role may change many times and is specific to only one domain of life. Sex roles are also learned much earlier than are work roles, and they entail a wide variety of diffuse skills and abilities. Work roles, on the other hand, call for more specific skills and abilities.

The important point here is that being sexual and being a sex object are aspects of the female sex role that frequently are carried over to the workplace by both men and women. A variety of subtle pressures may encourage women to behave in a sexual manner at work, and this then confirms their supposedly essential sexual nature. Because it is expected, people notice female sexuality, and they believe it is normal, natural, an outgrowth of being female.

Unfortunately, women do not seem to be able to be sex objects and analytical, rational, competitive, and assertive at the same time because femaleness is viewed as "not-maleness," and it is the men who are viewed as analytic, logical, and assertive. Despite the fact that the model of male and female as polar opposites has been severely criticized on several grounds, a dichotomy is used by researchers and laypersons alike (for example, we speak of the "opposite" sex). This is an important part of sex-role spillover. Not only are the sexual aspects of the female role carried over to work, but also they swamp or overwhelm a view of women as capable, committed workers. This is especially true in an environment where sexual jokes, innuendos, posters, and small-talk are common. A recent study by Mohr and Zanna showed that sex-role traditional men exposed to sexually explicit material behaved in a significantly more sexual and obtrusive manner toward women than men who did not see sexually explicit material. As Kanter noted, a woman's perceived sexuality can "blot out" all other characteristics, particularly in a sexualized work environment. Thus, sex role interferes with and takes precedence over work role.

What is doubly troublesome about this inability to be sexual and a worker at the same time is that women are not the ones who usually choose between the two. A female employee might decide to be a sex object at work, especially if her career or job is not very important to her. More often, however, the working woman chooses not to be a sex object but may be so defined by male colleagues or supervisors anyway, regardless of her own actions. A woman's sexual behavior is noticed and labeled sexual even if it is not intended as such. In order to avoid being cast into the role of sex object, a woman may have to act completely asexual. Then she is subject to the charge of being a "prude," an "old maid," or "frigid," and in her attempt to avoid being a sex object, she is still stereotyped by her sexuality, or more accurately, by her perceived lack of sexuality.

The situation for men is entirely different. Benefiting from the stereotype of men as natural inhabitants of organizations—goal oriented, rational, analytic, competitive, assertive, strong, or, as Deaux puts it, "active, work-oriented"—men may be able to behave in a blatantly sexual manner, seemingly with impunity. Even when a man goes so far as to say that he encourages overtures from women by unzipping his pants at work, he may escape being viewed as sexual or more interested in sex than work by supervisors and colleagues. While the image of women acting in a seductive manner and distracting men from work is viewed as a detriment to the organization, many executives know of men in their employ who are "playboys" and harassers, yet they may not see that these men are a detriment to the organization. Although these men may hire the wrong women for the wrong reasons, make poor use of female human resources in the organization, squander the organization's resources in their quests for new sexual partners, and make elaborate attempts to impress potential sexual partners, all this may escape the notice of employers. In short, men's sexual behavior at work often goes unnoticed. At least two reasons for this can be cited. First, as noted above, there is no strongly recognized sexual component of the male sex role. Thus, men's sexual behavior is neither salient nor noticed. Second, perhaps sexual pursuits and conquests, jokes and innuendos can be subsumed under the stereotype of the organizational man—goal-oriented, rational, competitive, and assertive—which are expected and recognized as male traits. Men may make sexual overtures in an assertive, competitive manner. Likewise, sexual jokes, metaphors, and innuendos may be seen as part of competitive male horseplay. Thus the traits of competitiveness, assertiveness, and goal orientation are noticed, whereas the sexual component is not.

To recapitulate, expectations about male and female behavior that are derived from stereotypes (clusters of beliefs) about men and women spill over, or are carried over, into work roles for a variety of reasons. While the female stereotype has a sexual component (sex object), the male stereotype revolves around competence and achievement. The stereotype declares men to be asexual and women to be sexual. People attend to behavior that is expected, and behavior that is consistent with a stereotype is expected. Beliefs (stereotypes) take precedence over behaviors. Thus, men's sexual behavior is not noticed, and even some men's sexually intended behavior is not interpreted by target women or their employers as such. On the other hand, women's behavior is interpreted as sexual even when it is not intended as such.

IX. The Spillover Perspective: Behaviors, Impacts, and Beliefs Concerning Sex at Work

How does the sex-role spillover perspective enrich our understanding of sex at work or integrate the diverse findings about sexual harassment? This perspective leads to an examination of both men's and women's behavior at work and stereotypes or beliefs about how men and women behave at work. It helps to explain the apparent paradox that women are perceived as using sex to their advantage, while, in practice, they are hurt by sex at work. On the other hand, while men are not perceived as sexual at work, they may display more sexual behavior and may benefit from it.

Sex-role spillover is further useful in explaining why sexual harassment remained invisible for so long. In the absence of data on the subject, women were labeled as sexy, men as asexual. Sexual overtures including harassment were elicited by the sexy women; men who are normally active and work-oriented, "all-business," could be distracted by seductively behaving women, but these distractions were considered a trivial part of men's overall work behavior. If the woman subsequently felt uncomfortable with the situation, it was her problem. If she could not handle the problem and complained about it, it was at least partially her fault. Men and women, including women victims, shared this belief. Thus a woman who complained might be labeled a troublemaker and be asked to leave the job or the company.

It should be noted that although the spillover perspective is not incompatible with a power perspective, it falls short when attempting to account for hostile sexual coercion at work. To take an extreme (but not unknown) case, one would hardly say that rape in the office is a spillover from externally imposed sex roles. Rather, it might best be construed as aggression or power, and a power perspective of sexual harassment may be a better explanatory model.

X. Closing Remarks

Much of the research on sexual harassment was inspired by the innovations and developments in law and policy and researchers have drawn directly from them in developing a research agenda. So far it has focused primarily on two issues, definition and prevalence, although topics such as consequences to victims and conditions under which harassment occurs have also been studied.

Recently, Terpstra and his colleagues have engaged in a program of research in a new area: the factors which affect the outcome of decisions in sexual harassment cases. Terpstra and Baker studied Illinois state EEOC cases and examined the factors associated with the outcomes of sexual harassment charges; only thirty-one percent of formal charges (20 of 65 cases) resulted in a settlement favorable to the complainant. Using the same set of EEOC cases, Terpstra and Cook found that employment-related consequences experienced by the complainant were the most critical factor in filing a charge. Other research, for example, on men who harass and the way men respond to women when sexually explicit material is or is not available, represent other new and important areas of research.

Overall, the research on sexual harassment and sex at work has provided data showing that many of the common beliefs about sexual behavior at work are false. The contribution of research toward understanding and explaining sex at work has been valuable. A domain of human behavior that was largely invisible a decade ago is now visible, numerous misconceptions have been uncovered, and some facts have been exposed as myths by researchers.

42. Exaggerating the Extent of Sexual Harassment

Ellen Frankel Paul

Ellen Frankel Paul argues that sexual harassment has been exaggerated to include everything from rape to "looks." She argues that the extortion of sexual favors by a supervisor from a subordinate by threatening to penalize, fire, or fail to reward is sexual harassment. But she argues that a hostile working environment should be regarded as sexual harassment only when the "reasonable man" of tort law would find the working environment offensive. She contends that given this understanding of sexual harassment, scatological jokes, leers, unwanted offers of dates, and other sexual annoyances would no longer have their day in court.

Women in American society are victims of sexual harassment in alarming proportions. Sexual harassment is an inevitable corollary to class exploitation; as capitalists exploit workers, so do males in positions of authority exploit their female subordinates. Male professors, supervisors, and apartment managers in ever increasing numbers take advantage of the financial dependence and vulnerability of women to extract sexual concessions.

Valid Assertions?

These are the assertions that commonly begin discussions of sexual harassment. For reasons that will be adumbrated below, dissent from the prevailing view is long overdue. Three recent episodes will serve to frame this disagreement.

Valerie Craig, an employee of Y & Y Snacks, Inc., joined several co-workers and her supervisor for drinks after work one day in July of 1978. Her supervisor drove her home and proposed that they become more intimately acquainted. She refused his invitation for sexual relations, whereupon he said that he would "get even" with her. Ten days after the incident she was fired from her job. She soon filed a complaint of sexual harassment with the Equal Employment Opportunity Commission (EEOC), and the case wound its way through the courts. Craig prevailed,

From "Bared Buttocks and Federal Cases," *Society* (1991). Reprinted by permission.

the company was held liable for damages, and she received back pay, reinstatement, and an order prohibiting Y & Y from taking reprisals against her in the future.

Carol Zabowicz, one of only two female forklift operators in a West Bend Co. warehouse, charged that her co-workers over a four-year period from 1978–1982 sexually harassed her by such acts as: asking her whether she was wearing a bra; two of the men exposing their buttocks between ten and twenty times; a male co-worker grabbing his crotch and making obscene suggestions or growling; subjecting her to offensive and abusive language; and exhibiting obscene drawings with her initials on them. Zabowicz began to show symptoms of physical and psychological stress, necessitating several medical leaves, and she filed a sexual harassment complaint with the EEOC. The district court judge remarked that "the sustained, malicious, and brutal harassment meted out . . . was more than merely unreasonable; it was malevolent and outrageous." The company knew of the harassment and took corrective action only after the employee filed a complaint with the EEOC. The company was, therefore, held liable, and Zabowicz was awarded back pay for the period of her medical absence, and a judgment that her rights were violated under the Civil Rights Act of 1964.

On September 17, 1990, Lisa Olson, a sports reporter for the *Boston Herald,* charged five football players of the just-defeated New England Patriots with sexual harassment for making sexually suggestive and offensive remarks to her when she entered their locker room to conduct a post-game interview. The incident amounted to nothing short of "mind rape," according to Olson. After vociferous lamentations in the media, the National Football League fined the team and its players $25,000 each. The National Organization of Women called for a boycott of Remington electric shavers because the owner of the company, Victor Kiam, also owns the Patriots and who allegedly displayed insufficient sensitivity at the time when the episode occurred.

Utopian Treatment for Women

All these incidents are indisputably disturbing. In an ideal world—one needless to say far different from the one that we inhabit or are ever likely to inhabit—women would not be subjected to such treatment in the course of their work. Women, and men as well, would be accorded respect by co-workers and supervisors, their feelings would be taken into account, and their dignity would be left intact. For women to expect reverential treatment in the workplace is utopian, yet they should not have to tolerate outrageous, offensive sexual overtures and threats as they go about earning a living.

One question that needs to be pondered is: What kinds of undesired sexual behavior women should be protected against by law? That is, what kind of actions are deemed so outrageous and violate a woman's rights to such extent that the law should intervene, and what actions should be considered inconveniences of life, to be morally condemned but not adjudicated? A subsidiary question concerns the type of legal remedy appropriate for the wrongs that do require redress. Before directly addressing these questions, it might be useful to diffuse some of the hyperbole adhering to the sexual harassment issue.

Harassment Surveys

Surveys are one source of this hyperbole. If their results are accepted at face value, they lead to the conclusion that women are disproportionately victims of legions of sexual harassers. A poll by the Albuquerque *Tribune* found that nearly 80 percent of the respondents reported that they or someone they knew had been victims of sexual harassment. The Merit Systems Protection Board determined that 42 percent of the women (and 14 percent of men) working for the federal government had experienced some form of unwanted sexual attention between 1985 and 1987, with unwanted "sexual teasing" identified as the most prevalent form. A Defense Department survey found that 64 percent of women in the military (and 17 percent of the men) suffered "uninvited and unwanted sexual attention" within the previous year. The United Methodist Church established that 77 percent of its clergywomen experienced incidents of sexual harassment, with 41 percent of these naming a pastor or colleague as the perpetrator, and 31 percent mentioning church social functions as the setting.

A few caveats concerning polls in general, and these sorts of polls in particular, are worth considering. Pollsters looking for a particular social ill tend to find it, usually in gargantuan proportions. (What fate would lie in store for a pollster who concluded that child abuse, or wife beating, or mistreatment of the elderly had dwindled to the point of negligibility!) Sexual harassment is a notoriously ill-defined and almost infinitely expandable concept, including everything from rape to unwelcome neck massaging, discomfiture upon witnessing sexual overtures directed at others, yelling at and blowing smoke in the ears of female subordinates, and displays of pornographic pictures in the workplace. Defining sexual harassment, as the United Methodists did, as "any sexually related behavior that is unwelcome, offensive or which fails to respect the rights of others," the concept is broad enough to include everything from "unsolicited suggestive looks or leers [or] pressures for dates" to "actual sexual assaults or rapes." Categorizing everything from rape to "looks" as sexual harassment makes us all victims, a state of affairs satisfying to radical feminists, but not very useful for distinguishing serious injuries from the merely trivial.

Yet, even if the surveys exaggerate the extent of sexual harassment, however defined, what they do reflect is a great deal of tension between the sexes. As women in ever increasing numbers entered the workplace in the last two decades, as the women's movement challenged alleged male hegemony and exploitation with ever greater intemperance, and as women entered previously all-male preserves from the board rooms to the coal pits, it is lamentable, but should not be surprising, that this tension sometimes takes sexual form. Not that sexual harassment on the job, in the university, and in other settings is a trivial or insignificant matter, but a sense of proportion needs to be restored and, even more important, distinctions need to be made. In other words, sexual harassment must be de-ideologized. Statements that paint nearly all women as victims and all men and their patriarchal, capitalist system as perpetrators, are ideological fantasy. Ideology blurs the distinction between being injured—being a genuine victim—and merely being offended. An example is this statement by Catharine A. MacKinnon, a law professor and feminist activist:

> Sexual harassment perpetuates the interlocked structure by which women have been kept sexually in thrall to men and at the bottom of the labor market. Two forces of American society converge: men's control over women's sexuality and capital's control over employees' work lives. Women historically have been required to exchange sexual services for material survival, in one form or another. Prostitution and marriage as well as sexual harassment in different ways institutionalize this arrangement.

Such hyperbole needs to be diffused and distinctions need to be drawn. Rape, a nonconsensual invasion of a person's body, is a crime clear and simple. It is a violation of the right to the physical integrity of the body (the right to life, as John Locke or Thomas Jefferson would have put it). Criminal law should and does prohibit rape. Whether it is useful to call rape "sexual harassment" is doubtful, for it makes the latter concept overly broad while trivializing the former.

Extortion of Sexual Favors

Intimidation in the workplace of the kind that befell Valerie Craig—that is, extortion of sexual favors by a supervisor from a subordinate by threatening to penalize, fire, or fail to reward—is what the courts term *quid pro quo* sexual harassment. Since the mid-1970s, the federal courts have treated this type of sexual harassment as a form of sex discrimination in employment proscribed under Title VII of the Civil Rights Act of 1964. A plaintiff who prevails against an employer may receive such equitable remedies as reinstatement and back pay, and the court can order the company to prepare and disseminate a policy against sexual harassment. Current law places principal liability on the company, not the harassing supervisor, even when higher management is unaware of the harassment and, thus, cannot take any steps to prevent it.

Quid pro quo sexual harassment is morally objectionable and analogous to extortion: The harasser extorts property (i.e., use of the woman's body) through the leverage of fear for her job. The victim of such behavior should have legal recourse, but serious reservations can be held about rectifying these injustices through the blunt instrument of Title VII. In egregious cases the victim is left less than whole (for back pay will not compensate her for ancillary losses), and no prospect for punitive damages are offered to deter would-be harassers. Even more distressing about Title VII is the fact that the primary target of litigation is not the actual harasser, but rather the employer. This places a double burden on a company. The employer is swindled by the supervisor because he spent his time pursuing sexual gratification and thereby impairing the efficiency of the workplace by mismanaging his subordinates, and the employer must endure lengthy and expensive litigation, pay damages, and suffer loss to its reputation. It would be fairer to both the company and the victim to treat sexual harassment as a tort—that is, as a private wrong or injury for which the court can assess damages. Employers should be held vicariously liable only when they know of an employee's behavior and do not try to redress it.

Defining Harassment Is Difficult

As for the workplace harassment endured by Carol Zabowicz—the bared buttocks, obscene portraits, etc.—that too should be legally redressable. Presently, such incidents also fall under the umbrella of Title VII, and are termed hostile environment sexual harassment, a category accepted later than *quid pro quo* and with some judicial reluctance. The main problem with this category is that it has proven too elastic: cases have reached the courts based on everything from off-color jokes to unwanted, persistent sexual advances by co-workers. A new tort of sexual harassment would handle these cases better. Only instances above a certain threshold of egregiousness or outrageousness would be actionable. In other words, the behavior that the plaintiff found offensive would also have to be offensive to the proverbial "reasonable man" of the tort law. That is, the behavior would have to be objectively injurious rather than merely subjectively offensive. The defendant would be the actual harasser, not the company, unless it knew about the problem and failed to act. Victims of scatological jokes, leers, unwanted offers of dates, and other sexual annoyances would no longer have their day in court.

A distinction must be restored between morally offensive behavior and behavior that causes serious harm. Only the latter should fall under the jurisdiction of criminal or tort law. Do we really want legislators and judges delving into our most intimate private lives, deciding when a look is a leer, and when a leer is a Civil Rights Act offense? Do we really want courts deciding, as one recently did, whether a school principal's disparaging remarks about a female school district administrator was sexual harassment and, hence, a breach of Title VII, or merely the act of a spurned and vengeful lover? Do we want judges settling disputes such as the one that arose at a car dealership after a female employee turned down a male

co-worker's offer of a date and his colleagues retaliated by calling her offensive names and embarrassing her in front of customers? Or another case in which a female shipyard worker complained of an "offensive working environment" because of the prevalence of pornographic material on the docks? Do we want the state to prevent or compensate us for any behavior that someone might find offensive? Should people have a legally enforceable right not to be offended by others? At some point, the price for such protection is the loss of both liberty and privacy rights.

No Perfect Working Environment Exists

Workplaces are breeding grounds of envy, personal grudges, infatuation, and jilted loves, and beneath a fairly high threshold of outrageousness, these travails should be either suffered in silence, complained of to higher management, or left behind as one seeks other employment. No one, female or male, can expect to enjoy a working environment that is perfectly stress-free, or to be treated always and by everyone with kindness and respect. To the extent that sympathetic judges have encouraged women to seek monetary compensation for slights and annoyances, they have not done them a great service. Women need to develop a thick skin in order to survive and prosper in the workforce. It is patronizing to think that they need to be recompensed by male judges for seeing a few pornographic pictures on a wall. By their efforts to extend sexual harassment charges to even the most trivial behavior, the radical feminists send a message that women are not resilient enough to ignore the run-of-the-mill, churlish provocation from male co-workers. It is difficult to imagine a suit by a longshoreman complaining of mental stress due to the display of nude male centerfolds by female co-workers. Women cannot expect to have it both ways: equality where convenient, but special dispensations when the going gets rough. Equality has its price and that price may include unwelcome sexual advances, irritating and even intimidating sexual jests, and lewd and obnoxious colleagues.

Egregious acts—sexual harassment per se—must be legally redressable. Lesser but not trivial offenses, whether at the workplace or in other more social settings, should be considered moral lapses for which the offending party receives opprobrium, disciplinary warnings, or penalties, depending on the setting and the severity. Trivial offenses, dirty jokes, sexual overtures, and sexual innuendoes do make many women feel intensely discomfited, but, unless they become outrageous through persistence or content, these too should be taken as part of life's annoyances. The perpetrators should be either endured, ignored, rebuked, or avoided, as circumstances and personal inclination dictate. Whether Lisa Olson's experience in the locker room of the Boston Patriots falls into the second or third category is debatable. The media circus triggered by the incident was certainly out of proportion to the event.

As the presence of women on road gangs, construction crews, and oil rigs becomes a fact of life, the animosities and tensions of this transition period are likely to abate gradually. Meanwhile, women should "lighten up," and even dispense a few risqué barbs of their own, a sure way of taking the fun out of it for offensive male bores.

43. Reflections on the Confirmation of Clarence Thomas

Nancy Fraser

Nancy Fraser analyzes the Senate Judiciary Committee hearings on Anita Hill's claim that Clarence Thomas had sexually harassed her as a struggle with three phases. In the first gender-dominated phase, Fraser claims that Anita Hill was not able to prevent intensive examination of her private life whereas Clarence Thomas was able to declare key areas of his private life as off-limits, even though in the first round of hearings he had substituted his personal life story for a discussion of his political, legal, and constitutional views. In the second race-dominated phase, Fraser claims that Thomas was able to characterize the attack on him as motivated by the stereotypes of black men as male studs and rapists, whereas Hill became functionally white. In this phase of the struggle, Fraser claims that the black woman's perspective was never taken into account. In the third class-dominated phase of the struggle, Fraser claims that class resentment was mobilized in favor of Thomas through his "working class" supporter J. C. Alvarez whereas Hill, despite her lower class origins and the fact that Thomas had been her boss, was associated with her "upper class" supporter Susan Hoerchner.

1. Introduction

The recent struggle over the confirmation of Clarence Thomas and the credibility of Anita

From *Critical Inquiry* 18 (Spring 1992). © 1992 by The University of Chicago. All rights reserved. Reprinted by permission.

Hill raises in a dramatic and pointed way many of the issues at stake in theorizing the public sphere in contemporary society. At one level, the Senate Judiciary Committee hearings on Hill's claim that Thomas sexually harassed her constituted an exercise in democratic publicity as it has been understood in the classical liberal theory of the public sphere. The hearings opened to public scrutiny a function of government, namely, the nomination and confirmation of a Supreme Court justice. They thus subjected a decision of state officials to the force of public opinion. Through the hearings, in fact, public opinion was constituted and brought to bear directly on the decision itself, affecting the process by which the decision was made as well as its substantive outcome. As a result, state officials were held accountable to the public by means of a discursive process of opinion and will formation.

Yet that classical liberal view of the public sphere does not tell the whole story of these events. If we examine the Thomas confirmation struggle more closely, we see that the very meaning and boundaries of the concept of publicity were at stake. The way the struggle unfolded, moreover, depended at every point on who had the power to successfully and authoritatively define where the line between the public and the private would be drawn. It depended as well on who had the power to police and defend that boundary.

Consider how those issues underlay many of the questions that were explicitly debated: Was the public disclosure on 6 October 1991 of Anita Hill's accusations against Clarence Thomas a leak that represented a breach of proper procedure and confidentiality, or was it an act of whistle-blowing that exposed a cover-up? Was Anita Hill's failure to go public with her accusations prior to 6 October grounds for doubting her account, or was it consistent with her story? Should the behavior Hill ascribed to Thomas be considered innocent comradery or abuse of power? Is such behavior "normal" or "pathological"?

Moreover, do men and women have different views of these issues, and are they positioned differently with respect to privacy and publicity? Did the efforts of Thomas's supporters to undermine the credibility of Anita Hill constitute an invasion of her privacy or a proper exercise of public scrutiny? Were there significant differences in the ability of Thomas and Hill respectively to define and defend their privacy?

Was the injection of the issue of race by Clarence Thomas a mere smoke screen, or did the convening of an all-white public tribunal to adjudicate on television a dispute between two blacks signal the existence of real racial-ethnic differences in relation to privacy and public-

ity? Is "sexual harassment" a figment of the fevered imagination of puritanical, sexually repressed, elite white feminists or an instrument of gender, race, and class power? Does the vindication in this case of a black man's ability to defend his privacy against a white-dominated public represent an advance for his race or a setback for black women?

Did the hearings themselves constitute an unseemly circus that degraded the democratic process, or were they a rare exercise in democratic publicity, a national teach-in on sexual harassment? Was the airing in public hearings of the charge of sexual harassment another case of the American obsession with the private lives of public figures, an obsession that displaces real politics onto questions of character? Or was it instead a historic breakthrough in an ongoing struggle to achieve a more equitable balance in the social relations of privacy and publicity?

Finally, is democratic publicity best understood as a check on the public power of the state, or should it be understood more broadly as a check against illegitimate "private" power as well? And what is the relationship between various publics that emerged here: for example, the official public sphere within the state (the hearings); the extragovernmental public sphere constituted by the mass media; various counterpublics associated with oppositional social movements like feminism and with ethnic enclaves like the black community (the feminist press, the black press); various secondary associations active in forming public opinion (interest groups, lobbies); the ephemeral but intense constitution of informal public spheres at various sites in everyday life—at workplaces, restaurants, campuses, street corners, shopping centers, private homes, wherever people gathered to discuss the events? In each of those public arenas, whose words counted in the conflict of interpretations that determines the official public story of what "really" happened? And why?

Underlying all these questions are two more general problems that are centered on power and inequality: Who has the power to decide where to draw the line between public and private? What structures of inequality underlie the hegemonic understandings of these categories as well as the struggles that contest them?

2. Gender Struggle

The first phase of the struggle was played out as a gender struggle, and it laid bare important gender asymmetries concerning privacy and publicity. These were not the familiar orthodoxies of an earlier stage of feminist theory, which protested women's alleged confinement to the private sphere. Rather, the asymmetries here concerned women's greater vulnerability to unwanted, intrusive publicity and lesser ability to define and defend their privacy.

These issues first emerged when the public at large learned of a struggle that had been waged behind closed doors for several weeks between Anita Hill and members of the Senate Judiciary Committee over the handling of her accusations against Clarence Thomas. In her first public news conference after her charges had been publicly reported, Hill focused on what she called her lack of "control" over the routing, timing, and dissemination of her information. She was already having to defend herself against two apparently contradictory charges: first, that she had failed to make public her allegations in a timely fashion, as any bona fide victim of sexual harassment supposedly would have; but second, that in making these charges she was seeking publicity and self-aggrandizement. Hill sought to explain her actions, first, by insisting that "control" over these disclosures "had never been with me," and second, by acknowledging her difficulty in balancing her need for privacy against her duty to disclose information in response to the committee's inquiry. As it turned out, she never succeeded in fully dispelling many Americans' doubts on these points.

For its part, the committee's initial decision not to publicize her sexual harassment charges against Thomas represented an effort to delimit the scope of the first round of public hearings in September and to contain public debate about the nomination. Once Hill's charges were made public, however, the com-

mittee lost control of the process. Instead, its members became embroiled in a public struggle with feminists who objected to the privatization of an important gender issue and accused the senators of "sexism" and "insensitivity."

This gender struggle was widely reported in the media in counterpoint with a counterdiscourse of outrage over "the leak." These two themes of "The Senate and Sexism" and leaks were for a time the two principal contenders in the battle for preeminence in interpreting the events, as the struggle over whether or not to delay the Senate vote on the nomination was being waged. The vote *was* of course delayed, and the feminists succeeded in broadening the space of the official national political public sphere to encompass, for the first time, the subject of sexual harassment.

Getting an issue on the public agenda, however, does not guarantee success in controlling the discussion of it. Even as it was being decided that the vote on Thomas's nomination would be delayed and that public hearings on the sexual harassment charges would be held, there began a fierce backstage contest to shape the public debate over the issues. While public debate focused on the question of the Senate's "insensitivity," White House strategists worked behind the scenes to shape the focus of the hearings and the interpretation of events.

As it turned out, the administration's plan to shape public debate and limit the scope of the hearings had three crucial features. First, the White House sought to prevent or marginalize any new allegations of sexual harassment by other victims in order to shape the hearings as a he-said-she-said affair. Second, they sought to rule off-limits any interrogation of what was defined as Thomas's "private life," including what the *New York Times* called his "well-documented taste for watching and discussing pornographic movies while he was at Yale Law School." Third, and last, they sought to exclude expert testimony about the nature of sexual harassment and the characteristic responses of victims, so that, in the words of one administration spin doctor, they could "prevent this from turning into a referendum on 2000 years of male dominance and sexual harassment."

Together these three moves cast Clarence Thomas and Anita Hill in very different relations to privacy and publicity. Thomas was enabled to declare key areas of his life "private" and therefore off-limits. Hill, in contrast, was cast as someone whose motives and character would be subjects of intense scrutiny and intrusive speculation, since her "credibility" was to be evaluated in a conceptual vacuum. When the Senate Judiciary Committee adopted these ground rules for the hearings, they sealed in place a structural differential in relation to publicity and privacy that worked overwhelmingly to Thomas's advantage and to Hill's disadvantage.

Once these ground rules were in place, the administration could concentrate on its hardball attempt to undermine Hill. They sought to insure, as Senator Alan K. Simpson presciently predicted, that "Anita Hill will be sucked right into the maw, the very thing she wanted to avoid most. She will be injured and destroyed and belittled and hounded and harassed, real harassment, different from the sexual kind."

While open season was being declared on Hill, Clarence Thomas was attempting to define and defend his privacy. His attempts had a certain ironic flavor, to be sure, given his insistence in the first round of hearings on substituting his personal life story—or at least his version thereof—for discussion of his political, legal, and constitutional views. Having first tried to make his private character the public issue, he was nearly undone by the focus on his character when Hill's accusation was made public.

In the second round of hearings, Thomas responded to Hill's charges by trying to define what he thought was or should be his private life. He refused to accept questions that breached his privacy as he defined it. And he objected to "reporters and interest groups . . . looking for dirt" as un-American and Kafkaesque.

I am not here . . . to put my private life on display for prurient interests or other reasons. I will not allow this committee or anyone else to probe into my private life. . . . I will not provide the rope for my

own lynching or for further humiliation. I am not going to engage in discussions nor will I submit to roving questions of what goes on in the most intimate parts of my private life, or the sanctity of my bedroom. These are the most intimate parts of my privacy, and they will remain just that, private.

Certainly, Thomas was not entirely successful in enforcing his definitions of privacy and publicity, as the mere airing of Hill's charges attested. Yet within the limits imposed by the fact of the hearings, he was more successful than not. His questioners on the committee generally accepted his definition of privacy, and their questions did not trespass on that space as he had defined it. They didn't inquire into his sexual history or his fantasy life, and he was not in fact questioned about his practice of viewing and discussing pornographic films. The one time when this subject was broached, at the session of 12 October 1991, Thomas successfully repulsed the inquiry:

[Senator Leahy]:   Did you ever have a discussion of pornographic films with . . . any other women [than Professor Hill]?

[Thomas]:   Senator, I will not get into any discussions that I might have about my personal life or my sex life with any person outside of the workplace.

The question was not pursued. Later, after the Senate confirmed the nomination, Democratic members of the Judiciary Committee defended their failure to cross-examine Thomas vigorously by saying that he had put up a "wall" and refused to answer questions about his private life.

The relative success of Thomas's efforts to define and defend his privacy can be seen in the fact that while the country was awash in speculation concerning the character, motives, and psychology of Anita Hill, there was no comparable speculation about him. No one wondered, it seemed, what sort of anxieties and hurts could lead a powerful and successful self-made black man from a very poor background to sexually harass a black female subordinate from a similar background.

Anita Hill also sought to define and defend her privacy, but she was far less successful than Thomas. Events constantly eluded her efforts to keep the focus on her complaint and on the evidence that corroborated it. Instead, the principal focus soon became *her* character. During the course of the struggle, it was variously suggested that Hill was a lesbian, a heterosexual erotomaniac, a delusional schizophrenic, a fantasist, a vengeful spurned woman, a perjurer, and a malleable tool of liberal interest groups. Not only the Republican hit men, Arlen Specter, Orrin Hatch, and Alan Simpson, but even her female coworkers from the Equal Employment Opportunity Commission tarred her with many of the classical sexist stereotypes: "stridently aggressive," "arrogant," "ambitious," "hard," "tough," "scorned," "opinionated." Nor did any of the Democratic committee members succeed, or for that matter even try, to limit the scope of inquiry into her "privacy."

Hill's lesser success in drawing the line between public and private testifies to the gendered character of these categories and to the way their constitution reflects the asymmetry or hierarchy of power along gender lines. That asymmetry is reflected in the phenomenon of sexual harassment as well. Consider the following account by Hill in response to the questioning of Howell Heflin, who first read to her portions of her own opening statement:

> I sense[d] that my discomfort with [Thomas's] discussions [of pornography] only urged him on as though my reaction of feeling ill at ease and vulnerable was what he wanted.

Then, in response to Heflin's request for elaboration, Hill replied: "It was almost as though he wanted me at a disadvantage . . . so that I would have to concede to whatever his wishes were. . . . I would be under his control. I think it was the fact that I had said no to him that caused him to want to do this." As Hill saw it, then, Thomas's behavior had been an assertion (or reassertion) of power, aimed simultaneously at compensating himself and punishing her for rejection. She herself had lacked the power to define the nature of their interaction: he, in contrast, had had the power to inject what liberals consider private sexual elements into the public sphere of the workplace against her wishes and over her objections.

Given the gender differential in ability to define and protect one's privacy, we can understand some of the deeper issues at stake in Thomas's insistence on avoiding the "humiliation" of a "public probe" into his "privacy." This insistence can be understood in part as a defense of his masculinity; to be subject to having one's privacy publicly probed is to risk being feminized.

Women's difficulty in defining and defending their privacy is also attested by an extremely important absence from the hearings: the non-appearance of Angela Wright, a second black woman who claimed to have been sexually harassed by Thomas and whose testimony to that effect was to have been corroborated by another witness, Rose Jordain, in whom Wright had confided at the time. Given that disbelief of Hill was often rationalized by the claim that there were no other complainants, the non-appearance of Wright was significant. We can speculate that had she testified and proved a credible witness, the momentum of the struggle might have shifted decisively. Why then did Angela Wright not appear? Both sides had reasons to privatize her story. Thomas's supporters feared a second accusation would be extremely damaging and threatened to discredit her by introducing information concerning her personal history. Thomas's opponents may have feared that a woman described in the press as presenting "a more complex picture than Professor Hill" would appear to lack credibility and undermine Hill's as well. Thus, the silencing of a complainant who was thought to lack Hill's respectability was a crucial and possibly

even decisive factor in the dynamics and outcome of the struggle.

3. The Struggle over Race

During the first, gender-dominated phase of
the struggle, the issue of race was barely discussed, despite repeated, but unelaborated
references to the Senate as an all-white body.
The relative silence about race was soon
shattered, however, when Thomas himself
broached the issue. Moving quickly to occupy
an otherwise vacant discursive terrain, he and
his supporters managed to establish a near-
monopoly on "race" talk, and the result
proved disastrous for Hill.

Thomas claimed that the hearings were a
"high-tech lynching" designed to stop "uppity
Blacks who in any way deign to think for
themselves." He also spoke repeatedly about
his defenselessness before charges that played
into racial stereotypes of black men as having
large penises and unusual sexual prowess.

Here it is important to note that by combining references to lynching with references to
stereotypes about black men's sexual prowess,
Thomas artfully conflated two stereotypes,
which, although related, are far from identical. The first is the stereotype of the black man
as sexual stud, highly desired by women and
capable of providing them great sexual pleasure. This was the figure that emerged from
Hill's testimony, according to which Thomas
bragged to her about his heterosexual virtuos-
ity. The second stereotype is that of the black
man as rapist, a lust-driven animal, whose
sexuality is criminal and out of control. There
was no hint of that stereotype in Hill's testimony.

It is possible that at an unconscious level
there are affinities between these two stereotypes. But they differ importantly in at
least one crucial respect. While both have been
embraced by white racists, the first, but not the
second, has also been embraced by some black
men. Thus, while it may be inconceivable that
Thomas would have elected to affect the persona of black man as rapist, it is not inconceivable that he would have affected the persona

of the black male sexual stud. Yet by conflat-
ing these two stereotypes, Thomas was able to
suggest that Hill's reports of his behavior as a
would-be stud were equivalent to southern
white racist fabrications of criminal sexuality
and rape. This turned out to be a rhetorical
master stroke. The Democrats on the committee were too cowed by the charge of racism
to question the nominee's logic. Many leading
black liberals seemed caught off guard and
unable to respond effectively; most simply denied that race had any relevance in the case at
all.

The mainstream press contributed to the
confusion. For example, the *New York Times*
printed solemn quotations from Harvard psychiatrist Alvin Poussaint about the effects of
Hill's charges on black men:

> "Black men will feel [her allegations] rein-
> force negative stereotypes about them as
> sexual animals out of control. . . . It will in-
> crease their level of tension and vulnerabil-
> ity around charges of this type. . . . There's
> a high level of anger among black men . . .
> that black women will betray them; that
> black women are given preference over
> them; that white men will like to put black
> women in between them to use them.
> Black men feel that white men are using
> this black woman to get another black
> man."

I have no way of knowing whether or to what
extent Poussaint is accurately reporting the
views and feelings of black men. What is clear
however is the lack of any comparable discussion of the effects of the case on black women.
In the absence of such discussion, moreover,
the fears ascribed to black men seem to acquire legitimacy. They are not contextualized
or counterpointed by any other perspective.
The press coverage of the racial dimensions of
the struggle generally slighted black women. It
focused chiefly on questions such as whether
or not all black men would be tarred in the
eyes of white America, and whether or not
another black man would get a shot at a seat
on the Supreme Court.

One of the most important features of the
entire struggle was the absence from the hear-

ings and from the mainstream public sphere debate of a black feminist analysis. No one who was in a position to be heard in the hearings or in the mainstream mass media spoke about the historic vulnerability of black women to sexual harassment in the United States and about the use of racist-misogynist stereotypes to justify such abuse and to malign black women who protest.[1] As a result, black women were yet again "asked to choose . . . whether to stand against the indignities done them as women, sometimes by men of their own race, or to remember that black men take enough of a beating from the white world and to hold their peace." In other words, there was no widely disseminated perspective that persuasively integrated a critique of sexual harassment with a critique of racism. At this stage the struggle was cast as either a gender struggle or a race struggle. It could not, apparently, be both at once.

The result was that it became difficult to see Anita Hill as a black woman. She became, in effect, functionally white. Certainly, Thomas's references to lynching had the effect of calling into question her blackness. The lynching story requires a white woman as "victim" and pretext. To my knowledge, no black man has ever been lynched for the sexual exploitation of a black woman. Thomas's charge thus implied that Hill might not really be black. Perhaps because she was a tool of white interest groups. Or perhaps because she had internalized the uptight, puritanical sexual morality of elite white feminists and had mistaken his lower class, black courting style for abuse, a view propounded by Orlando Patterson. Or perhaps most ingeniously of all, because, like Adela Quested, the white female protagonist of E. M. Forster's *A Passage to India,* Hill was an erotomaniacal spinster who fantasized abuse at the hands of a dark-skinned man out of the depths of her experiences of rejection and sexual frustration, a view apparently originated by John Doggett, but more effectively—because less self-servingly—presented by Hatch and other Thomas supporters.

Whichever of these scenarios one chose to believe, the net effect was the same: Anita Hill became functionally white. She was treated, consequently, very differently from the way

that Angela Wright would probably have been treated had *she* testified. Wright might very well have been cast as Jezebel, opposite Hill's Adela Quested, in a bizarre melodramatic pastiche of traditional and nontraditional casting.

The "whitening" of Anita Hill had much broader implications, however, since it cast black women who seek to defend themselves against abuse at the hands of black men as traitors or enemies of the race. Consequently, when the struggle was cast exclusively as a racial struggle, the sole black protagonist became the black man. He was made to stand synecdochically for the entire race, and the black woman was erased from view.

A recent development holds out some hope for redressing this erasure and for overcoming the definition of the struggle as either a gender or a race struggle. This is the founding of a group called African American Women in Defense of Ourselves, whose inaugural statement is worth quoting at some length:

Many have erroneously portrayed the allegations against Clarence Thomas as an issue of either gender or race. As women of African descent, we understand sexual harassment as both. We further understand that Clarence Thomas outrageously manipulated the legacy of lynching in order to shelter himself from Anita Hill's allegations. To deflect attention away from the reality of sexual abuse in African American women's lives, he trivialized and misrepresented this painful part of African American people's history. This country, which has a long legacy of racism and sexism, has never taken the sexual abuse of Black women seriously. Throughout U.S. history Black women have been sexually stereotyped as immoral, insatiable, perverse; the initiators in all sexual contacts—abusive or otherwise. The common assumption in legal proceedings as well as in the larger society has been that Black women cannot be raped or otherwise sexually abused. As Anita Hill's experience demonstrates, Black women who speak of these matters are not likely to be believed.

In 1991, we cannot tolerate this type of dismissal of any one Black woman's experience or this attack upon our collective character without protest, outrage, and resistance. . . . No one will speak for us but ourselves.

What is so important about this statement is its rejection of the view, held by many supporters of Anita Hill, that race was simply irrelevant to this struggle, apart from Thomas's manipulation of it. Instead, the statement implies that the categories of privacy and publicity are not simply gendered categories; they are racialized categories as well. Historically blacks have been denied privacy in the sense of domesticity. As a result, black women have been highly vulnerable to sexual harassment at the hands of masters, overseers, bosses, and supervisors. At the same time, they have lacked the public standing to claim state protection against abuse, whether suffered at work or at home. Black men, meanwhile, have lacked the rights and prerogatives enjoyed by white men, including the right to exclude white men from "their" women and the right to exclude the state from their "private" sphere.

Perhaps, then, it is worth exploring the hypothesis that in making his case before the white tribunal, Clarence Thomas was trying to claim the same rights and immunities of masculinity that white men have historically enjoyed, especially the right to maintain open season on black women. Or perhaps he was not claiming *exactly* the same rights and immunities as white men. Perhaps he was not seeking these privileges vis-à-vis all women. After all, no white woman claimed to have been sexually harassed by him. Is that because in fact he never sexually harassed a white woman, although he married one? And if so, is *that* because he felt less of a sense of entitlement in his interactions with his white female subordinates at work? If so, then perhaps his references to lynching were not *merely* a smoke screen, as many people assumed. Perhaps they were also traces of the racialization of his masculinity. In any event, we need more work that theorizes the racial subtext of the categories of privacy and publicity and its intersection with the gender subtext.

4. Class Struggle?

Sexual harassment is not only a matter of gender and racial domination but one of status and class domination as well. The scene of harassment is the workplace or educational institution; the protagonists are bosses, supervisors, or teachers, on the one hand, and employees or students, on the other; the effect of the practice is to maintain the power of the former over the latter.[2] Sexual harassment, therefore, implicates the classic issues of workers' power in the workplace and student power in the school. It should be high on the agenda of every trade union, labor organization, and student association.

Yet the class and status dimensions of the struggle over Thomas's confrontation were not aired in the public sphere debates. No trade unionist or workers' or students' representative testified in the hearings. Nor did any publish an op-ed piece in the *New York Times*. In general, no one in a position to be widely heard articulated support for Anita Hill grounded in class or status solidarity. No one foregrounded the accents of class to rally workers and students to her side.

The absence of a discourse of class conflict in the United States is no surprise. What is surprising perhaps was the deployment in the final phase of the struggle of a counterdiscourse of class resentment to mobilize support for Thomas.

On the day before the Senate confirmation vote, the *New York Times* printed an op-ed piece by that longtime friend of labor, former speech-writer for presidents Reagan and Bush, Peggy Noonan. Noonan predicted victory for Thomas based on a "class division" between the "chattering classes" supporting Hill and the "normal humans," who believed Thomas. She also glossed this as a division between the "clever people who talk loudly in restaurants and those who seat them":

> You could see it in the witnesses. For
> Anita Hill, the professional, movement-y
> and intellectualish Susan Hoerchner, who
> spoke with a sincere, unmakeupped face
> of inherent power imbalances in the

workplace. For Clarence Thomas, the straight-shooting Maybellined J. C. Alvarez, who once broke up a mugging because she hates bullies and paid $900 she doesn't have to get there because she still hates 'em. . . . Ms. Alvarez was the voice of the real, as opposed to the abstract, America: she was like a person who if a boss ever sexually abused her would kick him in the gajoobies and haul him straight to court.

Here Noonan appealed in familiar terms to the "real American" workers (tough and macho, even if wearing eyeliner) to resist the effeminate (albeit make-up-free) intellectuals who impersonate them and feign concern for their interests, but whose Americanness is suspect (shades of Communism). The scenario thus appeared to oppose "the real worker," J. C. Alvarez, to "the intellectual," Susan Hoerchner. Yet Alvarez here actually represented Thomas, the boss, while the actual aggrieved subordinate, Anita Hill, disappeared altogether behind the representation of Hoerchner. Moreover, by painting "the worker" as a Maybellined tough guy, Noonan simultaneously updated and perpetuated masculinist stereotypes. It became hard to see most women, who do not repay sexual harassment with a kick to the groin, as "workers."

Noonan's rhetoric mobilized class resentment in support of Thomas by disappearing Anita Hill as a worker. A similar tack was taken by Orlando Patterson, whose own *New York Times* op-piece appeared the following week in the guise of a more analytical postmortem. Although Patterson acknowledged Hill's lower class origins, he nonetheless treated her as an instrument of "elitist" (read: "bourgeois") forces. In his scenario she was a tool, not simply of whites or of feminists, but of *elite, upper-class* white feminists bent on using the law to impose a class-specific sexual morality on poor and working-class populations with different, less repressive norms. Workers were in effect called to defend their class culture—by siding with the boss against his assistant.

Both Noonan and Patterson in effect bourgeoisified Anita Hill, just as Thomas had earlier whitened her. Her actual social origins in

rural poverty, which she had stressed in her opening statement to the committee, had by the end of the affair become so clouded by the rhetoric of class resentment that to many she was just another yuppie. The way, once again, was paved by Thomas. Very early on, even before the sexual harassment story broke, he staked out a strong claim to the discourse of impoverished origins. And as in the case of race, here too he retained a near-monopoly.

The "class struggle" in this affair, then, was largely a matter of manipulating the signifiers of class to mobilize resentment in the interests of management. But was class not relevant in any other sense? Were there no class differences in the way Americans viewed these events and in the way they chose sides?

Some news reports following closely on Thomas's confirmation portrayed white working-class women and women of color of all classes as unsympathetic to Hill. For example, in a story titled "Women See Hearing from a Perspective of Their Own Jobs," the *New York Times* reported that blue-collar women were put off by her soft-spokenness and what they construed as her inability to take care of herself. The story contrasted this "blue-collar" view with the views of female "lawyers, human service professionals, and politicians," who strongly sympathized with and believed Hill. Despite the title of the article, the *Times* did not consider the possibility that these putative class differences could be rooted in different class work cultures. It could be the case, for example, that working-class people who felt that Hill should simply have told Thomas off and quit and found another job were not attuned to professional career structures, which require cultivation of one's reputation in the profession via networking and long-term maintenance of relationships.

There was another sense in which class affected this struggle, but it remained largely unspoken and implicit. Polls taken on the last night of the hearings showed that party affiliation was the most statistically significant factor distinguishing Thomas's supporters from Hill's. This suggests that a large part of what was at stake in the confirmation of this and other recent Supreme Court nominees was the continuation—or not—of the Reagan-Bush agenda, broadly conceived. For a moment, the question of sexual harassment became the condensation point for a host of anxieties, resentments, and hopes about who gets what and who deserves what in America. In our current political culture, those anxieties, resentments, and hopes are often articulated in terms of gender and race, but they are also necessarily about status and class. Noonan and Patterson notwithstanding, class remains the great unarticulated American secret. As such, it remains highly susceptible to manipulation and abuse.

5. Conclusion: Some Morals of the Story

This extraordinary series of struggles proves the continuing importance of the public sphere in relation to state power. However, it also shows the need to revise the standard liberal view of the public sphere, since the categories of publicity and privacy are multivalent and contested, and not all understandings of them promote democracy.

For example, male-supremacist constructions enshrine gender hierarchy by privatizing practices of domination like sexual harassment. They enforce men's privacy rights to harass women with impunity in part by smearing in public any woman who protests. As a result, women are in effect asked to choose between quiet abuse in private and noisy discursive abuse in public.

However, the gendered character of the categories publicity and privacy cannot today be understood in terms of the Victorian separate-spheres ideology, as some feminists have assumed. It is not the case now, and never was, that women are simply excluded from public life; nor that men are public and women are private; nor that the private sphere is women's sphere and the public sphere is men's; nor that the feminist project is to collapse the boundaries between public and private. Rather, feminist analysis shows the political, ideological nature of these categories. And the feminist project aims in part to overcome the gender hierarchy that gives men more power than women to draw the line between public and private.

Yet even that more complicated view is still too simple because the categories of public and private also have a racial-ethnic dimension. The legacy of American slavery and racism has denied black women even the minimal protections from abuse that white women have occasionally managed to claim, even as their disadvantaged economic position has rendered them more vulnerable to sexual harassment. That same legacy has left black men without white men's privacy rights; they have sometimes tried to claim them in ways that endanger black women. That suggests the need to develop an antiracist project that does not succeed at black women's expense, one that simultaneously attacks the racial and gender hierarchy embedded in hegemonic understandings of privacy and publicity.

Recognizing how these categories become defined by gender and race points up several inadequacies of the liberal theory of the public sphere. For one thing, it is not correct to view publicity as always and unambiguously an instrument of empowerment and emancipation. For members of subordinate groups, it will always be a matter of balancing the potential political uses of publicity against the dangers of loss of privacy. Likewise, it is not adequate to analyze these categories as supports for and challenges to state power exclusively. Rather, we need also to understand the ways in which discursive privatization supports the "private" power of bosses over workers, husbands over wives, and whites over blacks. Publicity, then, is not only a weapon against state tyranny, as its bourgeois originators and current Eastern European devotees assume. It is also potentially a weapon against the extrastate power of capital, employers, supervisors, husbands, fathers, among others. There was no more dramatic proof of the emancipatory potential of publicity in relation to "private" power than the way in which these events momentarily empowered many women to speak openly for the first time of heretofore privately suffered humiliations of sexual harassment.

Yet these events also show that publicity as a political weapon cannot be understood simply in terms of making public what was previously private. They demonstrate that merely publicizing some action or practice is not always sufficient to discredit it; that is only the case where the view that the practice is wrong is already widely held and uncontroversial.

Where, in contrast, the practice is widely approved or contested, publicity means staging a discursive struggle over its interpretation. Certainly, a key feature of the Thomas-Hill confrontation was the wider struggle it sparked over the meaning and moral status of sexual harassment.

The way that struggle played out, moreover, reflected the current state of American political culture. The drama unfolded at a point at which a feminist vocabulary for naming and interpreting the behavior ascribed to Thomas had already been created in the feminist counterpublic sphere and disseminated to a broader public. Not only was that vocabulary thus available and ready to hand, but it was also even encoded in law. However, the feminist interpretation of sexual harassment was neither deeply rooted nor widely accepted in the culture at large. Consequently, it was contested and resisted throughout these events despite its official legal standing. In fact, it was precisely the disjuncture between its official legal acceptance, on the one hand, and the widespread popular resistance it met, on the other, that helped determine the shape of the struggle. Much of the disbelief of Anita Hill may well have been a disguised rejection of the feminist view of sexual harassment as a wrong, a rejection that could not easily be openly expressed and that was displaced onto doubts about Hill. Moreover, because the feminist understanding had legal legitimacy before it had widespread popular legitimacy, it could become a target for the expression of class, ethnic, and racial resentments. While it is not the case, in other words, that the feminist perspective is elitist, white, upper class, and so forth, it was vulnerable to being coded as such. Consequently, people with any number of a range of class, ethnic, or racial resentments, as well as those with gender resentments, could express them by disbelieving Hill. Yet the result was a sharpening and broadening of the battle of interpretation.

If one result of this struggle was some increased consciousness-raising about sexual harassment, another was the fracturing of the myth of homogeneous "communities." "The black community," for example, is now fractured into black feminists versus black conservatives versus black liberals versus various other strands of opinion that are less easy to fix with ideological labels. The same fracturing holds for "the women's community." This struggle showed that women don't necessarily side with women just because they are women. Rather, the polls, for what they are worth (and it may not be much), showed that a plurality of women in every age, income, and education group said they believed Clarence Thomas more than Anita Hill. Perhaps these events should lead us to consider replacing the homogenizing, ideological category of "community" with the potentially more critical category of "public" in the sense of a discursive arena for staging conflicts.

This last point suggests that if these events expose some weaknesses in the liberal theory of the public sphere, they also point in the direction of a better theory. Such a theory would need to take as its starting point the multivalent, contested character of the categories of privacy and publicity with their gendered and racialized subtexts. It would have to acknowledge that in highly stratified late capitalist societies, not everyone stands in the same relation to privacy and publicity; some have more power than others to draw and defend the line. Further, an adequate theory of the public sphere would need to theorize both the multiplicity of public spheres in contemporary late capitalist societies and also the power differentials among them. It would need to distinguish, for example, official governmental public spheres, mass-mediated mainstream public spheres, counterpublic spheres, and informal public spheres in everyday life; and it would have to show how some of these publics marginalize others. Such a theory would certainly help us better understand discursive struggles like the Clarence Thomas-Anita Hill confrontation. Perhaps it could also help inspire us to imagine, and to fight for, a more egalitarian and democratic society.

Notes

1. The one exception was Ellen Wells, a witness who corroborated Hill's version of events by testifying that Hill had told her that Thomas was

harassing her at the time. In the course of her testimony, Wells explained why Hill might have nonetheless maintained contact with Thomas:

> My mother told me, and I'm sure Anita's mother told her. When you leave,
> make sure you leave friends behind, because you don't know who you may need later on. And so you do at least want to be cordial. I know I get Christmas cards from people that I . . . quite frankly do not wish to [see]. And I also return their cards and will return their calls. And these are people who have insulted me and done things which perhaps have degraded me at times. But these are things that you have to put up with. And being a black woman you know you have to put up with a lot. And so you grit your teeth and you do it.

2. There is in addition another variety of sexual harassment, in which male workers harass female coworkers who are not formally under their supervisory authority. This sort of harassment is frequent when very small numbers of women enter heavily male-dominated and masculinized occupations such as construction, fire fighting, and military service. Women in these fields are often subject to harassment from coworkers who are technically their peers in the occupational hierarchy—in the form, for example, of the display of pornography in the workplace, sexual taunts, noncooperation or sabotage, and even having male coworkers urinate in front of them. This sort of "horizontal" harassment differs significantly from the "vertical" variety discussed in the present essay, which involves harassment of an occupational subordinate by a superordinate. "Horizontal" harassment merits a different sort of analysis.

Suggestions for Further Reading

Bravo, Ellen, and Casedy, Ellen. *The 9 to 5 Guide to Combating Sexual Harassment*. New York: Wiley, 1992.

Copeland, Lois, and Wolfe, Leslie R. *Violence Against Women as Bias Motivated Hate Crime: Defining the Issues*. Washington, D.C.: Center for Women Policy Studies, 1991.

Dziech, Billie Wright, and Weiner, Linda. *The Lecherous Professor: Sexual Harassment on Campus*. Champaign: University of Illinois Press, 1992.

Fields, Suzanne. "Is It Really Harassment?" *Insight*. December 9, 1991. Available from 3600 New York Ave. NE, Washington, D.C. 20002.

Hooks, Bell. "A Feminist Challenge: Must We Call All Women Sister?" *Z Magazine*, February 1992.

McKenzie, Richard B. "The Thomas/Hill Hearings: A New Legal Harassment." *The Freeman*, January 1992. Available from the Foundation for Economic Education, Irvington-on-Hudson, N.Y. 10533.

MacKinnon, Catharine A. *Sexual Harassment of Working Women: A Case of Sex Discrimination*. New Haven: Yale University Press, 1979.

Marin, Richard. "It's Not Just a Woman Thing: Many Men Do Understand." *The Washington Post National Weekly Edition*, October 14–20, 1991.

Morgenson, Gretchen. "Watch That Leer, Stifle That Joke," *Forbes*, May 15, 1989.

Munson, Naomi. "Harassment Blues," *Commentary*, February 1992.

Niven, David. "The Case of the Hidden Harassment." *Harvard Business Review*, March–April 1992.

Paludi, Michele, ed. *Working 9 to 5: Women, Men, Sex, and Power*. Albany: State University of New York Press, 1991.

Phelps, Timothy M., and Winternitz, Helen. *Capital Games: Clarence Thomas, Anita Hill, and the Story of a Supreme Court Nomination*. Westport, Conn.: Hyperion, 1992.

Repa, Barbara Kate, and Petrocelli, William. *Sexual Harassment on the Job*. Berkeley, Calif.: Nolo Press, 1992.

Sharp, Rochelle. "Capitol Hill's Worst Kept Secret: Sexual Harassment." *Ms.*, January/February 1992.

Sunrall, Amber Coverdale. *Sexual Harassment: Women Speak Out*. Freedom, Calif.: The Crossing Press, 1992.

Webb, Susan L. *Step Forward: Sexual Harassment in the Workplace*. New York: Mastermedia, 1991.

Privacy, Drug Testing, and AIDS

Introduction

Basic Concepts

Do programs for drug testing and testing for AIDS violate people's right to privacy? In order to answer this question, we need first to get clear about what sort of privacy it is to which we can claim a right. Privacy, as defined by W. A. Parent (Selection 44), is the condition of not having undocumented personal knowledge about one possessed by others. Parent criticizes a number of other definitions. First, he contends that privacy does not consist of simply being let alone because we can fail to let people alone by forcefully interfering with them or insulting them without invading their privacy. Second, he argues that privacy is not a form of autonomy or control over significant personal matters because we can have this form of autonomy even when we choose to give up our privacy by revealing all sorts of undocumented personal information about ourselves. Third, Parent argues that privacy is not a limitation on access to oneself. Rather, he contends that such a limitation would protect privacy while not itself being privacy.

Yet notice that it is not the disclosure of just any undocumented information about oneself, such as one's hat size, that interferes with privacy. Rather, privacy is at issue when the information that is disclosed is important to one's personal life. So, for example, if someone were to reveal accounts of friends and associates found in your diary, that would clearly infringe on your privacy. Nor is privacy interfered with only when undocumented information that is important to one's personal life is made public. Some documented information may only be known to a small number of people, so that bringing that information to a larger audience may also infringe upon privacy.

But obviously other things can have an important impact on one's personal life than other people's knowledge of it, and some of these other ways of affecting one's personal life have been thought to infringe on privacy as well. For example, the Supreme Court considered prohibiting the use of contraceptives an unjustified infringement on people's privacy in *Griswold v. Connecticut,* and the Court also considered anti-abortion laws an unjustified infringement on the privacy of women in *Roe v. Wade.* So it would seem that the question of whether one's privacy has been infringed on turns on whether there has been a significant negative impact on one's personal life either by the disclosure of personal information or by direct interference with one's life.

Alternative Views

Once we know what constitutes an infringement of privacy, the next question is when such infringements are unjustified because they violate a person's right to privacy. Currently, this question is being debated in the area of drug testing and testing for AIDS. In Selection 45, Susan Dentzer and coauthors survey various examples of job testing that are presently in use, such as honesty tests, drug tests, personality tests, and tests for AIDS, bringing out the conflicting interests of employees and employers in each case. The authors claim that society has much to gain from careful and sophisticated testing, but the challenge, as they see it, is whether this gain can be attained without unwarranted encroachment on the rights and freedoms that Americans hold dear.

In Selection 46, James Felman and Christopher Petrini argue that drug testing as it is practiced in public employment violates the Fourth Amendment's prohibition on unreasonable searches and seizures. They present a statistical overview of the nature and scope of illegal drug use in the United States. Although drug use has been declining since 1979, it was estimated in 1982 that 3 to 5 percent of the U.S. work force used drugs regularly. It has also been determined that poverty and affluence correlate with drug use, but not race and ethnicity.

Felman and Petrini discuss two types of drug tests: the EMIT and the GC/MS. The EMIT is inexpensive and easy to administer on the job, but is inherently inaccurate. The GC/MS is more expensive and requires laboratory conditions to evaluate, but is highly accurate. Yet even when EMIT positive results are confirmed by GC/MS testing, the likelihood that a given positive result is correct depends entirely on the extent to which the testing group actually uses drugs. If one assumes that 5 percent of a group of employees uses illegal drugs and an employer uses a drug testing program with 95 percent accuracy to screen the group, the program will yield one false positive for every true positive. If only 2 percent of the group uses illegal drugs, three out of every four positives will be false.

Felman and Petrini point out that the main governmental interests in drug testing are to maintain (1) the safety and efficiency in the workplace and (2) the integrity of the employment institution as perceived by the public. Yet they argue that a general drug testing program is both an overinclusive and underinclusive means of reaching these goals. They argue that, in general, a better and less intrusive means of reaching these goals is a supervision program that focuses on employees who make more mistakes, are frequently absent, and suffer from drug-related health problems.

Yet the courts seem less concerned with whether drug testing programs are a good means of reaching these goals as they are with whether the programs violate anyone's rights. Since the courts do not consider a job something to which people have a right, imposing drug testing as a condition for initial or continued employment does not seem objectionable to them.* By contrast in criminal cases where people's rights to life and liberty are clearly at issue, "probable cause" is generally required to justify search and seizure. Of course, it could be argued that what the courts are failing to appreciate in these cases is the extent to which a person's right to privacy is at issue.

Obviously, testing for AIDS raises somewhat different questions than testing for illegal drugs. In Selection 47, Theresa L. Crenshaw argues for widespread voluntary HIV testing and for mandatory or routine HIV testing under certain circumstances. She contends that HIV testing is reliable, cost effective, and need not violate privacy or lead to

quarantine. The crucial question, of course, is when should HIV testing be voluntary and when should it be mandatory and what should be the consequences of testing positive? For example, should insurance companies be allowed to require a test for AIDS as a condition for getting insurance? And, if so, should they be able to refuse insurance to those who test positive? In general, what should be the consequences of testing positive? If one is HIV positive should one be excluded from certain jobs? Which jobs? In addition, is confidentiality required when there is an unsuspecting sexual or needle-sharing partner in immediate danger of contracting HIV?

Practical Application

In *Schaill v. Tippecanoe School Corporation* (Selection 48), the issue before the United States Court of Appeals was whether a random urinalysis program at a school operated by the Tippecanoe County School Corporation violated the right of student athletes not to be subjected to unreasonable searches and seizures under the Fourth Amendment. The court argues that the urinalysis program was a search and seizure under the Fourth Amendment, but that it was justified because a standard of reasonableness rather than "probable cause" is all that has to be met by such a program. Here the court is arguing in much the same way that other courts have argued with respect to drug testing for employment and insurance. The court contends that because participation in interscholastic athletics is a good to which student athletes do not have a right, "reasonable" restrictions on access to that good do not violate a right to privacy. So it would seem that as the court interprets a right to privacy, it rides "piggy-back," so to speak, on other rights. If then, as libertarians claim, people do not have a right to employment, insurance, or participation in interscholastic athletics, restricting access to these goods does not violate their right to privacy. But if welfare liberals or socialists are correct that people do have a right to employment and insurance and maybe even to participate in interscholastic athletics, then it would seem that what the courts have permitted in these cases does violate a right to privacy.

---

*Notice that this is the same type of reasoning that was used by the Supreme Court in *Wyman v. James*, an earlier Fourth Amendment case concerning welfare.

In Selection 49, the issue before the U.S. Court of Appeals was whether a preliminary injunction to preserve the status quo should be granted to Vincent Chalk who was being relieved of his classroom duties and reassigned to an administrative position because he was diagnosed as having AIDS. The Court ruled that the District Court had erred in failing to grant Chalk a preliminary injunction because Chalk had provided ample evidence that he would pose no appreciable risk of transmitting the AIDS virus to his students as well as evidence that he would suffer irreparable loss if he were reassigned to administrative duties. But would a libertarian agree? Would a welfare liberal or socialist?

44. Privacy, Morality, and the Law

W. A. Parent

According to W. A. Parent, privacy is the condition of not having undocumented personal knowledge about one possessed by others. Parent criticizes a number of other definitions of privacy and then argues that privacy, as he defines it, is a fundamental moral value that people have a right to have protected. Finally, he develops a set of questions for determining when a right to privacy has been wrongfully invaded.

The Definition of Privacy

Defining privacy requires a familiarity with its ordinary usage, of course, but this is not enough since our common ways of talking and using language are riddled with inconsistencies, ambiguities, and paradoxes. What we need is a definition which is by and large consistent with ordinary language, so that capable speakers of English will not be genuinely surprised that the term "privacy" should be defined in this way, but which also enables us to talk consistently, clearly, and precisely about the family of concepts to which privacy belongs. Moreover the definition must not usurp or encroach upon the basic meanings and functions of the other concepts within this family. Drawing useful and legitimate distinctions between different values is the best antidote to exploitation and evisceration of the concept of privacy.

Let me first state and then elaborate on my definition. Privacy is the condition of not having undocumented personal knowledge about one possessed by others. A person's privacy is diminished exactly to the degree that others possess this kind of knowledge about him. I want to stress that what I am defining is the condition of privacy, not the right to privacy. I will talk about the latter shortly. My definition is new, and I believe it to be superior to all of the other conceptions that have been proffered when measured against the desiderata of conceptual analysis above.

A full explication of the personal knowledge definition requires that we clarify the concept of personal information. My suggestion is that it be understood to consist of *facts* about a person which most individuals in a given society at a given time do not want widely known about themselves. They may not be concerned that a few close friends, relatives, or professional associates know these facts, but

W. A. Parent, "Privacy, Morality, and the Law," *Philosophy and Public Affairs* 12, no. 4 (Fall 1983). Copyright © 1983 by Princeton University Press. Excerpts reprinted with permission of Princeton University Press.

they would be very much concerned if the information passed beyond this limited circle. In contemporary America facts about a person's sexual preferences, drinking or drug habits, income, the state of his or her marriage and health belong to the class of personal information. Ten years from now some of these facts may be a part of everyday conversation; if so their disclosure would not diminish individual privacy.

This account of personal information, which makes it a function of existing cultural norms and social practices, needs to be broadened a bit to accommodate a particular and unusual class of cases of the following sort. Most of us don't care if our height, say, is widely known. But there are a few persons who are extremely sensitive about their height (or weight or voice pitch). They might take extreme measures to ensure that other people not find it out. For such individuals height is a very personal matter. Were someone to find it out by ingenious snooping we should not hesitate to talk about an invasion of privacy.

Let us, then, say that personal information consists of facts which most persons in a given society choose not to reveal about themselves (except to close friends, family, . . .) or of facts about which a particular individual is acutely sensitive and which he therefore does not choose to reveal about himself, even though most people don't care if these same facts are widely known about themselves.

Here we can question the status of information belonging to the public record, that is, information to be found in newspapers, court proceedings, and other official documents open to public inspection. (We might discover, for example, that Jones and Smith were arrested many years ago for engaging in homosexual activities.) Should such information be excluded from the category of personal information? The answer is that it should not. There is, after all, nothing extraordinary about public documents containing some very personal information. I will hereafter refer to personal facts belonging to the public record as documented.

My definition of privacy excludes knowledge of documented personal information. I do this for a simple reason. Suppose that A is browsing through some old newspapers and happens to see B's name in a story about child prodigies who unaccountably failed to succeed as adults. B had become an obsessive gambler and an alcoholic. Should we accuse A of invading B's privacy? No. An affirmative answer blurs the distinction between the public and the private. What belongs to the public domain cannot without glaring paradox be called private; consequently it should not be incorporated within our concept of privacy.

But, someone might object, A might decide to turn the information about B's gambling and drinking problems over to a reporter who then publishes it in a popular news magazine. Isn't B's privacy diminished by this occurrence? No. I would certainly say that his reputation might well suffer from it. And I would also say that the publication is a form of gratuitous exploitation. But to challenge it as an invasion of privacy is not at all reasonable since the information revealed was publicly available and could have been found out by anyone, without resort to snooping or prying. In this crucial respect, the story about B no more diminished his privacy than would have disclosures about his property interests, say, or about any other facts concerning him that belonged to the public domain.

I hasten to add that a person does lose a measure of privacy at the time when personal information about him first becomes a part of the public record, since the information was until that time undocumented. It is also important not to confuse documented facts as I define them here with facts about individuals which are kept on file for special purposes but which are not available for public consumption, for example, health records. Publication of the latter does imperil privacy; for this reason special precautions are usually taken to ensure that the information does not become public property.

I believe the personal knowledge definition isolates the conceptual one of privacy, its distinctive and unique meaning. It does not appropriate ideas which properly belong to other concepts. Unfortunately the three most popular definitions do just this, confusing privacy with quite different values.

Privacy Consists of Being Let Alone

Warren and Brandeis were the first to advocate this broad definition. Brandeis movingly appealed to it again in his celebrated dissent to the U.S. Supreme Court's majority ruling in *Olmstead v. U.S.* Objecting to the Court's view that telephone wiretapping does not constitute a search and seizure, Brandeis delivered an impassioned defense of every citizen's right to be let alone, which he called our most cherished entitlement. Several other former U.S. Supreme Court Justices have endorsed this conception of privacy, among them Douglas, Fortas, and Steward. And a number of distinguished law professors have done likewise.

What proponents of the Brandeis definition fail to see is that there are innumerable ways of failing to let a person alone which have nothing to do with his privacy. Suppose, for instance, that A clubs B on the head or repeatedly insults him. We should describe and evaluate such actions by appeal to concepts like force, violence, and harassment. Nothing in the way of analytical clarity and justificatory power is lost if the concept of privacy is limited, as I have suggested that it be, to cases involving the acquisition of undocumented personal knowledge. Inflationary conceptions of privacy invite muddled reasoning.

Privacy Consists of a Form of Autonomy or Control over Significant Personal Matters

"If the right to privacy means anything, it is the right of the individual, married or single, to be free from unwarranted government invasion into matters so fundamentally affecting a person as the decision whether to bear or beget a child." With these words, from the Supreme Court case of *Eisenstadt v. Baird*, Mr. Justice Brennan expresses a second influential theory of privacy.

Indeed, definitions of privacy in terms of control dominate the literature. Perhaps the most favored among them equates privacy with the control over personal information about oneself. Fried, Wasserstrom, Gross, and Beardsley all adopt it or a close variation of it. Other lawyers and philosophers, including

Van Den Haag, Altman, and Parker, identify privacy with control over access to oneself, or in Parker's words, "control over when and by whom the various parts of us can be sensed by others."

All of these definitions should be jettisoned. To see why, consider the example of a person who voluntarily divulges all sorts of intimate, personal, and undocumented information about himself [sic] to a friend. She is doubtless exercising control, in a paradigm sense of the term, over personal information about herself as well as over (cognitive) access to herself. But we would not and should not say that in doing so she is preserving or protecting her privacy. On the contrary, she is voluntarily relinquishing much of her privacy. People can and do choose to give up privacy for many reasons. An adequate conception of privacy must allow for this fact. Control definitions do not.

I believe the voluntary disclosure counterexample is symptomatic of a deep confusion underlying the thesis that privacy is a form of control. It is a conceptual confusion, the mistaking of privacy for a part of liberty. The defining idea of liberty is the absence of external restraints or coercion. A person who is behind bars or locked in a room or physically pinned to the ground is unfree to do many things. Similarly a person who is prohibited by law from making certain choices should be described as having been denied the liberty or freedom to make them. The loss of liberty in these cases takes the form of a deprivation of autonomy. Hence we can meaningfully say that the right to liberty embraces in part the right of persons to make fundamentally important choices about their lives and therewith to exercise significant control over different aspects of their behavior. It is clearly distinguishable from the right to privacy, which condemns the unwarranted acquisition of undocumented personal knowledge.

Privacy Is the Limitation on Access to the Self

This definition, defended by Garrett and Gavison among others, has the virtue of separating privacy from liberty. But it still is unsatisfactory. If we understand "access" to mean something like "physical proximity," then the difficulty becomes that there are other viable concepts which much more precisely describe what is at stake by limiting such access. Among these concepts I would include personal property, solitude, and peace. If, on the other hand, "access" is interpreted as referring to the acquisition of personal knowledge, we're still faced with a seemingly intractable counterexample. A taps B's phone and overhears many of her conversations, including some of a very intimate nature. Official restraints have been imposed on A's snooping, though. He must obtain permission from a judge before listening in on B. This case shows that limitation of cognitive access does not imply privacy.

A response sympathetic with the Garrett-Gavison conception to the above criticism might suggest that they really meant to identify privacy with certain kinds of limitations on access to the self. But why then didn't they say this, and why didn't they tell us what relevant limitations they had in mind?

Let us suppose that privacy is thought to consist of certain normal limitations on cognitive access to the self. Should we accept this conception? I think not, since it confuses privacy with the existential conditions that are necessary for its realization. To achieve happiness I must have some good luck, but this doesn't mean that happiness is good luck. Similarly, if I am to enjoy privacy there have to be limitations on cognitive access to me, but these limitations are not themselves privacy. Rather privacy is what they safeguard.

The Value of Privacy

Is privacy a basic human value? There are many unpersuasive arguments that it is. Consider one of the most well-known, that given by Fried: "to respect, love, trust, feel affection for others, and to regard ourselves as the objects of love, trust, and affection is at the heart of our notion of ourselves as persons among persons, and privacy is the necessary atmosphere for these attitudes and actions, as oxygen is for combustion." Privacy is essential for intimate relationships because, in Fried's view,

their defining mark is the sharing of information about oneself that is not shared with others, and without privacy this would be impossible.

The difficulty with Fried's argument is that it relies on a skewed conception of intimacy. Intimacy involves much more than the exclusive sharing of information. It also involves the sharing of one's total self—one's experiences, aspirations, weaknesses, and values. This kind of emotional commitment, and concomitant giving, is entirely overlooked by Fried. He furnishes no argument for the claim that it cannot survive the loss of privacy.

Several so-called functional arguments on behalf of privacy also fail. Thus it is sometimes said that privacy is needed for relaxation, emotional release, self-reflection, and self-analysis, but this account confuses privacy with solitude, that is, the condition of being physically alone. Granted A might not be able to relax or think about her life unless she is left by herself, we are still not being told why *privacy* is important. Of course A might have to believe that her privacy is being respected if she is to relax and reflect successfully, but this still doesn't show that privacy itself (as opposed to the belief that we have it) is necessary to do these things.

Nor should we buy the thesis that privacy is necessary for individuality and freedom. It is easy to imagine a person who has little or no privacy but who nonetheless possesses the determination and strength of will to think and act individually. Even those lacking in such determination might still be able to think and act for themselves so long as they believe (rightly or wrongly) that their privacy is intact. Similarly, persons without privacy might still enjoy considerable freedom. This will be true in cases where A is not aware of and has no reason for thinking that someone else is watching her every move and so is not deterred from pursuing various activities. It will also be true in cases where A simply doesn't care whether anyone else is watching her.

Lest you now begin to wonder whether privacy has any value at all, let me quickly point to several very good reasons why people in societies like ours desire privacy as I have defined it. First of all, if others manage to obtain sensitive personal knowledge about us they will by that very fact acquire power over us. Their power could then be used to our disadvantage. The possibilities for exploitation become very real. The definite connection between harm and the invasion of privacy explains why we place a value on not having undocumented personal information about ourselves widely known.

Second, as long as we live in a society where individuals are generally intolerant of life styles, habits, and ways of thinking that differ significantly from their own, and where human foibles tend to become the object of scorn and ridicule, our desire for privacy will continue unabated. No one wants to be laughed at and made to feel ashamed of himself. And we all have things about us which, if known, might very well trigger these kinds of unfeeling and wholly unwarranted responses.

Third, we desire privacy out of a sincere conviction that there are certain facts about us which other people, particularly strangers and casual acquaintances, are not entitled to know. This conviction is constitutive of "the liberal ethic," a conviction centering on the basic thesis that individuals are not to be treated as mere property of the state but instead are to be respected as autonomous, independent beings with unique aims to fulfill. These aims, in turn, will perforce lead people down life's separate paths. Those of us educated under this liberal ideology feel that our lives are our own business (hence the importance of personal liberty) and that personal facts about our lives are for the most part ours alone to know. The suggestion that all personal facts should be made available for public inspection is contrary to this view. Thus, our desire for privacy is to a large extent a matter of principle.

For most people, this desire is perfectly innocent. We are not seeking to hurt or disadvantage anyone by exercising it. Unquestionably some people at times demand privacy for fraudulent purposes, for example, to hide discreditable facts about themselves from future employers who are entitled to this information. Posner emphasizes this motive for privacy. But not everyone values privacy for this reason, and, even for those who do, misrepresentation is most often not the only or the overriding motive.

So there are several good reasons why we hold privacy to be an important value, one worth arguing for, and defending from unwarranted invasion. Now I want to suggest that anyone who deliberately and without justification frustrates or contravenes our desire for privacy violates the distinctively liberal, moral principle of respect for persons. Let us say that A frustrates B's desire for privacy if he invades B's privacy and B knows it. A acts in contravention of B's desire for privacy if he invades B's privacy without B's knowing it. Assuming that A has no justification for doing either, we can and should accuse him of acting in disregard of B's own desires and interests. A's action displays contempt for B in the sense that it is undertaken with no effort to identify with her life purposes or to appreciate what the fulfillment of these purposes might mean to her. Specifically by gratuitously or indiscriminately invading B's privacy (I will explain these terms shortly) A manifests disrespect for B in the sense that he ignores or counts as having no significance B's desire, spawned and nurtured by the liberal values of her society, not to have personal facts about herself known by ingenious or persistent snooping.

The Moral Right to Privacy

The above argument establishes that privacy is indeed a moral value for persons who also prize freedom and individuality. That we should seek to protect it against unwarranted invasion should come, then, as no surprise. Advocating a moral right to privacy comprises an integral part of this effort. It expresses our conviction that privacy should only be infringed under exigent circumstances and for the most compelling reasons, for example, law enforcement and health care provision.

The moral right to privacy does not embody the rule "privacy may never be invaded." It is important to emphasize that there are such things as justifiable invasions of privacy. Our concern is not to condemn invasions but to declare our right not to become the victims of wrongful invasions. Discussion of a right to privacy presupposes that privacy is a good, vulnerable to loss by human contrivance. It does not presuppose that such loss is always bad.

Davis and Thomson have recently tried to deflate the right to privacy. The latter's essay is the better known so I will now discuss it. Thomson wants us to believe that there is no one independently identifiable right to privacy. Instead there are a number of diverse rights under "privacy" each of which is a right of some other kind. Moreover, the right to privacy is derivative in the sense that we can explain why we possess each of the rights subsumable under privacy without ever mentioning the right of privacy itself. And we can also explain the wrongness of every violation of the right to privacy without once mentioning it. So according to Thomson we really don't need to talk about a distinct right to privacy at all. She supports her argument with the following analyses.

(1) A owns a pornographic picture which he keeps locked up in a safe. B trains his special X-ray device on the safe and sees the picture. Thomson concedes that B has violated A's right to privacy, but she thinks a more fundamental explanation of why B acted wrongly is in terms of A's right that others not do certain things with what he owns. These include looking at them and selling them. These are property rights and it is by infringing one of them that B wrongs A.

(2) B finds out by entirely legitimate means that A owns the pornographic picture. He proceeds to publish this fact in a newspaper. If anyone thinks that B has invaded A's right to privacy, a very simple explanation is available: A has the right not to be caused mental distress, and it is this right that B's action violates.

(3) A doesn't want her face looked at and so keeps it covered. B uses his X-ray device to look at A's face through the covering. In doing so B violates A's right that her face not be looked at (how simple!). This is one of the rights over our person that we possess.

(4) A is a great opera singer who no longer wants to be listened to. She only sings quietly behind closed doors and soundproof walls. B trains an amplifier on A's home and listens to her sing. In so doing B transgresses A's right not to be listened to, which according to Thomson is another one of those basic rights

over the person we possess. Here, as in each of the preceding cases, we have no need to invoke the right to privacy.

Thomson's attempt to diminish the status of the right to privacy fails to persuade. It requires that we recognize a plethora of rights whose status is certainly more problematic than that of the right whose significance she wants to impugn. Do we really think of ourselves as possessing the rights not to be looked at and listened to? Must we talk about a right not to have our property looked at? Thomson's claim that we waive these rights all the time—a claim she has to make to avoid the absurd implication that our rights are violated thousands of times every day—flies in the face of common sense and common experience. Just ask whether you thought of yourself as having waived the right not to be listened to before speaking with people today. The idea seems preposterous. I certainly didn't conceive of myself as waiving a right not to be looked at before entering the classroom this morning. And I venture to add that it would bemuse my students to hear me speak of my right not to be looked at.

Thomson's simplifying strategy is unmistakably convoluted. It is possible to deal in a much less ad hoc and tortuous manner with her examples once we have settled on an adequate definition of privacy.

(1) If B's looking at A's picture is unjustified, and if A is entitled to possess the pornographic picture, then by my account of the moral right to privacy B does violate this right in A. We could also say that A has a concrete moral right that her picture not be looked at which can be deduced from the more fundamental right of privacy when applied to the particular circumstances of this case.

(2) If B has no justification for publishing the fact that A possesses a pornographic picture, then he has violated A's right to privacy. And it is by virtue of violating this right that B causes A mental distress.

(3) If A has no evil intention in covering her face and if B has no substantial reason for peeking at it, then B's intrusion violates A's right to privacy. We could express this point by saying that A's right to privacy when applied to the particular circumstances of this

case yields her concrete right not to be looked at. (Remember that a person's physical appearance can constitute personal information.)

(4) If B's snooping is without justification it should be condemned as a violation of A's right to privacy.

The basic failing of Thomson's essay is that she makes no attempt to define privacy. We have good reason to ask how she hopes to convince anyone that the right to privacy is derivative and quite dispensable without first telling us what the right means. My position is that once the meaning of privacy is clarified and its value articulated no one will have cause to question the legitimacy of our talk about a fundamental right of privacy.

Criteria of Wrongful Invasion

Which invasions of privacy are justifiable and which are not? A complete conception of the right to privacy must address this question, providing general criteria of wrongful invasion, which will then have to be applied to specific cases. Whether the right to privacy has been violated in a specific case can often only be answered through a process of making difficult and controversial value judgments. No conception of the right to privacy, no matter how detailed and sophisticated, will allow us to eliminate or bypass this process.

The following questions are central to assessing alleged violations of the right to privacy:

1. For what purpose(s) is the undocumented personal knowledge sought?

2. Is this purpose a legitimate and important one?

3. Is the knowledge sought through invasion of privacy relevant to its justifying purpose?

4. Is invasion of privacy the only or the least offensive means of obtaining the knowledge?

5. What restrictions or procedural restraints have been placed on the privacy-invading techniques?

6. What protection is to be afforded the personal knowledge once it has been acquired?

The first four questions all have to do with the rationale for invading privacy. We can say that the right to privacy is violated by *gratuitous* invasions and that these occur when: there is no purpose at all to them; when the purpose is less than compelling; when the personal facts sought have nothing to do with the justifying purposes; when the personal information could have been obtained by less intrusive measures. Among the legitimate purposes for acquiring undocumented personal information are efficient law enforcement, confirmation of eligibility criteria set forth in various government welfare programs, and the compilation of statistical data concerning important behavioral trends.

Question (5) pertains to the actual invasion of privacy itself. We can say that the right to privacy is violated by *indiscriminate* invasions and that these occur when insufficient procedural safeguards have been imposed on the techniques employed so that either: all sorts of personal information, some germane to the investigation but some totally irrelevant thereto, are obtained; or persons with no business knowing the personal facts acquired are allowed to gain cognitive access to them. One can argue against a proposed invasion of privacy on the grounds that it is too likely to be indiscriminate in either of these two senses.

Question (6) pertains to postinvasion safeguards. We can say that the right to privacy is violated when the undocumented personal information acquired is not adequately protected against unwarranted cognitive intrusion or unauthorized uses. It is also violated, of course, by actual instances of such intrusions and uses.

Let us look at a concrete example. Suppose a large city is faced with the growing problem of welfare fraud. It decides that to combat this problem an elaborate system of surveillance must be initiated. Personal information regarding welfare recipients' income, family status, sexual habits, and spending habits is to be obtained. Search warrants are obtained permitting unlimited surveillance and specifying the kind of information being sought.

Once obtained the information is to be stored on magnetic tapes and kept in the welfare department.

Any person who takes the right to privacy seriously will raise the following questions and make the following observations about this city's (C's) action:

i. C presents no arguments or evidence in support of its belief that the problem of welfare fraud can be solved by resorting to large-scale surveillance. We should demand that C do so.

ii. C presents no arguments or evidence showing that surveillance is the only way to acquire the relevant personal information. Did it first try to obtain knowledge of welfare recipients' life styles by asking them about it or sending them questionnaires? Were there other, less intensive measures available for acquiring this knowledge?

iii. Search warrants permitting unlimited surveillance are insufficiently discriminating. So are warrants which do not particularly describe the places to be observed and the facts to be gathered. C should have insisted that the warrants place restrictions on the time periods of surveillance as well as on its scope.

iv. Why is it necessary to acquire information about welfare recipients' sexual habits? How is this knowledge relevant to the objective of eradicating fraud?

v. What kind of security does C intend to provide for the magnetic tapes containing the acquired information? Who will enjoy access to these tapes? Will they eventually be erased or destroyed? C has the duty to guard against the potential abuse of the stored facts.

I hope this brief analysis is helpful in isolating some of the crucial issues and difficult questions that must be confronted when applying the right of privacy to particular cases. Often there will be strong disagreement over whether proposed programs of physical, psychological, and data surveillance are gratuitous or indiscriminate. This is to be expected. The results of these disputes will determine the contours of the privacy right.

45. Can You Pass the Job Test?

Susan Dentzer, Bob Cohn, George Raine, Ginny Carroll, and Vicki Quade

In this selection the authors survey various examples of job testing that are currently in use, such as honesty tests, drug tests, personality tests, and tests for AIDS, and bring out the conflicting interests of employees and employers with respect to each case.

When Arlo Guthrie sang his Vietnam-era ballad "Alice's Restaurant," his tormentor was that era's answer to Big Brother—the military draft board. Today John Sexton might cast someone else in the role of snooping archvillain: his former employer. Last year [1985]

From *Newsweek* (5 May 1986): 46–53; story prepared by Susan Dentzer, Bob Cohn, George Raine, Ginny Carroll, and Vicki Quade. © 1986 Newsweek, Inc. All rights reserved. Reprinted by permission.

Sexton, then a $30,000-a-year dispatcher at Federal Express Corp. in Atlanta, was one of a group of employees ordered to submit urine samples for a drug test. Sexton tested positive; he says he had smoked marijuana at a party two weeks earlier, but he didn't appear impaired at the time of the test. Next he was ordered to take a lie-detector test or face suspension—but when he denied using drugs on the job or knowing anyone who did, the polygrapher running the test concluded he was holding something back. Fired last May, the 29-year-old college graduate hasn't been able to land another job since. Federal Express declines to comment on the episode but suggests that Sexton's firing was appropriate. Sexton, meanwhile, is preparing to sue Federal for wrongful discharge—and the American Civil Liberties Union (ACLU) of Georgia says he has a strong case.

Sexton's situation isn't unusual: in corporations across the United States, a frenzy of inspecting, detecting, selecting and rejecting is under way. Plans to test baseball players for illegal drug use have created a stir, but nearly a third of the corporations in the Fortune 500 also screen employees for abuse of even casual intake of such substances as marijuana and cocaine. Countless other firms monitor workers' honesty with lie detectors or written exams or probe their psyches with an array of personality tests. Some corporations have begun monitoring employees for diseases such as AIDS. And in quest of the perfect employee, many firms may one day be able to screen out workers with hundreds of genetic traits that could predispose them to serious and costly illnesses.

The boom in testing is fueling the growth of what was once a cottage industry: an array of labs, consulting firms, security specialists and other testing companies that together take in hundreds of millions of dollars in revenue each year. At the same time, it pits employees against management in a debate over whose interests tip the scales of justice. Which set of rights is paramount: those of companies seeking a productive and safe work force—or those of employees trying to protect their privacy? Does testing really identify drug abusers, in-house thieves and other undesirables, or are the innocent and employable also caught in the net? Is testing of employees the key to U.S. industrial competitiveness, or is it worsening labor-management relations at a time when more cooperation is needed? Does testing protect the commonweal, or does it run against the grain of American society— smacking of the oppressive utopias of Aldous Huxley's *Brave New World* or George Orwell's *1984*?

. . . Lawsuits and union grievances challenging the use of drug testing are on the rise;

California has barred testing for the AIDS virus or antibody as a condition of employment, and Congress may soon approve legislation to outlaw the use of lie detectors by most private employers. But whether these developments will dampen the current enthusiasm for testing is unclear. Many companies, alarmed by growing drug use and fearful of everything from wrongful-discharge suits to liability for faulty products, are embracing the use of testing as a vital defense. And advances in technology have made testing almost irresistible, yielding procedures that are "good enough and cheap enough that they are now an [inexpensive] management tool," says Bill Maher, a San Francisco supervisor who helped draft a city ordinance that bars most blanket drug testing.

Testing employees and job applicants is hardly new; in fact, the 1950s may have marked an earlier zenith of testing, as companies gathered reams of information on their prospective workers through psychological profiles, employment histories, criminal records and personal data. The shifting values and mores of the 1960s and 1970s changed all that, says Columbia University professor of public law Alan Westin. Federal equal-employment-opportunity guidelines put the onus on employers to ensure that testing was a scientifically valid selection tool and that it didn't discriminate against specific racial or social groups. As privacy laws were passed to protect the public from intrusive or discriminatory data collection by government and institutions such as credit agencies, private employers also began weeding out their personnel files and testing less.

Now that companies are turning to testing again, the privacy issue is back with a vengeance. Through the Fourth Amendment, only government workers have constitutional protection against unreasonable searches and seizures by their employer—a by-product of the Founding Fathers' fear that unchecked government posed the greatest threat to citizens' rights. Nonetheless, many legal scholars believe that there also exists in society "a certain essential right of individuals to be left alone, and not to be subjected to . . . invasive activities without justification," as Geoffrey Stone, a professor of constitutional law at the

University of Chicago, puts it. "Can you imagine the Founding Fathers saying that the major source of authority in [your] life"—your employer—"can make you drop your pants and urinate as a condition of getting or keeping a job?" asks Gene Guerrero, director of the Georgia ACLU. "It's ludicrous." But while employers argue that it's necessary, that's in a sense what many are compelling employees to do.

Honesty Tests: Are They Valid?

The late Sen. Sam Ervin called them "20th-century witchcraft," but that hasn't stopped many employers from administering lie detectors, or polygraph tests. Almost 2 million are given to employees and job applicants each year—and they can be "a very effective tool in stopping employee crime," says Mark A. de Bernardo, a labor lawyer at the U.S. Chamber of Commerce. Brokerage firms such as E. F. Hutton and banks like Citicorp routinely give polygraphs—Hutton to all employees and Citicorp to most workers who physically handle money. Days Inns of America, a national motel chain based in Atlanta, testified in Congress last year that use of lie detectors helped cut its losses from employee crime to $115,000 in 1984, down from $1 million in 1975.

But polygraphs are undoubtedly more of a deterrent to crime than an effective means of determining an employee's guilt or innocence. The federal Office of Technology Assessment determined in 1983 that the scientific validity of lie-detector results couldn't be established. The American Psychological Association charges that polygraphs turn up "an unacceptable number of false positives"—that is, the subjects had not been lying. Because of these and other factors, few American courts will admit polygraph data as evidence.

Following the pattern of similar legislation in about 20 states, the House of Representatives last March passed the Polygraph Protection Act, which would prohibit private employers from giving lie-detector tests to most current or prospective employees. (Many utility workers, pharmaceutical workers handling controlled substances, day-care workers and employees of private security companies could still be polygraphed.) Last week hearings were held on a similar measure introduced in the Senate by Republican Orrin Hatch of Utah, a conservative, and liberal Democrat Ted Kennedy. Opposed by the likes of attorney F. Lee Bailey—as well as polygraphers and many employers, who would prefer tighter regulation of the polygraph industry—the measure seems likely to pass.

To avoid the cost (about $40 to $50 per test) and ambiguity of polygraph tests, many companies have turned instead to written honesty tests. John E. Reid & Associates of Chicago, a pioneer in the field, markets its $9 tests to about 2,000 clients nationwide: Stanton Corp., based in Charlotte, N.C., sells about a million tests each year to hotel chains, clothing retailers, convenience stores and other companies whose workers regularly handle money or merchandise for sale. Jim Walls, vice president of Stanton, contends that such screening is a necessity in an age when people move or change jobs frequently. "There's no way that [companies] can ever get to know the people they're hiring before they're hired," he says.

Many honesty-test questions are almost disarmingly ingenuous. Dr. Homer B. C. Reed, a neuropsychologist at Tufts University's New England Medical Center and a consultant to Stanton, singles out one sample question: "The amount I stole from my employer was (a) 0 (b) $5 (c) $25 (d) $100 (e) $500," accompanied by a space for an explanation. Reed says many job applicants actually circle one of the last four answers. "You would think you can't identify scoundrels by asking them if they're scoundrels, but you can," he says.

Prompted by concerns that employers would use written tests to pry too much into employees' backgrounds, as some lie-detector tests have done, a new Massachusetts state law prohibits employers from giving honesty tests that amount to "paper and pencil" polygraphs. Many experts are troubled for different reasons, calling some tests a useless tool that could actually screen out capable, honest employees. Columbia Professor Westin derides the absolutism of some tests in requiring "a Fearless Fosdick, Dick Tracy response to every situation"; he thinks they may be used to screen out "people more likely to join a union or challenge something on a job as being morally or ethically improper." Michael Merbaum, a psychologist with St. Louis–based Psychological Associates Inc., a management-consulting and training firm, concurs. He believes that the "correct" answers to many tests are too often based on strict definitions of honesty that may not be shared by test takers: for example, an employee who admits he once took office supplies may not believe he did anything wrong. A far better approach, says Merbaum, is interviewing prospective employees carefully to determine their level of emotional maturity—and to discover whether they have "the capability to appraise situations . . . judiciously so they will make the proper decisions."

Drug Tests: Legal Challenges

When guards conducted an early-morning drug sweep of the Albuquerque Publishing Co. last January, company officials said it was for good reason: an estimated 20 percent of the firm's employees have "an abuse problem," says company president Thompson Lang—and of all the job applicants who've taken drug tests in recent months, "no one has passed." Few companies face problems quite so dramatic, but drug use does take a serious toll: the U.S. Chamber of Commerce estimates that drug and alcohol abuse among workers costs employers $60 billion a year—the total tab for lost productivity, accidents, higher medical claims, increased absenteeism and theft of company property (the means by which many workers finance their drug habits). Relatively few companies seem to be tackling alcohol abuse with as much conviction, but concern about drugs is plainly growing, and it has spread well beyond the private workplace. Last week Boston's police commissioner called for mandatory drug testing of all officers, and in a recommendation hotly disputed by some panel members, President Reagan's Commission on Organized Crime recently called for testing of all federal workers in an attempt to control the spread of drugs.

To root out drug abusers among applicants or employees, meanwhile, companies such as Michigan-based Consumers Power Co., Westinghouse Electric Corp., the Du Pont Co. and Albuquerque Publishing have turned to relatively inexpensive urine tests, such as the EMIT (Enzyme Multiplied Immunoassay Test) manufactured by Syva Co., a subsidiary of Syntex Corp. of Palo Alto, Calif. But whether use of these tests does much to control drug abuse is a matter of fierce debate. A major flaw of the most widely used tests is that they don't measure an employee's degree of impairment or level of job performance at the time of the test but show only traces of drugs in the urine. Cocaine may show up as much as three days after consumption; marijuana may be present from five days to three weeks afterward. A drug test, then, may nab even drug users who don't use them at the workplace. "What someone does outside the job isn't a concern for the employer unless it affects what they do on the job," argues Erwin Chemerensky, professor of constitutional law at the University of Southern California (USC).

An even bigger problem is that the tests aren't always accurate. Results can vary widely with the skills of the individuals carrying out the tests or the laboratories analyzing the results. Over-the-counter drugs such as Advil and Nuprin have shown up as illegal drugs on some tests, notes Kerry Shannon, marketing director of Bio-Analytical Technologies, a Chicago lab that conducts urinalysis tests. The most widely used tests claim a 95 to 99 percent accuracy rate; in companies where blanket testing is carried out, this means that, on average, 1 to 5 out of every 100 tests will produce inaccurate results. A recent Northwestern University study suggests an even worse record: it found that 25 percent of all EMIT tests that came up positive were really "false positives." And James Woodford, a forensic chemist in Atlanta and a consultant to the U.S. Public Health Service, contends that urinalysis tests may be racially biased. The reason: test results may be skewed by blacks' higher concentrations of the pigment melanin, which has an ion identical to THC, the active ingredient in marijuana—and which may also soak up body substances similar to THC.

Manufacturers of urine tests acknowledge some of their deficiencies. Michelle Klaich, a spokeswoman for Syntex, stresses that a positive reading on one test shouldn't by itself be a ground for firing: she says Syntex recommends follow-up tests and other measures to verify the results. To improve accuracy, meanwhile, some companies are at work on the next generation of testing devices. National Patent Analytical Systems, Inc., of Roslyn Heights, N.Y., is awaiting results of clinical tests of its Veritas 100 Analyzer, which uses computer hardware and software to analyze the electrical stimuli given off by the brain in the presence of certain drugs. Company president Joseph Boccuzi says the device measures only the presence of drugs at the time of the test and cuts the false-positive rate to less than 5 percent.

But Ira Glasser, executive director of the ACLU, worries that the growing testing industry will become its own reason for being, propounding the use of testing to justify its existence. He recommends "an unused method for detecting [drug abuse]—it's called 'two eyes'." Most employees who are drug abusers reveal telltale signs of their problem, such as erratic behavior or inability to concentrate. A watchful supervisor, says Glasser, should be able to spot drug use and help an employee into a drug-rehabilitation program—an approach that ultimately may be most helpful in eliminating drug abuse.

Despite a growing number of lawsuits, courts so far have generally upheld the legality of drug testing. But some state and local legislatures are moving to restrict and regulate it. California Assemblyman Johan Klehs has proposed a bill that would require a company's testing policy to be in writing; test results would be kept confidential, and all labs that analyze tests of employees and job applicants would be licensed. The Civil Liberties Union of Massachusetts is drafting a bill that would allow testing of only those employees whose performance had a bearing on public safety—nuclear-plant operators, school-bus drivers and the like—and who show some signs of impairment. Similarly, in San Francisco, a new ordinance prohibits drug testing by private employers unless there is a high degree of what's known as individualized suspicion—that the employees to be tested are not only impaired but also pose a "clear and present danger" to themselves or others. Only through such measures will companies be barred from

"rummaging through another person's biology," says San Francisco supervisor Maher, unless testing is absolutely necessary.

Personality Tests: Probing the Psyche

Wanted: people with "kinetic energy," "emotional maturity" and the ability to "deal with large numbers of people in a fairly chaotic situation." No, not to be cohost of "Wheel of Fortune"; American Multi Cinema, the third largest theater chain in America, wants to hire candidates with these qualities to manage its movie houses. To identify the right employees, AMC is one of an increasing number of companies that administer personality or psychological tests to job applicants. Meanwhile, dozens of others such as General Motors, American Cyanamid, J. C. Penney and Westinghouse now rely on personality-assessment programs to evaluate and promote many current employees.

The tests that companies administer run the gamut. Some are standard psychological tests such as the 46-year-old MMPI (Minnesota Multiphasic Personality Inventory). Long used by psychiatrists and psychologists to test individuals for an array of personality traits, the MMPI consists of up to 566 statements and requires the answers "true," "false" or "cannot say" to questions such as "I avoid getting together with people" or "I have a great deal of self-confidence." Simpler tests include AMC's timed personality-profile exam, known as the PEP test, which among other things examines an applicant's level of mechanical interest and aptitude; people who score well "will be more likely to cope if the butter machine or the projection equipment develops problems," says an AMC district manager, Mario Marques.

Praendix Inc. of Wellesley Hills, Mass., produces a personality-assessment test that consists of a list of phrases and adjectives—including "life of the party," "sympathetic" and "aggressive"—and two questions: "Which of these adjectives describes how you think you are expected to act by others?" and

"Which of these adjectives describes who you really are?" Arnold Daniels, founder of Praendix, explains that people who select "patient" as an apt description of themselves might be good "detail" workers, such as researchers, and comfortable reporting to a higher authority. But those who select "impatient"—and think others expect them to be less so—might be good managers, focused on the big picture and eager to see tasks completed.

Many companies swear by the tests. Bobbi Ciarfella, an administrator of Yankee Cos., Inc., an oil-and-gas firm based in Massachusetts, says the Praendix test has helped the firm cut its high turnover rate and hire employees who thrive in a fast-paced environment. "You can't afford to make a mistake when you're hiring somebody in the $45,000 range," she says. Others insist the objectivity of many tests benefits applicants by being even fairer than the typically subjective job interview.

Yet some employees may not fare so well. "For a large number of people, [tests] can predict" roughly who will perform a given job well, says Alexandra Wigdor of the National Research Council, which is currently conducting a study to devise an advanced testing system for the U.S. military. But for any one person, especially one who doesn't test well, "they can be hopeless," she concedes. Moreover, the human personality is so complex that not even the MMPI—considered by many psychiatrists to be the most objective of psychological tests—can give anything like a full and accurate reflection of the individual, says New York psychologist Juliet Lesser. Finally, there's the danger that employers will substitute test results for background checks or even old-fashioned intuition. "Anyone relying too much on tests is abdicating his responsibility as a manager," says New York industrial psychologist Brian Schwartz.

Genetic Tests: Screening for Diseases

At Enserch Corp., a diversified energy company based in Dallas, officials were horrified:

last summer the *maître d'hôtel* of the executive dining room was discovered to have AIDS. When the company summarily ordered mandatory AIDS tests for its other food-service workers, another was discovered to have the AIDS antibody. Both employees were suspended with full pay and medical benefits and escorted from the premises.

The consternation that followed among gay-rights groups and civil libertarians pointed up the controversy around a growing area of testing: monitoring employees' health. Examining blood or tissue samples for signs of disease or certain genetic traits could protect employees and the public from health risks—while sparing employers higher medical-insurance costs and reduced productivity. But as tests get increasingly sophisticated, they could also provide a powerful tool for discrimination against homosexuals, women, those predisposed to diseases or other groups of employees.

Testing for AIDS is especially problematic. Most of the tests offered have high rates of both false positives and "false negatives" (incorrect negative results)—traumatic with AIDS. Nor is it clear just what AIDS testing accomplishes, given most experts' belief that the disease isn't spread through the casual contact typical of the workplace but through sexual relations or contact with AIDS-contaminated blood. Yet so far, only California has acted to prohibit AIDS testing as a condition of employment.

Looming on the horizon is genetic testing. Each year 390,000 workers contract occupational illnesses including lung, bladder and other cancers; about 100,000 die. The belief that some workers possessed genetic "hypersusceptibility" to some of these conditions that could be triggered by exposure to toxins in the workplace led companies like Du Pont and Dow Chemical to conduct tests on workers beginning in the 1970s. But "after a number of years we were not seeing what we thought we might find," says Dr. John Venable, medical director of Dow. Negative publicity about tests—particularly Du Pont's testing of workers for sickle-cell trait, which leads to a condition that affects many blacks—further dampened corporate enthusiasm for testing. By the time a 1983 report by the Office of Technology Assessment determined that existing genetic tests couldn't predict what might happen on the job, most companies had quit the field.

Recently, however, biologists have discovered genetic "markers" for a number of genetic diseases such as cystic fibrosis and are now searching for others for more commonplace conditions such as Alzheimer's disease and breast cancer. "We're still many years away" from the time when genetic tests for such conditions could come into widespread use, asserts Alexander Morgan Capron, professor of law and medicine at USC. But since so many people may be prone to these diseases, there is the distant prospect that companies could one day undertake genetic screening—declining to hire employees who seem likely to become sick on the job, use up expensive medical benefits or die young.

As the technology of testing advances, say the experts, so must the public's attention to the range of economic, ethical and legal issues it raises. Columbia's Westin is confident that such awareness will increase; as a consequence, he predicts, within 10 years a "latticework of legislation" will be in place to balance employers' aims with employees' rights. Society has much to gain from careful and sophisticated testing—a potentially more productive corps of workers whose skills more closely match the requirements of their jobs. But the preeminent challenge for on-the-job testing will be whether it can avoid unwarranted encroachment on the rights and freedoms Americans hold dear.

46. Drug Testing and Public Employment

James Felman and Christopher Petrini

James Felman and Christopher Petrini present a statistical overview of the nature and scope of illegal drug use in America. They also examine the prevalence of drug testing in the workplace and describe the forms and accuracy of drug testing. They then consider the major constitutional issue: whether drug testing of a public employee without any individualized suspicion of drug use is an unreasonable search and seizure in violation of the Fourth Amendment. They argue that it is.

I. Introduction

In the absence of legislative action, the fourth amendment to the Constitution provides the most important barrier to "the progress of science." Fourth amendment analysis inevitably involves a balancing of competing interests— the collective needs of the society must be tempered by the interests of individual human

Reprinted with permission from *Law and Contemporary Problems* (Winter 1988), copyright © 1988, Duke University School of Law.

dignity and privacy. As these interests change and science progresses, new balances must be struck. The issue of drug testing in public employment presents a controversial example of such a new balance to be struck.

Significant societal interests are advanced in support of drug testing of public employees. Drug testing may increase employee safety and efficiency, enhance the perceived integrity of the particular public entity, as well as help reduce society's overall demand for illegal drugs. The individual interests implicated by drug testing are also formidable. Being told by the government to urinate into a jar brushes up against normal expectations of individual privacy. Moreover, the tests are sometimes inaccurate, falsely implicating innocent employees, and they reveal a broad array of private facts, such as pregnancy, medication for a psychological condition, and other similar information that is not of legitimate concern to employers.

This article focuses on the fourth amendment issues presented by the drug testing of public employees. This issue, in a nutshell, is whether an individual may be subjected to a highly intrusive bodily search in the absence of any individualized suspicion to ensure that she does not use drugs, whether at home or on the job. If upheld, drug testing will represent the first instance in the history of the fourth amendment in which a highly intrusive bodily search has been permitted without any measure of individualized suspicion. Such an erosion of the fourth amendment should not be allowed without a critical inquiry into the interests at stake, and the extent to which they are served by drug testing. The authors believe that this inquiry leads to the conclusion that testing public employees should be impermissible in the absence of individualized suspicion.

Even if the reader disagrees with the authors' conclusion, however, perhaps the more important point is that a critical examination of the competing interests involved should be used to draw the fourth amendment line between permissible and impermissible bodily searches in the absence of individualized suspicion. If this critical analysis is not adhered to, there may be no further fourth amendment lines left to draw, and the "progress of science" is surely not complete.

Part II of the article presents a brief statistical overview of the nature and scope of illegal drug use in America. It discusses how many illegal drug users there are, who they are, and what costs they are estimated to impose upon American society. Part II also examines the prevalence of drug testing in the workplace, describes the forms of drug testing, and details the accuracy of drug testing. Part III of the article presents the major constitutional issue: whether drug testing of a public employee without any individualized suspicion of drug use is an unreasonable search and seizure in violation of the fourth amendment. . . .

II. The Lines of Battle: Drug Use and Drug Testing in the Public Workplace

A. The Nature and Scope of the American Drug Problem

1. *How Many Drug Users Are There?* Unfortunately, there is a dearth of reliable scientific evidence detailing the extent of illegal drug use in America, although it is undoubtedly a serious problem. Illicit drug use per capita in this country is estimated to exceed that of any other industrialized nation. The permissiveness and experimentation of the 1960s included the use and acceptance of numerous illegal drugs. American illicit drug use increased throughout the 1960s and the 1970s, peaking by some estimates in 1979. Between 1979 and 1986 there was a statistically significant decline in illegal drug use. Accurate measurement of illicit drug use is difficult, however, because the relative popularity of illegal drugs fluctuates when inexpensive substitutes or new, more potent varieties of existing drugs reach the market. In 1982, narcotics officials estimated that 3 to 5 percent of the American workforce used drugs regularly.

To some extent, persons of all races, ethnicities, and socioeconomic backgrounds use illegal drugs. Ironically, however, studies identify the two extremes of poverty and affluence as characteristics often correlating with drug abuse. In a study examining whether particular ethnic and racial groups are more prone to alcohol or drug abuse, it was found that the percentage breakdown of ethnic and racial groups in drug or alcohol treatment programs merely reflected their percentage in the general population. In fact, prior use of alcohol or drugs was found to be a stronger predictor of abuse than race or ethnicity.

2. *At What Cost?* Employees who use illegal drugs regularly may use drugs on the job or report to work under the influence of drugs. There is little evidence regarding the number of employees who may be impaired on the job, but those who use drugs on the job undoubtedly inflict upon employers increased

costs from inefficiency, greater absenteeism, accidents, and insurance claims. The workplace costs of employee drug use are, however, difficult to estimate, in part because it is not always clear whether drug use by employees is a cause of inefficiency or merely a symptom of an already inefficient employee. The only study of the issue seems to have overlooked this difficulty, assuming all costs imposed by drug-using employees to have been caused by the drugs, not the employee. This study, by the Research Triangle Institute, estimated that employee drug use cost American industry $25.7 billion in 1980, and that alcohol and drug use together cost American society as a whole an estimated $136.4 billion. One drug consulting firm has reported that the average drug user is likely to be tardy three times as often as nonusers, request time off during work 2.2 times more often, and have 2.5 times as many absences of eight days or more. Other experts, however, dispute these statistics.

Drug use on the job is also believed to increase workplace accidents. One writer suggests that drug users are three times as likely as nonusers to injure themselves or someone else on the job. Since 1975, investigators have attributed about fifty train accidents to workers impaired by drugs or alcohol. Medical and property insurance claims are estimated to be somewhat higher because of employee drug use. There may also be a connection between employee drug use and increased workplace theft and embezzlement. Authorities have uncovered several large-scale drug selling operations in employment settings.

Although illegal drug use is a serious problem, its significance must be kept in proper perspective. By any standard of measurement, the more pervasive national drug problem is the abuse of alcohol, tobacco, and legal prescription and over-the-counter drugs. Each year 15,000 Americans die from misuse of legal prescription drugs. The National Institute on Drug Abuse (NIDA) estimates that legal prescription drugs cause 60 percent of emergency room admissions for drug overdoses and 70 percent of all drug-related deaths. Compared to the staggering number of deaths caused each year by alcohol and tobacco abuse, the yearly number of deaths attributable to illegal drug use appears small

indeed. The Research Triangle Institute estimates that the costs imposed upon American industry by employee alcohol use are nearly two times that caused by illegal drug use. Employees with an alcohol problem are an estimated 21 percent less productive than other employees. Yet despite the tremendous costs of alcohol use to American industry, very few drug testing programs currently screen employees for alcohol abuse.

B. The Employers' Response: The Use and Variety of Drug Testing

1. *The Increased Implementation of Drug Testing Programs.* Many employers have responded to workplace costs of employee drug use by implementing drug testing programs. Currently, about 40 percent of the Fortune 500 companies have instituted such programs or plan to do so, and some professional sports leagues have proposed player drug testing programs.

Federal, state, and local public employers have increasingly developed employee drug testing programs. Such programs for all federal agencies are currently being developed in response to an Executive Order issued by President Reagan. This order seeks to make the federal workforce a model for eliminating drug use in the national workplace by requiring implementation of such programs. In addition, drug testing programs are already in place in all four branches of the military, the Coast Guard, and several administrative agencies.

In addition to requiring testing of certain public employees, government regulations require some private companies in highly regulated industries to test their employees for illegal drug use. For example, most railroads now test employees under regulations issued by the Federal Railroad Administration, and 90 percent of all nuclear power plants have instituted testing programs on a voluntary basis under guidelines issued by the Nuclear Regulatory Commission. In addition, many public utilities such as electric power companies and gas companies have voluntarily established drug testing programs, and a 1986 study revealed that nearly three-fourths of major police departments surveyed require urine testing for all job applicants.

2. *The Variety of Drug Testing Programs.* When employers test and what they do with the results varies significantly among employers. Testing may be conducted randomly or upon a possible drug-related incident, such as an accident. Testing may be required for all job applicants, for all promotions, or as part of periodically required physicals. Some programs focus upon only specific types of employees. Of the Fortune 500 companies with testing programs, 80 percent test job applicants, 47 percent test employees after accidents, and 13 percent test employees at random.

Drug testing programs also vary in terms of the actions taken toward employees testing positive for illegal drug use. Many simply dismiss all employees who test positive. A few testing programs, however, require employees who test positive to enter drug treatment or counseling programs paid for by the company or employee health insurance. About 30 percent of Fortune 500 companies with testing programs have established in-house employee assistance programs which refer drug abusing employees to hospitals or clinics for treatment.

3. *The Variety of Urine Tests.* Drug testing programs may employ a variety of different types of tests to evaluate the physiological components of urine. Two of the most commonly used tests are the enzyme multiplied immunoassay test (EMIT), and the gas chromatography-mass spectrometer test (GC/MS). The tests differ significantly in chemical evaluation process, accuracy, and cost.

The EMIT is highly popular because it is inexpensive and because it is portable, easy to administer on the job location. The EMIT relies upon a process known as competitive displacement and bonding, in which metabolites of illegal drugs present in the subject's urine displace preexisting bonds in the testing reagent and create new molecular configurations which indicate prior illegal drug use. For reasons discussed below, the EMIT suffers from inherent inaccuracy problems that make reliance on its results ill-advised without confirmation by GC/MS testing.

The much more expensive GC/MS test requires laboratory conditions to evaluate, but is highly accurate. In the GC/MS test, compounds present in urine are classified in a gas chromatographer and fragmented by bombarding them with high energy particles in a mass spectrometer. Different compounds split apart at different times, and the fragments' ionic weights vary. The time of fragmentation and the fragments' ionic weights are then compared to data stored in a computer library of compounds. If the fragmentation time and ionic weights match the computer data for a particular compound, a molecular "fingerprint" exists which is regarded as a highly accurate confirmation of that compound's presence. For optimum efficiency and accuracy, the EMIT should be used for initial screening. Positive EMIT results should then be subjected to GC/MS testing for more reliable confirmation.

C. A Critical Review of the Employers' Response: The Scientific Limitations of Drug Testing Programs

Is drug testing a reasonable response by employers to the problem of employee drug use? To answer this question, one must examine the scientific limitations of drug testing programs.

1. *The Inherent Inaccuracy of EMIT Testing.* While the GC/MS test is quite accurate, the EMIT is to some degree inherently inaccurate, even when properly administered. The EMIT may yield a "false positive" by mistaking legal substances for illegal drugs due to "cross-reactivity," which occurs when compounds present in urine react with the testing solution and displace its preexisting chemical bonds in the same manner as by-products of the targeted drug. Courts examining testing programs have recognized the serious accuracy problems of the EMIT, and many have suggested the need for confirmation by a more accurate test.

The substances that the EMIT may mistake for various illegal drugs are numerous. Legal prescription and over-the-counter drugs such as aspirin, Contac, and Nyquil may cause a false positive result. Also, certain foods may trigger a false positive EMIT finding. For example, poppy seeds may be mistaken for opiates such as heroin and morphine, and herbal teas may be confused with cocaine. Bodily enzymes with which the EMIT testing reagent may react are excreted through the urine. If an individual happens to discharge above-average amounts of those enzymes, the EMIT may register a false positive. The same problem may occur with the polar acids present in urine. The concentration and bonding properties of these acids vary with the body chemistry of the subject, and they may cross-react with the EMIT testing reagent. Some scientific evidence also suggests that higher concentrations of the pigment melanin present in the bodies of blacks and Hispanics may cause false positives. Because of cross-reactivity, it is estimated that 5 percent to 25 percent of the positive results indicated by EMIT testing are incorrect, even if the EMIT is properly administered and evaluated. The EMIT may also register false *negative* readings, thus failing to identify those subjects who have used illegal drugs.

2. *The Administrative Inaccuracy of Drug Testing.* While the EMIT is inaccurate even when properly administered, an EMIT positive result confirmed by GC/MS testing is quite reliable. This level of scientific accuracy, however, may be obtained only if testing administrators carefully observe strict processing procedures. Administrative errors may result from incorrect collection processes, sample mislabeling, improper training of administrators and lab technicians, dirty or uncalibrated laboratory equipment, or failure to keep urine specimens at the proper temperature. Since even the most accurate test is administered by fallible humans, errors are bound to occur in any large-scale testing program.

The Centers for Disease Control (CDC) in Atlanta conducted a nine-year study of thirteen independent laboratories which revealed that some field testing programs had a false-positive rate ranging from 6 to 60 percent depending upon the drug being tested for. The error rate for false negatives was even higher. The factors of operator error, in-

adequate testing protocol, and poor laboratory quality control are, of course, to some extent correctable. Nevertheless, the CDC study indicates that even established companies with professional technicians and comprehensive testing controls remain subject to remarkably high rates of error. The study concluded that these randomly selected laboratories displayed "serious shortcomings" in quality control even though they knew they were being monitored.

3. *Limitations on the Probative Value of Drug Testing.* Having discussed the extent to which drug tests are able to detect illicit substances, it is useful, in order to assess the probative value of urinalysis, to examine what the tests do *not* show. First, even a correct positive test result for marijuana use does not prove that the test subject ever used marijuana himself. Depending upon what concentration of an illicit substance metabolite constitutes a positive test result, a positive result could be caused by the subject's passive inhalation of smoke from marijuana used by someone else.

Second, urine testing shows neither intoxication nor actual job impairment. Rather, it indicates only that the subject ingested the detected drug within the preceding days or weeks. The tests cannot identify the presence of an illicit drug directly; instead, they determine prior use of an illicit drug inferentially by screening for the presence of its by-products in the urine.

For instance, prior use of marijuana is determined by screening not for the intoxicating chemical itself, tetrahydrocannabinol (THC), but for its by-product metabolite, which appears only after THC breaks down and its intoxicating effects disappear. Because the target metabolite does not appear until intoxication passes, testing "can establish only marijuana *use,* not *intoxication.*" The metabolite is detectable in the body of a casual user for several days and even longer in the chronic user. The use of other drugs can have a similar effect, permitting detection of by-products long after intoxication has passed.

Because urine testing cannot detect present intoxication or the time that the illegal drugs were taken, it cannot measure job impairment accurately. These serious shortcomings necessarily permit an employer's drug testing to scrutinize an employee's off-duty drug use, whether or not that use impairs her job performance.

In addition, testing may fail to identify those drug-using employees who avoid or manipulate tests. If employees learn of the testing date, drug users may merely abstain from drug use in order to test negative. Drug users may also neutralize evidence of drug use by adulterating their samples with substances as common as table salt. A drug-using employee may even substitute a drug-free urine sample for her own.

The most telling limitation on the probative value of drug testing is its statistical unreliability. The likelihood that a given positive result is correct depends entirely upon the extent to which the tested group actually uses drugs. If one assumes that 5 percent of a group of employees uses illegal drugs and that an employer uses a drug testing program with 95 percent accuracy to screen the group, the employer's "accurate" program will yield one false positive result for every correct positive result. If only 2 percent of the group uses illegal drugs, three out of every four positive results will be incorrect.* If all 2.8 million federal workers are tested as suggested by the President's Commission on Organized Crime, an estimated 140,000 workers will be accused and disciplined unjustly.

III. Drug Testing and the Fourth Amendment

But even if the front door of the house is no longer protected by the Constitution, surely it had been thought until now that the bathroom door is.

*This analysis is illustrated by the following table:

Prevalence, %	Predictive Value of a Positive Result, %
0.1	2
1.0	16
2.0	28
5.0	50
10.0	68
50.0	95

A. The Purpose and Scope of the Fourth Amendment

Against this factual background, careful application of fourth amendment doctrine to random drug testing programs in the public sector reveals that such programs are unconstitutional searches and seizures under most circumstances. The fourth amendment to the United States Constitution provides:

> The right of the people to be secure in their persons, houses, papers, and effects, against unreasonable searches and seizures, shall not be violated, and no Warrants shall issue, but upon probable cause, supported by Oath or affirmation, and particularly describing the place to be searched and the persons or things to be seized.

"The fundamental command of the Fourth Amendment is that searches and seizures be reasonable. . . ." The amendment prohibits only *unreasonable* searches and seizures. What is reasonable, however, depends on the context of the search. The prevailing test for "reasonableness" was set forth by the Supreme Court in *Bell v. Wolfish:* "The test of reasonableness under the Fourth Amendment is not capable of precise definition or mechanical application. In each case it requires a balancing of the need for the particular search against the invasion of personal rights that the search entails."

It is difficult to predict with certainty, however, the exact test the Supreme Court will use when confronted with the testing of public employees. Most recently, in *O'Connor v. Ortega,* the Court indicated that searches of

> government employees for noninvestigatory, work-related purposes, as well as for investigations of work-related misconduct, should be judged by the standard of reasonableness under all the circumstances. Under this reasonableness standard, both the inception and the scope of the intrusion must be reasonable.

The Court explicitly did not, however, "address the proper Fourth Amendment analysis for drug and alcohol testing of employees." It is difficult to discern what independent meaning is communicated by this most recent formulation of the test. Depending upon the context, it may be impossible to determine whether a search is justified at its inception without first considering the scope of the search. For example, the "scope" of a drug test is the compelled tender of a urine specimen. It may be compelled under direct or indirect observation. All of these considerations seem appropriate to take into account when determining whether the drug test was justified at its inception.

Whether the inception and scope of a search are reasonable would seem in the final analysis to depend upon a balancing of the interests outlined in *Bell*. Even if the Court utilizes the recent *O'Connor* formulation, it appears inevitable that the same balancing of governmental interests against individual privacy rights articulated in *Bell* will in the end determine the constitutionality of public employee drug testing programs. Thus, to determine the constitutionality of such drug testing, the state interests advanced by testing must be balanced against its intrusiveness upon employees' privacy interests; the greater the intrusion occasioned by the search, the greater must be the governmental interest in conducting the search.

B. The Threshold Issue: A Drug Test Is a Search

The threshold issue in fourth amendment analysis is whether a drug test is a search. If the test is not a search, then no fourth amendment objection arises, which obviates the need to balance state and individual privacy interests. Whether a drug test is a search generally depends upon whether there exists a "reasonable expectation of privacy" in the act of urination.

Evaluating reasonable expectations of privacy for purposes of determining whether an intrusion constitutes a fourth amendment search is an abstract, non-case-specific inquiry which focuses upon whether society is prepared to recognize that the employee has a legitimate expectation of privacy from drug tests. In response to this question, the courts have uniformly found that a drug test is a

search within the meaning of the fourth amendment. Despite the novelty of the technology, the courts have recognized that drug testing implicates central fourth amendment values, and that individuals have legitimate expectations of privacy in the act of urination.

C. The Individual Interests: The Intrusiveness of Drug Testing

Once courts determine that a drug test is a search, they must balance the intrusiveness of the search against the government's need for the information that the search will reveal. In focusing on the intrusiveness of a search, courts first examine the context of an individual's expectation of privacy. What is reasonable in one context may not be reasonable in another. Although most public employees legitimately have very strong expectations of privacy both in the act of urination and in its contents, an employee's expectations of privacy may be diminished if she enters an occupation which requires significant preparedness and discipline, such as the military, intensely regulated industries, nuclear power plants, prisons, public transportation, or law enforcement. On the other hand, public employees whose occupations do not directly implicate public safety or other similar governmental interests retain the same level of privacy enjoyed by the ordinary citizen.

After courts assess the context of the employee's expectations of privacy, they examine the intrusiveness of the search. Because an individual generally has the highest expectations of privacy in her body, searches violating the integrity of the body are greater invasions of privacy than inspections of personal effects. The Supreme Court has observed that "even a limited search of the person is a substantial invasion of privacy."

There are three compelling reasons why drug tests are very intrusive, even when compared with other bodily searches. First, the tests reveal not only past drug use, but also numerous other physiological facts that are of no legitimate interest to the employer. While exposing past illegal drug use, drug tests also expose the use of legally prescribed medications, including oral contraceptives and medication to treat physical and psychiatric conditions previously recognized as within the traditional confidentiality of medical records. Drug testing also exposes otherwise private medical conditions, including diabetes, epilepsy, urinary tract infections, venereal disease, and pregnancy.

Second, drug tests necessarily scrutinize a broad array of off-duty activities. As observed in *American Federation of Government Employees v. Weinberger*, "[t]hese tests enable the individual or organization administering them to monitor the off-duty conduct of employees, and represent a technological advance that . . . could threaten much of the privacy most citizens now take for granted."

Third, the manner in which urine specimens are obtained is quite intrusive. Urination is a personal bodily function usually performed in solitude. In fact, many municipal ordinances prohibit the act in public. Some testing programs require a government official's direct observation of the act of urination to assure the accuracy of the test and to prevent adulteration of the samples. Urination under the direct observation of another "necessarily includes exposing one's private parts, an experience which even if courteously supervised can be humiliating and degrading."

Even if urine samples are not collected under direct observation, many testing programs require at least indirect observation, which may be equally embarrassing and insulting. Regardless of whether testing requires any observation, the experience of being forced to produce a urine sample at the behest of an employer offends normal expectations of dignity. As one court noted, "the very taking of the sample makes for a quite substantial intrusion that could not be negated even if an employee were allowed to produce his urine sample in the privacy of an executive washroom, with no observation whatsoever." Drug tests have been described as more intrusive than a search of the home; equal to or more intrusive than a blood test; and equal to the intrusiveness of a strip search or even a body cavity search. In light of the private bodily information that drug testing can reveal, the potential days of off-duty activity it can scrutinize, and the highly offensive and degrading process of collecting the specimen itself, it is fair to con-

clude that drug testing is a highly invasive search that requires a proportionally weighty state interest to justify it.

D. The Governmental Interests

The magnitude of the invasion upon individual liberties caused by drug testing must be balanced against the governmental interests furthered by the tests. Three distinct governmental interests have been advanced in support of drug testing: (1) the identification of drug-using employees to further efficiency and safety in the workplace; (2) the integrity of the particular employment institution as perceived by the public; and (3) the enforcement of the criminal laws against drug trade and use by reducing the demand for illegal drugs. While these are certainly legitimate objectives of governmental action, the fourth amendment question is not the legitimacy of the goals themselves, but whether the goals properly may be achieved by means of drug testing. Each of the asserted governmental interests must be examined critically with this question in mind.

1. *The Safety/Efficiency Interest.* The governmental interest most commonly advanced in support of drug testing is to increase efficiency and safety in the workplace through detection of employees who use drugs on the job. Mistakes made by drug-using employees may endanger themselves or others, and under some circumstances, may result in the employer's liability. But while the governmental interest in efficiency and safety is an important one, the extent to which drug testing promotes this interest is limited for three reasons.

First, it is worthwhile to note that the safety/efficiency interest suggests a great deal more than testing for illegal drugs. If the efficiency of the workforce is the issue, employers should logically test for other influences that affect efficiency. Recently, Representative Patricia Schroeder argued:

[I]f [efficiency and on-the-job performance] is the reason for the [proposed urine testing], why did the Commission [on organized crime] not recommend testing for off-duty use of the two most addictive and destructive drugs known to society—alcohol and tobacco? Alcoholism has ruined the careers and families of hundreds of thousands of Americans. As for smoking, the Surgeon General has documented that cigarette smoking results in greater illness and use of sick leave. If our goal is to regulate off-duty conduct which could hurt performance, alcohol and tobacco would be prime candidates. I, however, along with most Americans, would find such restrictions abhorrent.

Second, the governmental interest in safety varies greatly with the context. The government has a significant safety interest in preventing the use of drugs by employees whose drug use would ordinarily pose situations of grave public danger, such as air traffic controllers and police officers. But this safety interest is not significant in other contexts, where danger to life does not result, as a matter of course, from the conduct of drug-using employees.

Third, the strength of the government's safety/efficiency interest depends upon the extent to which employees now engage in drug use. If drug use is widespread, then some additional efficiency and safety might be achieved by drug testing. On the other hand, if no employees use drugs, then drug testing will not enhance efficiency or safety *at all*. The courts should not rest content with the mere assertion that a drug problem exists; given the intrusiveness of drug testing, the employer should be required to produce evidence on the extent of employee drug use to justify drug testing. Without such evidence, ordering drug testing is "an act of pure bureaucratic caprice."

Even in those circumstances in which the employer has a strong safety and efficiency interest in identifying drug users, the question remains whether drug testing is a reasonable means of furthering that interest. As Judge Vietor explained:

There is no doubt about it—searches and seizures can yield a wealth of information useful to the searcher. (That is why King George III's men so frequently searched the colonists.) That potential, however, does not make a governmental employer's search of an employee a constitutionally reasonable one.

Even where an employer is able to assert a strong safety/efficiency interest, drug testing is both an over- and underinclusive means of advancing that interest. Drug testing is overinclusive because the tests do not reveal whether or when the illicit substance was ingested. Drug testing does not indicate whether an individual was intoxicated or impaired on the job or at the time the test was given. It does not indicate whether an individual is drug-dependent, a regular user, or likely to ingest the drug during working hours. If employers discipline an employee based upon a positive urine test, the employer in effect regulates the employee's off-duty behavior. In these respects, drug testing is no less overinclusive than random searches of employees' homes or wiretaps placed on employees' phones.

Drug testing to detect on-the-job drug use by employees is also an underinclusive means of advancing safety and efficiency, due to its inaccuracy. Tests may be manipulated, and studies show that properly administered urine tests have very high rates of false negatives. Even those employees who have used drugs immediately prior to a test may not be detected.

Finally, drug testing is not only extremely overinclusive and somewhat underinclusive, but also is not the least intrusive means of furthering the governmental interest. A properly designed and implemented program of employee supervision will in many contexts lead to the detection of virtually all drug-using employees. Given that scientific studies are able to generate statistical and scientific evidence of the absenteeism, mistakes, and health problems caused by drug use, one wonders why employers do not simply take disciplinary action against those employees who make more mistakes, are frequently absent, or suffer from drug-related health problems? "Certainly one so under the influence of drugs as to impair the performance of his or her duties must manifest some outward symptoms. . . ." While it is possible that an employee on drugs may escape detection for a while, risking injury to himself or another, there is certainly no guarantee that drug testing would prevent such an accident.

Drug testing is a much more intrusive action than is necessary to serve the governmental safety/efficiency interest. To the extent that it does so, it is both over- and underinclusive. Accordingly, the governmental interest in safety and efficiency in the workplace has only a marginal nexus with drug testing.

2. *The Integrity Interest.* Wholly apart from the actual effects of drug use, the government's ability to do its job may be impaired if the public perceives governmental workers as drug users. Under this line of reasoning, the imposition of drug testing will comfort the public and contribute to the perception that public employees are drug-free. Because of this perception the government arguably will be able to carry out its duties more effectively.

The strength of the integrity interest, like the safety/efficiency interest discussed above, depends entirely upon context. Only in some employment situations is the public's perception critical to the ability of an employee to do his job effectively. The integrity interest is most commonly advanced as a justification for testing law enforcement officers.

The argument that the perceived use of drugs by law enforcement officers will affect their ability to carry out their duties is attenuated at best. In the absence of any empirical evidence to the contrary, it is equally plausible to infer that most citizens obey law enforcement officers even if they have some vague suspicion that some officers, although not necessarily the officers they are dealing with, use illegal drugs. Furthermore, the establishment by way of testing that law enforcement officers do not use drugs can only serve to heighten respect for the officers to the extent that it is already perceived that the officers use drugs. That is, if no one thinks law enforcement officers use drugs, then confirming that they do not serves little purpose. Accordingly, the mere assertion of an unfavorable public perception must not suffice to trigger the government's integrity interest. To prove that drug testing is needed to preserve the integrity of law enforcement officers, the government must be required to make at least some evidentiary showing that perceived drug use

actually has compromised law enforcement integrity.

Even if the public actually perceives that its law enforcement officers use illegal drugs, it is doubtful that drug testing will eliminate that perception. Although it is true that drug testing may serve to comfort the public, this comforting effect inevitably will be to some extent undermined by the report of positive test results, which will likely receive a lot of attention and strengthen the public's impression that the public employees are drug users.

The governmental interest in employee integrity does not exist in other contexts where the performance of its employees is not affected by public perception. In those areas of employment, the integrity interest should never be allowed as a justification for drug testing.

3. *Policing Drug Use.* The government occasionally asserts that it should be permitted to conduct employee drug testing programs to advance its interest in eliminating the use and trade of illegal drugs. While it may be true, at the margin, that drug use and trade may be attacked by reducing demand for drugs through employee drug testing, the extent to which demand and trade may be reduced by drug testing is certainly speculative. The difficulty with this justification for drug testing is that it presents no reason to stop with public employees. If the elimination of drug demand is the goal, then there is no rational basis for testing only employees, let alone public employees. An equal state interest would support random drug testing at roadway blockades, election booths, street corners, and so on. Because there is no reason to believe that public employees are more likely to support the drug trade than any other citizen, random drug testing for this purpose limited to public employees as a class raises profound equal protection problems. Government cannot legitimately promote its interest in eliminating drug use and trade by testing public employees only.

E. Balancing the Competing Interests

After examining the intrusiveness of drug testing and the countervailing state interests, courts must balance these competing values to arrive at the appropriate level of suspicion or cause required to make the testing of an individual employee reasonable under the fourth amendment. Unfortunately, courts have given rather hasty treatment to this portion of the analysis, arriving at results in a rather conclusory fashion. While only a few courts have allowed drug testing without any individualized suspicion, none has gone so far as to require probable cause. Most of the courts have instead held that "reasonable suspicion" is the constitutionally required standard. "Reasonable suspicion" is often defined as suspicion that is based on specific objective facts and reasonable inferences that a particular employee has used drugs on the job. That so many courts have adopted the reasonable suspicion standard without any detailed analysis when confronted with many different factual scenarios suggests that a spirit of compromise is in the air. Though many courts oppose random testing plans, they do not want to appear to promote employee drug use by requiring probable cause. The lesser "reasonable suspicion" standard allows courts to stop random testing programs while politically saving face. Because the governmental interests in testing necessarily vary with the context, constitutional standards which reflect these factual distinctions would be more analytically satisfying. The authors offer the following framework as a rough guide to achieve a more thoughtful balancing of interests.

When the governmental interest in integrity is irrelevant because the public's perception of the institution does not affect its ability to function, and when the governmental interest in safety is less important, as in situations where drug use would not inevitably present public danger, the government should not be allowed to test an employee for illegal drug use without *probable cause* to believe that she uses illegal drugs on the job. In such a situation, absent evidence of widespread drug use among employees, there is simply no compelling reason to alter the probable cause standard.

When the government demonstrates a strong integrity interest, by proving that (1) public perception is critical to the ability of the employees to perform their functions, and (2) there is an accurate general public perception of drug use among those employees, then the government should be allowed to test an employee based on *reasonable suspicion* of drug use on the job. However, courts must not accept mere assertions of unfavorable public perception. Without proof that such a perception impairs the employee's performance, drug testing is a remedy without a wrong.

Alternatively, when the government shows a strong safety interest by demonstrating that employee drug use would as a matter of course present situations of grave public danger, then the government should be permitted to test an employee based upon *reasonable suspicion*. As with the integrity interest, however, courts must require evidence of extensive employee drug use on the job and accurate confirmatory test procedures. Without such evidence, the government may advance its safety interest adequately by implementing a well-designed program of supervision.

Drug testing is so intrusive, over- and underinclusive, and of such limited utility in detecting drug use on the job that testing without reasonable suspicion must not be allowed under any circumstances.

F. Consent?

Even if a testing program violates the fourth amendment, an employer could attempt to obtain employee consent to the search. In several drug testing programs challenged in the courts, employees were required to sign consent forms before testing.

There are two reasons why these consent forms may not validate an otherwise unreasonable search. First, consent is not voluntary where each employee knows that her refusal to consent will result in disciplinary action. Second, even if employees signed the forms voluntarily, the government should never be allowed to condition public employment upon the waiver of constitutional rights.

Whether the consent of an employee is voluntary, and not the result of duress or coercion, express or implied, is a question of fact to be determined from all the circumstances. The critical consideration in consent form situations is what the employee reasonably believes will happen if she does not sign the form. If it is obvious under the circumstances that disciplinary action will result from a failure to sign the form, then clearly any decision to sign results from coercion.

Regardless of the voluntariness with which consent is given, the government should not be permitted to require a waiver of fourth amendment rights as a condition of public employment. If government could do this, it could by the same reasoning require the relinquishment of other fundamental rights. In *Frost & Frost Trucking Company v. Railroad Commission,* the Supreme Court observed:

> If the state may compel the surrender of one constitutional right as a condition of its favor, it may, in like manner, compel a surrender of all. It is inconceivable that guarantees embedded in the Constitution of the United States may thus be manipulated out of existence.

The point is perhaps best captured by Judge Vietor in *McDonell v. Hunter:* "Advance consent to future *unreasonable* searches is not a reasonable condition of employment."

G. The Government As Employer

A separate but related argument that has been advanced in support of drug testing is that the government in its role as employer, as contrasted with its role as law enforcer, should be given the same latitude in dealing with its employees as any other employer in the private sector. Upon first examination this argument appears seductively simple and sound: Because private employers generally may institute employee drug testing programs, the government as employer arguably should be permitted to do the same. Upon closer analysis, however, the argument is compelling only from the government's perspective; from the employee's perspective, his fourth amendment rights may depend upon whether his employer suspects him of criminal activity. Nevertheless, several courts have adopted some form of the "government-as-employer" rationale in upholding drug testing programs. The courts' utilization of the rationale, however, has been analytically confusing; some courts view the doctrine as rendering the fourth amendment totally inapplicable to governmental searches for work-related misconduct while others view the fourth amendment as applicable to such searches, but to a lesser extent.

In *Allen v. City of Marietta,* for example, the court considered a fourth amendment challenge by a public employee to a drug test imposed on reasonable suspicion of drug use. The *Allen* court determined at the outset that the drug test was a "search" within the meaning of the fourth amendment. Further, the court recognized that "[g]overnment employees do not surrender their fourth amendment rights merely because they go to work for the government. They have as much of a right to be free from warrantless government searches as any other citizens." Nevertheless, the court drew a distinction between governmental searches for evidence of crime and searches for noncriminal work-related misconduct. As to the latter type of search, the court stated: "Because the government as employer has the same rights to discover and prevent employee misconduct relevant to the employee's performance of her duties [as a private employer], the employee cannot really claim a legitimate expectation of privacy from searches of that nature." Although the *Allen* court stated that fourth amendment protection extends to government employees, the logical result of its holding that government employees have no reasonable expectation of privacy from searches for work-related misconduct is that the fourth amendment does *not* protect government employees from work-related searches. This is because where there is no legitimate expectation of privacy to be free from a search, there is no fourth amendment protection. Accordingly, the *Allen* court's analysis, focusing on the government as employer's need to search, leads to the conclusion that the fourth amendment has no application *at all* to searches for employment-related misconduct. This holding would appear to be squarely at odds with Supreme Court precedent, particularly the Court's latest pronouncement in *O'Connor v. Ortega* that "[s]earches and seizures by government employers or supervisors of the private property of their employees . . . are subject to the restraints of the Fourth Amendment."

The government-as-employer argument was stated somewhat differently in *National Treasury Employees Union v. Von Raab*. In that case, the court seemed to focus on the employee's need to be free from governmental searches: "While the fourth amendment protects against invasions for civil as well as criminal investigatory purposes, *the need for protection against governmental intrusion diminishes if the investigation is neither designed to enforce criminal laws nor likely to be used to bring criminal charges against the person investigated*." Under the Fifth Circuit's view, the fourth amendment continues to apply to governmental searches for work-related misconduct, but in a somewhat less robust form.

At least two criticisms of this position may be made. First, it is entirely unclear *why* the need to be free from searches "diminishes" where the search is not intended to enforce criminal laws. It is equally plausible that a citizen's "need" to be free from a search depends upon the intrusiveness of the search itself, rather than upon whether the evidence sought is proscribed by a statute instead of an employment regulation.

Second, it is unclear why the focus of inquiry should be on the employee's "need for protection *against* governmental intrusion" rather than on the government's need *for* the intrusion. That is, the *Von Raab* court's proposition seems no more inherently appealing than the proposition that "the need for [the governmental intrusion itself] diminishes if the investigation is neither designed to enforce criminal laws nor likely to be used to bring criminal charges. . . ." This is because it is difficult to classify the "need" for a search (or to be free from one) by whether the object of the search is to be used in civil or criminal proceedings. On the civil side, the government-as-employer may have a great need to discover whether an air traffic controller is impaired by alcohol, whereas it may have little need to discover that he is double parked. On the other hand, searching an employee's car for a murder weapon will be of greater necessity than a search of the car for a box of pencils taken from the office.

The civil/criminal distinction is equally unavailing when viewed from an employee's perspective. Many employees would prefer to have a search yield evidence of a minor criminal infraction than evidence causing their employment to be terminated. As this brief discussion indicates, it is of little help in determining the reasonableness of a search to focus on whether the evidence sought to be obtained relates to criminal or civil matters.

Regardless of the manner in which the government-as-employer theory is applied, however, it rests upon an extremely problematic interpretation of the fourth amendment. The doctrine makes sense, if at all, only from the perspective of the government. From an employee's perspective, the theory allows fourth amendment protections "to fluctuate with the 'intent' of the invading officers." If an employee is subjected to a drug test because he is suspected of criminal activity, the test is illegal. But if a test is administered merely to evaluate his fitness for a job, the same urine test is legal. Clearly, this turns the fourth amendment on its head. As the Supreme Court commented in *Camara v. Municipal Court*, "It is surely anomalous to say that the individual and his private property are fully protected by the Fourth Amendment only when the individual is suspected of criminal behavior."

This anomaly should be foreclosed by the language of the amendment itself. As Justice Brennan noted:

> The Amendment states its own purpose, the protection of the privacy of the individual and of his property against the incursions of officials: the "right of the people to be secure in their persons, houses, papers, and effects." Like most of the Bill of Rights it was not designed to be a shelter for criminals, but a basic protection for everyone; to be sure, it must be upheld when asserted by criminals, in order that it may be at all effective, but it "reaches all alike, whether accused of crime or not."

H. Administrative Searches

Several courts have upheld the drug testing of public employees under the administrative search exception to the warrant requirement. This exception is based upon a line of Supreme Court decisions allowing warrantless searches of commercial premises in closely regulated industries. In these decisions the Court has recognized significant state interests in regulating industries such as coal mining, firearms sales, junkyards, and the sale of alcoholic beverages. Because such regulation tends to reduce expectations of privacy, the Court has allowed warrantless searches of commercial property where authorized by specific statutory authority. The Court has made it clear, however, that the exception does not excuse warrantless searches of personal property outside of the commercial context, especially warrantless searches of private homes. In *Donovan v. Dewey,* the Court explicitly distinguished searches of private residences from searches of commercial premises for purposes of the administrative search exception.

The Court's most recent case on administrative searches, *New York v. Burger,* set forth three criteria which must be met in order for a warrantless search of commercial premises to be permissible. There must be a "substantial" government interest supported by the regulatory scheme permitting the search; "warrantless inspections must be 'necessary to further [the] regulatory scheme'"; and "the statute's inspection program, in terms of the certainty and regularity of its application, [must] provid[e] a constitutionally adequate substitute for a warrant." The Court has also required a nexus between the purposes for the regulation and the interests involved in the search, although it did not articulate it as a formal criterion.

On its face, the administrative search exception to the warrant requirement does not apply to bodily searches of public employees. The Court has taken great pains to explicitly limit the doctrine to searches of commercial *property*. Nevertheless, several courts have extended the doctrine to apply to drug testing employees in regulated industries. In effect, these courts have taken a relatively narrow doctrine permitting warrantless searches of commercial property in a few historically and pervasively regulated industries and applied it to highly intrusive bodily fluid searches of individual employees who work in regulated industries. There is little that can be said

about this development except that it represents a radical departure from precedent. The Sixth Circuit has noted this point quite forcefully:

> To allow widespread mandatory drug testing of individuals by analogizing it to the relaxed standards governing the less intrusive searches of places allowed under the administrative search warrant exception fundamentally misapprehends that doctrine.
>
> Given the origins of the administrative search warrant exception, it seems incredible that the argument in favor of mandatory drug testing should be based on this doctrine.

The application of the administrative search doctrine to bodily searches is particularly unfortunate in view of the relaxation of the doctrine itself in *Burger.* There, the Court found a "substantial" state interest in the regulation of junkyards. Warrantless searches were considered necessary to further the regulatory scheme because a warrant requirement might impair the "surprise" found crucial to the Court in order to enforce the regulatory scheme. Finally, the Court found that the regulatory scheme provided a "constitutionally adequate substitute for a warrant." As Justice Brennan noted in his dissent, however, the only real restriction on the searches was that they must occur during the business hours of junkyards. That the search actually conducted was unrelated to the administrative regulations that initially justified the search, but rather was aimed at criminal law enforcement, was not viewed as a sufficient difficulty to remove the search from the administrative search exception.

In the wake of *Burger,* it becomes clear that almost any regulatory scheme may validly authorize a warrantless search as long as the legislature is able to articulate some plausible significant interest and at least one restriction on the time, place, and scope of the authorized searches. Moreover, the search will not be objectionable merely because its sole purpose is criminal law enforcement. As Justice Brennan observed, "[t]he implications of the

Court's opinion, if realized, will virtually eliminate Fourth Amendment protection of commercial entities in the context of administrative searches." Applying the administrative search doctrine to bodily searches of individual employees will have the further effect of virtually eliminating fourth amendment protection of individuals employed in commercial entities. The implications of this result may be to allow a legislature to effectively abrogate much of traditional fourth amendment protection by regulatory fiat.

---

47. HIV Testing: Voluntary, Mandatory, or Routine?

Theresa L. Crenshaw

Theresa L. Crenshaw argues for widespread voluntary HIV testing and for mandatory or routine HIV testing under certain circumstances. She contends that HIV testing is reliable, cost effective, and need not violate privacy or lead to quarantine.

The AIDS virus is formidable. For a preventable disease, it continues to spread at an alarming rate. As long as 90 percent of those who are infected—1.5 million people or more in the United States—don't know it and continue to spread it to others, we have little hope of controlling this epidemic.

Yet, there are many dilemmas and questions that face us as individuals and as a society. Isn't it better for a person who is infected not to know? How can one expect an infected person to stop having sex when he or she is already suffering more than a human being can bear? Are condoms sufficient protection? Is testing dependable? How can we protect the civil rights of the ill and the civil rights of the healthy?

There is no simple solution. Testing alone is not enough. We need all of our resources: common sense, sexual integrity, compassion, love, exclusivity, education, discipline, testing, condoms, and spermicides—to name just a few. We also need an emphatic, positive message that promotes *quality* sex rather than *quantity* sex. Multiple partners and casual sex are not in the best interest of health, but within an exclusive relationship quality sex can thrive.

In this context, perhaps we could take an in-depth look at the controversial issue of HIV-testing. Widespread voluntary testing, if encouraged by health officials and physicians, will most probably be successful, making widespread mandatory testing unnecessary. The general population will cooperate. However, under certain circumstances, required or routine testing might be considered and could be implemented whenever common sense dictates without the feared repercussions of quarantine and discrimination. Regardless of whether testing is voluntary, required or routine, maintaining confidentiality is critical. It is vitally important to understand that public health officials are trained to maintain confidentiality in all cases; they do not put advertisements in the newspaper or call a person's employer.

Confidentiality is nonetheless a genuine concern. Lists of infected persons have been stolen. There is probably no way humanly possible to ensure against any and all breaches of confidentiality throughout the United States and the world. It would be unrealistic to falsely assure individuals that confidentiality would be 100 percent secure. On the other hand, we must do everything within our power to come as close as possible to 100 percent confidentiality and to assure those who are concerned that these efforts are being made. There are many things we can do to improve our recording and to improve confidentiality

From *The Humanist,* January/February 1988, pp. 29–34. Reprinted by permission.

systems. These aspects are being investigated and will hopefully be implemented by federal, state, and local authorities.

An encouraging point is that in Colorado, where HIV-positive status is reportable and contact tracing is routine, *there has not been one episode of breach of confidentiality*, demonstrating that when extra care is taken there can be great success. Often forgotten is the fact that confidentiality is equally important for voluntary, required, and routine testing. It must be applied to *all* forms of testing, and it must not be used to distinguish between them.

Mandatory testing brings to mind visions of concentration camps and human beings subjected to arbitrary and insensitive public health tactics. In practice, however, nothing could be further from the truth. Urine tests and blood counts are routinely required upon hospital admission. If a patient refuses, he or she will generally not be accepted by the hospital and certainly won't be allowed to undergo surgery. That's mandatory testing, but we take it in stride. And it has no hint of repressiveness; it is simply a reasonable measure for the protection and well-being of both the patient and the hospital.

Likewise, tests for syphilis are mandatory in many states. In many countries, certain tests and inoculations are required before one can travel. In the not-so-distant past, health cards had to be carried by travelers along with their passports, proving that they had had certain immunizations. There is also required testing of school children for childhood diseases, which includes the tuberculin skin test, and various inoculations, without which they are not permitted to enter school. These are just a few examples of mandatory testing or treatments that are routine in our everyday lives— and that do not compromise our civil rights. However, since the term *mandatory* is emotionally charged, substituting the term *required* might more accurately reflect the intent.

Our society takes in stride sensible, necessary tests and treatments which in many circumstances are required in order to travel abroad or to perform certain jobs. However, strenuous arguments against any form of required testing for AIDS persist. The following are some of the issues most commonly raised by opponents of mandatory testing. I have attempted to analyze each argument.

Mandatory testing will drive infected individuals underground. They will hide out and refuse to be tested.

Since 90 percent of the 1.5 million or more individuals who are infected within the United States don't even know it, *they are already underground*. While certain numbers of people may use creative methods to avoid testing procedures, we would be able to reduce that percentage of people who do not know their HIV status to 10 percent instead of 90 percent, because most people would cooperate voluntarily.

Testing would cause more problems than it solves because huge numbers of people would receive false positive test results. Their lives would be destroyed by such test results.

The enzyme linked immunosorbent assay, or ELISA test, does have a high percentage of false positives, just as the tuberculin skin test has a high percentage of false positives. *That does not mean it is without value.* Whenever a test such as this is performed, a physician never stops at screening tests. Follow-up studies are required to confirm a positive test result. For example, with tuberculosis, chest X-rays and sputum cultures are performed until a positive diagnosis of tuberculosis can be made. The tuberculin skin test is used to determine whether there are indications for further studies. The AIDS antibody test is used in the same fashion. If the ELISA is positive, it should be repeated again and the Western Blot test performed. If these are all positive, the likelihood of the result being a false positive approaches zero (per 400,000, according to Dr. James Curran of the Centers for Disease Control). Immune system studies can then be done and, although it is expensive and somewhat logistically difficult, a patient who wants additional proof of infection can request actual viral cultures. Since recent research demonstrates that there can be a year or more during which the virus is present but antibodies have not yet developed—the so-called window in time—the far greater problem with testing is the high number of false negatives that still will be missed. Another study by A. Ranki et al., in the September 12, 1987, issue of *Lancet,* indicates that up to 36 percent of ELISAs are false negatives in those individuals who have had sex with an infected person. As you see, the screening test is not perfect. There will be false negatives that escape detection, so the test should be repeated periodically. All false positives would be followed up with additional tests until a confirmed positive result can be established. In the near future, we will have a test for the virus itself, solving some of the problems we now face, especially the "window in time" between infection and antibody development.

There is no point in having yourself tested because there is no cure.

Although there is no cure, and indeed *because* there is no cure, it is even more essential to be tested and to know what your antibody status is, because, if you test positive, you must take every precaution not to infect another person. If this disease were curable, perhaps we could be more cavalier. But since we must protect individuals in society from it, we must motivate those who are already infected not to infect anyone else. To assume that everyone should and will behave as though they were infected is optimistic and unreasonable, although I think many can achieve this end. It is unlikely, however, for an individual to take complete responsibility for his or her actions without definitive knowledge of infection. Even then it is a challenge.

There are other reasons for being tested. Someone who tests positive will live longer if counseled not to become exposed unnecessarily to other infections by visiting sick friends at home or in the hospital or by traveling extensively to countries where foreign organisms can cause unusual infections. Additional health counseling can lead to a healthier lifestyle, the avoidance of other opportunistic infections or cofactors, improved nutrition, and planning for the future—which includes estate planning, a will, and making other practical arrangements as indicated.

Perhaps the most important reason for being tested early is that many of the treatments becoming available are more effective the earlier they are instituted. If you know you are HIV-positive, you can apply for research projects for experimental protocols or arrange to take AZT (which is now available) or other similar drugs when they become approved for clinical use. In short, the reasons for being tested far outweigh the reasons for not being tested.

Testing is undesirable for many individuals who are unable to cope with knowledge that they are infected. These people are better off not being tested.

Anyone who is asked whether or not they think they will be able to cope with the news of an HIV-positive test result would ordinarily say no. It is normal not to be able to cope well with a deadly, incurable disease. Most people who are tested receive pretest counseling. Often pretest counseling, advertently or inadvertently, dissuades individuals from being tested. At a recent conference in New York cosponsored by the American Medical Association and the Centers for Disease Control, one physician said that, with just three minutes on the telephone with someone inquiring about being tested, he succeeds in talking 57 percent of potential patients out of being tested. In the anonymous testing centers, we need only look at the numbers of people who show up for testing compared to those who leave without being tested to assess the effectiveness of some counseling in discouraging testing.

Yet, imagine an analogous situation for a woman needing a breast biopsy. If the physician asked, "Are you sure you want this biopsy? Do you realize that the results could show that you have cancer? Are you prepared to live with that? If the biopsy is positive, you'll need to have your breast removed. Do you think you can cope? How do you think your husband will feel about you sexually? What if the cancer is incurable and you're given a short time to live? Do you think you can handle that?" Of course, the answer to most of these questions would be "no," and many women needing breast biopsies would not pursue them. Instead, doctors help a woman confront the need for the biopsy. They support her in helping her to deal with the natural reluctance and fear involved and help her to find the courage and determination to proceed.

We must do the same with AIDS testing. Instead of asking, "Are you sure you want this test?" and "Do you think you can cope?" the physician, psychologist, or therapist must take the same kind of approach they do with other necessary or valuable medical procedures. Assume it is a good idea to be tested. Compliment the person for his or her courage and self-responsibility in pursuing the test. Let each person know that you intend to help him or her get through some of the difficulties and will be there to talk in detail about the issues should that person's test turn out to be positive. Let patients know that you appreciate the courage it takes for them to proceed with the test. Emphasize that the test will be of value to them whether it turns out to be negative or positive. By taking the approach that it is valuable and worthwhile to be tested, counselors can help patients deal with their fear and discomfort rather than contribute to it. Many counseling centers are beginning to change to this approach, but too many still follow the one that effectively discourages testing.

Testing isn't cost effective except in high-risk populations. Required testing will simply waste a lot of money getting nothing but negative results.

A negative result is exceedingly valuable and can be utilized to maintain health. Any individual who tests negative should be given written, taped, or individual information on how to remain uninfected so that they are motivated to protect that fortunate status. Some studies have found that an HIV-negative result alone is sometimes not sufficient to motivate a change in sexual behavior. It is exceedingly worthwhile to test negative, especially if it can be combined with some information or counseling so that the individual can be given an opportunity to remain HIV-negative for life.

The cost of testing the entire population and counseling those who are HIV-positive on how not to spread the disease is a fraction of the cost that would be required to care for those who would otherwise become infected.

Testing is no good. The day after someone has the test they could become infected. That's why safe sex cards don't work.

It is true that moments after blood has been drawn for an AIDS test the person could have sex and become infected. There is no question that the test is only as good as the behavior that follows it. On the other hand, if a person gets tested fairly regularly (every six months or once a year) and you meet that person five years after their first test and learn that that person has had the discipline and the concern about his or her health to remain negative for that period of time, it tells you something about that person's judgment and health status. One test may not carry a great deal of meaning, except to the individual who knows whether or not his or her behavior has been risky since the last test. On the other hand, a series of tests that are negative makes a statement of great importance.

It is also important to emphasize that testing is not enough. I do not support safe sex cards if they are used in singles clubs with the recommendation that anyone who tests negative and carries a card can have sex with anyone else holding a similar card. Multiple partners multiplies the possible error. On the other hand, I think that one or more tests are very valuable if used as a prerequisite to a monogamous relationship and if condoms and spermicide are also used until at least a year has passed to protect against the window in time mentioned earlier.

If you institute mandatory testing, what are you going to do with the individuals who test positive? Isolate them? Quarantine them?

Society will do the same thing with individuals who test HIV-positive on mandatory testing that they will do with any individuals who test HIV-positive on widespread voluntary testing. Most people who are fighting mandatory testing are actually fighting quarantine, afraid that one will lead to the other. I would much prefer that they support the valuable and meaningful step of testing and fight the issue of quarantine, rather than fight step two to avoid step three.

You should not test because some people will panic when they are told of a positive result and commit suicide.

This is one of the most worrisome consequences of testing. It is understandable that someone who tests positive would fleetingly consider taking his or her own life, and some individuals might progress to actually doing so. This is one of the reasons a positive test result should never be given by phone. A patient should be called to see his or her physician or counselor or to the anonymous testing center so that he or she can be counseled extensively at that moment.

There are no guarantees that will ensure that someone would not commit suicide, but we must do everything humanly possible to prevent it—short of not testing. The reason for this is simple: if that person were not tested and did not know that he or she were HIV-positive, the odds are good that that person would take someone else's life unknowingly through continued sexual activity. So, even in this case, informing and counseling the individual are preferable to allowing that person to remain ignorant and perhaps infect not one but many others, thereby sentencing them to death.

Contact tracing is of no value, requires too much manpower, and violates privacy.

Contact tracing is *always* voluntary. A patient must be willing to identify sexual partners for it to be successful. When the public health department performs contact tracing, it contacts the sexual partner without giving him or her the name of the person involved. Instead, health officials say, "It has come to our attention that you have been exposed to the AIDS virus and it is important that you be tested in order to determine whether you have become infected." It is true that if the individual has had only one sexual partner in his or her entire life he or she will be able to deduce who the person was. Since this is the exception rather than the general rule, and since the incubation period of this disease might go back a decade or more, in most cases it would be very difficult to identify the other individual involved.

Under what circumstances could required testing be instituted, and what rationale would justify implementing this system?

Hospital admission is an important opportunity for mandatory or required testing. In order to give the best care to a patient who is HIV-positive, a physician must know the patient's antibody status. A physician would treat a post-operative infection or any other infection far more aggressively with antibiotics in a patient that the physician knew to be HIV-positive than in one who did not have the potential for immune system compromise. Anyone admitted with an infection would be watched more closely if HIV-positive and would probably be treated earlier than someone whose immune system was more dependable.

Many argue that the doctor should use his or her discretion on whom to test. I argue that that feeds into a discriminatory bias suggesting that one can prejudge who might be suspiciously gay. There are no indicators in the healthy HIV-positive person to cause a physician to suspect which person needs testing.

One case history was particularly convincing that physicians need the test to help make a proper diagnosis. A woman called a television program in San Francisco. She said that she had AIDS. Several months before, she had flown to San Diego to donate blood for her mother's elective surgery. Subsequently, she returned to San Francisco, had several additional sexual partners, and eventually was admitted to San Francisco General Hospital for acute respiratory distress. She was treated for allergies and asthma but almost died. During the time that she was in the hospital, she received a letter from the blood bank informing her that her blood had tested HIV-positive. She asked her roommate to open the letter. The doctors then made the diagnosis of Pneumocystis pneumonia, treated her, and she was discharged from the hospital a few days later.

San Francisco General is one of the hospitals that has the most experience in diagnosing and dealing with the AIDS virus. They missed this diagnosis and might not have made it without the aid of the mandatory AIDS test performed by the blood bank. The patient would have died without a change in treatment approach. It seems to me that if such a sophisticated treatment center can miss the diagnosis it would be common in less experienced hospitals. Physicians need the assistance of this kind of testing to guide them.

This also pertains to mental hospital admissions. AIDS dementia and central nervous system infection are proving to be more common than uncommon. Some researchers believe that over 90 percent of those infected manifest some degree of central nervous system involvement. Most psychologists and psychiatrists would still not suspect organic disease due to AIDS when a patient manifests acute or chronic depression, psychoses, schizophrenia, sociopathy, or aggressive or violent behavior. The virus can infect any part of the brain and, depending upon the location of infection, the resultant behavioral changes can be quite varied.

Should HIV testing be required for any special jobs?

Another challenging aspect of HIV infection not yet confronted by our society is the otherwise asymptomatic individual who has extensive central nervous system or brain infection causing impaired judgment and interference with fine motor coordination. Pilots, air traffic controllers, and those in similar professions could be affected. Testing for the AIDS virus under these circumstances is common sense, not discrimination.

Mandatory or routine testing has been suggested for many other situations and occupations. Testing is already common in the military, prisons, and during immigration. Other situations becoming more common opportunities for testing are during prenatal examinations and in substance abuse programs. Other situations being heatedly debated are premarital testing and testing for food handlers, teachers, health care workers, and business travelers. . . .

Having reviewed the common arguments against mandatory or required testing, we have only to devise methods that will alleviate the concerns of those who oppose mandatory testing. The two greatest obstacles are concerns about confidentiality and fear of quarantine. Everything possible must be done to improve the security of our record-keeping systems. Simultaneously, society must be taught that everyone who is ill deserves our compassion, care, and respect, regardless of the source of infection.

The issue of testing must be separated from the issue of quarantine. We have tested and reported people with AIDS to the public health department for many years, and there has been no hint of quarantining unless violent or aggressive behavior put others in danger. The issue of quarantining is independent, but related, and should be fought on a different front.

Mandatory, or preferably "required," testing under certain circumstances incorporates all the virtues of voluntary testing without the drawbacks. We do not now have widespread compliance with voluntary testing. Many individuals still prefer not to know. If only one person's health were at stake, this privilege could persist. However, the ostrich approach has never demonstrated itself to be of much value. In order to deal with reality, one must face it. Self-responsibility and responsibility to others require it.

There would be widespread voluntary compliance with required testing just as there is for blood counts and tuberculin tests once it becomes widely recognized as a matter of common sense for health—for the benefit of every individual—and not an issue of coercion.

Voluntary testing is ideal but unrealistic in many situations. Required testing under certain circumstances is best for all concerned if handled with confidentiality and consideration. Routine testing in other circumstances will naturally evolve out of the preceding two. Should these trends materialize, being tested for AIDS will become a way of life. The challenge then becomes how to preserve the quality of life for everyone—the healthy and the ill.

48. *Schaill v. Tippecanoe School Corporation*

Court of Appeals of the United States

The issue before the United States Court of Appeals was whether a random urinalysis program at a school operated by the Tippecanoe County School Corporation violated the right of student athletes not to be subject to unreasonable searches and seizures under the Fourth Amendment. The court argued that the urinalysis program was a search and seizure under the Fourth Amendment, but that it was justified because a standard of reasonableness rather than "probable cause" is all that has to be met by such a program. In this case, the court claimed that this standard was met because, among other things, there is a much diminished expectation of privacy in interscholastic athletics.

The essential facts of this case are undisputed, and can be stated quite briefly. TSC operates Harrison and McCutcheon High Schools in Indiana. In the spring of 1986, based on information concerning possible drug use by athletes on the McCutcheon High School baseball team, the team's coach ordered sixteen team members to provide urine samples. Of the sixteen students tested, five students' tests produced positive results for the presence of marijuana. Based on these results, other reports of drug use among participants in the TSC athletic program, and their concern over the high incidence of drug abuse among high school students nationwide, the board of trustees of TSC decided to institute a random urine testing program for interscholastic athletes and cheerleaders in the TSC school system.

Under the program, all students desiring to participate in interscholastic athletics and their parent or guardian are required to sign a consent form agreeing to submit to urinalysis if chosen on a random basis. Each student selected for an athletic team is assigned a number. The athletic director and head coach of each athletic team are authorized to institute random urine tests during the athletic season. In order to select individuals to be tested, the number assigned to each athlete is placed in a box, and a single number is drawn.

The student selected for testing is accompanied by a school official of the same sex to a bathroom, where the student is provided with an empty specimen bottle. The student is then allowed to enter a lavatory stall and close the door in order to produce a sample. The student is not under direct visual observation while producing the sample; however, the water in the toilet is tinted to prevent the student from substituting water for the sample, the monitor stands outside the stall to listen for normal sounds of urination and the monitor checks the temperature of the sample by hand in order to assure its genuineness.

The chain of custody of the sample is designed to insure the accuracy and anonymity of the testing procedure. The sample is sent to a private testing laboratory, where it is initially tested for the presence of controlled substances or performance-enhancing drugs using the enzyme multiplied immunoassay technique ("EMIT"). Any sample which tests positive is then retested using the more accurate, and more expensive, gas chromatography/mass spectrometry ("GC/MS") method.

If a sample tests positive under both the EMIT and GC/MS analyses, the student and his or her parent or guardian are informed of the results. They then have the opportunity to have the remaining portion of the sample tested at a laboratory of their choice. The student and his or her parent or guardian may also present the athletic director with any evidence which suggests an innocent explanation for the positive result, such as the fact that the athlete legally takes prescription or over-the-counter medication.

Barring a satisfactory explanation, the student is then suspended from participation in a portion of the varsity competitions held during the athletic season. A first positive urinalysis test results in a suspension from 30% of the athletic contests, a second positive results in a 50% suspension, a third positive causes a suspension for a full calendar year and a fourth positive results in the student's being barred from all interscholastic athletic competitions during the remainder of the student's high school career. No other penalties are imposed, and a student may decrease the specified punishment by participating in an approved drug counselling program.

In the spring of 1987, appellants Darcy Schaill and Shelley Johnson were 15-year-old sophomores at Harrison High School. Shelley had been a member of the varsity swim team as a freshman. Both appellants attended an organizational meeting for students desiring to participate in interscholastic athletics in the fall of 1987, at which time they were first informed of the proposed implementation of the TSC urinalysis program. Both appellants were offended by the thought of having to undergo urinalysis as a condition of participation in interscholastic athletics, and both decided that they would forego the opportunity to compete in interscholastic athletics if required to sign a form consenting to random urine testing. . . .

As a threshold matter, we must consider whether TSC's random urine testing program involves a "search" as that term is employed in the fourth amendment. The Supreme Court has held that "[a] 'search' occurs when an expectation of privacy that society is prepared to consider reasonable is infringed." . . .

There can be little doubt that a person engaging in the act of urination possesses a reasonable expectation of privacy as to that act, and as to the urine which is excreted. In our society, it is expected that urination be performed in private, that urine be disposed of in private and that the act, if mentioned at all, be described in euphemistic terms. . . .

The fact that urine is voluntarily discharged from the body and treated as a waste product does not eliminate the expectation of privacy which an individual possesses in his or her urine. While urine is excreted from the body, it is not "knowingly expose[d] to the public," . . . ; instead, the highly private manner by which an individual disposes of his or her urine demonstrates that it is not intended to be inspected or examined by anyone. . . .

Having determined that urine testing constitutes a "search" in the constitutional sense, we must consider what level of suspicion is required to authorize urinalysis of any particular student. Appellants first argue that individual student's urine may not be tested unless TSC officials have probable cause to believe that the particular student has consumed the drugs which the test is designed to detect, and have obtained a warrant authorizing the test from a neutral and detached judicial officer.

Determining the level of suspicion required before the government may conduct a search requires "balanc[ing] the nature and quality of the intrusion on the individual's Fourth Amendment interests against the importance of the governmental interests alleged to justify the intrusion." . . . Unfortunately for appellants, we believe that the Supreme Court has already struck the appropriate balance in the context of school searches, and has determined that the probable cause and warrant requirements do not apply. . . .

In the present case, TSC plans to conduct a search not only without probable cause or a warrant, but in the absence of any individualized suspicion of drug use by the students to be tested. In these circumstances, TSC bears a heavier burden to justify its contemplated actions. In a criminal law enforcement context, the Supreme Court has been extremely hesitant to condone searches performed without any articulable basis for suspecting the particular individual of unlawful conduct. However, in several carefully defined situations, the Court has recognized that searches may be conducted in the absence of any grounds to believe that the individual searched has violated the law. The Court has stressed that "[i]n those situations in which the balance of interests precludes insistence upon 'some quantum of individualized suspicion,' other safeguards are generally relied upon to assure that the individual's reasonable expectation of privacy is not 'subject to the discretion of the officer in the field.' " . . .

In general, there is a substantial expectation of privacy in connection with the act of urination. However, the privacy considerations are somewhat mitigated on the facts before us because the provider of the urine sample enters a closed lavatory stall and the person monitoring the urination stands outside listening for the sounds appropriate to what is taking place. The invasion of privacy is therefore not nearly as severe as would be the case if the monitor were required to observe the subject in the act of urination.

We also find great significance in the fact that the drug testing program in this case is being implemented solely with regard to participants in an interscholastic athletic program. In the first place, in athletic programs in general there is a much diminished expectation of privacy and, in particular, privacy with respect to urinalysis. There is an element of "communal undress" inherent in athletic participation, which suggests reduced expectations of privacy. In addition, physical examinations are integral to almost all athletic programs. In fact, athletes and cheerleaders desiring to participate in the TSC athletic program have long been required to produce a urine sample as part of a mandatory medical examination. This sample is not produced under monitored conditions, is only tested for the presence of sugar in the urine and is given to the athlete's physician of choice rather than a school official; however, the fact that such samples are required suggests that legitimate expectations of privacy in this context are diminished.

Further, in the case before us, we are dealing with *interscholastic* athletics. In these programs the Indiana High School Athletic Association has extensive requirements which it imposes upon schools and individuals participating in interscholastic athletics. These include minimum grade, residency and eligibility requirements. In addition to IHSAA regulations, participants in interscholastic athletics are also subject to training rules, including prohibitions on smoking, drinking and drug use both on and off school premises.

Perhaps even more demonstrative of the special characteristics of athletics is the high visibility and pervasiveness of drug testing in professional and collegiate athletics in this country and in the Olympic Games. The suspension and disqualification of prominent athletes on the basis of positive urinalysis results has been the subject of intense publicity all over the world. . . .

The combination of these factors makes it quite implausible that students competing for positions on an interscholastic athletic team would have strong expectations of privacy with respect to urine tests. We can, of course, appreciate that monitored collection and subsequent testing of urine samples may be distasteful (although plaintiffs' subjective evidence on this point was not powerful), but such procedures can hardly come as a great shock or surprise under present-day circumstances. For this reason, we believe that sports are quite distinguishable from almost any other activity. Random testing of athletes does not necessarily imply random testing of band members or the chess team. . . .

The convergence of several important factors convinces us that the searches involved here take place in one of the relatively unusual environments in which suspicionless searches are permissible: interscholastic athletes have diminished expectations of privacy, and have voluntarily chosen to participate in an activity which subjects them to pervasive regulation of off-campus behavior; the school's interest in preserving a drug-free athletic program is substantial, and cannot adequately be furthered by less intrusive measures; the TSC program adequately limits the discretion of the officials performing the search; and the information sought is intended to be used solely for noncriminal educational and rehabilitative purposes. Based on a careful and considered weighing of these factors, we conclude that the TSC urinalysis program does not violate the fourth amendment. . . .

Appellants' final contention is that the procedures provided in the TSC program for a student to challenge a positive urinalysis test are insufficient under the due process clause of the fourteenth amendment. . . .

Appellants fault the TSC program for placing on the student the burden of proving that the twice-confirmed test result is erroneous, for requiring the student to hire his own toxicologist or testing laboratory to conduct a further evaluation of the TSC urine test and for allowing the athletic director, who was personally involved in the collection, labeling and storage of the initial sample, to serve as the adjudicator of the student's claim that the initial result was erroneous.

There was evidence before the district court indicating that TSC's urine testing program, which requires confirmation of any positive result using the gas chromatography/mass spectrometry method, would produce results with a 95% confidence level. Based on this evidence, the district court concluded that the "possible pitfalls involved in EMIT screening have been avoided, as much as possible, by [GC/MS] followup." . . . Given the high degree of accuracy inhering in TSC's testing procedures, we cannot conclude that the school system has violated the due process clause by placing the burden to disprove a confirmed positive result on the student. Further, after providing a confirmatory test using the most accurate technology available at no cost to the student, TSC cannot be faulted for requiring a student to bear the cost of any further testing which the student may desire to perform. . . .

In our consideration and decision of this case, we have been mindful of the Supreme Court's admonition that public school students "do not shed their constitutional rights . . . at the schoolhouse gate." . . . We are also cognizant of the trenchant observation of Justice Jackson: "That [schools] are educating the young for citizenship is reason for scrupulous protection of Constitutional freedoms of the individual, if we are not to strangle the free mind at its source and teach youth to discount important principles of our government as mere platitudes." . . .

However, we recognize that, if students are to be educated at all, an environment conducive to learning must be maintained. The plague of illicit drug use which currently threatens our nation's schools adds a major dimension to the difficulties the schools face in fulfilling their purpose—the education of our children. If the schools are to survive and prosper, school administrators must have reasonable means at their disposal to deter conduct which substantially disrupts the school environment. In this case, we believe that the Tippecanoe County School Corporation has chosen a reasonable and limited response to a serious evil. In formulating its urinalysis program, the school district has been sensitive to the privacy rights of its students, and has sought to emphasize rehabilitation over punishment. We cannot conclude that this approach is inconsistent with the mandates of the Constitution. The judgment of the district court is therefore
Affirmed.

---

49. *Chalk v. U.S. District Court of California*

United States Court of Appeals

The issue before the U.S. Court of Appeals was whether a preliminary injunction to preserve the status quo should be granted to Vincent Chalk who because he was diagnosed as having AIDS was being relieved of has classroom duties and reassigned to an administrative position. The Court ruled that the District Court had erred in failing to grant Chalk a preliminary injunction.

The Court judged that Chalk had submitted ample evidence that he would pose no appreciable risk of transmitting the AIDS virus to his students. The Court also judged that he would suffer irreparable loss if he were reassigned to administrative duties.

Petitioner Vincent L. Chalk is a certified teacher of hearing-impaired students in the Orange County Department of Education. In February of 1987, Chalk was diagnosed as having Acquired Immune Deficiency Syndrome (AIDS). Subsequently, the Department reassigned Chalk to an administrative position and barred him from teaching in the classroom. Chalk then filed this action in the district court, claiming that the Department's action violated § 504 of the Rehabilitation Act of 1973, . . . which proscribes recipients of federal funds from discriminating against otherwise qualified handicapped persons.

Chalk's motion for a preliminary injunction ordering his reinstatement was denied by the district court, and Chalk brought this appeal.
. . .

Petitioner Chalk has been teaching hearing-impaired students in the Orange County schools for approximately six years. In February 1987, Chalk was hospitalized with pneumocystis carinii pneumonia and was diagnosed as having AIDS. On April 20, after eight weeks of treatment and recuperation, he was found fit for duty and released to return to work by his personal physician, Dr. Andrew Siskind. The Department, however, placed him on administrative leave pending the opinion of Dr. Thomas J. Prendergast, the Director of Epidemiology and Disease Control for the Orange County Health Care Agency. On May 22, Dr. Prendergast informed the Department that "[n]othing in his [Chalk's] role as a teacher should place his students or others in the school at any risk of acquiring HIV infection."

Chalk agreed to remain on administrative leave through the end of the school year in June. On August 5, Chalk and representatives of the Department met to discuss his return to the classroom. The Department offered Chalk an administrative position at the same rate of pay and benefits, with the option of working either at the Department's offices or at his home, and informed him that if he insisted on returning to the classroom, it would file an action for declaratory relief. Chalk refused the offer. On August 6, the Department filed an action in the Orange County Superior Court, and Chalk filed this action in the district court seeking a preliminary and permanent injunc-

tion barring the Department from excluding him from classroom duties. . . .

Chalk submitted in evidence to the district court, and that court accepted, more than 100 articles from prestigious medical journals and the declarations of five experts on AIDS, including two public health officials of Los Angeles County. Those submissions reveal an overwhelming evidentiary consensus of medical and scientific opinion regarding the nature and transmission of AIDS. AIDS is caused by infection of the individual with HIV, a retrovirus that penetrates chromosomes of certain human cells that combat infection throughout the body. Individuals who become infected with HIV may remain without symptoms for an extended period of time. When the disease takes hold, however, a number of symptoms can occur, including swollen lymph nodes, fever, weight loss, fatigue and night sweats. Eventually, the virus destroys its host cells, thereby weakening the victim's immune system. When the immune system is in a compromised state, the victim becomes susceptible to a variety of so-called "opportunistic infections," many of which can prove fatal.

Transmission of HIV is known to occur in three ways: (1) through intimate sexual contact with an infected person; (2) through invasive exposure to contaminated blood or certain other bodily fluids; or (3) through perinatal exposure (i.e., from mother to infant). Although HIV has been isolated in several body fluids, epidemiologic evidence has implicated only blood, semen, vaginal secretions, and possibly breast milk in transmission. Extensive and numerous studies have consistently found no apparent risk of HIV infection to individuals exposed through close, non-sexual contact with AIDS patients.

Based on the accumulated body of medical evidence, the Surgeon General of the United States has concluded:

> There is no known risk of non-sexual infection in most of the situations we encounter in our daily lives. We know that family members living with individuals who have the AIDS virus do not become infected except through sexual contact. There is

no evidence of transmission (spread) of AIDS virus by everyday contact even though these family members shared food, towels, cups, razors, even toothbrushes, and kissed each other. . . .

The Surgeon General also specifically addressed the risk of transmission in the classroom setting:

None of the identified cases of AIDS in the United States is known or is suspected to have been transmitted from one child to another in school, day care or foster care settings. Transmission would necessitate exposure of open cuts to the blood or other body fluids of the infected child, a highly unlikely occurrence. Even then, routine safety procedures for handling blood or other body fluids . . . would be effective in preventing transmission from children with AIDS to other children in school. . . .

Casual social contact between children and persons infected with the AIDS virus is not dangerous.

. . . These conclusions are echoed by such medical authorities as the United States Centers for Disease Control, the American Medical Association and the Institute of Medicine of the National Academy of Sciences. In its *amicus* brief in support of Chalk's appeal, the American Medical Association summarized the medical evidence and concluded that "there is *no* evidence in the relevant medical literature that demonstrates any appreciable risk of transmitting the AIDS virus under the circumstances likely to occur in the ordinary school setting." . . .

The only opposing medical opinion submitted by the Department was that of one witness, Dr. Steven Armentrout, that "there is a probability, small though it is, that there are vectors of transmission as yet not clearly defined." . . . He elaborated on his opinion as follows:

I believe, sincerely believe that there is a significant, and significant here—it's significant even though it's small, potential

for transmission of AIDS in ways which we have not yet determined and, therefore, may pose a risk . . . If they don't occur now, it is my firm belief that with the almost inevitable mutation of the virus, they will occur. And when that does occur, they certainly could be—there can be a potential threat.

. . . Asked whether there was a scientific basis for such a hypothesis, Dr. Armentrout indicated that he had "no scientific evidence that would enable me to answer that or to have an opinion. . . . What we're saying is that we haven't proved scientifically a vector." . . .

The district judge addressed each of the four *Arline* factors in his ruling. He found that the duration of the risk was long and the severity was "catastrophic," but that scientifically established methods of transmission were unlikely to occur and that the probability of harm was minimal. . . . He therefore concluded that Chalk "may very well win ultimately." . . . Nonetheless, the district judge expressed skepticism about the current state of medical knowledge. He was troubled that there might be something yet unknown to science that might do harm. He said:

Now, here, according to present knowledge, the risk probably is not great because of the limited ways that medical science believes the disease is transmitted. But, of course, if it is transmitted the result is horrendous.

It seems to me the problem is that we simply do not know enough about AIDS to be *completely certain*. The plaintiff has submitted massive documentation tending to show a minimal risk. . . . But in any event, the risk is small—risk of infection through casual contact. . . . The incubation period is reported to be seven years. We have been studying this only for six. And I do not in any sense mean to be an alarmist. I—I reiterate, I think the risk is small. The likelihood is that the medical profession knows exactly what it's talking about. But I think it's too early to draw a definite conclusion, as far as this case is concerned, about the extent of the risk. . . .

This language demonstrates that the district court failed to follow the legal standards set forth in *Arline* and improperly placed an impossible burden of proof on the petitioner. Little in science can be proved with complete certainty, and section 504 does not require such a test. As authoritatively construed by the Supreme Court, section 504 allows the exclusion of an employee only if there is "a *significant* risk of communicating an infectious disease to others." . . . In addition, *Arline* admonishes courts that they "should defer to the reasonable medical judgments of public health officials." . . . The district judge ignored these admonitions. Instead, he rejected the overwhelming consensus of medical opinion and improperly relied on speculation for which there was no credible support in the record.

That Chalk demonstrates a strong probability of success on the merits is supported by the three published opinions brought to our attention dealing with AIDS discrimination under section 504. In *Thomas v. Atascadero Unified School Dist.,* . . . the court granted a preliminary injunction prohibiting the school district from excluding a child with AIDS from the classroom, despite the child's involvement in a biting incident. The court found that:

> The overwhelming weight of medical evidence is that the AIDS virus is not transmitted by human bites, even bites that break the skin. Based upon the abundant medical and scientific evidence before the Court, Ryan poses no risk of harm to his classmates and teachers. Any theoretical risk of transmission of the AIDS virus by Ryan in connection with his attendance in regular kindergarten class is so remote that it cannot form the basis for any exclusionary action by the School District. . . .

In *Ray v. School Dist. of DeSoto County,* . . . the court followed *Thomas* and granted a preliminary injunction prohibiting the district from excluding three seropositive brothers from the classroom. The court rejected the "future theoretical harm" of transmission of the AIDS virus in the classroom as unsupported by the weight of medical evidence.

. . . Significantly, Dr. Armentrout was one of two doctors who testified for the defendants in *Ray,* . . . and his opinion was implicitly rejected.

The third case, *District 27 Community School Bd. v. Board of Educ.,* . . . concerned the New York City Board of Education's policy of determining on a case-by-case basis whether the health and development of children with AIDS permitted them to attend school in an unrestricted setting. Two school districts challenged the policy, seeking an injunction prohibiting the Board from admitting any child with AIDS into the classroom. After a five-week trial, the court unheld the policy in an exhaustive opinion. One of the central conclusions was that the transmission of the AIDS virus in the classroom setting was "a mere theoretical possibility" and that exclusion of AIDS victims on that basis would violate section 504. . . .

Plaintiff's position is also supported by *New York State Ass'n of Retarded Children v. Carey,* . . . in which the Second Circuit affirmed a district court ruling that the segregation of carriers of hepatitis B by the New York City Board of Education violated section 504. The court said:

> [T]he Board was unable to demonstrate that the health hazard posed by the hepatitis B carrier children was anything more than a remote possibility. There has never been any definite proof that the disease can be communicated by nonparenteral routes such as saliva. Even assuming there were, the activities that occur in classroom settings were not shown to pose any significant risk that the disease would be transmitted from one child to another.

. . . Chalk presented evidence to the district court here that hepatitis B and AIDS are tramsmitted in similar ways, but that hepatitis B is transmitted much more easily. . . .

Viewing Chalk's submissions in light of these cases, it is clear that he has amply demonstrated a strong probability of success on the merits. We hold that it was error to require that every theoretical possibility of harm be disproved.

Irreparable Injury

Having demonstrated a strong probability of success on the merits, Chalk next had to demonstrate that he was threatened with the possibility of irreparable injury. . . . The district court held that Chalk's proof on this element was insufficient:

> I cannot conclude that there is any irreparable injury to plaintiff if he must wait pending trial. He has a job offered and he can do that job until we can determine by medical testimony the extent of the risk and whether or not it's justified for the court to order the school board to put this man back in the classroom. But I cannot—I simply cannot do it on the basis of the present record. . . .

We believe this determination was clearly erroneous. In making its finding, the court focused on the momentary loss to Chalk and concluded that he was no worse off than before the reassignment. This approach failed to consider the nature of the alternative work offered Chalk. Chalk's original employment was teaching hearing-impaired children in a small-classroom setting, a job for which he developed special skills beyond those normally required to become a teacher. His closeness to his students and his participation in their lives is a source of tremendous personal satisfaction and joy to him and of benefit to them. The alternative work to which he is now assigned is preparing grant proposals. This job is "distasteful" to Chalk, involves no student contact, and does not utilize his skills, training or experience. Such nonmonetary deprivation is a substantial injury which the court was required to consider. . . .

Several cases support petitioner's claim that his non-monetary deprivation is irreparable. The most striking parallel is *E.E.O.C. v. Chrysler Corp.,* . . . where the court granted a preliminary injunction ordering reinstatement of employees terminated in violation of the Age Discrimination in Employment Act. The court acknowledged that the loss of income and its effects were compensable after trial and did not constitute irreparable harm. . . . Nonetheless, irreparable injury was found in the consequent emotional stress, depression and reduced sense of well-being, which constituted "psychological and physiological distress . . . the very type of injury Congress sought to avert." . . .

Chalk's injury here is quite similar, and it likewise falls within the realm of noncompensable injury which Congress contemplated in enacting section 504. As stated by the Supreme Court in *Arline:*

> Congress acknowledged that society's accumulated myths and fears about disability and disease are as handicapping as are the physical limitations that flow from actual impairment. Few aspects of a handicap give rise to the same level of public fear and misapprehension as contagiousness. Even those who suffer or have recovered from such noninfectious diseases as epilepsy or cancer have faced discrimination based on the irrational fear that they might be contagious. The Act is carefully structured to replace such reflexive reactions to actual or perceived handicaps with actions based on reasoned and medically sound judgments. . . .

An additional factor favoring a preliminary injunction here arises from the very nature of Chalk's affliction. Studies and statistics of etiology and terminus of AIDS show that although the time during which such a person may be quick and productive varies, the virus is fatal in all recorded cases. Presently Chalk is fully qualified and able to return to work; but his ability to do so will surely be affected in time. A delay, even if only a few months, pending trial represents precious, productive time irretrievably lost to him.

We therefore conclude that the district court's finding that Chalk had not demonstrated any possibility of irreparable injury was clearly erroneous and must be reversed.

The Balance of Hardships

Having demonstrated a strong probability of success on the merits and the possibility of irreparable injury, Chalk has shown all that is necessary for a preliminary injunction to issue. Nonetheless, we will also briefly address the claimed injury on the part of the Department, since "at least a minimal tip in the balance of hardships must be found even when the strongest showing on the merits is made." . . .

Even under the balance of hardships standard, plaintiff's injury outweighs any harm to the defendant. Defendant's asserted injury is based entirely on the risk to others posed by plaintiff's return to the classroom. As discussed above, this theoretical risk is insufficient to overcome plaintiff's probability of success on the merits, and it is likewise insufficient to outweigh the injury which plaintiff is likely to suffer. . . .

In denying the preliminary injunction, the district court concluded that Chalk's injury was outweighed by the fear that his presence in the classroom was likely to produce:

> The plaintiff desires to teach despite all these circumstances. . . . Counsel has recognized that he doesn't have a constitutional right to do so. On the other hand, he has a statutory right not to be discriminated against. He has a statutory right to go back to the school if he is otherwise qualified.
>
> But I think I have a right—in fact, an obligation to compare on the one hand the trauma on the plaintiff if he is held out from the school for a period of months until we can have a trial in this action. The trauma on him, on the one hand, with the trauma on the children and parents in being required to submit to what they are likely to conclude is an unacceptable risk.*
> . . .

*The district court apparently miscalculated the reaction of at least some of Chalk's students and their parents. The mothers of five of Chalk's students joined amicus Disability Rights Education and Defense Fund in support of Chalk's appeal, and Chalk was greeted with hugs and homemade gifts upon his return to work following our order of November 18.

We recognize that the public interest is one of the traditional equitable criteria which a court should consider in granting injunctive relief. . . . Here, however, there is no evidence of any significant risk to children or others at the school. To allow the court to base its decision on the fear and apprehension of others would frustrate the goals of section 504. "[T]he basic purpose of § 504 [is] to ensure that handicapped individuals are not denied jobs or other benefits because of the prejudiced attitudes or ignorance of others." . . . The Supreme Court recognized in *Arline* that a significant risk of transmission was a legitimate concern which could justify exclusion if the risk could not be eliminated through reasonable accommodation; however, it soundly rejected the argument that exclusion could be justified on the basis of "pernicious mythologies" or "irrational fear." . . .

> The Court recognizes the concern and fear which is flowing from this small community, particularly from the parents of school age children in DeSoto County. However, the Court *may not* be guided by such community fear, parental pressure, and the possibility of lawsuits. "These obstacles, real as they may be, cannot be allowed to vitiate the rights . . ." of [the Ray children]. . . .

Nonetheless, we recognize that the parties and the district court will have to deal with the apprehensions of other members of the school community, as well as with the inexorable progress of Chalk's disease. Although the time frame is unpredictable, given the current state of medical knowledge, the course of petitioner's condition is reasonably certain. Chalk's immune system will deteriorate over time, leaving him increasingly susceptible to opportunistic infections. These infections do not cause AIDS, nor do they increase the risk of transmission of the AIDS virus, but some of them may themselves be communicable to others in a classroom setting. The district court is in the best position, guided by qualified medical opinion, to determine what reasonable procedures, such as periodic reports from petitioner's doctors, will best give assurance to the Department, the community and the court that no significant risk of harm will arise in the future from Chalk's continued presence in the classroom.

Conclusion

We conclude that petitioner met all of the requirements necessary to receive a preliminary injunction. We therefore reverse the district court's order and remand this action with direction to enter a preliminary injunction ordering defendants forthwith to restore petitioner to his former duties as a teacher of hearing-impaired children in the Orange County Department of Education. This panel will retain jurisdiction over any subsequent appeal.

Reversed and remanded

Suggestions for Further Reading

Anthologies

Biskup, Michael, and Swisher, Karins. *AIDS: Opposing Viewpoints*. San Diego: Greenhaven Press, 1992.

Pennock, J. R., and Chapman, J. *Privacy*. New York: Atherton Press, 1971.

Pierce, C., and Van DeVeer, D. *AIDS: Ethics and Public Policy*. Belmont: Wadsworth Publishing Co., 1988.

"What Science Knows About AIDS." *Scientific American*, October, 1988.

Alternative Views

Arthur, J. *The Unfinished Constitution*. Belmont: Wadsworth Publishing Co., 1989.

Hollowell, E., and Eldridge, J. "AIDS and the Insurance Industry." *The Journal of Legal Medicine* (1989), pp. 77–87.

Husak, Douglas. *Drugs and Rights*. Cambridge: Cambridge University Press, 1992.

Oppenheimer, G., and Padgug, R. "AIDS: The Risks to Insurers, the Threat to Equity." *Hastings Center Report* (1986), pp. 18–22.

Research Triangle Institute. *Economic Costs to Society of Alcohol and Drug Abuse*. Research Triangle Park, N.C., 1984.

Rubenfeld, J. "The Right to Privacy." *Harvard Law Review* (1989), pp. 737–807.

Winston, M. "AIDS, Confidentiality and the Right to Know." *Public Affairs Quarterly* (1988), pp. 91–104.

Practical Applications

Boggan, C. *The Rights of Gay People: The Basic ACLU Guide to a Gay Person's Rights*. New York: Avon, 1975.

Gay and Lesbian Rights

Introduction

Basic Concepts

Prohibitions against homosexuality have ancient roots, but the enforcement of such prohibitions has most always been haphazard at best. This is because when one is dealing with acts between consenting adults, it can be difficult to find a complainant. Even so, twenty-four states and the District of Columbia still have statutes on the books prohibiting homosexual acts. Penalties range from three months in prison or one year's probation to life imprisonment.

Moreover, what these statutes prohibit is sodomy, which involves more than just homosexual acts. For example, the Georgia statute whose constitutionality was upheld by the Supreme Court in *Bowers v. Hardwick* (see Selection 54) holds that "a person commits the offense of sodomy when he performs or submits to any sexual act involving the sex organs of one person and the mouth or anus of another." The reason why sodomy is defined so broadly here is that the main complaint against homosexual acts—that they are unnatural—also applies to a range of other acts. More specifically, the complaint applies to oral and anal intercourse between heterosexuals, masturbation, and bestiality, as well as homosexual acts.

Now it is important to understand what is considered unnatural about these acts. One sense of *natural* refers to what is found in nature as contrasted with what is artificial or the product of human artifice. In this sense, homosexuality would seem to be natural because it is found in virtually every human society. But even if homosexuality is understood to be a product of a certain type of upbringing or socialization and hence artificial, that would hardly seem to be grounds for condemning it, because a great deal of human behavior has a similar origin.

Another sense of natural refers to what is common or statistically normal as contrasted with what is uncommon or statistically abnormal. In this sense, homosexuality would not be natural because most people are not homosexuals, despite the fact that according to one study about half of all American males have engaged in homosexual acts at some time of their lives. But being unnatural in this sense could not be grounds for condemning homosexuality because many traits we most value in people are also statistically abnormal and, hence, unnatural in this sense.

Still another sense of natural refers to a thing's proper function, and it is this sense of natural that is frequently used to condemn homosexuality. Because if we maintain that the proper function of human sexual organs is simply procreation, then any use of those organs for a purpose other than procreation would be unnatural. Hence, homosexuality, contraception, masturbation, and bestiality would all be unnatural. But clearly the proper function of human sexual organs is not limited to procreation. These organs are also used to express love and to provide pleasure for oneself and others. Given that our sexual organs can be properly used for these other purposes, we would need to argue that every use of these organs must serve their procreative function in order to be able to condemn homosexuality. But no nontheologically based argument has succeeded in establishing this conclusion.* Moreover, once we grant that, for example, contraception and masturbation can be morally permissible, there seems to be no ground left, based on the proper functioning of our sexual organs, for denying that homosexuality can be morally permissible as well.

Alternative Views

Michael Levin argues that homosexuality is abnormal on the grounds that it is a misuse of bodily parts because the penis and the vagina are made for each other (Selection 50). To misuse either of these bodily parts, Levin claims, is likely to lead to unhappiness. For that reason, he argues that homosexuals can be legally restricted in order to reduce the incidence of homosexuality.

In Selection 51, Timothy F. Murphy directly challenges Levin's argument against homosexuality. Murphy argues that even if a

*Clearly if there is to be freedom of religion, a nontheologically based argument is needed here.

particular use of our sexual organs leads to adaptive success, it doesn't follow that we are bound to pursue that success. He further argues that even adaptive success itself is compatible with a minority's pursuit of beneficial departures from the natural adaptive order. As for Levin's concern about the unhappiness suffered by homosexuals, Murphy contends that we could reduce that unhappiness simply by removing the social and legal restrictions that we impose on homosexuals.

Another argument against homosexuality that does not depend on characterizing it as unnatural or abnormal is developed by Paul Cameron in Selection 52. Cameron begins with the assumption that human sexuality is totally learned. According to Cameron, homosexuality and heterosexuality are equally the products of socialization. Cameron further argues that there are a number of factors favoring the adoption of homosexuality: (1) the extreme homosociality of children starting around age five, (2) the greater attraction males have for sex than females, (3) the superiority of homosexual sex as sex, and (4) the self-servingness/egocentricity of the young. Cameron argues that we need to overcome these factors because heterosexuality leads to more permanent social relationships, greater altruism, and more social cohesion than homosexuality.

Yet although the social problems that Cameron focuses on are real enough, these problems can be combated without criminalizing homosexuality. First, homosexuals would probably form more permanent social relationships among themselves if they were not denied the social and legal means for maintaining such relationships. Second, the extreme homosociality of children can be effectively combated by providing the same socialization for girls and boys. Third, the egocentricity of the young, which manifests itself not in harming but simply in failing to benefit others, is probably best combated with positive altruistic ideals rather than threatened criminalization, except where the basic needs of others are at stake.

In Selection 53, Richard D. Mohr surveys various ways in which homosexuals are discriminated against in our society. Mohr cites one study in which 90 percent of gays and lesbians report that they have been victimized because of their sexual orientation. In opposition to Cameron, Mohr argues that being gay or lesbian is not a matter of choice, making it difficult, if not impossible to change one's sexual orientation. Obviously then, what sodomy statutes demand of homosexuals is that they not act as they are. A difficult charge indeed! Moreover, it is a charge that does not appear to be supported by a defensible account of what is wrong with homosexual behavior.

Practical Application

The most recent Supreme Court case dealing with homosexuality is *Bowers v. Hardwick* (1986). In this case, the issue before the Supreme Court was whether the Georgia sodomy statute violates the federal Constitution. In delivering the opinion of the court, Justice White argues that the statute does not violate the Constitution because the Constitution does not confer a fundamental right on homosexuals to engage in sodomy. While in previous cases, the Constitution was interpreted to confer a right to decide whether or not to beget or bear a child and a right not to be convicted for possessing and reading obscene material in the privacy of one's home, White argues that the Constitution cannot analogously be interpreted to confer a fundamental right on homosexuals to engage in sodomy. Justice Burger concurs, stressing the ancient roots of sodomy statutes. Justice Blackmun, joined by Justices Brennan and Marshall, argues that notwithstanding the ancient roots of prohibitions against homosexuality, a right to be let alone that is the underpinning of previous court decisions justifies in this case a right to engage in sodomy at least in the privacy of one's home.

In this case, the majority of the Supreme Court seem to reach their conclusion by interpreting previous decisions in an excessively literal manner in much the same way that the majority of the court ruled in *Olmstead v. United States* (1928) that warrantless wiretapping did not violate the Fourth Amendment prohibitions against search and seizure because the framers of the amendment were not explicitly prohibiting this method of obtaining incriminating evidence. One can only hope that just as the Supreme Court later repudiated it decision in *Olmstead v. United States*, the Supreme Court will someday return to the issue of the criminalization of homosexuality and address the relevant privacy concern it raises.

In Selection 55, Ken Corbett tries to explain the fear and hatred that was expressed regarding ending the ban against gays and lesbians in the military. He contends that the fear that some men express is the fear of being desired in the way most men feel only a woman should be desired—as a sexual object. Does this suggest that being desired as a sexual object is not so great after all?

It is also important to note that adherents of all three of our political ideals generally tend to favor granting homosexuals the same rights as heterosexuals. Libertarians favor this view because to do otherwise would deny homosexuals important basic liberties. Welfare liberals favor this view because to do otherwise would deny homosexuals fundamental fairness. Socialists favor this view because to do otherwise would deny homosexuals basic equality.

50. Homosexuality Is Abnormal

Michael Levin

Michael Levin argues that homosexuality is abnormal because it is a misuse of bodily parts. He further argues that homosexuality is likely to lead to unhappiness, and, for that reason, he contends that homosexuals can be legally restricted to reduce the incidence of homosexuality.

Introduction

This paper defends the view that homosexuality is abnormal and hence undesirable—not because it is immoral or sinful, or because it weakens society or hampers evolutionary development, but for a purely mechanical reason. It is a misuse of bodily parts. Clear empirical sense attaches to the idea of *the use* of such bodily parts as genitals, the idea that they are *for* something, and consequently to the idea of their misuse. I argue on grounds involving natural selection that misuse of bodily parts can with high probability be connected to unhappiness. I regard these matters as prolegomena to such policy issues as the rights of homosexuals, the rights of those desiring not to associate with homosexuals, and legislation

From "Why Homosexuality Is Abnormal" (1984), *The Monist.* © 1984, *The Monist,* La Salle, Illinois 61301. Reprinted by permission.

concerning homosexuality, issues which I shall not discuss systematically here. However, I do in the last section draw a seemingly evident corollary from my view that homosexuality is abnormal and likely to lead to unhappiness. . . .

Despite the publicity currently enjoyed by the claim that one's "sexual preference" is nobody's business but one's own, the intuition that there is something unnatural about homosexuality remains vital. The erect penis fits the vagina, and fits it better than any other natural orifice; penis and vagina seem made for each other. This intuition ultimately derives from, or is another way of capturing, the idea that the penis is not *for* inserting into the anus of another man—that so using the penis is not the way it is *supposed,* even *intended,* to be used. Such intuitions may appear to rest on an outmoded teleological view of nature, but recent work in the logic of functional ascription shows how they may be explicated, and justified, in suitably naturalistic terms. . . .

On "Function" and Its Cognates

To bring into relief the point of the idea that homosexuality involves a misuse of bodily parts, I will begin with an uncontroversial case of misuse, a case in which the clarity of our intuitions is not obscured by the conviction that they are untrustworthy. Mr. Jones pulls all his teeth and strings them around his neck because he thinks his teeth look nice as a necklace. He takes puréed liquids supplemented by intravenous solutions for nourishment. It is surely natural to say that Jones is misusing his teeth, that he is not using them for what they are for, that indeed the way he is using them is incompatible with what they are for. Pedants might argue that Jones's teeth are no longer part of him and hence that he is not misusing any bodily parts. To them I offer Mr. Smith, who likes to play "Old MacDonald" on his teeth. So devoted is he to this amusement, in fact, that he never uses his teeth for chewing—like Jones, he takes nourishment intravenously. Now, not only do we find it perfectly plain that Smith and Jones are misusing their teeth, we predict a dim future for them on purely physiological grounds; we expect the muscles of Jones's jaw that are used for—that *are* for—chewing to lose their tone, and we expect this to affect Jones's gums. Those parts of Jones's digestive tract that are for processing solids will also suffer from disuse. The net result will be deteriorating health and perhaps a shortened life. Nor is this all. Human beings enjoy chewing. Not only has natural selection selected in muscles for chewing and favored creatures with such muscles, it has selected a tendency to find the use of those muscles reinforcing. Creatures who do not enjoy using such parts of their bodies as deteriorate with disuse, will tend to be selected out. Jones, product of natural selection that he is, descended from creatures who at least tended to enjoy the use of such parts. Competitors who didn't simply had fewer descendants. So we expect Jones sooner or later to experience vague yearnings to chew something, just as we find people who take no exercise to experi-

ence a general listlessness. Even waiving for now my apparent reification of the evolutionary process, let me emphasize how little anyone is tempted to say "each to his own" about Jones or to regard Jones's disposition of his teeth as simply a deviation from a statistical norm. This sort of case is my paradigm when discussing homosexuality.

The main obstacle to talk of what a process or organic structure is for is that, literally understood, such talk presupposes an agent who intends that structure or process to be used in a certain way. Talk of function derives its primitive meaning from the human use of artifacts, artifacts being for what purposive agents intend them for. Indeed, there is in this primitive context a natural reason for using something for what it is for: to use it otherwise would frustrate the intention of some purposeful agent. Since it now seems clear that our bodily parts were not emplaced by purposeful agency, it is easy to dismiss talk of what they are for as "theologically" based on a faulty theory of how we came to be built as we are:

> The idea that sex was designed for propagation is a theological argument, but not a scientific one. . . . To speak of the "fit" of penis and vagina as proof of nature's intention for their exclusive union is pure theological reasoning—imposing a meaning or purpose upon a simple, natural phenomenon.

Barash—who elsewhere uses its cognates freely—dismisses "unnatural" as a mere term of abuse: "people with a social or political axe to grind will call what they don't like 'unnatural' and what they do, 'natural.' " Hume long ago put the philosopher's case against the term 'natural' with characteristic succinctness: " 'Tis founded on final Causes; which is a consideration, that appears to me pretty uncertain & unphilosophical. For pray, what is the End of Man? Is he created for Happiness or for Virtue? For this Life or the next? For himself or for his Maker?". . .

An organ is for a given activity if the organ's performing that activity helps its host or organisms suitably related to its host, *and* if this contribution is how the organ got and stays where it is. . . . This definition . . . distinguishes what something is *for* from what it may be *used* for on some occasion. Teeth are for chewing—we have teeth because their use in chewing favored the survival of organisms with teeth—whereas Jones is using his teeth for ornamentation.

[This account of what it is for an organ to be *for* a certain activity] explains our intuition that, since their efficacy in chewing got them selected in, teeth are for masticating and Jones is preventing his teeth from doing their proper job. . . . Nature is interested in making its creatures like what is (inclusively) good for them. A creature that does not enjoy using its teeth for chewing uses them less than does a toothed competitor who enjoys chewing. Since the use of teeth for chewing favors the survival of an individual with teeth, and, other things being equal, traits favorable to the survival of individuals favor survival of the relevant cohort, toothed creatures who do not enjoy chewing tend to get selected out. We today are the filtrate of this process, descendants of creatures who liked to chew. . . .

Jones's behavior is ill-advised not only because of the avertible objective consequences of his defanging himself, but because he will feel that something is missing. Similarly, this is why you should exercise. It is not just that muscles are for running. We have already heard the sceptic's reply to that: "So what? Suppose I don't mind being flabby? Suppose I don't give a hang about what will propagate my genetic cohort?" Rather, running is good because nature made sure people like to run. This is, of course, the prudential "good," not the moral "good"—but I disavowed at the outset the doctrine that misuse of bodily parts is *morally* bad, at least in any narrow sense. You ought to run because running was once necessary for catching food: creatures who did not enjoy running, if there ever were any, caught less food and reproduced less frequently than competitors who enjoyed running. These competitors passed on their appetites along with their muscles *to you*. This is not to say that those who suffer the affective consequences of laziness must recognize them as such, or even be able to identify them against their general background feeling-tone. They may not realize they would feel better if they exercised.

They may even doubt it. They may have allowed their muscles to deteriorate beyond the point at which satisfying exercise is possible. For all that, evolution has decreed that a life involving regular exercise is on the whole more enjoyable than a life without. The same holds for every activity that is the purpose of an organ.

Applications to Homosexuality

The application of this general picture to homosexuality should be obvious. There can be no reasonable doubt that one of the functions of the penis is to introduce semen into the vagina. It does this, and it has been selected in because it does this. . . . Nature has consequently made this use of the penis rewarding. It is clear enough that any proto-human males who found unrewarding the insertion of penis into vagina have left no descendants. In particular, proto-human males who enjoyed inserting their penises into each other's anuses have left no descendants. This is why homosexuality is abnormal, and why its abnormality counts prudentially against it. Homosexuality is likely to cause unhappiness because it leaves unfulfilled an innate and innately rewarding desire. And should the reader's environmentalism threaten to get the upper hand, let me remind him again of an unproblematic case. Lack of exercise is bad and even abnormal not only because it is unhealthy but also because one feels poorly without regular exercise. Nature made exercise rewarding because, until recently, we had to exercise to survive. Creatures who found running after game unrewarding were eliminated. Laziness leaves unreaped the rewards nature has planted in exercise, even if the lazy man cannot tell this introspectively. If this is a correct description of the place of exercise in human life, it is by the same token a correct description of the place of heterosexuality.

It hardly needs saying, but perhaps I should say it anyway, that this argument concerns tendencies and probabilities. Generalizations about human affairs being notoriously "true by and large and for the most part" only, saying that homosexuals are bound to be less happy than heterosexuals must be understood as short for "Not coincidentally, a larger proportion of homosexuals will be unhappy than a corresponding selection of the heterosexual population." There are, after all, genuinely jolly fat men. To say that laziness leads to adverse affective consequences means that, because of our evolutionary history, the odds are relatively good that a man who takes no exercise will suffer adverse affective consequences. Obviously, some people will get away with misusing their bodily parts. Thus, when evaluating the empirical evidence that bears on this account, it will be pointless to cite cases of well-adjusted homosexuals. I do not say they are non-existent; my claim is that, of biological necessity, they are rare. . . .

Talk of what is "in the genes" inevitably provokes the observation that we should not blame homosexuals for their homosexuality if it is "in their genes." True enough. Indeed, since nobody decides what he is going to find sexually arousing, the moral appraisal of sexual object "choice" is entirely absurd. However, so saying is quite consistent with regarding homosexuality as a misfortune, and taking steps—this being within the realm of the will—to minimize its incidence, especially among children. Calling homosexuality involuntary does not place it outside the scope of evaluation. Victims of sickle-cell anemia are not blameworthy, but it is absurd to pretend that there is nothing wrong with them. Homosexual activists are partial to genetic explanations and hostile to Freudian environmentalism in part because they see a genetic cause as exempting homosexuals from blame. But surely people are equally blameless for indelible traits acquired in early childhood. And anyway, a blameless condition may still be worth trying to prevent. . . .

Utilitarians must take the present evolutionary scenario seriously. The utilitarian attitude toward homosexuality usually runs something like this: even if homosexuality is in some sense unnatural, as a matter of brute fact homosexuals take pleasure in sexual contact with members of the same sex. As long as they don't hurt anyone else, homosexuality is as great a good as heterosexuality. But the matter cannot end here. Not even a utilitarian doctor would have words of praise for a degenerative disease that happened to foster a certain kind of pleasure (as sore muscles uniquely conduce to the pleasure of stretching them). A utilitarian doctor would presumably try just as zealously to cure diseases that feel good as less pleasant degenerative diseases. A pleasure causally connected with great distress cannot be treated as just another pleasure to be toted up on the felicific scoreboard. Utilitarians have to reckon with the inevitable consequences of pain-causing pleasure. . . .

On Policy Issues

Homosexuality is intrinsically bad only in a prudential sense. It makes for unhappiness. However, this does not exempt homosexuality from the larger categories of ethics—rights, duties, liability. Deontic categories apply to acts which increase or decrease happiness or expose the helpless to the risk of unhappiness.

If homosexuality is unnatural, legislation which raises the odds that a given child will become homosexual raises the odds that he will be unhappy. The only gap in the syllogism is whether legislation which legitimates, endorses or protects homosexuality does increase the chances that a child will become homosexual. If so, such legislation is *prima facie* objectionable. The question is not whether homosexual elementary school teachers will molest their charges. Prohomosexual legislation might increase the incidence of homosexuality in subtler ways. If it does, and if the protection of children is a fundamental obligation of society, legislation which legitimates homosexuality is a dereliction of duty. I am reluctant to deploy the language of "children's rights," which usually serves as one more excuse to interfere with the prerogatives of parents. But we do have obligations to our children, and one of them is to protect them from harm. If, as some have suggested, children have a right to protection from a religious education, they surely have a right to protection from homosexuality. So protecting them limits somebody else's freedom, but we are often willing to protect quite obscure children's rights at the expense of the freedom of others. There is a movement to ban TV commercials for sugar-coated cereals, to protect children from the relatively trivial harm of tooth decay. Such a ban would restrict the freedom of advertisers, and restrict it even though the last clear chance of avoiding the harm, and thus the responsibility, lies with the parents who control the TV set. I cannot see how one can consistently support such legislation and also urge homosexual rights, which risk much graver danger to children in exchange for increased freedom for homosexuals. (If homosexual behavior is largely compulsive, it is falsifying the issue to present it as balancing risks to children against the freedom of homosexuals.) The right of a homosexual to work for the Fire Department is not a negligible good. Neither is fostering a legal atmosphere in which as many people as possible grow up heterosexual.

It is commonly asserted that legislation granting homosexuals the privilege or right to be firemen endorses not homosexuality, but an expanded conception of human liberation. It is conjectural how sincerely this can be said in a legal order that forbids employers to hire whom they please and demands hours of paperwork for an interstate shipment of hamburger. But in any case legislation "legalizing homosexuality" cannot be neutral because passing it would have an inexpungeable speech-act dimension. Society cannot grant unaccustomed rights and privileges to homosexuals while remaining neutral about the value of homosexuality. Working from the assumption that society rests on the family and its consequences, the Judaeo-Christian tradition has deemed homosexuality a sin and withheld many privileges from homosexuals. Whether or not such denial was right, for our society to grant these privileges to homosexuals *now* would amount to declaring that it has rethought the matter and decided that homosexuality is not as bad as it had previously supposed. . . .

Up to now, society has deemed homosexuality so harmful that restricting it outweighs putative homosexual rights. If society reverses itself, it will in effect be deciding that homosexuality is not as bad as it once thought.

---

51. Homosexuality and Nature

Timothy F. Murphy

Timothy F. Murphy argues that even if a particular use of our sexual organs leads to adaptive success, it doesn't follow that we are bound to use our sexual organs in that adaptive way. He further argues that even adaptive success itself is compatible with a minority's pursuit of beneficial departures from the natural adaptive order. Those who are truly concerned about the unhappiness suffered by homosexuals, Murphy contends, could reduce that unhappiness simply by removing the social and legal restrictions that we impose on homosexuals.

The nature and legitimacy of homosexual behaviour continue to generate considerable controversy. Since 1973, the American Psychiatric Association has formally professed that homosexuality per se is no disease entity,

From "Homosexuality and Nature: Happiness and the Law at Stake," *Journal of Applied Philosophy*. Reprinted by permission of the author and the publisher.

but one may still seek and find practitioners of sexual conversion therapy. While some religious thinkers have become more tolerant of it, others continue to conceptualize homosexuality as a sin of the first order, a sin said to be formally condemned in strong Old and New Testament language. While at present 26 states of the Union do *not* have criminal statutes for private consensual homosexual behaviour, the U.S. Supreme Court recently held that states may criminalize such behaviour if they so choose.

There are many ways used to argue against the moral legitimacy of homosexual behaviour, whether such behaviour is transient or exclusive. Some seek recourse to concepts of sinfulness, disease or crime in order to flesh out objections. Others appeal to the argument that homosexuality, its religious, medical, and criminal implications apart, is a kind of unnatural aberration which undermines its practitioners' prospects for happiness. I will consider this kind of argument here and contend that such an argument fails to establish that homosexuality is any significant abnormality and that neither its purported abnormality nor the unhappiness said to be associated with such behaviour can constitute a basis for criminalizing consensual homosexual behaviour or for failing to provide equal protections under the law for homosexuals in the area of public housing, service, jobs, and so on. I consider Michael Levin's "Why homosexuality is abnormal" as paradigmatic of the kind of argument I wish to investigate. Although I confine myself to his specific argument and frequently use its language, my position is applicable *a fortiori* to all similar kinds of position.

The Argument from Nature

Despite the effort which Levin takes to show that homosexual behaviour falls outside the behaviour upon which human adaptive success depended, I cannot say that I think this argument is even remotely convincing. Indeed, I believe it to be subject to a damning criticism. Even if it were certainly established that homosexuality was not part of originally adaptive behaviour, I do not see how that conclusion alone could establish the abnormality of homosexuality because there is neither a premise that natural selection has any kind of ultimate normative force nor a premise that human beings are bound to continue to be the kind of things that cosmic accident brought them to be. There is nothing in Levin's argu-

ment to sustain a claim that departures from a blind, accidental force of nature, or whatever metaphor of randomness is chosen, must be resisted. Without a logically prior and controlling premise that patterns of adaptive success possess ultimate, normative force, then it seems that human beings are completely at liberty to dispose of their world, their behaviour, and even such things as their anatomy and physiology as they see fit. H. Tristram Engelhardt has made an argument along similar lines: that we human beings may choose our futures and are in no metaphysically binding sense bound to continue being the kind of persons blind determinants of nature have brought us to be. Violations of a random order of nature carry no inherent penalty for there is no ultimate enforcer, or at least none is specified by this argument. Levin believes that he can show the abnormality of homosexuality without having to show that it violates some cosmic principle, by showing its inherent obstacles to adaptive success. But I think it is because no cosmic principle is invoked that we can judge that adaptive success itself is no binding force. The only guide available for human beings in respect of their lives, sexuality, and future is their will and imagination. Should the entire population of the planet choose to become exclusive homosexuals, for example, leaving the business of reproduction to ectogenesis, I cannot think of a reason *derived from nature* why they should not do so.

Levin's argument, and others like it, ignore the prospects of beneficial departures from the naturally adaptive order. His argument assumes that each departure from our adaptive heritage will be unhappy in result. The argument, too, assumes that *all* behaviour of *all* persons must serve the purpose of adaption. Clearly, it is possible that some departures from the adaptive order are possible which do not threaten a species' survival as a whole. If a species can survive if only a majority of its members use their organs in a particular fashion, then it may enjoy a surplus of adaptive protection even for those who act in wholly non-procreative fashion. Homosexuality, then, might have served some beneficial advantage (as sociobiology asserts) or it may have been (and this is more important for my argument) no impediment to selective adaptation. If this is so, it is hard to see in what sense homosexuality would have to be reckoned as a natural aberration. . . .

Prospects for Happiness

Levin makes a great deal of the supposed link between homosexuality and unhappiness. One may assume that he would reply to my foregoing remarks by admitting that even if it were true that humans are not bound by any ultimate metaphysical sexual directive, then it would still remain true that prudential cautions obtain against homosexuality and that these cautions are sufficient to ground legal measures designed to minimize the occurrence of homosexuality. "Homosexuality," Levin says, "is likely to cause unhappiness because it leaves unfilfilled an innate and innately rewarding desire," a desire supposedly ingrained through millennia of evolutionary selection. One might find some happy homosexuals, but Levin believes that such exceptions are inconsequential and do not disable his argument. He does not say that happy homosexuals are non-existent, only that they are rare and that their lives will be inherently less rewarding than those of heterosexuals. . . .

To put specific quarrels about evidence aside, it seems to me that Levin fails almost culpably to imagine what a society would have to be like in order to be free of the oppressive elements which contribute to the putative unhappiness of homosexuals. In order to see the extent to which homosexual unhappiness is caused by social repressions and to what extent it is intrinsic, society would have to be completely free at every significant level of bias against homosexuals. To begin with—let's call this Phase I of the agenda: there should be no gratuitous assumption of heterosexuality in education, politics, advertising, and so on, just as a gender-neutral society would not presume the priority, real and symbolic, of males. For example, in education, texts and films ought to incorporate the experiences of gay men and lesbians. Educational measures should attempt to reduce anti-homosexuality in the same ways

and to the same extent they educate against racism. In a society reconstructed along these lines, moreover, there would also have to be no right of access or entitlement possessed by a heterosexual that could be denied to a homosexual. *Only* in such a radically restructured society would one be able to see if homosexual unhappiness were immune to social deconstruction. Even if it weren't, one could still argue that homosexuals are not necessarily unhappy but that their happiness requires social protections or accommodations unrequired by heterosexuals. That is, homosexuals might need, as Phase II of the agenda, entitlements which heterosexuals do not—in the way, for example, that legally mandated minority hiring quotas serve other specific populations. Of course, one might want to argue that such entitlements would be antidemocratic and therefore objectionable. This protestation however would not by itself diminish the point being made: that homosexual unhappiness is perhaps adventitious and that the only way of discovering this is to protect homosexuals in their lives, jobs, and interests in ways that are not presently served. . . .

Issues at Law

Levin believes that the abnormality of homosexuality and its attendant unhappiness are warrant enough to ground legal enactments against homosexuality and this is a matter of protecting citizens from lives impoverished by the loss of heterosexual rewards. Any legislation therefore that raises the odds that a child will become homosexual ought to be rejected as prima facie objectionable, as a dereliction of the duty of protecting children from the unhappy homosexual selves they might become. The U.S. Supreme Court recently ruled in *Bowers v. Hardwick* that states may enact, if they choose, statutes proscribing private consensual homosexual behaviour since, according to the opinion, there is nothing in the Constitution making such behaviour a fundamental right. Levin's argument would presumably extend further since private consensual homosexual behaviour is socially invisible and unlikely as such to influence persons to become homosexual. Although he does not specifically mention what kinds of laws ought to be called for, or what kinds of laws ought to be rejected, presumably he means denying homosexuals protections in jobs, housing, foster-parenting, and so on. In short, the law would presumably have to serve the function of rendering homosexuality entirely invisible else there would continue to exist subtle promptings to homosexuality by virtue of degree of acceptance extended to it. Levin says he does not believe that this legal scenario would put any undue burden on any actual homosexual since, unlike members of racial minorities, he or she can always stay in the closet while applying for jobs, housing and the like. Therefore to give homosexuals protections they don't really need would have to be interpreted as a de facto social legitimation of homosexuality. This implied approval might be causally involved in the production of more homosexuals and therefore ought to be rejected.

I do not believe that this argument is convincing. First of all, the "cause" or "causes" of homosexuality are a matter of continuing controversy. There are metaphysical arguments that homosexuality is the result of some cosmic principle of world ordering; Plato's *Symposium* depicts homosexuals (and heterosexuals) as the result of an angry god's punishment. Biological theories hold homosexuality to be the result of some developmental variance or organismal dysfunction. Genetic theories try to locate the origins of homosexuality at the lowest level of biological causality, the gene. The most numerous kinds of theories are psychosocial theories which see homoeroticism as the result of either original psychical constitution or some developmental influences. Even the briefest perusal of the literature of the "cause" of homosexuality leaves one with the conclusion that the "cause" is an essentially disputed concept. There is not even agreement that homosexuality is a reifiable trait (any more than, say, courage) that can be explained by reference to a universally preexisting set of conditions. This dispute is important to consider since Levin seems to hold, without justification (at least without explanation), a developmental theory of homosexuality, a

theory that homosexuals are made not born. This may or may not be true, but it seems wrong-headed to establish legal policy on the basis of one particular speculative theory of the origins of homosexual behaviour. If homosexuality is primarily a function of biological variance, for example, such laws and forbearances that Levin would see as desirable would have no effect whatever on the production of more homosexuals. Even if the law diligently erased all evidence of homosexual behaviour and persons from public view, one could not automatically assume a reduced number of homosexuals or a decrease in homosexual behaviour. I suspect that most persons are homosexual and become homosexual in ways completely immune to the written or enforced statutes of the various states. Children who never hear a word about homosexuality in their youth nevertheless become homosexuals. Children who walk past homosexual clubs and persons in the streets of certain American cities do not thereby automatically become homosexuals. Would it really be the case that there are more homosexuals spawned in West Virginia because there are no laws against private, consensual homosexual behaviour there than in Virginia where there are such laws? The net result of efforts to criminalize and reduce the visibility of homosexuality then would be to impose burdens on those who are perhaps involuntarily homosexual. At the very least, Levin's theory gratuitously supposes a developmental theory of homosexuality, a theory which has its insistent critics. One should also point out that even if some developmental theory of homosexuality were true, it is not necessarily the case that changing statutes would halt the flow of homosexuals since there may be other pathways to homosexuality. It is also the suspicion of many psychologists that homosexual tendencies are established very early on in childhood, in which case one presumes fairly that statutes criminalizing sodomy and lacks of protection in housing on the basis of sexual orientation have little to do with either ingraining or stifling homosexual dispositions.

If the reason that Levin suggests antihomosexual measures is to contain human unhappiness, then his argument may be turned on its head. If the reason, or part of the reason that homosexuals are unhappy is because of the existence of certain legally permissible discriminations (or what comes to the same thing: fear of such), then it can certainly be suggested that laws ought to be changed in order to protect and enlarge the happiness of homosexuals, whether their homosexuality is elective or involuntary. In the name of their happiness, they ought to be afforded protections under the law, freedom from fear of prosecution for their private consensual behaviour and freedom to occupy jobs as the persons they are, not as the persons others would have them be. The law could further protect them by saving them from blackmailers who would expose their homosexuality to employers, landlords, and so on. It is eminently clear that the law could at least enlarge the happiness of gay men and lesbians in these respects even if it cannot vouchsafe them absolute satisfaction in their lives.

Interestingly enough, even if all the unhappiness said to be associated with being homosexual were not eliminated by a dogged social reconstruction that achieved full parity between homosexuality and heterosexuality, it would still not follow that the law ought to be put to the purpose of eliminating homosexuality (assuming it could). Life, sad to say, is in some of its aspects inherently tragic. For example, in some important ways, law or society could never fully compensate the atheist for the lost rewards of religion. Atheism can discover in the world no incentives to conduct, no promise of the eventual recompense for injustices borne, and no guarantee that the heart's desires will be met. Society might provide such consolations as it can, but it is certainly the case that a certain tragedy antagonis-

tic to human happiness is an irreducible element of atheistic thought. That atheism leads to this measure of unhappiness would certainly not be a reason for instituting social and legal barriers to atheism on the theory that children ought to be glowingly happy (if self-deceived) theists rather than unhappy atheists. Human dignity is not automatically overthrown by a position of atheism; the atheist accepts and honours those satisfactions that are within his or her power. That homosexuality too might lead to a certain amount of unhappiness does not thereby overthrow the dignity of homosexual persons. One realizes merely that the law is no unfailing conduit to human happiness.

Levin's conclusions that legal measures ought to be taken to minimize the possibility that children become themselves the sad new recruits of homosexuality therefore cannot stand. I believe, on the contrary, that the law ought to do what it can to protect homosexuals from socially inflicted unhappiness. Levin's point that to decriminalize homosexual behaviour and to provide legal protections for homosexual persons would be seen as social legitimization of homosexuality (and not just tolerance) is correct. But this is no point over which to despair, for this inference is precisely compatible with the underlying metaphysics of gay activism, that homosexuality is no degrading impoverishment of human life. On the contrary, it has an integrity of its own apart from invidious comparison with heterosexuality. Therefore, lest society be a political enforcer of sexual ideology, homosexuals ought to be afforded equal standing and protections under the law, and this in the name of serving human happiness. . . .

52. A Case against Homosexuality

Paul Cameron

Beginning with the assumption that human sexuality is totally learned, Paul Cameron argues that there are a number of factors favoring the adoption of homosexuality: (1) the extreme homosociality of children starting around age five, (2) the greater attraction males have for sex than females, (3) the superiority of homosexual sex as sex, and (4) the self-servingness/egocentricity of the young. To overcome these factors, Cameron argues that discrimination against homosexuals is justified, especially in view of the fact that heterosexuality leads to more permanent social relationships, greater altruism, and more social cohesion.

In some segments of the mass media, the homosexuality issue takes on the appearance of a struggle between orange juice peddlers and bathhouse owners. At a different level individual rights versus the interests of society provide the conflict. Some argue that adult homosexuals ought to be allowed to do what they want behind closed doors. Others, often seeing the issue in terms of rights, honesty, and overpopulation, seek to grant homosexuality equal status with heterosexuality. The school system of San Francisco, apparently resonating with the latter tack, is offering a course including "homosexual life-styles." Liberals attempt to shame as unenlightened all who oppose complete equality as vigorously as conservative Bible-thumpers threaten wrath from above.

No known human society has ever granted equal status to homo- and heterosexuality. What information do those who desire social equivalence for these two sexual orientations possess that assures them that this new venture in human social organization is called for at this time? Have the cultures of the past practiced discrimination against homosexuality out of a mere prejudice, or was there substance to their bias? At the risk of seeming rather out of step with the academic community, no new information has surfaced that would lead me to discount the social policies of the past. On the contrary, the policies of the past in regard to homosexuality appear generally wise, and considerable discrimination against homosexuality and for heterosexuality, marriage and parenthood appears needful for the social good.

Discrimination

Discrimination is something all humans and all human communities do. Individually we discriminate for certain things and against others, e.g., movies over T.V. Collectively we discriminate for and against selected: (1) acts (pleasantries, sharing versus murder, robbery), (2) traits (generous, kind versus whiny, hostile) and (3) life-styles (independent, productive versus gambling, indolent). Prejudice is unwarranted discrimination. The issue is not whether discrimination should exist—for human society to exist, it must. The issues are always: (1) is discrimination called for? and (2) how much is necessary? Reasonable people can and do disagree on what ought to be discriminated for and against, to what degree, and even if discrimination is prejudicial rather than called for. But reasoned opinion *can* hold that homosexuality and homosexuals ought to be discriminated against. . . .

From the *Human Life Review* (1978), pp. 17–49. Reprinted by permission of the Human Life Foundation and the author.

The Case against Homosexuality/Wisdom of the Ages

No contemporary society accords homosexuality equivalent status with heterosexuality. No known society has accorded equivalent status in the past (Karlen, 1971). No current or ancient religion of any consequence has failed to teach discrimination against homosexuality. The Judeo-Christian tradition is no exception to this rule. The Old Testament made homosexuality a capital offense, and while the New Testament writers failed to invoke capital punishment for any offense, they did manage to consign homosexuals to eternal hell for the practice. Church fathers and traditions have stayed in line with this position until recently. To the degree that tradition and agreed-upon social policy ought to carry weight in our thinking about issues, the weight of tradition is preponderately on the side of discrimination. The same is true if we "poll" famous thinkers of the past: Plato, for instance, who at one time of his life provided some endorsement of homosexuality, but switched to a strongly negative vote by the end of his career. Aristotle simply considered homosexuality a depravity and Plutarch noted that "no wise father would permit a notable Greek philosopher near his sons." St. Augustine condemned homosexuality and St. Thomas Aquinas ranked homosexuality just a rung above bestiality.

While it is somewhat fashionable to claim that the ancient Greeks legalized and practiced homosexuality, it rather appears that this was, at most, true for only a short time, and only for the leisure class (Karlen, 1971). Similarly, while a number of American Indian societies had a place for the homosexual, it was, all in all, a rather unpleasant one (the Mohave interchanged the word for "coward" and "queer"). Most of the anthropological information that alludes to common practicing of homosexuality among males of various tribes neglects to note that the members of the tribe didn't consider what they were doing sexual, much less homosexual (various touching customs among males featured no erections,

etc). Further, the common anti-female bias of the Greeks and other philosophic systems is not fairly construed as homosexuality. Aristotle claimed that the best forms of friendship and love were found "between men," but condemned homosexuality. One can be pro-male without necessitating elimination of copulation between the sexes. It is quite possible to keep love and sex, or friendship and sex, almost completely separate.

While one cannot carry the "wisdom of the ages" argument too far—just because all peoples up to a certain point in time believed something does not necessarily mean that it was so—yet it appears more than a little injudicious to cast it aside as merely "quaint." Probably no issue has occupied man's collective attentions more than successful living together. That such unanimity of opinion and practice should exist must give one pause. Certainly such congruence "puts the ball in the changer's court." As in so many spheres of human endeavor, when we know that we can get on in a particular way, the burden of proof that we can get on as well or better by following a different custom falls upon those seeking the change. The "fallacy of the ages" is that we "got here because we did X" (we might have gotten here just as well, thank you, by doing K) but that we are regarding fallacy rather than wisdom must still be *proven* by those seeking change.

To date, those seeking change have not been flush with scientific evidence that homosexuality is not socially disruptive. On the contrary, the arguments that have been advanced have been little more than "people ought not to be discriminated against; homosexuals are people; ergo homosexuals ought not to be discriminated against" shouted larger and louder. No one to my knowledge has ever claimed that homosexuals were not people, and one would have to be a dunce to believe that being a person qualifies one, *ipso facto,* for nondiscrimination. Aside from this argument repeated in endless variations and *ad nauseam,* the evidence is simply not there. I'll admit to a charm in residing in a society undergoing dramatic change. You get to stand at the end of the tunnel of history and help dig a new hole (something that particularly excites the modern scholar and local news team). But let us be sure we are not digging new holes just for our amusement. Meddling with procreation and heterosexuality is considerably more than a parlor game in which the stakes are but a trifle. Because what we are about is so very serious, if anything, an even better set of evidence needs to be produced by those seeking change, not, as is the case today, mere syllogistic flatus.

Homosociality Coupled with Increasing Self-Centeredness Could Lead to Widespread Homosexuality

. . . Jimmy Carter said: "I don't see homosexuality as a threat to the family." . . . His sentiments probably echo those of the educated class of our society. They trust that "only deviants" are really into homosexuality anyway, and, more important, that "mother nature" will come through in the last analysis. Biology, they assume, has a great deal to do with sexuality and sexual attraction, and millions of years of heterosexuality has firmly engraved itself on the genetic code.

Such thinking betrays a lack of appreciation of the enormous component of learning that goes into human sexuality. The point that anthropology has made over the past hundred years is the *tremendous diversity of human social organization.* Marvelously varied are the ways man rears his young, honors his dead, plays the game of procreation, or practices dental hygiene. While the onset of the events of puberty vary relatively little from one society to another, the onset of copulation varies over a full quarter of the lifespan—from 5 or 6 years of age to mid-20s. While three-spine stickle-backs predictably go into paroxysms of delight over a given colored shape, the object of man's sexual desires varies from car mufflers, to animals, to various ages, and sexes of his own kind. Many mammals practice sex for only a few days or weeks in the year, but man varies from untrammeled lust to studied virginity. While I have enumerated my reasons more fully elsewhere (Cameron, 1977), I believe that

the most reasonable construal of the evidence to date suggests that *human sexuality is totally learned.*

There are really only three ways for human sexuality to develop. Humans are among, if not *the,* most gregarious creatures. We are reared by our kind, schooled with and by our kind, and just generally like to be around other humans (my research into the contents of consciousness suggests that, worldwide, *the* most frequent topic of thought is other humans). We prefer to do just about anything with one or more other humans. We prefer to eat with another human, we would rather go to the movies, picnic, take walks with another, etc. We are firmly gregarious. The same is true for sexuality. For all but the kinkiest of us, we would rather "do it" with another human. Bestiality, necrophilia, vacuum cleaners, dolls, you name it, none of these sexual aberrations will ever become modal sex—they will always appeal to only a few. Since modal human sexuality must needs be confined to other humans, the three ways to "fly" are obvious modes: heterosexuality, homosexuality, or bisexuality. Because human sexuality is totally learned, humans must be pointed in the "right" direction, and taught how and with whom to perform. And there's the rub. Homosexuality and heterosexuality do not start off on the same footing. *Au contraire,* one gets a number of important boosts in the scheme of things. In our society the developmental process is decidedly *tilted toward the adoption of homosexuality!*

Part of the homosexual tilt is the extreme homosociality of children starting around the age of 5. As everyone is aware, boys want to play with boys and girls with girls, and they do so with a vengeance. It's quite reasonable, on their part. First, boys' and girls' bodies are different and they are aware that their bodies-to-be will differ still more. In part because of this the games, sports and skills they practice differ. As if in anticipation of the differing roles they will have, their interests and proclivities differ. Even if they try, few girls can do as well as most boys at "boy things" and few boys can do as well as girls at "girl things." They almost inhabit different worlds. Not surprisingly for members of two different "races," poles apart psychologically, socially,

and physically, they "stick to their own kind."
. . .

There are three other components that contribute to the homosexual tilt. First, on the average in our society, males are considerably more taken with sex than females are. In my 1975 survey of 818 persons on the east coast of the United States, respondents were asked to rate the degree of pleasure they obtained from 22 activities including "being with one's family," "listening to music," "being out in nature," "housework," and "sexual activity." Between the late teens through middle age, sexual activity topped the male list as the "most pleasurable activity." It did manage to rank as high as fifth place for young adult women (aged 18 to 25), but, overall for the female life span, was outscored by almost everything including "housework" (which, incidentally ranked dead last among males). . . .

How well suited are "hot" males to "cool" females? Not very. One of (if not *the*) most common problems in marital counseling is sexual incompatibility. *Females pay sex as the price of love/companionship and males pay love for sex.* While this is rather too aphoristic to capture all that goes on in the male-female struggle, there is a great deal of truth to it. Even among homosexuals, the males probably outsex lesbians by a factor of 5 to 1 (see Tripp's sympathetic treatment for elaboration on this theme). Where is a male most apt to find his counterpart, among maledom or femaledom? If he wants hot, dripping sex, what better place to find it than with another of similar bent? If she wants tender companionship, which sex is most apt to provide the partner? The answers are obvious.

The second part of the homosexual tilt derives from the fact that *homosexual encounter offers better sex*, on the average, *than heterosexual sex.* If pleasure is what you are after, who better to fulfill you than a partner who has a body and predilections like yours? One of the things that both the male homosexual and lesbian societies advertise is that "they satisfy." The Greek literature of yore also contains the "better sex" claim of homosexuals. And why not? A male, who has the same basic equipment and rhythms is most able to satisfy— particularly initially (heterosexual "one nite stands" are frequently exciting, but just as fre-

quently lacking in sexual satisfaction for both participants—not so homosexual "one niters"). Who better to understand "what you need" than someone whose needs are as your own? From a sexual standpoint, a female can offer little extra orifice as compensation for her: ignorance, timidity, desire for companionship first, etc. Further, sex between members of a sex assures that there will be no pregnancy problems further on down the line.

Another developmental boost for homosexuality comes from the self-servingness/egocentricity of the young. Humans are born with, at best, rudimentary consciousness. Then, over time and experience, they learn to differentiate themselves from the environment. From about the age of 5 or 6 onward for the next decade or so of life, they are engrossed in themselves, in the service of themselves, their pleasures, their interests, their ways. Reciprocity of interaction is rendered begrudgingly, certainly far from spontaneously. My research, involving the interviewing of over 8,000 respondents from the United States and five other nations, in which we asked persons to tell us: (1) whose interests they had just been thinking about serving— their own or another's or others' and (2) whether they had just been thinking about themselves, things, or other people, indicated that younger persons more frequently reported themselves in a self-serving attitude and thinking about themselves than adults did. In the United States, adults of both sexes typically reported themselves in an other-serving attitude. But U.S. males "switched" from self-servingness to other-servingness around age 26 while for females the switch occurred in the middle teens. If one is after self-fulfillment, pleasure for self, which sexual orientation "fits" better? Homosexuality, obviously. One can have his homosociality and sex too. One can comfortably neglect the painful transformation from self-interest to other-interest. Me and mine to the fore.

Which kind of sexuality is the more compelling? The one that can say "come, sex my way and I will show you a life of complexity. Of children and responsibility. Of getting on with 'that other kind.' I will offer you poorer sex initially, and, who knows, perhaps you will just have to satisfy yourself with poorer sex permanently. But you will be able to 'glimpse immortality in your children' (Plato)." Or "come, sex my way and I will give it to you straight and hot. Pleasures of the best quality, almost on demand, with persons with whom you already share a great deal, and I will enable you to share more. It will not be difficult, in fact, it will be fun. You will not have to change or adapt your personality style or your egocentric orientation. You'll fit right in immediately. None of this hemming and hawing—you'll get what you want when you want it. Motto? Pleasure—now. The future? Who knows, but the present is going to be a dilly." Which kind of sexuality is the more compelling? Does anyone doubt which way most youth would turn if equivalent social status attended homosexuality and heterosexuality? . . .

The myths about love and romance that grace our society have been almost 100 percent heterosexual. From children's readers to tube fare, heterosexuality has been the "only game in town." Tom and Jane live with their parents Dick and Sue, *not* Tim and Jim. Dagwood has Blondie, and the odd couple is squarely heterosexual. Yet even in the glare of the massive efforts of religions, customs, laws, and example, about 2 percent of the citizenry fail to accomplish the mental gymnastic of separating sexual object from social object. They go the developmentally "easy way," and add sexuality to homosociality. What if society offered an honest to goodness *choice* between the two sexual orientations? The current lock on the myth-making, image-providing process by heterosexuality may be an instance of overkill. Perhaps an 80/20 hetero-homosexuality split would still result in 96 percent heterosexuality. Maybe even a 60/40 split would. But we've got 2 percent now with something like a 99/1 split, and somewhere up the line, growth in homosexual mythology and literature *has* to have an effect (unless one can seriously believe that that to which people are exposed does not influence them).

It appears that once a solid choice for either homo- or heterosexuality is made, the "other way" becomes unlikely, and, in fact, disgusting. True, with the current pro-heterosexual bias in the psychiatric community, about a third of homosexuals in treatment can, with

considerable effort, be "switched." But as "even-steven" literature grows and becomes incorporated into the psychiatric community's consciousness, the attempt to convert will be made less frequently. Tripp's *The Homosexual Matrix* is a well-received work that melds the myths of love, sex, homo- and heterosexuality. It certainly constitutes a solid start toward "even-steven" in myth-making. The resolutions of the American Psychiatric and American Psychological Associations calling for equality or near equality of treatment of professionals and clients with either homo or hetero orientations, further movement toward equality of the sexual orientations. Pre-teens and teens are the battle ground. With the exception of the San Francisco school system, students' official fare is still 100 percent heterosexual. In my opinion, heterosexuality "needs all the help it can get," and these current developments portend a much more homosexual future. . . .

A Cluster of Undesirable Traits Is Disproportionately Associated with Homosexuality

---

Though some may shriek that "my personality traits are my business," let us acknowledge that some traits are society's business. A person's traits can lead to actions which affect the collectivity. Megalomania often proves socially disruptive, and sometimes, as in the case of Hitler, leads to incredible human destruction. It is obviously in society's interest to encourage those social roles and traits that tend to social cohesion and betterment. Similarly, it is in the social interest to discourage those that tend to produce disruption and harm. Any life-style that leads to, or is more frequently associated with, undesirable personality traits suitably receives discouragement. Most traits, e.g. intelligence, appear unsystematically related to either homo- or heterosexuality, but those that are systematically related are socially important.

It would be as silly to contend that each of the following traits is associated with each homosexual as to argue that none of these appear in heterosexuals (or even worse, that the obverse of these traits always accompanies heterosexuality). However, for social policy formulation, it is enough to demonstrate disproportionate "loading" of undesirable traits within a given subgroup or subculture to justify social discrimination.

The Egocentric/ Supercilious/Narcissistic/ Self-Oriented/Hostile Complex

This cluster of traits appears to "go together" with homosexuality. . . . A person who, in part, seeks more of himself in his lover, is more apt to remain in the egocentric/self-centered orientation of youth. Such a person is more apt to gravitate toward those kinds of professions in which he can be a "star" and be noticed. . . .

The "star" lives for gratification of self. *My* way is his motto. . . . The star need not accommodate himself to the needs of others to the same degree as most folk. If a current love is "not working out" he can be discarded and a more suitable one found. . . .

Superciliousness—an attitude of aloof, hostile disdain—is also consonant with the egocentric person. If you will not realize his marvelous qualities and pay homage, he still has you one down. After all he treated you with contempt *first*. Even if you become hostile, his preceded yours. I am well aware that much of what I have written frequently applies to notable Hollywood and Broadway actors. Adoration-seekers disproportionately frequently make poor models for marriages. As the columnists often put it, "there was too much ego to go around." . . .

The greater component of the childish "I want it my way" associated with homosexuality stems, in part, from the greater ease connected with homosexual attachments. Developmentally, both hetero- and homosexuals want things "their way." But the kinds of accommodations and adjustment necessary for successful heterosexuality assure participants that it won't be all their way. Just because

so much of the time things don't work out perfectly in the face of such effort helps wean one from the coddled security of childhood. Parents and the rest of society work to "make the world nice" for children. Every childhood painting is worthy of note, as is every musical note. But adulthood is strewn with disappointments. Heterosexuality is a "maturing" sexual orientation. . . .

. . . It appears to me that homosexuality leads to a shallower commitment to society and its betterment. Such shallowness comes about both because of a lack of children and the ease of sexual gratification. The *effort* involved in being heterosexual, the *effort* expended in being a parent—these are denied the homosexual. As he *has* less responsibility and commitment, so he *is* or becomes less responsible and committed. It is difficult to develop personality characteristics that fail to resonate with one's environment. While we are not totally creatures of our environment, it is far easier to "swim with the tide."

It is difficult to find anything like "hard" scientific evidence to substantiate the notion that homosexuals are on the average, less responsible/trustworthy than heterosexuals. The Weinberg and Williams sample of homosexuals was asked a question that bears upon the issue. Do you agree or disagree with the statement "most people can be trusted?" To a degree, since a person cannot know "most people" it appears reasonable to assume that he might project his own personality onto "most people" and/or assume that those people with whom he comes in contact are like "most people." While 77 percent of a reasonably representative sample of the U.S. population chose "agree," only 47 percent of the homosexuals ticked the same response. Because of the ambiguity of such items, I would not make too much of the difference. But it could suggest that homosexuals are less trustworthy.

Homosexuality Is Associated with Personal Lethality

One of the more troubling traits associated with homosexuality is personal lethality. Extending back in time to classical Greece, a lethal theme shines through. In Greece, if historical sources are to be believed, companies of homosexual warriors were assembled because it was believed that they made better killers.

. . . In our society the childless are more apt to suicide and childless couples are more apt to be involved in homicide.

Heterosexuality Provides the Most Desirable Model of Love

Myths are created not only by storytellers but by people living within the myth. Almost all (95 percent or so) heterosexuals get married, and 75–80 percent stay married to their original partner till death. To be sure, there are marriage "hogs" within the heterosexual camp who play serial monogamy and assure that a third of all marriages end in divorce. Further, about half of all married men and about a third of all married women admit to one or more infidelities over the duration of their marriage (probably the greater bulk of the "cheaters" come from the serial monogamy camp). While heterosexuality's colors are far from simon pure, the relationship heterosexuality spawns is among, if not *the,* most enduring of human bonds. . . .

Homosexuality offers no comparison in durability. While "slam, bam, thank you ma'am" occurs in heterosexuality, few heterosexuals could more than fantasize about what occurs in homosexual bathhouses or tearooms. As Weinberg and Williams note, the homosexual community typically features "sex for sex's sake." Their survey in which two-thirds of their respondents chose to respond "no" to whether they had limited their ". . . sexual relationships primarily to (another)" is telling. Names and banter are typically neglected in bathhouses. . . .

When people are merely "getting their jollies," and fantasizing perfection while doing so, reduced communication is an asset. If you discover that your beautiful lover holds political views antithetical to your own, how can you really enjoy him/her? The "less known the bet-

ter" is fantasy sex. Communicating, mutually knowledgeable people often have to "work it out" before attempts at sex can even occur. But while typically short on durability, some homosexual relationships are more lasting. The quality of even these is often questionably desirable. Part of the problem lies in the lack of commitment that follows lower effort in the homosexual pairing. Tripp, for instance, opines that part ". . . of the reason many homosexual relationships do not survive the first serious quarrel is that one or both partners simply find it much easier to remarket themselves than work out conflicts (p. 155)." In heterosexuality, no matter how similar the participants, there is always a considerable gap between them. To stay together takes great effort, and the expenditure of this effort prompts both personal and social commitment to the partner.

. . . Because the heterosexual partners are so dissimilar, accommodation and adjustment are their key strategies. Because mutually satisfying heterosexual sexing takes so long and so much effort, both participants have to "hang in there" long after "sane people" would have toddled off in frustration. *We become the way we act. The heterosexual relationship places a premium on "getting on" and thus provides a model to smooth countless other human interactions.* The homosexual model is a considerably less satisfactory one upon which to build a civilization. Note Tripp again (p. 167): ". . . the problems encountered in balancing heterosexual and homosexual relationships are strikingly different. The *heterosexual blend tends to be rich in stimulating contrasts and short on rapport*—so much so that popular marriage counseling literature incessantly hammers home the advice that couples should develop common interests and dissolve their conflicts by increasing their "communication." By comparison, homosexual relationships are overclose, fatigue-prone, and are often adjusted to such narrow, trigger-sensitive tolerances that a mere whisper of disrapport can jolt the partners into making repairs, or into conflict." . . .

Our social system also features large components of delay of gratification. The heterosexual "carrot" is hard to get and requires a lot of input before successful outcome is achieved. The homosexual model is too immediate and influences people to expect instant results. . . .

In short, heterosexuality is effortful, durable, and demands delay of gratification. While any human relationship takes effort, homosexuality pales in comparison to heterosexuality on each count. . . .

No one is rich enough, powerful enough, or attractive enough to guarantee himself personal happiness. Incredibly wealthy, fabulously beautiful people have taken their lives in despair. *Nothing* guarantees happiness. On the other hand, extremely poor, grotesquely ugly people have achieved personal life-satisfaction. So it can likewise be said that nothing guarantees misery. More than any other single factor, happiness or life-satisfaction is an *achievement*. (The greatest "secret" to happiness is a dogged determination to wrest happiness from the cards life deals.)

Both degree of determination to be happy and the stage upon which happiness is pursued are influential in life-satisfaction. Since the stage is important, the prudent person attempts to include "props" that aid rather than hinder his pursuit of happiness. From the prudent perspective, it is foolish to neglect one's body or engage in needlessly hazardous pursuits. Similarly, it is wise to seek sufficient wherewithal to be free of nagging financial concern. From the prudent standpoint, homosexuality is an obstacle in the pursuit of happiness.

The best evidence on the question of homosexuals' happiness is, like most of what is known about homosexuality, not the best. But it is "fair" evidence from a social science standpoint. In their survey of 1,117 homosexuals, Weinberg and Williams asked respondents to answer "yes" or "no" to "I am a happy person." In an earlier poll of over 3,000 citizens, 92.8 percent had chosen "yes" to this question, but only 68.8 percent of the homosexuals did the same. Now I would not argue that 92.8 percent of Americans are "happy persons" because they chose "yes" rather than "no" to this kind of item—such questions probably can be used to suggest differences between groups of persons, but hardly deserve to be considered precise. Answering such questions is rather like being asked "do you like ice cream, yes or no?" Both the person who LOVES ice cream

and those who merely think it's "OK" probably check "yes" rather than "no." And those who HATE ice cream check "no" along with those who just feel indifferent to it. But even with this caveat, and it's an important one, the way the responses fell suggests that homosexuals *are* less happy, on the average, than heterosexuals are. My educated guess is that most homosexuals are "happy" with life, just as most heterosexuals are. It probably works both ways—that is, unhappy people may be attracted to homosexuality and/or homosexuality may be a "negative prop" on the "life-satisfaction stage." But, either way, evidence such as Weinberg and Williams report cannot just be tossed aside. Even if their findings only mean that homosexuality attracts unhappy, less cheery sorts of people, a person "buying into" homosexuality is going to have to run his "happiness play" on a stage disproportionately filled with "unhappy props."

Does homosexuality make being happy more difficult? In the Weinberg and Williams study, homosexuals were asked to respond "yes" or "no" to the statement "no one cares what happens to you." While a general population sample had chosen "yes" 23 percent of the time, 34 percent of homosexuals chose "yes." . . . Heterosexuality helps generate the very kinds of props and reasons that contribute toward making life-satisfaction more possible. *In the long run*, heterosexuality has a lot more to offer as a life-style than homosexuality. . . .

Summary

In sum, there are a number of reasons why homosexuality is best treated as a deviant sexual mode. I do not believe that homosexuality ought to be placed on an even keel with heterosexuality. Further, homosexuals ought not, in my opinion, to be permitted to openly ply their sexual orientation and retain influential positions in the social system. Thus teachers, or pastors who "come out," ought, in my opinion, to lose their claim to the roles they occupy.

Reasonable people can and do differ on the degree and kind of discrimination that is to be laid against undesirable life-styles. There are a number of issues that appear substantive and weigh against the liberalization of social policy toward homosexuality. The burden of proof always justly falls upon those who would change the social system. If the homosexual community and/or those who endorse the liberalization of social policy toward homosexuality have evidence that bears upon these points, by all means bring it forward and let us reason together. But mere cries of "we are being discriminated against" are not evidence. The collection of decent evidence takes organized time and effort. I am weary of those who feel that a case has been made just because they have gotten blisters on the streets or their voices are louder.

References

Allport, G. W. *The Person in Psychology.* New York: Beacon, 1961.

Atkins, J. *Sex in Literature.* New York: Grove Press, 1970.

Bergler, E. *Homosexuality: Disease or Way of Life?* New York: Macmillan, 1956.

Bieber, I. *Homosexuality: A Psychoanalytic Study.* New York: Basic Books, 1962.

Cameron, P. "Immolations to the Juggernaut." *Linacre Quarterly,* 1977, *44,* 64–74.

Cameron, P. *The Life-Cycle: Perspectives and Commentary.* New York: General Health, 1977.

Cameron, P. & Oeschger, D. "Homosexuality in the Mass Media as Indexed by Magazine Literature over the Past Half Century in the U.S." Paper presented at Eastern Psychological Association Convention, New York, April 4, 1975.

Davis, N. & Graubert, J. *Heterosexual.* New York: Vantage Press, 1975.

Freud, S. "Three Contributions to Sexual Theory." *Nervous and Mental Disease Monograph Series,* 1925, 7.

Gubrium, J. F. "Being Single in Old Age." *International Journal of Aging and Human Development,* 1975, *6,* 29–41.

Hunt, M. *Sexual Behavior in the 1970s.* Chicago: Playboy Press, 1974.

Karlen, A. *Sexuality and Homosexuality.* New York: Norton, 1971.

Kastenbaum, R. J. & Costa, P. T. "Psychological Perspectives on Death." *Annual Review of Psychology,* 1977, *28,* 225–49.

Maugham, S. *El Greco.* New York: Doubleday, 1950.

Sears, R. R. "Sources of Life Satisfactions of the Terman Gifted Man." *American Psychologist,* 1977, *32,* 119–128.

Tripp, C. A. *The Homosexual Matrix.* New York: McGraw-Hill, 1975.

Weinberg, M. S. & Williams, C. J. *Male Homosexuals: Their Problems and Adaptations.* New York: Oxford University Press, 1974.

53. Prejudice and Homosexuality

Richard D. Mohr

Richard D. Mohr begins by noting that although gays are a significant percentage of the American population, they are characterized by stereotypes based on false generalizations. He cites one study in which 90 percent of gays and lesbians report that they have been victimized because of their sexual orientation. Mohr also questions whether a correct understanding of Christianity would condemn homosexuality, and he denies that any argument from nature supports such a condemnation. He further argues that if gays were socially accepted, society would be enriched and a step closer to its goal of "liberty and justice for all."

Who are gays anyway? A 1993 *New York Times*–CBS poll found that only one-fifth of Americans suppose that they have a friend or family member who is gay or lesbian. This finding is extraordinary given the number of practicing homosexuals in America. In 1948, Alfred Kinsey published a study of the sex lives of 12,000 white males. Its method was so rigorous that it set the standard for subsequent statistical research across the social sciences, but its results shocked the nation: thirty-seven percent of the men had at least one homosexual experience to orgasm in their adult lives; an additional thirteen percent had homosexual fantasies to orgasm; four percent were exclusively homosexual in their practices; another five percent had virtually no heterosexual experience, and nearly one fifth had at least as many homosexual as heterosexual experiences. Kinsey's 1953 study of the sex lives of 8000 women found the occurrence of homosexual behavior at about half the rates for men.

Every second family in the country has a member who is essentially homosexual and many more people regularly have homosexual experiences. Who are homosexuals? They are your friends, your minister, your teacher, your bankteller, your doctor, your mailcarrier, your officemate, your roommate, your congressional representative, your sibling, parent, and spouse. They are we. We are everywhere, virtually all ordinary, virtually all unknown.

Ignorance about gays, however, has not stopped people from having strong opinions about them. The void which ignorance leaves has been filled with stereotypes. Society holds two oddly contradictory groups of antigay stereotypes. One revolves around an individual's allegedly confused gender identity: lesbians are females who want to be, or at least look and act like, men—bull dykes, diesel dykes; while gay men are males who want to be, or at least look and act like, women—queens, fairies, nances, limp-wrists, nellies, sissies, aunties. These stereotypes of mismatches between biological sex and socially defined gender provide the materials through which lesbians and gay men become the butts of ethnic-like jokes. These stereotypes and jokes, though derisive, basically view gays as ridiculous: "How do you identify a bull dyke?" Answer: "She kick-starts her vibrator and rolls her own tampons." Or, "How many fags does it take to change a light bulb?" Answer: "Eight—one to replace it and seven to scream 'Faaaaaabulous!'"

The other set of stereotypes revolves around gays as a pervasive sinister conspiratorial threat. The core stereotype here is that of the gay person—especially gay man—as child molester, and more generally as sex-crazed maniac. Homosexuality here is viewed as a vampire-like corruptive contagion. These stereotypes carry with them fears of the very destruction of family and civilization itself. Now, that which is essentially ridiculous can hardly have such a staggering effect. Something must be afoot.

Sense can be made of this incoherent amalgam if the nature of stereotypes is clarified. Stereotypes are not simply false generalizations from a skewed sample of cases examined. Admittedly, false generalizing plays some part in the stereotypes society holds about gays and other groups. If, for instance, one takes as one's sample gay men who are in psychiatric hospitals or prisons, as was done in nearly all early investigations, not surprisingly one will probably find them to be of a crazed or criminal cast. Such false generalizations, though, simply confirm beliefs already held on independent grounds, ones that likely led the investigator to the prison and psychiatric ward to begin with. Evelyn Hooker, who in the late 1950s carried out the first rigorous studies of nonclinical gay men, found that psychiatrists, when presented with case files including all the standard diagnostic psychological profiles—but omitting indications of sexual orientation—were unable to distinguish gay files from nongay ones, even though they believed gay men to be crazy and supposed themselves to be experts in detecting craziness. These studies proved a profound embarrassment to the psychiatric establishment, the financial well-being of which has been substantially enhanced by "curing" allegedly insane gays. The studies led the way to the American Psychiatric Association's finally, in 1973, dropping homosexuality from its registry of mental illnesses. Nevertheless, the stereotype of gays as sick continues apace in the mind of America.

False generalizations help maintain stereotypes, they do not form them. As the story of Hooker's discoveries shows, stereotypes have a life beyond facts; their origins lies in a culture's ideology—the general system of beliefs by which it lives—and they are sustained across generations by diverse cultural transmissions, hardly any of which, including slang and jokes, even purport to have a scientific basis. Stereotypes, then, are not the products of bad science, but reflections of society's conception of itself.

On this understanding, it is easy to see that stereotypes about gays as gender-confused reinforce still powerful gender roles in society. If, as these stereotypes presume and condemn, one is free to choose one's social roles independently of one's biological sex, many guiding social divisions, both domestic and commercial, might be threatened. Blurred would be the socially sex-linked distinctions between breadwinner and homemaker, boss and secretary, doctor and nurse, protector and protected, even God and His world. The accusations "fag" and "dyke" serve in significant part to keep women in their place and to prevent men from breaking ranks and ceding away theirs.

The stereotypes of gays as civilization destroyers function to displace (possibly irresolvable) social problems from their actual source to a remote and (society hopes) manageable one. For example, the stereotype of child molester functions to give the traditionally defined family unit a false sheen of innocence. It keeps the unit from being examined too closely for incest, child abuse, wife-battering, and the terrorizing of women and children by a father's constant threats. The stereotype teaches that the problems of the family are not internal to it, but external.

One can see these cultural forces at work in society's and the media's treatment of current reports of violence, especially domestic violence. When a husband kills his wife or a father rapes his daughter—regular Section B fare even in major urban papers—this is never taken by reporters, columnists, or pundits as evidence that there is something wrong with heterosexuality or with traditional families. These issues are not even raised. But when a homosexual child molestation is reported, it is taken as confirming evidence of the way homosexuals are. One never hears of "heterosexual murders," but one regularly hears of "homosexual" ones.

If this account of stereotypes holds, society has been profoundly immoral. For its treatment of gays is a grand-scale rationalization, a moral sleight-of-hand. The problem is not that society's usual standards of evidence and procedure in decision making have been misapplied to gays, rather when it comes to gays, the standards themselves have simply been ruled out of court and disregarded in favor of mechanisms that encourage unexamined fear and hatred.

Partly because lots of people suppose they don't know any gay people and partly through the maintaining of stereotypes, society at large is unaware of the many ways in which gays are subject to discrimination in consequence of widespread fear and hatred. Contributing to this social ignorance of discrimination is the difficulty for gay people, as an invisible minority, even to complain of discrimination. For if one is gay, to register a complaint would suddenly target oneself as a stigmatized person, and so, especially in the absence of any protection against discrimination, would simply invite additional discrimination. So, discrimination against gays, like rape, goes seriously underreported. Even so, known discrimination is massive.

Annual studies by the National Gay and Lesbian Task Force have consistently found that over ninety percent of gay men and lesbians have been victims of violence or harassment in some form on the basis of their sexual orientation. Greater than one in five gay men and nearly one in ten lesbians have been punched, hit, or kicked; a quarter of all gays have had objects thrown at them; a third have been chased; a third have been sexually harassed, and fourteen percent have been spit on, all just for being perceived to be gay.

The most extreme form of antigay violence is queerbashing—where groups of young men target a person who they suppose is a gay man and beat and kick him unconscious and sometimes to death amid a torrent of taunts and slurs. Few such cases with gay victims reach the courts. Those that do are marked by inequitable procedures and results. Frequently judges will describe queerbashers as "just All-American Boys." A District of Columbia judge handed suspended sentences to queerbashers whose victim had been stalked, beaten, stripped at knife point, slashed, kicked, threatened with castration, and pissed on, because the judge thought the bashers were good boys at heart—they went to a religious prep school. In 1989, a judge in Dallas handed a sentence he acknowledged as light to the eighteen-year-old murderer of two gay men, because the murderer had killed them in a gay cruising zone, where the judge said they might be molesting children. The judge thereby justified a form of vigilantism that bears an eerie resemblance to the lynching of black men on the grounds that they might molest white women. Indeed, queerbashing has the same function that past lynchings of blacks had—to keep a whole stigmatized group in line. As with lynchings, society has routinely averted its eyes, giving its permission or even tacit approval to violence and harassment.

Police and juries will simply discount testimony from gays; they frequently construe assaults on and murders of gays as "justified" self-defense. The killer simply claims his act was an understandably panicked response to a sexual overture. Alternatively, when guilt seems patent, juries will accept highly implausible "diminished capacity" defenses, as in the case of Dan White's 1978 assassination of openly gay San Francisco city councilman Harvey Milk. Hostess Twinkies made him do it, or so the successful defense went. These inequitable procedures collectively show that the life and liberty of gays, like those of blacks, simply count for less than the life and liberty of members of the dominant culture.

The equitable rule of law is the heart of an orderly society. The collapse of the rule of law for gays shows that society is willing to perpetrate the worst possible injustices against them. As the ethnic and religious wars in the former Yugoslavia have made clear, there is only a difference in degree between the collapse of the rule of law and systematic extermination of members of a population simply for having some group status. In the Nazi concentration camps, gays were forced to wear pink triangles as identifying badges, just as Jews were forced to wear yellow stars. In remembrance of that collapse of the rule of law, the pink triangle has become the chief symbol of the gay rights movement.

Gays are also subject to widespread discrimination in employment. Governments are leading offenders here. They do a lot of discriminating themselves, require that others do it, and set precedents favoring discrimination in the private sector. Lesbians and gay men are barred from serving in the armed forces. The federal government has also denied gays employment in the CIA, FBI, National Security Agency, and the state department. The government refuses to give security clearances to gays and so forces the country's considerable private sector military and aerospace contractors to fire employees known to be gay and to avoid hiring those perceived to be gay. State and local governments regularly fire gay teachers, policemen, firemen, social workers, and anyone who has contact with the public. Further, state licensing laws (though frequently honored only in the breech) officially bar gays from a vast array of occupations and professions—everything from doctors, lawyers, accountants, and nurses to hairdressers, morticians, even used car dealers.

Gays are subject to discrimination in a wide variety of other ways, including private-sector employment, public accommodations, housing, insurance of all types, custody, adoption, and zoning regulations that bar "singles" or "nonrelated" couples from living together. A 1988 study by the congressional Office of Technology Assessment found that a third of America's insurance companies openly admit that they discriminate against lesbians and gay men. In nearly half the states, same-sex sexual behavior is illegal, so that the central role of sex to meaningful life is officially denied to lesbians and gay men.

Illegality, discrimination and the absorption by gays of society's hatred of them all interact to impede and, for some, block altogether the ability of gay men and lesbians to create and maintain significant personal relations with loved ones. Every facet of life is affected by discrimination. Only the most compelling reasons could justify it.

Many people think society's treatment of gays is justified because they think gays are extremely immoral. To evaluate this claim, different senses of "moral" must be distinguished. Sometimes by "morality" is meant the values generally held by members of a society—its mores, norms, and customs. On this understanding, gays certainly are not moral: lots of people hate them, and social customs are designed to register widespread disapproval of gays. The problem here is that this sense of morality is merely a descriptive one. On this understanding, every society has a morality—even Nazi society, which had racism and mob rule as central features of its "morality" understood in this sense. What is needed in order to use the notion of morality to praise or condemn behavior is a sense of morality that is prescriptive or normative.

As the Nazi example makes clear, that a belief or claim is descriptively moral does not entail that it is normatively moral. A lot of people in a society saying something is good, even over aeons, does not make it so. The rejection of the long history of socially approved and state-enforced slavery is another good example of this principle at work. Slavery would be wrong even if nearly everyone liked it. So consistency and fairness require that one abandon the belief that gays are immoral simply because most people dislike or disapprove of gays.

Furthermore, recent historical and anthropological research has shown that opinion about gays has been by no means universally negative. It has varied widely even within the larger part of the Christian era and even within the Church itself. There are even societies—current ones—where homosexual behavior is not only tolerated but is a universal compulsory part of male social maturation. Within the last thirty years, American society has undergone a grand turnabout from deeply ingrained, near total condemnation to near total acceptance on two emotionally charged "moral" or "family" issues—contraception and divorce. Society holds its current descriptive morality of gays not because it has to, but because it chooses to.

If popular opinion and custom are not enough to ground moral condemnation of homosexuality, perhaps religion can. Such arguments usually proceed along two lines. One claims that the condemnation is a direct revelation of God, usually through the Bible. The other claims to be able to detect condemnation in God's plan as manifested in nature; homosexuality (it is claimed) is "contrary to nature."

One of the more remarkable discoveries of recent gay research is that the Bible may not be as univocal in its condemnation of homosexuality as many have believed. Christ never mentions homosexuality. Recent interpreters of the Old Testament have pointed out that the story of Lot at Sodom is probably intended to condemn inhospitality rather than homosexuality. Further, some of the Old Testament condemnations of homosexuality seem simply to be ways of tarring those of the Israelites' opponents who happen to accept homosexual practices when the Israelites themselves did not. If so, the condemnation is merely a quirk of history and rhetoric rather than a moral precept.

What does seem clear is that those who regularly cite the Bible to condemn an activity like homosexuality do so by reading it selectively. Do ministers who cite what they take to be condemnations of homosexuality in Leviticus maintain in their lives all the hygienic and dietary laws of Leviticus? If they cite the story of Lot at Sodom to condemn homosexuality, do they also cite the story of Lot in the Cave to praise incestuous rape? It seems then not that the Bible is being used to ground condemnations of homosexuality as much as society's dislike of homosexuality is being used to interpret the Bible.

Even if a consistent portrait of condemnation could be gleaned from the Bible, what social significance should it be given? One of the guiding principles of society, enshrined in the Constitution as a check against the government, is that decisions affecting social policy are not made on religious grounds. The Religious Right has been successful in stymieing sodomy-law reform, in defunding gay safe-sex literature and gay art, and in blocking the introduction of gay materials into school curriculums. If the real ground of the alleged immorality invoked by governments to discriminate against gays is religious (as it seems to be in these cases), then one of the major commitments of our nation is violated. Religious belief is a fine guide around which a person might organize his own life, but an awful instrument around which to organize someone else's life.

People also try to justify society's treatment of gays by saying they are unnatural. Though the accusation of unnaturalness looks whimsical, when applied to homosexuality, it is usually delivered with venom of forethought. It carries a high emotional charge, usually expressing disgust and evincing queasiness. Probably it is nothing but an emotional charge. For people get equally disgusted and queasy at all sorts of things that are perfectly natural, yet that could hardly be fit subjects for moral condemnation. Two typical examples in current American culture are some people's responses to mothers' suckling in public and to women who do not shave body hair. Similarly people

fling the term "unnatural" against gays in the same breath and with the same force as when they call gays "sick" and "gross." When people have strong emotional reactions, as they do in these cases, without being able to give good reasons for them, they are thought of not as operating morally, but as being obsessed and manic. So the feelings of disgust that some people have toward gays will hardly ground a charge of immorality.

When "nature" is taken in technical rather than ordinary usages, it also cannot ground a charge of homosexual immorality. When unnatural means "by artifice" or "made by humans," it can be pointed out that virtually everything that is good about life is unnatural in this sense. The chief feature that distinguishes people from other animals is people's very ability to make over the world to meet their needs and desires. Indeed people's well-being depends on these departures from nature. On this understanding of human nature and the natural, homosexuality is perfectly unobjectionable; it is simply a means by which some people adapt nature to fulfill their desires and needs.

Another technical sense of natural is that something is natural and so, good, if it fulfills some function in nature. On this view, homosexuality is unnatural because it violates the function of genitals, which is to produce babies. One problem with this view is that lots of bodily parts have lots of functions and just because some one activity can be fulfilled by only one organ (say, the mouth for eating), this activity does not condemn other functions of the organ to immorality (say, the mouth for talking, licking stamps, blowing bubbles, or having sex). So the possible use of the genitals to produce children does not, without more, condemn the use of the genitals for other purposes, say, achieving ecstasy and intimacy.

The functional view of nature will only provide a morally condemnatory sense to the unnatural if a thing that might have many uses has but one proper function to the exclusion of other possible functions. But whether this is so cannot be established simply by looking at the thing. For what is seen is all its possible functions. The notion of function seemed like it might ground moral authority, but instead it turns out that moral authority is needed to define proper function.

Some people try to fill in this moral authority by appeal to the "design" or "order" of an organ, saying, for instance, that the genitals are designed for the purpose of procreation. But these people cheat intellectually if they do not make explicit who the designer and orderer is. If the "who" is God, we are back to square one—holding others accountable to one's own religious beliefs.

Further, ordinary moral attitudes about childbearing will not provide the needed supplement which would produce a positive obligation to use the genitals for procreation. Though there are local exceptions, society's general attitude toward a childless couple is that of pity not censure—even if the couple could have children. The pity may be an unsympathetic one, that is, not registering a course one would choose for oneself, but this does not make it a course one would require of others. The couple who discovers they cannot have children are viewed not as having thereby had a debt cancelled, but rather as having to forgo some of the richness of life, just as a quadriplegic is viewed not as absolved from some moral obligation to hop, skip, and jump, but as missing some of the richness of life. Consistency requires then that, at most, gays who do not or cannot have children are to be pitied rather than condemned. What *is* immoral is the willful preventing of people from achieving the richness of life. Immorality in this regard lies with those social customs, regulations, and statutes that prevent lesbians and gay men from establishing blood or adoptive families, not with gays themselves.

Many gays would like to raise or foster children—perhaps those alarming number of gay kids who have been beaten up and thrown out of their "families" for being gay. And indeed many lesbian and gay male couples are now raising robust, happy families where children are the blessings of adoption, artificial insemination, or surrogacy. The country is experiencing something approaching a gay and lesbian babyboom.

Sometimes people attempt to establish authority for a moral obligation to use bodily parts in a certain fashion simply by claiming that moral laws are natural laws and vice versa.

On this account, inanimate objects and plants are good in that they follow natural laws by necessity, animals follow them by instinct, and persons follow them by a rational will. People are special in that they must first discover the laws that govern them. Now, even if one believes the view—dubious in the post-Newtonian, post-Darwinian world—that natural laws in the usual sense ($e = mc^2$, for instance) have some moral content, it is not at all clear how one is to discover the laws in nature that apply to people.

On the one hand, if one looks to people themselves for a model—and looks hard enough—one finds amazing variety, including homosexual relations as a social ideal (as in upper-class fifth-century Athens) and even as socially mandatory (as in some Melanesian initiation rites today). When one looks to people, one is simply unable to strip away the layers of social custom, history, and taboo in order to see what's really there to any degree more specific than that people are the creatures that make over their world and are capable of abstract thought. That this is so should raise doubts that neutral principles are to be found in human nature that will condemn homosexuality.

On the other hand, if one looks to nature apart from people for models, the possibilities are staggering. There are fish that change sex over their lifetimes: should we "follow nature" and be operative transsexuals? Orangutans, genetically our next of kin, live completely solitary lives without social organization of any kind among adults: ought we to "follow nature" and be hermits? There are many species where only two members per generation reproduce: shall we be bees? The search in nature for people's purpose far from finding sure models for action is likely to leave one morally rudderless.

But (it might also be asked) aren't gays willfully the way they are? It is generally conceded that if sexual orientation is something over which an individual—for whatever reason—has virtually no control, then discrimination against gays is presumptively wrong, as it is against racial and ethnic classes.

Attempts to answer the question whether or not sexual orientation is something that is reasonably thought to be within one's own control usually appeal simply to various claims of the biological or "mental" sciences. But the ensuing debate over genes, hormones, hypothalamuses, twins, early childhood development, and the like is as unnecessary as it is currently inconclusive. All that is needed to answer the question is to look at the actual experience of lesbians and gay men in current society and it becomes fairly clear that sexual orientation is not likely a matter of choice.

On the one hand, the "choice" of the gender of a sexual partner does not seem to express a trivial desire which might as easily be fulfilled by a simple substitution of the desired object. Picking the gender of a sex partner is decidedly dissimilar, that is, to such activities as picking a flavor of ice cream. If an ice cream parlor is out of one's flavor, one simply picks another. And if people were persecuted, threatened with jail terms, shattered careers, loss of family and housing and the like for eating, say, rocky road ice cream, no one would ever eat it. Everyone would pick another easily available flavor. That gay people abide in being gay even in the face of persecution suggests that being gay is not a matter of easy choice.

On the other hand, even if establishing a sexual orientation is not like making a relatively trivial choice, perhaps it is relevantly like making the central and serious life-choices by which individuals try to establish themselves as being of some type or having some occupation. Again, if one examines gay experience, this seems not to be the general case. For one virtually never sees anyone setting out to become a homosexual, in the way one does see people setting out to become doctors, lawyers, and bricklayers. One does not find gays-to-be picking some end—"At some point in the future, I want to become a homosexual"—and then setting about planning and acquiring the ways and means to that end, in the way one does see people deciding that they want to become lawyers, and then sees them plan what courses to take and what sort of temperaments, habits, and skills to develop in order to become lawyers. Typically gays-to-be simply find themselves having homosexual encounters and yet, at least initially, resisting quite strongly the identification of being homosexual. Such a person even very likely resists having such encounters, but ends up having them

anyway. Only with time, luck, and great personal effort, but sometimes never, does the person gradually come to accept her or his orientation, to view it as a given material condition of life, coming as materials do with certain capacities and limitations. The person begins to act in accordance with his or her orientation and its capacities, seeing its actualization as a requisite for an integrated personality and as a central component of personal well-being. As a result, the experience of coming out to oneself has for gays the basic structure of a discovery, not the structure of a choice. And far from signaling immorality, coming out to others affords one of the few remaining opportunities in ever more bureaucratic, technological, and socialistic societies to *manifest* courage.

How would society at large be changed if gays were socially accepted? Suggestions to change social policy with regard to gays are invariably met with claims that to do so would invite the destruction of civilization itself: after all isn't that what did Rome in? Actually, Rome's decay paralleled not the flourishing of homosexuality but its repression under the later Christianized emperors. Predictions of American civilization's imminent demise have been as premature as they have been frequent. Civilization has shown itself to be rather resilient here, in large part because of the country's traditional commitments to respect for privacy, to individual liberties, and especially to people minding their own business. These all give society an open texture and the flexibility to try out things to see what works. And because of this, one now need not speculate about what changes reforms in gay social policy might bring to society at large. For many reforms have already been tried.

Half the states have decriminalized lesbian and gay male sex acts. Can you guess which of the following states still have sodomy laws: Wisconsin, Minnesota; New Mexico, Arizona; Vermont, New Hampshire; Nebraska, Kansas. One from each pair does and one does not have sodomy laws. And yet one would be hard pressed to point out any substantial social differences between the members of each pair. (If you're interested: it is the second of each pair with them.) Empirical studies have shown that there is no increase in other crimes in states that have decriminalized.

Neither has the passage of legislation barring discrimination against gays ushered in the end of civilization. Nearly a hundred counties and municipalities, including some of the country's largest cities (like Chicago and New York City) have passed such statutes, as have eight states: Wisconsin, Connecticut, Massachusetts, Hawaii, New Jersey, Vermont, California, and Minnesota. Again, no more brimstone has fallen in these places than elsewhere. Staunchly antigay cities, like Miami and Houston, have not been spared the AIDS crisis.

Berkeley, California, followed by a couple dozen other cities including New York, has even passed "domestic partner" legislation giving gay couples at least some of the same rights to city benefits as are held by heterosexually married couples, and yet Berkeley has not become more weird than it already was. A number of major universities (like Stanford and the University of Chicago) and respected corporations (like Levi Strauss and Company, the Montefiore Medical Center of New York, and Apple Computer, Inc.) are also following Berkeley's lead.

Seemingly hysterical predictions that the American family would collapse if such reforms would pass proved false, just as the same dire predictions that the availability of divorce would lessen the ideal and desirability of marriage proved unfounded. Indeed if current discrimination, which drives gays into hiding and into anonymous relations, ended, far from seeing gays destroying American families, one would see gays forming them.

Virtually all gays express a desire to have a permanent lover. But currently society and its discriminatory impulse make gay coupling very difficult. It is difficult for people to live together as couples without having their sexual orientation perceived in the public realm and so becoming targets for discrimination. Life in hiding is a pressure-cooker existence not easily shared with another. Members of nongay couples are here asked to imagine what it would take to erase every trace of their own sexual orientation for even just one week.

Even against oppressive odds, gays have shown an amazing tendency to nest. And those gay couples who have survived the odds show that the structure of more usual couplings is not a matter of destiny, but of personal responsibility. The so-called basic unit of society turns out not to be a unique immutable atom, but can adopt different parts, be adapted to different needs, and even be improved. Gays might even have a thing or two to teach others about divisions of labor, the relation of sensuality and intimacy, and the stages of development in such relations.

If discrimination ceased, gay men and lesbians would enter the mainstream of the human community openly and with self-respect. The energies that the typical gay person wastes in the anxiety of leading a day-to-day existence of systematic disguise would be released for use in personal flourishing. From this release would be generated the many spin-off benefits that accrue to a society when its individual members thrive.

Society would be richer for acknowledging another aspect of human diversity. Families with gay members would develop relations based on truth and trust rather than lies and fear. And the heterosexual majority would be better off for knowing that they are no longer trampling their gay friends and neighbors.

Finally and perhaps paradoxically, in extending to gays the rights and benefits it has reserved for its dominant culture, America would confirm its deeply held vision of itself as a morally progressing nation, a nation itself advancing and serving as a beacon for others—especially with regard to human rights. The words with which our national pledge ends—"with liberty and justice for all"—are not a description of the present, but a call for the future. America is a nation given to a prophetic political rhetoric that acknowledges that morality is not arbitrary and that justice is not merely the expression of the current collective will. It is this vision that led the black civil rights movement to its successes. Those senators and representatives who opposed that movement and its centerpiece, the 1964 Civil Rights Act, on obscurantist grounds, but who lived long enough and were noble enough came in time to express their heartfelt regret and shame at what they had done. It is to be hoped and someday to be expected that those who now grasp at anything to oppose the extension of that which is best about America to gays will one day feel the same.

54. *Bowers v. Hardwick*

The Supreme Court of the United States

The issue before the Supreme Court was whether the Georgia sodomy statute violates the Federal Constitution. In delivering the opinion of the Court, Justice White argues that the statute does not violate the Constitution because the Constitution does not confer a fundamental right on homosexuals to engage in sodomy. While in previous cases, the Constitution was interpreted to confer a right to decide whether or not to beget or bear a child and a right not to be convicted for possessing and reading obscene material in the privacy of one's home, White argues that the Constitution cannot be analogously interpreted to confer a fundamental right on homosexuals to engage in sodomy. Justice Burger concurs, stressing the ancient roots of sodomy statutes. Justice Blackmun joined by Justices Brennan and Marshall argues that notwithstanding the ancient roots of prohibitions against homosexuality, a right to be let alone that is the underpinning of previous court decision justifies in this case a right to engage in sodomy at least in the privacy of one's home.

Justice *White* delivered the opinion of the Court.

In August 1982, respondent Hardwick . . . was charged with violating the Georgia statute criminalizing sodomy by committing that act with another adult male in the bedroom of respondent's home. After a preliminary hearing, the District Attorney decided not to present the matter to the grand jury unless further evidence developed.

Respondent then brought suit in the Federal District Court, challenging the constitutionality of the statute insofar as it criminalized consensual sodomy. He asserted that he was a practicing homosexual, that the Georgia sodomy statute, as administered by the defendants, placed him in imminent danger of arrest, and that the statute for several reasons violates the Federal Constitution. . . .

This case does not require a judgment on whether laws against sodomy between consenting adults in general, or between homosexuals in particular, are wise or desirable. It raises no question about the right or propriety of state legislative decisions to repeal their laws that criminalize homosexual sodomy, or of state-court decisions invalidating those laws on state constitutional grounds. The issue presented is whether the Federal Constitution confers a fundamental right upon homosexuals to engage in sodomy and hence invalidates the laws of the many States that still make such conduct illegal and have done so for a very long time. The case also calls for some judgment about the limits of the Court's role in carrying out its constitutional mandate.

We first register our disagreement with the Court of Appeals and with respondent that the Court's prior cases have construed the Constitution to confer a right of privacy that extends to homosexual sodomy and for all intents and purposes have decided this case. . . . [Three] cases were interpreted as construing the Due Process Clause of the Fourteenth Amendment to confer a fundamental individual right to decide whether or not to beget or bear a child. . . .

Accepting the decisions in these cases . . . we think it evident that none of the rights announced in those cases bears any resemblance to the claimed constitutional right of homosexuals to engage in acts of sodomy that is asserted in this case. No connection between family, marriage, or procreation on the one hand and homosexual activity on the other has been demonstrated, either by the Court of Appeals or by respondent. Moreover, any claim that these cases nevertheless stand for the proposition that any kind of private sexual conduct between consenting adults is constitutionally insulated from state proscription is unsupportable. . . .

Precedent aside, however, respondent would have us announce, as the Court of Appeals did, a fundamental right to engage in homosexual sodomy. This we are quite unwilling to do. It is true that despite the language of the Due Process Clauses of the Fifth and Fourteenth Amendments, which appears to focus only on the processes by which life, liberty, or property is taken, the cases are legion in which those Clauses have been interpreted to have substantive content, subsuming rights that to a great extent are immune from federal or state regulation or proscription. Among such cases are those recognizing rights that have little or no textual support in the constitutional language. . . .

Striving to assure itself and the public that announcing rights not readily identifiable in the Constitution's text involves much more than the imposition of the Justices' own choice of values on the States and the Federal Government, the Court has sought to identify the nature of the rights qualifying for heightened judicial protection. In *Palko v. Connecticut*, . . . it was said that this category includes those fundamental liberties that are "implicit in the concept of ordered liberty," such that "neither liberty nor justice would exist if [they] were sacrificed." A different description of fundamental liberties appeared in *Moore v. East Cleveland*, . . . where they are characterized as those liberties that are "deeply rooted in this Nation's history and tradition." . . .

It is obvious to us that neither of these formulations would extend a fundamental right to homosexuals to engage in acts of consensual sodomy. Proscriptions against that conduct have ancient roots. . . . Sodomy was a criminal offense at common law and was forbidden by the laws of the original thirteen States when they ratified the Bill of Rights. In 1868, when the Fourteenth Amendment was ratified, all but 5 of the 37 States in the Union had criminal sodomy laws. In fact, until 1961, all 50 States outlawed sodomy, and today, 24 States and the District of Columbia continue to provide criminal penalties for sodomy performed

in private and between consenting adults. . . . Against this background, to claim that a right to engage in such conduct is "deeply rooted in this Nation's history and tradition" or "implicit in the concept of ordered liberty" is, at best, facetious.

Nor are we inclined to take a more expansive view of our authority to discover new fundamental rights imbedded in the Due Process Clause. The Court is most vulnerable and comes nearest to illegitimacy when it deals with judge-made constitutional law having little or no cognizable roots in the language or design of the Constitution. That this is so was painfully demonstrated by the face-off between the Executive and the Court in the 1930s, which resulted in the repudiation of much of the substantive gloss that the Court had placed on the Due Process Clauses of the Fifth and Fourteenth Amendments. There should be, therefore, great resistance to expand the substantive reach of those Clauses, particularly if it requires redefining the category of rights deemed to be fundamental. Otherwise, the Judiciary necessarily takes to itself further authority to govern the country without express constitutional authority. The claimed right pressed on us today falls far short of overcoming this resistance.

Respondent, however, asserts that the result should be different where the homosexual conduct occurs in the privacy of the home. He relies on *Stanley v. Georgia*, . . . where the Court held that the First Amendment prevents conviction for possessing and reading obscene material in the privacy of one's home: "If the First Amendment means anything, it means that a State has no business telling a man, sitting alone in his house, what books he may read or what films he may watch." . . .

Stanley did protect conduct that would not have been protected outside the home, and it partially prevented the enforcement of state obscenity laws; but the decision was firmly grounded in the First Amendment. The right pressed upon us here has no similar support in the text of the Constitution, and it does not qualify for recognition under the prevailing principles for construing the Fourteenth Amendment. Its limits are also difficult to discern. Plainly enough, otherwise illegal conduct is not always immunized whenever it occurs in the home. Victimless crimes, such as the possession and use of illegal drugs, do not escape the law where they are committed at home. *Stanley* itself recognized that its holding offered no protection for the possession in the home of drugs, firearms, or stolen goods. . . . And if respondent's submission is limited to the voluntary sexual conduct between consenting adults, it would be difficult, except by fiat, to limit the claimed right to homosexual conduct while leaving exposed to prosecution adultery, incest, and other sexual crimes even though they are committed in the home. We are unwilling to start down that road.

Even if the conduct at issue here is not a fundamental right, respondent asserts that there must be a rational basis for the law and that there is none in this case other than the presumed belief of a majority of the electorate in Georgia that homosexual sodomy is immoral and unacceptable. This is said to be an inadequate rationale to support the law. The law, however, is constantly based on notions of morality, and if all laws representing essentially moral choices are to be invalidated under the Due Process Clause, the courts will be very busy indeed. Even respondent makes no such claim, but insists that majority sentiments about the morality of homosexuality should be declared inadequate. We do not agree, and are unpersuaded that the sodomy laws of some 25 States should be invalidated on this basis.

Accordingly, the judgment of the Court of Appeals is
Reversed.

Chief Justice *Burger,* concurring.

I join the Court's opinion, but I write separately to underscore my view that in constitutional terms there is no such thing as a fundamental right to commit homosexual sodomy.

As the Court notes, . . . the proscriptions against sodomy have very "ancient roots." Decisions of individuals relating to homosexual conduct have been subject to state intervention throughout the history of Western civilization. Condemnation of those practices is firmly rooted in Judaeo-Christian moral and ethical standards. Homosexual sodomy was a capital crime under Roman law. . . . During the En-

glish Reformation when powers of the ecclesiastical courts were transferred to the King's Courts, the first English statute criminalizing sodomy was passed. . . . Blackstone described "the infamous *crime against nature*" as an offense of "deeper malignity" than rape, a heinous act "the very mention of which is a disgrace to human nature," and "a crime not fit to be named." . . . The common law of England, including its prohibition of sodomy, became the received law of Georgia and the other Colonies. In 1816 the Georgia Legislature passed the statute at issue here, and that statute has been continuously in force in one form or another since that time. To hold that the act of homosexual sodomy is somehow protected as a fundamental right would be to cast aside millennia of moral teaching.

This is essentially not a question of personal "preferences" but rather of the legislative authority of the State. I find nothing in the Constitution depriving a State of the power to enact the statute challenged here. . . .

Justice *Blackmun,* with whom Justice *Brennan,* Justice *Marshall,* and Justice *Stevens* join, dissenting.

This case is no more about "a fundamental right to engage in homosexual sodomy," as the Court purports to declare, . . . than *Stanley v. Georgia* . . . was about a fundamental right to watch obscene movies, or *Katz v. United States,* . . . was about a fundamental right to place interstate bets from a telephone booth. Rather, this case is about "the most comprehensive of rights and the right most valued by civilized men," namely, "the right to be let alone." . . .

The statute at issue, . . . denies individuals the right to decide for themselves whether to engage in particular forms of private, consensual sexual activity. The Court concludes that [the statute] is valid essentially because "the laws of . . . many States . . . still make such conduct illegal and have done so for a very long time." . . . But the fact that the moral judgments expressed by statutes like . . . [the Georgia statute] may be " 'natural and familiar . . . ought not to conclude our judgment upon the question whether statutes embodying them conflict with the Constitution of the United States.' " . . . Like Justice Holmes, I believe that "[i]t is revolting to have no better reason for a rule of law than that so it was laid down in the time of Henry IV. It is still more revolting if the grounds upon which it was laid down have vanished long since, and the rule simply persists from blind imitation of the past." . . . I believe we must analyze Hardwick's claim in the light of the values that underlie the constitutional right to privacy. If that right means anything, it means that, before Georgia can prosecute its citizens for making choices about the most intimate aspects of their lives, it must do more than assert that the choice they have made is an " 'abominable crime not fit to be named among Christians.' " . . .

In its haste to reverse the Court of Appeals and hold that the Constitution does not "confe[r] a fundamental right upon homosexuals to engage in sodomy," . . . the Court relegates the actual statute being challenged to a footnote and ignores the procedural posture of the case before it. A fair reading of the statute and of the complaint clearly reveals that the majority has distorted the question this case presents.

. . . [T]he Court's almost obsessive focus on homosexual activity is particularly hard to justify in light of the broad language Georgia has used. Unlike the Court, the Georgia Legislature has not proceeded on the assumption that homosexuals are so different from other citizens that their lives may be controlled in a way that would not be tolerated if it limited the choices of those other citizens. . . . Rather, Georgia has provided that "[a] person commits the offense of sodomy when he performs or submits to any sexual act involving the sex organs of one person and the mouth or anus of another." . . . The sex or status of the persons who engage in the act is irrelevant as a matter of state law. In fact, to the extent I can discern a legislative purpose for Georgia's 1968 enactment . . . that purpose seems to have been to broaden the coverage of the law to reach heterosexual as well as homosexual activity. I therefore see no basis for the Court's decision to treat this case . . . solely on the grounds that it prohibits homosexual activity. Michael Hardwick's standing may rest in significant part on Georgia's apparent willingness to enforce against homosexuals a law it seems not to have any desire to enforce against heterosexuals. . . . But his claim that . . . [the Georgia statute] involves an unconstitutional intrusion into his privacy and his right of intimate association does not depend in any way on his sexual orientation. . . .

"Our cases long have recognized that the Constitution embodies a promise that a certain private sphere of individual liberty will be kept largely beyond the reach of government." . . . In construing the right to privacy, the Court has proceeded along two somewhat distinct, albeit complementary, lines. First, it has recognized a privacy interest with reference to certain *decisions* that are properly for the individual to make. . . . Second, it has recognized a privacy interest with reference to certain *places* without regard for the particular activities in which the individuals who occupy them are engaged. . . . The case before us implicates both the decisional and the spatial aspects of the right to privacy.

The Court concludes today that none of our prior cases dealing with various decisions that individuals are entitled to make free of governmental interference "bears any resemblance to the claimed constitutional right of homosexuals to engage in acts of sodomy that is asserted in this case." . . . While it is true that these cases may be characterized by their connection to protection of the family, . . . the Court's conclusion that they extend no further than this boundary ignores the warning in *Moore v. East Cleveland,* . . . against "clos[ing] our eyes to the basic reasons why certain rights associated with the family have been accorded shelter under the Fourteenth Amendment's Due Process Clause." We protect those rights not because they contribute, in some direct and material way, to the general public welfare, but because they form so central a part of an individual's life. "[T]he concept of privacy embodies the 'moral fact that a person belongs to himself and not others nor to society as a whole.' " . . . And so we protect the decision whether to marry precisely because marriage "is an association that promotes a way of life, not causes; a harmony in living, not political faiths; a bilateral loyalty, not commercial or social projects." . . . We protect the decision whether to have a child because parenthood alters so dramatically an individual's self-definition, not because of demographic considerations or the Bible's command to be fruitful and multiply. . . . And we protect the family because it contributes so powerfully to the happiness of individuals, not because of a preference for stereotypical households. . . . The Court recognized in *Roberts* . . . that the "ability independently to define one's identity that is central to any concept of liberty" cannot truly be exercised in a vacuum; we all depend on the "emotional enrichment from close ties with others."

Only the most willful blindness could obscure the fact that sexual intimacy is "a sensitive, key relationship of human existence, central to family life, community welfare, and the development of human personality," . . . The fact that individuals define themselves in a significant way through their intimate sexual relationships with others suggests, in a Nation as diverse as ours, that there may be many "right" ways of conducting those relationships, and that much of the richness of a relationship will come from the freedom an individual has to *choose* the form and nature of these intensely personal bonds. . . .

In a variety of circumstances we have recognized that a necessary corollary of giving individuals freedom to choose how to conduct their lives is acceptance of the fact that different individuals will make different choices. For example, in holding that the clearly important state interest in public education should give way to a competing claim by the Amish to the effect that extended formal schooling threatened their way of life, the Court declared: "There can be no assumption that today's majority is 'right' and the Amish and others like them are 'wrong.' A way of life that is odd or even erratic but interferes with no rights or interests of others is not to be condemned because it is different." . . . The Court claims that its decision today merely refuses to recognize a fundamental right to engage in homosexual sodomy; what the Court really has refused to recognize is the fundamental interest all individuals have in controlling the nature of their intimate associations with others.

The behavior for which Hardwick faces prosecution occurred in his own home, a place to which the Fourth Amendment attaches special significance. The Court's treatment of this aspect of the case is symptomatic of its overall refusal to consider the broad principles that have informed our treatment of privacy in specific cases. Just as the right to privacy is more than the mere aggregation of a number of entitlements to engage in specific behavior, so too, protecting the physical integrity of the home is more than merely a means of protecting specific activities that often take place there. Even when our understanding of the contours of the right to privacy depends on "reference to a 'place,' " . . . "the essence of a Fourth Amendment violation is 'not the breaking of [a person's] doors, and the rummaging of his drawers,' but rather is 'the invasion of his indefeasible right of personal security, personal liberty and private property.' " . . .

The Court's interpretation of the pivotal case of *Stanley v. Georgia,* . . . is entirely unconvincing. *Stanley* held that Georgia's undoubted power to punish the public distribution of constitutionally unprotected, obscene material did not permit the State to punish the private possession of such material. According to the majority here, *Stanley* relied entirely on the First Amendment, and thus, it is claimed, sheds no light on cases not involving printed materials. . . . But that is not what *Stanley* said. Rather, the *Stanley* Court anchored its holding in the Fourth Amendment's special protection for the individual in his home:

"The makers of our Constitution undertook to secure conditions favorable to the pursuit of happiness. They recognized the significance of man's spiritual nature, of his feelings and of his intellect. They knew that only a part of the pain, pleasure and satisfactions of life are to be found in material things. They sought to protect Americans in their beliefs, their thoughts, their emotions and their sensations."

"These are the rights that appellant is asserting in the case before us. He is asserting the right to read or observe what he pleases—the right to satisfy his intellectual and emotional needs in the privacy of his own home." . . . quoting *Olmstead v. United States* . . .

The central place that *Stanley* gives Justice Brandeis' dissent in *Olmstead*, a case raising *no* First Amendment claim, shows that *Stanley* rested as much on the Court's understanding of the Fourth Amendment as it did on the First. Indeed, in *Paris Adult Theatre I v. Slaton*, . . . the Court suggested that reliance on the Fourth Amendment not only supported the Court's outcome in *Stanley* but actually was *necessary* to it: "If obscene material unprotected by the First Amendment in itself carried with it a 'penumbra' of constitutionally protected privacy, this Court would not have found it necessary to decide *Stanley* on the narrow basis of the 'privacy of the home,' which was hardly more than a reaffirmation that 'a man's home is his castle.' " . . . "The right of the people to be secure in their . . . houses," expressly guaranteed by the Fourth Amendment, is perhaps the most "textual" of the various constitutional provisions that inform our understanding of the right to privacy, and thus I cannot agree with the Court's statement that "[t]he right pressed upon us here has no . . . support in the text of the Constitution," . . . Indeed, the right of an individual to conduct intimate relationships in the intimacy of his or her own home seems to me to be the heart of the Constitution's protection of privacy. . . .

. . . Petitioner asserts that the acts made criminal by the statute may have serious adverse consequences for "the general public health and welfare," such as spreading communicable diseases or fostering other criminal activity. . . . Inasmuch as this case was dismissed by the District Court on the pleadings, it is not surprising that the record before us is barren of any evidence to support petitioner's claim. In light of the state of the record, I see no justification for the Court's attempt to equate the private, consensual sexual activity at issue here with the "possession in the home of drugs, firearms, or stolen goods," . . . to which *Stanley* refused to extend its protection. . . . None of the behavior so mentioned in *Stanley* can properly be viewed as "[v]ictimless," . . . : drugs and weapons are inherently

dangerous, . . . and for property to be "stolen," someone must have been wrongfully deprived of it. Nothing in the record before the Court provides any justification for finding the activity forbidden [by the Georgia statute] to be physically dangerous, either to the persons engaged in it or to others.

The core of petitioner's defense . . . however, is that respondent and others who engage in the conduct prohibited . . . interfere with Georgia's exercise of the " 'right of the Nation and of the States to maintain a decent society,' " . . . Essentially, petitioner argues, and the Court agrees, that the fact that the acts described . . . "for hundreds of years, if not thousands, have been uniformly condemned as immoral" is a sufficient reason to permit a State to ban them today. . . .

I cannot agree that either the length of time a majority has held its convictions or the passions with which it defends them can withdraw legislation from this Court's scrutiny. . . . As Justice Jackson wrote so eloquently . . . "we apply the limitations of the Constitution with no fear that freedom to be intellectually and spiritually diverse or even contrary will disintegrate the social organization. . . . [F]reedom to differ is not limited to things that do not matter much. That would be a mere shadow of freedom. The test of its substance is the right to differ as to things that touch the heart of the existing order." . . . It is precisely because the issue raised by this case touches the heart of what makes individuals what they are that we should be especially sensitive to the rights of those whose choices upset the majority.

The assertion that "traditional Judeo-Christian values proscribe" the conduct involved, . . . cannot provide an adequate justification. . . . That certain, but by no means all, religious groups condemn the behavior at issue gives the State no license to impose their judgments on the entire citizenry. The legitimacy of secular legislation depends instead on whether the State can advance some justification for its law beyond its conformity to religious doctrine. . . . Thus, far from buttressing his case, petitioner's invocation of Leviticus, Romans, St. Thomas Aquinas, and sodomy's heretical status during the Middle Ages undermines his suggestion that [the

Georgia statute] represents a legitimate use of secular coercive power. A State can no more punish private behavior because of religious intolerance than it can punish such behavior because of racial animus. "The Constitution cannot control such prejudices, but neither can it tolerate them. Private biases may be outside the reach of the law, but the law cannot, directly or indirectly, give them effect." . . . No matter how uncomfortable a certain group may make the majority of this Court, we have held that "[m]ere public intolerance or animosity cannot constitutionally justify the deprivation of a person's physical liberty." . . .

. . . Reasonable people may differ about whether particular sexual acts are moral or immoral, but "we have ample evidence for believing that people will not abandon morality, will not think any better of murder, cruelty and dishonesty, merely because some private sexual practice which they abominate is not punished by the law." . . . Petitioner and the Court fail to see the difference between laws that protect public sensibilities and those that enforce private morality. Statutes banning public sexual activity are entirely consistent with protecting the individual's liberty interest

in decisions concerning sexual relations: the same recognition that those decisions are intensely private which justifies protecting them from governmental interference can justify protecting individuals from unwilling exposure to the sexual activities of others. But the mere fact that intimate behavior may be punished when it takes place in public cannot dictate how States can regulate intimate behavior that occurs in intimate places. . . .

This case involves no real interference with the rights of others, for the mere knowledge that other individuals do not adhere to one's value system cannot be a legally cognizable interest, . . . let alone an interest that can justify invading the houses, hearts, and minds of citizens who choose to live their lives differently.

. . . I can only hope that . . . the Court soon will reconsider its analysis and conclude that depriving individuals of the right to choose for themselves how to conduct their intimate relationships poses a far greater threat to the values most deeply rooted in our Nation's history than tolerance of nonconformity could ever do. Because I think the Court today betrays those values, I dissent.

---

55. Gays in the Military: Between Fear and Fantasy

Ken Corbett

Ken Corbett tries to explain the fear and hatred that was expressed regarding ending the ban against gays and lesbians in the military

Military officials and Congressional leaders cite the possible threat of violence to homosexuals as a reason to continue discriminating against gays in the military. This raises the obvious question of whether we should be governed by threat. But we also are left to ask what fuels such aggression.

Throughout the debate, straight military

From *The New York Times,* February 3, 1993. © 1993 by The New York Times Company. Reprinted by permission.

men keep voicing concern that they will not be able to control their aggression against gay men. Gay soldiers and sailors are threatened with the prospect of being beaten, even murdered. As if to prove the point, three marines beat a homosexual man outside a gay bar in Wilmington, N.C., Saturday morning while shouting, "Clinton must pay!"

Why is this aggression almost exclusively focused on gay men? Newspaper articles are full of the anger and concerns of male soldiers. Talk shows feature verbal slugfests between gay and straight military men. Women are almost never mentioned. This no doubt reflects military demographics, but it also reflects the manner in which the hatred of male homosexuality is founded on fears of femininity. The equation is simple: male homosexuality equals femininity, which produces fear, which produces aggression.

More specifically, hatred of gay men is based on fear of the self, not of an alien other. This was expressed by Martin Jones, a 22-year-old airman quoted in this paper as saying he wouldn't be able to sleep at night if the ban were lifted because he would be "worried that some homosexual is going to sneak over and make a pass."

Seemingly unaware of the slippery slope between fear and fantasy, he conveyed a suspicion that gay men will not be able to control their sexual appetite, and rape will ensue. Leaving aside the fact that rape is largely a heterosexual phenomenon (and a prevalent heterosexual male fantasy), Airman Jones's concern smacks of the pernicious misconception that gay men and women have a devouring sexual appetite—that they are hungry sirens eager to bite.

More to the point, Mr. Jones imagines himself the object of a man's desire. He anxiously pictures himself wanted in a way that most men feel only a woman should be wanted. In so fantasizing, he must, if ever so briefly, put himself in the place of a man who desires another man.

But Mr. Jones quickly sheds this threatening desire: He and his like-minded colleagues turn the object of desire into a hated, threatening object. Mr. Jones creates a distinct border between "them" and "us." He is not one of them, he hates them.

Hatred thrives on rigid order. Armed with hatred and protected by institutional values, Mr. Jones doesn't have to take responsibility for his aggressive impulses. Mr. Jones, his commanders and many in Congress would have us believe this kind of phobic behavior should guide military policy. But what kind of policy is built on a phobic solution? What kind of law is built on hatred?

Apparently these are not questions that Mr. Jones is asking himself when he can't fall asleep. He thinks sneaky homosexuals cause his insomnia. But it is really his own fears and fantasies that keep him awake.

Suggestions for Further Reading

Anthologies

Batchelor, E. *Homosexuality and Ethics.* New York: Pilgrim Press, 1980.

Dudley, William. *Homosexuality—Opposing Viewpoints.* San Diego: Greenhaven Press, 1993.

Marmor, J. *Homosexual Behavior.* New York: Basic Books, 1980.

Basic Concepts

"Survey on the Constitutional Right to Privacy in the Context of Homosexual Activity." *Miami Law Review* (1986), pp. 521–657.

Alternative Views

du Mas, F. *Gay Is Not Good.* Nashville, Tenn.: Thomas Nelson Publishers, 1979.

Friedman, R. *Male Homosexuality.* New Haven, Ct.: Yale University Press, 1988.

Harrigan, J. *Homosexuality: The Test Case for Christian Ethics.* Mahwah, N.J.: Paulist Press, 1988.

Malloy, E. *Homosexuality and the Christian Way of Life.* Lanham, Md.: University Press of America, 1981.

Mohr, R. *Gays/Justice.* New York: Columbia University Press, 1988.

Animal Liberation and Environmental Justice

Introduction

Basic Concepts

The problem of animal liberation and environmental justice has begun to attract widespread public attention. Beginning with the 1973 publication of Peter Singer's article, "Animal Liberation," in the *New York Review of Books,* followed by the publication two years later of his book of the same title, people have become increasingly concerned with two of the most serious forms of animal exploitation: animal experimentation and factory farming.

Animal experimentation is a big business, involving 60 to 100 million animals a year. Two experiments alone—the rabbit-blinding Draize eye test and the LD50 toxicity test designed to find the lethal dose for 50 percent of a sample of animals—cause the deaths of more than 5 million animals per year in the United States alone. In factory farming, millions of animals are raised in such a way that their short lives are dominated by pain and suffering. Veal calves are put in narrow stalls and tethered with a chain so that they cannot turn around, lie down comfortably, or groom themselves. They are fed a totally liquid diet to promote rapid weight gain, and they are given no water because thirsty animals eat more than those who drink water.

In recent years, environmental concern has focused on a myriad of problems from acid rain to the destruction of the rain forests and the ozone layer. For example, the acidity of rainfall over the northeastern United States has quadrupled since 1900. Moreover, just last year, an estimated 12,350 square miles of Brazilian rain forest—an area larger than Belgium—was reduced to ashes, and over the past decade, ozone levels over Antarctica have diminished by 50 percent. In many cases, resolving these problems will require extensive programs and international cooperation. For example, in the Montreal protocol of 1987, dozens of nations agreed to cut their chlorofluorocarbon emissions (which are thought to be the major cause of ozone depletion) in half by the end of the century, and several countries and the major chlorofluorocarbon manufacturers have more recently announced their intentions to eliminate the chemicals by that deadline.

At the most general level, the problem of animal liberation and environmental concern raises the question of what should be our policies for treating animals and preserving the environment, or alternatively, what is the moral status of nonhuman living things. One possible answer is that nonhuman living things have no independent moral status at all, but that their moral status depends completely on the impact they have on human welfare. Another possible answer is that nonhuman living things have an independent moral status such that their welfare has to be weighed against, and at least sometimes outweigh, considerations of human welfare.

Obviously, supporters of animal liberation favor the view that animals have independent moral status, but they disagree as to the grounds for this independent moral status. Some claim that animals have independent moral status because taking their welfare into account would maximize overall utility. Others claim that the independent moral status of animals rests on a nonutilitarian foundation.

This conflict among supporters of animal liberation reflects a general conflict among utilitarians and nonutilitarians with respect to a wide range of practical problems (see the General Introduction to this anthology). However, with respect to this particular problem, supporters of animal liberation cannot rely on some form of a Kantian theory to reach an acceptable resolution because most animals are incapable of forming either an actual or hypothetical contract with human beings for the purpose of securing their common welfare. Kantian theory, however, is only a means to a goal, which is to achieve a fair resolution of morally relevant interests. Consequently, if nonhuman living things do have morally relevant interests, then to achieve that goal some means other than Kantian theory will have to be employed.

This is not to say that Kantian theory is not useful for achieving a fair resolution of conflicts when only human interests pertain. In fact, it would seem that a fair resolution of conflicts among human and nonhuman interests would mirror a fair resolution of conflicts among purely human interests. For example, if a utilitarian (or a nonutilitarian) resolution were fair when only human interests are taken into account, a utilitarian (or a nonutilitarian) resolution would seem to be fair when both human and nonhuman interests are considered.

With respect to environmental concern, supporters do not agree that all nonhuman living things have independent moral status. Those who maintain that only sentient beings have independent moral status attempt to ground human concern for other living things on the impact they have on the welfare of sentient beings. Accordingly, to resolve the problem of animal liberation and environmental concern, we must determine which living beings have independent moral status and what sort of justification best accounts for that status.

Alternative Views

In Selection 56, R. D. Guthrie defends an anthropocentric environmental ethics according to which nonhuman living things have no independent moral status. Instead their moral status depends entirely on the impact they have on the human community. Guthrie argues that it is both illogical and impractical to extend moral concern beyond the human community. Given that we already recognize the relationships of nonhuman organisms to each other and to ourselves to be nonmoral, Guthrie claims that it is illogical to think our relationship to nonhuman organisms was anything but nonmoral as well. Moreover, he argues that it would be impractical for us when making decisions as to what to do to have to weigh the effects our actions have on nonhuman organisms.

Yet although it is true that only moral agents like ourselves can recognize moral value, why should we think that we are the only ones to have moral value? Surely things can have moral value without being able to recognize moral value, in fact, some humans are like that. Of course, weighing the welfare of nonhuman organisms against our own will make our deliberations more complicated, but it need not render them impractical if we can

devise some reasonable weighing principles as James P. Sterba argues we can in Selection 59.

In Selection 57, Peter Singer argues for the independent moral status of animals by comparing the bias against animals, which he calls "speciesism," with biases against blacks and women. According to Singer, the grounds we have for opposing racism and sexism are also grounds for opposing speciesism because all forms of discrimination run counter to the principle of equal consideration. Racists violate this principle by giving greater weight to the interests of members of their own race in cases of conflict; sexists violate this principle by favoring the interests of their own specific sex; and speciesists violate this principle by allowing the interests of their own species to override the greater interests of other species.

Animals have interests, Singer maintains, because they have a capacity for suffering and enjoyment. According to the principle of equal consideration, there is no justification for regarding the pain animals feel as less important than the same amount of pain (or pleasure) humans feel. As for the practical requirements of this view, Singer contends that we cannot go astray if we give the same respect to the lives of animals that we give to the lives of humans at a similar mental level. In the end, Singer thinks, this requires a utilitarian weighing of both human and animal interests.

Singer's view has been challenged on the grounds that utilitarianism does not ultimately support a strong case for animal rights for several reasons. First of all, by Singer's own admission, it is permissible to eat farm animals, typically cattle and sheep, that are reared and killed without suffering. Second, Singer's objection to the suffering inflicted on animals in factory farms can be overcome by reforming the practices used on such farms rather than by requiring that we become vegetarians. Third, a radical turn to vegetarianism would probably result in the elimination of most farm animals as we know them because they certainly cannot survive in the wild. This would seriously disrupt and/or eliminate many industries and social practices, resulting in significant disutility.

Responding to these criticisms in an article

in the *New York Review of Books,* Singer makes two points. He first claims that adopting vegetarianism would improve people's general health, eliminate Third World poverty, and create new and beneficial industries and social practices. Second, Singer claims that in political campaigning, opposition to the current techniques of factory farming is not taken seriously unless one is also a committed vegetarian. According to Singer, only vegetarians can silence that invariable objection to reforming our treatment of animals: But don't you eat them?

Nevertheless, Singer's response turns on the political effectiveness of being a vegetarian and the effects vegetarianism would have on human welfare rather than its effects on animal welfare. However, it is in terms of animal welfare that the case for animal rights must ultimately be made.

In Selection 58, Paul W. Taylor argues that all living beings have independent moral status. He grounds his view on two central claims: (1) that each individual organism is a teleological center of life, pursuing its own good in its own way, and (2) that whether we are concerned with standards of merit or with the concept of inherent worth, there is no grounds for believing that humans by their very nature are superior to other species. Taylor's argument for his second claim is similar to the argument used in the General Introduction to support morality against rational egoism. Both claim that their view represents a non-question-begging solution.

The main difficulty with Taylor's view concerns how we are to weigh human welfare against the good of other living beings if we were to grant that human beings are not superior to other species. In a later book that develops the argument of this essay, Taylor distinguishes between basic and nonbasic interest of living beings, but because he doesn't hold that the basic interests always have priority over nonbasic interests, it is difficult to know how decisions should be made when there is conflict between human and nonhuman interests.

In Selection 59, James P. Sterba seeks to resolve a central debate in contemporary environmental ethics between those who defend an anthropocentric ethics and those who defend a nonanthropocentric ethics by showing that when the most morally defensible versions of each of these perspectives are laid out, they do not lead to different practical recommendations. He develops a set of principles for weighing human against nonhuman welfare, contending that should be acceptable to defenders of both anthropocentric and nonanthropocentric environmental ethics. Obviously, the crucial question is whether these principles do represent common ground between these opposing perspectives and whether they can be effectively applied.

Practical Applications

The next two selections come from the only federal law in the United States pertaining to the treatment of animals. The provisions of the Animal Welfare Act (Selection 60) pertain only to the transportation of animals and the treatment of animals for research and experimentation. The act does not mention the treatment of animals in factory farms. The amendments to the Animal Welfare Act (Selection 61) passed in 1985 represent a considerable strengthening of the original act. Specifically, the amendments call for a national data bank that will list the results of all animal experiments and thus prevent needless repetition. All laboratories using live animals are also required, under the amendments, to set up animal-care committees and submit to annual inspections. Facilities housing dogs must let them exercise, and those housing primates must provide for their "psychological well-being." Unfortunately, the implementation of these amendments is currently held up by the federal budget office.

In *Tennessee Valley Authority v. Hill* (Selection 62), the issue before the Supreme Court is whether the Endangered Species Act of 1973 prohibited the completion of a dam whose operation would destroy the habitat of the snail darter, an endangered species, despite the fact that the dam was virtually completed and that Congress continued to appropriate large sums of money to the project even after the congressional appropriations committees were apprised of the project's apparent impact on the survival of the snail darter. The Court held that the Endangered Species Act did prohibit the completion of the dam because the language of the act and the history that led to its passage required that its provisions be applied without exceptions. Immediately after this Supreme Court decision, however, Congress amended the Endangered Species Act to provide a "review" process designed to relax the protection accorded endangered species in some circumstances. In the case of the snail darter, protection was relaxed because it was possible to transport snail darters to another river. It was also discovered that additional populations of snail darters existed in other rivers. An interesting sidelight to this case, however, was that an economic study conducted in the interim revealed that the construction of the dam was a pork barrel project. Its benefits to the Tennessee economy could have been achieved in much less costly ways while at the same time preserving the natural state of the river.

Although there is no denying that existing federal laws protecting animals and the environment are quite limited in scope, it seems clear that any solution to the problem of animal liberation and environmental concern that gives independent moral status to all living beings, or even just to all sentient beings will, if implemented, have a significant impact on the way we live and work and, accordingly, on how we will be able to solve the other practical problems discussed in this anthology.

56. Anthropocentrism

R. D. Guthrie

R. D. Guthrie argues that it is both illogical and impractical to extend moral concern beyond the human community. He argues that it is illogical to think that our relationship to nonhuman organisms is moral when we already recognize that the relationships of nonhuman organisms to each other and to ourselves are nonmoral. He argues that it is impractical for us to have to weigh the effect that our actions are having on nonhuman organisms when we are deciding what to do.

The nature of our responsibilities toward other organisms is certainly no new issue, but the controversy has been reignited recently by legislative action to regulate the care and maintenance of laboratory stock. Although this specific issue involves a decision of immediate concern to scientists, it also raises the even more basic question as to the general role that other organisms should occupy in our ethical system. It seems prudent that we should first examine the problem in its broadest context before further legislative action and the firm lines of political alignment are drawn.

An analysis of one aspect of our ethical

From "The Ethical Relationship between Humans and Other Organisms." *Perspectives in Biology and Medicine.* Vol. II (1967–1968).

system necessarily involves some dealings with the system as a whole. Unfortunately, the area of ethical theory can sometimes be an ideological quagmire from which few return enlightened. Much of the difficulty arises from our being drawn, by tradition, into thinking that our moral scaffolding is suspended from some outside agency. Rather, I would subscribe to the concept that moral principles, and the standards by which they are judged, are human constructs and thus can be evaluated on an empirical basis, even though the criteria are complex and the judgments sometimes difficult. Inherent in this position is the idea that our judgments are dependent upon generalizations from past experiences and may have to be altered as new situations are encountered. The only aprioristic element is the underlying assumption that man's rules of conduct are to be to his benefit. For the limited purposes of this essay, I will thus assume that the most desirable rules governing human behavior are those which, now and in the future, promote the welfare of the human population as an aggregate of individuals and contribute to the smooth functioning of its social machinery, while at the same time allowing for the greatest freedom of individual expression and fulfilment. Such a conceptual distillation necessarily includes academic deficiencies with which philosophers of ethical theory will quibble; but, by and large, this has become the gauge by which we evaluate political systems, economic policies, codes of sexual behavior, technological innovations, planned parenthood, and so forth. This assumption of the most desirable code of conduct forms the basis of the idea that I wish to present.

My thesis is that the inclusion of other organisms as primary participants in our ethical system is both logically unsound and operationally unfeasible. It is illogical because we cannot consider other organisms as moral bodies and amoral bodies simultaneously. By *moral bodies* I mean those entities ultimately to be considered in evaluating the action. As an example of this categorization, let us say that, as part of an experiment, a mineralogist wishes to dissolve a unique crystal. On what basis does he decide that the destruction will be worthwhile? The judgment has to be made on the effect of his action on living and future humans—the immediate benefits derived from the crystal's destruction weighed against the assets of its continued existence. The rare crystal is an amoral body, since our concern is with the ultimate effect on humans (the moral bodies which made this a moral question) and not with the welfare of the rock per se.

The relationships among non-human organisms are also not generally defined as moral or immoral. Most would agree that a wild wolf killing a wild deer is, in and of itself, not subject to moral analysis. We as humans may wish to keep the wolf from killing a game species, or the weeds from stunting the turnips, but we do not contend that the wolves and weeds are immoral for so doing. We wish to curtail the wolf and weed population, not ultimately for the sake of the deer and turnips,

but for our own ends. In my categorization, then, rare crystals, wolves, deer, weeds, and turnips are all amoral bodies. Likewise, an act of another organism toward humans, say a mosquito bite, could also be classified as amoral. The mosquito is an amoral body, and we do not hold it morally responsible for having bitten us. Thus, at two bonds of a triangular relationship, we recognize the amoral nature of the non-human's act toward another non-human organism and, second, a non-human organism's act toward a human as being amoral. It is difficult not to conclude that the final bond—a human's act toward other organisms—is, in and of itself, an amoral one. It becomes a moral act only when humans are affected, because our moral codes are rules of human behavior, as I assumed in the beginning, and, as such, exclude other organisms as primary participants.

The fallacy of giving other organisms the status of moral bodies and amoral bodies simultaneously leads us into what we might refer to as "Schweitzer's dilemma." In his *reverence for life* philosophy, Schweitzer considered each organism as an individual whose suffering and death were to be avoided if at all possible. If one supports this philosophy—that it is the organism's discomfort, the welfare of the organism itself, that is our concern—he is confronted with the perplexing situation of having to regard pain that occurs "in the wild" as bad. Since it is an individual organism's discomfort that is emphasized and not the effect upon the human causing it, the pain will be just as real no matter what the origin. One is, as Schweitzer was, forced to regard predators as evil. However, predators avoid the pains of starvation and eventual death by causing pain and death to other organisms. This relationship is an inherent part of the community structure where energy is transferred from one trophic level to the next, ergo, the dilemma. Failure to have reverence for the predator's life is itself a contradiction of the basic tenet of Schweitzer's philosophy, yet to have reverence for the predator's life is to revere those processes which result in pain and death. Furthermore, if it is the organism's pain, in and of itself, that we wish to prevent, we incur responsibilities beyond our own species' actions. The Schweitzerian philosophy implies that the billions of non-human animals (and plants?) which are being mutilated and killed in nature are the unattended wards of humankind.

Within our own species, if a fellow member becomes mentally or physically incapacitated to function within the moral code, we make corresponding adjustments by withholding some of those freedoms which are given to others (we confine him to a mental institution or hospital ward or require glasses while driving). To extend a similar sliding scale of conduct toward, or expected conduct from, other organisms is operationally unfeasible. First of all, we would have to formulate some sort of discriminatory system which would define the nature and extent of preferential moral treatment. Which organisms would we include in our moral system, and to what degree?

Some who apply our moral code to other organisms do so only to higher organisms. However, the concept of a "higher" organism is a rather nebulous affair. Which is "higher," a bee, apple tree, elephant, sailfish, or winter wheat? The ideas of "progressive," "advanced," or "higher" may be applied, with meaning, to a phylogenetic sequence—the older being more primitive—or with reference to one particular character—horses exhibiting a more advanced state of digit reduction than man. However, as a generalized concept, "higher" is interlaced with teleological overtones that are rejected by virtually all evolutionists.

The concept of phylogenetic proximity has also been suggested as a discriminatory basis for evaluating the behavior of other organisms. As well as having anthropocentric underwear, this idea also involves other problems; for example, sewer rats are probably just as close phylogenetically to humans as are cocker spaniels. Relying on something like the potential for learned behavior seems just as arbitrary and shallow. All organisms which rely more on the equally successful "instinctive" behavior would be whimsically bypassed.

Not only do we face absurd decisions as to what organisms we are to apply the code among the different taxa, but the question can also be posed as to how individual variation within each species is to be regarded. There is

even the problem of the fluctuation of our code through time. Does the evaluation of what constitutes "indecent exposure" also change for other organisms? These and many other questions arise. If, however, we are to consider our morality as an entirely human phenomenon, and apply it only to humans, many problems are eliminated, and the system is workable. We need not cringe in sin every time we bite into a pork chop, trim the hedge, or order the pooch to get the paper. The human ramifications of any deed are ponderous enough.

My contention that human acts committed toward other organisms can only be evaluated by their human effects should be interpreted in its broadest sense. One could even argue that a highly pathogenic species of bacteria should not be driven to extinction. It may be wise to maintain the species as a protected laboratory culture in the event that future development may be able to utilize the species as a valuable source of information or a unique research tool. Although hunting, fishing, butterfly collecting, and wildflower picking provide immediate recreation, these species must also be managed with regard to their recreational use by future generations of humans. The health of our livestock, both those in the private laboratory and those raised for commercial purposes, must necessarily have high priority because our health as consumers and the information that we as scientists derive from them depend upon their physical condition. In the management of livestock and game species, our concern is mainly with population parameters and not with specific individuals. This is not the case with pets. Since one of the chief functions of a pet is to provide companionship, the owner must be concerned about his pet as an individual—an organism from which he receives pleasure by exchanging affection—and should be able to expect that other people will treat his pet with this in mind. I do not wish to imply in the presentation of this philosophy of our relationships with other organisms that the owner should look upon his Rover without emotion or affection, for to do so would destroy the relationship from which the owner is receiving satisfaction. However, he should not deceive himself by thinking that he is giving the dog attention solely for the dog's sake. The motivation for domesticating and continuing to raise pets is not the improvement of these animals' welfare.

In general practice, we do not bring laboratory and domestic animals under the same moral consideration that we do other humans. We regulate their diet, decide on breeding time and specific mate, compel them to do tasks against their volition, eat them, and put them to death when they become senile. Only in rare instances have human slaves received similar treatment.

The basic distinction in the human interpretation of the two phenomena, slavery of other humans and slavery of other organisms, is rather revealing. We do not hesitate in our discrimination against those organisms who are not our own species. The categorization is discrete and operationally meaningful in its broadest application. Those times in the past when human slavery has been condoned, and those sentiments among us today that are sympathetic with human enslavement, can be tied to the idea that the subjugated are "other"— something else radically different from me and mine. A fairer criticism of the mistake of the *apartheid* attitude is not so much a breach of the moral code as it is bad taxonomy. The growing world pressure against racial discrimination is perhaps due to the increasing recognition that we are all one species with very little, if any, interpopulational variation in potential ability to accumulate information, to formulate ideas, and to experience the varied forms of social interaction.

Although it is but a small minority of humans that wish to extend such moral codes as "freedom from servitude" to other organisms, many rebel in revulsion when they witness other organisms experiencing pain. This, I believe, is because we have stronger emotions relating to the prevention of human pain than we do for preventing such things as freedom infringements, and have been more thorough in our anthropomorphic transference of these to other organisms. Yet, in the attempt to incorporate the pain experienced by other organisms directly into our moral judgments, we are courting the same logical and practical difficulties which we encounter in any consideration of them as moral bodies.

A current example will bring the question into better focus. Suppose society is faced with the decision whether to permit students the freedom to experiment with live laboratory animals, bred and maintained for that purpose, or to withhold this freedom by law on the basis that the animal's pain and ensuing death caused by the inexperienced hands of the student is not worth the information and experience that the student derives. It is difficult to imagine any basis of equivalency by which we could evaluate education in terms of some translatable value of rat pain. I contend that there is no common denominator. Even the problems that we face within our own moral system, in attempting to weigh the immediate discomforts of the varied forms of child discipline, and the dangers of testing a new drug, against their long-term advantages, border on being insurmountable. However, we still have a common foundation for our judgments—human welfare.

A recurrent thread in most discussions on the relationship of our ethics to other animals is the concept that none should be hurt or caused to die unnecessarily. Certainly all would agree with this in theory. However, we have no common basis to judge *necessity* in this context. One group contends that all vivisection is unnecessary; another feels that most is necessary. How does one judge if it is necessary to kill or cause other organisms pain for the aesthetic enjoyments of fishing, recovering from a mild parasitic infection, training a retriever dog, or having a mosquito-free back yard? What unresolvable quandaries we are led into! The act that is unnecessary to one is quite necessary to another, and we eventually return to the *effect upon humans* as the final basis of evaluation.

Also, if one wishes to assume the position that killing and causing other organisms pain is "justified when necessary for sustenance," but nevertheless immoral, then we must surely classify meat-eating societies, like the Eskimos, as more evil than some vegetarian agriculturists. Our own meat-eating habits would also have to be abandoned, for who among us would take the hypocritical position that we eat prime T-bone only for the necessary protein? We, by heritage and necessity, are organisms with heterotrophic habits and tastes and, therefore, are tethered to continued existence by the inexorable expenditure of the lives of other organisms. Our heterotrophic nature precludes any philosophy which would judge killing of other organisms as a sinful act against those organisms.

Throughout the evolution of social thought, man has not always visualized himself as separate from other organisms, just as he drew no distinct line between animate and inanimate objects. But the growing trend in the modern world to anthropomorphize the acts of other organisms arises from a rather different source. Early man had an intimate contact with other organisms, and his incorporation of these other species into his philosophy and religion no doubt was a result of this dependency upon and fear of other species. In the process of our self-domestication we have removed ourselves farther and farther from our contact with other species, and it is because of this lack of firsthand understanding and familiarity that we attribute human feelings and motivations to other organisms. Although science has enabled us to place ourselves in the proper phylogenetic scheme, it has also removed humanity as a whole from the firsthand contact with, and appreciation of, some basic ecological processes. We have seldom seen the organisms that we eat, when they were alive. It is not uncommon to meet people who are upset at the thought of eating the same lobster that they chose from the live-box earlier in the evening. Although perhaps small by comparison, the price that we pay for the benefits of modern society is the loss in breadth of experience gained from seeing ourselves "in the system," as direct participants in the life and death of other organisms somewhat similar to ourselves. Moreover, we can expect further increases in this price as society's relationship with other organisms becomes even more indirect. Perhaps the current boom and rising influence of animal suffrage groups exemplifies this trend.

One can identify the changes in attitude within this century as we grade from a rural to an urban society. On the farm there was a sharper line between humans and other organisms. The pigs were butchered and the peas canned. As urbanites, our contact with other organisms is usually with pets or even the more humanized cartoon characters. Children reared in our urban society may misread "roast duck" on the menu as roast Donald, and bears are those furry people who wear ranger hats in ads that tell you to use care with matches. Our increasingly limited experience with other organisms has caused us to extend further our moral code outside its sphere of applicability. What a black day for the nation if Alfred the alligator ended up in the last frame of Tuesday's Special chomping a half-skinned, intestines-dangling, Pogo—but, of course, that is part of the real relationship between alligators and opossums.

We have generated a phobia of seeing viscera of other organisms and of seeing them killed. The idea that insides are repugnant, and our distaste for non-human death, probably originated as extensions of the fear of human death or witnessing human viscera. Relating emotionally to other organisms is no doubt a natural by-product of the breakdown of our sharp value delineation between humans and non-humans, resulting from our increasing lack of contact with other organisms. However, this transference of our fears and concerns about humans to other species may detract from the welfare of our own species. If we are to sterilize our view of life by editing the realities of nature to suit our anthropomorphic attitudes, we can anticipate attendant limitations in our potential for understanding ourselves and the real world about us. To become involved in the births and deaths of other organisms in the laboratory or in the field, if it can be done without any recognizable loss to human welfare, may help us understand or at least feel more deeply the natural processes of life and death, of which we are a part. Also, witnessing the inner complexities of individual function surely contributes to our appreciation of the phenomenon of life. Denying ourselves these perspectives by letting our emotions completely humanize other organisms may be no trivial loss.

If we are to accept the idea that our moral system was designed by man for regulating the behavior of his own species and that it is improper to apply it to other organisms, we can then attempt to deal with a related issue—the nature of our moral obligation to other humans as it relates to our conduct toward other organisms. How must we behave if our treatment of a non-human organism offends others who empathize more than we do? In its extreme form, one pressure group attempts to legislate its tastes or emotional sensitivities on the minority group. Consider bullfighting and live pigeon shoots, both of which are illegal in the United States. Those who wish to outlaw these events have two alternative arguments, assuming that they themselves are not forced to experience or witness the event: they can take the position that it is detrimental either to the bull's welfare or to the welfare of those who are attending. In the case of the first position, one courts some of the problems that I have been reviewing. The basis of the second position has yet to be demonstrated. We are told by some who attend these events that they can be enjoyable and rewarding experiences, and in those countries where they occur now, we can but conclude that they are enjoyed by many people. Those who disagree take the position that an emphasis on the "humane" treatment of other organisms will further nurture those qualities in our relationship with other humans. In some situations this is probably true, but, unfortunately, blurring this difference also invites the other part of the association; and disposing of an intestinal parasite would be a poor analogy to our disposition toward a fellow human drawing unemployment compensation. I would rather take the other view, that it is the distinction between human welfare and the welfare of other things that will provide deeper meaning to the preciousness of the human individual. Debasing the value of human relationships by a loose analogy with our relationship to other organisms has affected, and no doubt could further affect, the esteem of human worth.

I refer again to the criteria for evaluating moral actions, stated in the beginning, that the rules governing human behavior should be constructed to regard the welfare of humans not only as a group but also as individuals. This necessitates maintaining the greatest possible latitude of individual behavior without markedly encroaching on the welfare of the unit as a whole. We must then make sure that to allow one segment to perform an act does not, in consequence, detract materially from the freedom of another segment, and, if so, some mutual compromise will have to be made. Performing a physiology experiment with the exposed viscera of a live horse in the middle of a public park does not show moral regard for the individuals who, by witnessing it, would experience considerable discomfort. Even though the physiologist may feel that the squeamishness of the lady passerby is unjustified, he nevertheless has the responsibility to consider her emotional sensitivities. Likewise, the same lady must allow other segments of society to use other organisms in their education and enjoyment, so long as she is not personally forced to experience or witness those acts. This is, of course, the same principle that we use in other matters of individual taste (e.g., nudity, intoxication, and loud parties).

The classroom is a slightly different situation. The teacher has been given the responsibility to aid people in their education in the best way he knows. The teacher's judgment to require the student to work on living organisms (or to read *Catcher in the Rye*, for that matter) may be intended to give the student a more intimate contact with other perspectives that cannot be communicated by just reading a lab manual or a literary review. Thus a teacher has a less restricted license to expose his students to other ways of feeling and thinking than does one stranger to another. But certainly there are still limitations. Interestingly enough, almost all of the opposition to vivisection in schools has been directed, not toward the question of the students' rights and discomforts, but of the animals'.

The error of extending moral judgment outside the system is widespread among scientists. Biologists are particularly susceptible. Most biologists were attracted to their discipline because they were fascinated with animals in their youth, and in the modern world this fascination is generally on an individual basis with pets, cartoon characters, circus performers, and zoo inhabitants. We as biologists are hesitant to accord other organisms the same moral status as inorganic objects because of the striking kinship we share morphologically, physiologically, and behaviorally (those areas with which biologists are most familiar). And, of course, the philosophical tendency to include other organisms directly in human codes of behavior stems, indirectly, from these phylogenetic bonds. However, our ethical constructs apply to an entirely different level of organization, a level with which biologists typically do not deal professionally. Value judgments of human conduct are in the same realm as concepts such as citizenship and taxation where we do categorize other animate objects in the same set with inorganic ones, and would consider as ludicrous the application of an idea such as proportional representation—"one individual, one vote"—to include gophers.

Although many other species have, like the human species, evolved their own codes of social behavior, they have only done so directly or indirectly to increase the welfare of the members of their own species. Not unexpectedly, these codes are not the same ones that we have constructed for ourselves.

The key theme of this essay is that the human species, or for that matter any species, is under no moral obligation to extend its own internal code of behavior to other species and that it can be a serious error to do so; however, it would be an equal or greater error to take the short-sighted view that a species' welfare is merely an intraspecific matter. Any species is a segment of the entire community, and its integrity and continued existence cannot be evaluated aside from the larger community unit. The quality of our future as humans will depend on the quality of our management of the community of organisms of which we are an integral part. To impede this management by misunderstanding the nature of *either* our ecological or moral relationships can only be to the human detriment.

---

57. All Animals Are Equal

Peter Singer

Peter Singer begins his defense of animal liberation by comparing the bias against animals with biases against blacks and women. According to Singer, all of these forms of discrimination violate the principle of equal consideration. According to this principle, there is no justification for regarding the pain that animals feel as less important than the same amount of pain (or pleasure) felt by humans.

"Animal Liberation" may sound more like a parody of other liberation movements than a serious objective. The idea of "The Rights of Animals" actually was once used to parody the case for women's rights. When Mary Wollstonecraft, a forerunner of today's feminists, published her *Vindication of the Rights of Women* in 1792, her views were widely regarded as absurd, and before long an anonymous publication appeared entitled *A Vindication of the Rights of Brutes*. The author of this satirical work (now known to have been Thomas Taylor, a distinguished Cambridge philoso-

From *Animal Liberation* (New York: New York Review, 1975), pp. 1–22. Reprinted by permission of Peter Singer.

pher) tried to refute Mary Wollstonecraft's arguments by showing that they could be carried one stage further. If the argument for equality was sound when applied to women, why should it not be applied to dogs, cats, and horses? The reasoning seemed to hold for these "brutes" too; yet to hold that brutes had rights was manifestly absurd; therefore the reasoning by which this conclusion had been reached must be unsound, and if unsound when applied to brutes, it must also be unsound when applied to women, since the very same arguments had been used in each case.

In order to explain the basis of the case for the equality of animals, it will be helpful to start with an examination of the case for the equality of women. Let us assume that we wish to defend the case for women's rights against the attack by Thomas Taylor. How should we reply?

One way in which we might reply is by saying that the case for equality between men and women cannot validly be extended to nonhuman animals. Women have a right to vote, for instance, because they are just as capable of making rational decisions about the future as men are; dogs, on the other hand, are incapable of understanding the significance of voting, so they cannot have the right to vote. There are many other obvious ways in which men and women resemble each other closely, while humans and animals differ greatly. So, it might be said, men and women are similar beings and should have similar rights, while humans and nonhumans are different and should not have equal rights.

The reasoning behind this reply to Taylor's analogy is correct up to a point, but it does not go far enough. There *are* important differences between humans and other animals, and these differences must give rise to *some* differences in the rights that each have. Recognizing this obvious fact, however, is no barrier to the case for extending the basic principle of equality to nonhuman animals. The differences that exist between men and women are equally undeniable, and the supporters of Women's Liberation are aware that these differences may give rise to different rights. Many feminists hold that women have the right to an abortion on request. It does not follow that since these same feminists are campaigning for equality between men and women they must support the right of men to have abortions too. Since a man cannot have an abortion, it is meaningless to talk of his right to have one. Since a dog can't vote, it is meaningless to talk of its right to vote. There is no reason why either Women's Liberation or Animal Liberation should get involved in such nonsense. The extension of the basic principle of equality from one group to another does not imply that we must treat both groups in exactly the same way, or grant exactly the same rights to both groups. Whether we should do so will depend on the nature of the members of the two groups. The basic principle of equality does not require equal or identical *treatment;* it requires equal *consideration.*

Equal consideration for different beings may lead to different treatment and different rights.

So there is a different way of replying to Taylor's attempt to parody the case for women's rights, a way that does not deny the obvious differences between humans and nonhumans but goes more deeply into the question of equality and concludes by finding nothing absurd in the idea that the basic principle of equality applies to so-called "brutes." At this point such a conclusion may appear odd; but if we examine more deeply the basis on which our opposition to discrimination on grounds of race or sex ultimately rests, we will see that we would be on shaky ground if we were to demand equality for blacks, women, and other groups of oppressed humans while denying equal consideration to nonhumans. To make this clear we need to see, first, exactly why racism and sexism are wrong.

When we say that all human beings, whatever their race, creed, or sex, are equal, what is it that we are asserting? Those who wish to defend hierarchical, inegalitarian societies have often pointed out that by whatever test we choose it simply is not true that all humans are equal. Like it or not we must face the fact that humans come in different shapes and sizes; they come with different moral capacities, different intellectual abilities, different amounts of benevolent feeling and sensitivity to the needs of others, different abilities to communicate effectively, and different capacities to experience pleasure and pain. In short, if the demand for equality were based on the actual equality of all human beings, we would have to stop demanding equality.

Still, one might cling to the view that the demand for equality among human beings is based on the actual equality of the different races and sexes. Although, it may be said, humans differ as individuals there are no differences between the races and sexes *as such.* From the mere fact that a person is black or a woman we cannot infer anything about that person's intellectual or moral capacities. This, it may be said, is why racism and sexism are wrong. The white racist claims that whites are superior to blacks, but this is false—although there are differences among individuals, some blacks are superior to some whites in all of the capacities and abilities that could conceivably be relevant. The opponent of sexism would say the same: a person's sex is no guide to his or her abilities, and this is why it is unjustifiable to discriminate on the basis of sex.

The existence of individual variations that cut across the lines of race or sex, however, provides us with no defense at all against a more sophisticated opponent of equality, one who proposes that, say, the interests of all those with IQ scores below 100 be given less consideration than the interests of those with ratings over 100. Perhaps those scoring below the mark would, in this society, be made the slaves of those scoring higher. Would a hierarchical society of this sort really be so much better than one based on race or sex? I think not. But if we tie the moral principle of equality to the factual equality of the different races or sexes, taken as a whole, our opposition to racism and sexism does not provide us with any basis for objecting to this kind of inegalitarianism.

There is a second important reason why we ought not to base our opposition to racism and sexism on any kind of actual equality, even the limited kind that asserts that variations in capacities and abilities are spread evenly between the different races and sexes: we can have no absolute guarantee that these capacities and abilities really are distributed evenly, without regard to race or sex, among human beings. So far as actual abilities are concerned there do seem to be certain measurable differences between both races and sexes. These differences do not, of course, appear in each case, but only when averages are taken. More important still, we do not yet know how much of these differences is really due to the different genetic endowments of the different races and sexes, and how much is due to poor schools, poor housing, and other factors that are the result of past and continuing discrimination. Perhaps all of the important differences will eventually prove to be environmental rather than genetic. Anyone opposed to racism and sexism will certainly hope that this will be so, for it will make the task of ending discrimination a lot easier; nevertheless it would be dangerous to rest the case against racism and sexism on the belief that all significant differences are environmental in origin. The opponent of, say, racism who takes this line will be unable to avoid conceding that *if* differences in ability do after all prove to have some genetic connection with race, racism would in some way be defensible.

Fortunately there is no need to pin the case for equality to one particular outcome of a scientific investigation. The appropriate response to those who claim to have found evidence of genetically based differences in ability between the races or sexes is not to stick to the belief that the genetic explanation must be wrong, whatever evidence to the contrary may turn up: instead we should make it quite clear that the claim to equality does not depend on intelligence, moral capacity, physical strength, or similar matters of fact. Equality is a moral idea, not an assertion of fact. There is no logically compelling reason for assuming that a factual difference in ability between two people justifies any difference in the amount of consideration we give to their needs and interests. *The principle of the equality of human beings is not a description of an alleged actual equality among humans: it is a prescription of how we should treat humans.*

Jeremy Bentham, the founder of the reforming utilitarian school of moral philosophy, incorporated the essential basis of moral equality into his system of ethics by means of the formula: "Each to count for one and none for more than one." In other words, the interests of every being affected by an action are to be taken into account and given the same weight as the like interests of any other being. A later utilitarian, Henry Sidgwick, put the point in this way: "The good of any one individual is of no more importance, from the point of view (if I may say so) of the Universe, than the good of any other." More recently the leading figures in contemporary moral philosophy have shown a great deal of agreement in specifying as a fundamental presupposition of their moral theories some similar requirement which operates so as to give everyone's interests equal consideration—although these writers generally cannot agree on how this requirement is best formulated.[1]

It is an implication of this principle of equality that our concern for others and our readiness to consider their interests ought not to depend on what they are like or on what abilities they may possess. Precisely what this concern or consideration requires us to do may vary according to the characteristics of those affected by what we do: concern for the well-being of a child growing up in America would require that we teach him to read; concern for the well-being of a pig may require no more than that we leave him alone with other pigs in a place where there is adequate food and room to run freely. But the basic element—the taking into account of the interests of the being, whatever those interests may be —must, according to the principle of equality, be extended to all beings, black or white, masculine or feminine, human or nonhuman.

Thomas Jefferson, who was responsible for writing the principle of the equality of men into the American Declaration of Independence, saw this point. It led him to oppose slavery even though he was unable to free himself fully from his slaveholding background. He wrote in a letter to the author of a book that emphasized the notable intellectual achievements of Negroes in order to refute the then common view that they had limited intellectual capacities:

> Be assured that no person living wishes more sincerely than I do, to see a complete refutation of the doubts I have myself entertained and expressed on the grade of understanding allotted to them by nature, and to find that they are on a par with ourselves . . . but whatever be their degree of talent it is no measure of their rights. Because Sir Isaac Newton was superior to others in understanding, he was not therefore lord of the property or person of others.[2]

Similarly when in the 1850s the call for women's rights was raised in the United States a remarkable black feminist named Sojourner Truth made the same point in more robust terms at a feminist convention:

> . . . they talk about this thing in the head; what do they call it? ["Intellect," whispered someone near by.] That's it. What's that got to do with women's rights or Negroes' rights? If my cup won't hold but a pint and yours holds a quart, wouldn't you be mean not to let me have my little half-measure full?[3]

It is on this basis that the case against racism and the case against sexism must both ultimately rest; and it is in accordance with this principle that the attitude that we may call "speciesism," by analogy with racism, must also be condemned. Speciesism—the word is not an attractive one, but I can think of no better term—is a prejudice or attitude of bias toward the interests of members of one's own species and against those of members of other species. It should be obvious that the fundamental objections to racism and sexism made by Thomas Jefferson and Sojourner Truth apply equally to speciesism. If possessing a higher degree of intelligence does not entitle one human to use another for his own ends, how can it entitle humans to exploit nonhumans for the same purpose?[4]

Many philosophers and other writers have proposed the principle of equal consideration of interests, in some form or other, as a basic moral principle; but not many of them have recognized that this principle applies to members of other species as well as to our own. Jeremy Bentham was one of the few who did realize this. In a forward-looking passage written at a time when black slaves had been freed by the French but in the British dominions were still being treated in the way we now treat animals, Bentham wrote:

> The day *may* come when the rest of the animal creation may acquire those rights which never could have been withholden from them but by the hand of tyranny. The French have already discovered that the blackness of the skin is no reason why a human being should be abandoned without redress to the caprice of a tormentor. It may one day come to be recognized that the number of the legs, the villosity of the skin, or the termination of the *os sacrum* are reasons equally insufficient for abandoning a sensitive being to the same fate. What else is it that should trace the insuperable line? Is it the faculty of reason, or perhaps the faculty of discourse? But a full-grown horse or dog is beyond comparison a more rational, as well as a more conversable animal, than an infant of a day or a week or even a month, old. But suppose they were otherwise, what would it avail? The question is not, Can they *reason?* nor Can they *talk?* but, *Can they suffer?*[5]

In this passage Bentham points to the capacity for suffering as the vital characteristic that gives a being the right to equal consideration. The capacity for suffering—or more strictly, for suffering and/or enjoyment or happiness—is not just another characteristic like the capacity for language or higher mathematics. Bentham is not saying that those who try to mark "the insuperable line" that determines whether the interests of a being should be considered happen to have chosen the wrong characteristic. By saying that we must consider the interests of all beings with the capacity for suffering or enjoyment Bentham does not arbitrarily exclude from consideration any interests at all—as those who draw the line with reference to the possession of reason or language do. The capacity for suffering and enjoyment is *a prerequisite for having interests at all,* a condition that must be satisfied before we can speak of interests in a meaningful way. It would be nonsense to say that it was not in the interests of a stone to be kicked along the road by a schoolboy. A stone does not have interests because it cannot suffer. Nothing that we can do to it could possibly make any difference to its welfare. A mouse, on the other hand, does have an interest in not being kicked along the road, because it will suffer if it is.

If a being suffers there can be no moral justification for refusing to take that suffering into consideration. No matter what the nature of the being, the principle of equality requires that its suffering be counted equally with the like suffering—in so far as rough comparisons can be made—of any other being. If a being is not capable of suffering, or of experiencing enjoyment or happiness, there is nothing to be taken into account. So the limit of sentience (using the term as a convenient if not strictly accurate shorthand for the capacity to suffer and/or experience enjoyment) is the only defensible boundary of concern for the interests of others. To mark this boundary by some other characteristic like intelligence or rationality would be to mark it in an arbitrary manner. Why not choose some other characteristic, like skin color?

The racist violates the principle of equality by giving greater weight to the interests of members of his own race when there is a clash between their interests and the interests of those of another race. The sexist violates the principle of equality by favoring the interests of his own sex. Similarly the speciesist allows the interests of his own species to override the greater interests of members of other species. The pattern is identical in each case.

Most human beings are speciesists. . . . Ordinary human beings—not a few exceptionally cruel or heartless humans, but the overwhelming majority of humans—take an active part in, acquiesce in, and allow their taxes to pay for practices that require the sacrifice of the most important interests of members of other species in order to promote the most trivial interests of our own species.

There is, however, one general defense of these practices . . . that needs to be disposed of. . . . It is a defense which, if true, would allow us to do anything at all to nonhumans for the slightest reason, or for no reason at all, without incurring any justifiable reproach. This defense claims that we are never guilty of neglecting the interests of other animals for one breathtakingly simple reason: they have no interests. Nonhuman animals have no interests, according to this view, because they are not capable of suffering. By this is not meant merely that they are not capable of suffering in all the ways that humans are—for instance, that a calf is not capable of suffering from the knowledge that it will be killed in six months time. That modest claim is, no doubt, true; but it does not clear humans of the charge of speciesism, since it allows that animals may suffer in other ways—for instance, by being given electric shocks, or being kept in small, cramped cages. The defense I am about to discuss is the much more sweeping, although correspondingly less plausible, claim that animals are incapable of suffering in any way at all; that they are, in fact, unconscious automata, possessing neither thoughts nor feelings nor a mental life of any kind.

Although . . . the view that animals are automata was proposed by the seventeenth-century French philosopher René Descartes, to most people, then and now, it is obvious that if, for example, we stick a sharp knife into the stomach of an unanesthetized dog, the dog will feel pain. That this is so is assumed by the laws in most civilized countries which prohibit wanton cruelty to animals. Readers whose common sense tells them that animals do suffer may prefer to skip the next few paragraphs . . . since they do nothing but refute a position which they do not hold. Implausible as it is, though, for the sake of completeness this skeptical position must be discussed.

Do animals other than humans feel pain? How do we know? Well, how do we know if anyone, human or nonhuman, feels pain? We know that we ourselves can feel pain. We know this from the direct experiences of pain that we have when, for instance, somebody presses a lighted cigarette against the back of our hand. But how do we know that anyone else feels pain? We cannot directly experience anyone else's pain, whether that "anyone" is our best friend or a stray dog. Pain is a state of consciousness, a "mental event," and as such it can never be observed. Behavior like writhing, screaming, or drawing one's hand away from the lighted cigarette is not pain itself; nor are the recordings a neurologist might make of activity within the brain observations of pain itself. Pain is something that we feel, and we can only infer that others are feeling it from various external indications.

In theory, we *could* always be mistaken when we assume that other human beings feel pain. It is conceivable that our best friend is really a very cleverly constructed robot, controlled by a brilliant scientist so as to give all the signs of feeling pain, but really no more sensitive than any other machine. We can never know, with absolute certainty, that this is not the case. But while this might present a puzzle for philosophers, none of us has the slightest real doubt that our best friends feel pain just as we do. This is an inference, but a perfectly reasonable one, based on observations of their behavior in situations in which we would feel pain, and on the fact that we have every reason to assume that our friends are beings like us, with nervous systems like ours that can be assumed to function as ours do, and to produce similar feelings in similar circumstances.

If it is justifiable to assume that other humans feel pain as we do, is there any reason why a similar inference should be unjustifiable in the case of other animals?

Nearly all the external signs which lead us to infer pain in other humans can be seen in other species, especially the species most closely related to us—other species of mammals, and birds. Behavioral signs—writhing, facial contortions, moaning, yelping or other forms of calling, attempts to avoid the source of pain, appearance of fear at the prospect of its repetition, and so on—are present. In addition, we know that these animals have nervous systems very like ours, which respond physiologically as ours do when the animal is in circumstances in which we would feel pain: an initial rise of blood pressure, dilated pupils, perspiration, an increased pulse rate, and, if the stimulus continues, a fall in blood pressure. Although humans have a more developed cerebral cortex than other animals, this part of the brain is concerned with thinking functions rather than with basic impulses, emotions, and feelings. These impulses, emotions, and feelings are located in the diencephalon, which is well developed in many other species of animals, especially mammals and birds.[6]

We also know that the nervous systems of other animals were not artificially constructed to mimic the pain behavior of humans, as a robot might be artificially constructed. The nervous systems of animals evolved as our own did, and in fact the evolutionary history of humans and other animals, especially mammals, did not diverge until the central features of our nervous systems were already in existence. A capacity to feel pain obviously enhances a species' prospects of survival, since it causes members of the species to avoid sources of injury. It is surely unreasonable to suppose that nervous systems which are virtually identical physiologically, have a common origin and a common evolutionary function, and result in similar forms of behavior in similar circumstances should actually operate in an entirely different manner on the level of subjective feelings.

It has long been accepted as sound policy in science to search for the simplest possible explanation of whatever it is we are trying to explain. Occasionally it has been claimed that it is for this reason "unscientific" to explain the behavior of animals by theories that refer to the animal's conscious feelings, desires, and so on—the idea being that if the behavior in question can be explained without invoking consciousness or feelings, that will be the simpler theory. Yet we can now see that such explanations, when placed in the overall context of the behavior of both human and nonhuman animals, are actually far more complex than their rivals. For we know from our own experience that explanations of our own behavior that did not refer to consciousness and the feeling of pain would be incomplete; and it is simpler to assume that the similar behavior of animals with similar nervous systems is to be explained in the same way than to try to invent some other explanation for the behavior of nonhuman animals as well as an explanation for the divergence between humans and nonhumans in this respect.

The overwhelming majority of scientists who have addressed themselves to this question agree. Lord Brain, one of the most eminent neurologists of our time, has said:

I personally can see no reason for conceding mind to my fellow men and denying it to animals. . . . I at least cannot doubt that the interests and activities of animals are correlated with awareness and feeling in the same way as my own, and which may be, for aught I know, just as vivid.[7]

While the author of a recent book on pain writes:

Every particle of factual evidence supports the contention that the higher mammalian vertebrates experience pain sensations at least as acute as our own. To say that they feel less because they are lower animals is an absurdity; it can easily be shown that many of their senses are far more acute than ours—visual acuity in certain birds, hearing in most wild animals, and touch in others; these animals depend more than we do today on the sharpest possible awareness of a hostile environment. Apart from the complexity of the cerebral cortex (which does not directly perceive pain) their nervous systems are almost identical to ours and their reactions to pain remarkably similar, though lacking (so far as we know) the philosophical and moral overtones. The emotional element is all too evident, mainly in the form of fear and anger.[8]

In Britain, three separate expert government committees on matters relating to animals have accepted the conclusion that animals feel pain. After noting the obvious behavioral evidence for this view, the Committee on Cruelty to Wild Animals said:

. . . we believe that the physiological, and more particularly the anatomical, evidence fully justifies and reinforces the commonsense belief that animals feel pain.

And after discussing the evolutionary value of pain they concluded that pain is "of clear-cut biological usefulness" and this is "a third type of evidence that animals feel pain." They then went on to consider forms of suffering other than mere physical pain, and added that they were "satisfied that animals do suffer from acute fear and terror." In 1965, reports by British government committees on experiments on animals, and on the welfare of animals under intensive farming methods, agreed with this view, concluding that animals are capable of suffering both from straightforward physical injuries and from fear, anxiety, stress, and so on.[9]

That might well be thought enough to settle the matter; but there is one more objection that needs to be considered. There is, after all, one behavioral sign that humans have when in pain which nonhumans do not have. This is a developed language. Other animals may communicate with each other, but not, it seems, in the complicated way we do. Some philosophers, including Descartes, have thought it important that while humans can tell each other about their experience of pain in great detail, other animals cannot. (Interestingly, this once neat dividing line between humans and other species has now been threatened by the discovery that chimpanzees can be taught a language.)[10] But as Bentham pointed out long ago, the ability to use language is not relevant to the question of how a being ought to be treated—unless that ability can be linked to the capacity to suffer, so that the absence of a language casts doubt on the existence of this capacity.

This link may be attempted in two ways. First, there is a hazy line of philosophical thought, stemming perhaps from some doctrines associated with the influential philosopher Ludwig Wittgenstein, which maintains that we cannot meaningfully attribute states of consciousness to beings without language. This position seems to me very implausible. Language may be necessary for abstract thought, at some level anyway; but states like pain are more primitive, and have nothing to do with language.

The second and more easily understood way of linking language and the existence of pain is to say that the best evidence that we can have that another creature is in pain is when he tells us that he is. This is a distinct line of argument, for it is not being denied that a non-language-user conceivably *could* suffer, but only that we could ever have sufficient reason to *believe* that he is suffering. Still, this line of argument fails too. As Jane Goodall has pointed out in her study of chimpanzees, *In the Shadow of Man*, when it comes to the expressions of feelings and emotions language is less important than in other areas. We tend to fall back on nonlinguistic modes of communication such as a cheering pat on the back, an exuberant embrace, a clasp of the hands, and so on. The basic signals we use to convey pain, fear, anger, love, joy, surprise, sexual arousal, and many other emotional states are not specific to our own species.[11]

Charles Darwin made an extensive study of this subject, and the book he wrote about it, *The Expression of the Emotions in Man and Animals,* notes countless nonlinguistic modes of expression. The statement "I am in pain" may be one piece of evidence for the conclusion that the speaker is in pain, but it is not the only possible evidence, and since people sometimes tell lies, not even the best possible evidence.

Even if there were stronger grounds for refusing to attribute pain to those who do not have a language, the consequences of this refusal might lead us to reject the conclusion. Human infants and young children are unable to use language. Are we to deny that a year-old child can suffer? If not, language cannot be crucial. Of course, most parents understand the responses of their children better than they understand the responses of other animals; but this is just a fact about the relatively greater knowledge that we have of our own species, and the greater contact we have with infants, as compared to animals. Those who have studied the behavior of other animals, and those who have pet animals, soon learn to understand their responses as well as we understand those of an infant, and sometimes better. Jane Goodall's account of the chimpanzees she watched is one instance of this, but the same can be said of those who have observed species less closely related to our own. Two among many possible examples are Konrad Lorenz's observations of geese and jackdaws, and N. Tinbergen's extensive studies of herring gulls.[12] Just as we can understand infant human behavior in the light of adult human behavior, so we can understand the behavior of other species in the light of our own behavior—and sometimes we can understand our own behavior better in the light of the behavior of other species.

So to conclude: there are no good reasons, scientific or philosophical, for denying that animals feel pain. If we do not doubt that other humans feel pain we should not doubt that other animals do so too.

Animals can feel pain. As we saw earlier, there can be no moral justification for regarding the pain (or pleasure) that animals feel as less important than the same amount of pain (or pleasure) felt by humans. But what exactly does this mean, in practical terms? To prevent misunderstanding I shall spell out what I mean a little more fully.

If I give a horse a hard slap across its rump with my open hand, the horse may start, but it presumably feels little pain. Its skin is thick enough to protect it against a mere slap. If I slap a baby in the same way, however, the baby will cry and presumably does feel pain, for its skin is more sensitive. So it is worse to slap a baby than a horse, if both slaps are administered with equal force. But there must be some kind of blow—I don't know exactly what it would be, but perhaps a blow with a heavy stick—that would cause the horse as much pain as we cause a baby by slapping it with our hand. That is what I mean by "the same amount of pain" and if we consider it wrong to inflict that much pain on a baby for no good reason then we must, unless we are speciesists, consider it equally wrong to inflict the same amount of pain on a horse for no good reason.

There are other differences between humans and animals that cause other complications. Normal adult human beings have mental capacities which will, in certain circumstances, lead them to suffer more than animals would in the same circumstances. If, for instance, we decided to perform extremely painful or lethal scientific experiments on normal adult humans, kidnaped at random from public parks for this purpose, every adult who entered a park would become fearful that he would be kidnaped. The resultant terror would be a form of suffering additional to the pain of the experiment. The same experiments performed on nonhuman animals would cause less suffering since the animals would not have the anticipatory dread of being kidnaped and experimented upon. This does not mean, of course, that it would be right to perform the experiment on animals, but only that there is a reason, which is *not* speciesist, for preferring to use animals rather than normal adult humans, if the experiment is to be done at all. It should be noted, however, that this same argument gives us a reason for preferring to use human infants—orphans perhaps—or retarded humans for experiments, rather than adults, since infants and retarded humans would also have no idea of what was going to happen to them. So far as this argument is concerned nonhuman animals and infants and retarded humans are in the same category; and if we use this argument to justify experiments on nonhuman animals we have to ask ourselves whether we are also prepared to allow experiments on human infants and retarded adults; and if we make a distinction between animals and these humans, on what basis can we do it, other than a barefaced—and morally indefensible—preference for members of our own species?

There are many areas in which the superior mental powers of normal adult humans make a difference: anticipation, more detailed memory, greater knowledge of what is happening, and so on. Yet these differences do not all point to greater suffering on the part of the normal human being. Sometimes an animal may suffer more because of his more limited understanding. If, for instance, we are taking prisoners in wartime we can explain to them that while they must submit to capture, search, and confinement they will not otherwise be harmed and will be set free at the conclusion of hostilities. If we capture a wild animal, however, we cannot explain that we are not threatening its life. A wild animal cannot distinguish an attempt to overpower and confine from an attempt to kill; the one causes as much terror as the other.

It may be objected that comparisons of the sufferings of different species are impossible to make, and that for this reason when the interests of animals and humans clash the principle of equality gives no guidance. It is probably true that comparisons of suffering between members of different species cannot be made precisely, but precision is not essential. Even if we were to prevent the infliction of suffering on animals only when it is quite certain that the interests of humans will not be affected to anything like the extent that animals are affected, we would be forced to make radical changes in our treatment of animals that would involve our diet, the farming methods we use, experimental procedures in many fields of science, our approach to wildlife and to hunting, trapping and the wearing of furs, and areas of entertainment like circuses, rodeos, and zoos. As a result, a vast amount of suffering would be avoided.

So far I have said a lot about the infliction of suffering on animals, but nothing about killing them. This omission has been deliberate. The application of the principle of equality to the infliction of suffering is, in theory at least, fairly straightforward. Pain and suffering are bad and should be prevented or minimized, irrespective of the race, sex, or species of the being that suffers. How bad a pain is depends on how intense it is and how long it lasts, but pains of the same intensity and duration are equally bad, whether felt by humans or animals.

The wrongness of killing a being is more complicated. I have kept, and shall continue to keep, the question of killing in the background because in the present state of human tyranny over other species the more simple, straightforward principle of equal consideration of pain or pleasure is a sufficient basis for identifying and protesting against all the major abuses of animals that humans practice.

Nevertheless, it is necessary to say something about killing.

Just as most humans are speciesists in their readiness to cause pain to animals when they would not cause a similar pain to humans for the same reason, so most humans are speciesists in their readiness to kill other animals when they would not kill humans. We need to proceed more cautiously here, however, because people hold widely differing views about when it is legitimate to kill humans, as the continuing debates over abortion and euthanasia attest. Nor have moral philosophers been able to agree on exactly what it is that makes it wrong to kill humans, and under what circumstances killing a human being may be justifiable.

Let us consider first the view that it is always wrong to take an innocent human life. We may call this the "sanctity of life" view. People who take this view oppose abortion and euthanasia. They do not usually, however, oppose the killing of nonhumans—so perhaps it would be more accurate to describe this view as the "sanctity of *human* life" view.

The belief that human life, and only human life, is sacrosanct is a form of speciesism. To see this, consider the following example.

Assume that, as sometimes happens, an infant has been born with massive and irreparable brain damage. The damage is so severe that the infant can never be any more than a "human vegetable," unable to talk, recognize other people, act independently of others, or develop a sense of self-awareness. The parents of the infant, realizing that they cannot hope for any improvement in their child's condition and being in any case unwilling to spend, or ask the state to spend, the thousands of dollars that would be needed annually for proper care of the infant, ask the doctor to kill the infant painlessly.

Should the doctor do what the parents ask? Legally, he should not, and in this respect the law reflects the sanctity of life view. The life of every human being is sacred. Yet people who would say this about the infant do not object to the killing of nonhuman animals. How can they justify their different judgments? Adult chimpanzees, dogs, pigs, and many other species far surpass the brain-damaged infant in their ability to relate to others, act independently, be self-aware, and any other capacity that could reasonably be said to give value to life. With the most intensive care possible, there are retarded infants who can never achieve the intelligence level of a dog. Nor can we appeal to the concern of the infant's parents, since they themselves, in this imaginary example (and in some actual cases), do not want the infant kept alive.

The only thing that distinguishes the infant from the animal, in the eyes of those who claim it has a "right to life," is that it is, biologically, a member of the species Homo sapiens, whereas chimpanzees, dogs, and pigs are not. But to use *this* difference as the basis for granting a right to life to the infant and not to the other animals is, of course, pure speciesism.[*] It is exactly the kind of arbitrary difference that the most crude and overt kind of racist uses in attempting to justify racial discrimination.

This does not mean that to avoid speciesism we must hold that it is as wrong to kill a dog as it is to kill a normal human being. The only position that is irredeemably speciesist is the one that tries to make the boundary of the right to life run exactly parallel to the boundary of our own species. Those who hold the sanctity of life view do this because while distinguishing sharply between humans and other animals they allow no distinctions to be made within our own species, objecting to the killing of the severely retarded and the hopelessly senile as strongly as they object to the killing of normal adults.

To avoid speciesism we must allow that beings which are similar in all relevant respects have a similar right to life—and mere mem-

---

[*]I am here putting aside religious views, for example the doctrine that all and only humans have immortal souls, or are made in the image of God. Historically these views have been very important, and no doubt are partly responsible for the idea that human life has a special sanctity. Logically, however, these religious views are unsatisfactory, since a reasoned explanation of why it should be that all humans and no nonhumans have immortal souls is not offered. This belief too, therefore, comes under suspicion as a form of speciesism. In any case, defenders of the "sanctity of life" view are generally reluctant to base their position on purely religious doctrines, since these doctrines are no longer as widely accepted as they once were.

bership in our own biological species cannot be a morally relevant criterion for this right. Within these limits we could still hold that, for instance, it is worse to kill a normal adult human, with a capacity for self-awareness, and the ability to plan for the future and have meaningful relations with others, than it is to kill a mouse, which presumably does not share all of these characteristics; or we might appeal to the close family and other personal ties which humans have but mice do not have to the same degree; or we might think that it is the consequences for other humans, who will be put in fear of their own lives, that makes the crucial difference; or we might think it is some combination of these factors, or other factors altogether.

Whatever criteria we choose, however, we will have to admit that they do not follow precisely the boundary of our own species. We may legitimately hold that there are some features of certain beings which make their lives more valuable than those of other beings; but there will surely be some nonhuman animals whose lives, by any standards, are more valuable than the lives of some humans. A chimpanzee, dog, or pig, for instance, will have a higher degree of self-awareness and a greater capacity for meaningful relations with others than a severely retarded infant or someone in a state of advanced senility. So if we base the right to life on these characteristics we must grant these animals a right to life as good as, or better than, such retarded or senile humans.

Now this argument cuts both ways. It could be taken as showing that chimpanzees, dogs, and pigs, along with some other species, have a right to life and we commit a grave moral offense whenever we kill them, even when they are old and suffering and our intention is to put them out of their misery. Alternatively one could take the argument as showing that the severely retarded and hopelessly senile have no right to life and may be killed for quite trivial reasons, as we now kill animals.

Since the focus of this book is on ethical questions concerning animals and not on the morality of euthanasia I shall not attempt to settle this issue finally. I think it is reasonably clear, though, that while both of the positions just described avoid speciesism, neither is entirely satisfactory. What we need is some mid-

dle position which would avoid speciesism but would not make the lives of the retarded and senile as cheap as the lives of pigs and dogs now are, nor make the lives of pigs and dogs so sacrosanct that we think it wrong to put them out of hopeless misery. What we must do is bring nonhuman animals within our sphere of moral concern and cease to treat their lives as expendable for whatever trivial purposes we may have. At the same time, once we realize that the fact that a being is a member of our own species is not in itself enough to make it always wrong to kill that being, we may come to reconsider our policy of preserving human lives at all costs, even when there is no prospect of a meaningful life or of existence without terrible pain.

I conclude, then, that a rejection of speciesism does not imply that all lives are of equal worth. While self-awareness, intelligence, the capacity for meaningful relations with others, and so on are not relevant to the question of inflicting pain—since pain is pain, whatever other capacities, beyond the capacity to feel pain, the being may have—these capacities may be relevant to the question of taking life. It is not arbitrary to hold that the life of a self-aware being, capable of abstract thought, of planning for the future, of complex acts of communication, and so on, is more valuable than the life of a being without these capacities. To see the difference between the issues of inflicting pain and taking life, consider how we would choose within our own species. If we had to choose to save the life of a normal human or a mentally defective human, we would probably choose to save the life of the normal human; but if we had to choose between preventing pain in the normal human or the mental defective—imagine that both have received painful but superficial injuries, and we only have enough painkiller for one of them—it is not nearly so clear how we ought to choose. The same is true when we consider other species. The evil of pain is, in itself, unaffected by the other characteristics of the being that feels the pain; the value of life is affected by these other characteristics.

Normally this will mean that if we have to choose between the life of a human being and the life of another animal we should choose to save the life of the human; but there may be special cases in which the reverse holds true, because the human being in question does not have the capacities of a normal human being. So this view is not speciesist, although it may appear to be at first glance. The preference, in normal cases, for saving a human life over the life of an animal when a choice *has* to be made is a preference based on the characteristics that normal humans have, and not on the mere fact that they are members of our own species. This is why when we consider members of our own species who lack the characteristics of normal humans we can no longer say that their lives are always to be preferred to those of other animals. . . . In general, though, the question of when it is wrong to kill (painlessly) an animal is one to which we need give no precise answer. As long as we remember that we should give the same respect to the lives of animals as we give to the lives of those humans at a similar mental level, we shall not go far wrong.

Notes

1. For Bentham's moral philosophy, see his *Introduction to the Principles of Morals and Legislation*, and for Sidgwick's see *The Methods of Ethics* (the passage quoted is from the seventh edition, p. 382). As examples of leading contemporary moral philosophers who incorporate a requirement of equal consideration of interests, see R. M. Hare, *Freedom and Reason* (New York: Oxford University Press, 1963) and John Rawls, *A Theory of Justice* (Cambridge: Harvard University Press, Belknap Press, 1972). For a brief account of the essential agreement on this issue between these and other positions, see R. M. Hare, "Rules of War and Moral Reasoning," *Philosophy and Public Affairs*, vol. 1, no. 2 (1972).

2. Letter to Henri Gregoire, February 25, 1809.

3. Reminiscences by Francis D. Gage, from Susan B. Anthony, *The History of Woman Suffrage*, vol. 1; the passage is to be found in the extract in Leslie Tanner, ed., *Voices from Women's Liberation* (New York: Signet, 1970).

4. I owe the term "speciesism" to Richard Ryder.

5. *Introduction to the Principles of Morals and Legislation*, chapter 17.

6. Lord Brain, "Presidential Address," in C. A. Keele and R. Smith, eds., *The Assessment of Pain in Men and Animals* (London: Universities Federation for Animal Welfare, 1962).

7. Ibid., p. 11.

8. Richard Serjeant, *The Spectrum of Pain* (London: Hart-Davis, 1969), p. 72.

9. See the reports of the Committee on Cruelty to Wild Animals (Command Paper 8268, 1951), paragraphs 36–42; the Departmental Committee on Experiments on Animals (Command Paper 2641, 1965), paragraphs 179–182; and the Technical Committee to Enquire into the Welfare of Animals Kept under Intensive Livestock Husbandry Systems (Command Paper 2836, 1965), paragraphs 26–28 (London: Her Majesty's Stationery Office).

10. One chimpanzee, Washoe, has been taught the sign language used by deaf people, and acquired a vocabulary of 350 signs. Another, Lana, communicates in structured sentences by pushing buttons on a special machine. For a brief account of Washoe's abilities, see Jane van Lawick-Goodall, *In the Shadow of Man* (Boston: Houghton Mifflin, 1971), pp. 252–254; and for Lana, see *Newsweek*, 7 January 1974, and *New York Times*, 4 December 1974.

11. *In the Shadow of Man*, p. 225; Michael Peters makes a similar point in "Nature and Culture," in Stanley and Roslind Godlovitch and John Harris, eds., *Animals, Men and Morals* (New York: Taplinger Publishing Co., 1972).

12. Konrad Lorenz, *King Solomon's Ring* (New York: T. Y. Crowell, 1952); N. Tinbergen, *The Herring Gull's World*, rev. ed. (New York: Basic Books, 1974).

58. The Ethics of Respect for Nature

Paul W. Taylor

According to Paul W. Taylor, the ethics of respect for nature is made up of three elements: a belief system, an ultimate moral attitude, and a set of rules of duty and standards of character. The belief system is said to justify the adoption of the attitude of respect for nature, which in turn requires a set of rules and standards of character. Two central elements of the belief system are (1) that each individual organism is a teleological center of life, pursuing its own good in its own way, and (2) that whether we are concerned with standards of merit or with the concept of inherent worth, the claim that humans by their very nature are superior to other species is groundless.

Human-Centered and Life-Centered Systems of Environmental Ethics

In this paper I show how the taking of a certain ultimate moral attitude toward nature, which I call "respect for nature," has a central place in the foundations of a life-centered system of environmental ethics. I hold that a set of moral norms (both standards of character and rules of conduct) governing human treatment of the natural world is a rationally grounded set if and only if, first, commitment to those norms is a practical entailment of adopting the attitude of respect for nature as an ultimate moral attitude, and second, the adopting of that attitude on the part of all rational agents can itself be justified. When the basic characteristics of the attitude of respect for nature are made clear, it will be seen that a life-centered system of environmental ethics need not be holistic or organicist in its conception of the kinds of entities that are deemed the appropriate objects of moral concern and consideration. Nor does such a system require that the concepts of ecological homeostasis,

From "The Ethics of Respect for Nature," *Environmental Ethics* (1986), pp. 197–218. Reprinted by permission of the publisher. Notes renumbered.

equilibrium, and integrity provide us with normative principles from which could be derived (with the addition of factual knowledge) our obligations with regard to natural ecosystems. The "balance of nature" is not itself a moral norm, however important may be the role it plays in our general outlook on the natural world that underlies the attitude of respect for nature. I argue that finally it is the good (well-being, welfare) of individual organisms, considered as entities having inherent worth, that determines our moral relations with the Earth's wild communities of life.

In designating the theory to be set forth as life-centered, I intend to contrast it with all anthropocentric views. According to the latter, human actions affecting the natural environment and its nonhuman inhabitants are right (or wrong) by either of two criteria: they have consequences which are favorable (or unfavorable) to human well-being, or they are consistent (or inconsistent) with the system of norms that protect and implement human rights. From this human-centered standpoint it is to humans and only to humans that all duties are ultimately owed. We may have responsibilities *with regard to* the natural ecosystems and biotic communities of our planet, but these responsibilities are in every case based on the contingent fact that our treatment of those ecosystems and communities of life can further the realization of human values and/or human rights. We have no obligation to promote or protect the good of nonhuman living things, independently of this contingent fact.

A life-centered system of environmental ethics is opposed to human-centered ones precisely on this point. From the perspective of a life-centered theory, we have prima facie moral obligations that are owed to wild plants and animals themselves as members of the Earth's biotic community. We are morally bound (other things being equal) to protect or promote their good for *their* sake. Our duties to respect the integrity of natural ecosystems, to preserve endangered species, and to avoid environmental pollution stem from the fact that these are ways in which we can help make it possible for wild species populations to achieve and maintain a healthy existence in a natural state. Such obligations are due those living things out of recognition of their inherent worth. They are entirely additional to and independent of the obligations we owe to our fellow humans. Although many of the actions that fulfill one set of obligations will also fulfill the other, two different grounds of obligation are involved. Their well-being, as well as human well-being, is something to be realized *as an end in itself*.

If we were to accept a life-centered theory of environmental ethics, a profound reordering of our moral universe would take place. We would begin to look at the whole of the Earth's biosphere in a new light. Our duties with respect to the "world" of nature would be seen as making prima facie claims upon us to be balanced against our duties with respect to the "world" of human civilization. We could no longer simply take the human point of view and consider the effects of our actions exclusively from the perspective of our own good.

The Good of a Being and the Concept of Inherent Worth

What would justify acceptance of a life-centered system of ethical principles? In order to answer this it is first necessary to make clear the fundamental moral attitude that underlies and makes intelligible the commitment to live by such a system. It is then necessary to examine the considerations that would justify any rational agent's adopting that moral attitude.

Two concepts are essential to the taking of a moral attitude of the sort in question. A being which does not "have" these concepts, that is, which is unable to grasp their meaning and conditions of applicability, cannot be said to have the attitude as part of its moral outlook. These concepts are, first, that of the good (well-being, welfare) of a living thing, and second, the idea of an entity possessing inherent worth. I examine each concept in turn.

(1) Every organism, species population, and community of life has a good of its own which moral agents can intentionally further or damage by their actions. To say that an entity has a good of its own is simply to say that, without reference to any *other* entity, it can be benefited or harmed. One can act in its overall interest or contrary to its overall interest, and environmental conditions can be good for it (advantageous to it) or bad for it (disadvantageous to it). What is good for an entity is what "does it good" in the sense of enhancing or preserving its life and well-being. What is bad for an entity is something that is detrimental to its life and well-being.[1]

We can think of the good of an individual nonhuman organism as consisting in the full development of its biological powers. Its good is realized to the extent that it is strong and healthy. It possesses whatever capacities it needs for successfully coping with its environment and so preserving its existence throughout the various stages of the normal life cycle of its species. The good of a population or community of such individuals consists in the population or community maintaining itself from generation to generation as a coherent system of genetically and ecologically related organisms whose average good is at an optimum level for the given environment. (Here *average good* means that the degree of realization of the good of *individual organisms* in the population or community is, on average, greater than would be the case under any other ecologically functioning order of interrelations among those species populations in the given ecosystem.)

The idea of a being having a good of its own, as I understand it, does not entail that the being must have interests or take an interest in what affects its life for better or for worse. We can act in a being's interest or contrary to its interest without its being interested in what we are doing to it in the sense of wanting or not wanting us to do it. It may, indeed, be wholly unaware that favorable and unfavorable events are taking place in its life. I take it that trees, for example, have no knowledge or desires or feelings. Yet is is undoubtedly the case that trees can be harmed or benefited by our actions. We can crush their roots by running a bulldozer too close to them. We can see to it that they get adequate nourishment and moisture by fertilizing and watering the soil around them. Thus we can help or hinder them in the realization of their good. It is the good of trees themselves that is thereby affected. We can similarly act so as to further the good of an entire tree population of a certain species (say, all the redwood trees in a California valley) or the good of a whole community of plant life in a given wilderness area, just as we can do harm to such a population or community.

When construed in this way, the concept of a being's good is not coextensive with sentience or the capacity for feeling pain. William Frankena has argued for a general theory of environmental ethics in which the ground of a creature's being worthy of moral consideration is its sentience. I have offered some criticisms of this view elsewhere, but the full refutation of such a position, it seems to me, finally depends on the positive reasons for accepting a life-centered theory of the kind I am defending in this essay.[2]

It should be noted further that I am leaving open the question of whether machines—in particular, those which are not only goal-directed, but also self-regulating—can properly be said to have a good of their own.[3] Since I am concerned only with human treatment of wild organisms, species populations, and communities of life as they occur in our planet's natural ecosystems, it is to those entities alone that the concept "having a good of its own" will here be applied. I am not denying that other living things, whose genetic origin and environmental conditions have been produced, controlled, and manipulated by humans for human ends, do have a good of their own in the same sense as do wild plants and animals. It is not my purpose in this essay, however, to set out or defend the principles that should guide our conduct with regard to their good. It is only insofar as their production and use by humans have good or ill effects upon natural ecosystems and their wild inhabitants that the ethics of respect for nature comes into play.

(2) The second concept essential to the moral attitude of respect for nature is the idea of inherent worth. We take that attitude toward wild living things (individuals, species populations, or whole biotic communities) when and only when we regard them as entities possessing inherent worth. Indeed, it is only because they are conceived in this way that moral agents can think of themselves as having validly binding duties, obligations, and responsibilities that are *owed* to them as their *due*. I am not at this juncture arguing why they *should* be so regarded; I consider it at length below. But so regarding them is a presupposition of our taking the attitude of respect toward them and accordingly understanding ourselves as bearing certain moral relations to them. This can be shown as follows:

What does it mean to regard an entity that has a good of its own as possessing inherent worth? Two general principles are involved: the principle of moral consideration and the principle of intrinsic value.

According to the principle of moral consideration, wild living things are deserving of the concern and consideration of all moral agents simply in virtue of their being members of the Earth's community of life. From the moral point of view their good must be taken into account whenever it is affected for better or worse by the conduct of rational agents. This holds no matter what species the creature belongs to. The good of each is to be accorded some value and so acknowledged as having some weight in the deliberations of all rational agents. Of course, it may be necessary for such agents to act in ways contrary to the good of this or that particular organism or group of organisms in order to further the good of others, including the good of humans. But the principle of moral consideration prescribes that, with respect to each being an entity having its own good, every individual is deserving of consideration.

The principle of intrinsic value states that, regardless of what kind of entity it is in other respects, if it is a member of the Earth's community of life, the realization of its good is something *intrinsically* valuable. This means that its good is prima facie worthy of being preserved or promoted as an end in itself and for the sake of the entity whose good it is. Insofar as we regard any organism, species population, or life community as an entity having inherent worth, we believe that it must never be treated as if it were a mere object or thing whose entire value lies in being instrumental to the good of some other entity. The well-being of each is judged to have value in and of itself.

Combining these two principles, we can now define what it means for a living thing or group of living things to possess inherent worth. To say that it possesses inherent worth is to say that its good is deserving of the concern and consideration of all moral agents, and that the realization of its good has intrinsic value, to be pursued as an end in itself and for the sake of the entity whose good it is.

The duties owed to wild organisms, species populations, and communities of life in the Earth's natural ecosystems are grounded on their inherent worth. When rational, autonomous agents regard such entities as possessing inherent worth, they place intrinsic value on the realization of their good and so hold themselves responsible for performing actions that will have this effect and for refraining from actions having the contrary effect.

The Attitude of Respect
for Nature

Why should moral agents regard wild living things in the natural world as possessing inherent worth? To answer this question we must first take into account the fact that, when rational, autonomous agents subscribe to the principles of moral consideration and intrinsic value and so conceive of wild living things as

having that kind of worth, such agents are *adopting a certain ultimate moral attitude toward the natural world.* This is the attitude I call "respect for nature." It parallels the attitude of respect for persons in human ethics. When we adopt the attitude of respect for persons as the proper (fitting, appropriate) attitude to take toward all persons as persons, we consider the fulfillment of the basic interests of each individual to have intrinsic value. We thereby make a moral commitment to live a certain kind of life in relation to other persons. We place ourselves under the direction of a system of standards and rules that we consider validly binding on all moral agents as such.[4]

Similarly, when we adopt the attitude of respect for nature as an ultimate moral attitude we make a commitment to live by certain normative principles. These principles constitute the rules of conduct and standards of character that are to govern our treatment of the natural world. This is, first, an *ultimate* commitment because it is not derived from any higher norm. The attitude of respect for nature is not grounded on some other, more general, or more fundamental attitude. It sets the total framework for our responsibilities toward the natural world. It can be justified, as I show below, but its justification cannot consist in referring to a more general attitude or a more basic normative principle.

Second, the commitment is a *moral* one because it is understood to be a disinterested matter of principle. It is this feature that distinguishes the attitude of respect for nature from the set of feelings and dispositions that comprise the love of nature. The latter stems from one's personal interest in and response to the natural world. Like the affectionate feelings we have toward certain individual human beings, one's love of nature is nothing more than the particular way one feels about the natural environment and its wild inhabitants. And just as our love for an individual person differs from our respect for all persons as such (whether we happen to love them or not), so love of nature differs from respect for nature. Respect for nature is an attitude we believe all moral agents ought to have simply as moral agents, regardless of whether or not they also love nature. Indeed, we have not truly taken the attitude of respect for nature ourselves unless we believe this. To put it in a Kantian way, to adopt the attitude of respect for nature is to take a stance that one wills it to be a universal law for all rational beings. It is to hold that stance categorically, as being validly applicable to every moral agent without exception, irrespective of whatever personal feelings toward nature such an agent might have or might lack.

Although the attitude of respect for nature is in this sense a disinterested and universalizable attitude, anyone who does adopt it has certain steady, more or less permanent dispositions. These dispositions, which are themselves to be considered disinterested and universalizable, comprise three interlocking sets: dispositions to seek certain ends, dispositions to carry on one's practical reasoning and deliberation in a certain way, and dispositions to have certain feelings. We may accordingly analyze the attitude of respect for nature into the following components. (a) The disposition to aim at, and to take steps to bring about, as final and disinterested ends, the promoting and protecting of the good of organisms, species populations, and life communities in natural ecosystems. (These ends are "final" in not being pursued as means to further ends. They are "disinterested" in being independent of the self-interest of the agent.) (b) The disposition to consider actions that tend to realize those ends to be prima facie obligatory *because* they have that tendency. (c) The disposition to experience positive and negative feelings toward states of affairs in the world *because* they are favorable or unfavorable to the good of organisms, species populations, and life communities in natural ecosystems.

The logical connection between the attitude of respect for nature and the duties of a life-centered system of environmental ethics can now be made clear. Insofar as one sincerely takes that attitude and so has the three sets of dispositions, one will at the same time be disposed to comply with certain rules of duty (such as nonmaleficence and noninterference) and with standards of character (such as fairness and benevolence) that determine the obligations and virtues of moral agents with regard to the Earth's wild living things. We can say that the actions one performs and the character traits one develops in fulfilling these

moral requirements are the way one *expresses* or *embodies* the attitude in one's conduct and character. In his famous essay, "Justice as Fairness," John Rawls describes the rules of the duties of human morality (such as fidelity, gratitude, honesty, and justice) as "forms of conduct in which recognition of others as persons is manifested."[5] I hold that the rules of duty governing our treatment of the natural world and its inhabitants are forms of conduct in which the attitude of respect for nature is manifested.

The Justifiability of the Attitude of Respect for Nature

I return to the question posed earlier, which has not yet been answered: why *should* moral agents regard wild living things as possessing inherent worth? I now argue that the only way we can answer this question is by showing how adopting the attitude of respect for nature is justified for all moral agents. Let us suppose that we were able to establish that there are good reasons for adopting the attitude, reasons which are intersubjectively valid for every rational agent. If there are such reasons, they would justify anyone's having the three sets of dispositions mentioned above as constituting what it means to have the attitude. Since these include the disposition to promote or protect the good of wild living things as a disinterested and ultimate end, as well as the disposition to perform actions for the reason that they tend to realize that end, we see that such dispositions commit a person to the principles of moral consideration and intrinsic value. To be disposed to further, as an end in itself, the good of any entity in nature just because it is that kind of entity, is to be disposed to give consideration to *every* such entity and to place intrinsic value on the realization of its good. Insofar as we subscribe to these two principles we regard living things as possessing inherent worth. Subscribing to the principles is what it *means* to so regard them. To justify the attitude of respect for nature, then, is to justify commitment to these principles and thereby to justify regarding wild creatures as possessing inherent worth.

We must keep in mind that inherent worth is not some mysterious sort of objective property belonging to living things that can be discovered by empirical observation or scientific investigation. To ascribe inherent worth to an entity is not to describe it by citing some feature discernible by sense perception or inferable by inductive reasoning. Nor is there a logically necessary connection between the concept of a being having a good of its own and the concept of inherent worth. We do not contradict ourselves by asserting that an entity that has a good of its own lacks inherent worth. In order to show that such an entity "has" inherent worth we must give good reasons for ascribing that kind of value to it (placing that kind of value upon it, conceiving of it to be valuable in that way). Although it is humans (persons, valuers) who must do the valuing, for the ethics of respect for nature, the value so ascribed is not a human value. That is to say, it is not a value derived from considerations regarding human well-being or human rights. It is a value that is ascribed to nonhuman animals and plants themselves, independently of their relationship to what humans judge to be conducive to their own good.

Whatever reasons, then, justify our taking the attitude of respect for nature as defined above are also reasons that show why we *should* regard the living things of the natural world as possessing inherent worth. We saw earlier that, since the attitude is an ultimate one, it cannot be derived from a more fundamental attitude nor shown to be a special case of a more general one. On what sort of grounds, then, can it be established?

The attitude we take toward living things in the natural world depends on the way we look at them, on what kind of beings we conceive them to be, and on how we understand the relations we bear to them. Underlying and supporting our attitude is a certain *belief system* that constitutes a particular world view or outlook on nature and the place of human life in it. To give good reasons for adopting the attitude of respect for nature, then, we must first articulate the belief system which underlies and supports that attitude. If it appears that the belief system is internally coherent and well ordered, and if, as far as we can now tell, it is consistent with all known scientific truths relevant to our knowledge of the object of the attitude (which in this case includes the whole set of the Earth's natural ecosystems and their communities of life), then there remains the task of indicating why scientifically informed and rational thinkers with a developed capacity of reality awareness can find it acceptable as a way of conceiving of the natural world and our place in it. To the extent we can do this we provide at least a reasonable argument for accepting the belief system and the ultimate moral attitude it supports.

I do not hold that such a belief system can be *proven* to be true, either inductively or deductively. As we shall see, not all of its components can be stated in the form of empirically verifiable propositions. Nor is its internal order governed by purely logical relationships. But the system as a whole, I contend, constitutes a coherent, unified, and rationally acceptable "picture" or "map" of a total world. By examining each of its main components and seeing how they fit together, we obtain a scientifically informed and well-ordered conception of nature and the place of humans in it.

This belief system underlying the attitude of respect for nature I call (for want of a better name) "the biocentric outlook on nature." Since it is not wholly analyzable into empirically confirmable assertions, it should not be thought of as simply a compendium of the biological sciences concerning our planet's ecosystems. It might best be described as a philosophical world view, to distinguish it from a scientific theory or explanatory system. However, one of its major tenets is the great lesson we have learned from the science of ecology: the interdependence of all living things in an organically unified order whose balance and stability are necessary conditions for the realization of the good of its constituent biotic communities.

Before turning to an account of the main components of the biocentric outlook, it is convenient here to set forth the overall structure of my theory of environmental ethics as it has now emerged. The ethics of respect for nature is made up of three basic elements: a belief system, an ultimate moral attitude, and a set of rules of duty and standards of character. These elements are connected with each other in the following manner. The belief system provides a certain outlook on nature which supports and makes intelligible an autonomous agent's adopting, as an ultimate moral attitude, the attitude of respect for nature. It supports and makes intelligible the attitude in the sense that, when an autonomous agent understands its moral relations to the natural world in terms of this outlook, it recognizes the attitude of respect to be the only *suitable* or *fitting* attitude to take toward all wild forms of life in the Earth's biosphere. Living things are now viewed as *the appropriate objects of the attitude of respect* and are accordingly regarded as entities possessing inherent worth. One then places intrinsic value on the promotion and protection of their good. As a consequence of this, one makes a moral commitment to abide by a set of rules of duty and to fulfill (as far as one can by one's own efforts) certain standards of good character. Given one's adoption of the attitude of respect, one makes that moral commitment because one considers those rules and standards to be validly binding on all moral agents. They are seen as embodying forms of conduct and character structures in which the attitude of respect for nature is manifested.

This three-part complex which internally orders the ethics of respect for nature is symmetrical with a theory of human ethics grounded on respect for persons. Such a theory includes, first, a conception of oneself and others as persons, that is, as centers of autonomous choice. Second, there is the attitude of respect for persons as persons. When this is adopted as an ultimate moral attitude it involves the disposition to treat every person as having inherent worth or "human dignity." Every human being, just in virtue of her or his humanity, is understood to be worthy of moral consideration, and intrinsic value is placed on the autonomy and well-being of each. This is what Kant meant by conceiving of persons as ends in themselves. Third, there is an ethical system of duties which are acknowledged to be owed by everyone to everyone. These duties are forms of conduct in which public recognition is given to each individual's inherent worth as a person.

This structural framework for a theory of human ethics is meant to leave open the issue of consequentialism (utilitarianism) versus nonconsequentialism (deontology). That issue concerns the particular kind of system of rules defining the duties of moral agents toward persons. Similarly, I am leaving open in this paper the question of what particular kind of system of rules defines our duties with respect to the natural world.

The Biocentric Outlook on Nature

The biocentric outlook on nature has four main components. (1) Humans are thought of as members of the Earth's community of life, holding that membership on the same terms as apply to all the nonhuman members. (2) The Earth's natural ecosystems as a totality are seen as a complex web of interconnected elements, with the sound biological functioning of each being dependent on the sound biological functioning of the others. (This is the component referred to above as the great lesson that the science of ecology has taught us.) (3) Each individual organism is conceived of as a teleological center of life, pursuing its own good in its own way. (4) Whether we are concerned with standards of merit or with the concept of inherent worth, the claim that humans by their very nature are superior to other species is a groundless claim and, in the light of elements (1), (2), and (3) above, must be rejected as nothing more than an irrational bias in our own favor. . . .

The Denial of Human Superiority

This fourth component of the biocentric outlook on nature is the single most important idea in establishing the justifiability of the attitude of respect for nature. Its central role is due to the special relationship it bears to the first three components of the outlook. This relationship will be brought out after the concept of human superiority is examined and analyzed.[6]

In what sense are humans alleged to be superior to other animals? We are different from them in having certain capacities that they lack. But why should these capacities be a mark of superiority? From what point of view are they judged to be signs of superiority and what sense of superiority is meant? After all, various nonhuman species have capacities that humans lack. There is the speed of a cheetah, the vision of an eagle, the agility of a monkey. Why should not these be taken as signs of *their* superiority over humans?

One answer that comes immediately to mind is that these capacities are not as *valuable* as the human capacities that are claimed to make us superior. Such uniquely human characteristics as rational thought, aesthetic creativity, autonomy and self-determination, and moral freedom, it might be held, have a higher value than the capacities found in other species. Yet we must ask: valuable to whom, and on what grounds?

The human characteristics mentioned are all valuable to humans. They are essential to the preservation and enrichment of our civilization and culture. Clearly it is from the human standpoint that they are being judged to be desirable and good. It is not difficult here to recognize a begging of the question. Humans are claiming human superiority from a strictly human point of view, that is, from a point of view in which the good of humans is taken as the standard of judgment. All we need to do is to look at the capacities of nonhuman animals (or plants, for that matter) from the standpoint of *their* good to find a contrary judgment of superiority. The speed of the cheetah, for example, is a sign of its superiority to humans when considered from the standpoint of the good of its species. If it were as slow a runner as a human, it would not be able to survive. And so for all the other abilities of nonhumans which further their good but which are lacking in humans. In each case the claim to human superiority would be rejected from a nonhuman standpoint.

When superiority assertions are interpreted in this way, they are based on judgments of *merit*. To judge the merits of a person or an organism one must apply grading or ranking standards to it. (As I show below, this distinguishes judgments of merit from judgments of inherent worth.) Empirical investigation then determines whether it has the "good-making properties" (merits) in virtue of which it fulfills the standards being applied. In the case of humans, merits may be either moral or nonmoral. We can judge one person to be better than (superior to) another from the moral point of view by applying certain standards to their character and conduct. Similarly, we can appeal to nonmoral criteria in judging someone to be an excellent piano player, a fair cook, a poor tennis player, and so on. Different social purposes and roles are implicit in the making of such judgments, providing the frame of reference for the choice of standards by which the nonmoral merits of people are determined. Ultimately such purposes and roles stem from a society's way of life as a whole. Now a society's way of life may be thought of as the cultural form given to the realization of human values. Whether moral or nonmoral standards are being applied, then, all judgments of people's merits finally depend on human values. All are made from an exclusively human standpoint.

The question that naturally arises at this juncture is: why should standards that are based on human values be assumed to be the only valid criteria of merit and hence the only true signs of superiority? This question is especially pressing when humans are being judged superior in merit to nonhumans. It is true that a human being may be a better mathematician than a monkey, but the monkey may be a better tree climber than a human being. If we humans value mathematics more than tree climbing, that is because our conception of civilized life makes the development of mathematical ability more desirable than the ability to climb trees. But is it not unreasonable to judge nonhumans by the values of human civilization, rather than by values connected with what it is for a member of *that* species to live a good life? If all living things have a good of their own, it at least makes sense to judge the merits of nonhumans by standards derived from *their* good. To use only standards based on human values is already to commit oneself to holding that humans are superior to nonhumans, which is the point in question.

A further logical flaw arises in connection with the widely held conviction that humans are *morally* superior beings because they possess, while others lack, the capacities of a moral agent (free will, accountability, deliberation, judgment, practical reason). This view rests on a conceptual confusion. As far as moral standards are concerned, only beings that have the capacities of a moral agent can properly be judged to be *either* moral (morally good) *or* immoral (morally deficient). Moral standards are simply not applicable to beings that lack such capacities. Animals and plants cannot therefore be said to be morally inferior in merit to humans. Since the only beings that can have moral merits *or be deficient in such merits* are moral agents, it is conceptually incoherent to judge humans as superior to nonhumans on the ground that humans have moral capacities while nonhumans don't.

Up to this point I have been interpreting the claim that humans are superior to other living things as a grading or ranking judgment regarding their comparative merits. There is, however, another way of understanding the idea of human superiority. According to this interpretation, humans are superior to nonhumans not as regards their merits but as regards their inherent worth. Thus the claim of human superiority is to be understood as asserting that all humans, simply in virtue of their humanity, have *a greater inherent worth* than other living things.

The inherent worth of an entity does not depend on its merits.[7] To consider something as possessing inherent worth, we have seen, is to place intrinsic value on the realization of its good. This is done regardless of whatever particular merits it might have or might lack, as judged by a set of grading or ranking standards. In human affairs, we are all familiar with the principle that one's worth as a person does not vary with one's merits or lack of merits. The same can hold true of animals and plants. To regard such entities as possessing inherent worth entails disregarding their merits and deficiencies, whether they are being judged from a human standpoint or from the standpoint of their own species.

The idea of one entity having more merit than another, and so being superior to it in merit, makes perfectly good sense. Merit is a grading or ranking concept, and judgments of comparative merit are based on the different degrees to which things satisfy a given standard. But what can it mean to talk about one thing being superior to another in inherent worth? In order to get at what is being asserted in such a claim it is helpful first to look at the social origin of the concept of degrees of inherent worth.

The idea that humans can possess different degrees of inherent worth originated in societies having rigid class structures. Before the rise of modern democracies with their egalitarian outlook, one's membership in a hereditary class determined one's social status. People in the upper classes were looked up to, while those in the lower classes were looked down upon. In such a society one's social superiors and social inferiors were clearly defined and easily recognized.

Two aspects of these class-structured societies are especially relevant to the idea of degrees of inherent worth. First, those born into the upper classes were deemed more worthy of respect than those born into the lower orders. Second, the superior worth of upper class people had nothing to do with their merits nor did the inferior worth of those in the lower classes rest on their lack of merits. One's superiority or inferiority entirely derived from a social position one was born into. The modern concept of a meritocracy simply did not apply. One could not advance into a higher class by any sort of moral or nonmoral achievement. Similarly, an aristocrat held his title and all the privileges that went with it just because he was the eldest son of a titled nobleman. Unlike the bestowing of knighthood in contemporary Great Britain, one did not earn membership in the nobility by meritorious conduct.

We who live in modern democracies no longer believe in such hereditary social distinctions. Indeed, we would wholeheartedly condemn them on moral grounds as being fundamentally unjust. We have come to think of class systems as a paradigm of social injustice, it being a central principle of the democratic way of life that among humans there are no superiors and no inferiors. Thus we have rejected the whole conceptual framework in which people are judged to have different degrees of inherent worth. That idea is incompatible with our notion of human equality based on the doctrine that all humans, simply in virtue of their humanity, have the same inherent worth. (The belief in universal human rights is one form that this egalitarianism takes.)

The vast majority of people in modern democracies, however, do not maintain an egalitarian outlook when it comes to comparing human beings with other living things. Most people consider our own species to be superior to all other species and this superiority is understood to be a matter of inherent worth, not merit. There may exist thoroughly vicious and depraved humans who lack all merit. Yet because they are human they are thought to belong to a higher class of entities than any plant or animal. That one is born into the species *Homo sapiens* entitles one to have lordship over those who are one's inferiors, namely, those born into other species. The parallel with hereditary social classes is very close. Implicit in this view is a hierarchical conception of nature according to which an organism has a position of superiority or inferiority in the Earth's community of life simply on the basis of its genetic background. The "lower" orders of life are looked down upon and it is considered perfectly proper that they serve the interests of those belonging to the highest order, namely humans. The intrinsic value we place on the well-being of our fellow humans reflects our recognition of their rightful position as our equals. No such intrinsic value is to be placed on the good of other animals, unless we choose to do so out of fondness or affection for them. But their well-being imposes no moral requirement on us. In this respect there is an absolute difference in moral status between ourselves and them.

This is the structure of concepts and beliefs that people are committed to insofar as they regard humans to be superior in inherent worth to all other species. I now wish to argue that this structure of concepts and beliefs is completely groundless. If we accept the first three components of the biocentric outlook and from that perspective look at the major philosophical traditions which have supported that structure, we find it to be at bottom nothing more than the expression of an irrational bias in our own favor. The philosophical traditions themselves rest on very questionable assumptions or else simply beg the question. I briefly consider three of the main traditions to substantiate the point. These are classical Greek humanism, Cartesian dualism, and the Judeo-Christian concept of the Great Chain of Being.

The inherent superiority of humans over other species was implicit in the Greek definition of man as a rational animal. Our animal nature was identified with "brute" desires that need the order and restraint of reason to rule them (just as reason is the special virture of those who rule in the ideal state). Rationality was then seen to be the key to our superiority over animals. It enables us to live on a higher plane and endows us with a nobility and worth that other creatures lack. This familiar way of comparing humans with other species is deeply ingrained in our Western philosophical outlook. The point to consider here is that this view does not actually provide an argument *for* human superiority but rather makes explicit the framework of thought that is implicitly used by those who think of humans as inherently superior to nonhumans. The Greeks who held that humans, in virtue of their rational capacities, have a kind of worth greater than that of any nonrational being, never looked at rationality as but one capacity of living things among many others. But when we consider rationality from the standpoint of the first three elements of the ecological outlook, we see that its value lies in its importance for *human* life. Other creatures achieve their species-specific good without the need of rationality, although they often make use of capacities that humans lack. So the humanistic outlook of classical Greek thought does not give us a neutral (nonquestion-begging) ground on which to construct a scale of degrees of inherent worth possessed by different species of living things.

The second tradition, centering on the Cartesian dualism of soul and body, also fails to justify the claim to human superiority. That superiority is supposed to derive from the fact that we have souls while animals do not. Animals are mere automata and lack the divine element that makes us spiritual beings. I won't go into the now familiar criticisms of this two-substance view. I only add the point that, even if humans are composed of an immaterial, un-extended soul and a material, extended body, this in itself is not a reason to deem them of greater worth than entities that are only bod-ies. Why is a soul substance a thing that adds value to its possessor? Unless some theological reasoning is offered here (which many, includ-ing myself, would find unacceptable on epis-temological grounds), no logical connection is evident. An immaterial something which thinks is better than a material something which does not think only if thinking itself has value, either intrinsically or instrumentally. Now it is intrinsically valuable to humans alone, who value it as an end in itself, and it is instrumentally valuable to those who benefit from it, namely humans.

For animals that neither enjoy thinking for its own sake nor need it for living the kind of life for which they are best adapted, it has no value. Even if "thinking" is broadened to in-clude all forms of consciousness, there are still many living things that can do without it and yet live what is for their species a good life. The anthropocentricity underlying the claim to human superiority runs throughout Carte-sian dualism.

A third major source of the idea of human superiority is the Judeo-Christian concept of the Great Chain of Being. Humans are supe-rior to animals and plants because their Creator has given them a higher place on the chain. It begins with God at the top, and then moves to the angels, who are lower than God but higher than humans, then to humans, positioned between the angels and the beasts (partaking of the nature of both), and then on down to the lower levels occupied by nonhu-man animals, plants, and finally inanimate ob-jects. Humans, being "made in God's image," are inherently superior to animals and plants by virtue of their being closer (in their es-sential nature) to God.

The metaphysical and epistemological diffi-culties with this conception of a hierarchy of entities are, in my mind, insuperable. Without entering into this matter here, I only point out that if we are unwilling to accept the meta-physics of traditional Judaism and Christian-ity, we are again left without good reasons for holding to the claim of inherent human superiority.

The foregoing considerations (and others like them) leave us with but one ground for the assertion that a human being, regardless of merit, is a higher kind of entity than any other living thing. This is the mere fact of the genet-ic makeup of the species *Homo sapiens*. But this is surely irrational and arbitrary. Why should the arrangement of genes of a certain type be a mark of superior value, especially when this fact about an organism is taken by itself, un-related to any other aspect of its life? We might just as well refer to any other genetic makeup as a ground of superior value. Clearly we are confronted here with a wholly arbitrary claim that can only be explained as an irration-al bias in our own favor.

That the claim is nothing more than a deep-seated prejudice is brought home to us when we look at our relation to other species in the light of the first three elements of the bio-centric outlook. Those elements taken con-jointly give us a certain overall view of the natural world and of the place of humans in it. When we take this view we come to un-derstand other living things, their environ-mental conditions, and their ecological rela-tionships in such a way as to awake in us a deep sense of our kinship with them as fellow members of the Earth's community of life. Humans and nonhumans alike are viewed together as integral parts of one unified whole in which all living things are functionally in-terrelated. Finally, when our awareness fo-cuses on the individual lives of plants and animals, each is seen to share with us the characteristic of being a teleological center of life striving to realize its own good in its own unique way.

As this entire belief system becomes part of the conceptual framework through which we understand and perceive the world, we come to see ourselves as bearing a certain moral relation to nonhuman forms of life. Our ethi-cal role in nature takes on a new significance. We begin to look at other species as we look at ourselves, seeing them as beings which have a good they are striving to realize just as we have a good we are striving to realize. We accord-ingly develop the disposition to view the world from the standpoint of their good as well as from the standpoint of our own good. Now if the groundlessness of the claim that humans are inherently superior to other species were brought clearly before our minds, we would not remain intellectually neutral toward that claim but would reject it as being fundamentally at variance with our total world outlook. In the absence of any good reasons for holding it, the assertion of human superiority would then appear simply as the expression of an irrational and self-serving prejudice that favors one particular species over several million others.

Rejecting the notion of human superiority entails its positive counterpart: the doctrine of species impartiality. One who accepts that doctrine regards all living things as possessing inherent worth—the *same* inherent worth, since no one species has been shown to be either "higher" or "lower" than any other. Now we saw earlier that, insofar as one thinks of a living thing as possessing inherent worth, one considers it to be the appropriate object of the attitude of respect and believes that attitude to be the only fitting or suitable one for all moral agents to take toward it.

Here, then, is the key to understanding how the attitude of respect is rooted in the biocentric outlook on nature. The basic connection is made through the denial of human superiority. Once we reject the claim that humans are superior either in merit or in worth to other living things, we are ready to adopt the attitude of respect. The denial of human superiority is itself the result of taking the perspective on nature built into the first three elements of the biocentric outlook.

Now the first three elements of the biocentric outlook, it seems clear, would be found acceptable to any rational and scientifically informed thinker who is fully "open" to the reality of the lives of nonhuman organisms. Without denying our distinctively human characteristics, such a thinker can acknowledge the fundamental respects in which we are members of the Earth's community of life and in which the biological conditions necessary for the realization of our human values are inextricably linked with the whole system of nature. In addition, the conception of individual living things as teleological centers of life simply articulates how a scientifically informed thinker comes to understand them as the result of increasingly careful and detailed observations. Thus, the biocentric outlook recommends itself as an acceptable system of concepts and beliefs to anyone who is clear-minded, unbiased, and factually enlightened, and who has a developed capacity of reality awareness with regard to the lives of individual organisms. This, I submit, is as good a reason for making the moral commitment involved in adopting the attitude of respect for nature as any theory of environmental ethics could possibly have.

Moral Rights and the Matter of Competing Claims

I have not asserted anywhere in the foregoing account that animals or plants have moral rights. This omission was deliberate. I do not think that the reference class of the concept, bearer of moral rights, should be extended to include nonhuman living things. My reasons for taking this position, however, go beyond the scope of this paper. I believe I have been able to accomplish many of the same ends which those who ascribe rights to animals or plants wish to accomplish. There is no reason, moreover, why plants and animals, including whole species populations and life communities, cannot be accorded *legal* rights under my theory. To grant them legal protection could be interpreted as giving them legal entitlement to be protected, and this, in fact, would be a means by which a society that subscribed to the ethics of respect for nature could give public recognition to their inherent worth.

There remains the problem of competing claims, even when wild plants and animals are not thought of as bearers of moral rights. If we accept the biocentric outlook and accordingly adopt the attitude of respect for nature as our ultimate moral attitude, how do we resolve conflicts that arise from our respect for persons in the domain of human ethics and our respect for nature in the domain of environmental ethics? This is a question that cannot adequately be dealt with here. My main purpose in this paper has been to try to establish a base point from which we can start working toward a solution to the problem. I have shown why we cannot just begin with an initial presumption in favor of the interests of our own species. It is after all within our power as moral beings to place limits on human population and technology with the deliberate intention of sharing the Earth's bounty with other species. That such sharing is an ideal difficult to realize even in an approximate way does not take away its claim to our deepest moral commitment.

Notes

1. The conceptual links between an entity *having* a good, something being good *for* it, and events doing good *to* it are examined by G. H. Von Wright in *The Varieties of Goodness* (New York: Humanities Press, 1963), chaps. 3 and 5.

2. See W. K. Frankena, "Ethics and the Environment," in K. E. Goodpaster and K. M. Sayre, eds., *Ethics and Problems of the 21st Century* (Notre Dame: University of Notre Dame Press, 1979), pp. 3–20. I critically examine Frankena's views in "Frankena on Environmental Ethics," *Monist*, (1981): 237–243.

3. In the light of considerations set forth in Daniel Dennett's *Brainstorms: Philosophical Essays on Mind and Psychology* (Montgomery, Vt.: Bradford Books, 1978), it is advisable to leave this question unsettled at this time. When machines are developed that function in the way our brains do, we may well come to deem them proper subjects of moral consideration.

4. I have analyzed the nature of this commitment of human ethics in "On Taking the Moral Point of View," *Midwest Studies in Philosophy*, vol. 3, *Studies in Ethical Theory* (1978), pp. 35–61.

5. John Rawls, "Justice As Fairness," *Philosophical Review* 67 (1958): 183.

6. My criticisms of the dogma of human superiority gain independent support from a carefully reasoned essay by R. and V. Routley showing the many logical weaknesses in arguments for human-centered theories of environmental ethics. R. and V. Routley, "Against the Inevitability of Human Chauvinism," in K. E. Goodpaster and K. M. Sayre, eds., *Ethics and Problems of the 21st Century* (Notre Dame: University of Notre Dame Press, 1979), pp. 36–59.

7. For this way of distinguishing between merit and inherent worth, I am indebted to Gregory Vlastos, "Justice and Equality," in R. Brandt, ed., *Social Justice* (Englewood Cliffs, N.J.: Prentice-Hall, 1962), pp. 31–72.

59. Environmental Justice

James P. Sterba

James P. Sterba seeks to resolve a central debate in contemporary environmental ethics between those who defend an anthropocentric ethics and those who defend a nonanthropocentric ethics by showing that when the most morally defensible versions of each of these perspectives are laid out, they do not lead to different practical recommendations. In this way he hopes to show how it is possible for defenders of anthropocentric and nonanthropocentric environmental ethics, despite their theoretical disagreement concerning whether humans are superior to members of other species, to agree on a common set of principles for achieving environmental justice.

From "Violence against Nature," in *Social Philosophy Today*, ed. Creighton Peden and Jeager Hudson (1993). Reprinted by permission.

A central debate, if not the most central debate, in contemporary environmental ethics is between those who defend an anthropocentric ethics and those who defend a nonanthropocentric ethics. This debate pits deep ecologists like George Sessions against reform or shallow ecologists like John Passmore.[1] It divides biocentric egalitarians like Paul Taylor from social ecologists like Murray Bookchin.[2] In this paper I propose to go some way toward resolving this debate by showing that when the most morally defensible versions of each of these perspectives are laid out, they do not lead to different practical requirements. In this way I hope to show how it is possible for defenders of anthropocentric and nonanthropocentric environmental ethics, despite their theoretical disagreement concerning whether humans are superior to members of other species, to agree on a common set of principles for achieving environmental justice.

Nonanthropocentric Environmental Ethics

Consider first the nonanthropocentric perspective. In support of this perspective it can be argued that we have no nonquestion-begging grounds for regarding the members of any living species as superior to the members of any other. It allows that the members of species differ in a myriad of ways, but argues that these differences do not provide grounds for thinking that the members of any one species are superior to the members of any other. In particular, it denies that the differences between species provides grounds for thinking that humans are superior to the members of other species. Of course, the nonanthropocentric perspective recognizes that humans have distinctive traits which the members of other species lack, like rationality and moral agency. It just points out that the members of nonhuman species also have distinctive traits that humans lack, like the homing ability of pigeons, the speed of the cheetah, and the ruminative ability of sheep and cattle.

Nor will it do to claim that the distinctive traits that humans have are more valuable than the distinctive traits that members of other species possess because there is no nonquestion-begging standpoint from which to justify that claim. From a human standpoint, rationality and moral agency are more valuable than any of the distinctive traits found in nonhuman species, since, as humans, we would not be better off if we were to trade in those traits for the distinctive traits found in nonhuman species. Yet the same holds true of nonhuman species. Pigeons, cheetahs, sheep and cattle would not be better off if they were to trade in their distinctive traits for the distinctive traits of other species.

Of course, the members of some species might be better off if they could retain the distinctive traits of their species while acquiring one or another of the distinctive traits possessed by some other species. For example, we humans might be better off if we could retain our distinctive traits while acquiring the ruminative ability of sheep and cattle. But many of the distinctive traits of species cannot be even imaginatively added to the members of other species without substantially altering the original species. For example, in order for the cheetah to acquire the distinctive traits possessed by humans, presumably it would have to be so transformed that its paws became something like hands to accommodate its humanlike mental capabilities, thereby losing its distinctive speed, and ceasing to be a cheetah. So possessing distinctively human traits would not be good for the cheetah. And with the possible exception of our nearest evolutionary relatives, the same holds true for the members of other species: they would not be better off having distinctively human traits. Only in fairy tales and in the world of Disney can the members of nonhuman species enjoy a full array of distinctively human traits. So there would appear to be no nonquestion-begging perspective from which to judge that distinctively human traits are more valuable than the distinctive traits possessed by other species. Judged from a nonquestion-begging perspective, we would seemingly have to regard the members of all species as equals.[3]

Nevertheless, regarding the members of all species as equals still allows for human preference in the same way that regarding all humans as equals still allows for self preference.

First of all, human preference can be justified on grounds of defense. Thus, we have

A Principle of Human Defense: Actions that defend oneself and other human beings against harmful aggression are permissible even when they necessitate killing or harming animals or plants.[4]

This principle is strictly analogous to the principle of self-defense that applies in human ethics and permits actions in defense of oneself or other human beings against harmful human aggression.[5] In the case of human aggression, however, it will sometimes be possible to effectively defend oneself and other human beings by first suffering the aggression and then securing adequate compensation later. Since in the case of nonhuman aggression, this is unlikely to obtain, more harmful preventive actions such as killing a rabid dog or swatting a mosquito will be justified.

Second, human preference can also be justified on grounds of preservation. Accordingly, we have

A Principle of Human Preservation: Actions that are necessary for meeting one's basic needs or the basic needs of other human beings are permissible even when they require aggressing against the basic needs of animals and plants.

Now needs, in general, if not satisfied, lead to lacks or deficiencies with respect to various standards. The basic needs of humans, if not satisfied, lead to lacks or deficiencies with respect to a standard of a decent life. The basic needs of animals and plants, if not satisfied, lead to lacks or deficiencies with respect to a standard of a healthy life.[6]

In human ethics, there is no principle that is strictly analogous to this Principle of Human Preservation. There is a principle of self-preservation in human ethics that permits actions that are necessary for meeting one's own basic needs or the basic needs of other people, even if this requires *failing to meet* (through an act of omission) the basic needs of still other people. For example, we can use our resources

to feed ourselves and our family, even if this necessitates failing to meet the basic needs of people in Third World countries. But, in general, we don't have a principle that allows us to aggress against (through an act of commission) the basic needs of some people in order to meet our own basic needs or the basic needs of other people to whom we are committed or happen to care about. Actually, the closest we come to permitting aggressing against the basic needs of other people in order to meet our own basic needs or the basic needs of people to whom we are committed or happen to care about is our acceptance of the outcome of life and death struggles in lifeboat cases, where no one has an antecedent right to the available resources. For example, if you had to fight off others in order to secure the last place in a lifeboat for yourself or for a member of your family, we might say that you justifiably aggressed against the basic needs of those whom you fought to meet your own basic needs or the basic needs of the member of your family.

Nevertheless, our survival requires a principle of preservation that permits aggressing against the basic needs of at least some other living things whenever this is necessary to meet our own basic needs or the basic needs of other human beings. Here there are two possibilities. The first is a principle of preservation that allows us to aggress against the basic needs of both humans and nonhumans whenever it would serve our own basic needs or the basic needs of other human beings. The second is the principle, given above, that allows us to aggress against the basic needs of only nonhumans whenever it would serve our own basic needs or the basic needs of other human beings. The first principle does not express any general preference for the members of the human species, and thus it permits even cannibalism provided that it serves to meet our own basic needs or the basic needs of other human beings. In contrast, the second principle does express a degree of preference for the members of the human species in cases where their basic needs are at stake. Happily, this degree of preference for our own species is still compatible with the equality of all species because favoring the members of one's own species to this extent is characteristic of the members of all the species with which we interact and is thereby legitimated. The reason it is legitimated is that we would be required to sacrifice the basic needs of members of the human species only if the members of other species were making similar sacrifices for the sake of the members of the human species. In addition, if we were to prefer consistently the basic needs of the members of other species whenever those needs conflicted with our own (or even if we do so half the time), given the characteristic behavior of the members of other species, we would soon be facing extinction, and, fortunately, we have no reason to think that we are morally required to bring about our own extinction. For these reasons, the degree of preference for our own species found in the above Principle of Human Preservation is justified, even if we were to adopt a nonanthropocentric perspective.

Nevertheless, preference for humans can go beyond bounds, and the bounds that are compatible with a nonanthropocentric perspective are expressed by the following:

> A Principle of Disproportionality: Actions that meet nonbasic or luxury needs of humans are prohibited when they aggress against the basic needs of animals and plants.

This principle is strictly analogous to a principle in human ethics that prohibits meeting some people's nonbasic or luxury needs by aggressing against the basic needs of other people.[7]

Without a doubt, the adoption of such a principle with respect to nonhuman nature would significantly change the way we live our lives. Such a principle is required, however, if there is to be any substance to the claim that the members of all species are equal. We can no more consistently claim that the members of all species are equal and yet aggress against the basic needs of some animals or plants whenever this conflicts with our own nonbasic or luxury needs than we can consistently claim that all humans are equal and yet aggress against the basic needs of some other human beings whenever this conflicts with our nonbasic or luxury needs.[8] Consequently, if species equality is to mean anything, it must be the case that the basic needs of the members of

nonhuman species trump the nonbasic needs of humans in these cases of conflict.

So while a nonanthropocentric perspective allows for a degree of preference for the members of the human species, it also significantly limits that preference.

Nevertheless, animal liberationists may wonder about the further implications of this nonanthropocentric perspective for the treatment of animals. Obviously, a good deal of work has already been done on this topic. Initially, philosophers thought that humanism could be extended to include animal liberation and eventually environmental concern.[9] Then Baird Callicott argued that animal liberation and environmental concern were as opposed to each other as they were to humanism.[10] The resulting conflict Callicott called "a triangular affair." Agreeing with Callicott, Mark Sagoff contended that any attempt to link together animal liberation and environmental concern would lead to "a bad marriage and a quick divorce."[11] Yet more recently, such philosophers as Mary Ann Warren, have tended to play down the opposition between animal liberation and environmental concern, and even Callicott now thinks he can bring the two back together again.[12] There are good reasons for thinking that such a reconciliation is possible.

Right off, it would be good for the environment if people generally, especially people in the First World, adopted a more vegetarian diet of the sort that animal liberationists are recommending. This is because a good portion of livestock production today consumes grains that could be more effectively used for direct human consumption. For example, 90 percent of the protein, ninety-nine percent of the carbohydrate, and 100 percent of the fiber value of grain is wasted by cycling it through livestock, and currently 64 percent of the U.S. grain crop is fed to livestock.[13] So by adopting a more vegetarian diet, people generally, and especially people in the First World, could significantly reduce the amount of farmland that has to be kept in production to feed the human population. This, in turn, could have beneficial effects on the whole biotic community by eliminating the amount of soil erosion and environmental pollutants that result from raising livestock. For example, it has been estimated that 85 percent of U.S. topsoil lost from cropland, pasture, range land and forest land is directly associated with raising livestock.[14]

But even though a more vegetarian diet seems in order, it is not clear that the interests of farm animals would be well served if all of us became complete vegetarians. Sagoff assumes that in a completely vegetarian human world people would continue to feed farm animals as before.[15] But it is not clear that we would have any obligation to do so. Moreover, in a completely vegetarian human world, we would probably need about half of the grain we now feed livestock to meet people's nutritional needs, particularly in Second and Third World countries. There simply would not be enough grain to go around. And then there would be the need to conserve cropland for future generations. So in a completely vegetarian human world, it seems likely that the population of farm animals would be decimated, relegating many of the farm animals that remain to zoos. On this account, it would seem to be more in the interest of farm animals generally that they be maintained under healthy conditions, and then killed relatively painlessly and eaten, rather than that they not be maintained at all. So a completely vegetarian human world would not seem to serve the interest of farm animals.

Nor, it seems, would it be in the interest of wild species who no longer have their natural predators not to be hunted by humans. Of course, where possible, it may be preferable to reintroduce natural predators. But this may not always be possible because of the proximity of farm animals and human populations, and then if action is not taken to control the populations of wild species, disaster could result for the species and their environments. For example, deer, rabbits, squirrels, quails and ducks reproduce rapidly, and in the absence of predators can quickly exceed the carrying capacity of their environments. So it is in the interest of certain wild species and their environments that humans intervene periodically to maintain a balance. Of course, there will be many natural environments where it is in the interest of the environment and the wild animals that inhabit it to be simply left alone. But here, too, animal liberation

and environmental concern would not be in conflict. For these reasons, animal liberationists would have little reason to object to the proposed three principles for a nonanthropocentric environmental ethics.

Anthropocentric Environmental Ethics

But suppose we were to reject the central argument of the nonanthropocentric perspective and deny that the members of all species are equal. We might claim, for example, that humans are superior because they, through culture, "realize a greater range of values" than members of nonhuman species or we might claim that humans are superior in virtue of their "unprecedented capacity to create ethical systems that impart worth to other life-forms."[16] Or we might offer some other grounds for human superiority.[17] Suppose, then, we adopt this anthropocentric perspective. What follows?

First of all, we will still need a principle of human defense. However, there is no need to adopt a different principle of human defense from the principle favored by a nonanthropocentric perspective. Whether we judge humans to be equal or superior to the members of other species, we will still want a principle that allows us to defend ourselves and other human beings from harmful aggression, even when this necessitates killing or harming animals or plants.

Second, we will also need a principle of human preservation. But here, too, there is no need to adopt a different principle from the principle of human preservation favored by a nonanthropocentric perspective. Whether we judge humans to be equal or superior to the members of other species, we will still want a principle that permits actions that are necessary for meeting our own basic needs or the basic needs of other human beings, even when this requires aggressing against the basic needs of animals and plants.

The crucial question is whether we will need a different principle of disproportionality. If we judged humans to be superior to the members of other species, will we still have grounds for preferring in this way the basic needs of animals and plants over the nonbasic or luxury needs of humans?

Here it is important to distinguish between two degrees of preference that we noted earlier. First, we could prefer the basic needs of animals and plants over the nonbasic or luxury needs of humans when to do otherwise would involve *aggressing against* (by an act of commission) the basic needs of animals and plants. Second, we could prefer the basic needs of animals and plants over the nonbasic or luxury needs of humans when to do otherwise would involve simply *failing to meet* (by an act of omission) the basic needs of animals and plants.

Now in human ethics when the basic needs of some people are in conflict with the nonbasic or luxury needs of others, the distinction between failing to meet and aggressing against basic needs seems to have little moral force. In such conflicting cases, both ways of not meeting basic needs are objectionable.[18]

But in environmental ethics, whether we adopt an anthropocentric or a nonanthropocentric perspective, we would seem to have grounds for morally distinguishing between the two cases, favoring the basic needs of animals and plants when to do otherwise would involve *aggressing against* those needs in order to meet our own nonbasic or luxury needs, but not when it would involve simply *failing to meet* those needs in order to meet our own nonbasic or luxury needs. This degree of preference for the members of the human species would be compatible with the equality of species insofar as members of nonhuman species also fail to meet the basic needs of members of the human species.

Even so, this theoretical distinction would have little practical force since most of the ways that we have of preferring our own nonbasic needs over the basic needs of animals and plants actually involve aggressing against their basic needs to meet our own nonbasic or luxury needs rather than simply failing to meet their basic needs.[19]

Yet even if most of the ways that we have of preferring our own nonbasic or luxury needs do involve aggressing against the basic needs of animals and plants, wouldn't human superiority provide grounds for making such

sacrifices? Or put another way, shouldn't human superiority have more theoretical and practical significance than I am allowing? Not, I claim, if we are looking for the most morally defensible position to take.

For consider: The claim that humans are superior to the members of other species, if it can be justified at all, is something like the claim that a person came in first in a race where others came in second, third, fourth, and so on. It would not imply that the members of other species are without intrinsic value. In fact, it would imply just the opposite—that the members of other species are also intrinsically valuable, although not as intrinsically valuable as humans, just as the claim that a person came in first in a race implies that the persons who came in second, third, fourth, and so on are also meritorious, although not as meritorious as the person who came in first.

This line of argument draws further support once we consider the fact that many animals and plants are superior to humans in one respect or another, e.g., the sense of smell of the wolf or the acuity of sight of the eagle or the photosynthetic power of plants. So any claim of human superiority must allow for the recognition of excellences in nonhuman species, even for some excellences that are superior to their corresponding human excellences. In fact, it demands that recognition.

Moreover, if the claim of human superiority is to have any moral force, it must rest on nonquestion-begging grounds. Accordingly, we must be able to give a nonquestion-begging response to the nonanthropocentric argument for the equality of species. Yet for any such argument to be successful, it would have to recognize the intrinsic value of the members of nonhuman species. Even if it could be established that human beings have greater intrinsic value, we would still have to recognize that nonhuman nature has intrinsic value as well. So the relevant question is: How are we going to recognize the presumably lesser intrinsic value of nonhuman nature?

Now if human needs, even nonbasic or luxury ones, are always preferred to even the basic needs of the members of nonhuman species, we would not be giving any recognition to the intrinsic value of nonhuman nature. But what if we allowed the nonbasic or luxury needs of humans to trump the basic needs of nonhuman nature half the time, and half the time we allowed the basic needs of nonhuman nature to trump the nonbasic or luxury needs of humans. Would that be enough? Certainly, it would be a significant advance over what we are presently doing. For what we are presently doing is meeting the basic needs of nonhuman nature, at best, only when it serves our own needs or the needs of those we are committed to or happen to care about, and that does not recognize the intrinsic value of nonhuman nature at all. A fifty-fifty arrangement would be an advance indeed. But it would not be enough.

The reason it would not be enough is that the claim that humans are superior to nonhuman nature no more supports the practice of aggressing against the basic needs of nonhuman nature to satisfy our own nonbasic or luxury needs than the claim that a person came in first in a race would support the practice of aggressing against the basic needs of those who came in second, third, fourth and so on to satisfy the nonbasic or luxury needs of the person who came in first. A higher degree of merit does not translate into a right of domination, and to claim a right to aggress against the basic needs of nonhuman nature in order to meet our own nonbasic or luxury needs is clearly to claim a right of domination. All that we would be justified in doing, I have argued, is not meeting the basic needs of nonhuman nature when this conflicts with our nonbasic or luxury needs. What we are not justified in doing is aggressing against the basic needs of nonhuman nature when this conflicts with our nonbasic or luxury needs. But this is no more than is justified assuming the equality of species.

In sum, I argue that whether we endorse an anthropocentric or a nonanthropocentric environmental ethics, we should favor the very same principles: a Principle of Human Defense, a Principle of Human Preservation, and a Principle of Disproportionality as I have interpreted them. Taken together these three principles strike the right balance between concerns of human welfare and the welfare of nonhuman nature.

Of course, the practical implications of these three principles would include proposals for conserving existing resources, particularly nonrenewable resources, proposals for converting to renewable resources, proposals for redistributing resources to meet basic needs of both humans and nonhumans, and proposals for population control, all implemented principally by educational changes and by changes in the tax and incentive structures of our society. In the longer work from which this paper is drawn, I go on to discuss these practical proposals in more detail. In this paper, I have sought to provide the nonanthropocentric and anthropocentric grounding for such proposals in a common set of conflict resolution principles that are required for achieving environmental justice.

Notes

1. See John Passmore, *Man's Responsibility for Nature* (London: Charles Scribner's Sons, 1974) and George Sessions and Bill Devall, *Deep Ecology* (Salt Lake City: Glibb Smith, 1985).

2. See Paul Taylor, *Respect for Nature* (Princeton: Princeton University Press, 1987) and Murray Bookchin, *The Ecology of Freedom* (Montreal: Black Rose Books, 1991). It is also possible to view Passmore as pitted against Taylor and Bookchin as pitted against Sessions, but however one casts the debate, those who defend an anthropocentric ethics are still opposed to those who defend a nonanthropocentric ethics.

3. I am assuming here that either we treat humans as superior overall to other living things or we treat them as equal overall to other living things. Accordingly, if there is no self-evident or nonquestion-begging grounds for claiming that humans are superior overall to other living things, then, I claim that we should treat humans as equal overall to all other living things.

4. For the purposes of this paper, I will follow the convention of excluding humans from the class denoted by "animals."

5. Of course, one might contend that no principle of human defense applied in human ethics because either "nonviolent pacifism" or "nonlethal pacifism" is the most morally defensible view. However, I have argued elsewhere that this is not the case, and that still other forms of paci-

fism more compatible with just war theory are also more morally defensible than either of these forms of pacifism. See Selection 67.

6. For further discussion of basic needs, see *How to Make People Just* (Totowa, N.J.: Rowman & Littlefield, 1988), pp. 45–50.

7. This principle is clearly acceptable to welfare liberals and socialists, and it can even be shown to be acceptable to libertarians. See Selection 4.

8. Of course, libertarians have claimed that we can recognize that people have equal basic rights while failing to meet, but not aggressing against, the basic needs of other human beings. However, I have argued that this claim is mistaken. See Selection 4.

9. Peter Singer's *Animal Liberation* (New York: New York Review, 1975) inspired this view.

10. Baird Callicott, "Animal Liberation: A Triangular Affair," *Environmental Ethics* (1980), 311–328.

11. Mark Sagoff, "Animal Liberation and Environmental Ethics: Bad Marriage, Quick Divorce," *Osgood Hall Law Journal* (1984), 297–307.

12. Mary Ann Warren, "The Rights of the Nonhuman World," in *Environmental Philosophy*, edited by Robert Elliot and Arran Gare (London,

1983), 109–134, and Baird Callicott, *In Defense of the Land Ethic* (Albany: SUNY Press, 1989), chapter 3.

13. *Realities for the 90's* (Santa Cruz, 1991), p. 4.

14. Ibid., p. 5.

15. Mark Sagoff, op. cit., pp. 301–305.

16. Holmes Rolston, *Environmental Ethics* (Philadelphia: Temple University Press, 1988), pp. 66–68; Murray Bookchin., op. cit., p. xxxvi.

17. See the discussion of possible grounds of human superiority in Taylor, pp. 135–152 and in Byran Norton, *Why Preserve Natural Variety?* (Princeton: Princeton University Press, 1987), 135–150.

18. This is clearly true for welfare liberals and socialists, and it can even be shown to be true for libertarians because most failings to meet the basic needs of others really turn out to be acts of aggressing against the basic needs of others. See *How To Make People Just,* chapter 7.

19. The same holds true in human ethics where most of the ways that we have of preferring our own nonbasic needs over other humans actually involve aggressing against their needs to meet our own nonbasic or luxury needs rather than simply failing to meet them. See the previous note.

60. From the Animal Welfare Act

Congress of the United States

"Sec. 13. The Secretary shall promulgate standards to govern the humane handling, care, treatment, and transportation of animals by dealers, research facilities, and exhibitors. Such standards shall include minimum requirements with respect to handling, housing, feeding, watering, sanitation, ventilation, shelter from extremes of weather and temperatures, adequate veterinary care, including the appropriate use of anesthetic, analgesic or tranquilizing drugs, when such use would be proper in the opinion of the attending veterinarian of such research facilities, and separation by species when the Secretary finds such separation necessary for the humane handling, care, or treatment of animals. In promulgating and enforcing standards established pursuant to this section, the Secretary is authorized and directed to consult experts, including outside consultants where indicated. Nothing in this Act shall be construed as authorizing the Secretary to promulgate rules, regulations, or orders with regard to design, outlines, guidelines, or performance of actual research or experimentation by a research facility as determined by such research facility: *Provided* That the Secretary shall require, at least annually, every research facility to show that professionally acceptable standards governing the care, treatment, and use of animals, including appropriate use of anesthetic, analgesic, and tranquilizing drugs, during experimentation are being followed by the research facility during actual research or experimentation."

61. Amendments to the Animal Welfare Act

Congress of the United States

The bill amends the Animal Welfare Act as follows:

1. Expands the definition of the term "research facility" to include each department, agency or instrumentality of the United States which uses animals for research or experimentation; defines the term "Federal agency" to mean any Executive agency from which a research facility has received or may receive Federal funds to support the conduct of research, experimentation, or testing involving the use of animals; and, makes it clear that the definition of "animal" is the same as that provided under the current Act.

2. Deletes the language stating that minimum requirements be applied to the standards promulgated by the Secretary of Agriculture to govern the humane handling, care, treatment, and transportation of animals by dealers, research facilities and exhibitors; adds exercise for dogs as a standard; and, allows the Secretary to make exceptions to the standards, but only when such exceptions are specified by the research protocol.

3. Requires the Secretary to promulgate standards for research facilities, including requirements for animal care, treatment, and practices in experimental procedures, to ensure that animal pain and distress are minimized. Requires each research facility, in its annual statement of compliance, to provide the Secretary of Agriculture with assurances that such standards are being followed. Also requires the research facility to provide annual training sessions for personnel involved with animal care and treatment.

4. Provides that any State (or political subdivision of that State) may promulgate standards in addition to those promulgated by the Secretary.

5. Mandates the establishment and makeup of an animal research committee of three or more members within each research facility. Makes it unlawful for any member of the committee to release trade secrets or confidential information. The committee must make inspections at least semiannually of all animal study areas of the research facility and file an inspection report which must remain on file at the research facility for three years. The committee must notify, in writing, the Animal and Plant Health Inspection Service (APHIS) of the Department of Agriculture and the funding Federal agency of any unacceptable conditions that are not corrected despite notification. Federal support for a particular project can be suspended or revoked for continued failure by a research facility to comply with the standards of animal care, treatment or practices; such suspension or revocation may be appealed.

6. The inspection results of the animal research committee must be available to the Department of Agriculture's inspectors for review during inspection. These inspectors must forward to APHIS and the funding Federal agency any inspection records of the committee which include reports of any deficient conditions of animal care or treatment and any deviations of research practices from the originally approved proposal that adversely affect animal welfare.

7. Prohibits the Secretary from promulgating rules, regulations, or orders that may require a research facility to disclose trade secrets or commercial or financial information which is privileged or confidential.

8. Mandates the establishment of an information service on improved methods of animal experimentation at the National Agricultural Library. . . .

62. *Tennessee Valley Authority v. Hill*

Supreme Court of the United States

The issue before the Supreme Court was whether the Endangered Species Act of 1973 prohibited the completion of a dam whose operation would destroy the habitat of the snail darter, an endangered species, even though the dam was virtually completed and Congress continued to appropriate large sums of money to the project even after the congressional appropriations committees were apprised of the project's apparent impact on the survival of the snail darter. Chief Justice Burger, delivering the opinion of the Court, held that the Endangered Species Act did prohibit the completion of the dam because the language of the act and the history that led to its passage required that its provisions be applied without exceptions.

We begin with the premise that operation of the Tellico Dam will either eradicate the known population of snail darters or destroy their critical habitat. Petitioner does not now seriously dispute this fact. In any event, . . . the Secretary of the Interior is vested with exclusive authority to determine whether a species such as the snail darter is "endangered" or "threatened" and to ascertain the factors which have led to such a precarious existence. . . . Congress has authorized—indeed commanded—the Secretary to "issue such regulations as he deems necessary and advisable to provide for the conservation of such species." . . . As we have seen, the Secretary promulgated regulations which declared the snail darter an endangered species whose critical habitat would be destroyed by creation of the Tellico Dam. Doubtless petitioner would prefer not to have these regulations on the books, but there is no suggestion that the Secretary exceeded his authority or abused his discretion in issuing the regulations. Indeed, no judicial review of the Secretary's determinations has ever been sought and hence the validity of his actions are not open to review in this Court. . . .

It may seem curious to some that the survival of a relatively small number of three-inch fish among all the countless millions of species extant would require the permanent halting of a virtually completed dam for which Congress has expended more than $100 million. The paradox is not minimized by the fact that Congress continued to appropriate large sums of public money for the project, even after congressional Appropriations Committees were apprised of its apparent impact upon the survival of the snail darter. We conclude, however, that the explicit provisions of the Endangered Species Act require precisely that result. . . .

. . . By 1973, when Congress held hearings on what would later become the Endangered Species Act of 1973, it was informed that species were still being lost at the rate of about one per year, . . . and "the pace of disappearance of species" appeared to be "accelerating." Moreover, Congress was also told that the primary cause of this trend was something other than the normal process of natural selection:

> [M]an and his technology has [*sic*] continued at an ever-increasing rate to disrupt the natural ecosystem. This has resulted in a dramatic rise in the number and severity of the threats faced by the world's wildlife. The truth in this is apparent when one realizes that half of the recorded extinctions of mammals over the past 2,000 years have occurred in the most recent 50-year period. . . .

That Congress did not view these developments lightly was stressed by one commentator:

The dominant theme pervading all Congressional discussion of the proposed [Endangered Species Act of 1973] was the overriding need *to devote whatever effort and resources were necessary* to avoid further diminution of national and worldwide wildlife resources. Much of the testimony at the hearings and much debate was devoted to the biological problem of extinction. Senators and Congressmen uniformly deplored the irreplaceable loss to aesthetics, science, ecology, and the national heritage should more species disappear. . . .

The legislative proceedings in 1973 are, in fact, replete with expressions of concern over the risk that might lie in the loss of *any* endangered species. Typifying these sentiments is the Report of the House Committee on Merchant Marine and Fisheries on . . . a bill which contained the essential features of the subsequently enacted Act of 1973; in explaining the need for the legislation, the Report stated:

As we homogenize the habitats in which these plants and animals evolved, and as we increase the pressure for products that they are in a position to supply (usually unwillingly) we threaten their—and our own—genetic heritage.
The value of this genetic heritage is, quite literally, incalculable.
From the most narrow possible point of view, *it is in the best interests of mankind to minimize the losses of genetic variations.* The reason is simple: they are potential resources. They are keys to puzzles which we cannot solve, and may provide answers to questions which we have not yet learned to ask.
To take a homely, but apt, example: one of the critical chemicals in the regulation of ovulations in humans was found in a common plant. Once discovered, and analyzed, humans could duplicate it synthetically, but had it never existed—or had it been driven out of existence before we knew its potentialities—we would never have tried to synthesize it in the first place.
Who knows, or can say, what potential cures for cancer or other scourges, present or future, may lie locked up in the structures of plants which may yet be undiscovered, much less analyzed? . . . Sheer self-interest impels us to be cautious. . . .

As the examples cited here demonstrate, Congress was concerned about the *unknown* uses that endangered species might have and about the *unforeseeable* place such creatures may have in the chain of life on this planet. . . .
. . . Representative Dingell provided an interpretation of what the Conference bill would require, making it clear that the mandatory provisions . . . were not casually or inadvertently included:

. . . A recent article . . . illustrates the problem which might occur absent this new language in the bill. It appears that the whooping cranes of this country, perhaps the best known of our endangered species, are being threatened by Air Force bombing activities along the gulf coast of Texas. Under existing law, the Secretary of Defense has some discretion as to whether or not he will take the necessary action to see that this threat disappears . . . . [O]nce the bill is enacted, [the Secretary of Defense] *would be required to take the proper steps.* . . .
Another example . . . [has] to do with the continental population of grizzly bears which may or may not be endangered, but which is surely threatened. . . . Once this bill is enacted, the appropriate Secretary, whether of Interior, Agriculture or whatever, *will have to take action* to see that this situation is not permitted to worsen, and that these bears are not driven to extinction. The purposes of the bill included the conservation of the species and of the ecosystems upon which they depend, and *every agency of government is committed* to see that those purposes are carried out. . . . [T]he agencies of Government can no longer plead that they can do nothing about it. *They can, and they must. The law is clear.* . . .

Notwithstanding Congress's expression of intent in 1973, we are urged to find that the continuing appropriations for Tellico Dam constitute an implied repeal of the 1973 Act, at least insofar as it applies to the Tellico Project. In support of this view, TVA points to the statements found in various House and Senate Appropriations Committees' Reports. . . . Since we are unwilling to assume that these latter Committee statements constituted advice to ignore the provisions of a duly enacted law, we assume that these Committees believed that the Act simply was not applicable in this situation. But even under this interpretation of the Committees' actions, we are unable to conclude that the Act has been in any respect amended or repealed. . . .

. . . The starting point in this analysis must be the legislative proceedings leading to the 1977 appropriations since the earlier funding of the dam occurred prior to the listing of the snail darter as an endangered species. In all successive years, TVA confidently reported to the Appropriations Committees that efforts to transplant the snail darter appeared to be successful; this surely gave those Committees some basis for the impression that there was no direct conflict between the Tellico Project and the Endangered Species Act. Indeed, the special appropriation for 1978 of $2 million for transplantation of endangered species supports the view that the Committees saw such relocation as the means whereby collision between Tellico and the Endangered Species Act could be avoided. . . .

. . . Here we are urged to view the Endangered Species Act "reasonably," and hence shape a remedy "that accords with some modicum of common sense and the public weal." . . . But is that our function? We have no expert knowledge on the subject of endangered species, much less do we have a mandate from the people to strike a balance of equities on the side of the Tellico Dam. Congress has spoken in the plainest of words, making it abundantly clear that the balance has been struck in favor of affording endangered species the highest of priorities, thereby adopting a policy which it described as "institutionalized caution."

Our individual appraisal of the wisdom or unwisdom of a particular course consciously selected by the Congress is to be put aside in the process of interpreting a statute. Once the meaning of an enactment is discerned and its constitutionality determined, the judicial process comes to an end. We do not sit as a committee of review, nor are we vested with the power of veto. The lines ascribed to Sir Thomas More by Robert Bolt are not without relevance here:

> The law, Roper, the law. I know what's legal, not what's right. And I'll stick to what's legal. . . . I'm *not* God. The currents and eddies of right and wrong, which you find such plain-sailing, I can't navigate, I'm no voyager. But in the thickets of the law, oh there I'm a forester. . . . What would you do? Cut a great road through the law to get after the Devil? . . . And when the last law was down, and the Devil turned round on you—where would you hide, Roper, the laws all being flat? . . . This country's planted thick with laws from coast to coast—Man's laws, not God's—and if you cut them down . . . d'you really think you could stand upright in the winds that would blow then? . . . Yes, I'd give the Devil benefit of law, for my own safety's sake.
> R. Bolt, *A Man for All Seasons*

We agree with the Court of Appeals that in our constitutional system the commitment to the separation of powers is too fundamental for us to pre-empt congressional action by judicially decreeing what accords with "common sense and the public weal." Our Constitution vests such responsibilities in the political branches.

Suggestions for Further Reading

Anthologies

Armstrong, Susan, and Botzler, Richard. *Environmental Ethics.* New York: McGraw Hill, 1993.

Regan, T., and Singer, P. (eds.). *Animal Rights and Human Obligation.* Englewood Cliffs, N.J.: Prentice-Hall, 1976.

Sterba, James P. *Earth Ethics.* New York: Macmillan, 1993.

Alternative Views

Atfield, R. *The Ethics of Environmental Concern.* New York: Columbia University Press, 1983.

Dombrowski, D. *The Philosophy of Vegetarianism.* Amherst, MA: University of Massachusetts Press, 1984.

Frey, R. G. *Rights, Killing and Suffering.* Oxford, England: Basil Blackwell, 1983.

Hargrove, Eugene. *The Foundations of Environmental Ethics.* Englewood Cliffs, N.J.: Prentice-Hall, 1988.

Regan, T. *The Case for Animal Rights.* Berkeley: University of California Press, 1984.

Singer, P. *Animal Liberation.* New York: New York Review, 1975.

Stone, C. *Earth and Other Ethics.* New York: Harper & Row, 1987.

Taylor, P. *Respect for Nature.* Princeton: Princeton University Press, 1988.

Practical Applications

Akers, K. *A Vegetarian Sourcebook.* New York: G. P. Putnam and Sons, 1983.

Boas, M., and Chain, S. *Big Mac: The Unauthorized Story of McDonald's.* New York: New American Library, 1976.

Gore, Al. *Earth in the Balance.* New York: Houghton Mifflin, 1992.

Swanson, W., and Schultz, G. *Prime Rip.* Englewood Cliffs, N.J.: Prentice-Hall, 1982.

National Health Care

Introduction

Basic Concepts

At present there is widespread agreement that the U.S. health care system is in crisis. The United States spends 14 percent of its GNP on health care while Canada spends only 9 percent for its national health care program, and health care costs in the United States are expected to rise to 17 percent of GNP by the year 2000. At the same time, by one estimate, 30 million people are uninsured and 100 million others are underinsured. So our health care system seems to both cost more and benefit a smaller percentage of our population when compared to the Canadian health care system. Obviously, our health care system needs to be improved, but how should we improve it?

If we assume that libertarian, welfare liberal, and socialist conceptions of justice all require a right to welfare (see Section I), then, in order to determine the morally appropriate level of health care, we would need to determine what provision of health care would be required by this right. Since a right to welfare is usually associated with a welfare liberal conception of justice, it would seem reasonable to use John Rawls's original position decision procedure, a procedure favored by welfare liberals, to determine what level of health care would be required by a right to welfare.

Let us then imagine people behind a veil of ignorance trying to determine how they should allocate health care services over their lifetimes, but not knowing whether they are young or old. When characterized in this way, the hypothetical choosers will tend to favor death-preventing health care for the young because they clearly have more to lose if such health care is not in place. Accordingly, they may choose a certain level of health care that reduces the death-preventing health care for the old in order to provide greater death-preventing health care for the young. Nor would this be unjust, since, as they are characterized, the hypothetical choosers would still want a measure of death-preventing health care for the old.

So the consequences of using a Rawlsian decision procedure to determine the morally appropriate level of health care required by a right to welfare is:

1. A focus on a death-preventing level of health care for the young.

2. A focus on a life-enhancing health care for both young and old.

3. A willingness to cut back on death-preventing health care for the old to some extent when it conflicts with (1) and possibly when it conflicts with (2) as well.

Yet these consequences remain indeterminate until we can specify the amount of resources that are to be devoted to health care rather than to meeting the various other needs and wants that people have. In this regard, it won't do simply to have each person choose the level of health care that he or she prefers because we can't assume that everyone will have sufficient income to purchase whatever level of health care they want or need. Instead, we seem to have two options.

One option is to specify an optimal and affordable level of health care and then guarantee this same level of health care to all legitimate claimants. The other option is to specify a decent minimal level of health care, guarantee that level of health care to all legitimate claimants, but then allow higher levels of health care to be purchased by whomever has the income and desire to do so. Of course, both of these options will leave some people dissatisfied. The equal health care option will leave dissatisfied those people who would have preferred and could have afforded a higher level of health care that would have been available under the multitiered health care option. The multitiered health care option will leave dissatisfied those people who would only receive the decent minimum level of health care under that option but who want or need more health care than they will be receiving. Is there any just resolution of this conflict?

Assuming again that we are trying to determine the morally appropriate level of health care required by a right to welfare, it is surely the case that nothing less than a guaranteed decent minimum level of health care to all legitimate claimants would be morally acceptable. But is a multitiered option for health care morally permissible or is an equal-level-of-health-care option morally required?

The answer to this question requires taking into account all the morally legitimate claimants to our available resources. This is because the class of morally legitimate claimants to our available resources includes not only the members of the particular society to which we happen to belong, but also distant peoples and future generations as well. (See Section II.) So once we recognize how numerous are the morally legitimate claimants on our available resources, it becomes clear that all that we can hope to do is provide a decent minimal level of health care to all claimants. Given the morally legitimate claims that distant peoples and future generations make on our available resources, it is unlikely that we will have sufficient resources to allow people to purchase higher levels of health care (the multitiered option). Morally, we would seem to have no other choice than to favor the same level of health care for everybody (the equal health care option).

Yet notice that in preferring the equal health care option we did not appeal to the ideal of equality itself, but rather to the goal of providing all legitimate claimants with a decent minimum level of health care. Given that available resources are limited, to meet the goal of providing a decent minimum of health care to all legitimate claimants, equality of health care for all legitimate claimants is required. In this context, no one can have more than equality if everyone is to have enough. This choice would clearly be favored by people behind a Rawlsian veil of ignorance, assuming that the hypothetical choosers are understood to represent all morally legitimate claimants.

Nevertheless, there remains the question of how to specify this minimum level of health care that all legitimate claimants are to receive. The problem is how to specify how much of the available resources should go to providing everyone with a decent minimum of health care rather than providing for the satisfaction of people's other needs and wants. Yet here, too, the question seems resolvable using a Rawlsian hypothetical choice procedure. We simply need to introduce behind the veil of ignorance the knowledge of the relevant technology for meeting people's basic needs and the knowledge of available resources in order to decide how many resources should be devoted to providing a decent minimum level of health care and how many resources should be devoted to meeting the other needs and wants that people have.

In this way, we should be able to determine what specific requirements of health care are gounded in a right to welfare. Morevoer, these specific requirements of just health care would be further supported *if* it can be shown that the right to welfare from which these health care requirements are derived is itself a shared practical requirement of libertarian, welfare liberal, socialist conceptions of justice.

Alternative Views

In Selection 63, Michael Walzer provides a historical perspective on the distribution of health care, pointing out that during the Middle Ages the cure of souls was public and the cure of bodies was private, whereas today, in most European countries, the situation is reversed—the cure of bodies is public and the cure of souls is private. Walzer goes on to argue that recognizing health care as a basic need should lead us to constraining and/or abolishing a free market in medical care so as to make it equally available to all citizens. Of course, to establish this result would require showing that libertarian, welfare liberal, and socialist conceptions of justice all require a right to welfare, which, in turn requires equality of health care for all legitimate claimants, as I argued above.

In Selection 64, Nancy Watzman argues that the United States should use the Canadian health care system as a model for improvement. In so doing, she assumes that every U.S. citizen has a right to decent health care. Watzman argues that if the United States were to adopt a Canadian-like health care system, it would save conservatively $68 billion in administrative cases compared to its present system. Using these savings, Watzman claims that the United States would be able both to care for its uninsured and underinsured and avoid the longer waiting times for certain forms of treatment that exist within the Canadian health care system.

John C. Goodman disagrees (Selection 65). He claims that the support for national health care is encouraged by a number of myths he hopes to expose. For example, he claims that it is a myth that the United States does not get better health care for the extra dollars it spends and that it is a myth that countries with national health care have solved the problem of long waiting times for certain forms of treatment. However, Goodman does not explain how we can meet the needs of the millions of uninsured and underinsured people in the United States without going to a national health care system.

Practical Application

Selection 66 is a proposal recently put forward by the Health Insurance Association of Amer-

ica. The proposal calls for a new federal law that would require coverage for all Americans, define a basic set of benefits, and try to contain health care costs by limiting tax breaks for the purchase of insurance. The Health Insurance Association of America represents 270 commercial insurers. This proposal signals that the insurance industry is willing to accept sweeping changes in the U.S. health care system, many of them similar to those proposed by President Clinton. Is this an indication that we are reaching consensus on a right to adequate health care? If so, what impact should it have on the solutions to other practical moral problems? Should it lead to the recognition of an adequate right to welfare? Or will it be easier to reach consensus on health care than welfare?

63. The Case of Medical Care

Michael Walzer

> Michael Walzer provides a historical perspective on the distribution of medical care. He points out that during the Middle Ages the cure of souls was public and the cure of bodies was private, whereas today, in most European countries, the situation is reversed—the cure of bodies is public and the cure of souls is private. Walzer argues that recognizing medical care as a basic need should lead us to constraining and/or abolishing a free market in medical care so as to make it equally available to all citizens.

. . . Until recent times, the practice of medicine was mostly a matter of free enterprise. Doctors made their diagnosis, gave their advice, healed or didn't heal their patients, for a fee. Perhaps the private character of the economic relationship was connected to the intimate character of the professional relationship. More likely, I think, it had to do with the relative marginality of medicine itself. Doctors could, in fact, do very little for their patients; and the common attitude in the face of disease (as in the face of poverty) was a stoical fatalism. Or, popular remedies were developed that were not much less effective, sometimes more effective, than those prescribed by established physicians. Folk medicine sometimes produced a kind of communal provision at the

From *Spheres of Justice* (1983). Reprinted by permission of Basic Books.

local level, but it was equally likely to generate new practitioners, charging fees in their turn. Faith healing followed a similar pattern.

Leaving these two aside, we can say that the distribution of medical care has historically rested in the hands of the medical profession, a guild of physicians that dates at least from the time of Hippocrates in the fifth century B.C. The guild has functioned to exclude unconventional practitioners and to regulate the number of physicians in any given community. A genuinely free market has never been in the interest of its members. But it is in the interest of the members to sell their services to individual patients; and thus, by and large, the well-to-do have been well cared for (in accordance with the current understanding of good care) and the poor hardly cared for at all. In a few urban communities—in the medieval Jewish communities, for example—medical services were more widely available. But they were virtually unknown for most people most of the time. Doctors were the servants of the rich, often attached to noble houses and royal courts. With regard to this practical outcome, however, the profession has always had a collective bad conscience. For the distributive logic of the practice of medicine seems to be this: that care should be proportionate to illness and not to wealth. Hence, there have always been doctors, like those honored in ancient Greece, who served the poor on the side, as it were, even while they earned their living from paying patients. Most doctors, present in an emergency, still feel bound to help the victim without regard to his material status. It is a matter of professional Good Samaritanism that the call "Is there a doctor in the house?" should not go unanswered if there is a doctor to answer it. In ordinary times, however, there was little call for medical help, largely because there was little faith in its actual helpfulness. And so the bad conscience of the profession was not echoed by any political demand for the replacement of free enterprise by communal provision.

In Europe during the Middle Ages, the cure of souls was public, the cure of bodies private. Today, in most European countries, the situation is reversed. The reversal is best explained in terms of a major shift in the common understanding of souls and bodies: we have lost confidence in the cure of souls, and we have come increasingly to believe, even to be obsessed with, the cure of bodies. Descartes's famous declaration that the "preservation of health" was the "chief of all goods" may be taken to symbolize the shift—or to herald it, for in the history of popular attitudes, Descartes's *Discourse on Method* came very early. Then, as eternity receded in the popular consciousness, longevity moved to the fore. Among medieval Christians, eternity was a socially recognized need; and every effort was made to see that it was widely and equally distributed, that every Christian had an equal chance at salvation and eternal life: hence, a church in every parish, regular services, catechism for the young, compulsory communion, and so on. Among modern citizens, longevity is a socially recognized need; and

increasingly every effort is made to see that it is widely and equally distributed, that every citizen has an equal chance at a long and healthy life: hence doctors and hospitals in every district, regular check-ups, health education for the young, compulsory vaccination, and so on.

Parallel to the shift in attitudes, and following naturally from it, was a shift in institutions: from the church to the clinic and the hospital. But the shift has been gradual: a slow development of communal interest in medical care, a slow erosion of interest in religious care. The first major form of medical provision came in the area of prevention, not of treatment, probably because the former involved no interference with the prerogatives of the guild of physicians. But the beginnings of provision in the area of treatment were roughly simultaneous with the great public health campaigns of the late nineteenth century, and the two undoubtedly reflect the same sensitivity to questions of physical survival. The licensing of physicians, the establishment of state medical schools and urban clinics, the filtering of tax money into the great voluntary hospitals: these measures involved, perhaps, only marginal interference with the profession—some of them, in fact, reinforced its guildlike character; but they already represent an important public commitment. Indeed, they represent a commitment that ultimately can be fulfilled only by turning physicians, or some substantial number of them, into public physicians (as a smaller number once turned themselves into court physicians) and by abolishing or constraining the market in medical care. But before I defend that transformation, I want to stress the unavoidability of the commitment from which it follows.

What has happened in the modern world is simply that disease itself, even when it is endemic rather than epidemic, has come to be seen as a plague. And since the plague can be dealt with, it *must* be dealt with. People will not endure what they no longer believe they have to endure. Dealing with tuberculosis, cancer, or heart failure, however, requires a common effort. Medical research is expensive, and the treatment of many particular diseases lies far beyond the resources of ordinary citizens. So the community must step in, and any democratic community will in fact step in, more or less vigorously, more or less effectively, depending on the outcome of particular political battles. Thus, the role of the American government (or governments, for much of the activity is at the state and local levels): subsidizing research, training doctors, providing hospitals and equipment, regulating voluntary insurance schemes, underwriting the treatment of the very old. All this represents "the contrivance of human wisdom to provide for human wants." And all that is required to make it morally necessary is the development of a "want" so widely and deeply felt that it can plausibly be said that it is the want not of this or that person alone but of the community generally—a "human want" even though culturally shaped and stressed.

But once communal provision begins, it is subject to further moral constraints: it must provide what is "wanted" equally to all the members of the community; and it must do so in ways that respect their membership. Now, even the pattern of medical provision in the United States, though it stops far short of a national health service, is intended to provide minimally decent care to all who need it. Once public funds are committed, public officials can hardly intend anything less. At the same time, however, no political decision has yet been made to challenge directly the system of free enterprise in medical care. And so long as that system exists, wealth will be dominant in (this part of) the sphere of security and welfare; individuals will be cared for in proportion to their ability to pay and not to their need for care. In fact, the situation is more complex than that formula suggests, for communal provision already encroaches upon the free market, and the very sick and the very old sometimes receive exactly the treatment they should receive. But it is clear that poverty remains a significant bar to adequate and consistent treatment. Perhaps the most telling statistic about contemporary American medicine is the correlation of visits to doctors and hospitals with social class rather than with degree or incidence of illness. Middle- and upper-class Americans are considerably more likely to have a private physician and to see him often, and considerably less likely to be seriously ill, than are their poorer fellow citizens. Were medical care a luxury, these discrepancies would not matter much; but as soon as medical care becomes a socially recognized need, and as soon as the community invests in its provision, they matter a great deal. For then deprivation is a double loss—to one's health and to one's social standing. Doctors and hospitals have become such massively important features of contemporary life that to be cut off from the help they provide is not only dangerous but also degrading.

But any fully developed system of medical provision will require the constraint of the guild of physicians. Indeed, this is more generally true: the provision of security and welfare requires the constraint of those men and women who had previously controlled the goods in question and sold them on the market (assuming, what is by no means always true, that the market predates communal provision). For what we do when we declare this or that good to be a needed good is to block or constrain its free exchange. We also block any other distributive procedure that doesn't attend to need—popular election, meritocratic competition, personal or familial preference, and so on. But the market is, at least in the United States today, the chief rival of the sphere of security and welfare; and it is most importantly the market that is pre-empted by the welfare state. Needed goods cannot be left to the whim, or distributed in the interest, of some powerful group of owners or practitioners.

Most often, ownership is abolished, and practitioners are effectively conscripted or, at least, "signed up" in the public service. They serve for the sake of the social need and not, or not simply, for their own sakes: thus, priests for the sake of eternal life, soldiers for the sake of national defense, public school teachers for the sake of their pupils' education. Priests act wrongly if they sell salvation; soldiers, if they set up as mercenaries; teachers, if they cater to the children of the wealthy. Sometimes the conscription is only partial, as when lawyers are required to be officers of the court, serving the cause of justice even while they also serve their clients and themselves. Sometimes the conscription is occasional and temporary, as when lawyers are required to act as "assigned counsels" for defendants unable to pay. In these cases, a special effort is made to respect the personal character of the lawyer-client relationship. I would look for a similar effort in any fully developed national health service. But I see no reason to respect the doctor's market freedom. Needed goods are not commodities. Or, more precisely, they can be bought and sold only insofar as they are available above and beyond whatever level of provision is fixed by democratic decision making (and only insofar as the buying and selling doesn't distort distributions below that level).

It might be argued, however, that the refusal thus far to finance a national health service constitutes a political decision by the American people about the level of communal care (and about the relative importance of other goods): a minimal standard for everyone—namely, the standard of the urban clinics; and free enterprise beyond that. That would seem to me an inadequate standard, but it would not necessarily be an unjust decision. It is not, however, the decision the American people have made. The common appreciation of the importance of medical care has carried them well beyond that. In fact, federal, state, and local governments now subsidize different levels of care for different classes of citizens. This might be all right, too, if the classification were connected to the purposes of the care—if, for example, soldiers and defense workers were given special treatment in time of war. But the poor, the middle class, and the rich make an indefensible triage. So long as communal funds are spent, as they currently are, to finance research, build hospitals, and pay the fees of doctors in private practice, the services that these expenditures underwrite must be equally available to all citizens. . . .

64. Socialized Medicine Now—Without the Wait

Nancy Watzman

Nancy Watzman argues that we in the United States should use the Canadian health care system as a model for improving our own. Watzman argues that our adoption of a Canadian-like health care system would save conservatively $68 billion in administrative costs when compared with our present system. Using this savings, Watzman claims that we will be able to both care for the uninsured and underinsured and avoid the longer waiting times for certain forms of treatment that exist within the Canadian health care system.

By now, you've seen a million stories on the Canadian health care system, and perhaps even read a few. If so, you've discovered that they all apply the same formula. First, like a slap in the face, comes the horror story: In Orange County, California, a woman goes into business for herself, giving up her health insurance—and discovers she has breast cancer.

From Nancy Watzman, "Socialized Medicine Now—Without the Wait," *Washington Monthly*, vol. 23, no. 10 (October 1991). Copyright © 1991 by The Washington Monthly Company, 1611 Connecticut Avenue, NW, Washington, D.C. 20009; (202) 462-0128. Reprinted by permission of the *Washington Monthly*.

She takes to selling flowers from her garden in a desperate effort to keep up with her bills. Next come the terrifying statistics: Americans spend more than $750 billion—or nearly 14 percent of the GNP—on health care each year. If costs continue to rise at current rates, they'll eat up 37 percent of the GNP by 2030. Yet 28 percent of U.S. citizens lack basic health care; 35 billion are uninsured—and nearly two-thirds of them have jobs.

Now the emergency is clear, and the stage is set for a hero. But as he comes into focus, our savior looks a lot less like a chiseled Mountie on a galloping steed than a . . . "Worthwhile

Canadian Initiative," to borrow the inspirational title for a Most Boring Headline contest in *The New Republic* a few years back. The stories, you see, are carefully "balanced." On the plus side, they point out that "our neighbors to the north" spend only 9 percent of their GNP on a tax-financed national health program, yet everybody is covered, from the wealthiest businesswoman to the poorest, unemployed IV-drug user. Then comes the downside: Canadians must wait longer than Americans do for high-tech treatments such as coronary bypasses, MRIs, CAT scans, and even cancer treatments. It appears to be a trade-off, conclude the *Washington Post,* the *New York Times,* the *Miami Herald,* and Walter Cronkite. Who can say, they shrug, which system is better? Will America ever reform its health care system, and will Canada be the model? One thing is certain: Only time will tell.

Hey! How about a little American initiative? If our system's broke—as everyone from Physicians for a National Health Program to the Heritage Foundation agrees—let's fix it. That means choosing the best model we've got—the Canadian system—and eliminating the bugs. After all, the Canadians don't have to give us a blueprint, just a beginning.

Despite the utopian claims of universal health care advocates, the problems with the Canadian system are real. Making it right for us will take hard work and above all, brutal honesty about its flaws. But the end result will be advanced, humane medical care for all Americans. That it will also be billions of dollars cheaper than the jury-rigged, inequitable system we've got now—well, that's just added incentive to do the right thing.

Wealth Care

On New York City's Park Avenue, doctors understand the subtleties of putting together a practice. The artwork is understated but expensive, the *New Yorkers* uncreased and up-to-date. The nurse is as gentle as a Swedish masseuse, the gown as ample as your backside. And the doctor, one of the best in his field, gives you his undivided attention for an hour.

At $200 a visit, this is American medicine at its best. For the worst, walk 30 blocks uptown, to the "Medicaid mills" of Harlem. These "doctors' offices," which actually boast no doctors except on the requisite city licenses, serve thousands of New York's poorest people. A recent *Washington Post* story described the care provided at one such institution: A clerk collects a patient's Medicaid card, scribbles out an Rx, and sends him on his way. Given this sham service, why do dozens of people pass through these revolving doors every day? Because many doctors in the city refuse to accept patients on Medicaid.

Now head northwest to the village of Tofino in the Pacific Rim region of Canada's Vancouver Island—one of the few places on earth that harbors more eagles than people. It also harbors the only hospital in 100 miles: a low-slung green building with one doctor, one nurse, one ambulance, one helipad, and nine clean yellow rooms. Inside tonight are an elder of the Ucluelets, an impoverished fishing tribe located several miles away; two injured loggers; and one affluent, 30-year-old ecotourist who escaped from Vancouver to hike the coast and promptly broke his leg. His starchy wife sits, reading Barry Lopez's *Arctic Dreams,* by the bed.

Universal access like this is the chief rationale for the Canadian system: Instead of some Americans receiving miserable treatment or none at all while others enjoy the best in the world, all would be taken care of. The rub is that universal access also means *equal* access—that all Americans will meet somewhere in the medical middle, sharing the same waiting room, the same doctor, the same equipment, the same quality of care. That leveling effect is wonderful if you're among the millions of Americans without insurance. It may not be so wonderful if you are accustomed to the Park Avenue touch.

But if you are, you're in a class virtually by yourself. Only 10 percent of Americans approve of their health care system. Meanwhile, according to a recent Harvard study, *56 percent* of Canadians approve of theirs. That shouldn't be surprising, since all Canadians enjoy not just access to health care but choice about whom they're going to see to get it.

Opponents of "socialized medicine" always

trot out the British system as the prime example of how state control can lead to consumer misery. And they're right—but only because the Brits made the mistake of depriving patients of any say over who peers in their ears, prods their stomachs, or cuts them open. Canadians can make an appointment with any doctor they choose. And what those doctors do for them is clearly working. Canadians are much healthier than Americans. They're less likely to die as babies or from surgical complications, and they live longer.

Mary Lou and Robert Dunn of Brampton, Ontario, have alternated medical crises through the years. Twenty years ago, she was in a car accident that left "the windshield with an imprint of my face." She had nine operations to fix multiple fractures and rebuild her nose, lips, and eyes. Robert's medical history includes one operation for hemorrhoids and several for his back. He's about to go in for an operation on his shoulder. Quality of care? The Dunns' praise is unqualified. Waiting time for an appointment? Just the other day, when they both woke up sick, "I called our doctor at about 9:30 a.m. and she said 'Come right on in, I have an opening in 15 minutes,'" says Mary Lou.

Even by south-of-the-border standards, that's good service. But it gets better. In all those operations, through vaccines and infections and a dozen bouts of flu, the Dunns have never seen a hospital bill. The only money they ever hand over for health care is what goes to the government in taxes—and, believe it or not, it's less than what it costs to supply the average American with health care. According to *Consumer Reports,* a Canadian who earns the equivalent of $26,000 pays about $1,300 for health care. People in the U.S.—or their employers, who pass the costs along as lower wages or higher prices—pay about $2,500.

The Canadian system is actually several different systems, as each province administers its own health plan using federal and local funds. What's constant is the way the system is structured to keep costs down. First, hospitals and clinics receive fixed amounts of money to cover day-to-day expenses, such as Q-tips and syringes. If administrators want more money to make capital investments—for a new CAT scanner, for example—they must apply to the province. Second, the provinces negotiate with medical associations to establish how much doctors are allowed to charge for certain services. This is not too different from the established reimbursement rates used by U.S. health insurers and government programs, except that U.S. doctors can always charge their patients more than what insurers are willing to pay. Canadian doctors are simply not allowed to do that.

The government-issued health plan cards that the Dunns carry in their pockets entitle them to care in every province in Canada and every country in the world. Their province will pick up the bill. That generosity ensures they won't end up stranded without coverage in some medical hellhole . . . like Washington, D.C., where their niece, 24-year-old Mamie Stobie, has been turned down for coverage by over 30 health insurance companies.

The reason? Mamie's diabetic. In health insurance jargon, that's a "pre-existing condition," a term that roughly translates to: Because Mamie needs health care, she can't have any insurance to help pay for it. That's the American way.

Home of the Fee

One reason we'll be able to afford Mamie's insurance under a Canadian-style plan is that such a system would put an end to several perversions and inefficiencies in the U.S. medical market. Critics of the Canadian approach may rail about creeping socialism, but right now, American medicine turns the laws of supply and demand on their head.

Let's say, for example, you've had a heart attack. To dissolve the clots forming in your blood, you need to start taking one of two equally effective drugs. One costs $76 to $300 a dose, the other $2,200. So you take the cheaper one, right? Wrong. *Because* one of the drugs costs more, your doctor would probably prescribe it to you. As Andrew Pollack showed in the *New York Times* last summer, Genentech, the company behind the more expensive drug, pumps enormous amounts of money into studies and aggressive marketing (performed by 278 salespeople) to push its product. The other drug has been around for decades, is unprotected by patents—and so is too cheap to make marketing worthwhile. That's how the free market functions in American medicine: The development of more expensive, high-tech treatments creates the demand for more expensive, high-tech treatments; likewise, more doctors means higher fees, and that means—you guessed it—more doctors. And even higher fees.

Estimates vary among surveys, but there is no doubt that each year huge numbers of Americans undergo treatments they don't need. A 1988 *New England Journal of Medicine* study, for example, concluded that two-thirds of patients who receive heart surgery do so for either "equivocal" or "inappropriate" reasons. Perhaps this is because the American medical establishment helps them decide that they want it. . . .

We Need Our Hips

Under the Canadian system, the government doesn't step in just to iron out inefficiencies in the health care market. It actually takes control of supply, and therefore of demand, through rationing, a notion Canadians accept but Americans shudder to consider. Of course, some rationing decisions are fairly easy (like which of the two equally effective heart drugs doctors should be allowed to offer). In vitro fertilization, cosmetic surgery, and sex change operations are among the services for which Canadians most often have to dip into their own pockets. But the calls quickly get tougher. It's much easier to turn away than to confront hard rationing decisions, to trust in the invisible hand and our tattered patchwork of support programs rather than in some new government bureaucracy—a federal Department For Whether We Feel Like Saving Your Life.

Trouble is, the invisible hand isn't known for its compassion. As a result of the laissez-faire approach to medical care, we already have a rationing system in place—one based

not on need but on ability to pay. A new study in the *Journal of the American Medical Association (JAMA)* found that the uninsured were 25 to 75 percent less likely to undergo each of five high-cost, discretionary procedures, including certain biopsies, colonoscopies, and CAT scans. Even after controlling for the severity of illness at the time of admission, the study discovered that the uninsured were far more likely than the insured to die before leaving the hospital. Coincidence? Not likely. Take the MRI again. The AHA explicitly recommends that MRI centers keep an eye on what's called the "funding mix"—in other words, making the MRI more available to those more able to pay.

So there's a strong social justice argument to be made for the rational rationing of health care. So what? That high-minded reasoning would be mighty small comfort if you found yourself waiting six months to get your hip replaced, like the Canadians do. It's rare that a procedure performed in the United States is not covered at all in the Canadian health care system. Instead, where rationing shows it dark side in Canada is in the wait you must endure for non-emergency care. Some cheerleaders for the Canadian system gloss over this problem, but no patient should have to wait six times longer to get his hip replaced under a new health care system than he would today at Georgetown University Hospital. Under our modification of the Canadian plan, no one—including those Americans who today have no hope of ever receiving the treatment in the first place—will have to.

Paper Tigers

How it that possible? Because for once, more government involvement means less paperwork. Consider D.C. General Hospital, where armed guards escort men in shackles to the overtaxed HIV clinic. Ninety percent of the men and women who come through the doors lack health insurance—not to mention jobs, homes, and families. Dying or not, they wait more than an hour to see a doctor for ten minutes. If there seem to be few staff members in this massive complex, take a turn down the stairs and through the hall. There are hundreds of health care workers here at D.C. General. Unfortunately, most of them are filling out forms.

Patients here have enough to worry about without paperwork. But the Medicaid forms they're required to fill out are so complicated that many just can't keep up. One U.S. government estimate states that about a million Medicare enrollees a year don't seek reimbursement because they find the forms too complicated. And don't think just the poor get confused. A recent *Washington Post* editorial lamented that you need a personal CPA to keep track of all the forms that pour in when you suffer from a serious illness—the health insurance claim forms, the hospital bills, doctor bills, the abstruse notices from Medicare that need deciphering to find out what's covered. This paperwork isn't just tiresome for would-be patients—it's incredibly expensive. Thankfully, the Canadian national health program actually involves *less*—much, much less—bureaucracy than ours.

Think about it. Since every citizen is automatically covered in Canada, there's no need to employ armies of people to determine whether Mamie's diabetes is a "pre-existing condition"—there's no such thing. Fewer people are needed to work in doctors' or hospitals' billing departments, because those facilities bill the government directly for all services. Doctors aren't forced to hire professional staff to manage the intricacies of insurance status and the collections process. They don't have to keep track of exactly how many Tylenol tablets one patient swallowed during a hospital stay in order to bill him for them later; they need only track how many Tylenol tablets are being dispensed at the hospital on the whole, which requires a lot less paperwork.

Here's the bottom line: In Canada, just 11 cents out of every dollar spent on health care goes to administrative costs; across the border in the United States, up to *24 cents* goes to billing, form filing, and other advanced forms of paper shuffling performed by health administrators, whose ranks swelled nearly 400 percent from 1970 to 1987. In 1991 alone, we can expect to waste from $115 to $136 billion

on health administration—money we could be spending on health *care*.

Steffie Woolhandler and David Himmelstein, Harvard-based physicians who work with Physicians for a National Health Program, have estimated that as much as $83 billion could be saved in paperwork costs alone if the United States switched to a national health plan. The General Accounting Office (GAO) estimate is a little more conservative: $68 billion. Yet even that amount is more than enough to pay for basic health coverage for *all* the uninsured people in the United States, with enough left over to do more besides.

The key thing to remember about these estimates is that they cover administrative savings alone. They don't include any of the other cost-saving measures already discussed, such as cutting back on unnecessary procedures or starting up a rational rationing system. And they assume—this is crucial—that Americans *will not* start waiting longer for their heart or kidney transplant operations, or for anything else. The GAO points out that with the equipment we've already got, we'll be able to provide high-tech treatments for everyone without resorting to Canadian-style queuing.

Once that's understood, the question becomes: What do we do with the savings? The first thing, of course, it to extend the same level of care that insured Americans now receive to the uninsured; Himmelstein and Woolhandler estimate in a May *JAMA* article that this change would run us about $12 billion. If you take the GAO's $68 billion as a conservative estimate of administrative savings and subtract that $12 billion, then you're left with a full $56 billion for other goodies. What should we do with it?

Well, just to calm fears, let's take the worst case scenario, assume that we'll need to pay out some more money to fund high-tech treatments for all who need them, and do some seat-of-the-pants calculations. Consider the example of shock wave lithotripsy, a process that breaks up kidney stones. Canadians wait about six weeks to receive lithotripsy, while the average Washingtonian can get it in about three weeks at Georgetown University Hospital. Right now in the United States, about 23,000 people get lithotripsies per year.

Assuming that most of these people have health insurance, we can divide 23,000 by the number of insured Americans—214 million—and come up with a rough ratio showing how many lithotripsies should be performed per population. Then take that ratio, multiply it by the 35 million uninsured, and we get a rough number for how many lithotripsies we need to do if we want to cover the poor. Multiply that number by how much physicians earn for performing the procedure in Canada—U.S. $241—and voilà, we've got a figure for how much we would need to chop off the $56 billion savings budget—$906,642. Now, that figure underestimates some costs (it doesn't take into account hospitalization, for example) and overestimates others (it assumes that all Americans who now receive lithotripsy have health insurance, while some undoubtedly don't). So, just to be conservative, let's multiply by 10.

We can use the same formula for kidney, heart, and heart and lung transplants. Multiply by 10 and tack on the lithotripsy cost, and you get about $31,387,750—just 0.5 percent of the money we've got to spend. That $56 billion could go an awfully long way.

If you're an economist or a hypochondriac, you may well be thinking: All that's fine, but what about improving on the quality of treatments already offered? With the government trying to hold down costs, what incentive will there be for the kind of daring research and development only good old American capitalism can foster? One reason Canada is able to control its health care costs, some critics point out, is that it can rely on the United States to invest in coming up with new treatments and equipment. With the United States also going to a national system, health care could stagnate.

In the first place, there's still plenty of incentive for a truly daring health care entrepreneur to hit the laboratory; after all, if he can convince the American health care system to offer his treatment, he'll be a millionaire. But let's suppose that private corporations after nationalization do lose the will to invest in R&D. Who needs 'em? The federal government already plans to spend $8.7 billion in 1991 to fund health research—that amounts to 44 percent of all such research performed in the United States last year. Double that investment, kiss the private money goodbye, and we'll still have tens of billions of dollars in savings to spend on wart removal or herbal treatments or lollipops for the kids who don't cry.

Northern Light

Right now there are almost as many piecemeal health reform proposals floating around Capitol Hill as there are congressmen. The most inventive program the Democratic leadership has come up with is more of what we've already got: expansion of employer mandates and government programs in a "play or pay" scheme. Such a patchwork approach would actually be more expensive than our current system, let alone a Canada-type plan, because it adds benefits without cutting costs; estimates range from $24 to $60 billion worth of new taxes, much of which would go for more administrative bloat. This lack of vision springs partly from blind fear—a patent unwillingness to fight the AMA and an insurance industry facing annihilation. This is why the final thing we must take from Canada is courage.

The situation Canada faced back in 1964, right before the government enacted the universal program, may sound familiar. The Canadian Medical Association wasn't any more pleased with national health care proposals than the AMA is now—and neither were Canadian health insurance companies. Meanwhile, inflation was rising and the federal deficit worsening.

When the Medical Care Insurance Bill was introduced in July of that year, the parliamentary debate was fierce. "So strident were the tones, so angry the voices, and so vehement the opposition that one journalist summed up, 'The federal government's proposed legislation lies torn, tattered, and politically rejected,' " writes Malcolm Taylor, a public policy professor at York University and a former Canadian official. Yet the bill passed in the end, partly because of the boost it received from an official commission report, requested by the Canadian Medical Association, that to the doctors' chagrin came out in favor of a national program.

Congress should listen less to campaign contributors and more to the facts. We *can* provide both basic, preventative medicine and sophisticated high-tech care to every American—for less money than we now spend to coddle the few while leaving tens of millions vulnerable. In fact, with some political courage and a little hard work, we could probably teach Canada a thing or two about the right way to run a national health care program.

---

65. An Expensive Way to Die

John C. Goodman

John C. Goodman opposes national health care. He claims that the support for national health care is encouraged by a number of myths that he seeks to expose.

Countries with national health insurance spend less on health care than the United States does. It is all too easy to assume that the United States can therefore control health-care costs through national health insurance without any loss of benefits. And this mistake is encouraged by a number of myths.

Myth #1: Although the United States spends more on health care per capita than countries with national health insurance, the United States does not get better health care for the extra dollars it spends.

This myth rests upon the fact that life expectancy hardly differs among the developed countries and that infant mortality in the United States is actually higher than in most other developed countries.

In fact, a population's general mortality is affected by a great many factors over which doctors and hospitals have little influence. For those diseases and injuries for which modern medicine can affect the outcome, however, which country the patient lives in really matters. Life expectancy is not the same among developed countries for premature babies, for children born with spina bifida, or for people who have cancer, a brain tumor, heart disease, or chronic renal failure. Their chances of survival are best in the United States.

From John C. Goodman, "An Expensive Way to Die," *National Review* (April 16, 1990). Copyright © 1990 by National Review, Inc., 150 East 35th Street, New York, NY 10016. Reprinted by permission.

Consider the availability of modern technology in the United States and in Canada, a country with comprehensive national health insurance. There are eight times more magnetic-resonance-imaging units (the latest improvement on X-rays), seven times more radiation-therapy units (used in the treatment of cancer), about six times more lithotripsy units (used for nonsurgical removal of kidney stones), and about three times more open-heart surgery units and cardiac-catheterization units per capita in the United States than in Canada.

It is sometimes argued that countries with national health insurance delay the purchase of expensive technology in order to see if it really works and is cost effective. Even if true, patients will be denied access to life-saving treatment while government bureaucracies evaluate it. For example, during the 1970s, life-saving innovations were made in the fields of renal dialysis, CAT-scan technology, and pacemaker technology. Yet the implant rate of pacemakers in the United States during the mid 1970s was more than four times the rate in Britain, and almost twenty times the rate in Canada (see Table 1). The availability of CAT scanners in the United States was more than three times that in Canada and almost six times that in Britain. The treatment rate of kidney patients in the United States was more than 60 percent greater than in Canada and Britain.

Table 1. Use of Modern Medical Technology in the 1970s

Country	Pacemakers per 100,000 Population, 1976	CAT Scanners per Million Population, 1979	Kidney Dialysis and/ or Transplants per Million Population, 1976
Australia	7.3	1.9	65.8
Canada	2.3	1.7	73.4
France	22.6	0.6	111.3
West Germany	34.6	2.6	105.0
Italy	18.8	NA	102.0
Japan	2.7	4.6	NA
United Kingdom	9.8	1.0	71.2
United States	44.2	5.7	120.0

Source: National Center for Policy Analysis

There is considerable evidence that cost effectiveness is not what drives the bias against modern medical technology abroad. CAT-scan technology was invented in Britain, and until recently Britain exported about half the CAT scanners used in the world. Yet the British government has purchased only a handful of CAT scanners for use in the National Health Service [NHS]. British scientists also co-developed kidney dialysis. Yet Britain has one of the lowest dialysis rates in all of Europe, and as many as nine thousand British kidney patients per year are denied the treatment.

In the United States we pay more for health care. But we also get more. And what we get saves lives.

Myth #2: Countries with national health insurance have solved the problem of access to health care.

In Britain and New Zealand, hospital services are completely paid for by government. Yet both countries have long waiting lists for hospital surgery. In Britain, with a population of about 55 million, the number of people waiting for surgery is almost eight hundred thousand. In New Zealand, with a population of three million, the waiting list is about fifty thousand. In both countries, elderly patients in need of a hip replacement can wait in pain for years. Patients waiting for heart surgery are often at risk of their lives.

In response to rationing by waiting, both Britain and New Zealand have witnessed a growing market in private health insurance—where citizens willingly pay for prompt private surgery, rather than wait for "free" surgery in public hospitals. In Britain, the number of people with private insurance has more than doubled in the last ten years, to about 12 percent of the population. In New Zealand, one-third of the population has private health insurance, and private hospitals now perform 25 percent of all surgical procedures.

Canada has had a national health program for only a few decades. But because the demand for health care has proved insatiable, and because the Canadian government has resolutely refused to increase spending beyond about 8.5 percent of GNP, the waiting lines have been growing. In Newfoundland the wait for a hip replacement is about six to ten months, the wait for cataract surgery is two months, for pap smears up to five months, for "urgent" pap smears two months (see Table 2). All over Canada, heart patients must wait for coronary bypass surgery, and the Canadian press frequently reports episodes of heart patients dying while on the waiting list. Unlike Britain and New Zealand, however, Canada does not allow patients to turn to the private sector, although Canadian patients who can afford to do so sometimes travel to the U.S. for medical services they cannot get in their own country.

Myth #3: Countries with national health insurance hold down costs by operating more efficiently.

Table 2. Average Waiting Time in Newfoundland 1988

Procedure	Average Wait	
Mammogram	2½	months
Bone scan	1–1½	months
Myelogram	3–4	months
Brain shunt	5	months
Hip replacement	6–10	months
Cataract surgery	2	months
CAT scan	2	months
Pap smear	2–5	months
Urgent pap smear	2	months

Based on physician surveys by the Fraser Institute. Michael Walker, "From Canada: A Different Viewpoint," *Health Management Quarterly,* vol. XI, no. 1, 1989, p. 12.

By and large, countries that have succeeded in slowing the growth of health-care spending have done so by *denying people services,* not by making efficient use of resources.

How much does it cost a hospital to perform an appendectomy? Outside the United States it is doubtful that there is a public hospital anywhere in the world that could answer that question. One reason for [former British prime minister] Margaret Thatcher's health-care reforms is that even Britain's best hospitals did not keep adequate records, and it was not uncommon for the head of a hospital department to be unaware of how many people his department employed.

What about bed management? Consider that while fifty thousand people wait for surgery in New Zealand, one out of every five hospital beds is empty. While nearly eight hundred thousand people wait for surgery in Britain, at any point in time about one out of every four hospital beds is empty. In both Britain and New Zealand, about 25 percent of all acute beds, desperately needed for surgery, are clogged by chronically ill patients who are using the hospitals as nursing homes—often at six times the cost of alternative facilities. In Ontario about 25 percent of hospital beds are occupied by elderly chronic patients. Hospital administrators apparently believe chronic patients are less expensive than acute patients

(because they mainly use the "hotel" services of the hospital), and thus are less of a drain on limited budgets.

Myth #4: Under national health insurance money is allocated so that it has the greatest impact on health.

Even when resources are organized efficiently, they are still distributed with random extravagance under systems of national health insurance. These systems take millions of dollars that could be spent to save lives and cure diseases, and spend this money to provide a vast array of services to people who are not seriously ill. Take the ambulance service. English "patients" take more than 21 million ambulance rides each year—about one ride for every two people in all of England. About 91 percent of these rides are for non-emergency purposes (such as taking an elderly person to a pharmacy) and amount to little more than a free taxi service. Yet for genuine emergencies, the typical British ambulance has little of the life-saving equipment considered standard in most large American cities.

While tens of thousands who are classified as in "urgent need" of surgery wait for hospital beds, the NHS spends millions on items that have only marginal effects on health and which could well be financed either by charges on the patients or by a low-cost limited private insurance. On the average, the NHS spends more than $70 million each year on tranquilizers, sedatives, and sleeping pills; almost $19 million on antacids; and about $21 million on cough medicine. If the NHS did nothing more than charge patients the full costs of the sleeping pills and tranquilizers they consume, enough money would be freed to treat 10,000 to 15,000 additional cancer patients each year and save the lives of an additional three thousand kidney patients.

Myth #5: Under national health insurance the elderly in the United States will receive at least the same benefits they now receive under Medicare.

The elderly have the most to lose from the adoption of national health insurance. Take chronic kidney failure. Across Europe generally, in the late 1970s, 22 percent of dialysis centers reported that they refused to treat patients over 55 years of age. In Britain in 1978, 35 percent of the dialysis centers refused to treat patients over the age of 55; 45 percent refused to treat patients over the age of 65; and patients over the age of 75 rarely received treatment at all for this disease.

How pervasive is denial of life-saving medical technology to elderly patients in other countries? Lacking hard data, one can only speculate. However, a white 65-year-old male in the United States can expect to live 1.3 years longer than a 65-year-old British male. A white 65-year-old female in the United States can expect to live 1.4 years longer than a 65-year-old British female. For middle-aged males, U.S. mortality rates are higher than European ones. During the retirement years, however, when medical intervention can make much more of a difference, the U.S. mortality rate is significantly below that of European countries.

Myth #6: The defects of national health insurance schemes in other countries could be easily remedied by a few reforms.

The characteristics described above are not accidental byproducts of government-run health-care systems. Instead, they are the natural and inevitable consequences of politicizing medical practice.

Why are elderly and poor patients discriminated against in the rationing of acute care under national health insurance? Because national health insurance is always and everywhere a middle-class phenomenon. Prior to the introduction of national health insurance, every country had some government-funded program to meet the health-care needs of the poor. The middle-class working population not only had to pay for its own health care, but it was also paying taxes to fund health care for the poor. National insurance extends the "free ride" to the middle-class working population, and it is designed to serve the interests of this population.

Why do national health insurance schemes skimp on expensive services to the seriously ill while providing a multitude of inexpensive services to those who are only marginally ill? Because numerous services provided to the marginally ill create benefits for millions of people (read: millions of voters), while acute and intensive care services concentrate large amounts of money on a handful of patients (read: small number of voters). Democratic political pressures dictate the redistribution of resources from the few to the many.

Why are sensitive rationing decisions left to the hospital bureaucracies? Because the alternative is politically impossible. As a practical matter, no government can afford to make it a national policy that nine thousand people every year will be denied treatment for chronic kidney failure and die. Nor can any government announce that some people must wait for surgery so that elderly patients can use hospitals as surrogate nursing homes, or that elderly patients must be moved so that surgery can proceed. Budgetary decisions made by politicians and administrators are transformed into clinical decisions made by doctors.

Myth #7: Since national health insurance is very popular in other countries, it would also be popular in the United States.

National health insurance remains popular in other countries precisely because it does not function the way its advocates believe it should. It "works" in other countries for three reasons: (1) The wealthy, the powerful, and those who are most skilled at articulating their complaints find ways to maneuver to the front of the lines. (2) Those pushed to the end are generally unaware of the medical technologies denied to them. (3) There are no contingency fees, no generally recognized right of due process, and no lawyers willing to represent those who are systematically discriminated against—though these are beginning to develop, as, for instance, kidney patients learn the facts of their situation and organize into pressure groups on the AIDS model.

"Don't push me around" is a distinctively American phrase. In Europe, people have been pushed around for centuries. In the United States we have widespread access to information about modern medical technology, a legal system that encourages litigation, and a strong devotion to basic rights of due process. National health insurance, as it operates in other countries, would not survive the American cultural and legal system.

66. A Plan for Comprehensive Health Care

Health Insurance Association of America

Health Insurance Association of America recently put forward a proposal calling for a new federal law that would require coverage for all Americans, define a basic set of benefits and try to contain health care costs by limiting tax breaks for the purchase of insurance.

In a radical break from previous policy, the Health Insurance Association of America (HIAA) approved circulation of a discussion paper that would provide universal health care coverage and generate substantial revenue to help pay for health programs.

Under HIAA's draft reform proposal, the federal government would require all individuals to carry, and all employers to offer, an essential, continuous package of health care coverage. Funding to help pay for coverage for people below the poverty line would come from eliminating favorable tax treatment for benefits that go beyond the essential package.

The new proposal rests upon four cornerstones:

▪ *Universal coverage:* Under this program, everyone would be covered—by law—under an essential package of care, either through an employer or their own means. Private insurers would agree to provide coverage to everyone. The government would pay for health insurance for people below the poverty line. Private insurers and HMOs would provide managed care to the poor in order to encourage preventive treatment and wellness care.

▪ *An essential package of benefits:* Each individual would be guaranteed an essential package of benefits, which includes primary and preventive services as well as catastrophic coverage. Coverage will be designed to meet the essential needs of Americans, and consumers also would have the option to purchase supplemental coverage for additional benefits. People above the poverty line and people below the poverty line would receive the same package of benefits, and government would help define the essential package of coverage.

▪ *Cost control features:* Elimination of cost shifting from Medicare and Medicaid patients to privately insured individuals and new approaches designed to discourage excessive doctor visits, the unnecessary use of technology, and unnecessary hospital or specialist care.

▪ *An equitable tax policy:* To promote equitable tax policies, premiums paid for an essential package would be excluded from employee or individual taxable incomes. However, premiums paid by an employer for benefits in excess of the essential package could be deemed taxable to the employee. Monies generated from this tax preference would help finance health care coverage for the poor.

From the Health Insurance Association of America, December 3, 1992. Reprinted by permission.

Suggestions for Further Reading

Brody, Baruch A. "Health Care for the Haves and Have Nots: Toward a Just Basis of Distribution," in Earl Shelp, *Justice and Health Care*. Dordrecht: Reidal Publishing Co., 1981.

Buchanan, Alan. "A Right to a Decent Minimum of Health Care." *Philosophy and Public Affairs* (1984), 13:55–78.

Daniels, Norman. *Just Health Care*. Cambridge: Cambridge University Press, 1985.

———. *Am I My Parent's Keeper?* New York: Oxford University Press, 1988.

Gibbard, Alan. "The Prospective Pareto Principle and Its Application to Questions of Equity of Access to Health Care." *Milbank Memorial Fund Quarterly/Health and Society* (1982), 60: 399–428.

Guttmann, Amy. "For and Against Equal Access to Health Care." *Milbank Memorial Fund Quarterly/Health and Society* (1981), 59:4.

President's Commission for the Study of Ethical Problems in Medicine and Biomedical and Behavior Research. *Securing Access to Health Care*, vol. 1. Washington, D.C.: U.S. Government Printing Office, 1983.

War and Humanitarian Intervention

Basic Concepts

The problem of war and humanitarian intervention is simply the problem of determining the moral limits of the international use of force. *Just war theories* attempt to specify what these moral limits are. Such theories have two components: a set of criteria that establishes a right to go to war *(jus ad bellum)*, and a set of criteria that determines legitimate conduct in war *(jus in bello)*. The first set of criteria can be grouped under the label "just cause," the second under "just means."

Consider the following specification of just cause:

1. There must be substantial aggression.
2. Nonbelligerent correctives must be either hopeless or too costly.
3. Belligerent corrective must be neither hopeless nor too costly.

This specification of just cause excludes the criterion of legitimate authority, which has had a prominent place in just war theories. This criterion is excluded because it has the character of a second-order requirement; it is a requirement that must be satisfied whenever there is a question of group action with respect to any moral problem whatsoever. For example, with respect to the problem of the distribution of goods and resources in a society, we can certainly ask who has the (morally legitimate) authority to distribute or redistribute goods and resources in a society. But before we ask such questions with respect to particular moral problems, it is important to understand first what are the morally defensible solutions to these problems because a standard way of identifying morally legitimate authorities is by their endorsement of such solutions. With respect to the problem of war and humanitarian intervention, we first need to determine the nature and existence of just causes before we try to identify morally legitimate authorities by their endorsement of such causes.

Assuming that there are just causes, just war theorists go on to specify just means. Consider the following specification of just means:

1. The harm inflicted on the aggressor must not be disproportionate to the aggression.
2. Harm to innocents should not be directly intended as an end or a means.

The first criterion is a widely accepted requirement of just means. The second criterion is also widely accepted and contains the main requirement of the doctrine of double effect (see the introduction to Section III). Many philosophers seem willing to endorse the application of the doctrine in this context given that those to whom the doctrine applies are generally recognized to be persons with full moral status.

To evaluate these requirements of just war theory, we need to determine to what degree they can be supported by the moral approaches to practical problems presented in the General Introduction. Of course, one or more of these approaches may ultimately favor the pacifist position, but assuming that these approaches favored some version of a just war theory, which version would that be?

Obviously, a utilitarian approach would have little difficulty accepting the requirement of just cause and requirement (1) on just means because these requirements can be interpreted as having a utilitarian backing. However, this approach would only accept requirement (2) on just means conditionally, because occasions would surely arise when violations of this requirement would maximize net utility.

Unlike a Utilitarian Approach, an Aristotelian Approach is relatively indeterminate in its requirements. All that is certain, as I have interpreted the approach, is that it would be absolutely committed to requirement (2) on just means.[1] Of course, the other requirements on just cause and just means would be required by particular versions of this approach.

A Kantian Approach is distinctive in that it seeks to combine and compromise both the concern of a Utilitarian Approach for maximal net utility and the concern of an Aristotelian Approach for the proper development of each individual.[2] In its hypothetical choice situation, persons would clearly favor the requirement of just cause and requirement (1) on just means, although they would not interpret them in a strictly utilitarian fashion.

Yet what about the requirement (2) on just means? Because persons behind a veil of ignorance would not be committed simply to whatever maximizes net utility, they would want to put a stricter limit on the harm that could be inflicted on innocents in defense of a just cause than could be justified on utilitarian grounds alone. This is because persons behind a veil of ignorance would be concerned not only with what maximizes net utility, but also with the distribution of utility to particular individuals. Persons imagining themselves to be ignorant of what position they are in would be particularly concerned that they might turn out to be in the position of those who are innocent, and, consequently, they would want strong safeguards against harming those who are innocent, such as requirement (2) on just means.

Yet even though persons behind a veil of ignorance would favor differential restriction on harm to innocents, they would not favor an absolute restriction on intentional harm to innocents. They would recognize as exceptions to such a restriction cases where intentional harm to innocents is either:

1. Trivial (e.g., stepping on someone's foot to get out of a crowded subway).
2. Easily reparable (e.g., lying to a temporarily depressed friend to keep her from committing suicide).
3. Sufficiently outweighed by the consequences of the action (e.g., shooting one of two hundred civilian hostages to prevent in the only way possible the execution of all two hundred).

Accordingly, while persons behind a veil of ignorance would favor requirement (2) on just means, their commitment to this requirement would also have to incorporate the above exceptions. Even so, these exceptions are far more limited than those that would be tolerated by an Utilitarian Approach.

In sum, a Kantian Approach would strongly endorse the requirement of just cause and requirements (1) and (2) on just means. Yet its commitment to requirement (2) on just means would fall short of the absolute commitment that is characteristic of an Aristotelian Approach to practical problems.

It is clear, therefore, that our three moral approaches to practical problems differ significantly with respect to their requirements for a just war theory. A Utilitarian Approach strongly endorses the requirement of just cause and requirement (1) on just means, but only conditionally endorses requirement (2) on just means. An Aristotelian Approach endorses requirement (2) on just means as an absolute requirement, but is indeterminate with respect to the other requirements of just war theory. Only a Kantian Approach strongly endorses all of the basic requirements of a traditional just war theory, although it does not regard requirement (2) on just means as an absolute requirement. Fortunately for traditional just war theory, there are good reasons for favoring a Kantian Approach over each of the other two moral approaches to practical problems.

One reason for favoring a Kantian Approach over a Utilitarian Approach is that its requirements are derived from a veil of ignorance decision procedure that utilitarians and Kantians alike recognize to be fair. It is not surprising, therefore, to find such utilitarians as John Harsanyi and R. M. Hare simply endorsing this decision procedure and then trying to show that the resulting requirements would maximize utility.[3] Yet we have just seen how the concern of persons behind a veil of ignorance with the distribution of utility would lead them to impose a stricter limit on the harm that could be inflicted on innocents in defense of a just cause than could be justified on grounds of maximizing utility alone. At least with respect to just war theory, therefore, a Utilitarian Approach and a Kantian Approach differ significantly in their practical requirements.

Utilitarians who endorse this decision procedure are faced with a difficult choice: give up their commitment to this decision procedure or modify their commitment to utilitarian goals. Utilitarians cannot easily choose to give up their commitment to this decision procedure because the acceptability of utilitarianism as traditionally conceived has always depended on showing that fairness and utility rarely conflict, and that when they do, it is always plausible to think that the requirements of utility are morally overriding. Consequently, when a fair decision procedure significantly conflicts with utility—which it is not plausible to think can always be morally overridden by the requirements of utility—that procedure exposes the inadequacy of a Utilitarian Approach to practical problems.

These reasons for favoring a Kantian Approach over a Utilitarian Approach to practical problems are also reasons for favoring an Aristotelian Approach, because an Aristotelian Approach is also concerned with fairness and the distribution of utility to particular individuals. Nevertheless, there are other reasons for favoring a Kantian Approach over an Aristotelian Approach.

One reason is that a Kantian Approach does not endorse any absolute requirements. In particular, a Kantian Approach does not endorse an absolute requirement not to intentionally harm innocents. A Kantian Approach recognizes that if the harm is trivial, easily reparable, or sufficiently outweighed by the consequences, such harm can be morally justified.

Another reason for favoring a Kantian Approach over an Aristotelian Approach is that a Kantian Approach is determinate in its requirements; it actually leads to a wide range of practical recommendations. By contrast, an Aristotelian Approach lacks a deliberative procedure that can produce agreement with respect to practical requirements. This is evident because supporters of this approach tend to endorse radically different practical requirements. In this regard, the veil of ignorance decision procedure employed by a Kantian Approach appears to be just the sort of morally defensible device needed to achieve determinate requirements.

Finally, the particular requirements of just war theory endorsed by a Kantian Approach are further supported by the presence of analogous requirements for related areas of conduct. Thus, the strong legal prohibitions that exist against punishing the innocent provide support for the strong prohibition against harming innocents expressed by requirement

(2) on just means. This is the type of correspondence we would expect from an adequate moral theory; requirements in one area of conduct would be analogous to those in related areas of conduct.

Alternative Views

In the first selection (Selection 67), James P. Sterba argues that when pacifism and just war theory are given their most morally defensible interpretations, they can be reconciled both in theory and practice. He argues that the most morally defensible form of pacifism is antiwar pacifism (which prohibits participation in all wars) rather than nonviolent pacifism (which prohibits any use of violence against other human beings) or nonlethal pacifism (which prohibits any use of lethal force against other human beings). He also argues that when just war theory is given its most morally defensible interpretation, it favors a strong just means prohibition against intentionally harming innocents and favors the use of belligerent means only when such means (1) minimize the loss and injury to innocents lives overall; (2) threaten innocent lives only to prevent the loss of innocent lives; and (3) threaten or take the lives of unjust aggressors when it is the only way to prevent serious injury to innocents. He contends that the few wars and large-scale conflicts that meet these stringent requirements of just war theory (e.g., India's military action against Pakistan in Bangladesh and the Tanzanian incursion into Uganda during the rule of Idi Amin) are the only wars and large-scale conflicts to which antiwar pacifists cannot justifiably object. He calls the view that emerges from this reconciliation "just war pacifism."

In Selection 68, Michael Walzer argues that humanitarian intervention can be justified (1) to assist secessionist movements once they have demonstrated their representative character; (2) to balance the unjustified interventions of other powers; and (3) to rescue people threatened with massacre. Walzer further argues that humanitarian intervention requires that the intervening state enter, to some degree, into the purposes of the people on whose behalf it purports to be intervening. Applying this analysis, Walzer claims that the

U.S. intervention in Cuba in 1898 was not humanitarian intervention because the United States refused to aid the Cuban rebels in the way they requested and mounted an independent military campaign in Cuba. By contrast, he claims that India's intervention in East Pakistan in 1971 was humanitarian intervention because it did not conflict with the goals of the Bengali people.

In basic agreement with Walzer about the need for humanitarian intervention, Barbara Harff (Selection 69) argues that Bosnia, Somalia, and Iraqi Kurdistan exemplify three distinct types of crimes against humanity in which the international community has a legal and moral imperative to intervene. Harff further argues that the Bosnian crisis might never have assumed the proportions of genocide if a coherent strategy for intervention had been in place from the beginning. She examines various forms of response the international community can take to serious human rights violations ranging from early warning assessments of impending or escalating conflicts to collective military intervention and the establishment of interim trusteeships. She laments the fact that nations are allowing their political and domestic interests to outweigh the clear need for these various forms of humanitarian intervention. What would be interesting to determine is whether Sterba's "just war pacifism" would require the same forms of humanitarian intervention that Walzer and Harff favor.

Practical Applications

The readings in this section have already suggested a number of practical solutions to the problem of war and humanitarian intervention. However, a more sweeping solution is proposed by the final selection (Selection 70). In this selection, Robert S. McNamara argues that with the end of the Cold War, nations should move toward a system of collective security with conflict resolution and peace-keeping functions performed by multinational institutions. Agreeing with a recent proposal from President Yeltsin, McNamara also favors a return, insofar as practicable, to a nonnuclear world. Noting that the 1991 U.S. defense budget in constant dollars is still 40 percent higher than it was a decade ago, McNamara favors cutting military budgets throughout the world by 50 percent. It is significant that these recommendations come from the very person who was Secretary of Defense under Kennedy and Johnson and who presided over our increased military involvement in Vietnam.

Nevertheless, it is important to recognize that a solution to the problem of war and humanitarian intervention cannot stand alone; it requires solutions to the other practical problems discussed in this anthology as well. For example, a solution to the problem of the distribution of income and wealth may show that it is morally illegitimate to increase military security by sacrificing the basic needs of the less advantaged members of a society rather than by sacrificing the nonbasic needs of the more advantaged members of the society. Accordingly, it is impossible to reach a fully adequate solution to this or any other practical problem discussed in this anthology without solving the other practical problems as well.

Notes

---

1. See General Introduction.

2. See General Introduction.

3. See John Harsanyi, *Rational Behavior and Bargaining Equilibrium in Games and Social Situations* (Cambridge: Cambridge University Press, 1977), and R. M. Hare, "Justice and Equality," in *Justice: Alternative Political Perspectives*, ed. James P. Sterba (Belmont, Calif.: Wadsworth Publishing Co., 1991).

67. Reconciling Pacifists and Just War Theorists

James P. Sterba

James P. Sterba argues that when pacifism and just war theory are given their most morally defensible interpretations, they can be reconciled both in theory and practice. He argues that the most morally defensible form of pacifism is antiwar pacifism rather than nonviolent pacifism or nonlethal pacifism. He also argues that when just war theory is given its most morally defensible interpretation, it favors a strong just means prohibition against intentionally harming innocents and favors the use of belligerent means only when such means (1) minimize the loss and injury to innocent lives overall, (2) threaten innocent lives only to prevent the loss of innocent lives, and (3) threaten or take the lives of unjust aggressors when it is the only way to prevent serious injury to innocents. He contends that the few wars and large-scale conflicts that meet these stringent requirements of just war theory are the only wars and large-scale conflicts to which antiwar pacifists cannot justifiably object.

Traditionally pacifism and just war theory have represented radically opposed responses to aggression. Pacifism has been interpreted to rule out any use of violence in response to aggression. Just war theory has been interpreted to permit a measured use of violence in response to aggression. It has been thought that the two views might sometimes agree in particular cases—for example, that pacifists and just war theorists might unconditionally oppose nuclear war, but beyond that it has been generally held that the two views lead to radically opposed recommendations. In this paper, I hope to show that this is not the case. I will argue that pacifism and just war theory, in their most morally defensible interpretations, can be substantially reconciled both in theory and practice.

In traditional just war theory there are two basic elements: an account of just cause and an account of just means. Just cause is usually specified as follows:

1. There must be substantial aggression;
2. Nonbelligerent correctives must be either hopeless or too costly; and
3. Belligerent correctives must be neither hopeless nor too costly.

Needless to say, the notion of substantial aggression is a bit fuzzy, but it is generally understood to be the type of aggression that violates people's most fundamental rights. To suggest some specific examples of what is and is not substantial aggression, usually the taking of hostages is regarded as substantial aggression while the nationalization of particular firms owned by foreigners is not so regarded. But even when substantial aggression occurs, frequently nonbelligerent correctives are neither hopeless nor too costly. And even when nonbelligerent correctives are either hopeless or too costly, in order for there to be a just cause, belligerent correctives must be neither hopeless nor too costly.

Traditional just war theory assumes, however, that there are just causes and goes on to specify just means as imposing two requirements:

1. Harm to innocents should not be directly intended as an end or a means.
2. The harm resulting from the belligerent means should not be disproportionate to the particular defensive objective to be attained.

While the just means conditions apply to each defensive action, the just cause conditions must be met by the conflict as a whole.

It is important to note that these requirements of just cause and just means are not essentially about war at all. Essentially, they constitute a theory of just defense that can apply to war but can also apply to a wide range of defensive actions short of war. Of course, what needs to be determined is whether these requirements can be justified. Since just war theory is usually opposed to pacifism, to secure a non-question-begging justification for the theory and its requirements we need to proceed as much as possible from premises that are common to pacifists and just war theorists alike. The difficulty here is that there is not just one form of pacifism but many. So we need to determine which form of pacifism is most morally defensible.

Now when most people think of pacifism they tend to identify it with a theory of nonviolence. We can call this view "nonviolent pacifism." It maintains that:

> Any use of violence against other human beings is morally prohibited.

It has been plausibly argued, however, that this form of pacifism is incoherent. In a well-known article, Jan Narveson rejects nonviolent pacifism as incoherent because it recognizes a right to life yet rules out any use of force in defense of that right. The view is incoherent, Narveson claims, because having a right entails the legitimacy of using force in defense of that right at least on some occasions.

Given the cogency of objections of this sort, some have opted for a form of pacifism that does not rule out all violence but only lethal violence. We can call this view "nonlethal pacifism." It maintains that

> Any lethal use of force against other human beings is morally prohibited.

In defense of nonlethal pacifism, Cheyney Ryan has argued that there is a substantial issue between the pacifist and the nonpacifist concerning whether we can or should create the necessary distance between ourselves and other human beings in order to make the act of killing possible. To illustrate, Ryan cites George Orwell's reluctance to shoot at an enemy soldier who jumped out of a trench and ran along the top of a parapet half-dressed and holding up his trousers with both hands. Ryan contends that what kept Orwell from shooting was that he couldn't think of the soldier as a thing rather than a fellow human being.

However, it is not clear that Orwell's encounter supports nonlethal pacifism. For it may be that what kept Orwell from shooting the enemy soldier was not his inability to think of the soldier as a thing rather than a fellow human being but rather his inability to think of the soldier who was holding up his trousers with both hands as a threat or a combatant. Under this interpretation, Orwell's decision not to shoot would accord well with the requirements of just war theory.

Let us suppose, however, that someone is attempting to take your life. Why does that permit you, the defender of nonlethal pacifism might ask, to kill the person making the attempt? The most cogent response, it seems to me, is that killing in such a case is not evil, or at least not morally evil, because anyone who is wrongfully engaged in an attempt upon your life has already forfeited his or her right to life by engaging in such aggression.[1] So, provided that you are reasonably certain that the aggressor is wrongfully engaged in an attempt upon your life, you would be morally justified in killing, assuming that it is the only way of saving your own life.

There is, however, a form a pacifism that remains untouched by the criticisms I have raised against both nonviolent pacifism and nonlethal pacifism. This form of pacifism neither prohibits all violence nor even all uses of lethal force. We can call the view "antiwar pacifism" because it holds that

> Any participation in the massive use of lethal force in warfare is morally prohibited.[2]

In defense of antiwar pacifism, it is undeniable that wars have brought enormous amounts of death and destruction in their wake and that many of those who have perished in them are noncombatants or innocents. In fact, the tendency of modern wars has been to produce higher and higher proportions of noncombatant casualties, making it more and more difficult to justify participation in such wars. At the same time, strategies for nonbelligerent conflict resolution are rarely intensively developed and explored before nations choose to go to war, making it all but impossible to justify participation in such wars.

To determine whether the requirements of just war theory can be reconciled with those of antiwar pacifism, however, we need to consider whether we should distinguish between harm intentionally inflicted upon innocents and harm whose infliction on innocents is merely foreseen. On the one hand, we could favor a uniform restriction against the infliction of harm upon innocents that ignores the intended/foreseen distinction. On the other hand, we could favor a differential restriction which is more severe against the intentional infliction of harm upon innocents but is less severe against the infliction of harm that is merely foreseen. What needs to be determined, therefore, is whether there is any rationale for favoring this differential restriction on harm over a uniform restriction. . . .

Let us first examine the question from the perspective of those suffering the harm. Initially, it might appear to matter little whether the harm would be intended or just foreseen by those who cause it. From the perspective of those suffering harm, it might appear that what matters is simply that the overall amount of harm be restricted irrespective of whether it is foreseen or intended. But consider—don't those who suffer harm have more reason to protest when the harm is done to them by agents who are directly engaged in causing harm to them than when the harm is done incidentally by agents whose ends and means are good? Don't we have more reason to protest when we are being used by others than when we are affected by them only incidentally?

Moreover, if we examine the question from the perspective of those causing harm, additional support for this line of reasoning can be found. For it would seem that we as agents have more reason to protest a restriction against foreseen harm than we have reason to protest a comparable restriction against intended harm. This is because a restriction against foreseen harm limits our actions when our ends and means are good whereas a restriction against intended harm only limits our actions when our ends or means are evil or harmful, and it would seem that we have

greater grounds for acting when both our ends and means are good than when they are not. Consequently, because we have more reason to protest when we are being used by others than when we are being affected by them only incidentally, and because we have more reason to act when both our ends and means are good than when they are not, we should favor the foreseen/intended distinction that is incorporated into just means.

It might be objected, however, that at least sometimes we could produce greater good overall by violating the foreseen/intended distinction of just means and acting with the evil means of intentionally harming innocents. On this account, it might be argued that it should be permissible at least sometimes to intentionally harm innocents in order to achieve greater good overall.

Now it seems to me that this objection is well taken insofar as it is directed against an absolute restriction upon intentional harm to innocents. It seems clear that there are exceptions to such a restriction when intentional harm to innocents is:

1. Trivial (for example, as in the case of stepping on someone's foot to get out of a crowded subway);
2. Easily reparable (for example, as in the case of lying to a temporarily depressed friend to keep him from committing suicide); or
3. Greatly outweighed by the consequences of the action, especially to innocent people (for example, as in the case of shooting one of two hundred civilian hostages to prevent in the only way possible the execution of all two hundred).

Yet while we need to recognize these exceptions to an absolute restriction upon intentional harm to innocents, there is good reason not to permit simply maximizing good consequences overall because that would place unacceptable burdens upon particular individuals. More specifically, it would be an unacceptable burden on innocents to allow them to be intentionally harmed in cases other than the exceptions we have just enumerated. So allowing for these exceptions, we would have reason to favor a differential restriction against harming innocents that is more severe against the intentional infliction of harm upon innocents but is less severe against the infliction of harm upon innocents that is merely foreseen. Again, the main grounds for this preference is that we would have more reason to protest when we are being used by others than when we are being affected by them only incidentally, and more reason to act when both our ends and means are good than when they are not.

So far, I have argued that there are grounds for favoring a differential restriction on harm to innocents that is more severe against intended harm and less severe against foreseen harm. I have further argued that this restriction is not absolute so that when the evil intended is trivial, easily reparable, or greatly outweighed by the consequences, intentional harm to innocents can be justified. Moreover, there is no reason to think that antiwar pacifists would reject either of these conclusions. Antiwar pacifists are opposed to any participation in the massive use of lethal force in warfare, yet this need not conflict with the commitment of just war theorists to a differential but nonabsolute restriction on harm to innocents as a requirement of just means.[3] Where just war theory goes wrong, according to antiwar pacifists, is not in its restriction on harming innocents but rather in its failure to adequately determine when belligerent correctives are too costly to constitute a just cause or lacking in the proportionality required by just means. According to antiwar pacifists, just war theory provides insufficient restraint in both of these areas. Now to evaluate this criticism, we need to consider a wide range of cases where killing or inflicting serious harm on others in defense of oneself or others might be thought to be justified, beginning with the easiest cases to assess from the perspectives of antiwar pacifism and the just war theory and then moving on to cases that are more difficult to assess from these perspectives.

Case 1 where only the intentional or foreseen killing of an unjust aggressor would prevent one's own death.[4] This case clearly presents no problems. In the first place, antiwar pacifists adopted their view because they were convinced that there were instances of justified killing. And, in this case, the only person killed is an unjust aggressor. So surely antiwar pacifists would have to agree with just war theorists that one can justifiably kill an unjust aggressor if it is the only way to save one's life.

Case 2 where only the intentional or foreseen killing of an unjust aggressor and the foreseen killing of one innocent bystander would prevent one's own death and that of five other innocent people.[5] In this case, we have the foreseen killing of an innocent person as well as the killing of the unjust aggressor, but since it is the only way to save one's own life and the lives of five other innocent people, antiwar pacifists and just war theorists alike would have reason to judge it morally permissible. In this case, the intended life-saving benefits to six innocent people is judged to outweigh the foreseen death of one innocent person and the intended or foreseen death of the unjust aggressor.

Case 3 where only the intentional or foreseen killing of an unjust aggressor and the foreseen killing of one innocent bystander would prevent the death of five other innocent people. In this case, despite the fact that we lack the justification of self-defense, saving the lives of five innocent people in the only way possible should still provide antiwar pacifists and just war theorists with sufficient grounds for granting the moral permissibility of killing an unjust aggressor, even when the killing of an innocent bystander is a foreseen consequence. In this case, the intended lifesaving benefits to five innocent people would still outweigh the foreseen death of one innocent person and the intended or foreseen death of the unjust aggressor.

Case 4 where only the intentional or foreseen killing of an unjust aggressor and the forseen killing of five innocent people would prevent the death of two innocent people. In this case, neither antiwar pacifists nor just war theorists would find the cost and proportionality requirements of just war theory to be met. Too many innocent people would have to be killed to save too few. Here the fact that the deaths of the innocents would be merely foreseen does not outweigh the fact that we would have to accept the deaths of five innocents and the death of the unjust aggressor in order to be able to save two innocents.

Notice that up to this point in interpreting these cases, we have simply been counting the number of innocent deaths involved in each

case and opting for whichever solution minimized the loss of innocent lives that would
result. Suppose, however, that an unjust
aggressor is not threatening the lives of innocents but only their welfare or property.
Would the taking of the unjust aggressor's life
in defense of the welfare and property of innocents be judged proportionate? Consider
the following case.

Case 5 where only the intentional or foreseen
killing of an unjust aggressor would prevent serious
injury to oneself and/or five other innocent people.
Since in this case the intentional or foreseen
killing of the unjust aggressor is the only way
of preventing serious injury to oneself and five
other innocent people, then, by analogy with
Cases 1 through 3, both antiwar pacifists and
just war theorists alike would have reason to
affirm its moral permissibility. Of course, if
there were any other way of stopping unjust
aggressors in such cases short of killing them,
that course of action would clearly be required. Yet if there is no alternative, the intentional or foreseen killing of the unjust
aggressor to prevent serious injury to oneself
and/or five other innocent people would be
justified.

In such cases, the serious injury could be
bodily injury, as when an aggressor threatens
to break one's limbs, or it could be serious
psychological injury, as when an aggressor
threatens to inject mind-altering drugs, or it
could be a serious threat to property. Of
course, in most cases where serious injury is
threatened, there will be ways of stopping
aggressors short of killing them. Unfortunately, this is not always possible.

In still other kinds of cases, stopping an
unjust aggressor would require indirectly inflicting serious harm, but not death, upon innocent bystanders. Consider the following
cases.

Case 6 where only the intentional or foreseen
infliction of serious harm upon an unjust aggressor
and the foreseen infliction of serious harm upon one
innocent bystander would prevent serious harm to
oneself and five other innocent people.

Case 7 where only the intentional or foreseen
infliction of serious harm upon an unjust aggressor
and the foreseen infliction of serious harm upon one
innocent bystander would prevent serious harm to
five other innocent people.

In both of these cases, serious harm is indirectly inflicted upon one innocent bystander
in order to prevent greater harm from being
inflicted by an unjust aggressor upon other
innocent people. In Case 6, we also have the
justification of self-defense, which is lacking in
Case 7. Nevertheless, with regard to both
cases, antiwar pacifists and just war theorists
should agree that preventing serious injury to
five or six innocent people in the only way
possible renders it morally permissible to inflict serious injury upon an unjust aggressor,
even when the serious injury of one innocent
person is a foreseen consequence. In these
cases, by analogy with Cases 2 and 3, the foreseen serious injury of one innocent person and
the intended or foreseen injury of the unjust
aggressor should be judged proportionate
given the intended injury-preventing benefits
to five or six other innocent people.

Up to this point there has been the basis for
general agreement among antiwar pacifists
and just war theorists as to how to interpret
the proportionality requirement of just means,
but in the following case this no longer
obtains.

Case 8 where only the intentional or foreseen
killing of an unjust aggressor and the foreseen kill-
ing of one innocent bystander would prevent serious
injuries to the members of a much larger group of
people.

The interpretation of this case is crucial. In
this case, we are asked to sanction the loss of
an innocent life in order to prevent serious
injuries to the members of a much larger
group of people. Unfortunately, neither antiwar pacifists nor just war theorists have explicitly considered this case. Both antiwar
pacifists and just war theorists agree that we
can inflict serious injury upon an unjust
aggressor and an innocent bystander to prevent greater injury to other innocent people,
as in Cases 6 and 7, and that one can even
intentionally or indirectly kill an unjust
aggressor to prevent serious injury to oneself
or other innocent people as in Case 5. Yet
neither antiwar pacifists nor just war theorists
have explicitly addressed the question of
whether we can indirectly kill an innocent bystander in order to prevent serious injuries to
the members of a much larger group of innocent people. Rather they have tended to con-

fuse Case 8 with Case 5 where it is agreed that one can justifiably kill an unjust aggressor in order to prevent serious injury to oneself and/ or five other innocent people. In Case 8, however, one is doing something quite different: one is killing an innocent bystander in order to prevent serious injury to the members of a much larger group of people.

Now this kind of trade-off is not accepted in standard police practice. Police officers are regularly instructed not to risk innocent lives simply to prevent serious injury to other innocents. Nor is there any reason to think that a trade-off that is unacceptable in standard police practice would be acceptable in larger scale conflicts. Thus, for example, even if the Baltic republics could have effectively freed themselves from the Soviet Union by infiltrating into Moscow several bands of saboteurs who would then attack several military and government installations in Moscow, causing an enormous loss of innocent lives, such trade-offs would not have been justified. Accordingly, it follows that if the proportionality requirement of just war theory is to be met, we must save more innocent lives than we cause to be lost, we must prevent more injuries than we bring about, and we must not kill innocents, even indirectly, simply to prevent serious injuries to ourselves and others. Moreover, even when our lives and the lives of others are being threatened, we must save more innocent lives than we cause to be lost.

Of course, sometimes our lives and well-being are threatened together. Or better, if we are unwilling to sacrifice our well-being then our lives are threatened as well. Nevertheless, if we are justified in our use of lethal force to defend ourselves in cases where we will indirectly kill innocents, it is because our lives are also threatened, not simply our well-being. And the same holds for when we are defending others.

What this shows is that the constraints imposed by just war theory on the use of belligerent correctives are actually much more severe than antiwar pacifists have tended to recognize. In determining when belligerent correctives are too costly to constitute a just cause or lacking in the proportionality required by just means, just war theory under its most morally defensible interpretation:

1. Allows the use of belligerent means against unjust aggressors only when such means minimize the loss and injury to innocent lives overall;

2. Allows the use of belligerent means against unjust aggressors to indirectly threaten innocent lives only to prevent the loss of innocent lives, not simply to prevent injury to innocents; and

3. Allows the use of belligerent means to directly or indirectly threaten or even take the lives of unjust aggressors when it is the only way to prevent serious injury to innocents.

Now it might be objected that all that I have shown through the analysis of the above eight cases is that killing in defense of oneself or others is morally permissible, not that it is morally required or morally obligatory. That is true. I have not established any obligation to respond to aggression with lethal force in these cases, but only that it is morally permissible to do so. For one thing, it is difficult to ground an obligation to use lethal force on self-defense alone, as would be required in Case 1 or in one version of Case 5. Obligations to oneself appear to have an optional quality that is absent from obligations to others. In Cases 2 and 3 and 5 through 7, however, the use of force would prevent serious harm or death to innocents, and here I contend it would be morally obligatory if either the proposed use of force required only a relatively small personal sacrifice from us or if we were fairly bound by convention or a mutual defense agreement to come to the aid of others. In such cases, I think we can justifiably speak of a moral obligation to kill or seriously harm in defense of others.

Another aspect of Cases 1 through 3 and 5 through 7 to which someone might object is that it is the wrongful actions of others that put us into situations where I am claiming that we are morally justified in seriously harming or killing others. But for the actions of unjust aggressors, we would not be in situations where I am claiming that we are morally permitted or required to seriously harm or kill.

Yet doesn't something like this happen in a wide range of cases when wrongful actions are performed? Suppose I am on the way to the bank to deposit money from a fund-raiser, and someone accosts me and threatens to shoot if I don't hand over the money. If I do hand over the money, I would be forced to do something I don't want to do, something that involves a loss to myself and others. But surely it is morally permissible for me to hand over the money in this case. And it may even be morally required for me to do so if resistance would lead to the shooting of others in addition to myself. So it does seem that bad people, by altering the consequences of our actions, can alter our obligations as well. What our obligations are under nonideal conditions are different from what they would be under ideal conditions. If a group of thugs comes into this room and make it very clear that they intend to shoot me if each of you doesn't give them one dollar, I think, and I would hope that you would also think, that each of you now has an obligation to give the thugs one dollar when before you had no such obligation. Likewise, I think that the actions of unjust aggressors can put us into situations where it is morally permissible or even morally required for us to seriously harm or kill when before it was not.

Now it might be contended that antiwar pacifists would concede the moral permissibility of Cases 1–3 and 5–7 but still maintain that any participation in the massive use of lethal force in warfare is morally prohibited. The scale of the conflict, antiwar pacifists might contend, makes all the difference. Of course, if this simply means that many large-scale conflicts will have effects that bear no resemblance to Cases 1–3 or 5–7, this can hardly be denied. Still, it is possible for some large-scale conflicts to bear a proportionate resemblance to the above cases. For example, it can be argued plausibly that India's military action against Pakistan in Bangladesh and the Tanzanian incursion into Uganda during the rule of Idi Amin resemble Cases 3, 5, or 7 in their effects upon innocents.[6] What this shows is that antiwar pacifists are not justified in regarding every participation in the massive use of lethal force in warfare as morally prohibited. Instead, antiwar pacifists must allow that at least in some real-life cases, wars and other large-scale military operations both have been and will be morally permissible.

This concession from antiwar pacifists, however, needs to be matched by a comparable concession from just war theorists themselves, because too frequently they have interpreted their theory in morally indefensible ways. When just war theory is given a morally defensible interpretation, I have argued that the theory favors a strong just means prohibition against intentionally harming innocents. I have also argued that the theory favors the use of belligerent means only when such means (1) minimize the loss and injury to innocent lives overall; (2) threaten innocent lives only to prevent the loss of innocent lives, not simply to prevent injury to innocents; and (3) threaten or even take the lives of unjust aggressors when it is the only way to prevent serious injury to innocents.

Obviously, just war theory, so understood, is going to place severe restrictions on the use of belligerent means in warfare. In fact, most of the actual uses of belligerent means in warfare that have occurred turn out to be unjustified. For example, the U.S. involvement in Nicaragua, El Salvador, and Panama, the Soviet Union's involvement in Afghanistan, and Israeli involvement in the West Bank and the Gaza Strip all violate the just cause and just means provisions of just war theory as I have defended them. Even the recent U.S.-led war against Iraq violated both the just cause and just means provisions of just war theory.[7] In fact, one strains to find examples of justified applications of just war theory in recent history. Two examples I have already referred to are India's military action against Pakistan in Bangladesh and the Tanzanian incursion into Uganda during the rule of Idi Amin. But after mentioning these two examples it is difficult to go on. What this shows is that when just war theory and antiwar pacifism are given their most morally defensible interpretations, both views can be reconciled. In this reconciliation, the few wars and large-scale conflicts that meet the stringent requirements of just war theory are the only wars and large-scale conflicts to which antiwar pacifists cannot justifiably object.[8] We can call the view that emerges from this reconciliation "just war pacifism." It is the view which claims that due to the stringent requirements of just war theory, only very rarely will participation in a massive use of lethal force in warfare be morally justified. It is the view on which I rest my case for the reconciliation of pacifism and just war theory.[9]

Notes

1. Alternatively, one might concede that even in this case killing is morally evil, but still contend that it is morally justified because it is the lesser of two evils.

2. For two challenging defenses of this view, see Duane L. Cady, *From Warism to Pacifism* (Philadelphia: Temple University Press, 1989), and Robert L. Holmes, *On War and Morality* (Princeton: Princeton University Press, 1989).

3. This is because the just means restrictions protect innocents quite well against the infliction of intentional harm.

4. By an "unjust aggressor" I mean someone who the defender is reasonably certain is wrongfully engaged in an attempt upon her life or the lives of other innocent people.

5. What is relevant in this case is that the foreseen deaths are a relatively small number (one in this case) compared to the number of innocents whose lives are saved (six in this case). The primary reason for using particular numbers in this case and those that follow is to make it clear that at this stage of the argument no attempt is being made to justify the large-scale killing that occurs in warfare.

6. Although there is a strong case for India's military action against Pakistan in Bangladesh and the Tanzanian incursion into Uganda during the rule of Idi Amin, there are questions that can be raised about the behavior of Indian troops in Bangladesh following the defeat of the Pakistanian forces and about the regime Tanzania put in power in Uganda.

7. The just cause provision was violated because the extremely effective economic sanctions were not given enough time to work. It was estimated that when compared to past economic blockades, the blockade against Iraq had a near 100 percent chance of success if given about a year to work. (See the *New York Times*, January 14, 1991.) The just means provision was violated because the number of combatant and noncombatant deaths was disproportionate. As many as 120,000 Iraqi soldiers were killed, according to U.S. intelligence sources.

8. Of course, antiwar pacifists are right to point out that virtually all wars that have been fought have led to unforeseen harms and have been fought with less and less discrimination as the wars progressed. Obviously, these are considerations that in just war theory must weigh heavily against going to war.

9. Of course, more needs to be done to specify the requirements of just war pacifism. One fruitful way to further specify these requirements is to appeal to a hypothetical social contract decision procedure as has been done with respect to other practical problems. Here I have simply tried to establish the defensibility of just war pacifism without appealing to any such procedure. Yet once the defensibility of just war pacifism has been established, such a decision procedure will prove quite useful in working out its particular requirements.

68. Humanitarian Intervention

Michael Walzer

According to Michael Walzer, humanitarian intervention can be justified (1) to assist secessionist movements once they have demonstrated their representative character; (2) to balance the prior, unjustified interventions of other powers; and (3) to rescue people threatened with massacre. Walzer further argues that humanitarian intervention requires that the intervening state enter, to some degree, into the purposes of the people on whose behalf it purports to be helping. Applying this definition, Walzer claims that the U.S. intervention in Cuba in 1898 was not humanitarian intervention, but India's intervention in East Pakistan in 1971 was humanitarian intervention.

The principle that states should never intervene in the domestic affairs of other states follows readily from the legalist paradigm and, less readily and more ambiguously, from those conceptions of life and liberty that underlie the paradigm and make it plausible. But these same conceptions seem also to require that we sometimes disregard the principle; and what might be called the rules of disregard, rather than the principle itself, have been the focus of moral interest and argument. No state can admit to fighting an aggressive war and then defend its actions. But intervention is differently understood. The word is not defined as a criminal activity, and though the practice of intervening often threatens the territorial integrity and political independence of invaded states, it can sometimes be justified. It is more important to stress at the outset, however, that it always has to be justified. The burden of proof falls on any political leader who tries to shape the domestic arrangements or alter the conditions of life in a foreign country. And when the attempt is made with armed force, the burden is especially heavy—not only because of the coercions and ravages that military intervention inevitably brings, but also because it is thought that the citizens of a sovereign state have a right, insofar as they are to be coerced and ravaged at all, to suffer only at one another's hands. . . .

A legitimate government is one that can fight its own internal wars. And external assistance in those wars is rightly called counterintervention only when it balances, and does no more than balance, the prior intervention of another power, making it possible once again for the local forces to win or lose on their own. The outcome of civil wars should reflect not the relative strength of the intervening states, but the local alignment of forces. There is another sort of case, however, where we don't look for outcomes of that sort, where we don't want the local balance to prevail. If the dominant forces within a state are engaged in massive violations of human rights, the appeal to self-determination in the Millian sense of self-help is not very attractive. That appeal has to do with the freedom of the community taken as a whole; it has no force when what is at stake is the bare survival or the minimal liberty of (some substantial number of) its members. Against the enslavement or massacre of political opponents, national minorities, and religious sects, there may well be no help unless help comes from outside. And when a government turns savagely upon its own people, we must doubt the very existence of a political community to which the idea of self-determination might apply.

Examples are not hard to find; it is their plenitude that is embarrassing. The list of oppressive governments, the list of massacred peoples, is frighteningly long. Though an event like the Nazi holocaust is without precedent in human history, murder on a smaller

From *Just and Unjust Wars* (1977). Reprinted by permission of Basic Books.

scale is so common as to be almost ordinary. On the other hand—or perhaps for this very reason—clear examples of what is called "humanitarian intervention" are very rare. Indeed, I have not found any, but only mixed cases where the humanitarian motive is one among several. States don't send their soldiers into other states, it seems, only in order to save lives. The lives of foreigners don't weigh that heavily in the scales of domestic decision-making. So we shall have to consider the moral significance of mixed motives.* It is not necessarily an argument against humanitarian intervention that it is, at best, partially humanitarian, but it is a reason to be skeptical and to look closely at the other parts.

Cuba, 1898, and Bangladesh, 1971

Both these cases might be taken up under the headings of national liberation and counter-intervention. But they each have a further significance because of the atrocities committed by the Spanish and the Pakistani governments. The brutal work of the Spaniards is easier to talk about, for it fell short of systematic massacre. Fighting against a Cuban insurgent army that lived off the land and apparently had large-scale peasant support, the Spaniards first worked out the policy of forced resettlement. They called it, without euphemism, *la reconcentración*. General Weyler's proclamation required that:

All inhabitants of rural areas or areas outside the lines of fortified towns will be concentrated within the towns occupied by

---

*The case is different, obviously, when the lives at stake are those of fellow nationals. Interventions designed to rescue citizens threatened with death in a foreign country have conventionally been called humanitarian, and there is no reason to deny them that name when life and death are really at issue. The Israeli raid on Entebbe airport in Uganda (July 4, 1976) seems likely to become a classic case. Here there is, or ought to be, no question of mixed movies: the only purpose is to rescue *these* people towards whom the intervening power has a special commitment.

troops at the end of eight days. All individuals who disobey or who are found outside the prescribed areas will be considered as rebels and judged as such.

I will ask later on whether "concentration" in itself is a criminal policy. The immediate crime of the Spaniards was to enforce the policy with so little regard for the health of the people involved that thousands of them suffered and died. Their lives and deaths were widely publicized in the United States, not only in the yellow press, and undoubtedly figured in the minds of many Americans as the major justification for the war against Spain. Thus the Congressional resolution of April 20, 1898: "Whereas the abhorrent conditions which have existed for more than three years in the island of Cuba, so near our own borders, have shocked the moral sense of the people of the United States . . ." But there were other reasons for going to war.

The chief of these were economic and strategic in character, having to do, first, with American investment in Cuban sugar, a matter of interest to a section of the financial community; and second, with the sea approaches to the Panamanian Isthmus where the canal would one day be, a matter of interest to the intellectuals and politicians who championed the cause of American expansion. Cuba was a minor element in the plans of men like Mahan and Adams, Roosevelt and Lodge, who were more concerned with the Pacific Ocean than the Caribbean Sea. But the canal that would connect the two gave it a certain strategic value, and the war to win it was worthwhile insofar as it accustomed Americans to imperialist adventures (and led also to the conquest of the Philippines). By and large, the historical debate over the causes of the war has focused on the different forms of economic and political imperialism, the search for markets and investment opportunities, the pursuit of "national power for its own sake." It's worth remembering, however, that the war was also supported by anti-imperialist politicians—or rather, that Cuban freedom was supported and then, in consequence of Spanish brutality, the humanitarian intervention of American military forces. The war we actually fought, however, and the intervention urged by populists and radical Democrats were two rather different things.

The Cuban insurgents made three requests of the United States: that we recognize their provisional government as the legitimate government of Cuba, that we provide their army with military supplies, and that American warships blockade the Cuban coast and cut off the supplies of the Spanish army. Given such help, it was said, the insurgent forces would grow, the Spaniards could not long hold out, and the Cubans would be left to reconstruct their country (with American help) and manage their own affairs. This was also the program of American radicals. But President McKinley and his advisors did not believe the Cubans capable of managing their own affairs, or they feared a radical reconstruction. In any case, the United States intervened without recognizing the insurgents, invaded the island, and quickly defeated and replaced the Spanish forces. The victory undoubtedly had humane effects. Though the American military effort was remarkably inefficient, the war was short and added little to the miseries of the civilian population. Relief operations, also remarkably inefficient at first, began as soon as the battles were won. In his standard account of the war, Admiral Chadwick boasts of its relative bloodlessness: "War of itself," he writes, "cannot be the great evil; the evil is in the horrors, many of which are necessarily concomitant . . . The war now beginning between the United States and Spain was one in which these greater horrors were largely to be absent." The horrors were indeed absent; far more so, at least, than in the long years of the Cuban Insurrection. But the invasion of Cuba, the three years of military occupation, the eventual granting of a drastically limited independence (under the provisions of the Platt Amendment) go a long way toward explaining the skepticism with which America's professions of humane concern have conventionally been regarded. The entire course of action, from 1898 to 1902, might be taken as an example of benevolent imperialism, given the "piratical times," but it is not an example of humanitarian intervention.

The judgments we make in cases such as this don't hang on the fact that considerations other than humanity figured in the government's plans, or even on the fact that humanity was not the chief consideration. I don't know if it ever is, and measurement is especially difficult in a liberal democracy where the mixed motives of the government reflect the pluralism of the society. Nor is it a question of benevolent outcomes. As a result of the American victory, the *reconcentrados* were able to return to their homes. But they would have been able to do that had the United States entered the war on the side of the Spaniards and, together with them, decisively defeated the Cuban insurgents. "Concentration" was a war policy and would have ended with the war, whatever the war's end. The crucial question is a different one. Humanitarian intervention involves military action on behalf of oppressed people, and it requires that the intervening state enter, to some degree, into the purposes of those people. It need not set itself to achieve those purposes, but it also cannot stand in the way of their achievement. The people are oppressed, presumably, because they sought some end—religious toleration, national freedom, or whatever—unacceptable to their oppressors. One cannot intervene on their behalf and against their ends. I don't want to argue that the purposes of the oppressed are necessarily just or that one need accept them in their entirety. But it does seem that a greater attention is due them than the United States was prepared to pay in 1898.

This regard for the purposes of the oppressed directly parallels the respect for local autonomy that is a necessary feature of counter-intervention. The two revisionist principles reflect a common commitment: that intervention be as much like nonintervention as possible. In the one case, the goal is balance; in the other, it is rescue. In neither case, and certainly not in secessions and national liberation struggles, can the intervening state rightly claim any political prerogatives for itself. And whenever it makes such claims (as the United States did when it occupied Cuba and again when it imposed the Platt Amendment), we suspect that political power was its purpose from the start.

The Indian invasion of East Pakistan (Bangladesh) in 1971 is a better example of humanitarian intervention—not because of the singularity or purity of the government's motives, but because its various motives converged on a single course of action that was also the course of action called for by the Bengalis. This convergence explains why the Indians were in and out of the country so quickly, defeating the Pakistani army but not replacing it, and imposing no political controls on the emergent state of Bangladesh. No doubt, strategic as well as moral interests underlay this policy: Pakistan, India's old enemy, was significantly weakened, while India itself avoided becoming responsible for a desperately poor nation whose internal politics was likely to be unstable and volatile for a long time to come. But the intervention qualifies as humanitarian because it was a *rescue*, strictly and narrowly defined. So circumstances sometimes make saints of us all.

I shall not say very much about Pakistani oppression in Bengal. The tale is a terrible one and by now fairly well documented. Faced with a movement for autonomy in what was then its eastern province, the government of Pakistan, in March, 1971, literally turned an army loose on its own people—or rather, a Punjabi army loose on the Bengali people, for the unity of east and west was already a broken thing. The resulting massacre only completed the break and made it irreparable. The army was not entirely without direction; its officers carried "death lists" on which appeared the names of the political, cultural, and intellectual leaders of Bengal. There was also a systematic effort to slaughter the followers of these people: university students, political activists, and so on. Beyond these groups, the soldiers ranged freely, burning, raping, killing. Millions of Bengalis fled into India, and their arrival, destitute, hungry, and with incredible stories to tell, established the moral foundation of the later Indian attack. "It is idle to argue in such cases that the duty of the neighboring people is to look on quietly." Months of diplomatic maneuvering followed, but during that time, the Indians were already assisting Bengali guerrillas and offering sanctuary not only to refugees but also to fighting men and women. The two-week war of December 1971 apparently began with a Pakistani air strike, but the Indian invasion required no such prior attack; it was justified on other grounds.

The strength of the Bengali guerrillas and their achievements between March and De-

cember are matters of some dispute; so is their role in the two-week war. Clearly, however, it was not the purpose of the Indian invasion to open the way for the Bengali struggle; nor does the strength or weakness of the guerrillas affect our view of the invasion. When a people are being massacred, we don't require that they pass the test of self-help before coming to their aid. It is their very incapacity that brings us in. The purpose of the Indian army, then, was to defeat the Pakistani forces and drive them out of Bangladesh, that is, to win the war. The purpose was different from that of a counter-intervention, and for an important moral reason. People who initiate massacres lose their right to participate in the normal (even in the normally violent) processes of domestic self-determination. Their military defeat is morally necessary.

Governments and armies engaged in massacres are readily identified as criminal governments and armies (they are guilty, under the Nuremberg code of "crimes against humanity"). Hence humanitarian intervention comes much closer than any other kind of intervention to what we commonly regard, in domestic society, as law enforcement and police work. At the same time, however, it requires the crossing of an international frontier, and such crossings are ruled out by the legalist paradigm—unless they are authorized, I suppose, by the society of nations. In the cases I have considered, the law is unilaterally enforced; the police are self-appointed. Now, unilateralism has always prevailed in the international arena, but we worry about it more when what is involved is a response to domestic violence rather than to foreign aggression. We worry that, under the cover of humanitarianism, states will come to coerce and dominate their neighbors; once again, it is not hard to find examples. Hence many lawyers prefer to stick to the paradigm. That doesn't require them, on their view, to deny the (occasional) need for intervention. They merely deny legal recognition to that need. Humanitarian intervention "belongs in the realm not of law but of moral choice, which nations, like individuals must sometimes make . . ." But that is only a plausible formulation if one doesn't stop with it, as lawyers are likely to do. For moral choices are not simply *made;* they are also judged, and so there must be criteria for judgment. If these are not provided by the law, of if legal provision runs out at some point, they are nevertheless contained in our common morality, which doesn't run out, and which still needs to be explicated after the lawyers have finished.

Morality, at least, is not a bar to unilateral action, so long as there is no immediate alternative available. There was none in the Bengali case. No doubt, the massacres were a matter of universal interest, but only India interested itself in them. The case was formally carried to the United Nations, but no action followed. Nor is it clear to me that action undertaken by the UN, or by a coalition of powers, would necessarily have had a moral quality superior to that of the Indian attack. What one looks for in numbers is detachment from particularist views and consensus on moral rules. And for that, there is at present no institutional appeal; one appeals to humanity as a whole. States don't lose their particularist character merely by acting together. If governments have mixed motives, so do coalitions of governments. Some goals, perhaps, are cancelled out by the political bargaining that constitutes the coalition, but others are superadded; and the resulting mix is as accidental with reference to the moral issue as are the political interests and ideologies of a single state.

Humanitarian intervention is justified when it is a response (with reasonable expectations of success) to acts "that shock the moral conscience of mankind." The old-fashioned language seems to me exactly right. It is not the conscience of political leaders that one refers to in such cases. They have other things to worry about and may well be required to repress their normal feelings of indignation and outrage. The reference is to the moral convictions of ordinary men and women, acquired in the course of their everyday activities. And given that one can make a persuasive argument in terms of those convictions, I don't think that there is any moral reason to adopt that posture of passivity that might be called waiting for the UN (waiting for the universal state, waiting for the messiah . . .).

Suppose . . . that a great power decided that the only way it could continue to control a satellite state was to wipe out the satellite's entire population and recolonize the area with "reliable" people. Suppose the satellite government agreed to this measure and established the necessary mass extermination apparatus. . . . Would the rest of the members of the U.N. be compelled to stand by and watch this operation merely because [the] requisite decision of U.N. organs was blocked and the operation did not involve an "armed attack" on any [member state] . . . ?

The question is rhetorical. Any state capable of stopping the slaughter has a right, at least, to try to do so. The legalist paradigm indeed rules out such efforts, but that only suggests that the paradigm, unrevised, cannot account for the moral realities of military intervention.

The second, third, and fourth revisions of the paradigm have this form: states can be invaded and wars justly begun to assist secessionist movements (once they have demonstrated their representative character), to balance the prior interventions of other powers, and to rescue peoples threatened with massacre. In each of these cases we permit or, after the fact, we praise or don't condemn these violations of the formal rules of sovereignty, because they uphold the values of individual life and communal liberty of which sovereignty itself is merely an expression. The formula is, once again, permissive, but I have tried in my discussion of particular cases to indicate that the actual requirements of just interventions are constraining indeed. And the revisions must be understood to include the constraints. Since the constraints are often ignored, it is sometimes argued that it would be best to insist on an absolute rule of nonintervention (as it would be best to insist on an absolute rule of nonanticipation). But the absolute rule will also be ignored, and we will then have no standards by which to judge what happens next. In fact, we do have standards, which I have tried to map out. They reflect deep and valuable, though in their applications difficult and problematic, commitments to human rights.

69. The Need for Humanitarian Intervention: Bosnia and Somalia

Barbara Harff

Barbara Harff argues that Bosnia, Somalia, and Iraqi Kurdistan exemplify three distinct types of crimes against humanity in which the international community has a legal and moral imperative to intervene. Harff further argues that the Bosnian crisis might never have assumed the proportions of genocide if a coherent strategy for intervention had been in place from the beginning. She examines various forms of response the international community can take to serious human rights violations ranging from early warning assessments of impending or escalating conflicts to collective military intervention and the establishment of interim trusteeships.

Many legal scholars favor intervention against states that perpetrate massive human rights violations; their arguments are based upon moral principles and international standards of justice. But at present, policymakers and government leaders often allow their political interests to outweigh these other considerations. In affirming respect for the sovereignty of states, they fail to acknowledge that sovereignty is not necessarily absolute, and they ignore other provisions of international law that in some situations should be given priority. This short-sighted position has prevented the United States and Western Europe from mounting an effective cooperative effort to deal with the Bosnian conflict.

A number of newspaper columnists have contributed to the paralysis. Aware that the crisis in Bosnia has reached a point where a military commitment would be required to end the campaign of ethnic cleansing, they evoke the image of young Americans dying for the sake of nebulous policy objectives. But the sensible way to meet this concern is not to rule out intervention, but rather to insist that it combine precise policy goals, clear strategic objectives, and tactics that are suited to the desired end-state of the military involvement. It is illogical to conclude on the basis of an extreme case requiring an extensive military commitment that all forms of intervention are misguided in principle or are someone else's responsibility. If a coherent strategy for intervention had been in place from the beginning, the Bosnian crisis might never have assumed the proportions of genocide.

A multitude of ethnic conflicts may develop in the former Soviet Union and elsewhere in the next decade. Responses to these conflicts will, in turn, set the stage for the twenty-first century. In the early phases of ethnic conflict, will global leaders stand idly by while would-be dictators fight to expand their power base by killing their citizens, crossing internationally recognized boundaries, inflaming irredentist passions, and implementing ideologies of ethnic superiority?

It may prove to be a costly mistake if the last superpower and its friends (and sometime allies) become isolationist paper tigers once again. Explosions of ethnic passion rarely remain internal affairs. From a strategic perspective, it is clear that a future diffusion of ethnic passion, hatred, and rebellion will eventually call for much greater military measures than a maximum collective show of force with a minimum use of weapons in Bosnia. Failure to exert our capabilities may mean that we will lose our chance to build a world free from the forces that create global instability. From a cost-benefit perspective—as abhorrent as that

From "Bosnia and Somalia: Strategic, Legal and Moral Dimensions of Humanitarian Intervention," which appeared in the *Report from the Institute for Philosophy and Public Policy*, vol. 12, no. 4 (1992) Reprinted by permission of the publisher.

may seem, when we consider the loss of lives in Bosnia and similar theaters—early warning measures, a clear policy position, and a strategy with civil and military components are the best guarantees to forestall adventurers of the caliber of Saddam Hussein and Radovan Karadzic. From an American perspective, to be able to intervene with the knowledge that the United States is proceeding on a clearly plotted course that is strategically sound, morally correct, legally justified and internationally supported makes the task easier for the young men and women who have joined the military in order to fight for their country's just cause. Indeed, the more clearly designed the policy and tactical objectives are, the greater the likelihood that few if any American lives will be lost—provided action is taken swiftly in response to early signs of impending disaster.

The Legal Foundations of Humanitarian Intervention

Hersch Lauterpacht, one of the great scholars of international law, once asked whether law can promote the "realization of socially obtainable justice." My own answer is a qualified yes. We can achieve minimum standards of justice by affirming such essential goods as the right to live, and by enforcing sanctions against those who deprive people of those essential goods. Mass murder is unacceptable in all national legal systems and, in principle, states should apply their domestic laws to their own and others' external behavior. In other words, foreign policy should reflect the standards of national morality defined by domestic law.

In accordance with this principle, the Genocide Convention forbids governments to take steps to destroy any distinct national, ethnic, or religious group. Article 3 of the Universal Declaration of Human Rights asserts that "everyone has the right to life, liberty, and security of person." The large number of signatories to the human rights and genocide conventions attests to the fact that international morality in regard to the protection of fundamental human rights coincides with national moralities. These treaties con-

stitute, as Lauterpacht writes, "a recognition of fundamental rights superior to the law of the sovereign State."

Thus, when basic rights are violated to the degree we see at present in Somalia and Bosnia, international responses should follow, under the leadership of a United Nations that asserts and, ideally, enforces codified standards of morality. The most common argument against such action is based on Article 2, paragraph 7 of the U.N. Charter, which prohibits intervention in matters that are within the domestic jurisdiction of any state. In contrast, Article 34 identifies a competing principle by empowering the Security Council to investigate disputes that cause international friction, while Article 51 and Chapter VIII of the Charter offer regional organizations the legal justification for collective intervention.

The Bosnian situation is illustrative. If one accepts Bosnia's claim to being an independent state (as the U.N. did when it granted Bosnia a seat in the General Assembly), then under Article 51, the Bosnians have the right of self-defense, including the right to ask for outside help and to invite intervention by individual states, regional organizations, or the U.N. If one denies that Bosnia is an independent state (as does what remains of the federal Yugoslav government), then the situation is one of civil war between a state and a secessionist region. In this circumstance, the Security Council is empowered to execute collective measures, on the grounds that the situation is causing widespread abuse of human rights and international friction. Accordingly, in response to Serbian atrocities in Bosnia and Croatia, the first act of the General Assembly in the fall 1992 session was to deny membership to Serbia/Montenegro as the successor state to Yugoslavia.

Once it is established that international standards of human rights are being violated, the right to impose such standards should prevail over assertions of national sovereignty. But the path that leads from recognizing that a crime against humanity is being committed to the prescription of appropriate responses and sanctions is fraught with political difficulties. In principle, the U.N., as a collective body representing the great majority of states, is the entity that should delegate authority for any kind of intervention to willing and capable member states. Ideally, all full members would bear both the responsibility and the costs of the actions undertaken, even if the burden of action fell to the United States as perhaps the only country presently able to take a strong stand on such matters. Specific actions to be taken would be decided by the Security Council with the assistance of the Military Staff Committee (see Article 46).

The targets of international sanctions can be expected to complain that they are being victimized by a new brand of imperialism under the guise of the new world order. Given the archaic structure of the Security Council, in which the former imperial powers play a larger role than other states, such claims may have some prima facie plausibility. But such a claim by weaker states at no time and in no place mitigates the crimes of mass political murder, ethnic cleansing, or complicity in mass starvation of ethnic rivals.

What has been lacking, time and time again, on the part of states with the capacity to act is the political will to take a strong stand and accept the consequences of boldness. Standards of international morality and order are not achieved through timidity; precedent is never set through inaction. Violent ethnic conflicts in the Third World have steadily increased in frequency and intensity since the 1960s, as Ted Robert Gurr has demonstrated in a study tracking some 200 minorities during the entire postwar period. The disintegration of the Soviet, Yugoslav, and Ethiopian states has released the evil genies of nationalist xenophobia and ethnic hatred in vast new areas. Genocides—directed against people on the basis of their ethnic, racial, or social identity—and politicides—directed against people on the basis of their political beliefs—often follow war and revolution in poor countries. In my own work, I have identified more than forty such episodes since 1945 and have shown that they caused greater loss of life than all the wars fought *between* states during that period. For this reason, it is essential to demonstrate that building states on mass graves violates the moral standards of global society, and must lead with some certainty to sanctions proportional to the crimes.

In the absence of a formal international authority to monitor and police the human rights performances of states, communal and nationalist contenders seeking territory or autonomy often press their claims by force. Intimidation of opposing forces within states and assaults on less powerful neighbors are becoming more common, most acutely so in Eastern Europe. Yugoslavia in particular has regressed to a nineteenth-century mentality. Myths and memories of old injustices are invoked to mobilize young Serbs and Croats for war against one another, and together against Muslims. The territorial ambitions of the contenders take no account of Yugoslavia's carefully balanced heterogeneity; a resurgent nationalism calls instead for the creation of fictive homelands, purified of "alien peoples." The claims being made by the most militant of Serbs are reminiscent of Nazi ideology, and one can well imagine that in the future, nationalist Serbs, if unchecked, will assert their racial and cultural superiority over competing ethnic groups in a greater Serbia extending from Macedonia to Austria.

Civil Wars, Rebellion, Repression

Bosnia, Somalia, and Iraqi Kurdistan exemplify three distinct types of crimes against humanity in which the international community has a legal and moral imperative to intervene. Bosnia is a case that combines elements of civil and international war. On the civil side, Bosnia-Hercegovina's declaration of independence provoked uprisings by Bosnian Serbs concerned with their status in the new state. On the international side, they were armed by and acted as agents of "greater Serbian" nationalists. Recent events offer clear evidence of direct Serbian military support through air strikes and artillery barrages. The states of the European Community face a double responsibility, first because they helped precipitate the civil war by granting what many observers thought was premature recognition of Bosnian independence, and second because they have ample capacity to act. Yet EC leaders have largely behaved like bystanders, offering verbal condemnation and sending inadequate relief. It is clear that most European leaders find it politically more acceptable to condemn the participants and to talk about eventual war-crimes trials than to risk military casualties by trying to stop the war while it is still in progress.

Meanwhile, new civil wars and acts of aggression tragically similar to events in Bosnia are already under way or imminent in Macedonia, Moldova, the Caucasus, and some of the new republics of Central Asia. The international community has a compelling legal right and obligation to defend the civilian victims of such conflicts, not merely to provide them with minimal humanitarian assistance. The situation in Bosnia is all the more urgent because actions there will send a message to ambitious and potentially ruthless nationalists in all the states of the former Soviet bloc and elsewhere.

In Somalia, mass starvation is the result of the complete disintegration of political order. The process began in 1988 with a north-south civil war and massacres of northern civilians that attracted virtually no international attention. Since then, feuding clan leaders and warlords have made most of the country into a deadly wasteland in which humanitarian assistance, belatedly supplied, is seized at gunpoint. International pressure and diplomacy might have forestalled the crisis at an early stage. The immediate task must be to protect civilians against mass starvation, followed by restoration of critical elements of the transport infrastructure and preparation of the groundwork for an interim government. None of these tasks can be accomplished unless peacekeeping forces are authorized to use force. Somalia is a member of two regional organizations with the potential, in theory, to respond more forcefully: the Organization of African Unity and the Islamic Conference. Neither has acted decisively.

A similar situation existed in Lebanon and has now emerged in Liberia. The Liberian case is instructive: a West African peacekeeping force, operating under international auspices, temporarily stabilized the country and facilitated negotiations among the principal factions. The West African precedent for international intervention has been marred by the recent renewal of fighting in Liberia, but the peacekeeping effort undertaken so far appears preferable to the belated and inadequate international response to the Somali conflict. Other weak African states are at risk of similar crises.

Iraq exemplifies a more common kind of humanitarian crisis. Since the 1960s the Ba'athist regime in Baghdad has repeatedly used deadly force, including poison gas, against civilian Kurds suspected of rebellion. In the aftermath of the Gulf War, the Kurds revolted again and the Allies eventually responded with humanitarian aid in a Kurdish zone protected by Allied air cover. But for many Kurds, the response came too late. Allied leaders did not act until they were pressured by domestic and regional political considerations. Media coverage of atrocities mobilized public outrage in Western countries, and the Turkish government expressed its concern about the destabilizing effect of a flood of Kurdish refugees on its own Kurdish minority.

The main precedents for humanitarian intervention to end gross human rights violations like those in Iraq are unilateral ones: India in East Pakistan, now Bangladesh, in 1971; Vietnam in Cambodia, in 1978; and Tanzania in Uganda, in 1979. The intervenors' motives in these cases were politically suspect, but, on balance, unilateral action in each instance was better than inaction: it helped to end the killings and, except in Uganda, led to the establishment of regimes with a greater respect for human rights. The establishment of a security zone in Iraq was more easily achieved because it was done under international auspices in a pariah state that had lost credibility and clout in the Arab world; two previous decades of Iraqi abuse of Kurdish villagers had no significant international consequences.

Many future conflicts are likely to require international responses of the kind offered in Iraq. Chronic warfare and repression persist in Sudan and Myanmar (Burma); Ethiopia is at serious risk of renewed warfare that could be forestalled by international action. More distant crises can also be anticipated in such large Third World countries as Nigeria and Pakistan, where there are deep regional cleavages.

An Agenda for Peace: Responding to International Crises

The need for a more active role by the U.N. in such conflicts has been explicitly recognized by the new Secretary General, Boutros Boutros-Ghali. His *Agenda for Peace,* issued on June 17, 1992, focuses attention on threats to international security arising from "ethnic, religious, social, cultural or linguistic strife." The Agenda outlines four kinds of responses: preventive diplomacy, peacemaking, peacekeeping, and post-conflict peace-building. "Peace-building" refers to policies that address the root causes of conflict: "economic despair, social injustice and political oppression." The case of the Iraqi Kurds highlights the need to organize such responses to gross human rights violations at an early stage rather than wait for news of atrocities to create political pressures for action. The more quickly the U.N. acts, the less devastation communal conflicts will cause, whereas the longer that effective responses are delayed, the more difficult and costly peacekeeping and peace-building will be.

Let me conclude by examining the kinds of actions that the international community has at its disposal for responding to civil wars, repression, and anarchy that threaten the human rights and lives of large numbers of people. All have been used selectively to remedy past violations. The first are lowest in cost, and pose the least challenge to sovereignty. The last constitutes the revocation of a state's sovereignty. Military occupation and trusteeship are, or should be, the ultimate sanctions for states and local leaders that will not desist from mass killings.

1. Issue early-warning assessments of impending or escalating conflicts; send fact-finding missions and widely publicize their results. Establish a U.N.-sponsored news bureau with instant access to satellite telecommunications to assure global distribution of news and reports (a CNN for peace). These policies are particularly appropriate to civil wars and repression in their early stages. Fact-finding reports issued after six months of deadly and widely publicized conflict, as in Bosnia now, are little more than empty gestures.

2. Call on governments and their opponents to seek accommodation, provide international mediation and arbitration, offer political and material incentives to encourage contenders to reach agreements. These actions are well suited for the early and middle stages of civil wars.

3. Condemn putative violations of international law, issue formal warnings of impending sanctions, set deadlines for corrective action by the perpetrators. Such responses may help restrain states from gross human rights abuses. They are less likely to influence contenders in civil wars, especially those (like the Bosnian Serbs) whose moral and political ties to the international community are weak. More important, these symbolic acts help set the legal and political stage for more forceful international action.

4. Withdraw diplomatic recognition, apply sanctions, embargo military goods, energy supplies, and other commodities that prolong fighting. These actions can be applied to all armed contenders in civil wars and against state perpetrators of gross human rights violations. Of these options, embargoes are the most likely to be effective but are also the most difficult to enforce consistently. Implementing them is likely to require higher-order responses.

5. Use limited shows of force such as overflights by military aircraft, the stationing of warships offshore, and the introduction of moderately armed peacekeeping forces with sufficient firepower to defend themselves if attacked. These actions convey strong messages to belligerents and position international forces to respond more forcefully if warnings are not heeded.

6. Begin selective applications of force such as interdiction of military movements, air strikes on strategic targets, and the capture and disarming of combatants (individually or in small units). These actions require the international community to "take sides," which is politically feasible when one state or party is clearly the aggressor or perpetrator, as in Bosnia, but

which may be impossible in other civil war situations. Selective use of force also poses risks of escalation that may worsen and prolong conflict.

7. Use collective military intervention with the objectives of separating forces, disarming contenders, protecting neutral areas, and establishing secure procedures and zones for delivering and distributing humanitarian aid. This is the most decisive and costly form of international response, and seems to be the only one that might remedy the current situations in Bosnia and Somalia. The key is to use all means necessary to establish secure and defensible zones in which civilians can be supplied and protected. This is an interim strategy that must be complemented by diplomatic and political initiatives aimed at bringing about a political settlement. There is no denying the high-risk nature of such undertakings, but the consequences of inaction will ultimately lead to far greater cost and injustice.

8. Establish interim, internationally sponsored trusteeships, rebuild civil administration and basic services, provide material and technical assistance, supervise free elections. This form of wholesale intervention is equivalent to Allied policies in occupied Germany after 1945 and current U.N. actions in Cambodia, and is appropriate to Somalia's situation today. It requires a costly long-term commitment. Peacekeeping units must remain in place and be authorized to use force until authority can be transferred to elected local leadership.

Collective Responsibility

The international community has a wide range of options for responding to emerging communal conflicts and humanitarian crises. The choices are not restricted to passivity on the one hand and total war on the other. There are diverse and graduated responses that can be tailored to fit specific circum-

stances. Many of these responses have had demonstrably constructive effects in the recent past: belligerents have been separated by peacekeeping forces, abusive governments have been discouraged or prevented from continuing gross human rights abuses, humanitarian assistance has been delivered to victims of ongoing civil wars.

The central issue for timely and effective response is political will. The responses can be carried out under the direct auspices of the U.N. itself or under the authority of regional organizations. If international organizations default on their legal obligations to respond because of political paralysis, and if regional organizations are unable to act, then a strong argument can be made that individual states have the right to act unilaterally. But unilateral military intervention should not be used unless and until all collective remedies are exhausted. The intervenor must prove necessity and proportionality: military intervention has to be shown to be imperative and should remain the last resort.

International law provides the justification for all such actions. The U.N. was not founded so that it could impede progress by doggedly clinging to standards of absolute sovereignty. Instead, it was founded to limit the arbitrary rule of "sovereigns" and to imbue the world's citizens with a sense of collective responsibility for one another and for the survival of the species. The official *History of the United Nations War Crimes Commission* includes an appendix which is as compelling today as it was in 1948. After observing that "the idea of sovereignty paralyses the moral sense of humanity," the author points out that periods of growth in international law coincide with world upheavals. "The pressure of necessity stimulates the impact of natural law and of moral ideas and converts them into rules of law deliberately and overtly recognized by the consensus of civilized mankind." The humanitarian crises of the post–Cold War world point to the compelling necessity of translating international consensus into prompt and effective collective action.

70. A New World Security Order

Robert S. McNamara

Robert S. McNamara argues that with the end of the Cold War, nations have been slow to revise their foreign and defense policies. He argues that we should move toward a system of collective security with conflict resolution and peace-keeping functions performed by multinational institutions. He also favors a return, insofar as practicable, to a nonnuclear world and cutting military budgets throughout the world by 50 percent.

Although there has been clear evidence for several years that the Cold War was ending, nations across the globe have been slow to revise their foreign and defense policies, and slow to strengthen regional and international security organizations, to reflect that fact. This has been true of the United States.

In the United States, for example, in 1991, defense expenditures totaled $300 billion. In constant dollars that was 40 percent more than a decade ago, only 7 percent less than at the height of the Vietnam War. Moreover, the President's five-year defense program, presented to Congress in early 1992, projects that expenditures will decline only gradually from the 1991 levels. Defense outlays in 1997, in constant dollars, are estimated to be about 15 percent higher than 21 years earlier, under President Nixon, in the midst of the Cold War.

Such a defense program is not consistent with my view of the post–Cold War world.

Before we can respond to the changes in Soviet policy that ended the Cold War, we need a vision of a world no longer dominated by the East-West rivalry which for more than 40 years shaped the foreign policies and defense programs of Western nations.

As the Iraqi action demonstrated, the world of the future will not be a world without conflict, conflict among disparate groups within nations and conflict extending across national borders. Racial and ethnic differences will remain. Political revolutions will erupt as societies advance. Historical disputes over political boundaries will continue. Economic differentials among nations, as the technological revolution of the twenty-first century spreads unevenly across the globe, will increase.

In the past 45 years, 125 wars, leading to 40 million deaths, have taken place in the Third World. Third World military expenditures now approximate $200 billion per year. They have quintupled in constant dollars since 1960, increasing at an annual rate two to three times that of the industrialized countries. They are now only slightly less than the total amount the developing countries spend on health and education.

It is often suggested that the Third World was turned into an ideological battleground by the Cold War and the rivalries of the Great Powers. That rivalry was a contributing factor, but the underlying causes for Third World conflict existed before the origin of the Cold War and will almost certainly continue even though it has ended.

In those respects, therefore, the world of the future will not be different from the world of the past—conflicts within and among nations will not disappear.

But it is also clear that in the twenty-first century relations among nations will differ dramatically from those of the postwar decades. In the postwar years the United States had the power—and to a considerable degree it exercised that power—to shape the world as it chose. In the next century that will not be possible. While remaining the world's strongest nation, the United States will live in a multipolar world and its foreign policy and defense programs must be adjusted to that reality.

From "A Vision of a 'New World Security Order,'" *The Joan B. Kroc Institute for International Peace Studies Report* (1992). Reprinted by permission.

Japan is destined to play a larger and larger role on the world scene, exercising greater political power and, hopefully, assuming greater political and economic responsibility. The same can be said of Western Europe, which will take a giant step toward economic integration by the end of this year. From that is bound to follow greater political unity which will strengthen Europe's power in world politics.

And by the middle of the next century several of what we think of as Third World countries—in particular, China—will have so increased in size and economic power as to be major participants in decisions affecting relations among nations. India is likely to have a population of 1.6 billion, Nigeria 400 million, Brazil 300 million. If China achieves its economic goals for the year 2000, and if it then moves forward during the next 50 years at satisfactory but not spectacular growth rates, the income per capita of its approximately 1.6 billion people in 2050 may be roughly equal to that of the British in 1965. China's total Gross National Product would approximate that of the United States, Western Europe, or Japan, and very likely would substantially exceed that of Russia. These figures, are, of course, highly speculative. I point to them simply to emphasize the magnitude of the changes that lie ahead and the need to begin now to adjust our goals, our policies, and our institutions to take account of them.

In such a multipolar world, there clearly is need for developing new relationships both among the Great Powers and between the Great Powers and Third World nations. I believe that, at a minimum, the new order should accomplish four objectives. It should:

• Provide to all states guarantees against external aggression;
• Establish a mechanism for resolution of regional conflicts without unilateral action by the Great Powers;
• Commit the Great Powers to ending their military involvement in military conflicts among and within Third World nations;
• Increase the flow of both technical and financial assistance to the developing countries to help them accelerate their rates of social and economic advance.

In sum, we should strive to move toward a world in which relations among nations would be based on the rule of law, supported by a system of collective security, with conflict resolution and peace-keeping functions performed by multilateral institutions—a reorganized and strengthened United Nations and new and expanded regional organizations.

That is my vision of the post–Cold War world.

In contrast to my vision, many political theorists predict a return to the power politics of the nineteenth century. They claim that as ideological competition between East and West is reduced, there will be a reversion to more traditional relationships. They say that major powers will be guided by basic territorial and economic imperatives: that the United States, Russia, China, India, Japan, and Western Europe will seek to assert themselves in their own regions while competing for dominance in other areas of the world where conditions are fluid.

This view has been expressed, for example, by Michael J. Sandel, a political theorist at Harvard, and it underlies the recently leaked Defense Department conception of the post–Cold War world.

Professor Sandel has said: "The end of the Cold War does not mean an end of global competition between the Great Powers. Once the ideological dimension fades, what you are left with is not peace and harmony, but old-fashioned global politics based on dominant powers competing for influence and pursuing their internal interests."

Professor Sandel's conception of relations among nations in the post–Cold War world is historically well founded, but I would argue it is not consistent with the increasingly interdependent world—interdependent economically, environmentally, and in terms of security—into which we are now moving. In that interdependent world, I do not believe any nation will be able to stand alone. The U.N. Charter offers a far more appropriate framework for relations among nations in such a world than does the doctrine of power politics.

Such a world will, of course, need leaders. The leadership role may shift among nations depending on the issue at hand. Often it will be fulfilled by the United States. However, in such a system of collective security, whenever the United States plays a leadership role it must accept collective decision-making. Correspondingly, other nations—and that includes both Germany and Japan—should accept a sharing of the risks and the costs: the political risks, the financial costs, and the risk of casualties and bloodshed.

Had the United States and the other major powers made clear their conception of and support for such a system of collective security, and had they committed themselves both to pursuing their own interests without the use of force and to protecting Third World nations from external attack, the Iraqi action might well have been deterred.

While steps are being taken to establish a worldwide system of collective security, the arms reduction actions that have been under way should be expanded rapidly in scope and accelerated in time.

In recent days, there has been much discussion of reductions in nuclear forces. But the fact is that there are today approximately 50,000 nuclear warheads in the world, with a destructive power equivalent to well over one million times that of the Hiroshima bomb. Even assuming that the reductions called for by the START treaties and by the unilateral proposals of Bush, Gorbachev and Yeltsin are implemented, the stock of nuclear weapons will remain in the tens of thousands. The danger of nuclear war—the risk of destruction of our societies—will have been lowered but not eliminated. Can we go further? Surely the answer must be Yes.

More and more political and military leaders are accepting that basic changes in the world's approach to nuclear weapons are required. A few weeks ago, President Yeltsin went so far as to state that the long-term objective should be complete elimination of such weapons.

That is a very controversial proposition: leading Western security experts—both military and civilian—continue to believe that the threat of the use of nuclear weapons prevents war. And Zbigniew Brzezinski, President Carter's National Security Advisor, has said with reference to a proposal for eliminating nuclear weapons: "It is a plan for making the world safe for conventional warfare. I am therefore not enthusiastic about it." However, even if one accepts that argument, it must be recognized that the nuclear deterrent to conventional-force aggression carries a very high long-term cost: the risk of a nuclear exchange. Should we not begin immediately, therefore, to debate the merits of alternative long-term objectives for nuclear forces of existing nuclear powers, choosing, for example, from among three basic options:

- A continuation of the present strategy of "extended deterrence"—as recommended in a recent report to the Secretary of Defense—but with each side limited to approximately 5,000 warheads; or
- A minimum deterrent force—as recommended by a committee of the National Academy of Sciences—with each side retaining perhaps 1,000 warheads; or
- As I myself would prefer, a return, insofar as practicable, to a nonnuclear world.

And, should we not debate as well how best to deal with the proliferation of weapons of mass destruction and with the export of arms to the Third World? If we truly wish to stop proliferation and limit arms exports, I see no alternative to some form of collective, coercive action by order of the Security Council.

As we move toward a system providing for collective action against military aggression wherever it may occur, military budgets throughout the world—in both developed and developing countries—can be reduced substantially. They have totaled almost $1 trillion per year. I would say that amount could be cut in half. The huge savings—some $500 billion per year—could be used to address the pressing human and physical infrastructure needs across the globe.

That is my vision of a "New World Security Order" and it is an agenda I set before you for the twenty-first century.

It is not an agenda that any single nation can carry out by itself. But if together we are bold—if East and West and North and South dare break out of the mind-sets of the past four decades—we can reshape international institutions, as well as relations among nations, in ways that will lead to a far more peaceful world and a far more prosperous world for all the peoples of our interdependent globe.

It is the first time in my adult life we have had such an opportunity. Pray God we seize it.

Suggestions for Further Reading

Anthologies

Marrin, Albert. *War and the Christian Conscience.* Chicago: Henry Regnery Co., 1971.

Sterba, James P. *The Ethics of War and Nuclear Deterrence.* Belmont: Wadsworth, 1985.

Wakin, Malham. *War, Morality and the Military Profession.* Boulder: Westview Press, 1979.

Basic Concepts

Cady, Duane. *From Warism to Pacifism.* Philadelphia: Temple University Press, 1989.

Holmes, Robert. *On War and Morality.* Princeton: Princeton University Press, 1989.

Walters, LeRoy. *Five Classic Just-War Theories.* Ann Arbor: University Microfilms, 1971.

Walzer, Michael. *Just and Unjust Wars.* New York: Basic Books, 1977.

Alternative Views

Adelman, Howard. "The Ethics of Humanitarian Intervention." *Public Affairs Quarterly* (1992): 61–87.

Brzezinski, Zbigniew. "Selective Global Commitment." *Foreign Affairs* (1992): 1–20.

Falk, Richard. "Recycling Interventionism." *Journal of Peace Research* (1992): 129–134.

Luper-Foy, Steven. "Intervention and Refugees." *Public Affairs Quarterly* (1992): 45–60.

Pogge, Thomas. "An Institutional Approach to Humanitarian Intervention." *Public Affairs Quarterly* (1992): 89–103.

Powell, Colin. "U.S. Forces: Challenges Ahead." *Foreign Affairs* (1992): 32–45.